Tourism Economics and Policy

ASPECTS OF TOURISM TEXTS
Series Editors: Chris Cooper (*Oxford Brookes University, UK*),
C. Michael Hall (*University of Canterbury, New Zealand*) and
Dallen J. Timothy (*Arizona State University, USA*)

This new series of textbooks aims to provide a comprehensive set of titles for higher level undergraduate and postgraduate students. The titles will be focused on identified areas of need and reflect a contemporary approach to tourism curriculum design. The books are specially written to focus on the needs, interests and skills of students and academics. They will have an easy-to-use format with clearly defined learning objectives at the beginning of each chapter, comprehensive summary material, end of chapter review questions and further reading and websites sections. The books will be international in scope with examples and cases drawn from all over the world.

Full details of all the books in this series and of all our other publications can be found on http://www.channelviewpublications.com, or by writing to Channel View Publications, St Nicholas House, 31-34 High Street, Bristol BS1 2AW, UK.

ASPECTS OF TOURISM TEXTS
Series Editors: Chris Cooper (*Oxford Brookes University, UK*),
C. Michael Hall (*University of Canterbury, New Zealand*)
and Dallen J. Timothy (*Arizona State University, USA*)

Tourism Economics and Policy

Larry Dwyer, Peter Forsyth and Wayne Dwyer

CHANNEL VIEW PUBLICATIONS
Bristol • Buffalo • Toronto

Library of Congress Cataloging in Publication Data
Tourism Economics and Policy/Larry Dwyer, Peter Forsyth and Wayne Dwyer.
Aspects of Tourism Texts: 3
Includes bibliographical references and index.
1. Tourism—Forecasting.   2. Tourism—Management.   3. Tourism—Government policy.
I. Dwyer, Larry.   II. Forsyth, P. (Peter)   III. Dwyer, Wayne.   IV. Title.   V. Series.
G155.A1T58917 2010
338.4'791—dc22
2010026360

British Library Cataloguing in Publication Data
A catalogue entry for this book is available from the British Library.

ISBN-13: 978-1-84541-152-7 (hbk)
ISBN-13: 978-1-84541-151-0 (pbk)

Channel View Publications
UK: St Nicholas House, 31–34 High Street, Bristol BS1 2AW, UK.
USA: UTP, 2250 Military Road, Tonawanda, NY 14150, USA.
Canada: UTP, 5201 Dufferin Street, North York, Ontario M3H 5T8, Canada.

The policy of Multilingual Matters/Channel View Publications is to use papers that
are natural, renewable and recyclable products, made from wood grown in
sustainable forests. In the manufacturing process of our books, and to further support
our policy, preference is given to printers that have FSC and PEFC Chain of Custody
certification. The FSC and/or PEFC logos will appear on those books where full
certification has been granted to the printer concerned.

Typeset by Integra Software Services Pvt. Ltd, Pondicherry, India
Printed and bound in Great Britain by Gutenberg Press Ltd

CONTENTS

Measuring Tourism's Economic Contribution, Impacts and Net Benefits   237

PREFACE

This book has been some years in the making. This is not so much associated with particular difficulties with the writing of it, but more to do with the distractions that took the authors into other areas of research and scholarship at various times. These distractions were very much related to the volatility of tourism globally and its economic effects locally. They included such situations as the effects of SARS and the Global Financial Crisis (GFC) on tourism as well as proposals for deregulation of aviation, proposed changes in taxation that would affect particular tourism sectors and the potential effects of different carbon emissions mitigation policies on the tourism industry. The varied types of events that required the sometimes urgent attention of tourism economists reinforced our view of the importance of economics as a discipline of tourism research and also of educating students of its potential to inform government policy.

Larry Dwyer and Peter Forsyth have co-authored numerous articles on tourism economics over the years. Much of the book reflects the type of thinking that they have brought to tourism economics during their careers. Wayne Dwyer, a specialist in managerial economics, has brought to the team valuable expertise in pedagogy as well as sound insights into economic reasoning.

The authors wish to acknowledge the support and encouragement of many colleagues over the years. Many of the ideas in the book reflect the contributions that these persons have made to our thinking. Raul Hernandez-Martin, James Mak, Neelu Seetaram, Haiyan Song, Nada Kulendran, Tay Koo, Adam Blake, Leo Jago, Tien Duc Pham and Andreas Papatheodorou were kind enough to provide valuable feedback on the content of some chapters. Neelu Seetaram also prepared some of the material in the boxed summaries of articles that are a distinguishing feature of this book, and we acknowledge her valuable contribution in this activity. A special acknowledgement is also due to Ehsan Ahmed who expertly prepared most of the diagrams in the text. Every effort has been made to locate, contact and acknowledge copyright owners. Any errors will be rectified in future editions.

We extend our gratitude to these colleagues and to the large number of other colleagues that have influenced our views on tourism economics. Of this latter group we would like to single out Ray Spurr for special mention. Ray has, over a decade of collaboration with us on various projects, always brought special insights to the table in discussions about the findings of our studies and their implications for policy. We also wish to acknowledge the expert modelling work undertaken by Drs. Thiep Van Ho, Daniel Pambudi and Serajul Hoque which have underpinned many of our publications and have informed the content of this text.

At bottom it is the support of families that is most treasured. We would like to thank Libby, Eve, Joan, Ling, Enya and Jaime for their unfailing support for our work and their loving tolerance of living with workaholics. We promise henceforth to spend more time to smell the flowers and to linger longer over drinks. Larry and Wayne also wish to acknowledge the love and support they have always received from their mother, Iris, 88 years young and a daily user of the computer.

Larry Dwyer
Qantas Professor of Travel and Tourism Economics,
School of Marketing, Australian School of Business,
University of New South Wales, Australia

Peter Forsyth
Professor of Economics, Department of Economics,
Monash University, Victoria, Australia

Wayne Dwyer
Formerly Senior Lecturer, School of Economics and Finance,
University of Western Sydney, Australia

CHAPTER 1

OVERVIEW

Tourism is a major industry globally and a major sector in many economies. According to the United Nations World Tourism Organisation (UNWTO), over the past six decades, tourism has experienced continued growth and diversification to become one of the largest and fastest growing economic sectors in the world. Over time, an increasing number of destinations have opened up and invested in tourism development, turning modern tourism into a key driver for socio-economic progress (UNWTO, 2008).

The UNWTO emphasises that tourism has become one of the major international trade categories. The export income generated by international tourism ranks fourth after fuels, chemicals and automotive products. For many developing countries, it is one of the main income sources and the number one export category, creating much-needed employment and opportunities for development. Box 1.1 sets out the latest statistics that indicate the economic significance of tourism in the world economy (UNWTO, 2009a)

BOX 1.1 Statistics of world tourism

History
- From 1950 to 2008, international tourist arrivals grew from 25 million to 922 million.
- The overall export income generated by these arrivals (international tourism receipts and passengers Transport) grew to exceed US\$ 1.1 trillion in 2008, or over US\$ 3 billion a day.
- While, in 1950, the top 15 destinations absorbed 98% of all international tourist arrivals, in 1970 the proportion was 75%, and this fell to 57% in 2007, reflecting the emergence of new destinations, many of them in developing countries.
- Between 1995 and 2007 growth averaged over 4% a year, in spite of the stagnation between 2001 and 2003 due to terrorism, SARS and the economic downturn.

Current developments
- Worldwide, international tourist arrivals reached 922 million in 2008, up 1.9% on 2007.

- By region, Europe accounted for 53% of all international tourist receipts in 2008, and then came Asia and the Pacific (20%), the Americas (16%), the Middle East (6%), and Africa (5%).
- In order of growth rates sin international tourist arrivals, the Middle East lead with an 18.2% increase over 2007; then came Africa (4.1%), the Americas (3.0%), Asia and the Pacific (1.2%), and Europe (0.1%).
- By sub-region, the relative growth in international tourism arrivals was particularly strong in Central Asia (7.2%) and North Africa (5.4%) and particularly weak in Northern Europe (-1.9%), Western Europe (-1.1%) and Oceania (-1.0%).
- Worldwide, international tourist receipts reached US$ 944 billion in 2008, up 1.8% in real terms on 2007. This represented 30% of the world's export of services.
- By region, Europe accounted for 51% of all international tourist receipts in 2008, and then came Asia and the Pacific (22%), the Americas (20%), the Middle East (4%), and Africa (3%).

* In order of growth in international tourism receipts (2007–08), the Middle East lead with a 16.8% increase over 2007, the Americas (4.9%), Asia and the Pacific (3.4%), and Europe (-1.1%), and Africa (-2.0%).

- In 2007, interregional travel increased by 8% as against a growth of 6% for intraregional traffic. In terms of source markets, international tourism is still largely concentrated in the industrialized countries of Europe, the Americas and Asia and the Pacific. However, with rising levels of disposable income, many emerging economies have shown fast growth over recent years, in particular markets in North-East and South-East Asia, Central and Eastern Europe, the Middle East, Southern Africa and South America.
- In 2007, International tourism's biggest spenders were Germany (US$ 83 billion), followed by the USA, the UK, France and China. Outside the top ten, source countries that increased international tourism expenditure by over 15% were Saudi Arabia, Brazil, Egypt, Malaysia, Hungary, Argentina, Indonesia, South Africa, Turkey, the Czech Republic, Ireland and the Ukraine.
- The UNWTO estimates that international tourist arrivals are down 8% in early 2009 (January–April) on the corresponding period for 2008 but will moderate

to a fall of between 4% and 6% for the full year. The UNWTO attributes this downturn primarily to the GFC and the outbreak of Swine Flu (influenza A – H1N1 – virus). It also cites studies that suggest that global hotel investment is down 80% (on 2008).

Forecasts

- The UNWTO forecasts that international arrivals are expected to reach 1 billion (by 2010) and 1.6 billion (by 2020).
- Of the worldwide arrivals in 2020, 1.2 billion will be intraregional and 378 million will be long-haul travelers.
- The total tourist arrivals by region shows that by 2020 the top three receiving regions will be Europe (717 million tourists), East Asia and the Pacific (397 million) and Americas (282 million), followed by Africa, the Middle East and South Asia, East Asia and the Pacific. South Asia, the Middle East and Africa are forecasted to record growth at rates of over 5% per year, compared to the world average of 4.1%. The more mature regions, Europe and Americas, are anticipated to show lower than average growth rates. Europe will maintain the highest share of world arrivals, although there will be a decline from 60% in 1995 to 46% in 2020.
- Long-haul travel worldwide will grow faster, at 5.4% per year over the period 1995–2020, than intraregional travel at 3.8%.

Source: UNWTO (2008b) *Tourism Highlights 2008*, Facts and Figures section, and *United Nations World Tourism Barometer*, Vol. 7, No. 2, June 2009 at www.unwto.org.

The statistical data in Box 1.1 indicate the economic significance of tourism to the global economy and to individual economies. The substantial expenditure associated with tourism flows makes a substantial economic contribution to host countries. Changes in this expenditure resulting from shifting destination market shares will impact on countries' export earnings with further changes to Gross Domestic Product (GDP) and employment. This in itself indicates the importance of an understanding of the role that tourism economics can play in policy formulation.

However, in mid-2009, as this chapter was being written, the Global Financial Crisis (GFC) was affecting tourism worldwide. The world economy was in, or going into, recession. Financial, business and consumer confidence were at almost record low levels. Asset prices and wealth had declined substantially. International trade volumes had been adversely affected, with further declines likely. Unemployment was rising sharply, consumer spending was falling, businesses were collapsing, with investment reduced or cancelled. Inflation was slowing rapidly, commodity prices had collapsed, with deflation a real possibility in some countries. Currency values in many destinations had declined to historically low levels. Initially at least, attempts to halt the economic slide by policy stimuli were, at most, slowing the decline, not reversing it.

Broad solutions to restore conditions for growth all have serious consequences for tourism. Individuals and businesses need to reduce debt ('de-leverage'). Asset prices need to fall to more sustainable levels (to prices reflecting capitalised sustainable investment yields). In short, collectively we need to save more, consume less and accept wealth reductions as asset prices fall. Depressed consumer and business confidence is delivering all three at the present time.

Whatever the duration of the GFC, its effects on tourism are substantial. Reduced wealth, slowing or falling incomes, rising unemployment and low consumer and business confidence negatively affect consumer spending. Tourism spending, as part of discretionary consumer spending, can be expected to fall even more than other consumer spending. Price effects will not overcome income effects nor will exchange rate falls. Impacts on demand are happening with a lag, as many people make trip decisions well in advance. So, despite falling tourism flows across inbound, outbound and domestic markets in the initial months of the GFC, much worse is likely to follow.

It is not only tourism flows and associated expenditure that are being affected by the GFC. Declining asset values impact on the ability of firms to fund debt or invest and many capital projects (including fleet expansion, hotel projects, attractions, etc.) are being shelved due to financing difficulties. Credit availability and de-risking of bank balance sheets stifle tourism investment.

The GFC presents opportunities for both tourism operators and destination managers to undertake actions to enhance competitive advantage over the longer term. Thus tourism stakeholders can identify distortions that increase the costs of doing business, thereby reducing destination price competitiveness. They can assess areas for productivity improvement. They can carry out internal structural reforms which facilitate technological and organisational innovations. They can assess existing and future markets in light of changing consumer values and needs, including competitor analysis. They can identify demand-creating strategies, specifically those that *add value* rather than those that give price cuts to customers to maintain or improve market share. Investment should concentrate on maintaining or improving the quality of existing capacity to move up the yield curve. Business investments should be directed towards providing the basis for competitive advantage after the GFC ends, including staff training. Such initiatives will better position firms to access higher-yield visitors when the GFC ends.

The GFC is mentioned here to highlight the importance of economics in helping us to understand the tourism industry and to formulate policy that will lead to economic growth and employment. The GFC has both reinforced the importance of a knowledge of the economics of tourism and highlighted the gaps in our knowledge about this important industry.

The book aims to provide an overview of some of the most important areas of tourism economics. Much of the tourism literature today appreciates the importance of developing tourism 'sustainably'. Whatever the precise meaning of this term, an essential element of a sustainable tourism industry is economic viability. It is sometimes forgotten that the concept of sustainability has an economic dimension alongside its social and environmental dimensions. Economic efficiencies result in less use of resources with potentially less adverse social and environmental impacts from their use. While the focus of this book is clearly the economic dimension, the authors are mindful of the importance of the social and environmental effects of tourism development and tourist activity. The more comprehensive is our understanding of the economic issues associated with tourism, as reflected in the decisions made by tourism operators and policies enacted by destination managers, the more able are economic efficiencies to be achieved in the overall objective of sustainable development of the industry.

TOURISM DEMAND AND FORECASTING

Chapter 2 addresses the issue of tourism demand. Tourism demand refers to the willingness and ability of consumers to buy different amounts of a tourism product at different prices during some period of time. Tourism demand lies at the heart of tourism's economic contribution and economic impacts as it is the associated expenditure which determines its economic effects. There are particular problems estimating the demand for 'tourism' since 'tourism' is not a good or service like others.

The chapter distinguishes the demand for travel to a destination and the demand for a particular tourism-related product or service. Tourism demand may be influenced both by price and by a great many non-price factors. The price factors include the product price, the prices of other products and expectations regarding future price changes. The non-price factors include the size of the market, income, tastes, advertising and promotion, seasonality, buyer expectations of future income and wealth, product availability, the amount of leisure time available and other factors such as special events, immigration levels or random shocks.

An important concept much discussed in the tourism demand research literature is that of the elasticity of demand. Four main types of elasticity relevant for tourism policy are discussed: *price elasticity* (which reflects the sensitivity of the quantity demanded of some tourism product to changes in the price of that product itself), *income elasticity* (sensitivity to changes in the level of consumer income), *cross-price elasticity* (sensitivity to changes in the price of substitute goods and complementary goods) and *advertising elasticity* (sensitivity to changes in advertising expenditures on that product). The implications of the different elasticity measures for business strategy and destination management are discussed in the chapter. The relevance of these measures was evident in forecasts of the effects of the GFC on recent tourism flows. Reduced wealth, slowing or falling incomes, rising unemployment and shattered consumer and business confidence negatively affected consumer spending. Tourism spending in many countries, as part of discretionary consumer spending, typically fell even more than other consumer spending. Typically, price effects in destination markets did not overcome income effects or exchange rate falls. As a result, major origin markets delivered fewer tourists to the world and destinations worldwide experienced reduced tourism numbers and associated expenditure. The GFC has also highlighted the inadequacies of much of the research findings to explain consumer behaviour, since estimates of demand elasticities have generally been based on data accumulated over long time periods which have tended to 'smooth out' income variability in time-series analysis. Consumer response to short sharp shock in income remains a relatively neglected area of research.

A large number of research studies have attempted to model the factors that actually affect tourism demand, and the extent to which they do so. Demand modellers must consider carefully the issues of model specification, data collection, functional forms of the equation and evaluation of results. The relative importance of the various quantitative and qualitative factors found by researchers to influence the demand for international tourism arrivals is discussed. The more prominent factors include income, relative prices, transport cost, exchange rates, marketing expenses, migration levels in host destination and qualitative factors such as tourists' attributes, trade and cultural links between the countries, destination attractiveness, special events, natural disasters and social threats.

Over time, the modelling of tourism demand has become more sophisticated and more complex and different contexts of study, different data sets, use of different variables and different modelling techniques preclude generalisations. Given the importance of a better understanding of demand for destination management, marketing and policy purposes, tourism demand modelling is continually being refined with more input from the econometrics literature.

Chapter 3 addresses Tourism Forecasting. Forecasting is concerned with predicting the future, of estimating what will happen at some future time. Forecasting is undertaken by different tourism stakeholders, for different reasons, for different timeframes. The same forecasting techniques, however, will not be appropriate for all situations, for all markets and for all times.

This chapter reviews, compares and contrasts different demand-forecasting techniques, highlighting their implications for tourism policy. Forecasting is especially important in tourism because it aids long-term planning and is fundamental to the conduct of modern business and destination management. It is particularly challenging because the tourism product is perishable; tourism behaviour is complex; people are inseparable from the production–consumption process; customer satisfaction depends on complementary products and services; and tourism demand is extremely sensitive to natural and human-made disasters.

There are two broad approaches to tourism forecasting: qualitative tourism forecasting and quantitative tourism forecasting. Qualitative tourism forecasts are based on the judgements of persons sharing their experience, practical knowledge and intuition. These judgements are found through polling, expert opinion, panel consensus, surveys, Delphi technique and scenario writing and are often used for moderate or 'second-guess' quantitative forecasts. Qualitative forecasting is best applied when we face insufficient historical data, unreliable time series, rapidly changing macro environments, major disturbances, and when we desire long-term forecasts. Quantitative tourism forecasts are based on mathematical techniques using either cross-sectional data or time-series data. Time-series modelling employs either univariate models (that forecast a variable based on its own past movement in time) or multivariate (econometric) models that, in addition to time, include a number of non-time potential explanatory variables selected on the basis of economic theory.

A major focus of tourism forecasters has concerned forecasting international tourism arrivals. The typical method for forecasting with time-series models has been for the forecaster to choose a particular class of model and then use a set of objective criteria to choose the most suitable specific model within this class as appropriate to the data. Within the class of time-series models, there are many different forms that such models can take. While useful, time-series forecasts have their shortcomings in their assumption that the historical series will continue into the future, in their inability to predict turning points and in their inability to analyse causal relations. The chapter discusses these limitations.

For certain strategic business decisions, it may be more important to forecast correctly the direction of change in either tourism demand (i.e. whether tourism demand is likely to increase or decrease over a particular time period) or the rate of growth of tourism demand, rather than to minimise error magnitude. This gives a role for barometric techniques to be applied, highlighting the relationships between causal or coincident events to predict future events. A leading indicator series, in conjunction with other forecasting results, can help businesses, governments and destination managers predict and prepare for significant changes in the economic environment.

Econometric models actually seek to *explain* the variables being forecast. In the majority of business forecasting problems, management has a degree of control over some of the variables in the relationship being examined (e.g. price of product, level of advertising). Likewise, a destination manager may be able to use an econometric forecasting system to explore the consequences of alternative future policies on tourism demand. Only by thoroughly understanding the interrelations involved can management hope to forecast

The structure prevailing in any tourism market depends on numerous interlocking characteristics, among them: the number of sellers; the existence and extent of product differentiation; the cost structure; the presence of barriers to entry; and the extent of vertical and horizontal integration. The Structure–Conduct–Performance (SCP) paradigm is useful for gaining an overall picture of tourism markets, highlighting key features and capturing essential relationships. Within this framework, the market structure within which a tourism firm operates is held to affect the firm's conduct (decision-making processes), which, in turn, is held to affect the firm's performance (potential to make profit, to increase its market share and to achieve efficiency). This linearity may also work in reverse. Public policy (government involvement and influence in the marketplace) affects basic demand and supply conditions in the market, influencing market structure, rewarding or disparaging conduct and, ultimately, conditioning performance. Important ways through which government may differentially affect tourism markets include taxes and subsidies, regulation, price controls, competition laws and information provision to tourism stakeholders.

Chapter 5 discusses issues of pricing. The product price is not the only decision variable of importance to the tourism firm, but it is perhaps the most critical. Price is also the most adjustable of all the firm's decision variables.

Tourism firms differentiate their product in order to reduce its demand elasticity, and hopefully raise its price and total revenue. They divide their customers up into groups and price discriminate according to each group's willingness to pay (WTP). Pricing decisions, good and bad, have serious consequences for the firm. Given the inverse nature of the relationship between price and quantity sold, the firm must set its product prices carefully. The impacts of price changes on total revenue depend on the elasticity of demand for the product. Setting a higher price may result in fewer buyers and smaller potential total revenue if the product faces elastic demand. Setting a lower price may result in more buyers but, again, smaller potential total revenue if demand for the product is inelastic.

The price that a tourism firm sets for its products is governed by the interplay of a number of factors that are internal and external to the firm. These include the firm's objectives and ownership pattern, the market structure in which it operates, the degree of competition within the market and the firm's position within the market, seasonality, government policy, the macroeconomic environment, the price of other goods, capacity constraints, the degree of perishability of its products and so on.

Competitive profit maximising firms apply a variety of pricing strategies including uniform pricing, price discrimination, bundling, tying, peak load pricing and two-part tariffs as well as non-marginal pricing strategies involving penetration pricing, markup pricing and non-profit goals, as necessary. Each of these types of pricing strategies is discussed.

Firms tend to adopt the competition strategies of cost leadership, product differentiation and/or segment focus and set their prices by reference to one or a combination of these strategies. When firms become more interdependent in their pricing decisions, they tend to adopt price leadership strategies, especially when the option of a cartel arrangement is not available to them.

While firms can compete through the use of pricing strategies, they can also improve the quality of the characteristics of goods and services. Such quality improvements often enable the products to be sold for higher prices, effectively by making the demand curve more inelastic.

The hedonic pricing method has been used by tourism researchers to show how various supply-related factors explain the variation in overall accommodation and package tour prices, presenting tourism managers with an opportunity to enhance their strategic pricing through quality improvements and innovation.

DISTINGUISHING THE ECONOMIC CONTRIBUTION, ECONOMIC IMPACTS AND NET BENEFITS OF TOURISM

Chapter 6 is a capstone chapter which distinguishes between tourism's economic contribution, economic impacts and net benefits. It is widely acknowledged that both domestic and international tourism make an 'economic contribution' to a destination, that tourism has positive and negative 'economic impacts' and that it brings 'benefits and costs' to a destination. While often used in the literature, these terms are generally not well understood by researchers. Since these terms will be used throughout this book, we need to clarify them here since, to the economist, they mean different things.

The economic contribution of tourism refers to tourism's economic significance – to the contribution that tourism-related spending makes to key economic variables such as Gross Domestic (Regional) Product, household income, value added, foreign exchange earnings, employment and so on. The direct contribution is solely concerned with the immediate effect of expenditure made by tourists. As discussed in Chapter 7, countries are developing TSA to bring together basic data on the key economic variables that relate to tourism and to present them in a consistent and authoritative way using internationally endorsed concepts and definitions. The indirect economic contribution of tourism occurs when firms that sell goods and services to visitors purchase inputs from other firms and these other firms (suppliers) purchase inputs from other firms (suppliers). 'Indirect effects' are the production changes resulting from various rounds of re-spending of the tourism industry's receipts on products and services from other industries. Application of Input–Output (I–O) modelling, discussed in some detail in Chapter 8, allows the estimation of variables such as indirect tourism gross value added, indirect tourism GDP, indirect tourism output and indirect tourism employment. Tourism's total economic contribution (both direct and indirect) measures the size and overall significance of the tourism industry within an economy.

Tourism's economic impact refers to the changes in the economic contribution that result from specific events or activities that comprise 'shocks' to tourism demand. These changes in economic contribution (brought about by new tourism expenditure injected into a destination) generate three types of impacts or effects: direct impacts, indirect effects and induced effects. To estimate the economic impacts an economic model is needed. In Chapters 8 and 9, it is argued that the impact of higher visitor spending is highly sensitive to the assumptions one makes about the economy. It is argued that economy-wide effects must be taken into account in determining the impacts of increased tourism expenditure on a destination. An expanding tourism industry tends to 'crowd out' other sectors of economic activity. The extent of these 'crowding out' effects depends, in turn, on factor constraints, changes in the exchange rate, the workings of labour markets and the macroeconomic policy context.

Despite the common usage of the labels 'benefits' and 'costs' attached to tourism expenditure and its effects, they are very often misused. Prices seldom reflect full benefits from consumption or full costs of production. Since changes in national output resulting from inbound tourist expenditure reflect unadjusted market prices, gross revenues are an inaccurate measure of the real net benefits to a country from this activity. When additional resources are used to enable the extra activity resulting from a positive shock to tourism, the change in GDP exaggerates how much better off the country and, more precisely, its residents are. 'Net benefits' are a measure of the value of the gain in economic activity less the cost needed to enable this extra activity. The net benefits of tourism (benefits minus costs) are more fully explored in Chapter 10. Issues of concern in the measurement of net benefits associated with a change in tourism expenditure relate to terms of trade effects; government revenue and subsidies (Chapters 9 and 10); taxation (Chapter 15); market power, underemployment, foreign exchange effects and externalities (Chapter 6).

It is important that the net benefits from tourism (i.e. benefits less costs) be assessed accurately for policy reasons. Estimates of net benefits can help to determine such policy matters as the optimal level of tourism promotion and the extent of government involvement in promotion, and also such issues as appropriate aviation strategies, taxes on tourism, regulatory controls over the tourism industry and formulation of a National Tourism Strategy. For sound decision-making involving resource allocation, estimates of the *net* outcomes are required.

The issues addressed in Chapter 6 have substantial relevance to each of the remaining chapters of this book. Many of these issues will be discussed in greater detail below but they set out the basic approach which the authors take to economic analysis of tourism and policy formulation.

MEASURING TOURISM'S ECONOMIC CONTRIBUTION, IMPACTS AND NET BENEFITS

Chapter 7 addresses the issue of measuring tourism's economic contribution through the use of TSA. Tourism has grown substantially over recent decades as an economic and social phenomenon. Unfortunately, the development of statistical concepts and frameworks for tourism has not kept pace with the changes in the nature and significance of tourism worldwide and its potential for future growth. The problem with measuring the economic significance of tourism spending is that 'tourism' does not exist as a distinct sector in any system of economic statistics or of national accounts. As a result, tourism's value to the economy is not readily revealed. Tourism activity is 'hidden' in other industry activities (accommodation, transportation, telecommunications, etc.). TSA extract from the national accounts the contribution that tourism makes to each other sector of the economy allowing measurement of the true contribution of tourism to GDP or Gross State Product (GSP) and permitting comparison with other economic sectors listed in the national accounts. In TSA, the 'tourism industry' is identified from the demand side through demand for various commodities from tourism characteristic and connected industries.

TSA provide an internationally recognised and standardised method of assessing the scale and impact of tourism spending and its links across different sectors. TSA can provide a comprehensive database which identifies tourism's role in an economy and provides a rigorous and reliable basis for drawing comparisons between tourism and other sectors in terms of their contribution to the economy, as well as international comparisons. They provide an invaluable tool for measuring and monitoring the development of tourism and assessing its economic contribution. Countries in which TSA have been implemented are able to gain a much clearer picture of tourism's position within their economy and are thus able to evaluate more accurately the benefits it offers. Such information is the prerequisite to efficient and effective policy decisions to guide the future development of tourism. In addition, they provide a foundation for more sophisticated analyses of the impact of tourism and the assessment of different policy regimes using techniques such as Computable General Equilibrium (CGE) modelling.

TSA are now being developed at the sub-national level in some countries providing valuable data on tourism's economic contribution to regional destinations. TSA also provide a starting point for other more comprehensive approaches to analysing the overall economic impact of tourism. Several measures of tourism yield can be developed using the data contained in TSA. TSA can also be used to develop valuable economic performance indicators. These include measures of productivity, prices and profitability for the tourism industry as a whole. They can also be used to explore performance in individual sectors such as accommodation or motor vehicle hire. The measures can be used to explore the performance of individual tourism sectors or of tourism relative to that of other industries. A third use of TSA is to measure tourism's 'carbon footprint'. That is, if the relationship between industry production and Greenhouse Gas (GHG) emissions is known, then it is possible to calculate the emissions which are due to tourism as measured by the TSA.

Chapter 8 addresses issues involved in estimating the economic impacts of tourism. There is now an extensive literature on evaluating the economic impacts of tourism. This

13

literature seeks to show how the impacts of changes in tourism expenditure, due perhaps to improved promotion, development of special events or external shocks such as terrorist attacks, can be evaluated in economic terms. The more common applications of economic impact analysis to tourism have centred on the evaluation of the economic impacts of changes in tourism demand; the effects of policies and regulations which affect tourism activity either directly or indirectly; the effects on tourism demand from events beyond the direct control of the industry itself; public and private investment proposals; resource allocation, policy and management of tourism development strategies; and aspects of lobbying.

Expenditure by visitors to a destination represents an injection of 'new money' into that destination. This new expenditure gives rise to direct and secondary (indirect and induced) effects, leading to increases in economic activity at that destination. As typically employed in tourism research and policy analysis, economic impact analyses trace the flows of spending associated with tourism activity in an economy through business, households and government to identify the resulting changes in economic variables such as sales, output, government tax revenues, household income, value added and employment. The extent to which production, income and employment in the destination are affected by tourism expenditure depends importantly on the import content of consumption goods and inputs to production and the strengths of the business linkages between tourism and other industry sectors. Almost every industry in the economy is affected to some extent by the indirect and induced effects of the initial tourist expenditure. These flow-on effects are called multiplier effects. A multiplier is the number by which a given change in spending is multiplied in order to find the impact of that change on the economic variable under review. The size of the multiplier effects will determine the impact of a tourism shock (positive or negative) on important economic variables such as GDP (GSP), value added, factor incomes and employment.

There are two broad types of multipliers: Keynesian multipliers and multipliers based on I–O modelling. An I–O table illustrates, in matrix form, how transactions flow through the economy over a given time period. The rows of the matrix show the sales of the total output by each sector to every other sector. The columns show the inputs required by every sector from other sectors. The table provides a snapshot of the transactions occurring in an economy over a selected period, showing from which other industries a particular industry purchases and to which industries it sells.

I–O multipliers (relating to sales, output, income, value added and employment) can be decomposed into multiplier effects (initial, first round, industrial support, production-induced and consumption-induced). These multipliers can be derived from the direct requirements coefficient matrices based on I–O tables. Value added multipliers, which measure the change in net economic activity at each stage of production, are the preferred measure for the assessment of the contribution to the economy of some shock to final demand. Multipliers can be decomposed into their various effects: initial; first round and industrial support; and consumption-induced effects. Simple multipliers include only the direct and indirect effects of a demand shock while total multipliers include the induced effects as well.

Though widely used, I–O multipliers are based upon restrictive assumptions such as fixed factor proportion; output homogeneity; linear, homogeneous consumption functions; and no constraints on supply. They typically ignore the effects of input price changes including changes in real wages, changes in the exchange rate and the government fiscal policy stance. Invariably, by failing to account for crowding out effects and inter-industry interactions I–O modelling exaggerates the economic impacts of tourism shocks on the economy. I–O multipliers have often been used too uncritically in tourism policy formulation. Unfortunately, many researchers, destination managers and tourism policy makers often tend to ignore the limitations of multipliers based on I–O modelling. In truth, I–O multipliers have limited policy relevance for tourism.

Sometimes researchers employ a Social Accounting Matrix (SAM) to estimate the economic impacts of tourism. A SAM is a system of representing the economic and social structure of a country (region) at particular time, by defining its economic actors and recording their transactions. Although more comprehensive than I–O models in that they include inter-institutional transfers, as a tool for impact analysis, tourism multipliers including Type SAM have all of the limitations of I–O multipliers in general.

Tourism is not unique in its ability to increase incomes and jobs. All expenditure has multiplier effects and all industrial development generates economic benefits, although their precise impact on individuals and regions will vary from industry to industry. The discussion in the chapter emphasises moreover that multiplier analysis only tells part of the story of the impacts of tourism shocks. It has nothing to say on the costs and benefits of alternatives to tourism in generating income and employment in a particular region, or about the process of adjustment which must take place to respond to any changes in demand by tourists.

Chapter 9 discusses the most sophisticated technique for estimating the economic impacts of tourism shocks – CGE modelling.

In evaluating economic impacts, there is a need to model the economy, as far as is possible, as it really is, recognising other sectors and markets, and capturing feedback effects. Any analysis of the effects of a change in tourism demand on national or regional economies must not only contain information on the links between tourism and other industries but must also be able to account for resulting price and cost pressures that act as a brake to future economic expansion or contraction. Indeed, the increased output of the tourism industry may be more than offset by contractions in output elsewhere in the economy.

The study of the economic impacts of tourism shocks has recently undergone a 'paradigm shift' as a result of the use of CGE models in place of I–O models. CGE models are constructed as a series of markets (for goods, services and factors of production),

production sectors and demand groups (households). Each market, sector and household has its own set of economic rules that determine how it reacts to external changes. In this way, CGE models consist of a set of equations that characterise the production, consumption, trade and government activities of the economy. CGE models recognise resource constraints and consider the demand, price and income effects flowing from government policies and structural changes in the economy. They incorporate all I–O mechanisms; they incorporate mechanisms for potential crowding out of one activity by another, as well as for multiplier effects. CGE models can guide policy makers in a variety of scenarios arising from a range of domestic or international shocks or alternative policy scenarios. They can be tailored to allow for alternative conditions such as flexible or fixed prices, alternative exchange rate regimes, differences in the degree of mobility of factors of production and different types of competition.

CGE models represent a much more rigorous approach to estimating impacts than the use of I–O models, providing a much more informed basis for policy making. CGE models are widely employed by various national and international organisations (IMF, World Bank, OECD, etc.), the European Commission, research centres and universities for economic policy analysis at the sector level as well as the economy-wide level. They have become a standard tool for the quantitative analysis of policy formulation in many domains including fiscal policy, trade policy and environmental policy. CGE models are now increasingly used in tourism economics analysis and in policy formulation. Based on real data and mathematically specified key relationships within the economy, they are used to assess the economic impacts of changes in tourism expenditure. The development and application of this technique has major implications for the way that tourism economists think about the economic impacts of tourism and for the policy advice they give to decision makers in both public and private sectors.

The strengths of the CGE approach to assessing the economic impacts of changes in tourism expenditure are many and varied and include the ability to model business and household demand for goods and services, relative price changes and substitution effects; to take account of the interrelationships between tourism, other sectors in the domestic economy and foreign producers and consumers; to incorporate endogenous price determination mechanisms; to identify and test underlying assumptions; and to allow initial expenditure shocks to originate from anywhere in the economy.

Several studies of the use of CGE modelling to estimate the economic impacts of tourism are discussed in Chapter 9. These studies range over the economic impacts of changes in inbound tourism to nations and regions, the economic impacts of tourism crises, the economic impacts of climate change, the economic impacts on a destination of tourists from different market segments and the evaluation of economic policy measures affecting tourism. In Chapter 11, the use of CGE models in special event assessment is discussed. The discussion is intended to highlight the power of the approach in economic impact estimation in tourism. It is emphasised that CGE models are particularly helpful to tourism policy makers who seek to use them to provide guidance about a wide variety of 'what if?' questions, arising from a wide range of domestic or international expenditure shocks or alternative policy scenarios.

Chapter 10 discusses the use of Cost-Benefit Analysis (CBA) to evaluate tourism projects, developments, programmes or policies. As discussed in detail in Chapter 13, tourism development requires substantial investment in public infrastructure. In contrast to *financial evaluations* which are only concerned with cash flows in and out of the organisation, taking no account of external costs or benefits, *economic appraisal* considers the costs and benefits to society as a whole to determine whether the project will make society better or worse off. This requires estimating a wider range of costs and benefits than occurs in a financial appraisal, even estimating values where no direct price is charged.

In the public sector, the fundamental requirement is for an economic appraisal of projects, policies and programmes. The public sector is a major user of a destination's available resources and, as such, should ensure that it makes a significant positive contribution to the economy and society. More particularly, no new proposal, programme, project or policy should be adopted without first answering questions such as what are the specific outcomes sought? Do the gains to people exceed the costs the sacrifices required? Are there better ways to achieve these outcomes? Are there better uses for these resources? And is this an appropriate area of responsibility for government?

CBA is a tool of the decision maker in situations where an investment proposal or programme is expected to generate substantial costs and benefits that cannot be valued completely through market transactions. Its function is to generate information on the economic effects of alternative public expenditure decisions and to assist the decision maker to search for the set of alternatives that generates the greatest net benefit. CBA improves the political process by uncovering gains and losses which might otherwise be neglected in the bargaining process while encouraging decision makers to undertake a comprehensive search for alternative means of attaining their objectives. By quantifying all significant costs and benefits in monetary terms, it is possible to determine the net benefits or costs of a given proposal.

CBA is particularly important in the context of evaluating tourism policy, programmes, regulations, projects and developments. Specific examples include regional or local tourism plans; re-zoning of land for tourism purposes; and major tourism developments such as the creation of tourism shopping precincts, airport development, resorts and hotels, nature reserves and sporting facilities. Such projects, many of which involve private–public partnerships, generally have relatively wide economic, environmental and social implications for a community that are not captured in the basic financial analysis undertaken by project proponents. CBA is especially appropriate to tourism because there is often a clear trade-off between financial benefits and social or environmental costs. Tourism projects which might be financially beneficial may be rejected because of their adverse environmental and/or social impacts. Conversely, tourism projects that might not be financially viable may be accepted because of their social and environmental benefits.

Throughout the chapter, the emphasis is on CBA from a societal point of view in the use of social resources, rather than from an individual firm's point of view in the use of its own private resources. The chapter explains the what, why, how, when and where of CBA in tourism contexts, detailing the steps to be taken in conducting such an analysis, the issues to be clearly understood and the common errors to be avoided. The chapter also compares CBA with other forms of project evaluation such as Cost-Effectiveness Analysis (CEA). CBA is not without its problems: costs and benefits can be difficult to quantify, double counting is common and income distributional effects tend to be ignored. But, as an overall accounting technique, it can be used by government to determine the worth of tourism projects based on true (social) values.

Chapter 11 addresses the issue of assessment of the impacts of special events. Special events provide important recreational opportunities for local residents. In many destinations, they form a fundamental component of the destination's tourism development strategy. Special events increase the opportunities for new expenditure within a host region by attracting visitors to the region. They have the capacity to stimulate business activity, creating income and jobs in the short term and generating increased visitation and related investment in the longer term. On the other hand, events are recognised to generate adverse environmental impacts such as various forms of pollution and adverse social impacts such as disruption to local business and community backlash.

Governments are often asked to provide financial support for special events including the allocation of large expenditure to upgrade the required facilities and will therefore require credible forecasts of the event impacts and net benefits.

In recent years a growing number of researchers have been critical of the approach taken to assessing the economic impacts of special events. Three main types of criticism have been advanced. Some argue that the economic impacts of events are often exaggerated. These critics highlight some inappropriate practices in event assessment (e.g. inclusion of residents' expenditure as 'new money', exaggerating visitor numbers and expenditure, abuse of multipliers and inclusion of time switchers and casuals) as well as the tendency to ignore the various costs associated with special events (e.g. opportunity costs, costs borne by the local community and displacement costs). These issues are discussed in the text.

Other researchers have argued that the entire approach to event assessment needs a re-examination. At issue is the relevance of I–O modelling which for two decades has been the standard technique for converting event expenditure data into economic impacts. These critics argue that the economic assessment models used for estimating the economic impacts of major events should reflect contemporary developments in economic analysis, particularly regarding the use of CGE modelling. They argue that in most cases I–O modelling does not provide an accurate picture of the economic impacts of events and is thus incapable of informing event-funding agencies or governments of the 'return on investment' to be expected from event funding. They also argue that I–O modelling greatly exaggerates the economic impacts of events, providing inaccurate information to policy makers. These arguments are largely based on the types of arguments supporting the use of CGE modelling which were set out in Chapter 9.

A third group of researchers, comprising many of the advocates of CGE modelling, argues that event assessment which focuses only on economic impacts is too narrow in scope to provide sufficient information to policy makers and government funding agencies and that, where practical, a more comprehensive approach should be employed to embrace the importance of social and environmental impacts in addition to economic impacts. There are many potential effects of events that are often not accounted for in a standard economic impact analysis. Event assessments need to be broadened to take, where practicable, a more comprehensive approach embracing not only economic but also social and environmental factors. The standard tool of measurement of such effects in order to undertake a holistic or comprehensive evaluation of an event is CBA. Where public funds are to be provided to assist an event, it is necessary that the cost of these funds be compared to the benefits from the event via a CBA. Accepting the logic of this position, the text argues that a rational events strategy for government involves funding events at a level which is appropriate given the benefits they create, and which reflects the benefits which could be obtained by using the funds elsewhere. It also involves allocating the funds available to the events which create the greatest net benefits.

TOURISM INVESTMENT

Chapter 12 discusses issues of tourism investment. Investment refers to the spending on capital and financial assets undertaken by private firms and governments in the expectation of realising future returns. Strong, continuing tourism investment is vital to a strong, successful tourism industry. It is vital both to the individual firm, ensuring its future productive viability, and to the destination, adding strongly to the economy's overall capacity to satisfy tourism demand. The broader national and regional benefits that come from a more favourable tourism investment climate include economic growth; job creation; utilisation of domestic resources, particularly renewable resources; skills acquisition; expansion of exports; development of remote areas of the country; and facilitation of increased ownership of investment by the nation's citizens.

This chapter discusses the importance of tourism investment in its many forms, distinguishing capital investment from financial investment, private investment from public investment and domestic investment from foreign investment. It also discusses the elements of risk and uncertainty that accompany tourism investment decision-making generally and reviews the various techniques used to assess return on tourism investment.

Capital investment may be financed in several ways including from profits, borrowings, equity, securitisation, and grants and subsidies. It may be generated by several different motives including the need to replace capital assets, reduce production costs, expand output or expand into new product lines or markets, or by government regulation.

Successful capital budgeting depends on several steps. These include the accurate estimation of all future cash inflows and outflows (measured in terms of today's dollars) for each potential alternative capital investment project; the evaluation of these alternative projects; the choice of one or more of them for implementation; and the review after the investment projects have been implemented. Following the principles of marginal analysis, a tourism firm should undertake additional investment projects until the marginal return from the investment is equal to its marginal cost. The firm's actual decision as to whether to accept or reject any particular investment project will depend on its accept–reject criteria. Of the several different types of criteria, the net present value method is preferred on conceptual grounds.

Pitfalls for firms to avoid in capital budgeting include over-estimating the cost of capital; assuming that profits will be unaffected by new investment; omitting the effects on cash flows of factors that cannot be quantified; creating biases favouring small-scale incremental projects and discouraging more ambitious ones; and failing to estimate the average weighted cost of capital. The same as for other businesses, tourism firms in the tourism industry must be mindful of adhering to best practice to maximise net returns from investments.

Despite the tourism industry's impressive growth internationally, it continues to face challenges in attracting private-sector investment. A number of critical issues and areas of focus need to be addressed if tourism investment is to be appropriately harnessed not only to maintain a firm's current position in the market but more critically to meet growth forecasts. Impediments to new capital investment include trading volatility in some tourism sectors; poor past performance; misalignment of risk and return; misalignment of owner and management objectives; misalignment of investors and fund managers; misalignment of different sectors within the tourism industry; the illiquidity and capital-intensive nature of some tourism sectors; low barriers to entry within much of the tourism industry; lack of information on and understanding of tourism investment; the small size of some tourism sectors; and government distortions.

The importance of tourism investment became particularly evident during the recent GFC. Declining asset values impacted on the ability of firms to fund debt or invest and many capital projects (including fleet expansion, hotel projects, attractions, etc.) were shelved due to financing difficulties. Credit availability and de-risking of bank balance sheets stifled the volume of tourism investment needed to support tourism growth over time impacting adversely on destination competitiveness.

Chapter 13 addresses problems of provision of public infrastructure to support tourism development. Infrastructure refers to the basic physical and organisational structures needed for the operation of a society or the services and facilities necessary for an economy to function. The term typically refers to the technical structures and assets that support a society, such as networks, air services, airports, water supply, waste disposal systems, energy and power generation, post and telecommunications, recreational assets and so forth. In this chapter, infrastructure is used in the sense of technical structures or physical networks that support society. The operation of tourism facilities, services and amenities is heavily dependent on the available quantity and quality of public infrastructure.

Investment in tourism infrastructure is important for a number of reasons. Primarily, it is required for the development and growth of tourism capacity. The creation of tourism infrastructure assets creates jobs – both during the construction stage and in operations. Infrastructure increases the efficiency of privately producing and distributing tourism services and makes possible the supply of tourism services. The provision of tourism infrastructure is of particular importance for long-term tourism growth. Expanded facilities are needed to serve the needs of visitors and to maintain relatively uninterrupted service levels. The infrastructure on which a country's tourism industry relies, such as its roads, railways, airports and terminals, accommodation facilities, shopping, entertainment, restaurants, currency exchange facilities, telecommunications and so on are major determinants of its overall destination competitiveness including destination 'experience'.

Good infrastructure facilitates tourism development in a region or country and, in turn, enables the destination to maximise its economic and other benefits from tourism. If infrastructure is good, it is hardly noticed by the tourists, who can concentrate on experiencing what they came for. The developed countries tend to rank highly in respect of the quantity and quality of the different types of infrastructure, highlighting the inherent competitive advantages of developed economies across their industrial sectors. These basic infrastructure differences will take many years to overcome.

Tourism infrastructure may be provided by either the public sector or the private sector with the relative degree of provision between them dependent on prevailing domestic economic, social and political policies. Recent years have seen a growth in the West in the private provision of infrastructure, especially in airports, terminals, road links and rail. There has also been a proliferation of public–private partnerships in which the government sets the terms of the contract and may become the ultimate owner but the private sector builds, and perhaps operates, the facility. Newer forms of regulation encourage low-cost production, but they can also result in poor service quality, and inadequate investment.

Chapter 13 covers some of the main economic problems associated with ensuring the supply of tourism infrastructure. It outlines the changes that have been taking place in the institutional structure of infrastructure – the move from public to private provision. Many forms of tourism infrastructure are subject to congestion, and this makes ensuring efficient provision more difficult. Most tourism infrastructure is still government-regulated, and the problems in getting this regulation right are addressed. The chapter also examines the issues of how environmental constraints affect infrastructure, how provision of good infrastructure can stimulate tourism and, finally, the particular problems that developing countries face in ensuring that their infrastructure helps their tourism development.

Chapter 14 addresses issues involving Foreign Direct Investment (FDI) in tourism. FDI involves some element of ownership or control over tourism assets. The various motives for foreign direct tourism investment can be explained through the eclectic paradigm of international production which asserts that the extent, pattern and growth of value-adding activities undertaken by multinational enterprises outside their home countries are dependent on the value of and interaction between three main variables: ownership advantages, location advantages and market internalisation advantages.

It is widely held that FDI in any industry has the potential, *inter alia*, to contribute to growth and development; create jobs; build exports; provide additional sources of finance for commercial expansion; facilitate technology transfer and innovation; and increase opportunities for global networking. Many argue in particular that developing countries that lack capital, entrepreneurship and access to international brands, expertise and marketing networks need FDI to offset their disadvantages in tourism. Others, however, see FDI as disadvantageous to a country, resulting in a loss of profits that could have been kept at home, and also a reduction in local sourcing of inputs. FDI has some potential costs to the host country. These include its potential to crowd out domestic investment; increased leakages from tourist expenditure; reduced employment opportunities for locals; loss of equity and control of the tourism industry; and inappropriate form and scale of development.

In reality, FDI is associated with both benefits and costs to the host destination. The need for FDI in different countries depends on several factors including political orientation, general economic and tourism development and the type and scale of tourism development required. The question that any destination must ask is: do these benefits exceed the costs? The extent of costs and benefits will vary considerably from case to case and it is inappropriate to generalise too widely. On balance, unless distortions are such as to result in net costs arising from additional tourism (e.g. if goods and services bought by tourists are heavily subsidised), or foreign investment is associated with increase in market power which adversely affects the local economy, the net contribution of foreign investment is likely to be positive. The effect on tourism flows and net expenditure will be greater; and the net benefits will be greater as a result of the increased tourism flows and tourist expenditure.

Determination of the net benefits (costs) for any country is an empirical matter and two questions need to be answered: could the host nation do even better if its tourism operations were domestic-owned rather than foreign-owned? If so, should governments encourage and support domestic private tourism investment? Either way, foreign direct tourism investment is best seen as complementary to domestic tourism investment rather than as a substitute for it.

It is argued that FDI has the potential to help address some of the challenges facing developing countries in an increasingly interdependent, globalised world. Developing countries that seek to access foreign direct tourism investment as part of their overall economic development need to design and implement proper policy frameworks that will make themselves more attractive to tourists and improve the bargaining position of their tourism service suppliers. Governments reserve considerable power to determine how the industry performs. Policies can be enacted to increase local economic participation in order to reduce economic dependencies on other countries. Any such policies should be examined carefully within the framework of overall development strategies, weighing up the socio-economic benefits that result against the possible reduced contribution of tourism to the economy.

TAXATION AND TOURISM

Chapter 15 discusses issues in tourism taxation. This chapter examines the economics of taxing travel and tourism. It addresses the following questions: what are the types of tourist taxes? What are the effects of tourism taxation? What are the economic reasons for taxing travel and tourism? What are the arguments against tourism taxation? And is it economically 'efficient' and 'fair' to single out travel and tourism for special taxation?

As noted in Chapter 13, the tourism sector relies on the natural amenities in the destination and also on publically provided infrastructure and public goods. Tourism development is not a free good. Like residents, tourists and their suppliers demand public services which have to be paid for through taxes and user charges. As tourism continues to grow in many countries, the infrastructure of these countries is becoming increasingly overburdened. Unless efforts are made to fund travel and tourism infrastructure, destinations will not be capable of attracting and retaining global market share. Domestic taxpayers usually finance the provision of publicly provided goods and services. The influx of tourists imposes an extra cost on the government relating to the provision of items such as greater security and an improved environment. As non-residents, tourists do not pay to finance these extra costs, except for contributions made by way of such taxation schemes as a Goods and Services Tax (GST). A specific tax on tourism can, therefore, serve to redress the balance and impose the burden on those who are responsible for them. There are often user charges for some attractions, such as parks and safaris, but in other cases, such as with publicly provided services such as street lighting, waste disposal and security, enforcing payment is difficult. In such circumstances, taxing may be the only way of 'charging' tourists for the public goods they consume. Convention centre financing is a good example of the under-provision of infrastructure that is often corrected through appropriate taxation.

In recent years, there has been growing evidence that taxes on travellers and travel companies have been increasing as governments have viewed the expanding industry as a ready source of revenue. However, poorly conceived and implemented taxation leads to falls in tourism demand, lost output, lost growth, lost jobs and a worsening economy. Taxes are levied on both tourists and tourism businesses at rates that vary considerably from country to country. Many of these taxes tend to have been introduced in an *ad hoc* fashion, without serious consideration of their economic and social effects.

This chapter explains that there are sound economic reasons for taxing tourism beyond simply collecting revenues to provide public services to tourists and their suppliers. A well-designed system of tourist taxation can benefit the residents of destinations in a number of ways: it can broaden and increase the revenue elasticity of the destination's tax base, extract economic rents and protect the environment including reduction of negative externalities such as congestion (which also benefits tourism). Tourism taxes can help to finance the provision of public goods. More particularly, they can benefit tourism by generating funding for tourism promotion and for the construction and operation of convention centres. Moreover, levying higher taxes on goods and services that are largely purchased by tourists does not necessarily reduce economic efficiency or equity. Much or all of the tax burden can be paid by tourists who are not resident in the country in which the taxes are levied.

On the other hand, tourism taxes can impose costs on a destination. They can result in a contraction of economic activity with adverse effects on Gross Domestic Product, employment and foreign exchange earnings. The reduced price competitiveness of a tourism destination following the imposition of general or specific taxes may be such as to reduce the economic contribution of tourism to the wider economy. Additionally, taxes result in deadweight losses to destinations that impose them, reducing the welfare of resident consumers and producers. Taxes can also lead to retaliation by other destinations resulting in a lose-lose situation for the residents of each country. There is also some concern that international tourism is regarded by a growing number of countries as a 'tax revenue cash cow'. This results in a decline in tourism worldwide relative to other industries. Tourism taxes have proliferated around the world as governments have viewed the expanding tourism sector as a ready source of tax revenue. The taxes are levied on both tourists and tourism businesses at rates that vary considerably from country to country and have often been introduced in an *ad hoc* fashion, without serious consideration of their economic and social effects. The net benefit from tourism development depends critically on how a destination designs its public finance/revenue system to tax travel and tourism.

In estimating the effects of tourism taxes on the economy it needs to be acknowledged that if the government needs revenues and does not tax tourism, or some other industry, it will have to raise the tax somewhere else – and it will incur the similar negative effects on activity and employment. Alternatively, the government may not raise the tax revenue and may cut expenditure, but this too will have a negative impact on activity and employment. A tax on tourism will lower employment in the tourism industry and related industries, but not necessarily overall. To show that employment overall was lower than under an alternative revenue-raising policy, it would be necessary to show that taxes on tourism were more harmful to employment, directly and indirectly, than the alternative policy. There is no general reason why this should be the case, even if tourism is a labour-intensive industry, in terms of its direct labour inputs. It would be necessary to use CGE models of the economy, with all direct and indirect linkages between sectors, to explore this issue. Claims that specific taxes, such as taxes on tourism services, will affect employment adversely may be superficially convincing, but they are based on incomplete and misleading analysis and must be treated with caution.

The usual criteria for good taxation are that it should be efficient, equitable and administratively simple. Policy makers should be mindful of these criteria when formulating taxes affecting the tourism industry. Given the increasing importance of tourism taxation in both developed and developing countries, greater understanding of the economic underpinnings of tourism taxation and its effects is necessary, so that modelling of tourism taxation can be undertaken and appropriate policies for tourism taxation can be formulated.

TOURISM AND AVIATION

Chapter 16 addresses issues of aviation and tourism. Aviation and tourism are closely linked – for many tourists, especially international tourists, air transport is the preferred or only effective means of transport. Aviation and tourism are complementary industries. Aviation depends on tourist travel and tourists depend on air transport. The growth of tourism in the past 50 years has been greatly stimulated by developments in aviation.

However, there are conflicts of interest between tourism and aviation sectors – lower air fares stimulate tourism, but put pressure on airline profits. Thus, the restrictive regulation of earlier years may have ensured the profitability and stability of the aviation sector, but it discouraged tourism. Moves towards liberalisation have been taking place gradually but steadily over the past four decades. This has posed policy dilemmas for governments. Over time, however, governments have chosen to implement less restrictive regulation of air transport, and this has led to more competition, lower fares and more travel.

Up till the 1970s, air transport was a tightly regulated industry, and its products were primarily targeted at the business market. Air transport between different countries tended to be regulated in detail by the partner countries, and this regulation allowed little scope for competition and innovation. Over time, these regulations have been eased, allowing for the introduction of lower fares and new products, such as Low-Cost Carrier (LCC) airlines. The result has been a rapid growth in long-haul tourism alongside a growing market share of air transport in medium-haul and even short-haul travel. There have been several phases in these developments which have been critical, such as the development of charter markets in Europe, US domestic airline de-regulation and the emergence of LCC. The ways in which the limitations of air transport infrastructure have acted as a constraint on tourism growth are considered in the text.

Given that air transport is a key determinant of tourism flows, the technology of aviation will have an important impact on tourism. Technology determines costs, and thus it determines which destinations are price competitive and which are not. Improvements in aviation technology have impacted on tourism, notably by lowering costs, and they have also impacted on patterns of tourism. However, they have also had important impacts on patterns of tourism flows: for example, the changing strength of the economies of market density which are present in aviation has had implications for primary and secondary destinations, and increasing aircraft ranges have had implications for stopover destinations. Several issues in airline economics are associated with new technology. The text discusses cost structures, utilisation and pricing, booking systems, new aircraft types and the LCC phenomenon.

Aviation advances have given rise to the LCC phenomenon with its focus on low price and no frills. Competition from the LCC is creating problems for the major airlines, many of which are loss-making, and which find it difficult to match the fares of the LCC. The chief difference between LCC and traditional airlines fall into three groups: service savings, operational savings and overhead savings. The distinctive differences between LCC and legacy carriers is discussed in the text.

While aviation can help tourism to develop within a region by bringing in tourists, inadequate aviation infrastructure, such as limited airport capacity, can constrain tourism development. When limited airport capacity exists, usually for environmental reasons or simply through poor planning, the excess demand that can build up at the airport is handled through either air congestion or slot restriction. Here, government policy (taxation, subsidisation and regulation) need to be determined together.

Another aspect of the aviation–tourism connection concerns aviation and tourism taxes. Does a country wish to encourage tourism, and maximise economic benefits of tourism, by keeping taxes, on both aviation and ground tourism, low? Or does it wish to make use of its market power, and use foreign tourists as a source of revenue? Whichever of these options it chooses, it will need to determine at which level – aviation or ground tourism – such taxes are best levied.

Finally, the development of alliances between ostensibly independent airlines has allowed those airlines to create a wider network and services than they might otherwise be able to provide. Depending on the how and the where, such alliances can either encourage tourism through cheaper fares and improved networks or constrain it through raised fares and anti-competitive behaviour. There are costs to the individual airlines in forming alliances, usually centring on ensuring connecting flights and baggage handling, but in general the benefits appear to outweigh any costs involved. Competition authorities are now paying more attention to tourism implications of airline mergers and alliances.

TOURISM AND THE ENVIRONMENT

Chapter 17 explores issues in valuing the environment. Throughout the text it is emphasised that estimation of the social and environmental effects of tourism is essential for a comprehensive understanding of the industry and its role in society. The environment is important in attracting tourism flows with their attendant economic effects. Conservation of valued environmental features can help to maintain tourism visitation and tourism's contribution to the economy. Tourists, however, can also 'love the environment to death', impairing the very thing that attracts them and bringing about its deterioration and destruction. Satisfactorily resolving this problem is important to the tourist industry, especially given a limited (and dwindling) supply of pristine environments and with tourism demand expected to grow into the future. Determining, enumerating and measuring environmental costs and benefits can be very challenging. This chapter explores the broad positive and negative environmental impacts of tourism and examines the techniques by which these environmental effects are measured.

Tourism affects the environment through its interplay with *natural, human* and *built resources*. Tourism impacts on the environment are both direct and indirect and often are not easily observable. Conversely, the range and quality of such resources can influence tourism flows. Thus, attention to environmental features of the tourism experience can result in an outward shift of tourism demand thereby increasing producer surplus. Over-development, however, can impose costs on industry stakeholders as well as on the wider community.

Market prices serve as signals or incentives to guide resources and products into their most highly valued uses. If there are no markets for some valuable resources and products or if markets do not function properly, the resulting resource allocation will not be optimal. There are three major sources of market failure that are relevant to the environmental impacts associated with tourism. These relate to lack of property rights to environmental resources, public goods and externalities. The inevitable result is overuse, abuse, congestion and quality degradation of increasingly scarce environmental resources.

The text discusses how the 'public good' aspect of many environmental resources leads to their under-provision. Private markets will fail to allocate sufficient resources to the production of the so-called public goods, including environmental quality, resulting in a misallocation of resources. Collective action is needed to provide such goods in sufficient quantities.

The total economic value of a tourism environmental amenity is composed of its use value (actual use value) and non-use value. Components of non-use value are option, quasi-option, existence, bequest and vicarious value. Within this framework of thinking, the environmental impacts of tourism activity may be measured either directly (through their obvious price effects in the marketplace) or indirectly (through the construction of proxy prices).

The text discusses various measurement techniques available for valuing environments in tourism contexts and which can be used to inform policy making. The techniques available to measure the non-use of an environmental amenity include stated preferences (e.g. contingency valuation and contingent choice), revealed preferences (e.g. hedonic pricing and travel cost) and imputed valuation (e.g. replacement cost, damage cost avoided and production factor method). Revealed preference methods tend to be the more reliable, but stated preferences can be applied in more situations and can generate more data. Imputed valuation techniques are particularly useful when people actually spend money to prevent loss of an environmental amenity.

Non-direct use valuation techniques allow for planning and better management of environmental resources by affording resources non-market values that traditional resource economics has never had. The text discusses the use of these techniques in evaluating changes to natural environments associated with tourism development.

Chapter 18 describes and evaluates actual economic instruments that we use to try to forestall, or at least lessen, the adverse environmental impacts of tourism activity. The environmental impacts of visits to, say, a penguin colony, rainforest or heritage monument are all likely to be quite different. Moreover, the different resilience of different areas to tourism activity implies that similar activities will have different consequences in different locations. Such differential impacts raise the question as to what is the best way to avoid or reduce any adverse environmental impact. Economic theory informs us that because of market failure, the optimal level of pollution will seldom be achieved in the absence of government intervention. A wide variety of economic instruments have been developed to address this question.

Much of the focus in this chapter is on policies to reduce pollution resulting from tourism. The discussion allows us to introduce a number of concepts relevant to addressing other problems arising from the environmental effects of tourism activity. We now ask two questions for any given tourism activity, namely, how much pollution control is needed? and what will be the cost of achieving this? The economists' answer to each question is phrased in marginalist terms, namely, that the level of pollution should be reduced (i.e. environmental quality increased) until the marginal benefit from a further reduction in pollution equals the marginal costs of achieving it.

In theory, there is an optimal level of such environmental pollution. The text illustrates how the optimal level can be determined graphically. Graphically, this optimal level may be determined and shown through any of three approaches: the intersection of demand and supply curves for the final product; the intersection of the firm's marginal private gain curve and the marginal damage to society curve; and the intersection of the firm's marginal abatement cost curve and the marginal damage to society curve.

The types of economic instruments that may be used to reduce the environmental impacts of tourism include voluntary agreements, bargaining, merger, direct controls, tax on output, tax on pollution, subsidies, market for pollution rights and others such as technology development and energy efficiency, education and information and codes of conduct. There has been a gradual trend towards the use of market-based instruments for environmental policy. These are designed to influence either the *price* of an environmentally adverse activity (which in turn will affect the quantity of that activity) or its *quantity* (which in turn will affect the price of that activity). In determining the best policy mix for any destination, the overriding objective should be to achieve any given level of emissions abatement at least cost. Market-based instruments provide a strong ongoing incentive for investment in technology research, development and deployment, and in business efforts to improve energy efficiency.

There are several issues that attend the use of economic instruments in their protection of the environment from any adverse effects of tourism, including uncertainty, boundary problems, transaction costs and public good considerations.

In ideal conditions – perfectly competitive markets, perfect information and certainty, and no transaction costs – both taxes and quantity controls, if correctly designed, can be used to establish a common price signal across countries and sectors. Under uncertainty, price instruments are more efficient than quantity instruments when the marginal benefit curve is flat relative to the marginal social cost curve, but quantitative limits are more efficient the steeper is the marginal benefit curve relative to the marginal social cost curve.

Chapter 19 addresses the issue of climate change and tourism. Typically, tourism and climate change has been considered as 'a two-way street'. The same as for other industries, the tourism industry contributes to climate change through its generation of GHGs to meet tourist needs. Climate change, in turn, has increasing substantial effects on tourism flows, shifting market shares of domestic and international destinations.

Human-induced climate change is an externality on a global scale which, in the absence of policy intervention, is not 'corrected' through any institution or market. GHGs are negative externalities from industrial activity (including tourism). Economic activities that produce GHG emissions bring about climate change, thereby imposing costs on the world and on future generations. However, emitters typically do not directly face the full consequences of the costs of their actions. The discussion in the text emphasises that the climate is a public good. As discussed in Chapter 17, markets do not automatically provide the right type and quantity of public goods, since in the absence of public policy there are limited or no returns to private investors for doing so. Those who fail to pay for it cannot be excluded from enjoying its benefits and one person's enjoyment of the climate does not diminish the capacity of others to enjoy it also. Markets for relevant goods and services (energy, land use, innovation, etc.) do not reflect the full costs and benefits of different consumption and investment choices for the climate.

Climate change will directly impact on a country's tourism industry and the benefits it creates through loss or degradation of attractions, the costs of adaptation and replacement of capital infrastructure. Climate has a major influence on destination choice. As a result of changing climatic conditions, tourists are likely to entirely avoid some destinations in favour of others or else shift the timing of travel to avoid unfavourable climate conditions. Climate change generates both negative and positive impacts in the tourism sector and these impacts will vary substantially by market segment and geographic region. There are 'winners and losers' at the business, destination and nation level. Countries which rely heavily on nature-based tourism are likely to be a net losers from changing international patterns of tourism as a result of climate change.

Adaptation is a vital part of the response by the tourist industry to the challenge of climate change. Its objectives are to reduce tourism's vulnerability to climatic change and variability (thereby reducing their negative impacts) and to enhance tourism's capability to capture any benefits from climate change. Adaptation operates at two broad levels: building adaptive capacity (creating the information and regulatory, institutional and managerial conditions needed to support adaptation) and delivering adaptive actions (taking steps to help reduce vulnerability to climate risks or to exploit opportunities). Ignoring climate change is not a viable option for tourism stakeholders – over the long term inaction will be far more costly than adaptation. However, tourism is a footloose export industry, and both suppliers and consumers will cross borders to the extent that a destination becomes less attractive due to climate change.

Tourism generates a carbon footprint both directly (through GHG emissions associated with production of a tourism service) and indirectly (through GHG emissions associated with the supply of inputs into tourism production). The carbon *intensity* footprint of tourism refers to the GHGs directly and indirectly associated with tourism activity. The carbon *impact* footprint of tourism refers to how changes in tourism impact on overall GHGs – this depends on its carbon intensity and also on how other industries are impacted on by changes in tourism. Estimation of tourism's carbon impact requires CGE modelling to determine the net changes in the outputs of different industries in the economy. Most policy questions are questions about impact, not just intensity.

The text distinguishes four major mitigation strategies for addressing GHG emissions from tourism, namely, reducing energy use, improving energy efficiency, increasing the use of renewable or carbon neutral energy and sequestering CO_2. Tourism will be affected by the different types of climate change mitigation policies, all of which will increase the cost base of tourism firms. There are two main types of market-based instruments that play an important role in mitigating the effects of climate change on tourism: *carbon taxes* (in which a tax is imposed for each unit of emissions, thus setting a price and allowing the quantity of abatement to emerge from the market) and *Emissions Trading Schemes* (ETS, in which a total quota or ceiling for emissions is set, individual quota permits within that set are sold and the individual quotas are allowed to be traded, thereby setting their price). An ETS involves setting a target for the number of permits to be allocated, allocating them among conflicting users and then policing their use to ensure that firms create GHGs only to the extent that they have permits.

While the aviation sector is the largest emitter of GHGs in the tourism industry globally, no convincing case has been made for treating aviation differently, either more or less favourably (other than under general arrangements for footloose industries). Special taxes or restrictions on aviation, if they are included in the ETS, will be ineffective in reducing GHGs. When an effective and comprehensive ETS is in place, mandatory requirements or taxes imposed on specific industries such as aviation will be ineffective in reducing GHGs, given the quota imposed by the cap.

Although emissions trading is likely to be the key instrument used to reduce emissions over time, complementary policies will be needed. There is a role for governments in setting regulatory standards, supporting innovation of new low emission technology and encouraging changes in household behaviour. Destinations will tailor a package of measures that suits their specific circumstances, including the existing tax and governance system, participation in regional initiatives to reduce emissions (e.g. via trading schemes) and the structure of the economy and characteristics of specific sectors.

In practice, there are difficulties involved in identifying the optimum price of carbon and the optimum quantity of emissions. Over a particular time horizon, the most efficient market-based instrument for climate change mitigation policy will depend on how the total costs of abatement change with the level of emissions; how the total benefits of abatement change with the level of emissions; and the degree of uncertainty about both costs and benefits of abatement.

Tourism can and must play a significant role in addressing climate change as part of its broader commitment to sustainable development and the United Nations Millennium Development Goals. Economic analysis can contribute to our understanding of the different types of issues raised by climate change, in policy formulation, and in analysing the implications for tourism.

DESTINATION COMPETITIVENESS

Chapter 20 addresses issues of destination competitiveness. To achieve competitive advantage for its tourism industry, a destination must ensure that its overall attractiveness, and the tourist experience, is superior to that of the many alternative destinations available to potential visitors. Destination competitiveness is linked to the ability of a country or region to deliver goods and services that perform better than other destinations on those aspects of the tourism experience considered to be important by tourists.

Factors that determine the *market shares* of different destinations include the cost of tourism to the visitor. This includes the cost of transport services to and from the destination as well as the cost of ground content (accommodation, tour services, food and beverage, entertainment, etc.). Changing costs in particular destinations relative to others are an important economic influence on destination shares of total travel abroad. Qualitative factors are also important. These include such variables as transport access, health and safety issues, political stability, tourist appeal, destination image, quality of service, nature of attractions, effectiveness of tourism promotion and so on. The strength of some of these factors often reflects changing fashions and tastes.

It is important to know which factors determine the competitiveness of the tourism industry. It is useful for the industry and government to understand where a destination's competitive position is weakest and strongest. It is helpful for both industry and government to know how destination competitiveness (price and non-price) is changing and why these changes are occurring. Patterns of changes in demand need to be assessed in the light of changes in destination competitiveness.

The development of a model of destination competitiveness allows tourism stakeholders in both the private and the public sector to identify key strengths and weaknesses of their destination from the visitor perspective, highlight opportunities for tourism development and develop strategies to counter possible threats to future visitation.

Integrated models of destination competitiveness attempt to bring together the main elements of national and firm competitiveness into one such overall model of destination competitiveness. It is difficult, however, to develop such an overall model of destination competitiveness comprising both quantitative and qualitative variables. In particular, there is no single or unique set of competitiveness indicators that apply to all destinations at all times. For any given element of destination competitiveness, any number of attributes or indicators may be employed as measures. The importance of competitiveness indicators will vary across locations, depending on product mix and target market segments.

For specified market segments, it is possible to identify the most important attributes as perceived by tourists and to compare the performance of different destinations on the selected attributes. The approach offers a basis for strategy development and policy formulation for the different market segments of the destination tourism industry.

The Travel and Tourism Competitiveness Index, which covered 133 countries in 2009, is discussed in the text. This index is designed to help explore the factors that drive travel and tourism competitiveness worldwide, so providing a basis for implementing policies on a country-by-country basis. It is composed of 14 pillars organised into three sub-indexes capturing broad categories of variables that drive or facilitate travel and tourism competitiveness: regulatory framework; business environment and infrastructure; and human, cultural and natural resources. Despite some limitations this index is useful for highlighting the strengths and weaknesses of different destinations and can inform policy making to enhance destination competitiveness.

Factors that impinge on price competitiveness include exchange rates, inflation, the price of labour, productivity, export booms, tax structures and levels, infrastructure charges, fuel prices and environmental charges. The influence of each is discussed in the text.

Destination price competitiveness indices attempt to compare across different destinations the prices of goods and services that tourists actually buy (as opposed to general price indices that include goods and services that tourists seldom or never purchase).

The chapter discusses three measures recently developed by the authors. The Destination Price Competitiveness Index is the most comprehensive indicator of tourism price competitiveness. It measures only prices that enter the tourism bundle and thus is highly reflective of tourism. It enables cross-country comparisons at a point in time and can be calculated over time to indicate trends. With appropriate weights, it can be used to develop an indicator of changes in a country's overall tourism competitiveness. It is, however, the most data intensive of the measures. The Tourism Trade Weighted Index is an index of exchange rates with the weights being determined by the relative importance of the different countries in tourism inbound and outbound expenditures. It indicates effective exchange rates and provides policy makers with an ongoing monitor of the home country's price competitiveness, acting as a leading indicator of future tourism flows to and from the home country. In similar vein, the Aviation Trade Weighted Index provides an indicator of the change in the international competitive pressure on a country's aviation sector resulting from changes in exchange rates. It weights different currencies according to how important different countries' airlines are as competitors in markets operated in by home-country airlines.

The type of price competitiveness index employed depends on the research or policy needs at a given time. In some situations, quickly calculated, simple measures are most useful, while in others, more detailed and accurate measures are required. The measures used will also depend on the data available – some countries have very detailed tourism and price statistics, while statistics in other countries can be rudimentary.

Destination competitiveness is a goal that is achievable through informed decision-making and strategic choice. If the limitations of the various competitiveness indices are recognised, they can be valuable tools for policy formulation for any tourism destination to achieve and maintain competitive advantage over competitors, as well as empirical studies of tourism demand. The outcomes will be more informed policy making regarding the type of tourism development most likely to enhance resident quality of economic and social life.

DIRECTIONS FOR TOURISM RESEARCH

The topics discussed in the text are only some of the issues that could have been discussed in a book on tourism economics and policy. Clearly which topics to include and which to exclude come down to matters of judgement. We are aware of a number of important topics that have not been included in this volume. For example, despite discussion throughout the text on the importance of the workings of labour markets in estimating the impacts of shocks to tourism demand and supply, there is no chapter dedicated to a discussion of tourism employment. Another topic involves tourism transportation in modes other than air travel. The importance of land-based transport (train, bus, car, etc.) for tourist travel is well recognised as is the growing importance of cruise tourism globally. Others might point out that the book devotes insufficient space to issues of the role of tourism in the economic development of small countries and those with low GDP per capita. We plead guilty but one can do only so much in one text. What we have attempted to do is to consider each topic in some depth. This has rendered them each rather long but, we hope, of detailed content.

Another topic that might be regarded as relatively neglected in the book is that of sustainability. Increasingly one finds this concept discussed in the tourism literature as an ideal that should guide destination management and industry operations. A reading of the text would confirm, however, that issues relevant to sustainability are discussed in some detail throughout the text. We do not regard ourselves as having adopted a narrow economic stance regarding any of the topics addressed in the text. We are well aware that social and environmental effects are invariably present alongside the more purely economic effects associated with tourism shocks including policy initiatives. Our view of sustainability is the traditional one that acknowledges the importance of considering the social, environmental and economic effects of tourism development strategies and policy formulation. While recognising this, the focus of the text is on the economic issues. Our broader concern with issues beyond those that are more narrowly 'economic' is evident from the material on CBA and impact assessment as well as the general approach adopted in our exploration of the issues in and around each topic.

In each of the topics discussed in the book ongoing research is progressively expanding the boundaries of our knowledge. The final chapter attempts to highlight the specific directions that research on any given topic area might take. The directions for further research highlighted there are just some of those that arise in the topics covered in the book. Other research topics relate to areas that are important but not covered in the book. Changing global trends (economic, social, demographic, political, technological and environmental) will continually pose challenges to economic theory and policy and the ways we analyse tourism activity. Whatever the specific topics that researchers will address in the coming years, it is clear that tourism economics provides a fertile ground for research with the potential to inform policy making to improve socio-economic prosperity in all destinations worldwide.

TOURISM DEMAND AND FORECASTING

CHAPTER 2

DEMAND FOR TOURISM

LEARNING OBJECTIVES

After reading this chapter, you should be able to:

1. Define tourism demand, distinguishing between demand for travel to a destination and demand for a particular tourism product.

2. Differentiate between price and non-price determinants of tourism demand.

3. Evaluate the importance of each of price elasticity, income elasticity, cross-price elasticity and advertising elasticity as it relates to tourism demand.

4. Outline the important issues that must be addressed in modelling tourism demand.

5. Appreciate the relative importance of the various quantitative and qualitative factors found by researchers to influence the demand for international tourism arrivals.

6. Understand the strengths and weaknesses inherent in the present state of tourism demand modelling.

2.1 INTRODUCTION

Tourism demand refers to the willingness and ability of consumers to buy different amounts of a tourism product at different prices during any one period of time. Following standard theory, the demand for any good or service can be expected to be influenced by a myriad of price and non-price factors, including the size of the market (population), income, tastes, advertising and promotion, seasonality, buyer expectations of future prices, product availability, prices of substitute and complementary products, the amount of leisure time available and other factors such as special events, immigration levels or random shocks. As we shall discuss, there are particular problems estimating the demand for 'tourism' since 'tourism' is not a good or service like others.

2.2 FACTORS INFLUENCING TOURISM DEMAND

The market demand function for a product or service is the relationship between the quantity demanded of the product and the various factors that influence this quantity.

For tourism demand it is useful to distinguish between the demand for travel to a destination (e.g. visitor arrivals and expenditure) and the demand for a particular tourism-related products or services (e.g. hotel rooms, restaurant meals, cabins on cruiseships or sunglasses).

2.2.1 DEMAND FOR TRAVEL TO A DESTINATION

One helpful way of investigating the travel decision is to distinguish two broad determinants of the demand for tourism: *price* factors and *non-price* factors.

Price factors. The cost of tourism to the visitor includes the cost of *transport services* to and from the destination and the cost of *ground content* (accommodation, tour services, food and beverage, entertainment, etc.). The prices paid by an international tourist who must convert one currency into another will also be influenced by prevailing exchange rates, and prices in the destination as compared to prices in their home country.

Non-price factors. These include socio-economic and demographic factors such as population, income in origin country, leisure time, education, occupation, availability of leisure time, immigration stock and the like and qualitative factors including consumer tastes, tourist appeal, destination image, quality of tourist services, tourist preferences, special events, destination marketing and promotion, cultural ties, weather conditions and so on. Qualitative factors can have positive effects (boost tourism demand) or negative effects (reduce tourism demand) depending on the qualitative effect being studied. Thus, special events tend to boost tourism demand to a destination, while the incidence of terrorism tends to lessen it.

2.2.2 DEMAND FOR A TOURISM PRODUCT

Regarding the demand for a particular tourism product or service, the most important variables affecting the demand for any good include the price of the good (P_x), consumer's income (Y), the number of consumers in the market (N), the price of related products (substitutes P_s and complements P_c), consumer tastes (T), level of marketing/promotion expenditure (M) and other variables such as consumer price expectations, interest rates and so on.

Thus we can specify the following general function of the demand for the commodity (Q_x) measured in physical units, where the dots at the end of the equation refer to the other determinants of demand that are specific to the particular firm and product:

$$Q_x = f\,(P_x, Y, N, P_s, P_c, T, M, \ldots) \tag{2.1}$$

In a tourism context, Q_x might refer to visitor numbers, car rentals, tickets to attractions, number of airline passengers, and numbers of T-shirts sold, swimsuits, hotel rooms demanded and so forth.

2.2.2.1 Tourism demand and price

Economic theory suggests that price and tourism demand have an inverse relationship. As the price of a tourism product falls, the quantity demanded for it should rise, and as its price rises, the quantity demanded should fall. This negative relationship (commonly called the law of demand) captures the income effect and substitution effect evident in buyer behaviour.

Income effect: a price fall increases real incomes for consumers and therefore increases levels of consumption of most products. Thus, as the price of a tourism product falls, its price relative to consumer income falls and consumers can afford more of the tourism product given the same income.

Substitution effect: given their increased real income, consumers can buy more of this now relatively cheaper tourism product substituting it for other now relatively more expensive products.

By way of example, as the price of a particular travel destination falls (say, a particular promotion reduces the price of air fare/accommodation throughout the USA), a person may undertake more travel in the USA or longer travel or more expensive travel (income effect). The person may be inclined to visit the USA rather than other now relatively more expensive destinations (substitution effect). Figure 2.1a shows the inverse relationship between price and quantity demanded.

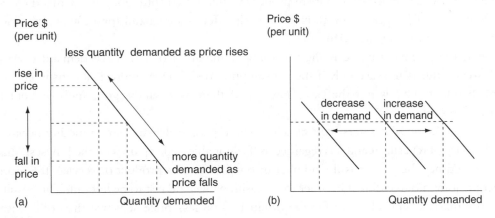

Figure 2.1 Changes in quantity demanded and in demand:(a) Price and quantity demanded (b) Non-price and demand

2.2.2.2 Tourism demand and non-price factors

The market demand curve for a good or service shows the various quantities of the commodity demanded in the market per unit of time at various alternative prices of the commodity while holding everything else constant. The things held constant in drawing the market demand curve for a commodity include those determinants of demand in Equation 2.1 – incomes, the prices of substitute and complementary goods, tastes and the number of consumers in the market. Changes in the price of a product, holding other things constant, change the quantity demanded and can be represented by a shift along the demand curve

Following standard theory, demand for a tourism product should increase and more of the product should be demanded at each price if non-price factors work in favour of the product. This could occur if population increases; income increases; tastes change in favour of the product; consumers expect the product's price to rise shortly; the amount of available leisure time increases; and the price of substitute products rises or the price of complementary products falls.

Conversely, demand for a tourism product should decrease and less of the product should be demanded at each price if non-price factors work against purchasing the product. This could occur if population decreases; income decreases; tastes change against the product; consumers expect the product's price to fall shortly; the amount of available leisure time decreases; and the price of substitute products falls or the price of complementary products rises. Figure 2.1b shows the effects of non-price influences on tourism demand. Changes in these factors cause the entire demand curve to shift left or right, indicating a reduction or increase in demand at any given price.

Tourism demand is affected by price and non-price factors. Changes in price will affect the quantity demanded of a tourism product resulting in a shift along the demand curve (Figure 2.1a). Changes in non-price factors will affect the demand for a tourism product at any given price (Figure 2.1b).

A market demand curve is the horizontal summation of individual demand curves. However, this is the case only if the consumption decisions of individual consumers are independent. This is not the case, however, if there is a bandwagon, snob or Veblen effect present.

The bandwagon effect refers to a situation where people demand a commodity because others are purchasing it and it is regarded as 'fashionable' to keep up with the Joneses. That is, sometimes the greater is the number of purchasers of a product or service, the more people join in purchasing it in order to be 'fashionable' and not to be left out. This results in the market demand curve for the product to be less price sensitive than otherwise. Some tourism destinations become fashionable for a time as tourism destination life cycle models indicate (Butler, 1980).

The snob effect is the opposite of the bandwagon effect as some consumers seek to be different and exclusive by demanding less of a product as more people consume it. Thus, as the price of some product falls and more people purchase the product, some people stop buying it in order to assert their independence 'from the mob'. This tends to make the market demand curve steeper with quantity demanded less sensitive to price reductions. In tourism, the demand for Low-Cost Carriers (LCC) may foster a snob effect among a proportion of travellers, who patronise the full-service carriers.

The Veblen effect refers to a situation where some individuals seek to impress others by demanding more of certain 'high status' products or services as their price rises. Also known as 'conspicuous consumption', tourism examples could include the demand for a stay at an expensive island resort whose facilities are no better than some other less expensive but less prestigious competitors. This results in a steeper market demand curve reflecting less price sensitivity by certain tourists.

Despite the presence of these effects in certain circumstances, researchers have tended to assume that the market demand curve for most tourism products and services can be obtained simply by the horizontal summation of the individual downward-sloping demand curves.

In tourism we often find examples of *joint demand*. This occurs when the demand for two or more products (or services) is interdependent, normally because they are used together. Thus, if the only means to access an island is by ferry, accommodation on the island and ferry tickets will be jointly demanded. While the quantity demanded of both will increase or decrease together, their prices may change at a different rate depending on the availability of substitutes (e.g. the opening up of an air route to compete with the ferry). To take another example, the demand for accommodation in an island resort may be associated with the demand for dive tours and parasailing. In such cases, the goods are also referred to as 'complements' (see below)

We also note the concept of derived demand wherein demand for one good or service occurs as a result of demand for another. Demand for transport is a good example of derived demand, as users of transport very often consume the service not because they benefit from consumption directly (except in cases such as pleasure cruises), but because they wish to partake in other consumption within a destination.

2.3 TOURISM DEMAND AND ELASTICITY

In broad terms, *elasticity* describes the sensitivity of one variable to changes in another variable. That is, it measures how much one variable changes in direct response to changes in another variable. Four forms of elasticity may be distinguished here.

1. *Price elasticity*: the extent to which demand for a tourism product changes because of a change in the price of that product itself. For example, an increase in air fares will, other things equal, result in reduced passenger numbers in air travel.

2. *Income elasticity*: the extent to which demand for a tourism product changes because of changes in the level of consumer income. For example, as individual and national wealth rises, more air travel or leisure cruising will result.

3. *Cross-price elasticity*: the extent to which demand for a tourism product changes because of changes in the price of substitute goods and complementary goods. For example, the demand for air travel in Europe will be affected by changes in the price of train or ship travel (substitute goods) or changes in the price of accommodation or car hire (complementary goods).

4. *Marketing elasticity*: the responsiveness of sales to changes in marketing/advertising expenditures. Thus a tour operator may advertise on radio or TV or a destination may promote itself in newspapers and magazines, generating increased visitation and sales revenues. The marketing elasticity measures the responsiveness of demand to a dollar change in marketing expenditure.

Broadly, demand for a tourism product is classified as either:

- *Elastic* when tourism demand is relatively sensitive to changes in prices or income. This tends to be the case when a particular tourism product faces competitive substitutes or is relatively expensive.
- *Inelastic* when tourism demand is relatively insensitive to a change in prices or income. This tends to be the case when the particular tourism product faces few, if any, substitutes or is relatively inexpensive.

2.3.1 PRICE ELASTICITY OF DEMAND

Figure 2.2 shows two demand curves faced by an airline. Suppose D_H is the demand for holiday travel and D_B is the demand for business travel. At price P_0 the demand by holiday and business travellers will be equal, with Q_0 air services demanded by each group. But if

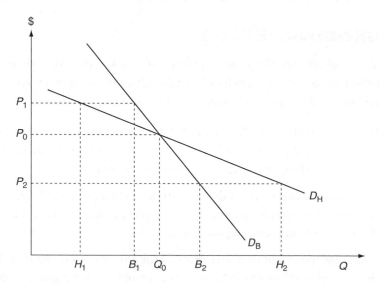

Figure 2.2 Price changes, elasticity and change in quantity demanded

the price of an air ticket were to increase to P_1, the quantity of air services demanded by holiday travellers would fall proportionately by much more than the quantity of air services demanded by business travellers. Following the price rise the demand by holiday travellers is H_1, while that of business travellers is B_1. If price were to fall to P_2, the quantity of air services demanded by holiday travellers would be H_2 and that by business travellers would be B_2. In this case, the increase in quantity demanded of air services by holiday travellers would increase proportionately by more than the quantity demanded by business travellers. This depicts a situation where the demand for holiday travel is more price elastic than the demand for business travel.

We can estimate price elasticity as an arc or point measure. The arc price elasticity of demand for any particular tourism product (ε) may be expressed as:

$$\varepsilon = \frac{\% \text{ change in the quantity demanded of the tourism product}}{\% \text{ change in the price of the tourism product}}$$

Suppose a boutique Paris hotel dropped the average price of its rooms by 10% and, as a consequence, its occupation rate increases by 20%, *ceteris paribus*.

$$\varepsilon = \frac{\% \text{ change in quantity demanded}}{\% \text{ change in price}} = \frac{20\%}{-10\%} = -2.0$$

The arc price elasticity of demand is 2.0. This simply means that for every 1% fall in the price there is a 2% rise in the demand, suggesting that customers are price sensitive to accommodation at that particular Parisian hotel (demand is price elastic). Given this, the hotel might maintain high sales or increase its total revenue in a competitive environment if it kept its room prices low.

Point elasticity of demand measures the price elasticity at a specific point on the demand curve. The point elasticity of demand is the slope of a demand curve at that price multiplied by the ratio of price to quantity. Because point elasticity is for an infinitesimally small change in price and quantity, it is defined in differentials as follows:

$$\frac{\mathrm{d}Q/Q}{\mathrm{d}P/P} = \frac{\mathrm{d}Q}{\mathrm{d}P}\frac{P}{Q}$$

Note: when discussing price elasticity of demand, we ignore the negative sign (the sign will always be negative for price elasticity of demand) and just focus on the absolute figure.

The price elasticity for a tourism product will vary depending on

- The *availability of substitutes*. The more substitutes faced by the product, the more sensitive its demand will be to price changes. Thus a large number of motels along a highway may help to keep prices low.

- The *product price relative to income*. The price elasticity of demand for a product depends on the importance of the product in consumer budgets. Demand tends to be more price elastic for more expensive products. For this reason, the demand for international holidays, for example, tends to be more price sensitive than the demand for domestic holidays.
- Whether the product is a *normal good* or a *luxury*. Demand tends to be more elastic for luxury products. The demand for four and five star accommodation (luxury), for example, tends to be more price elastic than the demand for lower-standard accommodation.
- *Time*. The price elasticity of demand is greater the longer the time period allowed for consumers to adjust to a change in price. Demand is less elastic in the short run (reflecting immediate needs and limited available choice) but more elastic in the long run. For example, travellers may pay a higher price to secure travel or accommodation if they are in a hurry (less elastic), but will look around to gain a lower price if they have time (more elastic). It takes time for consumers to learn about the availability of substitutes and to adjust their purchasing patterns to a price change.
- Whether a price change is considered to be permanent or temporary. For example, a 'one-day sale' of discounted hotel rooms will call forth a different demand response than a permanent decrease of the same magnitude

2.3.1.1 Elasticity and total revenue

Tourism managers need a good working knowledge of price elasticity of demand because it relates directly to total revenue. The price elasticity of demand indicates the effect that a change in price will have on the total revenue generated. This is because total revenue TR is equal to price (average revenue) times the number of units sold. The price elasticity of demand for a product or service is an important indicator of how TR received from the sale of that product varies as its price changes. Thus, a small percentage price increase in a tourism-related product:

(1) reduces TR if demand is elastic ($\varepsilon > 1$)

(2) leaves TR unchanged if the elasticity is unity ($\varepsilon = 1$)

(3) increases TR if demand is inelastic ($\varepsilon < 1$)

In the first case the percentage reduction in the quantity purchased is greater than the percentage increase in the price of the product, and in the last case, the relative reduction in quantity purchased is less than the relative rise in price.

Figure 2.3 shows the relationship between price elasticity of demand and total revenue from sales.

Marginal revenue (MR) is the extra revenue generated by a one-unit increase in sales. MR is positive where demand is elastic and negative when demand is inelastic. Since the MR

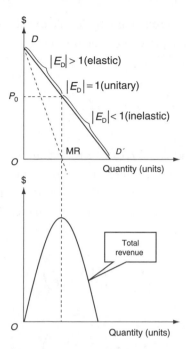

Figure 2.3 Elasticity of demand and total revenue

is positive for prices above P_0, this part of the demand curve has price elasticity greater than 1. Thus, rises in price above P_0 will result in reduced sales revenues as shown in the lower figure. Conversely, since the MR is negative for prices below P_0, this part of the demand curve has price elasticity less than 1. Thus, reductions in price below P_0 will result in reduced sales revenues. These relationships also hold true for non-linear demand curves. The point where MR is 0 always divides the elastic and inelastic regions of the demand curve.

The point of unitary elasticity on a demand curve corresponds to the point where the MR curve crosses the quantity axis. That is, MR is 0 where demand is unitary elastic (a 1% increase in price causes quantity demanded to decrease by 1%). This also implies that there is no change in total revenue. Sales revenue is maximised when the price of the product is set at P_0.

Knowledge of the price elasticity of demand for a product enables managers to answer questions such as the following: How much of an increase in sales can we expect if we reduce our prices by 5%? To increase the amount we sell by 15%, how much must we reduce price?

Because the price and quantity demand for any tourism product are inversely related, a firm will need to ensure that any rise in the price of its product will outweigh any fall in sales or it will lose total revenue, and that any fall in the price of its product will generate extra sales that outweigh the fall in price or it would again lose total revenue. That is, to

45

raise total revenue, firms should follow the basic rule of thumb that says: raise the price of inelastic products but lower the price of elastic products.

An estimation of the price elasticity of demand, ε, can also help to determine the optimal price of a product.

$$MR = P\left(1 - \frac{1}{\varepsilon}\right)$$

Marginal cost (MC) is the additional cost of producing one extra unit of output. A firm wishing to maximise its profit will therefore produce up to the point where the MC of the last unit produced is equal to the MR derived from its sale. The firm's profit-maximising condition will be discussed further in Chapter 4. Since MR equals MC if a firm is maximising profit, then

$$MC = P\left(1 - \frac{1}{\varepsilon}\right)$$

Solving for P we obtain

$$P = MC\left(\frac{1}{1 - \frac{1}{\varepsilon}}\right)$$

This is a very useful result. It indicates that the optimal price of a product depends on its MC and its price elasticity of demand.

Suppose that the MC of a ferry tour is $10 and that its price elasticity of demand equals 1.5. Thus its optimal price is $30. That is,

$$P = 10\left(\frac{1}{1 - \frac{1}{1.5}}\right) = \$30$$

The optimal price depends heavily on the price elasticity of demand. Holding the value of MC constant, a product's optimal price is inversely related to its price elasticity of demand. Thus if the ferry tour elasticity of demand were 2 rather than 1.5, its optimal price would be $20. That is,

$$P = 10\left(\frac{1}{1 - \frac{1}{2}}\right) = \$20$$

Estimates of the price elasticity of demand for tourism are important for destination managers as well as for private operators. For example, formulating an environmental policy of carbon taxes for aviation requires information on the price sensitivity of passengers to predict the effectiveness of the policy in both reducing demand for aviation and generating taxation revenues. If the airlines can charge all of the extra costs to the passengers without decreasing demand, the policy has no effect other than increasing prices paid by passengers and generating additional taxation revenues.

2.3.2 INCOME ELASTICITY OF DEMAND

An understanding of income elasticity is important for tourism organisations. Tourism, especially international tourism, can be a relatively expensive and even discretionary product the demand for which is responsive to income changes. As individual and national real income and wealth rise (or fall), the tourism firm will need to know the extent to which demand for its product will rise (or fall) with them.

Income elasticity of tourism demand (ε_y) is measured as:

$$\varepsilon_y = \frac{\text{percentage change in the quantity demanded of the tourism product}}{\text{percentage change in income}}$$

Tourism products may be classified as normal, luxuries, necessities and inferior depending on their income elasticity of demand

Normal goods reflect a positive relationship between income and tourism demand – demand for the tourism product rises as income rises, and vice versa. This is the case with most tourism products ($\varepsilon_y > 0$).

For instance, if a 15% rise in Thailand's household annual income brings about a 10% rise in overseas travel by Thais (*ceteris paribus*), then the elasticity of demand for overseas travel by Thais would be

$$\varepsilon_y = \frac{\% \text{ change in demand for overseas travel}}{\% \text{ change in income}} = \frac{10\%}{15\%} = +0.67$$

This suggests that for every 1% rise in real income there is a 0.67% rise in the demand by Thais for overseas travel. That is, outbound tourism by Thais is income elastic.

Luxury goods are those that have a high income elasticity of demand, exceeding 1 ($\varepsilon_y > 1$). This might include first class air travel or hotel accommodation.

Necessities have a low income elasticity of demand, either at 0 or marginally above 0. In a tourism context this might include the price of public transport.

Inferior goods imply a negative relationship between income and tourism demand. The income elasticity of demand is less than 0 ($\varepsilon_y < 0$). Examples might include holidays at a domestic caravan park (inferior good) as opposed to a hotel or motel (normal good), or five star resort (luxury good).

Figure 2.4 displays the relationships between income and tourism demand.

Tourism firms providing services with high income elasticities of demand (cruise tourism?) are likely to grow relatively rapidly as incomes rise in an expanding economy, whereas firms producing services with a low income elasticity of demand (domestic facilities?) are likely to experience more modest expansion. On the other hand, if the economy

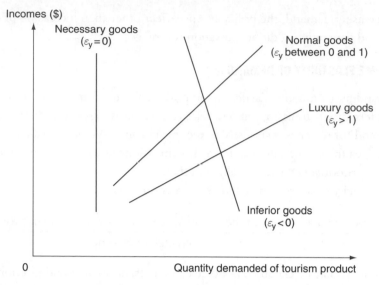

Incomes ($)

Necessary goods
($\varepsilon_y = 0$)

Normal goods
(ε_y between 0 and 1)

Luxury goods
($\varepsilon_y > 1$)

Inferior goods
($\varepsilon_y < 0$)

0

Quantity demanded of tourism product

Figure 2.4 Income elasticity of demand

experiences a recession, and incomes fall sharply, firms producing products and services with low income elasticities (caravan parks and campgrounds?) are likely to experience less reduction in sales than those delivering products with high income elasticities. There is a particular concern that the effects of the Global Financial Crisis (GFC) impact most severely on luxury tourism products and markets.

Income elasticity can also play an important role in the marketing activities of tourism organisations. If per capita or household income is found to be an important determinant of the demand for a particular product, this can affect the location of and nature of sales outlets (e.g. cheap eats vs gourmet restaurant).

Information on income elasticities is also useful in developing marketing strategies for products. Thus they can help to identify more precisely potential markets for products (which types of consumers are most likely to purchase the product) and to determine the most suitable media for promotional campaigns to reach the targeted audience. Thus, products having a high income elasticity of demand (business class travel?) can be promoted as being luxurious and stylish, whereas goods having a low income elasticity of demand (guesthouses and pensions) can be promoted as being economical.

2.3.3 CROSS-PRICE ELASTICITY OF DEMAND

In addition to setting the price of their own product correctly (price elasticity) and keeping an eye on changes in the level of national income (income elasticity), the tourism firm needs to appreciate the effects on demand for its products brought about by changes in the price of substitute and complementary products.

Cross-elasticity of demand between goods A and B

$$= \frac{\% \text{ change in the quantity demanded of A}}{\% \text{ change in the price of B}}$$

- *Substitute goods* are those that can be used in place of one another. The products exhibit positive cross-price elasticity – a rise in the price of one product will lead to a rise in the quantity demanded of the other product and vice versa. For example, a rise in the price of hotels may drive more tourists towards guesthouses and a fall in the price of package tours to Greece may result in less tourism to Turkey. Thus, if a 10% rise in the price of air fares from London to Paris brought about a 5% rise in the demand for train travel from London to Paris (*ceteris paribus*), the cross-price elasticity of air travel and train travel would be:

$$E_{\text{train/air fare}} = \frac{5\% \text{ (\% change in the demand for train travel from London to Paris)}}{10\% \text{ (\% change in the price of air fare from London to Paris)}}$$
$$= +0.5$$

This suggests that for every 1% rise in the price of air fares between London and Paris there is a 0.5% rise in the demand for train travel from London to Paris. Substitute products always have a positive relationship (price of one product and the demand for the other product always move in the same direction).

- *Complementary goods* are used in conjunction with one another. The products exhibit negative cross-price elasticity – a rise in the price of one product will lead to a fall in the quantity demanded of the other product, and vice versa. For example, a rise in the price of air travel to a destination resulting in less visitation may lead to a fall in the demand for hotel accommodation in that destination.

   For example, if a 10% rise in the price of airline travel from London to Paris brought about a 8% fall in the demand for hotel accommodation in Paris (*ceteris paribus*), then the cross-price elasticity of air travel and hotel accommodation would be:

$$E_{\text{train/air fare}} = \frac{-8\% \text{ (\% change in the demand for hotel accommodation in Paris)}}{10\% \text{ (\% change in the price of air fare from London to Paris)}}$$
$$= -0.8$$

Here, for every 1% rise in the price of air fare, which reduces the demand for airline travel to Paris, there is a 0.8% fall in the demand for hotel accommodation. Complementary products have a negative relationship (price of one product and the demand for the other product always move in opposite directions).

- *Independent goods* have no relationship with each other. The products exhibit zero cross-price elasticity – a rise in the price of one product will have no effect on the quantity demanded of the other product. For example, a rise in the price of air travel between Oslo and Dublin will have no effect on the demand for pizzas in Ottawa.

Figure 2.5 displays the relationship between consumption of one good and the price of a substitute or complement. If goods A and B are substitutes, the quantity demanded of A is directly related to the price of B.

If A and B are complements, the quantity demanded of A is inversely related to the price of B. Suppose that A is destination Macau and that B is the price of accommodation in Hong Kong. Reduced accommodation prices in Hong Kong would generate more visitors to Hong Kong, thereby generating more daytrippers and overnighters to Macau.

If A and B are substitutes, the quantity demanded of A is positively related to the price of B. Suppose that A is destination Greek Islands and B is accommodation prices in the Adriatic Islands. Reduced accommodation prices in the Adriatic Islands will generate more visitors to the Adriatic and less to Greece.

While there is extensive evidence on price elasticities of demand for tourism products, estimates of cross-elasticities are much more limited. One reason is that the effects of the price change of one mode on the demand for another may be small and, therefore, difficult to disentangle statistically from the background noise in any data set.

However, it is important for a firm to know how the demand for its product is likely to respond to changes in the prices of other goods and services. For example, if the cross-price elasticity of the demand for a product with respect to the price of a competitor's product is high, a firm should respond rapidly to a competitor's price reduction if it is to avoid a loss of its sales.

Information on cross-price elasticity is essential for formulating pricing strategy and analysis of the risks associated with various products, particularly for firms with extensive

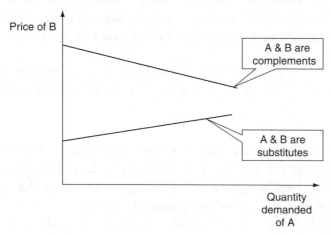

Figure 2.5 Substitute and complementary goods

product lines, where substantial substitute or complementary relations exist among the various products.

Cross-price elasticity also allows managers to measure the extent of competition in the industry. While a firm might be the sole supplier of some service within the local tourism industry, appearing to dominate some market segment, a high cross-elasticity of demand between the firm's products and products of firms in another industry indicates that the firm will not be able to raise its prices without losing sales to other firms in other industries. Tourism firms in the meetings industry, for example, may compete with firms in the communications industry, specialising in video-conferencing. Many tourism destinations compete for the same customer base (e.g. Greece and Turkey), and managers of tourism firms as well as destination managers must be mindful of prices on offer in the other tourism destination as this will affect their own sales.

Box 2.1 summarises a study of cross-elasticities of demand for ground transport in the UK.

BOX 2.1 Cross-elasticities of demand for travel in the UK

Acutt and Dodgson (1996) derive a set of cross-elasticities of demand for travel in the UK. Cross-elasticities are estimated between car travel and the fares on six different public transport modes, and between travel on these six modes and the price of petrol. The cross-elasticity values are calculated using previous estimates of own-price elasticities, data on modal traffic levels, and 'diversion factors' derived from a survey of transport experts.

The authors consider six public transport modes: British Rail InterCity services; British Rail Network South East services (commuter and other services around London and the rest of the South East region); British Rail Regional Railways (all other British Rail passenger services); the London Underground; London buses; and all other local buses.

Cross-elasticities of demand for car use with respect to the prices of public transport modes

The authors state that the cross-price elasticity of car use with respect to the price of a particular public transport mode is equal to the product of three components: the public transport mode's own-price elasticity, relative mode shares, and diversion factors. When the price of the public transport mode falls, there will be an increase in the demand for this mode, the size of which will depend on the mode's own-price elasticity. A part of this increase will be diverted from car travel. The resulting

51

percentage reduction in car travel can be deducted from the total traffic flow by scaling by relative traffic flows on the public transport and car modes.

The data used and elasticity estimations are shown in the Table.

		InterCity	NSE	Regional	Under-ground	London buses	Other local buses
1 Own-price elasticities	e_q	−1.0800	−0.4500	−0.9000	−0.4300	−0.6200	−0.4100
2 Passenger-miles share (public transport/car)	q_i/q_i	0.1563	0.1334	0.0298	0.2103	0.2120	0.1299
3 Passenger-miles share (car/public transport)	q_i/q_j	6.3980	7.4963	33.5570	4.7551	4.7170	7.6982
4 Diversion factors from survey	δ_{ji}	−0.2500	−0.2400	−0.2100	−0.1500	−0.1300	−0.1200
5 Specific market car cross-elasticities	e_{cj}	0.0422	0.0144	0.0056	0.0136	0.0171	0.0064
6 Specific market passenger-mile shares		0.2787	0.1775	0.3909	0.0429	0.0267	0.2893
7 Overall car cross-elasticities		0.0118	0.0026	0.0022	0.0006	0.0005	0.0018
8 Av. fare per public transport journey (£)	p_j	13.3000	1.9600	1.6600	0.8100	0.3800	0.5100
9 Av. length of trip (miles)		122.7900	16.6800	18.6500	4.9500	2.1600	3.1300
10 Av. price of petrol (£ per gallon)		2.2300	2.2300	2.2300	2.2300	2.2300	2.2300
11 Av. miles per gallon		32.5400	32.5400	32.5400	32.5400	32.5400	32.5400
12 Av. car occupancy		1.8200	1.5400	1.6000	1.5800	1.5800	1.5700
13 Petrol price per car journey (£)	p_w	4.6236	0.7423	0.7988	0.2147	0.0937	0.1366
14 Car/public transport price ratio	p_w/p_j	0.3476	0.3787	0.4812	0.2651	0.2465	0.2679
15 Public transport cross-elasticities	e_{jw}	0.0939	0.0409	0.0909	0.0171	0.0199	0.0132
16 Elasticity of car passenger-miles w.r.t. petrol price	e_{cw}	−0.1500	−0.1500	−0.1500	−0.1500	−0.1500	−0.1500
17 Specific market car diversion factors	δ_{jz}	−0.0978	−0.0364	−0.0181	−0.0240	−0.0281	−0.0114
18 Overall market car diversion factors		−0.0273	−0.0065	−0.0071	−0.0010	−0.0007	−0.0033

The car cross-elasticities are shown in row 7 of the Table. These are:

InterCity   0.0118

Network South East   0.0026

Regional Railways   0.0022

London Underground   0.0006

London buses   0.0005

Other local buses   0.0018

The authors note that these cross-elasticities can be added to give the percentage change in total car passenger-miles when all public transport fares change by the same proportion. The resulting car cross-elasticity of demand with respect to overall public transport fare is 0.0195.

Public transport cross-elasticities with respect to the price of petrol

As with the cross-elasticities of car demand with respect to public transport fares, it is possible to decompose the cross-elasticity of demand for a public transport mode with respect to the price of petrol into three components: these are the own-price elasticity of petrol, the relative modal shares of car and the public transport mode, and a diversion factor indicating the proportion of any change in car travel diverted from the particular public transport mode.

Public transport cross-elasticities with respect to the price of petrol are shown in row 15 of Table 1.

The 'specific market' diversion factors in terms of the proportion of any change in car passenger-miles of a particular type which divert to or from the particular public transport mode are shown in row 17 and are as follows (to nearest percentage):

		InterCity	NSE	Regional	Underground	London buses	Other local buses
17 Specific market car diversion factors	δ_{j1}	10%	4%	2%	2%	3%	1%

Thus, the figure of 10% indicates that if petrol prices increase, 10% of the resulting reduction in car travel on journeys over 50 miles will divert to InterCity. These diversion factors were multiplied by the proportion which each particular type of car travel represents of total car travel in order to find final 'overall' diversion factors which show the proportion of any total change in car travel which diverts to each public transport mode. These diversion factors are shown in row 18 thus:

	InterCity	NSE	Regional	Underground	London buses	Other local buses
18 Overall market car diversion factors	2.7%	0.6%	0.7%	0.1%	0.1%	0.3%

The figure of 2.7% indicates that if petrol prices increase, then 2.7% of the resulting total reduction in car travel will divert to InterCity. Adding these overall diversion factors gives the proportion of any total reduction in car travel as a result of a petrol price change which diverts to public transport as 4.7%.

Policy Implications

The estimates of cross-elasticities were undertaken as part of a study forecasting the effects of various policy options on the emission levels of greenhouse gases from all surface transport modes in Great Britain. The models required cross-elasticity estimates so that all the effects of modal split policies, such as subsidisation of a public transport mode, could be estimated.

The authors emphasise that cross-elasticity estimates are crucially important for many issues of transport policy. A knowledge of cross-elasticity estimates is required in order to assess the effects of any policy aimed at affecting modal split. Such policies could involve subsidization of public transport, pollution taxes on cars, road tolls etc. Without a comprehensive set of cross-elasticity estimates it is not possible to state with any degree of certainty the effects of many transport policies.

Source: Acutt, M.Z. and J.S. Dodgson (1996) 'Cross-elasticities of Demand for Travel', *Transport Policy*, 2(4), 271–277

2.3.4 MARKETING ELASTICITY OF DEMAND

Marketing elasticity (ε_a) measures the responsiveness of sales to changes in marketing/advertising expenditure. It is measured by the percentage change in sales to a percentage change in adverting expenditures.

$$\varepsilon_a = \frac{\text{percentage change in the quantity demanded of the tourism product}}{\text{percentage change in marketing expenditure}}$$

The higher the marketing elasticity value, the more responsive sales are to changes in the advertising budget. An awareness of this elasticity measure can assist advertising or marketing managers to determine appropriate levels of advertising outlays. This chapter will later discuss the impact of marketing and promotion expenditure on international tourism demand.

2.4 MODELLING TOURISM DEMAND

A large number of research studies have attempted to cast light on what factors actually affect tourism demand, and to what extent. Demand functions can be formulated for domestic or international tourism, or for particular tourism market segments, products or services. This section provides an overview of the research that has been undertaken, much of which is inaccessible to readers who lack quantitative research skills. This summary is not intended to be comprehensive but should provide the reader with an understanding of some of the main elements of the demand modelling literature and the directions that it is taking.

The most common method of estimating demand is regression analysis. Important issues that must be addressed include model specification, data collection, possible functional forms of the demand equation and the evaluation of the econometric results obtained.

2.4.1 MODEL SPECIFICATION

The first step in using regression analysis is to specify the model to be estimated. This involves identifying the most important variables that are considered to affect the demand for the product.

Suppose that our problem is to estimate the demand function for a tourism product (e.g. rooms in a four star hotel). The hotel manager might consider the most important variables to include: the price of a room (P_x), consumer's income (Y), the number of consumers in the market (N), the price of boutique hotels (substitute goods, P_s), air fares to the destination (complementary product, P_c), consumer tastes (T) and marketing expenditure (A).

$$Q_x = f(P_x, Y, N, P_s, P_c, T, A, \text{ dummy variables}, \dots) \tag{2.2}$$

The dots at the end of Equation 2.2 refer to any of the determinants of demand that are specific to the particular circumstances of a product or destination.

The researcher must avoid omitting important variables from the demand equation to be estimated; otherwise the results will be biased. On the other hand, including too many explanatory variables may lead to econometric difficulties and may be too expensive.

2.4.2 COLLECTING DATA ON THE VARIABLES

The second step in using regression analysis to estimate the demand for tourism visitation or the demand for a particular product is to collect the data for the variables in the model. Data can be collected for each of the variables over time (i.e. yearly, quarterly and monthly), or for different economic units (individuals, households, origin, etc.) at a particular point in time. The former is called 'time-series data' while the latter is called 'cross-sectional data'.

The type of data used in demand estimation is often dictated by availability. Sources of data for estimating tourism demand can come from a variety of sources including government statistics, industry reports and consumer surveys.

More recent studies evaluating a variety of tourism markets are using panel data techniques (Naudé & Saayman, 2005; Van Der Merwe *et al.*, 2007; Saayman & Saayman, 2008). When cross-sectional and time-series data are combined, as in panel data analysis, the quality and quantity of data are enhanced. Panel data techniques are particularly useful when cross-section data are also available over various time periods. They offer all the advantages of a larger number of observations, that is, more informative data, less multicollincarity, more degrees of freedom and more efficient estimates. In tourism demand studies, panel data techniques allow the inclusion of the variables that are mostly static for one region (such as distance), but which differ between regions, which is not possible with time-series data only.

2.4.3 SPECIFYING THE FORM OF THE DEMAND FUNCTION

The third step in estimating demand by regression analysis is to determine the form of the model to be estimated. The simplest model to deal with, and the one which is often the most realistic also, is the linear model.

Equation 2.2 can be written in explicit linear form as

$$Q_x = \alpha_0 + \beta_1 P_x + \beta_2 Y + \beta_3 N + \beta_4 P_s + \beta_5 P_c + \beta_6 T + \beta_7 A + \cdots + \mu \qquad (2.3)$$

Where,

α_0 is the intercept;

The βs are the parameters (coefficients) to be estimated;

μ is the error term.

In such a linear model, the change or marginal effect on the dependent variable (Q_x) for each 1 unit change in the independent or explanatory variables (given by the estimated coefficient for the variables) is constant regardless of the level of the particular variable (or other variables included in the demand equation). This makes for easy interpretation of the estimated coefficients of the regression as elasticities. We have seen that the formula for point elasticity of demand is $\varepsilon = (dP/dQ)(P/Q)$. By selecting a value for a price–quantity combination, the value of ε can be computed. Income and cross-price elasticities can be determined using the same general approach.

Various functional forms can be used for regression analysis. There are cases where a nonlinear relationship will fit the data better than any linear form. Other than the linear equation, the most common form is the multiplicative functional form or so-called power function. A demand equation in the form of a power function is expressed thus:

$$Q_x = \alpha(P_x^{\beta_1})(Y^{\beta_2})(N^{\beta_3})(P_s^{\beta_4})(P_c^{\beta_5})(A^{\beta_6})\mu \qquad (2.4)$$

In order to estimate the parameters (coefficients β_1 and β_2) of demand equation 2.4, we must first transform it into double log equation 2.5 which is linear in the logarithms, and then run a regression on the log variables.

$$\ln Q_x = \ln \alpha + \beta_1 \ln P_x + \beta_2 \ln Y + \beta_3 \ln N + \beta_4 \ln P_s$$
$$+ \beta_5 \ln P_c + \beta_6 \ln T + \beta_7 \ln A + \ln \mu \qquad (2.5)$$

Because this equation is linear in terms of the logarithms of the original variables, the coefficients can be estimated using the ordinary least squares method.

The estimated slope coefficients (i.e. β_1, β_2, etc.) in Equation 2.5 now represent percentage changes or average elasticities. Specifically:

β_1 is the price elasticity of demand;

β_2 is the income elasticity of demand;

β_3 is the elasticity of demand in respect of population growth;

β_4 is a cross-elasticity of demand (for a substitute);

β_5 is a cross-elasticity of demand (for a complement);

β_6 is the elasticity of demand with respect to changes in consumer tastes;

β_7 is the marketing or advertising elasticity of demand.

Thus, the advantage of the power formulation of the demand function is that the estimated coefficients give demand elasticities directly. Researchers often estimate both the linear and the power forms of the demand function, reporting the one that gives better results (i.e. fits the data better).

2.4.4 TESTING THE ECONOMETRIC RESULTS

The final step in the estimation of demand by regression analysis is to evaluate the regression results. Important items are the following:

- The sign of each estimated slope coefficient must be checked to see if it conforms to what is postulated on theoretical grounds.
- t-tests must be conducted on the statistical significance of the estimated parameters to determine the degree of confidence that we have in each of the estimated slope coefficients. The (adjusted) coefficient of determination $\bar{r}^2$ will then indicate the proportion of the total variation in the demand for the product that is 'explained' by the independent or explanatory variables included in the demand equation.
- The estimated demand equations must pass other econometric tests to ensure that such problems as multi-collinearity (when two or more explanatory variables are highly correlated), heteroscedasticity (when error terms do not have the same variance) and autocorrelation (when the error terms are correlated) are not present. If any of these problems are detected from the tests, measures must be applied to attempt to overcome them. More sophisticated tests are gradually being added in demand modelling to reflect the evolving econometrics literature.

Box 2.2 provides a hypothetical example of estimating the demand for air travel between two countries.

BOX 2.2 Demand for air travel between Origin X and Destination Y

Suppose that the following regression equation is estimated:

$$\ln Q_t = 2.737 - 1.247 \ln P_t + 1.905 \ln \text{GNP}_t$$

$$(-5.071) \qquad (7.286)$$

$r^2 = 0.97$, D-W = 1.83

Where

Q_t = number of passengers ('000) per year travelling between country X and country Y.

P_t = real average yearly fare between X and Y (weighted by the seasonal distribution of traffic and adjusted for inflation).

GNP_t = real gross national product of country X in each year.

The numbers in parentheses refer to the estimated t-statistics.

Since all the variables in the equation have been transformed into natural logarithms (a simple command in the regression package accomplishes this) and the regression is run on the transformed variables, the estimated coefficients give demand elasticities directly.

The estimated coefficient of -1.247 for variable $\ln P_t$ gives the price elasticity of demand. It implies that a 10% increase in real average airfares would reduce the number of airline passengers by 12.47% (demand is price elastic).

The estimated coefficient of 1.905 for variable GNP_t gives the income elasticity of demand. It is indicated that a 10% increase in real GNP would increase the number of passengers by 19.05% (the product is a luxury good).

We may have confidence in the estimated regression results for several reasons:

1. The signs of the estimated slope coefficients (elasticities) are as postulated by demand theory.

2. The very high t-statistics indicate that both are statistically significant at better than the 1% level.

3. The adjusted coefficient of determination (r^2) indicates that air fares explain 97% of the variation in the log of the number of passengers flying between country X and country Y.

4. The multi-collinearity problem between two independent variables seems to have been avoided by deflating both air fares and GNP by the price index.

5. The value of the Durbin–Watson (D-W) statistic indicates that the hypothesis of no autocorrelation cannot be rejected.

Source: Adapted from Salvatore, D. (1989) *Managerial Economics*, Case Study 6.2, New York: McGraw-Hill

2.5 MEASURING DEMAND FOR INTERNATIONAL TOURISM ARRIVALS

Perhaps the most effort of tourism researchers in measuring tourism demand has been on estimating the demand for tourism arrivals for different countries (Song & Li, 2008). Given the substantial literature on this in tourism demand modelling, it is appropriate to discuss some of the relevant issues.

Research suggests that the range of factors affecting the demand for tourism is very large. The more prominent factors that have been included in destination demand modelling are as follows (Crouch, 1994a; Lim, 2006; Saayman & Saayman, 2008):

- *Income*. Higher income in the origin country leads to a higher demand for travel and tourism.
- *Relative prices*. Price levels in the destination relative to competing destinations and relative to the tourists' home country influence its demand as a tourism destination (the real exchange rate or relative price indices are often used as proxies).
- *Transport cost*. Increased transportation cost between the origin and destination increases the cost of tourism to the destination.
- *Marketing/Promotion expenses*. Increased marketing spending and more effective marketing efforts strengthen the demand for the destination.
- *Migration levels* in a host destination can generate both inbound and outbound tourism flows.
- *Qualitative factors*. These include tourists' attributes which influence time available for travel, trade and ethnic ties between the countries; destination attractiveness (e.g. culture, climate, history, natural resources and tourism infrastructure); special events taking place at the destination; natural disasters; and social threats (e.g. political instability, health issues or terrorism).

A model of international tourism demand of the type that is typically estimated and tested can be written as:

$$Q_{ij} = f(Y_j, \mathrm{TC}_{ij}, \mathrm{RP}_{ij}, A_i, M_i) \tag{2.6}$$

Where,

Q_{ij} = demand for international travel services by origin j for destination i;

Y_j = income per capita in origin j;

TC_{ij} = transportation cost between destination i and origin j;

RP_{ij} = relative prices (i.e. the ratio of prices in destination i to prices in origin j and in alternative destinations, adjusted for exchange rate);

A_i = marketing/promotion expenditure by destination i;

M_i = migration levels in destination i.

Equation 2.6 can be written in explicit linear form as

$$Q_{ij} = \alpha_0 + \beta_1 Y_j + \beta_2 TC_{ij} + \beta_3 RP_{ij} + \beta_4 A_i + \beta_5 M_i + \text{dummy variables} + \mu \quad (2.7)$$

In Equation 2.7, α_0 is the intercept, the βs are the parameters (coefficients) to be estimated and μ is the error term. In such a linear model, the change or marginal effect on the dependent variable (Q_{ij}) for each 1 unit change in the independent or explanatory variables (given by the estimated coefficient for the variables) is constant regardless of the level of the particular variable (or other variables included in the demand equation). This leads to easy interpretation of the estimated coefficients of the regression.

2.5.1 DEPENDENT VARIABLES

Researchers use a variety of proxies to measure the dependent variable (Q_{ij}) in a tourism demand function. These include tourist arrivals and/or departures, tourist expenditures and/or receipts, travel exports and/or imports, tourist length of stay and the amounts of nights spent at tourist accommodation. Of these, data permitting, tourism receipts per capita (either nominal or real, or per diem) are perhaps the most appropriate measure of tourism demand given the importance of tourism expenditure for the economic contribution of the industry. The demand can be in total covering all travel motives or the demand from a particular market segment (e.g. business, Visits to Friends and Relatives (VFR), holiday, Japanese honeymooners, over 55s etc.).

The level of foreign tourism from a given origin will of course depend upon the origin population. While some past studies have included population as an explanatory variable, the effect of population is usually accommodated by taking the dependent variable to be international tourism demand per capita. The main justification for not having population as a separate explanatory variable is that its presence may cause multicollinearity problems, as population tends to be highly correlated with income (Witt & Witt, 1995).

Typically, demand modellers lag the tourism demand variable. A lagged dependent variable can be justified on the grounds of habit persistence and risk aversion on the part of repeat visitors. In general, tourists prefer to spend holidays in places that are already familiar to them or of which they have been informed about. There is much less uncertainty associated with a repeat visit to a destination compared with travelling to a previously unvisited destination. For these reasons the number of people choosing a given alternative in any year depends (positively) on the numbers who chose it in previous years (Song & Turner, 2006).

A second justification for the inclusion of a lagged dependent variable in tourism demand functions comes from the supply side. Supply constraints may involve shortages of hotel accommodation, passenger transportation capacity and numbers of trained staff, which typically cannot be increased rapidly (Song & Witt, 2000: 7–8). In several studies the lagged dependent variables have been found to be important factors that influence the demand for tourism. The exclusion of this variable in the modelling process can result in biased forecasts (Song & Turner, 2006).

2.5.2 INDEPENDENT (EXPLANATORY) VARIABLES

2.5.2.1 Income

International travel can be relatively expensive and depends importantly on the tourist's income. The purchasing power of people is an important influence on their decision to travel and helps explain tourism flows. An increase in real income provides consumers with greater spending power, resulting in the increased discretionary consumption of many types of products, including tourism. Wealthy countries and regions with strong currencies are important origin markets for international tourism.

The appropriate income variable is per capita personal disposable income or per capita private consumption expenditure in the origin country (in constant price terms). This corresponds to the specification of demand in per capita terms. Both of these variables measure people's living standards in the origin countries. Per capita income may be expected to have a positive influence on tourism demand. For leisure tourism and VFR, either private consumption or personal disposable income is the most appropriate measure. For retirees, permanent income based on wealth and retirement income may be the more appropriate (Alperovich & Machnes, 1994). For business tourism, a more general income variable such as Gross Domestic Product (GDP), Gross National Product (GNP) or National Disposable Income (NDI) is best used. Box 2.3 records some research findings on the influence of income on tourism demand.

It is interesting to observe that the focus on income as an influence on tourism flows has been associated with a relative neglect of wealth as a determining factor. The importance of wealth as a determinant of travel has been amply demonstrated as a result of the GFC. While the GFC certainly reduced incomes on average for millions of people, perhaps the greatest effect was on their level of wealth due to the decline in the value of their assets including superannuation payouts. While there has always been some recognition that wealth is important for some tourism markets, for example, seniors tourism, the issue remains under-researched.

BOX 2.3 Income and tourism demand. Some empirical results

- Per capita income is the single most important determinant of demand for international tourism (Crouch, 1992; Lim, 2006).
- The high income elasticities found in many studies indicate that international tourism is a luxury item and can be influenced greatly by the tourist origin country's economic growth cyclical pattern (Crouch, 1992: 648; Kulendran & Divisekera, 2007).
- In many developing countries, income is unevenly distributed, and so an increasing disposable income for the population as a whole is initially more likely to be translated into the purchase of consumer goods rather than travel. This suggests that the income elasticity for the major tourist-generating countries is likely to be higher than that of developing countries (Crouch, 1994a).
- Air travel exhibits procyclical behaviour and very few goods are as responsive to income as air transport is (Tretheway & Oum, 1992).
- Income elasticity varies as a function of the length of haul (Crouch, 1994b). As long-haul travellers tend to come from higher-income brackets, the demand for long-haul travel is likely to be less income sensitive than for short-haul travel (Anastasopoulos, 1984: 122).
- International tourism has become more income sensitive over time. In the early years of modern international tourism, only wealthier persons could afford to travel. Today, however, growing numbers of people can afford to travel (Crouch, 1994a).
- The income elasticity of demand for international travel from the UK was 1.9 compared to 0.6 for domestic travel, while the income elasticity of demand for air travel was 1.5 (Njegovan, 2006).
- Tremblay (1989) estimated that the income elasticities for tourism in 18 European destinations ranged between 0.33 for the UK and 11.35 for Portugal.
- Witt and Martin (1987) found that income elasticity values for UK travel to Europe ranged between 0.34 and 2.91 for independent travel and between 0.86 and 6.35 for package tours.
- Dargay and Hanly (2001) used a pooled time-series cross-section data which covered the years 1989–1998. They estimated a long-run income elasticity for UK outbound traffic of about +1.

2.5.2.2 Relative prices

In their destination choice decision, tourists will consider the price (cost of living) at the destination relative to the costs of living at the origin and substitute destinations. Thus, two types of prices must be considered in the demand function of tourism: the first one is relative price between the destination and the source country; the second is relative price between different competing destinations which generates the substitution price effect.

2.5.2.2.1 Cost of living at the destination relative to the origin

Tourists incur costs within the destination that they visit including, for example, accommodation, food, tours and shopping. They compare prices at the destination with those in their home country or region, deciding whether or not to visit that destination depending on the relative costs of living between the two areas. This comparison, of course, applies with more force to international travel than to domestic travel. While prices do change between cities and regions within a country, they differ more obviously and markedly between countries.

The relative price variable which is typically used in the demand for tourism function is the ratio of the consumer price indexes between the host and the origin countries adjusted by the bilateral exchange rate. A higher exchange rate in favour of the origin country's currency can result in a greater flow of outbound tourism to other destinations.

When the exchange rate-adjusted Consumer Price Index (CPI) ratio is used to measure the relative prices of goods and services in the destination, the impacts of inflation and exchange rate movements are measured through one 'relative price' variable, referred to as the 'real exchange rate' (Rosensweig, 1986).

That is,

$$RP_{it} = (CPI_{it}/CPI_{jt})ER_{it} \qquad (2.8)$$

Where,

RP$_{it}$ is relative price variable in destination i in period t;

CPI$_{it}$ is consumer price index in destination i in period t;

CPI$_{jt}$ is consumer price index in origin j in period t;

ER$_{it}$ is an index of the price of origin currency in terms of destination i currency in period t.

A rise in relative prices means that purchases in destination i are relatively more expensive for tourists from origin j, which could be either due to a higher inflation rate in the destination compared with the origin or due to the exchange rates having moved against the origin country, and vice versa.

The use of CPI as a relative cost of living measure, however, is only as good as its implicit assumption that the goods and services purchased by tourists are similar to those purchased by the representative household on which the CPI is constructed. However, because the expenditure pattern of a tourist is quite different from that of the average household, the CPIs of the origin country and the destination may not reflect the prices of goods which tourists actually purchase. Indeed, the basket of goods and services included in the price indices of a given country could differ significantly from the one consumed by its visitors.

Another assumption underlying the use of the CPI is that prices of tourism goods and services tend to move in the same direction as overall consumer prices. However, as Divisekera (2003) points out, trends in general price levels as implied by CPI measures may not necessarily coincide with that of tourism. The CPI can serve as a proxy for the cost of tourism at a destination, given lack of more suitable data. The issues are addressed in more detail in Chapter 20 which discusses destination price competiveness.

Researchers have argued that tourists are reasonably well-informed of changes in exchange rates, whereas information on price levels and price changes in destinations is generally not known in advance (Crouch, 1994a). Thus, exchange rates are sometimes included in tourism demand models in addition to the relative price variable (Lim, 1999). With imperfect knowledge, tourists may respond to exchange rate movements but not to changes in relative inflation rates when they make their decision to travel. Thus, some studies specifically examine the influence of nominal exchange rates on international tourism demand. Since the exchange rate is most important in costing tours and accommodation, and is a main component of price fluctuations, it may be an important proxy for the relative price of tourism in smaller open countries with floating exchange rates. However, the inclusion of both exchange rates and relative prices as explanatory variables may lead to multi-collinearity because the exchange rate is also a measure of relative prices (Lim, 2006).

2.5.2.2.2 Cost of living at other destinations

The impact of competing destinations has a positive influence on the demand for international tourism, meaning that a rise in price to one destination will boost visitor numbers to substitute destinations. Tourists may consider a range of competing destinations before choosing any particular one. They may compare changes in the cost of living in the choice destination with the changes in the cost of living in the competing destinations. Researchers model this consumer thinking in either of two ways.

One way to allow for the substitution between the destination and, separately, a number of possible competing destinations is by specifying the tourists' cost of living variable in the form of the possible destination value relative to the origin value (Song & Witt, 2000). This allows for substitution between tourist visits to the foreign destination under consideration and domestic tourism, therein acknowledging that domestic tourism may be the most important substitute for foreign tourism.

The other way is to calculate the cost of living at any substitute destination relative to a weighted average cost of living in the different competing destinations, adjusted by the relevant exchange rates. The weight assigned reflects the relative market share (arrivals or expenditures) in each competing destination. This approach allows for the impact of price changes in competing foreign destinations and is used more often in empirical studies as fewer variables are incorporated into the model, and therefore more degrees of freedom are available for the model estimation (Song & Turner, 2006).

Some destinations may be complements rather than substitutes and so may gain visitors if the cost of living in the other destination is low. Destinations that are complementary (e.g. India and Nepal; Hong Kong and China) may consider joint marketing programmes to increase visitation numbers and expenditure to both countries.

Box 2.4 records some research findings on the influence of price on international tourism demand.

BOX 2.4 Prices and tourism demand. Some empirical results

- Tourism demand is relatively responsive to price factors (Crouch, 1995; Lim, 1999). An increase in relative price is linked to a fall in market share in travel from the origin country, and a fall in relative price is linked to a rise in market share, in both the medium and the long term (Crouch, 1994a). This finding, while expected, suggests that there is a dominant substitution effect at work.
- Price elasticities vary depending on the definition of price; the form of the model used; the number of explanatory variables; whether prices have been adjusted for exchange rate changes; and whether the cost of transportation is included in the definition of price (Crouch, 1994a; Lim, 2006).
- Price elasticity varies as a function of the country of origin. The residents of large countries, offering a wider diversity of travel experiences, are likely to be more price sensitive in their international travel behaviour than tourists from geographically small countries whose choice of activities is much more limited (Crouch, 1995).
- Tourists have become less price sensitive over time. This may be a result of an increased emphasis on destination differentiation strategies (Crouch, 1994a).
- Price elasticity varies as a function of the destination country. The more unique the destination is, the less price elastic is its demand. A lower price elasticity is to be expected for more differentiated destinations (Anastasopoulos, 1984: 127; Bakkalsalihoglu, 1987: 178).

- A higher price elasticity is likely for destinations that compete closely with other substitute destinations. Significant substitution effects have been found between France and Spain (De Mello *et al.*, 2002) and between Italy and Turkey (Papatheodorou, 1999).
- Leisure travellers tend to be more sensitive to changes in relative prices than business travellers (BTCE, 1994).
- Little (1980) found that US demand for tourism was associated with a range of exchange rate elasticity values varying between -0.58 for Mexico and -3.15 for Canada.
- Martin and Witt (1988) estimated that the price elasticity values for outbound tourism from the UK ranged between -0.23 for Austria and -5.60 for Greece. For outbound travel from West Germany the values ranged between -0.06 for Spain and -1.98 for France.
- For tourism receipts by European countries, Tremblay (1989) found that exchange rate elasticities varied between 0.63 (West Germany) and 4.60 (Portugal).

2.5.2.3 Transportation costs

The demand for transportation is a derived demand, namely, to purchase tourism services.

Just as costs of living in substitute destinations are likely to influence the demand for tourism to a given destination, so transportation costs to substitute and complementary destinations are likely to influence travel flows. Transportation costs refer to the cost of round-trip travel between the origin and the destination. Unlike for other export goods, the consumer (tourist) must be transported to the product (destination) rather than the reverse.

Air travel has two major markets: leisure travel and business travel. Leisure travel tends to be price sensitive to changes in air fares, if only because air fares form a large proportion of total travel costs for leisure travellers. Leisure travel is generally based on discretionary spending and many goods and services compete with leisure travel for a share of the consumer's discretionary budget, for example, home entertainment systems, the family car, white goods, dining out and so on. Because leisure travel has many substitutes, individual travelling for leisure purposes tend to be price sensitive.

Business travel, however, is likely to be less sensitive to air fares than leisure travel for several reasons:

- The total cost of travel includes a value of time component and business travellers value time more highly than do leisure travellers.
- Business travellers may be more concerned to maximise their productivity while travelling and, therefore, may be more willing to pay for 'higher quality' services

that allow last-minute bookings, changes to itineraries and more comfortable seats.

- Business passengers generally have less substitute transport modes and itineraries available than leisure passengers.
- For business travellers, costs are absorbed by the firm, which makes the individual traveller less sensitive to price changes.

While estimation of the price of surface travel tends to be straightforward, whether for private vehicle, rental car, coach, train or ferry, estimating the cost of air travel can be quite difficult. Air fares often comprise a large proportion of total transportation costs for tourists, but they are difficult to measure accurately, given the pricing practices of airlines resulting in a variety of different fares for the same class of travel on the same flight. Indeed, data limitations have resulted in transportation costs being omitted altogether in most studies of tourism demand. In the few studies in which they have been included, the proxies for transportation cost have variously been the real economy air fare, real air travel cost, real average air fare, excursion air fare, cheapest air fare, distance and real revenue per passenger kilometre/mile of scheduled air fares. Some studies have attempted to include transportation costs of substitute travel modes in the demand function, though the majority does not (Witt & Witt, 1995).

Box 2.5 records some research findings on the influence of transportation costs on international tourism demand.

BOX 2.5 Transportation costs and tourism demand. Some empirical results

- In his meta-analysis of the tourism literature, Crouch (1995) finds central estimates of the travel cost elasticity of −0.85, with a standard deviation of 1.15; the underlying estimates range from 0.11 to −1.89 (Brons *et al.* 2002 estimated an average of −1.146).
- Pooled time-series cross-section data were used to estimate dynamic econometric models for air travel by British residents to 20 OECD countries and for residents of these 20 countries to the UK. Air fares were found to be an important determinant of demand, with long-run elasticities on the order of −0.3 to −0.6 (Dargay & Hanly, 2001).
- Brons *et al.* (2002) and Gillen *et al.* (2003) show empirical evidences that leisure travellers have a greater elasticity of demand to air fares than business travellers.
- Oum *et al.* (1992) surveyed 13 major empirical studies on the price demand elasticities of air passenger travel and found the price elasticities vary greatly between −0.4 and −4.51, with the majority falling between −0.8 and −2.0.

- International air travel by UK residents for leisure purposes is relatively price sensitive, suggesting that part of the increase in air travel over the 1990s can be explained by declining airfares. Air fare elasticity for business tourism is less than that for leisure tourism (Brons *et al.*, 2002; BTCE, 1994).

- Gillen *et al.* (2003) used 21 Canadian and international empirical studies and found mean elasticity values ranging between -0.7 and -1.52 for domestic travel.

- In a meta-analysis of studies on air travel demand, Gillen *et al.* (2003) found that business travellers are less responsive to changes in prices than are leisure travellers. Similarly, Dargay and Hanly (2001) found that business travel is fairly insensitive to fare changes and is driven mainly by other factors, particularly foreign trade.

- Dargay and Hanly (2001), in their study of UK outbound traffic, estimated fares elasticity of about -0.6. They found exchange rate (local currency per pound) and relative prices to be more influential than air fares with elasticity estimates of $+1$ and -0.8, respectively. This suggests that the estimates of the demand elasticity with respect to air fare alone may be biased in studies where the costs of other components of travel abroad are not taken into account.

- Alwaked (2005) estimated the fare and expenditure elasticities of demand for domestic air travel in the USA and found the uncompensated own-fare elasticities were between -0.7 and -1.09, with the compensated own-fare elasticities between -0.3 and -0.95.

- Njegovan (2006) examined elasticities of demand for leisure air travel in the UK and found -0.7 for the own-price elasticity in the Air Travel equation. He also found that the expenditure on tourism abroad was much more sensitive to changes in the price of domestic leisure (cross-price elasticity of 0.9) than to changes in air fares (cross-price elasticity of -0.2). The majority of estimates lie between -0.3 and -2, implying that air travel demand is elastic.

- In the long run, consumers and firms are better able to adjust to price signals than in the short run (Brons *et al.*, 2002; BTCE, 1994; Oum *et al.*, 1992). This may be due to three factors: (i) the relative lack of substitute modes on longer-distance flights; (ii) the fact that long-distance flights are usually more expensive to begin with than short-distance flights, so that an increase in costs will require a larger share of a passenger's budget – suggesting that long-haul travel may attract wealthier travellers who might be less price sensitive; and (iii) a lower awareness of prices in the more distant destinations and a lesser ability to change travel plans upon arrival (Crouch, 1994a).

The role of income and price factors in influencing tourism demand in the GFC is highlighted in Box 2.6.

BOX 2.6 Income and price factors and the Global Financial Crisis

The global financial crisis (GFC) refers to the world economy in recession. As of June 2009, financial, business and consumer confidence has been shattered. Asset prices and wealth have been slashed and may fall further. International trade volumes have been crushed, and further declines are likely. Unemployment is rising sharply, and consumer spending is falling. Businesses are collapsing, with investment reduced or cancelled. Inflation is slowing rapidly, commodity prices have collapsed, and there is talk of possible deflation. Currency values in many destinations have tumbled. Attempts to halt the economic slide by policy stimuli are, at most, slowing the decline, not reversing it, so far.

Reduced wealth, slowing or falling incomes, rising unemployment, and low consumer and business confidence, negatively influence consumer spending. Tourism spending, as part of discretionary consumer spending, is experiencing falls greater than other consumer spending. But precisely what impacts will the GFC have? Possible consumer responses to the GFC include: Spending less, travelling less (shifting to other products, debt reduction, savings?); switching to closer destinations?; taking shorter trips?; some shifting to domestic tourism?; some 'trading down' (e.g. towards low cost carriers, lower standard hotels, business class to economy class – – ?); become more sensitive to price signals and differentials? (increased elasticity of demand for tourism products)? We simply don't know enough about consumer travel behaviour to give definite answers to these questions.

The estimated income elasticities discussed in the text are averages, derived from analysis over a long run of years. They do not allow adequately for the sharp shocks reducing consumer and business confidence that the world is experiencing as a result of the GFC. Economic slow-downs or recessions, building as sharply as is currently the case, are likely to increase the negative effect on tourism spending from the measured slowing in economic growth. These confidence effects are likely to be particularly pronounced for discretionary spending such as tourism.

Like some other countries Australia has experienced a sharp decline in the value of its currency. Historically this has offered a major buffer against adverse tourism spending effects. During the 1997 Asian financial crisis, for example, much of the adverse growth impact of that crisis on Australian exports, including tourism, was offset by increased Australian competitiveness as a result of a decline in the value of the $A. However, part of the reason for that was that much of the developed Western world continued to grow solidly, so that its spending capacity was maintained as its currencies rose in value (and these countries switched to Australian-produced goods and services). The Asian financial crisis did reduce growth in Japan, and much of non-Japan Asia, but even here China and India were less affected. In the GFC, however, the advanced economies, having the highest per capita incomes which drive tourism demand, – are leading the whole world into recession. Australia will have to rely much more on China and other Asian economies to increase their demand for Australian tourism products. But even these economies are forecast to slow dramatically, and the latest IMF/World Bank warnings suggest the 'knock on' effects from the shock to developing country exports will have important adverse effects on growth for many developing countries as well.

In sum, tourism is a volatile industry. When general conditions are good, it can perform strongly. When conditions are bad and expected to get worse, it is likely to perform well below average. The tourism industry should plan on the basis that it will be disproportionately affected by these bad conditions associated with the GFC. There were good reasons to expect that, in the context of the GFC, the large negative income/wealth effects on global tourism demand, amplified by severe reductions in business and consumer confidence, would dominate, and Australia would not be fully insulated from this by the drop in the value of the $A. The consequences of the GFC have been that Australia (the same as for many other countries) has experienced reduced inbound, outbound and domestic tourism.

Source: Carmody, G. (2009) *Australia Tourism: How Deep the Recession? How Will Tourism Fare during the 'Great Recession' of 2009* (Report prepared by Geoff Carmody & Associates for the Tourism and Transport Forum, GCA tourism analysis note no. 2 – March 2009

While income and price factors are those that have been most tested by demand modellers, there are two further factors that have received attention in several studies. These are migration levels and tourism promotion

2.5.2.4 Marketing and promotion

Public agencies, together with private operators, spend substantial sums of money promoting cities, regions and countries as tourism destinations. Their objective is to create and increase awareness of the area as a tourist destination and to promote the desire to travel to that destination.

The extent to which marketing and promotion expenditure influence tourism demand is difficult to measure. Typically, researchers use the marketing budget of national tourism offices as a proxy. There are, however, great difficulties in modelling the impact of marketing and of separating its effect from the other major influences on tourism demand. Even if marketing expenditure can be estimated accurately across different origin countries (often difficult to do), marketing expenditure *per se* does not indicate that the promotion is effective. Different nationalities and cultures are likely to respond differently to marketing and different destinations vary in their ability to use marketing effectively to attract tourists. Few studies have attempted to model these differences in tourism and little is known about the likely directions of the differences (Crouch, 1995). Box 2.7 contains some empirical results.

BOX 2.7 Marketing expenditure and tourism demand. Some empirical results

- Marketing expenditure has a positive but small effect on international tourism demand (Kulendran & Divisekera, 2007). For instance, marketing expenditure elasticity for tourism to Australia from Japan, the UK, the USA and New Zealand is inelastic, varying between 0.05 and 0.37 (Kulendran & Dwyer, 2009).
- Marketing expenditure elasticity varies from country to country (Crouch *et al.*, 1992; Kulendran & Divisekera, 2007). In terms of tourist spending generated per dollar of marketing spent, the estimates for Australia are: New Zealand (36:1), Japan (8:1), the USA (7:1) and the UK (3:1) (Kulendran & Dwyer, 2009).
- The estimated aggregate dollar return per dollar invested in international tourism marketing by Australia's national tourism office is 13.5:1 (Kulendran & Dwyer, 2009).

At a destination management level it is important to know how responsive inbound tourism flows (and associated spending) are to destination promotion expenditure. Data permitting, a useful measure of marketing effectiveness, based on estimated elasticities, is the *return on marketing expenditure* developed by Crouch *et al.* (1992). This measures the expenditure return to a destination per dollar invested in tourism marketing in different origins. Kulendran and Dwyer (2009), using a dynamic modelling approach and cost-effectiveness analysis, estimated the return per dollar of marketing spend by Tourism Australia in Asian tourism origin markets. The results indicate that tourism marketing expenditure by Tourism Australia is associated with higher injected expenditure from the targeted inbound markets. Of the selected markets, New Zealand has the highest cost-effectiveness ratio (36:1), indicating the tourism expenditure return per dollar into the Australian economy of additional marketing activity. The next highest return is that of Asia (excluding Japan) where the estimated dollar return per dollar invested in tourism marketing is 17:1. On average, tourism receipts to Australia from the USA, Japan, the UK and New Zealand are $13.5 million per $1 million spent on tourism promotion in these markets. These measures show that the overall positive impact of tourism marketing expenditure is high and the ratio of tourism marketing expenditure to tourist expenditure return is greater than unitary.

2.5.2.5 Migration stock

The choice of destination is also influenced by ethnic and migration factors, which generate tourist flows for purposes of VFR in the various destinations. There are several possible ways in which immigration can affect tourism.

First, the greater the number of permanent migrants to a destination, the larger is the pool of friends and relatives in the home country who have an incentive to visit that destination. The primary impact here is when permanent residents communicate with kin, friends or associates in the home country, mentioning perhaps the attractions of their new homeland. This may result in potential tourists being attracted to that destination rather than another.

Second, permanent migrants who visit their former country for VFR purposes may explicitly and implicitly 'promote' the new homeland leading to an increased number of short-term visits.

Third, an increasing number of migrants to a destination mean that there is an increasing stock of accommodation for friends and relatives who visit from overseas. The lower cost of an international trip for those friends and relatives provides a price incentive to travel to a destination.

Fourth, permanent migrants enrich the local culture and render destinations more interesting and diverse for tourists. One obvious example (the 'Chinatown' example) is where various restaurants and shops locate in a particular area to sell a range of products reflecting arts, crafts and tastes from other lands. This factor has some importance as an influence in domestic tourism also.

Fifth, it may well be the case that, for some foreign tourists who have no friends or relatives in the destination, knowledge that numbers of their compatriots have settled there is a contributing factor to a visit to that country.

Finally, permanent migrants who retain or forge business links with their former country may influence the number of business travellers from their new homeland, resulting in expanded trading relations between their new homeland and the rest of the world.

Box 2.8 records some research findings on the influence of migration on tourism demand.

BOX 2.8 Migration and tourism demand

- The Bureau of Transport Economics found that the proportion of the Australian population born in a relevant overseas country is a significant determinant of demand for inbound leisure travel both for the country's sampled as a group and for the UK and New Zealand in particular, and also for outbound leisure travel both generally and for Italy, the UK and Germany (Smith & Toms, 1978).
- The Bureau of Industry Economics found that the number of migrants resident in Australia was associated with the demand for tourism to Australia from a group of selected countries and from New Zealand, the UK, the USA, Canada, Germany and Italy independently and demand for outbound tourism to the selected countries taken as a group (Hollander, 1982).
- The total flow of VFR as a proportion of the size of Country of Birth groups is significantly and directly related to the proportion of recent migrants (Jackson, 1990).
- The inflow of tourists to Australia is influenced by the presence of migrants, though only the Visiting Relatives (VR) category of tourist is influenced. Additional migration leads to additional VR tourists, though the relationship is not proportional, since some VR tourists are not visiting migrants (Dwyer *et al.*, 1993).
- Migration influences outbound tourism from Australia. Its impact on outbound VR tourism is greater than on inbound VR tourism. Most likely, again, it leads to an increase in the flow, not just a change in destination. Most, though not all, outbound VR tourism is likely to be migration-related. The length of residence has a slight negative impact on outbound VR travel (Dwyer *et al.*, 1993).
- Seetaram & Dwyer (2009) found that, overall, if the growth in the proportion of estimated resident population born overseas from a particular source rises by 10%, Australia can expect the total number of visitors from all countries to grow by an additional 4.5%. The effect on holiday travellers is stronger than that on VFR travellers. The coefficient for migration is insignificant in the regression for business travellers.

2.5.2.6 Qualitative factors

There are a large number of qualitative factors which have more or less influence on the demand for tourism. These include the following:

- Tourists' demographic attributes which may affect leisure time availability or similar constraints (gender, age, education level and employment/profession).

- Household size (composition of household and child/children age).
- Trip motive or frequency.
- Destination attractiveness (climate, culture, history and natural environment).
- Special events (Olympic Games, World Cup, religious festivals, World Expo, etc.).
- Political events (terrorism, political unrest, currency crises, grounding aircraft strike, oil crises, etc.).
- Natural events (tsunami, hurricanes, SARS, Avian Flu, etc.).

These types of factors have varying relevance depending on the destination selected. In order to account for the impacts of one-off events and tourist taste changes on the demand for tourism, dummy variables have been used in some studies. Qualitative variables (such as oil crisis vs no crisis, SARS vs no SARS) can be included in the regression analysis by assigning the value of 1 to one classification (e.g. tsunami) and 0 to the other (no tsunami). These dummy variables are treated as any other variables in regression analysis. Even though a dummy variable will simply take the value of 1 in some years and the value of 0 in other years, its coefficient can be estimated and evaluated just as any other variable in the linear regression model. If the value of the dummy variable is found to be statistically significant, it will then be added to the constant to determine the interception of the regression line for the years during which the dummy variable assumes the value of 1. The two oil crises in the 1970s have been shown to have the most significant adverse impacts on international tourism demand, followed by the Gulf War in the early 1990s and the global economic recession in the mid-1980s (Li *et al.*, 2005). A variety of dummy variables have been used in destination-specific studies.

Dummy variables may be used also to capture seasonal variations in travel demand. Seasonal patterns in tourist flows and expenditures are well-known characteristics of international tourism demand, but few studies have tried to account for seasonality in modelling tourism demand.

An example of demand modelling where qualitative factors play an important role as demand determinants is that of Bigano *et al.* (2005). These authors project the impacts of climate change on tourism flows to estimate holiday destination choice models for 45 countries from all levels of development and all climates. The tourists travel to 200-odd countries, including the home country. The modelling of the impacts of climate change clearly requires the inclusion of variables that might be omitted from other models.

$$\ln(A_i^j) = c^j + \alpha_1^j \ln(D_i^j) + \alpha_2^j \ln(y_i) + \alpha_3^j T_i + \alpha_4^j T_i^2 + \alpha_5^j H_i + \alpha_6^j C_i + \alpha_7^j A_i + \alpha_8^j S_i \quad (2.9)$$

Where,

A_i^j denotes the arrivals in country i from country j;

D_i^j is the great-circle distance between the two countries;

y_i is per capita income in the destination country;

T_i is the annual average temperature in the destination country;

H_i is the number of world heritage sites per million square kilometres in the destination country;

C_i is the length of the coast line of the destination country;

A_i is the land area of the destination country;

S_i is an index of the political stability of the destination country.

Among other things the findings were that tourists are deterred by distance, political instability and poverty, and attracted to coasts. Tourists prefer countries with a sunny yet mild climate, and avoid climates that are too hot or too cold. More modelling of tourism demand to reflect changing climatic conditions can be expected in future research. Chapter 19 discusses issues involving tourism and climate change.

2.5.2.7 Time trends

A trend variable may be used to capture specific household travel behaviour such as inertia, consumer's preferences and habits in this sector. Trend variables can also capture cyclical effects, demographic changes in the source country or supply improvements in the host country. However, a time trend tends to be highly correlated with the income variable and can cause a serious multi-collinearity problem in the model estimation. This is why most recent studies have avoided including a deterministic trend in the model specification (Song & Turner, 2006).

Box 2.9 summarises a study of modelling US tourism demand for European destinations.

BOX 2.9 Modelling US tourism demand for European destinations

Han *et al.* (2006) examine the economic determinants of US tourism demand for main European destinations, France, Italy, Spain and the UK. The authors use the almost ideal demand system (AIDS) model, in conjunction with cointegration analysis, to provide estimates of the price and income elasticities of tourism demand. Europe is the main destination for US tourists and has a market share of at least 40% of US tourists who travel abroad. Within Europe, France, Italy, Spain and the UK are particularly important destinations, together accounting for over 80% of the US tourism market in Europe. The authors investigate the determinants of each destination's share of US tourists' demand for the group of destinations, examining the role of changes in relative price competitiveness between the destinations and in the expenditure budget of US tourists.

The AIDS Model

The AIDS model is explicitly based on the microeconomics of consumer expenditure theory. Demand is specified as a function of the consumer's expenditure budget and the relative prices of the set of goods or services that the consumer can purchase. In contrast to the single equation models that have traditionally been used to estimate tourism demand, the AIDS model permits estimation of the complete set of price and expenditure elasticities, giving the sensitivities of tourism demand to changes in relative prices and expenditure. The system of equations in the AIDS model focuses on explaining changes in the budget shares of tourism expenditure, rather than changes in the levels of tourism demand. The model assumes that consumption and labour supply are not related, so that consumers' tourism budget shares do not vary in response to their work time and effort. Tourists' expenditure is separated into groups of destinations and the preferences within each group are not influenced by demand in other groups. It is assumed that US tourists first allocate total tourism expenditure between the top four destination countries and the rest of the world and then decide the budget shares between France, Italy, Spain and the UK.

Results

The AIDS model permits the derivation of the complete set of relevant elasticities, which supply crucial information about the interdependencies of competing products. The Table provides the values of the expenditure and uncompensated price elasticities using the budget share in 1990. The elasticities gives the percentage change in tourism demand in response to a 1% change in the variable under consideration.

	Expenditure and uncompensated price elasticities					
	Expenditure elasticities	*Uncompensated elasticities*				
		Own-price elasticities	*Cross-price elasticities*			
			France	*Italy*	*UK*	*Spain*
France $w_{90} = 0.206$	1.317	−1.755	–	0.748	−0.143	−0.167
Italy $w_{90} = 0.257$	1.249	−2.083	0.614	–	−0.090	0.310
UK $w_{90} = 0.441$	0.769	−0.892	0.046	0.071	–	0.006
Spain $w_{90} = 0.0096$	0.718	−1.554	−0.236	0.966	0.052	–

The own-price elasticity values indicate the extent to which an increase in relative prices, and hence a deterioration of price competitiveness, will reduce tourism demand for the destination. The authors emphasise that a change in the price of a destination sets two forces in motion. One is a substitution effect and the other is an income effect. The change in quantity demanded resulting from changing the price while simultaneously taking account of the change in real income brought about by the price changes (i.e. compensating the individual with income) is termed a compensated response. In contrast, an uncompensated response refers to a situation where the change in quantity demanded in response to a change in price is estimated without taking account of the effects of the price changes on real income. The authors estimate uncompensated price elasticities since these are often more suitable for price sensitivity analysis as consumers may not be aware of change in their real income. For France and Italy, the expenditure elasticities are greater than one, corresponding to the positive elasticity coefficients. Hence, these two countries could be regarded as 'luxuries' as tourism products and the share of US tourist expenditure in them is expected to increase as the total expenditure of US tourists increases. With regard to consumers' preferences, the authors categorise France and Italy as 'first choice' destinations for US tourists and the UK and Spain as 'second choice' destinations. This indicates that US tourists would prefer to direct additional expenditure towards France and Italy rather than the UK and Spain. Since the expenditure elasticities for the UK and Spain are less than one, these two countries will benefit/lose only marginally from an increase/decrease in US total tourism expenditure.

Negative values of uncompensated own-price elasticities indicate that an increase in price leads to reductions in demand. The most own-price responsive country is Italy with a price elasticity of −2.08. For Italy, Spain and France, a positive return could be gained from lower prices since the absolute value of the elasticities of these three countries are greater than one. This is particularly beneficial to Spain. The authors note that the price effect could be used to offset the loss of Spain's share due to an increase in US tourism expenditure. For all budget share equations except that for the UK, the own-price coefficient has the expected negative sign and is statistically significant. The negativity condition satisfies the law of demand. The results show that price competitiveness is important for US demand for France, Italy and Spain but is relatively unimportant for the UK.

The cross-price elasticity values indicate the extent to which tourism demand for competing destinations will change in response to a price increase. The income elasticity values indicate the extent to which tourism demand will change in response to changes in the total budget of US tourists for the destinations under consideration. France and Italy are regarded as substitutes by US tourists, as are Spain and Italy. As US expenditure rises, the market shares of Spain and the UK decline, while France and Italy benefit. The cross-price coefficient measures the absolute change in a destination's expenditure share following a unit proportional change in price other things equal. For example, if the UK increases its effective price by 1% (in log terms), Italy's budget share will increase by 0.171 percentage points. The underlying logic is that a higher than expected price level in one country may cause people to spend less there but more in another country. The authors note that all the expenditure per capita coefficients are significant. Italy appears to benefit from the increase in the real total expenditure of US tourists per capita as the positive coefficients show, while the UK and Spain are losers.

The estimated signs of the cross-price elasticities show large substitution effects are caused by changes in the prices of destination countries. For instance, when the price of visiting Italy increases, US tourists tend to substitute away from Italy towards France and Spain. The authors also note that the effects of an increase in the prices of visiting France and Spain are less than that of visiting Italy. Thus, the cross-price elasticities of the equations for France, Spain and Italy show that the shares of France and Spain are more sensitive to price changes in Italy than the share of Italy is to price changes in France and Spain. They regard this as expected given the differences in the quality and quantity of tourism infrastructures available in these countries. In contrast to these substitution effects, France is a complement to the UK and Spain, although the negative cross-price elasticities are not very large. The authors suggest that, given the complementary relationship existing between these destinations, policy makers in France may wish to co-operate or promote a joint marketing campaign with the other two countries.

Conclusions

The study provides policy makers with useful information concerning the sensitivity of tourism demand to changes in relative prices, exchange rates and expenditure. An important result is that maintaining price competitiveness matters greatly for France, Italy and Spain, as an increase in prices in each of the destinations will result in a significant reduction in US tourism demand for it. An increase (decrease) in prices in France results in an increase (decrease) in US tourists' demand for Italy, indicating that France and Italy are regarded as substitutes by US tourists. Similarly, an increase (decrease) in prices in Spain results in an increase (decrease) in prices in Italy, indicating that Spain and Italy are also regarded as substitutes. The UK is a different case in that changes in tourism demand result mainly from changes in US tourists' expenditure budget, as price competitiveness does not appear to be a key determinant of US tourists' decision-making in the UK case. As US tourists' budget for expenditure on all four destinations rises, the market shares of the UK and Spain tend to decline, while France and Italy benefit. This is a useful finding for policy makers in the UK and Spain who would like benefit from growth in the US market.

Source: Han Z., R. Durbarry and M.T. Sinclair (2006) 'Modelling US Tourism Demand for European Destinations', *Tourism Management*, 27, 1–10

2.6   CONCLUSIONS AND POLICY

- Tourism demand refers to the willingness and ability of consumers to buy different amounts of a tourism product at different prices during some period of time. In defining tourism demand, we need to distinguish the demand for travel to a destination and the demand for a particular tourism-related product or service.
- Following standard theory, tourism demand may be influenced by a myriad of price and non-price factors. The price factors include the product price, the prices of other products and expectations regarding future price changes. The non-price factors include the size of the market, income, tastes, advertising and promotion, seasonality, buyer expectations of future income and wealth, product availability, the amount of leisure time available and other factors such as special events, immigration levels or random shocks.
- Tourism demand exhibits four main types of elasticity relevant for policy: price elasticity (sensitivity to changes in the price of that product itself), income elasticity (sensitivity to changes in the level of consumer income), cross-price elasticity (sensitivity to changes in the price of substitute goods and complementary goods) and marketing/advertising elasticity (sensitivity to changes in advertising expenditures on that product).
- Broadly, tourism demand is classified as either elastic (relatively sensitive to changes in prices, income and/or advertising expenditure) or inelastic (relatively insensitive to changes in prices, income and/or advertising expenditure).
- Knowledge of price elasticity is important for tourism managers seeking to maximise sales revenues. Since total revenue for a tourism product is maximised when its price elasticity is unitary, managers should strive to raise the price of demand inelastic products but lower the price of demand elastic products. Price elasticity of tourism demand will vary with the availability of substitutes, the price relative to income, whether the product is a necessity or a luxury, and time.

- Knowledge of income elasticity of demand can help tourism managers to determine if their product is a normal good (demand for the product rises as income rises) or an inferior good (demand for the product falls as income rises). Such information can help tourism managers identify more precisely the potential markets for their products given anticipated changes in income over time.

- Knowledge of cross-price elasticity of demand can help tourism managers determine if their products have substitute goods, complementary goods or are independent of other products. Information on cross-price elasticity is essential for formulating pricing strategy and analysis of the risks associated with various products, particularly for firms with extensive product lines, where substantial substitute or complementary relations exist among the various products.

- Knowledge of marketing/advertising elasticity can assist tourism managers to determine appropriate levels of advertising outlays. At the destination level, estimates of marketing elasticities can inform the allocation of marketing expenditure between different market segments.

- The literature contains a large number of research studies that have attempted to model the factors that actually affect tourism demand, and the extent to which they do so. Demand modellers need to look carefully at the issues of model specification, data collection, functional forms of the equation and evaluation of results.

- The literature suggests that the range of factors that might affect the demand for international tourism is very large. The more prominent factors include income, relative prices, transport cost, exchange rates, marketing expenses, migration levels in host destination and qualitative factors such as tourists' attributes, trade and cultural links between the countries, destination attractiveness, special events, natural disasters and social threats. The GFC has reinforced the importance of wealth as a determinant of tourism flows.

- Over time, the modelling of tourism demand has become more sophisticated and more complex, and different contexts of study, different data sets, use of different variables and different modelling techniques preclude generalisations. Given the importance of a better understanding of demand for destination management, marketing and policy purposes, tourism demand modelling may be expected to continue to be refined with more input from the econometrics literature.

SELF-REVIEW QUESTIONS

1. Define tourism demand, distinguishing between demand for travel to a destination and demand for a particular tourism product.

2. Economic theory suggests that price and tourism demand should have an inverse relationship. Briefly explain why.

3. List the key non-price factors that might influence tourism demand for (i) land tour packages and (ii) cruise tours.

4. Discuss how each of the following might affect the demand for hotel accommodation at a destination.

   a. A rise in income in the origin country.
   b. A rise in the cost of transport fuel worldwide (distinguish between air and land transport).
   c. A successful marketing promotion by the destination country.

5. Use tourism examples to explain the possibility of bandwagon, snob and Veblen effects in tourism demand.

6. Briefly outline the four steps involved in modelling tourism demand through regression analysis.

7. Choose a tourism example and differentiate briefly between the possible quantitative and qualitative factors that might influence its demand.

8. List substitute and complementary products that might affect the demand for domestic air travel.

9. Using examples, explain why, over time, some tourism products that were once considered normal goods may come to be seen as inferior goods.

ESSAY QUESTIONS

1. Using examples, explain the income and substitution effects that underlie tourism consumer behaviour.

2. Discuss the factors that may affect demand for international air travel over (i) the next 5 years and (ii) over the next 20 years.

3. How might rising incomes in Asia affect the demand for tourism products, both domestically and internationally, in the coming decades? What types of tourism products may be most affected?

4. Determining exactly what factors influence tourism demand and to what extent is neither easy nor straightforward. How so?

5. Choose a tourism product and discuss each of the four main types of elasticity that might influence demand for it.

6. To maximise its total revenue, a tourism firm should strive towards unitary price elasticity of demand ($\varepsilon = 1$) for its product. Explain why.

7. Assess the relative importance of the independent variables found in the literature to influence the demand for international tourism arrivals.

8. Assess the strengths and weaknesses inherent in the present state of tourism demand modelling.

CHAPTER 3

FORECASTING TOURISM DEMAND

LEARNING OBJECTIVES

After reading this chapter you will be able to:

1. Explain who undertakes tourism forecasting and why.

2. Understand the difference in approach between qualitative tourism forecasting and quantitative tourism forecasting.

3. Describe the various techniques involved in qualitative and quantitative tourism forecasting.

4. Assess the appropriateness of different forecasting techniques in different tourism contexts.

5. Appreciate the move towards a more integrated approach in forecasting tourism demand.

3.1 INTRODUCTION

Forecasting is concerned with predicting the future, with estimating what will happen at some future time. Frechtling defines forecasting as 'a systematic way of organizing information from the past to infer the occurrence of an event in the future' (2001: 7). Demand forecasting may be characterised as predicting the most probable level of demand that is likely to occur given changing circumstances or, when alternative policies are implemented, to predict what different levels of demand may result (Archer, 1994).

Tourism forecasting, though, can be much like predicting the weather. Many factors come into play, not all at the one time and not all to the same degree of importance. The changing relationships between the factors make causality seem less direct and less certain. Tourism stakeholders will happily give you their predictions on the effects that, say, the latest change in government visa policy will have on inbound tourist numbers or what will be the effect that the opening of a theme park will have on coastal resort earnings and community employment. The problem is that such predictions often are not accurate, and decisions based on their assumed accuracy often lead to severe misallocation of resources on the part of both private and public decision makers.

3.2   THE IMPORTANCE OF FORECASTING IN TOURISM

Tourism researchers and practitioners are interested in tourism demand forecasting for several reasons. In a changing global tourism environment it is important, for both government policy development and business planning, to have reliable short-term and long-term forecasts of tourism activity. We can distinguish three different time horizons in tourism forecasting:

- The short run whose time span covers a year or less and decisions are made for current operations.
- The intermediate run, with a time horizon of 2–5 years for decisions on capacity expansions and changes in products and services.
- The long range, over 5 years for tourism planning and policy development.

Forecasts are essential for marketing, production and financial planning. Reliable forecasts are essential if managers, policy makers and planners are to avoid oversupply (leading to unnecessary excess costs) or undersupply (potential lost sales revenue). Forecasting is also an essential step in reducing disparities between the demand for, and supply of, services and facilities. However, tourism poses certain unique aspects which make forecasting particularly important but also problematic. We may highlight seven reasons why forecasting is of special importance in tourism (cf. Frechtling, 2001; Sheldon & Var, 1985).

1. *The tourist product is perishable*
Accurate forecasts of tourism demand are essential for efficient planning by tourism-related businesses, particularly given the perishable nature of many tourism products and services. As Archer (1980) has noted, unfilled airline seats and unused hotel rooms cannot be stockpiled. Any unused capacity at a particular point in time that cannot be stored or stockpiled for later use represents a loss of revenue that cannot be recovered. Once a plane has taken off or a ferry has left the dock, no additional revenue is possible from the potential customers who have not purchased the product or service. Firms use forecasts in order to supply goods and services to avoid both unsold inventory and unfilled demand.

2. *Tourism behaviour is complex*
Tourists display various motives for travel. These include relaxation, Visiting Friends and Relatives (VFR), business, attending conventions or special events, adventure, education and learning and so on. Each tourism market segment has different factors which influence tourism flows. Forecasting becomes an imperative if tourism organisations and destinations are to provide the different types of goods and services that are demanded by persons in tourism's different market segments. The complexity of tourist behaviour makes the task of forecasting more difficult since different demographic groups have different values that drive their quest for tourism experiences (Dwyer *et al.*, 2009) and demand by different

market segments may be affected quite differently by changes in price and non-price data affecting destination choice. Even short-term forecasting has become less accurate given the ever-shortening lead times between the decision to travel and the purchase of air travel, accommodation and other travel-related goods and services.

Consider how the complexities of human behaviour have affected forecasts of the effects of the Global Financial Crisis (GFC) on tourism. Our lack of knowledge about the possible consumer responses to the crisis places great impediments in the way of forecasting its effects on the tourism industry. Thus, consumers may spend less and travel less given the GFC, but to what extent do they shift to other products? Or reduce debt? Or save more? Estimates of the income elasticities of demand for tourism are typically based on data over several years and are not applicable to the sharp falls associated with the GFC. Do tourists switch to closer destinations? Do they exhibit shorter lengths of stay? What is the extent of any shifts to domestic tourism? Is there some 'trading down'? (e.g. towards lower-cost carriers, lower-standard hotels, business class to economy, etc.). Do such crises make consumers become more sensitive to price signals and differentials, thereby increasing the elasticity of demand for tourism products? What are the implications for particular destinations? What are the implications for particular tourism market segments (e.g. seniors tourism vs business tourism vs visiting friends and relatives vs cruise tourism).Will remote areas be differentially affected? To what extent do price level and exchange rate falls offset income falls to maintain tourism flows? There are many other related questions that could be asked. We simply do not know enough about consumer travel behaviour to give definite answers to these questions.

3. *People are inseparable from the production–consumption process*
Like other services, the production and consumption of tourist products typically take place simultaneously. Much of the production–consumption process involves people interacting as suppliers and consumers, for example, bar tenders, tour guides, chefs, diving instructors and shop assistants, and their customers. Thus, tour operators and restaurant managers will need to know how many staff to hire or lay off or how many facilities to open or close in line with predicted seasonal variations in the number and needs of their customers. A car hire firm will need to know how many cars to add to its rental fleet or how many temporary extra staff to hire over the coming holiday season. Short-term forecasts are used for making everyday strategic supply adjustment decisions. Firms use short-term forecasts to fine-tune their everyday marketing, production and financial planning decisions so as to enhance their profitability and efficiency.

4. *Customer satisfaction depends on complementary products and services*
The visitor experience depends on the satisfaction derived from a variety of different products and services offered by tourism characteristic and connected industries. The demand for a theme park, for example, may depend on the extent of air services to a location, accommodation facilities, other entertainments, the perceived safety and security offered

within the destination and so on. Forecasting can help to identify investment needs across different tourism sectors and potential impacts on firms' sales revenues of investments in complementary tourism sectors.

5. *Tourism demand is extremely sensitive to natural and human-made disasters*
The various influences on tourism demand were discussed in Chapter 2. While terrorist attacks, natural catastrophes and the incidence of pandemics such as SARS are almost impossible to predict, estimates of their projected impact on destinations can help to determine strategies that can be enacted to minimise their adverse effects. This is the essence of contingency planning which is of increasing importance in destination management. The inherent volatility of tourism demand, stemming from its predominantly discretionary nature, poses particular challenges to forecasting while at the same time requiring that it be undertaken. If, as Dwyer *et al.* (2009) suggest, we are witnessing a transformation of consumer values which can make tourist behaviour less predictable, then this volatility is likely to increase in the future.

The volatility of tourism demand constitutes an ongoing challenge for many destinations. The inherent cyclical and/or seasonal nature of tourism makes it difficult for stakeholders to match their future supply with demand and to meet consistent yield expectations. Improved forecasting techniques can help industry develop strategies for maximising yield and develop niche markets through the provision of appropriate data and research.

6. *Forecasting aids long-term planning*
Tourism supply requires large, long lead-time investments in plant, equipment and infrastructure. Forecasting lies at the heart of tourism planning and decision-making as policy makers, planners and managers strive to match supply with future demand.

Long-term forecasts provide the rationale for public sector strategic decisions such as investment in tourism infrastructure, highways, airports and allocation of budgets by national and local governments. Tourism investment, especially investment in destination infrastructure, such as airports, road networks, cruise ship terminals and rail-links, require long-term financial commitments at substantial cost. This applies equally to situations where expensive physical structures have to be put in place (e.g. airport terminals, rail links) or where skills need to be developed in the workforce through training programs (e.g. air traffic controllers, aeronautical engineers and hotel managers).

Similarly, future demand must often be anticipated up to several years in advance if destinations and their constituent firms are to avoid missed opportunities through inappropriate or under-utilised capacity. Accurate tourism forecasting can underpin efficient resource allocation over the longer term. Airlines, for example, given their long lead times for additional fleet, must estimate future passenger number several years ahead so as to be able to buy or lease planes. The raising of bank finance and investor capital depends strongly on projected earnings. Forecasting of tourist volume in the form of arrivals is

Table 3.1 Possible uses of forecasting and the consequences of poor forecasting

Uses of Demand Forecasts	Consequences of Poor Forecasting
Tourism marketers use demand forecasts to: • Set marketing goals, both for strategic and for annual marketing plan; • Explore potential markets for the feasibility of selling goods and services to them and expected volume of sales; • Simulate the impact of future events on demand, including alternative marketing programmes, changes in political, economic, social, technological or environmental conditions, and the actions of competitors.	• Over- or under-budgeting for marketing. • Marketing to low-yield segments. • Wrong marketing mix, for example, prices too high.
Managers use tourism demand forecasts to: • Determine operational requirements, such as staffing, supplies and capacity; • Study project feasibility of investment projects.	• Excess labour or customer dissatisfaction limited service. • Wasted financial resources, in meeting interest payments.
Planners and public agencies use tourism demand forecasts to: • Predict the economic, social/cultural and environmental effects of visitors; • Assess the potential impact of regulatory policies affecting tourism; • Project public revenues from tourism for the budgeting process; • Plan ahead and to develop contingency plans to cover possible future occurrences; • Ensure adequate capacity and supply of public infrastructure; • Help destination governments to formulate and implement appropriate medium- to long-term tourism strategies.	• Environmental and social/cultural degradation, inflation and unemployment. • Business losses, unemployment and inflation. • Budget deficits. • Costs of crises greater than necessary. • Inadequate provision of public infrastructure: traffic congestion, delays, accidents and shortages of essential services. • Inappropriate tourism development.

Source: Based on Frechtling (2001), pp. 10, 11

especially important since it is an indicator of the demand that can provide basic information for planning and policymaking (Chu, 1998). The prediction of long-term demand for tourism-related infrastructure is important to the appraisal of investment projects (see Chapters 10 and 13).

7. *Forecasting is fundamental to the conduct of modern business*
Forecasting provides a systematic basis for discovering and understanding the factors that influence the demand and supply of tourism products. Forecasts provide a basis for strategy development to deal with and changing situations. For example, the forecasts of tourism at the levels of both the firm and the destination as a whole depend on the performance of the overall economy, including the growth rate in GDP, the level of interest rates, the rate of unemployment, the value of the dollar in foreign exchange markets and the rate of inflation. They can help detect emerging opportunities and looming threats.

The success of many businesses depends importantly on the state of future tourism demand, and ultimate management failure is quite often due to the failure to match supply and market demand. Public and private organisations that seek to serve and manage tourism demand need to reduce the risk of future failures. This risk is intensified by the special characteristics of tourism demand and supply. The successful manager will seek ways to reduce this risk by organising knowledge about the past to better discern the future (Frechtling, 2001).

Most business decisions are made in the face of risk or uncertainty. A firm must decide how much of each product to produce, what prices to charge and how much to spend on advertising, and it must also plan for the future growth of the firm. All these decisions are based on some forecast of the level of future economic activity in general and demand for the firm's product(s) in particular. The aim of economic forecasting is to reduce the risk or uncertainty that the firm faces in its short-term operational decision-making and in planning for its long-term growth.

Table 3.1 sets out the possible uses of forecasting and the consequences of poor forecasting.

3.3 FORECASTING APPROACHES

There are two broad methods of forecasting: *qualitative forecasting* and *quantitative forecasting*. Mixed models contain elements of both these approaches.

Qualitative forecasting is based on the judgements of persons sharing their experience, practical knowledge and intuition. These judgements are often used to moderate or 'second-guess' quantitative forecasts. Qualitative methods are also called 'judgemental methods'. Past information about the forecast variable is organised by experts using their judgement rather than mathematical rules.

Quantitative forecasting employs mathematical techniques to predict the values of variables of interest. There are two major categories of quantitative models: *time series* and *causal*.

(1) *Time-series models* assume that a variable's past course is the key to predicting its future. A time-series model explains a variable with regard to its own past and a random disturbance term. Patterns in the data during the past are used to project or extrapolate future values. Time-series analysis assumes that a variable will follow its established path into the future and that its future behaviour can therefore be predicted through an analysis of its past behaviour. Causal relationships are ignored. As we shall see, there are many different forms that such models can take within the class of time-series models.

(2) *Causal (Econometric) methods* attempt to identify causal relationships between the tourism demand variable and its influencing factors. Causal models select explanatory variables on the basis of economic theory and attempt to develop the appropriate mathematical expression of this relationship. These relationships, together with forecasts of the explanatory variables, are then used to forecast the series of interest. Firstly, the approach relies on the ability to identify meaningful relationships between the explanatory variables, and secondly, on the accuracy of the estimates of the explanatory variables on which the forecasts are based. Causal forecasting models have the advantage of demonstrating the extent to which forecasts change as a result of changes in the variables that act as economic drivers of tourism (Blake *et al.*, 2004).

(3) *Mixed models.* Between the two extremes of time-series and causal models are mixed models which include both time-series and structural elements. The most widely used quantitative approach is for the forecaster to choose a particular class of model as indicated by the data and then use a set of objective criteria to choose the most suitable model within this class. Increasingly, both qualitative and quantitative judgements are used to make forecasts. This hybrid approach will be discussed below.

3.4 QUALITATIVE APPROACHES TO FORECASTING

Qualitative forecasting methods rely on the experience and judgement of individuals rather than on mathematical techniques.

Frechtling (2001) notes that qualitative forecasting (judgemental) methods are normally applied under one or more of the following conditions:

- *There are insufficient historical data.* In some cases, we do not have enough past data for use in a quantitative model to produce valid results, for example, new product, new service, new location, new technology and so on.
- *The time series available is not reliable or valid.* We may have a long time series of data, but its accuracy is not always assured, nor always relevant to what we wish to measure.

- *The macro environment is changing rapidly.* External macro-environmental factors are beyond control of the tourism marketer but affect tourism demand. Substantial change is taking place globally that will influence the types of experiences that tourists seek in the future. Major shifts in the leisure and tourism environment are occurring, reflecting changing consumer values, political forces, environmental changes and the explosive growth of information and communication technology (Dwyer *et al.*, 2009).
- *Major disturbances.* Although macro-environmental changes may be slow to develop and can last for years, disturbances are essentially unanticipated, short-term major changes in factors affecting tourism. These include wars, terrorism, political upheavals, labour strikes, natural disasters, infectious diseases and the like.
- *Long-term forecasts are desired.* Tourism managers and planners need to understand the possible shapes of a distant future. Reliable forecasts of periods of 3–5 years or more are difficult to generate from quantitative models, primarily because of the variety of factors that can affect demand over longer period. Questions asked for the long term include: what events may occur in the next decade that could critically affect our product or markets? What will be the implications for long-haul travel of an Emissions Trading Scheme (ETS)? By what year will a new technology be widely used? What will our visitor volume be in 10 years' time?

Qualitative forecasts are based on the informed views of tourism experts and are often used when quantitative numerical data is insufficient, inadequate or inappropriate, or the forecaster wishes to moderate or qualify a quantitative forecast. Qualitative techniques can be used by individual firms as well as by destination managers. They encompass one or more of the following approaches:

- Sales force polling
- Expert opinion
- Panel consensus
- Surveys
- Delphi technique
- Scenario writing.

These approaches are summarised in Box 3.1.

BOX 3.1 Qualitative forecasting techniques

Sales force polling
Some tourism organisations survey their own salespeople in the field about their expectations for future sales by specific geographical area and product line or service. An advantage of this type of forecasting is that the firm's salespeople are

aware of their clients' expected demand and of competitor tactics. The idea is that employees who are closest to the customer may have significant insights into the state of the future market.

Expert opinion

In this method, informed individuals use personal or organisational experiences as a basis for developing future expectations of tourism demand. Although the approach is highly subjective, the reasoned judgement of an informed individual often provides valuable insights.

Panel consensus

This technique relies on the interchange of ideas between experts. This interchange can be conducted face to face through meetings of top management, group meetings, think tanks, seminars and the like. Panel consensus pools the experience and judgement of those most familiar with the variable to be forecast. The collective judgement of knowledgeable persons can be an important source of information. Disadvantages are that often the opinions of the most forceful participants carry the most weight in the group discussion, resulting in a 'herd' or 'bandwagon' effect whereby individuals are reluctant to state views contrary to a developing consensus or those of 'recognised experts'. This jury of executive opinion method disperses responsibility for developing accurate forecasts with the result that some participants may not devote serious effort to the task. When a group is responsible, no single person can be held accountable for forecasting errors.

Surveys

Surveys are questionnaires conducted either face to face or by mail or phone that seek to determine the demand and supply intentions of households and businesses. The accuracy and reliability of forecasts based on surveys depend on the quality of the survey instrument, the quantity and quality of responses and the interpretation of those responses. Forecasts based on surveys are generally more reliable in the short to medium rather than longer term. Frechtling (2001: 227, 228) emphasises that even the most carefully designed surveys do not always predict consumer demand accurately. For one thing, respondents do not always have enough information to decide whether or not to purchase a product or service. In other situations, those surveyed may be pressed for time or be unwilling to devote much time to their answers. Sometimes the response may reflect a desire (conscious or unconscious) to put oneself in a favourable light or to gain approval from those conducting the survey. He notes three types of errors that can render intentions invalid as indicators of future tourism-related behaviour: sampling errors (resolved through applying statistical sampling theory); non-response errors (resolved through achieving high response rates); and response errors (resolved by encouraging respondents to answer carefully constructed, practicable questions honestly and objectively).

Delphi method

Surveys can be conducted in anonymity wherein participants do not meet or have contact with each other. The best known survey of this type is the Delphi method. The Delphi method is designed to produce a group consensus on forecasts while avoiding some of the problems of group forecasting methods. The Delphi method is a systematic, interactive forecasting method that relies on a panel of independent experts, sharing forecasts anonymously. The members of the expert panel respond to questions in two or more rounds. After each round, a facilitator provides an anonymous summary of the experts' forecasts from the previous round as well as the justifications for their judgements. Participants are encouraged to revise their earlier answers in light of the replies of other members of the group. During this process the range of the answers tends to decrease and the group tends to converge towards a 'common' answer. The process continues until a consensus is reached or until further iterations generate little or no change in forecasts. The value of the Delphi technique is that individual panel members are forced to consider why their judgement differs from that of others. It has three distinctive characteristics that set it apart from other judgemental techniques (Frechtling, 2001: 214):

- *Respondent anonymity.* Due to participant anonymity, reducing unwanted group discussion effects, the Delphi method does not suffer from the occasional bullying or deferential treatment of influential peoples' ideas that often accompany face-to-face panel discussion. Since only their anonymous ideas are passed around through questionnaire and feedback, there is no pressure on participants to conform to a particular view. As such, the Delphi method has the potential to gauge the participants' true beliefs.
- *Iteration and controlled feedback.* The researcher conducting the Delphi method transmits a summary of the emerging group consensus back to the judges who are encouraged to reassess their prior responses and provide new ones based on the feedback over several iterations or 'rounds'. In this way, the Delphi approach presents the spread of opinion as well as consensus points.
- *Statistical group response.* The group opinion is defined by certain statistics from each round.

When undertaken successfully, the Delphi method can provide a set of possible alternative medium- to long-term futures with their probability of occurrence. This allows planners, policy makers and managers to develop contingency plans. The method has proved more accurate than juries of executive opinion and traditional group meetings have. Importantly, the Delphi technique doesn't preclude presenting the group with time-series or other data of the variables to be forecast. Each participant can be asked to consider macro-environment factors (PEST analysis), industry-wide factors and others that might change the trend and by how much (Frechtling, 2001: 214).

A related technique is the Nominal Group Technique involving a group of participants, usually experts. After the participants respond individually to forecast-related questions, they rank their responses in order of perceived relative importance. The rankings are then collected and aggregated. Eventually, the group should reach a consensus regarding the priorities of the ranked issues.

Scenario writing

This technique uses a scripted scene or case study in order to generate ideas and open discussion. It is not a forecasting technique in itself but can be used to construct medium- to long-term scenarios whose likely eventualities can then be analysed for their potential effects upon tourism demand (van Doorn, 1984). Scenario writing is particularly useful for examining the likely effects of changes of greater magnitude, such as crises or large-scale policy changes. Ideally, destination managers or tourism operators should develop a relatively unconstrained approach to the generation of alternative scenarios, the assignment of notional probabilities to these scenarios and the planning of specific strategies for coping with each one. The value of using scenarios is that, by considering potential developments and responses in advance, the organisation will not be forced to make quick, ill-considered decisions when the unexpected occurs (Faulkner & Valerio, 1995).

Qualitative forecasting is growing in acceptance and usage. It is especially used today to moderate or 'second-guess' quantitative forecasts, due to the limitations of quantitative forecasting. Qualitative techniques can be useful for supplementing quantitative forecasts to anticipate changes in consumer tastes or business expectations about future economic conditions. They can also be invaluable in forecasting the demand for a product or service that the firm intends to introduce. In Section 3.9 we discuss the merits of a 'hybrid' approach which contains elements of both qualitative and quantitative forecasting.

3.5   TIME-SERIES APPROACHES TO FORECASTING

Data collected for use in forecasting the value of a particular variable may be classified into two major categories: cross-sectional and time-series. Cross-sectional data are an array of the values of an economic variable observed at the same one point in time. Time-series data are defined as a sequential array of the values of an economic variable at different points in time.

The time-series approach relates current values of a variable to its past values and to the values of current and past random disturbances, using extrapolation procedures. Time-series forecasting models are based solely on historical observations of the values of the variable being forecast. These models do not attempt to explain underlying causal relationships that produce the observed outcome. Time-series approaches are useful for providing forecasts based on relatively stable and predictable long-run relationships between tourism demand and its drivers.

Time-series analysis can be as simple as projecting or extrapolating the unadjusted trend. Applying either graphical analysis (by eye fitting) or least squares regression techniques, one can use historical data to determine the average increase or decrease in the series during each time period and then project this rate of change into the future.

Univariate analysis involves the projection of a variable based on its own past movement in time. For example, the demand for visitation to a resort island (Q) may be viewed as simply a function of time, t, such that $Q = f(t)$. This will provide a trend line that can be projected into the future (modified by cyclical and seasonal behaviour) in order to predict tourism numbers in the short-term future. Similarly, a beachfront shop may wish to predict next summer's demand for swimwear and the management of a city council might try to predict attendance at a local festival by projecting the trend line of past attendances. Time-series analysis can also be considerably more complex and sophisticated, allowing examination of seasonal and cyclical patterns as well as the basic trend.

In an analysis of time-series data, time (in years, months, etc.) is represented on the horizontal axis and the values of the dependent variable (e.g. sales) are on the vertical axis. Long-run changes in a time-series of data can follow a number of different types of trends. Three possible cases are shown in Figure 3.1.

Since extrapolation techniques assume that a variable will follow its established path, the problem is to determine the appropriate trend curve. In theory, one could fit any complex mathematical function to the historical data and extrapolate to estimate future values. Selection of the appropriate curve is guided by both empirical and theoretical considerations. Empirically, it is a question of finding the curve that best fits the historical movement in the data. Theoretical considerations intervene when logic or instinct dictates that a particular pattern of future events should prevail.

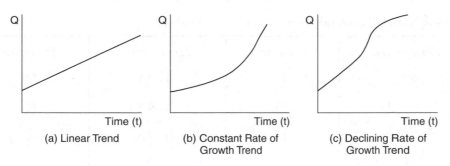

Figure 3.1 Time-series growth patterns of demand

A linear trend is shown in panel (a). The simplest form of time-series analysis is projecting the past trend by fitting a straight line to the data either visually or by regression analysis. In linear regression analysis the objective is to develop an equation that summarises the effects of the predictor (independent) variables upon the forecasted (dependent) variable. If the predictor variable were plotted, the object would be to obtain an equation of a straight line that minimises the sum of the squared deviations from the line (with deviation being the distance from each point to the line).

The linear regression will take the form

$$Q = a + bT \qquad (3.1)$$

Where,

Q is the value of the time series to be forecasted for period t;

a is the estimated value of the time series (the constant of the regression in the base period, time $t = 0$);

b is the absolute amount of growth per period;

T is the time period in which the time series is to be forecasted.

Once the coefficients of the model have been estimated, forecasting with a single-equation model consists of obtaining values for the independent variables in the equation and then evaluating the equation with those values. The suggested relationships between the variables may be written as *additive* or *multiplicative*, and therefore entered into the model in either *linear* or *log* form.

Table 3.2 shows the number of arrivals ('000's) of tourists to a resort island, by quarter, over a 4-year period.

Let us hypothesise that the demand equation for tourist arrivals is $Q_t = Q_0 + b_t$ where Q_t = number of arrivals ('000) in period t.

Table 3.2 Seasonal demand for tourism to a resort island

Time period	Quantity	Time period	Quantity
2007.1	11	2009.1	14
2007.2	15	2009.2	18
2007.3	12	2009.3	15
2007.4	14	2009.4	17
2008.1	12	2010.1	15
2008.2	17	2010.2	20
2008.3	13	2010.3	16
2008.4	16	2010.4	19

Fitting a regression line to the tourist arrivals data running from the first quarter of 2007 ($t = 1$) to the last quarter of 2010 ($t = 16$) given in Table 3.2 we get

$$Q_t = 11.90 + \underset{(4.00)}{0.39t} \tag{3.2}$$

$$R^2 = 0.50$$

Equation 3.2 is an example of univariate analysis which involves the projection of a variable based on its own past movements in time. In the last quarter of 2006, tourist arrivals on the island (i.e. Q_0) were 11.9 ('000). The regression equation indicates that visitor arrivals increase at an average rate of 0.39 per quarter. The trend variable is statistically significant at better than the 1% level (inferred from the value of 4 for the t-statistic given in parentheses below the estimated slope coefficient) and explains 50% of the variation in the quarterly variation in arrivals (R^2). Thus, based on past trends we can forecast tourist arrivals to the island in each quarter of 2011 to be

$Q_{17} = 11.90 + 0.394(17) = 18,600$ in the first quarter of 2011

$Q_{18} = 11.90 + 0.394(18) = 18,990$ in the second quarter of 2011

$Q_{19} = 11.90 + 0.394(19) = 19,390$ in the third quarter of 2011

$Q_{20} = 11.90 + 0.394(20) = 19,780$ in the fourth quarter of 2011

Equation 3.2 provides a trend line that can be used to project demand for tourism arrivals to the destination. In Figure 3.2, tourist arrivals to the island for the first, second, third and fourth quarters of 2011 can be read off the extended regression (trend)

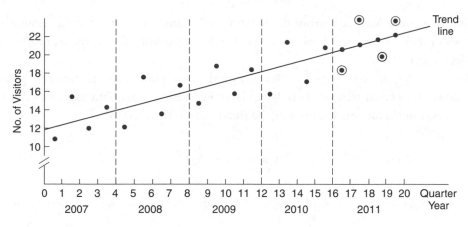

Figure 3.2 Actual and forecasted visitors to a resort island

line, the dots on the trend line, for quarters 17, 18, 19 and 20, respectively. Note, however, that the forecasted values are likely to be wide of the mark since they ignore the significant seasonal variation that appears to exist in the data. Techniques exist to incorporate this seasonal variation and substantially improve the forecast of tourist arrivals.

It is often assumed that relationships between variables are *linear* because

- linear relationships are the simplest non-trivial relationships that can be imagined (hence the easiest to work with);
- the 'true' relationships between the variables are often at least *approximately* linear over the range of values that are of interest to the forecaster;
- in any case, the forecaster can often *transform* the variables in such a way as to linearise the relationships.

Figures 3.1b and 3.1c depict non-linear trends.

In Figure 3.1b the time series follows a constant rate of growth path. While the assumption of a constant absolute amount of change per time period may be appropriate in many cases, there are situations where a constant percentage change is more appropriate and gives better forecasts.

When the data indicate a non-linear relationship, the regression equation may be derived as a linear equation in semi-logarithmic form

$$\ln Q = a + bT \tag{3.3}$$

The earnings of many new, innovative companies follow this type of trend, as do some emerging destinations that are in the high growth stage of their development.

Figure 3.1c shows a time series that exhibits a declining rate of growth. Sales of a new product may follow this pattern. As market saturation occurs, the rate of growth will decline over time. Mature tourism destinations and mature tourism products exhibit this pattern in their visitor arrivals as Butler has hypothesised in his Tourism Area Life Cycle model (Butler, 1980).

As Figure 3.1c shows, when the sales of a product are plotted against time, the growth of sales shows a linear trend that can be said to consist of two quadratic equations. During the stages of introduction and growth, the trend rises in the form of

$$Q = a + b_1 T + b_2 T^2 \tag{3.4}$$

Subsequently, the trend during the stages of maturity and decline can be approximated by

$$Q = a + b_1 T - b_2 T^2 \tag{3.5}$$

See Box 3.2 for an example of forecasting air travel between Japan and China.

BOX 3.2 Forecasting air travel between Japan and China

In Box 2.2 in Chapter 2 we reported the equation for air travel between Tokyo and Beijing as,

$\ln Q_t = 2.737 - 1.247 \ln P_t + 1.905 \ln GNP_t$ with $R^2 = 0.97$.

Where
Q_t = number of passengers ('000) per year travelling between Tokyo and Beijing
P_t = real average yearly fare between Tokyo and Beijing (weighted by the seasonal distribution of traffic and adjusted for inflation)
GNP_t = real Japanese gross national product in each year ($ billions)

Suppose that in 2010 an airline company forecasted that in 2011 air fares (adjusted for inflation) between Tokyo and Beijing would be $550 ($P_{t+1}$) and that Japanese real GDP would be $1480 billion. The natural log of 550 (i.e. ln 550) is 6.310 and ln 1480 is 7.300. Substituting these values into the above equation we get

$\ln Q_t + 1 = 2.737 - 1.247(6.310) + 1.905(7.300) = 8.775$

The antilog of 8.775 is 6470 or 6,470,000 passengers forecasted for 2011. The accuracy of this forecast depends on the accuracy of the estimated demand coefficients and on the accuracy of the forecasted values of the independent or explanatory values in the demand equation.

3.5.1 COMPONENTS OF A TIME SERIES

The variations that are evident in a time series can be decomposed into four components.

1. *Secular trend.* A trend is a relatively smooth long-term movement of a time series. It is the smooth or regular underlying movement of a series over a fairly long period of time. For example, in empirical demand analysis, such factors as increasing population, size and changing consumer tastes may result in general increases or decreases of a demand series over time. An example of a secular trend would be the growth in annual tourism arrivals to a particular destination over a 20-year period.

2. *Cyclical variation.* These are major expansions and contractions in an economic series that are usually greater than a year in duration. Cyclical variations are often related to the 'business cycle'. In most industries cyclical variations are not consistent or predictable over time. To make valid statistical adjustments for cyclical fluctuations in an economic series over time, one must assume that secular trend and cyclical fluctuations result from two different sets of causal factors. This is often difficult to establish. Since cyclical swings or business cycles can be of different duration and can arise from a variety of causes that may not be fully understood, they are often examined separately with qualitative techniques.

3. *Seasonal effects.* These are regularly recurring fluctuations in the data during each year. Seasonal variations recur each year with more or less the same intensity. They often reflect variations caused by weather patterns or social habits that produce an annual pattern in the time series. The data in Figure 3.2 show significant seasonal variation. For example, tourism arrivals to a destination will vary according to the particular season and even the month of the year.

4. *Random fluctuations.* A data series may be influenced by irregular, random factors that are by and large not predictable such as wars, natural disasters and government policies affecting the variable in question. Tourism arrivals to a destination can clearly be affected by such random factors.

These four patterns are illustrated in Figures 3.3a and 3.3b.

The total variation in the time series of some data (e.g. tourism arrivals, ticket sales of an attraction and ice creams purchased) is the result of all four factors operating together.

Seasonal and cyclical variations

Many important economic time series are influenced by seasonal and cyclical variations and thus will impact on tourism demand. Figures 3.3a and 3.3b illustrate how such variations can influence demand patterns for a tourism product. Controlling for seasonal and cyclical variations is an important aspect of time-series analysis and projection, and analyses of seasonal and cyclical fluctuations can greatly improve forecasting results, especially for short-run forecasting.

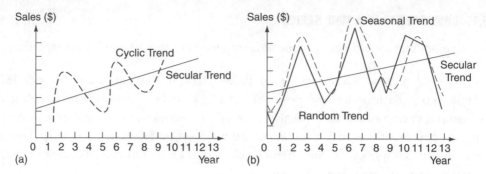

Figure 3.3 (a) Secular and cyclic trend (b) Secular, random and seasonal trends

Statistical problems make any breakdown of a time series into trend and cyclical components tenuous at best. Most analysts recognise that both secular trends and cycles are typically generated by common causal mechanisms and thus their separation leads to ambiguous forecasts. Moreover, the timing, size and duration of cycles change over time, making cyclical adjustments difficult.

In our example of forecasting tourist arrivals to the island, the arrivals data in Table 3.1 show strong seasonal variation with arrivals in the first and third quarters of each year consistently below the long-run trend, while arrivals in the second and fourth quarters are consistently above the trend values. By incorporating this seasonal variation, tourism managers can significantly improve the forecasted tourist arrivals.

There are several techniques for estimating seasonal variations. The most common are the ratio-to-trend method and the inclusion of dummy variables.

Ratio-to-Trend method

The ratio-to-trend method assumes that the trend value is multiplied by the seasonal effect. To adjust the trend forecast for the seasonal variation by the ratio-to-trend method, we simply find the average ratio by which the actual value of the time series differs from the corresponding estimated trend value in each time period, and then multiply the forecasted trend value by this ratio.

Using the ratio-to-trend method to adjust the trend forecast of tourist arrivals for the seasonal variation evident in Table 3.2 and Figure 3.2, we simply find the average ratio by which the actual value of the time series differs from the corresponding estimated trend value in each quarter during the period 2007–2010 and then multiply the forecasted trend value by this ratio. The predicted trend value for each quarter in the 2007–2010 period is obtained by simply substituting the value of t corresponding to the quarter under consideration into Equation 3.2 and solving for Q_t.

Table 3.3 shows the calculations for the seasonal adjustment of the tourist arrivals ('000) used to forecast arrivals for each quarter of 2011 from the extended trend line examined earlier.

Table 3.3 Estimation of the seasonal adjustment of the trend forecast by the ratio-to-trend method

Year	Forecasted (000)	Actual (000)		Actual/Forecasted
2007.1	12.29	11.00		0.895
2007.2	13.87	12.00		0.865
2007.3	15.45	14.00		0.906
2007.4	17.02	15.00		0.881
			Average	0.887
2008.1	12.69	15.00		1.182
2008.2	14.26	17.00		1.192
2008.3	15.84	18.00		1.136
2008.4	17.42	20.00		1.148
			Average	1.165
2009.1	13.08	12.00		0.917
2009.2	14.66	13.00		0.887
2009.3	16.23	15.00		0.924
2009.4	17.81	16.00		0.898
			Average	0.907
2010.1	13.48	14.00		1.039
2010.2	15.05	16.00		1.063
2010.3	16.63	17.00		1.022
2010.4	18.20	19.00		1.044
			Average	1.042

Multiplying the tourist arrivals forecasted earlier (from the simple extension of the linear trend) by the seasonal factors estimated in Table 3.2 (i.e. 0.887 for the first quarter, 1.165 for the second quarter, etc.) we get the following new forecasts for 2011 based on both the linear trend and the seasonal adjustment:

$Q_{17} = 18.60(0.887) = 16,500$ in the first quarter of 2011

$Q_{18} = 18.99(1.165) = 22,120$ in the second quarter of 2011

$Q_{19} = 19.39(0.907) = 17,590$ in the third quarter of 2011

$Q_{20} = 19.78(1.042) = 20,610$ in the first quarter of 2011

These forecasts are shown by the encircled points in Figure 3.2. With the inclusion of seasonal adjustment, the forecasted values for tourist arrivals closely replicate the past seasonal pattern in the time-series data along with the rising trend.

Seasonal adjustment can improve forecasts based on trend projection. However, trend projection still has some shortcomings:

- it is limited primarily to short-term predictions. If the trend is extrapolated much beyond the last data point, the accuracy of the forecast diminishes rapidly.
- factors such as changes in relative prices and fluctuations in the rate of economic growth are not considered. Rather, the trend projection assumes that historical relationships will not change.

Dummy variables

Another approach for incorporating seasonal effects into the linear trend analysis model is the use of *dummy variables*. A dummy variable normally takes on one of two values: either 0 or 1. With this method it is assumed that the seasonal effects are *added to* the trend value. If the time series consists of quarterly data, then the following model could be used to adjust for seasonal effects

$$\hat{Q}_t = \alpha + \beta_1 t + \beta_2 D_{1t} + \beta_3 D_{2t} + \beta_4 D_{3t} \qquad (3.6)$$

Where

$D_{1t} = 1$ for first-quarter observations and 0 otherwise,

$D_{2t} = 1$ for second-quarter observations and 0 otherwise and

$D_{3t} = 1$ for third-quarter observation and 0 otherwise, α and β are parameters to be estimated using least squares techniques.

In this model, the values of the dummy variables (D_{1t}, D_{2t} and D_{3t}) for observations in the fourth quarter of each year (base period) would be equal to 0.

The use of dummy variables in tourism forecasting is widespread, and the dummy variables selected can be quite diverse. For example, in the Song *et al.* (2003a) specification of individual models of the demand for tourism to Denmark from each of its six major origin countries – Germany, Netherlands, Norway, Sweden, the UK and the USA – the dummy variables comprised the two oil crisis dummies, a Gulf War dummy, a dummy for German unification and a dummy for Chernobyl/US bombing of Libya.

3.5.2 SMOOTHING TECHNIQUES

Data collected over time will normally comprise some random variation. In some time series, seasonal variation is strong enough to obscure any trends or cycles which are very important for the understanding of the process being observed. Smoothing techniques are used to reduce irregularities (random fluctuations) in time-series data. They provide a clearer view of the true underlying behaviour of the series. Smoothing can remove seasonality and highlight long-term fluctuations in the series. This technique, when properly applied, reveals more clearly the underlying trend, seasonal and cyclic components.

By taking some form of an average of past observations, smoothing techniques attempt to eliminate the distortions arising from random variation in the series and to base the forecast on a smoothed average of several past observations. In general, smoothing techniques work best when a data series tends to change slowly from one period to the next and when no frequent changes occur in the direction of the underlying pattern.

There are two distinct groups of smoothing methods:

- Moving average
- Exponential smoothing

Moving average

The simplest smoothing technique is the moving average. If a data series has a large random factor, a trend analysis forecast will tend to generate forecasts having large errors from period to period. To minimise the effects of this randomness, a series of recent observations can be averaged to arrive at a forecast. This is the moving average method. A number of observed values are chosen, their average is estimated and this average serves as a forecast for the next period. By reducing random fluctuations, moving average smoothing makes long-term trends clearer.

In general, a moving average may be defined as

$$\hat{Q}_{t+1} = \frac{Q_t + Q_{t-1} + \cdots + Q_{t-N+1}}{N} \tag{3.7}$$

Where,

$\hat{Q}_{t+1}$ = forecast value of Q for one period in the future;

Q_t, Q_{t-1} and Q_{t-N+1} = observed values of Q in these periods;

N = number of observations in the moving average.

The forecasted value of a time series in a given period (month, quarter and year) is equal to the average value of the time series in a number of previous periods. The greater the number of observations N used in the moving average, the greater the smoothing effect because each new observation receives less weight $(1/N)$ as N increases. Hence, generally, the greater the randomness in the data series and the slower the change in the underlying pattern, the more preferable it is to use a relatively large number of past observations in developing the forecast.

The choice of an appropriate moving average period, that is, the choice of N, should be based on a comparison of the results of the model in forecasting past observations. For example, the forecaster might try a three-period average and a five-period average and compare the accuracy of the alternatives. The best moving average is chosen on the basis of the value of N that minimises the Root Mean Squared Error (RMSE).

Table 3.4 shows the number of car rentals ('000 by quarter) made by the Haiyan Car Rental firm in its several locations in a tourist region. Suppose that the problem is to forecast the number of cars rented in the 13th quarter. With a three-period moving average, the forecasted value of the time series for the next period is given by the average value of the time series in the previous three periods. The three-quarter moving average forecast is 21,330 cars rented. In contrast, the five-quarter moving average is 20,600 vehicles rented in the 13th quarter. The greater the number of periods used in the moving average, the greater is the smoothing effect because each new observation receives less weight. This is more useful the more erratic or random is the time-series data.

The forecaster can use any number of time periods to calculate the moving average. In order to decide which of these moving average forecasts is better (i.e. closer to the actual data) we calculate the RMSE of each forecast and utilise the moving average that results in the smallest RMSE (weighted error in the forecast). The formula for the RMSE is

$$\text{RMSE} = \sqrt{\frac{\sum (A_t - F_t)^2}{n}}$$

Where,

A_t is the actual value of the time series in period t;

F_t is the forecasted value;

n is the number of time periods or observations.

The forecast difference or error (i.e. $A - F$) is squared in order to penalise larger errors proportionately more than smaller errors.

The RMSE for the three-quarter moving average is 2.95, while it is 2.99 for the five-quarter moving average. Thus, the three-quarter moving average forecast is marginally better than the corresponding five-quarter moving average forecast. That is, Haiyan Car Rentals can be slightly more confident in the forecast of 21,330 cars rented than 20,600 for the 13th quarter.

Table 3.4 Three-quarter and five-quarter moving average forecasts and comparison

(1) Quarter	(2) Firm's Actual Car Rental (A)	(3) Three-Quarter Moving Average Forecast (F)	(4) A–F	(5) (A–F)²	(6) Five-Quarter Moving Average (F)	(7) A–F	(8) (A–F)²
1	20	–	–	–	–	–	–
2	22	–	–	–	–	–	–
3	23	–	–	–	–	–	–
4	24	21.67	2.33	5.42	–	–	–
5	18	23.00	–5.00	25.00	–	–	–
6	23	21.67	1.33	1.76	21.4	1.6	2.56
7	19	21.67	–2.67	7.12	22.0	–3.0	9.00
8	17	20.00	–3.00	9.00	21.4	–4.4	19.36
9	22	19.67	2.33	5.42	20.2	1.8	3.24
10	23	19.33	3.67	13.46	19.8	3.2	10.24
11	18	20.67	–2.67	7.12	20.8	–2.8	7.84
12	23	21.00	2.00	4.00	19.8	3.2	10.24
			Total	78.35		**Total**	62.48
13	–	21.33			20.6		

An alternate measure is Mean Absolute Percentage Error (also known as MAPE). This measures the accuracy in a fitted time series value in statistics, specifically trending. It usually expresses accuracy as a percentage.

$$\text{MAPE} = \frac{1}{n} \sum_{t=1}^{n} \left| \frac{A_t - F_t}{A_t} \right|$$

The difference between actual value A_t and F_t is divided by the actual value A_t again. The absolute value of this calculation is summed for every fitted or forecast point in time and divided again by the number of fitted points n. This makes it a percentage error so one can compare the error of fitted time series that differ in level. The estimated MAPE is 2.04% for the three-quarter moving average forecasts and 2.62% for the five-quarter moving average forecasts. Thus, the MAPE estimates also indicate that the three-quarter moving average yields the more accurate forecasts.

Exponential smoothing

One criticism of moving averages as smoothing techniques is that they normally give equal weight $(1/N)$ to all observations used in preparing the forecast, even though it is likely that the most recent observations contain more immediately useful information than more distant observations. In contrast, exponential smoothing assigns exponentially decreasing weights as the observation get older. In other words, recent observations are given relatively more weight in forecasting than the older observations.

Consider the following forecasting model:

$$\hat{Q}_{t+1} = w\,Q_t + (1 - w)\hat{Q}_t \tag{3.8}$$

This model weights the most recent observations by w (some value between 0 and 1 inclusive), and the past forecast by $(1-w)$. A large w indicates that a heavy weight is being placed on the most recent observation. A w closer to 0 suggests little desire to adjust the current forecast for last period's error.

Exponential forecasting techniques can be easy to use. All that is required is last period's forecast, last period's observation and a value for the weighting factor w. The optimal weighting factor is normally determined by making successive forecasts using past data with various values of w and choosing the w that minimises the RMSE.

Exponential smoothing gives the forecaster great flexibility in choosing the appropriate weights for past values, w.

Using Equation 3.8 the forecast for $\hat{Q}$ may also be written as

$$\hat{Q}_t = w\,Q_{t-1} + (1 - w)\hat{Q}_{t-1} \tag{3.9}$$

Table 3.5 Exponential forecasts with $w = 0.3$ and $w = 0.5$, and comparison

(1) Quarter	(2) Firm's Actual Car Rental (A)	(3) Forecast with w = 0.3 (F)	(4) A–F	(5) (A–F)²	(6) Forecast with w = 0.5 (F)	(7) A–F	(8) (A–F)²
1	20	21.0	–1.0	1.00	21.0	–1.0	1.00
2	22	20.7	1.3	1.69	20.5	1.5	2.25
3	23	21.1	1.9	3.61	21.3	1.7	2.89
4	24	21.7	2.3	5.29	22.2	1.8	3.24
5	18	22.4	–4.4	19.36	23.1	–5.1	26.01
6	23	21.1	1.9	3.61	20.6	2.4	5.76
7	19	21.7	–2.7	7.29	21.8	–2.8	7.84
8	17	20.9	–3.9	15.21	20.4	–3.4	11.56
9	22	19.7	2.3	5.29	18.7	3.3	10.89
10	23	20.4	2.6	6.76	20.4	2.6	6.76
11	18	21.2	–3.2	10.24	21.7	–3.7	13.69
12	23	20.2	2.8	7.84	19.9	3.1	9.61
			Total	87.19		**Total**	101.50
13	–	21.0			21.5		

Applying the exponential smoothing technique to the problem of forecasting car rentals, we now apply these weights to the forecasts.

The RMSE for the exponential forecast using $w = 0.3$ is

$$\text{RMSE} = \sqrt{\frac{87.19}{12}} = 2.70$$

On the other hand, the RMSE for the exponential forecast using $w = 0.5$ is

$$\text{RMSE} = \sqrt{\frac{101.5}{12}} = 2.91$$

The RMSE for the exponential forecasts using $w = 0.3$ is 2.70, while the RMSE for the exponential forecasts using $w = 0.5$ is 2.91. Thus the management of Haiyan Car Rentals should be more confident in the exponential forecast of 21,000 cars rented for the 13th quarter obtained by using $w = 0.3$ than with the exponential forecast of 21,500 obtained by using $w = 0.5$.

Both exponential forecasts are also better than the three-quarters and five-quarters moving average forecasts. Since the best exponential forecast is usually better than the best moving average forecasts, the former is generally used.

An extension of exponential smoothing can be used when time-series data exhibits a linear trend. This method is variously called double smoothing; trend-adjusted exponential smoothing; Forecast Including Trend (FIT); and Holt's Model. Without adjustment, simple exponential smoothing results will lag the trend, that is, the forecast will always be low if the trend is increasing, or high if the trend is decreasing. With this model there are two smoothing constants, $\acute{\alpha}$ and β with β representing the trend component.

Tourism forecasters are paying increasing attention to the use of smoothing techniques in their analyses. Chen *et al.* (2003) discuss the advantages and disadvantages of different smoothing techniques for predicting seasonal visitor patterns depending on the quality and characteristics of the data available for analysis. Lim and McAleer (2001) evaluate various exponential smoothing models for accuracy in predicting quarterly tourist arrivals to Australia. Coshall (2009) applied univariate volatility models to UK outbound tourism flows to its most popular international destinations. These models are shown to generate highly accurate forecasts, but become optimal when combined with forecasts obtained from exponential smoothing models.

Evaluation of exponential smoothing

- Exponential smoothing allows more recent data to be given greater weight in analysing time-series data.
- As additional observations become available, it is easy to update the forecasts. There is no need to re-estimate the equations, as would be required with trend projection.

The main disadvantage is that it does not provide very accurate forecasts if there is a significant trend in the data. If the time trend is positive, forecasts based on exponential smoothing will be likely to be too low, while a negative time trend will result in estimates that are too high. Simple exponential smoothing works best when there is no discernible time trend in the data.

There are, however, more sophisticated forms of exponential smoothing that allow both trends and seasonality to be accounted for in making forecasts. An extension of Holt's Model, called Holt-Winter's Method, takes into account both trend and seasonality. There are two versions, multiplicative and additive, with the multiplicative being the most widely used. In the additive model, seasonality is expressed as a quantity to be added to or subtracted from the series average. The multiplicative model expresses seasonality as a percentage – known as seasonal relatives or seasonal indexes – of the average (or trend). A relative of 0.7 would indicate demand that is 70% of the average, while 1.05 would indicate demand that is 5% above the average. Such smoothing techniques have been used to forecast Canadian inbound tourism (Veloce, 2004).

3.5.3 FORECASTING TOURISM ARRIVALS USING TIME-SERIES ANALYSIS

Just as the most effort of tourism researchers in measuring tourism demand has been on estimating the demand for tourism arrivals for different countries, so too the primary effort of tourism forecasters has been concerned with forecasting international tourism arrivals. The typical and most generally accepted methodology for forecasting with time-series models is for the forecaster to choose a particular class of model and then use a set of objective criteria to choose the most suitable specific model within this class as appropriate to the data. Within the class of time-series models, there are many different forms that such models can take.

One sophisticated method of time-series analysis is called Autoregressive Moving Average (ARMA) models, sometimes called Box–Jenkins models (Box & Jenkins, 1976). The Box–Jenkins methodology applies moving average ARMA or ARIMA (Autoregressive Integrated Moving Average) models to find the best fit of a time series to past values of this time series, in order to make forecasts. This technique recognises that a stationary time series will contain a mixture of Autoregressive (AR) (an AR model expresses a time series as a linear function of its past values) and Moving Average (MA) components. This technique is one among a group of newer methods for time-series analysis which provide a sophisticated approach to analysing the various components – trend, seasonal, cyclical and random – that make up an economic time series. These techniques enable the analysis of complex patterns that exist in an ordered data set. For some forecasting applications they provide a substantial improvement over simpler extrapolation procedures.

Different versions of the ARIMA models have been applied in over two-thirds of the post-2000 studies that utilised the time-series forecasting techniques. Variants of the ARIMA model have recently been used in forecasting visitor arrivals to Singapore (Oh & Morzuch, 2005), Thailand (Song *et al.*, 2003b; Vu & Turner, 2006), Hong Kong (Cho, 2001), Spain (Garcia-Ferrer & Queralt, 1997), Korea (Kim & Song, 1998), Australia (Kulendran & Witt, 2003a), Denmark (Song *et al.*, 2003a), Balearic Islands (Rossello-Nadal, 2001) and the UK (Song *et al.*, 2000).

As seasonality is such a dominant feature of the tourism industry, forecasters are very much interested in the seasonal variation in tourism demand. The seasonal ARIMA model, which can be fitted to seasonal time series (in this case, monthly observations), consists of both seasonal and non-seasonal parts. Depending on the frequency of the time series, either simple ARIMA or seasonal ARIMA (i.e. SARIMA) models can be used with the latter gaining an increasing popularity over the last few years, given its high level of accuracy.

3.5.4 SHORTCOMINGS OF TIME-SERIES APPROACHES

Although trend projections can provide good estimates for some forecasting purposes, a number of serious shortcomings limit its usefulness in many situations:

- A simple trend projection technique lacks the ability to predict cyclical turning points or other short-term fluctuations.
- Trend projections implicitly assume that the historical relations involved in the time series will continue into the future. This is often not the case.
- Trend analysis does not analyse causal relations and hence offers no help in analysing either why a particular series moves as it does or what the effect of a particular policy decision would be on the future movement of the series. It is very difficult or impossible to consider cyclical and irregular forces. Trend analysis can discern the trend, cyclical fluctuations and seasonality in the data but cannot explain why the data act as they do.

Despite these limitations, time series can be useful in predicting future seasonal demand and in adjusting supply to anticipate seasonal fluctuations. Since time-series models only require historical observations of a variable, they are also less costly in data collection and model estimation. But, given its limitations, time-series analysis is seldom used alone and is most often useful in conjunction with other forecasting methods.

3.6 BAROMETRIC TECHNIQUES

Although cyclical patterns in most economic time series are so erratic that they make simple projection difficult, there is evidence that some relatively consistent relations exist between the movements of different economic variables over time. If so, then the variables in the second series are indicators of the variables in the first series. By observing changes in the second series, it may then be possible to predict changes in the first. Barometric techniques examine the relationships between causal or coincident events to predict future events. This approach is based on the logic that current economic indicators can serve as a barometer of the past, present and future and that the changes in the economic variables can be identified, measured and recorded as a statistical time series.

Economic indicators may be classified as leading, coincident or lagging indicators.

- *Leading indicators* are time series that tend to precede (lead) changes in the level of general economic activity. The peaks and troughs of a leading indicator series consistently occur before the peaks and troughs of the series of interest. This leading series can be used as a predictor or barometer for short-term changes in the series of interest.
- *Coincident indicators* move in step with or coincide with movements in general economic activity.
- *Lagging indicators* follow or lag movements in economic activity.

The relative positions of leading, coincident and lagging indicators in the business cycle are shown in Figure 3.4.

The figure shows that leading indicators precede business cycles turning points (i.e. peaks and troughs), coincident indicators move in step with business cycles, while lagging indicators follow or lag turning points in business cycles.

A leading indicator predicts 3–6 months into the future of another event. Examples of leading indicators include payroll employment, average weekly unemployment claims,

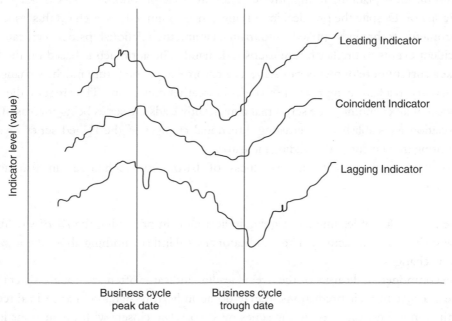

Figure 3.4 Leading, lagging and co-incident indicators

industrial material prices, personal income less transfer payments, an index of industrial production, stock prices, changes in business inventories, consumer expectations, new building permits, new orders for goods and materials and retail sales. A rise in leading economic indicators is used to forecast an increase in general business activity, and vice versa. Leading indicators normally tend to anticipate and are used to forecast turning points in the business cycle.

Tourism forecasting tends to concentrate on the projection of absolute numbers (arrivals, expenditure, etc.) rather than on the discovery of turning points in the data or changes in the growth rate of the data. Yet, these latter variables may be more appropriate for the development of risk management strategies. Rather than just focusing on directional accuracy, it may be desirable to examine turning point accuracy. It may be of most interest to the various sectors of the tourism industry to know whether there is likely to be a change in the trend of demand for their products. For certain strategic business decisions, it may be more important to forecast correctly the direction of change in either tourism demand (i.e. whether tourism demand is likely to increase or decrease over a particular time period) or the rate of growth of tourism demand, rather than to minimise error magnitude.

Prediction of the turning point or *directional change forecasting* is an important aspect in tourism forecasting research. It has a high practical value because tourism-related firms are keen to know not only the overall trends of tourism demand but also the timing of the directional change in tourism growth. This knowledge will contribute to the effectiveness of both business planning in the private sector and macroeconomic policy making in the public sector. Despite the practical importance, there is limited research on this issue.

Barometric techniques applied to tourism examine the relationships between causal or coincident events to predict future tourism demand. The approach is based on the logic that key current developments can serve as a barometer of the future much as changes in the mercury in a barometer precede changes in weather conditions. They require the identification of an economic time series that consistently leads the series being forecast. Once this relation is established, forecasting directional changes in the lagged series involves monitoring movement in the leading indicator.

Several problems affect the usefulness of barometric techniques in forecasting, including

- The main value of leading and lagging indicators is in predicting the *direction* of future change in economic activity. These indicators reveal little or nothing about the *magnitude* of the changes.
- The component indicators of the overall leading indicator often are not consistent with one another in their predictions. Rarely do all indicators signal a change in direction at the same time. Changes in one series must correlate closely with fluctuations in the series that it is intended to predict. However, few series always correctly indicate changes

in another economic variable. Even the best leading indicators of general business conditions forecast directional changes with less than complete accuracy.

- Even the indicators that have good records of forecasting directional changes generally fail to lead by a consistent period. If a series is to be an adequate barometer, it must not only indicate directional change but also provide a relatively constant lead time. Few series meet the test of lead-time consistency.
- The widespread use of a reasonably reliable leading indicator may, in itself, lead to less reliability in the indicator over time. This can happen if economic agents act on the forecast, changing either the economic outcome or the 'lead' time between the indicator and the associated economic variables.
- There should be a logical explanation as to why one series predicts another. Unless there is a causal relationship between the two series, the historical pattern may not be very useful in forecasting future events because there is no reason to expect the pattern to be repeated.
- An indicator's value is affected by the cost and time necessary for data collection. A time series that can be maintained only at high expense may not be worth the expense. Similarly, if there is a long delay before the data are available, the effective lead time of the indicator may be too short to be useful.

Two techniques that have been used with some success in partially overcoming the difficulties in barometric forecasting are composite indexes and diffusion indexes.

- *Composite indexes* are weighted averages of several leading indicators. Combining individual series into a composite index results in a series with less random fluctuations, or noise. The smoother composite series has less tendency to produce false signals of change in the predicted variable.
- *Diffusion indexes* are similar, but instead of combining a number of leading indicators into a single standardised index, the approach consists of noting the percentage of the total number of leading indicators that are rising at a given point in time. Forecasting with diffusion indexes typically involves projecting an increase in the economic variable if the index exceeds 50 and a decline when it is below 50. Greater confidence can be placed in the forecasts the closer the index is to 100.

There has been some attention to the potential of leading indicators in tourism forecasting (Kulendran & Witt, 2003b). Identification of leading indicators is very useful in predicting turning points in tourist arrival data and in forecasting the number of arrivals. Turner *et al.* (1997) examined various potential leading indicators (such as origin country income and exchange rate) in the context of forecasting the demand for tourism from Japan, New Zealand, the UK and the USA to Australia. They concluded that national macroeconomic indicators such as unemployment, the money supply and imports were all potential leading indicators of, and causally related to, the demand for tourist arrivals into Australia. Rossello-Nadal (2001) examined a wide range of potential leading indicators, which are taken to be indicative of economic activity, financial activity or prices, in the context of forecasting the demand for tourism from Germany and the UK to the Balearic Islands, Spain. He constructed regression models where the leading indicators appeared as independent variables and used the models to generate forecasts.

A leading indicator series, in conjunction with other forecasting results, can help businesses, governments and destination managers predict and prepare for significant changes in the economic environment. However, even with the use of composite and diffusion indexes, the barometric forecasting technique is a relatively poor tool for estimating the magnitude of change in any economic variable, including tourism demand. While it is an improvement over simple extrapolation techniques, for short-term forecasting in which calling the turning points is necessary, the barometric approach cannot stand alone as a forecasting technique.

3.7   ECONOMETRIC APPROACHES TO FORECASTING

Econometric or causal techniques involve the identification of variables that can be used to predict another variable of interest. For example, interest rates may be used to forecast the demand for holiday homes. Econometric techniques can relate general economic conditions to tourism demand and forecast conditions to derive tourism forecasts. They involve the regression of a number of variables over time in order to assess their influence on the variable to be forecast (independent variable) to arrive at a forecast (dependent variable).

Econometric methods typically use complex mathematical equations to show past relationships between demand and variables that influence the demand. An equation is derived and then tested and fine-tuned to ensure that it is as reliable a representation of the past relationship as possible. Once this is done, projected values of the influencing variables (income, prices, etc.) are inserted into the equation to make a forecast. If there is more than one predictor variable or if the relationship between predictor and forecast is not linear, simple linear regression will be inadequate. For situations with multiple predictors, multiple regression should be employed, while non-linear relationships call for the use of curvilinear regression.

Econometric models or *multivariate analysis* can include a large number of variables and use statistical techniques of correlation and regression analysis to test relationships and construct formulae. Econometric approaches are relevant to both business forecasting and the forecasting of tourism numbers.

Multivariate analysis is an advance on univariate analysis in that it allows the forecaster to examine outside influences on the variable under study. Thus it has the potential to explain *why* changes in some variables are expected to affect others. Because multivariate analysis is more complex than univariate analysis, it is also more prone to error.

There are three imperatives to framing a good multivariate model: inclusion of the right variables; timing the entry of the variables properly; and specification of the correct relationship between the variables.

3.7.1 SPECIFYING AN ECONOMETRIC MODEL

3.7.1.1 Single-equation model

Suppose the manager of Chuck's Duty Free Store wishes to forecast laptop computer sales next year. In constructing a model for forecasting the demand for laptop computers, the manager of the store might hypothesise that the demand for laptops, L, is determined by: price (P), the price of related software (P_c), a complement; the price of iPods (P_s), a substitute; disposable income (Y); population (N); interest rates (i); and advertising expenditures (A).

The *additive* form $Q = f(a_0 + P + P_c + P_s + Y + N + I + A)$ assumes that the explanatory influences are linear and are simply summed together to discover their individual and combined effects on the dependent variable.

The multiplicative form $Q = f(P, P_c, P_s, Y, N, I, A)$ transforms to log-linear form and assumes that the suspected relationship between each explanatory variables and the dependent variable is geometric in nature. A log-linear model expressing this relation would be

$$\log L = \alpha_0 + \ln \beta_1 P + \ln \beta_2 Y + \ln \beta_3 N + \ln \beta_4 P_c$$
$$+ \ln \beta_5 P_s + \ln \beta_6 i + \ln \beta_7 A + \mu \qquad (3.10)$$

Where,

α_0 is the Y-intercept on a data scatter plot;

$\beta_1, \ldots, \beta_7$ are the coefficients (parameters) that give the elasticity (degree of influence) of each explanatory variable on the dependent variable;

μ is the error term (assumes that the errors are random and the sum of their squares is equal to 0).

The forecasted values of the macroeconomic variables (e.g. national income, population) are usually obtained from government statistical agencies. The micro variables in the model not under the control of the firm (e.g. P_s, the price of substitutes, and P_c, the price of complements) might be forecasted by time-series analysis or smoothing techniques, and the firm can develop forecasting scenarios using alternative forecasted values of the independent policy variables under its control (P_{t+1}, A_{t+1}). The accuracy of this forecast depends on the accuracy of the estimated demand coefficients and on the accuracy of the forecasted values of the dependent or explanatory variables in the demand equation.

To forecast L_{t+1} (the demand for laptops in the next period), the firm must obtain the values for P_{t+1}, Y_{t+1}, N_{t+1}, P_{st+1}, P_{ct+1}, I_{t+1} and A_{t+1}. By substituting these forecasted values of the independent variable into the estimated equation, we obtain the forecasted value of the dependent variable L_{t+1}.

Once the regression equation is specified (additive, multiplicative, linear and log), the data is run through one of the many available statistical software packages. Typically, the regression procedure uses Ordinary Least Squares (OLS) to fit the specified model to the entered data. The technique draws an imaginary straight line (the regression line) through the data points on a scatter plot by minimising the sum of the squares of the deviations between the actual entered data and their values as suggested by the regression model. This determines the degree to which each explanatory variable in the model influences the dependent variable, statistically controlling for the other variables. As discussed in Chapter 2, one of the advantages of using a log-linear functional form is that the estimated coefficients of the explanatory variables can be interpreted directly as the demand elasticities, which provide useful information for policy makers in tourism destinations.

3.7.1.2 Multiple-equation systems

Consider again the problem of forecasting laptop computer sales. Equations 3.11–3.13 represent a simple three-equation model of the demand for laptops and related software sales and hardware equipment. Total revenues for Chuck's Duty Free Store would include not only sales of laptops but also sales of software programmes (including computer games) and sales of peripheral equipment (printers, scanners, etc.). The three equations are

$$Q = \alpha_0 + \alpha_1 \mathrm{TR}_t + \mu_1 \tag{3.11}$$

$$H_t = L_0 + \beta_1 L_{t-1} + \mu_2 \tag{3.12}$$

$$\mathrm{TR}_t = Q_t + H_t + L_t \tag{3.13}$$

Where,

Q is software sales;

H is hardware sales;

L is laptop sales;

TR is total revenue;

t is the current time period;

$t-1$ is the previous time period;

μ_1 and μ_2 are error, or residual, terms.

Equations 3.11 and 3.12 are behavioural hypotheses. The first hypothesises that current-period software sales are a function of the current level of total revenues; the second hypothesises that peripheral hardware sales depend on previous-period laptop sales. The last equation in the system (3.13) is an identity. It defines total revenue as equal to the sum of software, peripheral equipment and camera phone sales.

The stochastic disturbance terms in the behavioural equations, μ_1 and μ_2, are included because the hypothesised relations are not exact. That is, other factors that can affect software and peripheral hardware sales are not accounted for in the system. So long as these stochastic elements are random and their expected values are 0, they do not present a barrier to the empirical estimation of system parameters.

Since the endogenous variables of the system are both determined by, and, in turn, determine, the value of the other endogenous variables in the model, we cannot use the OLS approach to estimate the parameters of the structural equations. More advanced econometric techniques are required to estimate the coefficients of the model.

Empirical estimation of the parameters for multiple-equation systems (the α's and β's) in equations often requires the use of statistical techniques that go beyond the scope of this text. We can, however, illustrate the use of such a system for forecasting purposes after the parameters have been estimated.

To forecast next years' software and peripheral sales of hardware and total revenue for the firm, we must express S, H and TR in terms of those variables whose values can be estimated at the point in time when the forecast is made. In other words, each endogenous variable (S, H and TR) must be expressed in terms of the exogenous variables (L_{t-1} and L_t). Such relations are called reduced-form equations, because they reduce complex simultaneous relations to their most basic and simple form. Consider the reduced-form Equation 3.14.

$$\text{TR}_t = \frac{b_0 + a_0 + c_t C_{t-1} + C_t}{1 - b_1} \tag{3.14}$$

This equation relates current total revenues to previous and current-period laptop sales. It thus provides the firm with a forecasting model that takes into account the simultaneous relations expressed in our simple multiple-equation system. Of course in real-life situations, it is likely that laptop sales depend on the price, quantity and quality of available software and peripheral equipment (i.e. they are complements). Then, S, H and L, along with other important factors, may all be endogenous, involving a large number of relations in a highly complex multiple-equation system. Untangling the important but often subtle relations involved in such a system makes forecasting with multiple-equation systems very challenging. Box 3.3 illustrates use of a multiple-equation forecasting model to forecast tourism arrivals.

BOX 3.3 Forecasting tourism arrivals using econometric techniques

Witt *et al.* (2004) have examined the ability of various econometric and time-series models to generate accurate out-of-sample forecasts of inbound tourism to Denmark. Six major origin countries were examined: Germany, the Netherlands, Norway, Sweden, the UK and the USA. The models were estimated using annual data for 1969–93, and the estimated models were used to generate forecasts for 1994–99. Forecasting performance is assessed in terms of mean absolute percentage error (MAPE), which, as we have seen above, gives equal weight to all percentage errors, and root mean square percentage error (RMSPE), which gives more weight to avoiding large percentage errors.

Several models were specified to explain tourism demand. These were all special cases of a general autoregressive distributed lag model (ADLM). The form of the initial model was

$$\ln Q_{it} = a + f \ln Q_{it-1} + h_1 \ln Y_{it} + h_2 \ln Y_{it-1} + h_3 \ln P_{it}$$
$$+ h_4 \ln P_{it-1} + h_5 \ln P_{ist} + h_6 \ln P_{ist-1} + h_7 T + \text{dummies} + u_{it}$$

Where,

Q_{it} is the quantity of tourism consumed per capita measured by the expenditure-weighted number of nights spent by tourists from country i in Denmark (the weights reflect the different daily spending for tourists in different accommodation types in 1996) divided by the population of country i (1980 = 100);

Y_{it} is real private consumption expenditure per capita in country i (1980 = 100);

P_{it} represents the real cost of living for tourists in Denmark, and is measured by the Denmark CPI relative to the CPI in country i, adjusted by the exchange rate in order to transform the price variable into origin country currency;

P_{ist} represents tourism prices in substitute destinations and is measured by the tourists' cost of living in Denmark relative to a weighted average calculated for a set of alternative destinations for origin country i;

T is a time trend.

The dummy variables comprised two oil crisis dummies DOIL1 and DOIL2 (DOIL1 = 1 in 1974–75, = 0 otherwise; DOIL2 = 1 in 1979, = 0 otherwise), a Gulf War dummy (DGULF = 1 in 1990–91, = 0 otherwise), a dummy for German unification (applies to Germany model only) (DGERM = 1 in 1991, = 0 otherwise), and a dummy for Chernobyl/the US bombing of Libya

(DCHERNO $= 1$ in 1986, $= 0$ otherwise). u is an error term and $a, f, b_1, b_2,$ $\ldots, b_7$ are unknown parameters.

A travel cost variable, measured by the real economy airfare from the USA to Denmark, was also originally included in the USA model (as travel cost was thought to be potentially important for long haul travel), but it was found to be insignificant in the empirical analysis, and so was omitted from the Equation.

By imposing certain restrictions on the parameters in the above equation the authors derived six econometric models. These were a static (cointegration) model; two error correction models, one particularly appropriate for small samples and the other allowing for more than one cointegrating relationship; a reduced autoregressive distributed lag model; a time varying parameter model; and an unrestricted vector autoregressive model. Two time-series models were also included in the study as benchmark comparators: an ARIMA model based on the Box–Jenkins procedure and a simple naïve no-change (or random walk) model (Song & Witt, 2003). The model forecasts very different growth rates for tourist expenditure for the various markets. The highest average annual growth rates were recorded for Germany and Sweden (4%), followed by Norway (3%), the Netherlands (2%), the UK (1%) and the USA (−1%). Germany and Sweden dominated the Danish inbound tourism market and were forecast to account for 67% of inbound international tourist expenditure by 2010.

The empirical results showed that the most accurate forecasting method for the longer-term forecasting horizons (two and three years ahead) was the vector autoregressive model.

Source: Witt, S. F., H. Song, and S. Wanhill (2004) 'Forecasting Tourism-Generated Employment: The Case of Denmark', *Tourism Economics*, 10(2), 167–176

Given its potential to discover precisely what affects tourism demand, multivariate analysis has become the most common causal approach to tourism forecasting. Box 3.4 summarises the advantages and limitations of econometric forecasting models.

BOX 3.4 Advantages and limitations of econometric forecasting models

Advantages
- Econometric methods compel the forecaster to make explicit assumptions about the linkages among the variables being examined. The forecaster must

deal with causal relations, increasing the reliability and acceptability of the results.

- A major advantage of econometric methods lies in the consistency of the technique from period to period. The forecaster can compare forecasts with actual results and use the insights gained to improve the model. That is, by feeding past forecasting errors back into the model, one can develop new parameter estimates to improve future forecasting results.

- The type of output provided by econometric forecasts is another major advantage of this technique. Since econometric models provide estimates of actual values for forecasted variables, these models indicate not only the direction of change but also the magnitude of change. This represents a substantial improvement over the trend projection models, which fail to identify turning points, and the barometric models which do not forecast the magnitude of expected changes.

- The most important advantage of econometric models is that they actually seek to *explain* the variables being forecast. While destination managers may not be able to control many of the economic variables influencing tourist arrivals, in the majority of business forecasting problems, management has a degree of control over some of the variables in the relationship being examined (e.g. price of product, level of advertising). Likewise, a destination manager may be able to use an econometric forecasting system to explore the consequences of alternative future policies on tourism demand. Only by thoroughly understanding the interrelations involved can management hope to forecast accurately and to make optimal decisions as it selects values for controllable variables.

- Another advantage of econometric models is their adaptability. On the basis of a comparison between forecast values and actual values, the model can be modified (existing parameters may be re-estimated and new variables or relationships developed) to improve future forecasts. Econometric forecasting can incorporate or utilise the best features of other forecasting techniques, such as trend and seasonal variations, smoothing techniques and leading indicators.

Limitations

- Econometric models have much larger data requirements than the univariate models (on account of the explanatory variables). There may be some difficulty in forecasting tourism demand because the future values of the independent variables must first be known or predicted. This is of particular concern when a practitioner wishes to forecast many different tourism series.

- Because regression analysis assumes that the relationships between the variables remain constant, it only allows for short-term forecasting. Over the longer term, it can be expected that the relation between the variables will change given the wider economic, social and technological trends taking place.

- Single-equation approaches are incapable of analysing the interdependence of budget allocations to different consumer goods/services. For example, tourism decision-making normally involves a choice among a group of alternative destinations. A change of price in one destination may affect the tourists' decision as to where to travel, and also influence their expenditures within a destination. The single-equation methodology cannot adequately model the influence of a change in tourism price in a particular destination on the demand for travel to alternative destinations. This flags the need to use a systems demand approach.

- The single-equation approach depends heavily on the assumption that the endogenous tourism demand variable is related to a number of exogenous variables. If these variables are not independent, then multi-collinearity can skew the suggested relationships and undermine the accuracy and reliability of any forecast. If this assumption is violated, the researcher would have to model the economic relationships using a system (or simultaneous) equations method. This is called a systems demand approach (Li *et al.*, 2006).

- Econometric models require considerable user understanding and expertise as current regression techniques are becoming increasingly complex.

As econometric techniques advance, the above types of limitations are steadily being overcome.

Song and Witt (2000) were the first researchers to systematically introduce a number of modern econometric methods to tourism demand analysis. More recently, there has been increased attention to the application of modern econometric techniques to tourism demand modelling and forecasting, Modern econometric methods, such as the Autoregressive Distributed Lag Model (ADLM), the Error Correction Model (ECM), the Vector Autoregressive (VAR) model, the Almost Ideal Systems Approach (AIDS) and the Time Varying Parameter (TVP) models, have emerged as the main forecasting methods in the current tourism demand forecasting literature. These relate to a systems demand model approach that produces a set of simultaneous equations of tourism demand, rather than a single equation. The technical illustration of these methods is in Song and Witt (2000) and Li *et al.* (2006).

3.8 THE QUEST FOR FORECASTING ACCURACY

3.8.1 EVALUATING FORECASTS

There are several statistical methods available to evaluate forecast performance. Table 3.6 lists the commonly used measures. RMSE is the most widely used measure for its statistical properties.

All of these measures are subject to interpretation. While these tests provide useful information on the errors in forecasts, they will not provide commentary on the underlying forecast techniques. When forecasts are made in terms of growth rates, forecast errors are expressed in terms of percentage point difference and evaluated using average and absolute average of the errors.

The ability of the forecast to change quickly to respond to changes in data patterns is often considered to be more important than accuracy. Thus, the choice of forecasting method should reflect the relative balance of importance between accuracy and responsiveness, as determined by the forecaster.

3.8.2 NO SINGLE 'BEST APPROACH'

While some comparisons have been made of the forecasting accuracy of different models, there is no exclusive winner in the tourism demand forecasting competitions between the different quantitative approaches. That is, there is no single 'best' forecasting model. While there is no forecasting model that outperforms other approaches in all situations, the conclusions of recent research is that tourism practitioners should give serious consideration to using econometric models for generating forecasts of international tourism demand, given the demonstrated likely increase in forecasting accuracy (Witt & Witt, 1995; Witt *et al.*, 2003).

For the longer-term forecasting horizons, the methods that generate relatively accurate, unbiased forecasts vary markedly according to whether the objective is to minimise forecasting error magnitude or directional change forecasting error. This suggests that it is important to select a forecasting method that is appropriate for the particular objective of the forecast user (Witt *et al.*, 2003).

Theil's U-statistic is widely used to evaluate forecasts. Theil's statistic can be used in two ways. Firstly, to see how much two series (e.g. actuals and forecasts) are closer to each other, and secondly, whether forecasts produced by a model perform better than the naïve forecasts.

The formulas used to calculate Theil's U-statistics are

$$U_1 = \frac{\sqrt{\sum_{t=1}^{n} (a_t - f_t)^2}}{\sqrt{\sum_{t=1}^{n} a_t^2} + \sqrt{\sum_{t=1}^{n} f_t^2}}, \quad U_2 = \sqrt{\frac{\sum_{t=1}^{n-1} \left(\frac{f_{t+1} - a_{t+1}}{a_t}\right)^2}{\sum_{t=1}^{n-1} \left(\frac{a_{t+1} - a_t}{a_t}\right)^2}}$$

Table 3.6 Statistical techniques for error measurement

Technique	Abbreviation	Measures	Formula
Mean Squared Error	MSE	The average of squared errors over the sample period	$\text{MSE} = \frac{1}{n} \sum_{t=1}^{n} (a_t - f_t)^2$
Root Mean Squared Error	RMSE	A measure of total error defined as the square root of the sum of the variance and the square of the bias	$\text{RMSE} = \sqrt{\frac{\sum (a_t - f_t)^2}{n}}$
Mean Percentage Error	MPE	The average of percentage errors by which forecasts differ from outcomes	$\text{MPE} = \frac{1}{n} \sum_{t=1}^{n} \frac{(a_t - f_t)}{a_t} \times 100$
Mean Absolute Error	MAE	The average of absolute dollar amount or percentage points by which a forecast differs from an outcome	$\text{MAE} = \frac{1}{n} \sum_{t=1}^{n} |(a_t - f_t)|$
Mean Absolute Percentage Error	MAPE	The average of absolute percentage amount by which forecasts differ from outcomes	$\text{MAPE} = \frac{1}{n} \sum_{t=1}^{n} \frac{|(a_t - f_t)|}{a_t} \times 100$

a = actual outcome

f = forecast outcomes

t = time reference

n = number of time periods

e = error (defined as $a - f$)

$\sum$ = sum of

123

To interpret the U-statistics the general guide is:

- U_1 is bound between 0 and 1, with values closer to 0 indicating greater forecasting accuracy;
- if $U_2 = 1$, there is no difference between a naïve forecast and the technique used;
- if $U_2 < 1$ the technique is better than a naïve forecast; and
- if $U_2 > 1$ the technique is no better than a naïve forecast.

Some researchers have attempted to combine the forecasts generated from different models in order to improve the forecasting accuracy. Indeed, the general forecasting literature suggests that forecast combination can improve forecasting accuracy (Song *et al.*, 2003b).

Researchers and policy makers often approach forecasting differently. Researchers appear to be more interested in achieving high accuracy at the expense of losing simplicity while policy makers and practitioners emphasise achieving more accuracy with simple models. The choice of forecasting method depends on several considerations as listed in Box 3.5.

BOX 3.5 Choice of forecasting method

The choice of forecasting method depends on the following considerations:

- The level of accuracy required by the forecast. (There are at least three dimensions of accuracy: error magnitude accuracy, directional change accuracy and trend change or turning point accuracy).
- The ease of use of the forecasting technique.
- The cost of producing the forecasts compared with the potential gains from their use.
- The power of the forecasting technique to explain important relationships among key variables.
- The robustness of the technique (effect of extreme or outlier values in the historical series).
- The speed with which the forecasts can be produced.
- The lead time necessary for making decisions dependent on the variables estimated in the forecast model.
- The timeframe of the forecast (whether it is expected to generate short-term or long-term predictions).
- The availability of data on which the forecast is to be made.
- The quality of the available data on which the forecast is made.
- The complexity of the relationships to be forecast.

Despite the increasing sophistication of tourism forecasting approaches, we agree with Frechtling (2001) who notes that any model designed to forecast human behaviour will suffer from forecasting errors. Such errors are due to at least three factors that sometimes interact:

- *Omission of influential variables.* No forecasting model can include all of the variables that affect the one being forecast. Moreover, even if such a model could be built, it is unlikely that the forecaster could accurately estimate the true relationships between these and the forecast variable (due to weather, transport equipment failure, labour strikes, etc.).
- *Measurement error.* We often cannot measure visitor flows (or expenditure) completely accurately. Moreover, the variables that affect demand may be mis-measured as well. Some are inherently unmeasurable (e.g. 'attractiveness' of destination) and some are difficult to measure due to data collection difficulties (e.g. visitor expenditures).
- *Human indeterminateness.* Human beings do not always act in rational ways or even in their own best interests. They often ignore budget constraints when planning a vacation. Patterns of behaviour change. People, individually or in groups, cancel planned trips or schedule new ones. There is always a degree of randomness in human behaviour and this is reflected in forecast errors.

Of course, it is naïve to regard those forecasts that turn out to be accurate as necessarily superior. Faulkner and Valerio (1995) suggest that this may not necessarily be the case.

- The accurate forecast might be right for the wrong reasons. While this situation may not have negative planning implications in the short term, it will in the longer term if it results in too much faith being placed in an ostensibly 'proven' but potentially flawed approach.
- Under certain circumstances a good forecast may be one which does not eventuate. That is, if a forecast foreshadows the prospect of negative developments, and thereby triggers remedial action to prevent these from occurring, it will have served its purposes without being accurate in the long run.
- There are occasions when forecasts have such an influence on planning targets that they become self-fulfilling prophecies. This has a positive effect if it results in the infrastructure required to take up growth opportunities being put in place. On the other hand, unduly conservative forecasts can also become self-fulfilling prophecies if they discourage the development of capacity and, as a consequence, restrict growth in demand.

3.9 A HYBRID OR INTEGRATIVE APPROACH

Attempts have been made recently to further enhance forecast accuracy through forecast combination, and forecast integration of quantitative and qualitative approaches.

A growing number of researchers recommend that a broader 'hybrid' or 'integrative' approach to tourism analysis and forecasting is required, bringing together different methods of examining the future (Blake *et al.*, 2004; Faulkner & Valerio, 2000). This integrative approach is intended to be a more practical method of forecasting that takes into account data not available in any single approach.

The integrative approach emphasises that the ultimate purpose of tourism demand forecasting is to assist in management decision-making and the *process* of forecasting is as important as the *outcome*. Advocates of this approach observe that tourism demand forecasting, using quantitative approaches only, seems to have become an end in itself, with the forecasting process being divorced from the tourism management activities it is supposed to serve. By viewing forecasting as simply an attempt to anticipate the future, researchers have tended to forget that the forecasting process itself is an integral part of strategic management. These critics argue that such forecasting results in its alienation from the planning process and that a method that actively engages decision makers in the forecasting exercise can contribute more to the broader strategic planning process than one that does not.

Some basic tenets of the integrative approach are set out in the Box 3.6.

BOX 3.6 Basic elements of the integrative approach to forecasting

- Since all techniques currently employed for tourism forecasting have limitations, a combination of these techniques needs to be applied so that their respective strengths and weaknesses complement each other.
- By limiting analyses to the impact of quantifiable economic factors, most forecasting techniques overlook the numerous other factors involved in a potential tourist's decision-making process.
- A systematic approach to forecasting should be an integral part of the planning process, as this provides the basis for assessing emerging opportunities and threats.
- As a consequence, forecasting (and target setting) should be a consultative process and the approaches adopted should be 'transparent' from the point of view of all parties involved.
- Participants should be encouraged not to accept forecasts produced by the technicians uncritically. The assumptions on which forecasts are based should be scrutinised and challenged.
- While the integrative approach demands that managers and decision makers become more sophisticated, it also demands that the technicians involved become more effective in communicating with, and educating, users.

Source: Based on Faulkner and Valerio (2000)

Proponents of the integrative approach do not reject quantitative modelling techniques which, they agree, can provide a systematic basis for understanding relationships among variables and exploring the effects of alternative scenarios for the future. However, they claim that the integrative approach offers the dual advantage of enabling a broader range of quantifiable and non-quantifiable variables to be taken into account, while at the same time providing a framework for consultation. An example of the integrative approach is the forecasting process of Tourism Australia. The approach is summarised in Box 3.7. In this approach,

- dependence upon econometric modelling is reduced, with this approach being supplemented by others that take into account factors which are less amenable to quantitative analysis.
- more emphasis is being placed on a consultative approach which not only permits a more diverse range of factors to be taken into account but also facilitates the integration of forecasting with the management decision process.

BOX 3.7 Tourism Australia approach to integrative forecasting

- A step towards the development of a more open consultative approach to tourism forecasting has been taken in Australia with the establishment of the Federal Government's Tourism Forecasting Committee (TFC). The TFC is responsible for producing official 10-year forecasts for international visitor arrivals, domestic visitor activity, outbound departures, and export earnings. Forecasts are provided to inform investment and marketing planning within the tourism industry.
- The TFC provides a consultative framework which not only facilitates an industry input to the forecasting process, but enables the development of a broader understanding of the assumptions on which the forecasts are based and the insights produced by associated analyses.

First stage
- The process begins with the TFC Forecasting Unit preparing initial forecasts. The forecasts are derived from econometric and time series models that employ variables such as the relative price between Australia, and competitor markets; relative income; population; seasonal indicators; and significant event indicators. The models are based on quarterly data.

Second stage

- The second iteration requires the Forecasting Unit to present draft forecasts of tourism numbers and expenditure to a technical committee whose input is both technical and qualitative, addressing methodology and external factors influencing the forecast models. These factors include GDP growth projections, changes in relative prices and exchange rate changes.

- Data for the forecasts comes from an extensive range of sources such as the Australian Bureau of Statistics, Tourism Research Australia, the International Monetary Fund, the International Air Transport Association, the Pacific Asia Travel Association, and the World Tourism Organisation. Market intelligence is also gathered from an equally wide range of sources such as airlines, tourism operators and lobby groups, as well as local and international financial institutions.

- This stage of the process is critical in adjusting the forecasts by incorporating qualitative information such as travel fears, competitor marketing, and individual market conditions and factors existing and projected future travel propensities, aviation market trends and political/trade considerations such as agreements on the establishment of closer economic relations which no econometric model could encompass. Decisions regarding adjustments are made by consensus. These forecasts represent the most likely outcome given past trends, current information, and the impact of policy and industry changes.

Third stage

- The third (and final) iteration adjustment rests with the TFC which focuses on broader issues that will impact on the forecasts, such as the strategic direction of the industry. The focus at this stage is on broader issues that will impact on the forecasts, such as the strategic direction of the industry (alliances and recovery mechanisms or political decisions). In its decision process the TFC examines medium and long term industry responses based on short term fluctuations and concentrates on providing industry with the most likely growth rates and their contribution to the Australian economy. The decision for adjustment is by consensus and determines the final forecasts which are then published.

Source: Tourism Forecasting Council (1998) *Inbound Tourism Short-Term Scenarios* (Research Report No. 2). Canberra, Australia: Tourism Forecasting Council

Effective integration of tourism demand forecasting with management decision-making requires a meaningful dialogue between forecasters and users. This dialogue can lead to a more informed view of the nature and role of forecasting among all tourism stakeholders. A dialogue between the analysts who produce the forecasts and the decision makers who use them is essential if underlying assumptions are to be questioned and debated, and if insights generated by the analysis of trends are to be utilised in the management process. Furthermore, through the use of judgemental techniques, there will be more scope for bringing a range of alternative approaches to bear on the problem and the over-reliance on modelling techniques will be reduced.

3.10 CONCLUSIONS AND POLICY

- Tourism demand forecasting may be defined as the art of trying to predict future levels of demand for some tourism product or service.
- Forecasting is especially important in tourism because it aids long-term planning and is fundamental to the conduct of modern business and destination management. It is particularly challenging because the tourism product is perishable; tourism behaviour is complex; people are inseparable from the production–consumption process; customer satisfaction depends on complementary products and services; and tourism demand is extremely sensitive to both natural and human-made disasters.
- Forecasting is undertaken by different tourism stakeholders, for different reasons, for different timeframes. The same forecasting techniques, however, will not be appropriate for all situations, for all markets, for all times.
- There are two broad approaches to tourism forecasting: qualitative tourism forecasting and quantitative tourism forecasting.
- Qualitative tourism forecasts are based on the judgements of persons sharing their experience, practical knowledge and intuition. These judgements are found through sales force polling, expert opinion, panel consensus, surveys, Delphi technique and scenario writing and are often used to moderate or 'second-guess' quantitative forecasts.
- Qualitative forecasting is best applied when facing insufficient historical data; unreliable time series; rapidly changing macro environments; major disturbances; and when long-term forecasts are desired.
- Quantitative tourism forecasts are based on mathematical techniques using either cross-sectional data or time-series data. Time-series modelling employs either univariate models (which forecast a variable based on its own past movement in time) or multi-variate (econometric) models (which, in addition to time, include a number of non-time potential explanatory variables selected on the basis of economic theory).
- The variations that are evident in a time series can be decomposed into four components: secular trend, cyclical variation, seasonal effects and random events. Controlling for seasonal and cyclical variations is an important aspect of time-series analysis

and projection. An analysis of seasonal and cyclical fluctuations can greatly improve forecasting results, especially for short-run forecasting.

- A primary effort of tourism forecasters has been concerned with forecasting international tourism arrivals. The typical and most generally accepted methodology for forecasting with time-series models is for the forecaster to choose a particular class of model and then use a set of objective criteria to choose the most suitable specific model within this class as appropriate to the data. Within the class of time-series models, there are many different forms that such models can take.

- While useful, time-series forecasts have their shortcomings in their assumption that the historical series will continue into the future, in their inability to predict turning points and in their inability to analyse causal relations.

- Barometric techniques can be applied to discover turning points in time-series data and to highlight the relationships between causal or coincident events to predict future events. A leading indicator series, in conjunction with other forecasting results, can help businesses, governments and destination managers predict and prepare for significant changes in the economic environment.

- Econometric techniques seek to *explain* the variables being forecast. They involve the regression of a number of variables over time in order to assess their influence on the variable to be forecast. Econometric methods force the forecaster to make explicit assumptions about the linkages among the variables being examined. The forecaster must deal with causal relations, increasing the reliability and acceptability of the results.

- There are several statistical methods available to evaluate forecast performance. RMSE is perhaps the most widely used measure for its statistical properties. The different tests provide useful information on the errors in forecasts.

- There is no single quantitative technique that gives best forecasting results in all contexts. The choice of forecasting method depends on several considerations including the level of accuracy required; the ease of use of the forecasting technique; the cost of producing the forecasts compared with the potential gains from their use; the speed with which the forecasts can be produced; the timeframe of the forecast; the quality and availability of data on which the forecast is to be made; and the complexity of the relationships to be forecast.

- Recently, attempts have been made to enhance tourism forecasting accuracy through forecast combination and forecast integration of quantitative and qualitative approaches. Forecasts need to be justifiable with the forecasting process transparent and open to all to question and challenge. Combined forecasts tend to have greater explanatory power than single-approach forecasts and tend to be more accurate.

- Forecasting is not an end in itself. It needs to take place within a context as an integral part of management strategy. As such, forecasting should serve specific managerial

130

objectives. Forecasts are of no benefit to tourism stakeholders if the results cannot be acted on or are unrelated to their needs.

SELF-REVIEW QUESTIONS

1. What is meant by tourism forecasting? Why do researchers and practitioners engage in tourism forecasting?

2. Distinguish between the three different time horizons in tourism forecasting. Why is it essential to set a timeframe when tourism forecasting?

3. Briefly describe each of the seven reasons as to why forecasting is of special importance in tourism.

4. Differentiate between the two broad approaches to tourism forecasting: qualitative tourism forecasting and quantitative tourism forecasting. List the conditions that dictate when each of qualitative forecasting and quantitative forecasting might be undertaken.

5. Differentiate between the two major categories of quantitative tourism forecasting: time-series and cross-sectional. Describe the four components into which a time-series can be decomposed.

6. Why are data often smoothed in time-series analysis? How do moving averages and exponential smoothing each smooth time-series data?

7. Choose a tourism example and explain how relevant economic indicators may be classified as leading, coincident or lagging.

8. Briefly describe problems that may affect the usefulness of barometric tourism forecasting. How might these problems be mitigated?

9. Compare and contrast the advantages and limitations of the various econometric models used in tourism forecasting.

ESSAY QUESTIONS

1. Since any model designed to forecast human behaviour will suffer from forecasting errors, tourism forecasting is less than useful for destination managers. Discuss.

2. In a changing global tourism environment it is important for both government policy development and business planning to have reliable short-term and long-term forecasts of tourism activity. Why?

3. Using the airline industry as an example, distinguish between different qualitative and quantitative techniques that seek to forecast passenger demand.

4. Qualitative forecasting is more accurate and appropriate for short-term forecasting, while quantitative forecasting is better suited to intermediate and longer-term forecasting. Discuss.

5. Given its potential to discover precisely what affects tourism demand, multivariate analysis has become the most common causal approach to tourism forecasting. Explain why.

6. If it is fair to say that there is no exclusive winner in the tourism demand forecasting competitions between the quantitative approaches, that is, if there is no 'best' forecasting model, it does not matter which quantitative method is used. Discuss.

7. Tourism demand forecasts that turn out to be accurate are not necessarily superior. Argue for or against this statement.

8. The process of tourism demand forecasting is as important as the outcome. Why might this be so?

TOURISM SUPPLY AND PRICING STRATEGIES

CHAPTER 4

TOURISM SUPPLY

LEARNING OBJECTIVES

After reading this chapter, you should be able to:

1. Discuss the nature of tourism supply.

2. Understand the microeconomic foundation of tourism supply with its focus on production and costs.

3. Understand the nature and importance of diminishing marginal returns to short-run production within tourism and its relationship to variable costs.

4. Distinguish between explicit costs and implicit costs; between fixed costs and variable costs; and between total costs, average costs and marginal costs as they apply within tourism.

5. Understand the determinants of long-run economies of scale and diseconomies of scale within the tourism industry.

6. Appreciate the monopolistic competitive and oligopolistic natures of the tourism industry.

7. Understand the usefulness of the Structure–Conduct–Performance paradigm to gain an overall picture of tourism markets, highlighting key features and capturing essential relationships.

8. Distinguish between horizontal and vertical integration; and between integration and strategic alliances within tourism.

9. Appreciate the importance of effective supply chain management for tourism firms.

4.1 INTRODUCTION

In Chapters 2 and 3, we focused on tourism demand and on the factors that influence the patterns of tourism spending and demand forecasting. We now turn our attention to tourism supply: production, costs, market structure and supply chains.

135

Complicating the study of tourism supply are two issues. One is that unlike many other industries that manufacture products or produce services, there is no 'tourism industry'. The other is that the tourism product has several features that make it quite different from other products.

4.1.1 TOURISM IS NOT LIKE OTHER INDUSTRIES

Tourism is commonly thought of, and referred to, as an 'industry'. An industry is generally regarded as a group of establishments engaged in the same kind of productive activities. Typically, industries are classified in accordance with the goods and services that they produce. However, all industries are, in some degree, part of the aggregate activity of tourist expenditure, because tourists purchase goods and services from firms in all sectors of the economy. Thus, we note that

- The tourism 'industry' comprises outputs from a wide variety of different industry activities.
- In the case of tourism, the defining element is not the type of commodity produced, but the type of consumer. Visitor consumption is not restricted to a set of predefined goods and services produced by a predefined set of industries. Thus, whether the same product or service is or is not a tourism-related economic activity is based on certain characteristics of the consumer, rather than anything inherent in the product or service.

The second point implies that tourism is best seen statistically as a 'demand' side activity and is not an industry in the traditional sense. The demand concept of what constitutes tourism was adopted by the United Nations World Tourism Organisation (UNWTO) in 1993 as the international statistical standard. The UNWTO defines tourism as

> the activities of persons travelling to and staying in places outside their usual environment for not more than one consecutive year for leisure, business and other purposes not related to the exercise of an activity remunerated from within the place visited.

Tourism is more limited than travel as it refers to specific types of trips. Individuals when taking such trips are called visitors. Tourism is therefore a subset of travel and visitors are a subset of travellers (IRTS, 2008, paras. 2.6–2.13) both in an international context and in a domestic context.

This approach places great weight on the definition used for a tourist since the supply of any product or service to a person who is a tourist is a tourism activity, while the supply of the same product or service to a person who is not a tourist is not a tourism activity. It is the characteristics of the consumer that determine whether the production is included within the scope of tourism.

While tourism must retain the demand-side definition of its scope, there is also a need to delineate more clearly a supply-based conceptual structure for its activities because that is the source of most national economic statistics. When incorporated into the supply-based statistical structure, tourism's relationships to other economic sectors can be identified.

Tourism measurement and analysis from a supply perspective requires a particular classification of products and productive activities. By identifying the components of a 'tourism industry', it becomes possible to discover the type of main commodities purchased by visitors, the industries that benefit directly from tourism demand and the way in which those benefits are distributed. Supply-side definitions of tourism products and industries are listed in the Recommended Methodological Framework (TSA-RMF) developed by the Commission of the European Communities, the Organisation for Economic Cooperation and Development (OECD), the UNWTO and the World Travel and Tourism Council (WTTC), and approved by the United Nations Statistical Commission. The recommended framework identifies tourism's component products and industries through the concepts of Tourism Characteristic and Tourism Connected products and industries. Following the definitions in IRTS (2008), a *tourism industry* represents the grouping of those establishments whose main activity is the same tourism characteristic activity. Since they are integrally associated with the development of Tourism Satellite Accounts (TSA), they will be discussed in more detail in Chapter 7.

4.1.2 TOURISM PRODUCTS ARE NOT LIKE OTHER PRODUCTS

The 'outputs' of tourism firms are either 'goods' (e.g. shopping items) or 'services' (tour guiding) or, most likely, combinations of the two, since most tourism experiences are based on the consumption of a (tangible) product and an (intangible) service. Consider, for example, a restaurant meal that combines the food content with the service experience. Much of the supply of tourism operators and destinations as a whole is of 'services' rather than 'products' as the latter are usually conceived.

Services are intangible

Buyers cannot feel, see, smell, touch or taste a service before they agree to purchase it. Since goods are *made* while services are *delivered*, the output of services and cost per unit are often much more difficult to measure than for standard products. Goods are impersonal while services are *personal*.

Tourism experiences

Products possess physical characteristics we can evaluate before we buy; services *do not even exist* before they are purchased. Products are *used* while services are *experienced*. Tourism supply is generally not sampled before it is purchased. This generates a degree of uncertainty and risk for tourism buyers, especially in the destination and tour markets. Therefore, unless known to buyers through previous sampling or product description, the nature and quality of the tourism product cannot be determined precisely beforehand. Buyers must travel to the tourist location in order to consume it. That is, tourism products are 'experience products' rather than 'search products'.

To reduce uncertainty, buyers look for signals of service quality such as reputation and product reviews guide books, ratings organisations and the like.

Irreversibility

Once consumed, a service cannot be returned. While many manufactured products can be returned to the supplier or can be recalled by the manufacturer, once used, tourism services, such as tours and air travel, cannot be so returned.

Inseparability

Most services are provided by people. To purchase a service you must come into contact with someone who provides it. Tourism services are supplied and consumed simultaneously with buyers bringing their own experience to the supply. Since personal experience is part of the tourism product, tourism supply always faces the difficulty of ensuring consumer satisfaction.

Perishability

Services are perishable. Services supplied by people cannot be stored. Unlike most manufactured products much tourism supply cannot be stored for sale in the future. An unsold hotel room or airline seat remains forever unsold. For the firm, it is revenue foregone. This can lead tourism suppliers to engage in price wars when supply exceeds demand.

Interdependence

Tourism products are not supplied in isolation. Their supply (and their enjoyment by consumers) is often dependent on the presence of complementary products and services offered by other suppliers. The successful supply of tourist facilities, for instance, is dependent in large part on ready access to good infrastructure and transport links.

Seasonal fluctuations

Tourism supply fluctuates with seasons of the year (for holiday destinations), with weekends and weekdays (for hotels) and with the time of day (for airline flights) as it attempts to match demand. This leads to price adjustments (up or down) as tourism firms seek to manage short-run demand.

Spatial fixity

Tourism infrastructure such as accommodation, tourist attractions and destinations is place-sensitive. Location is an integral characteristic of supply as the buyer must travel to the supply.

Given the supply characteristics just outlined, our discussion of tourism supply now turns to the basic microeconomic theory that covers production, costs, market structure and supply chains.

4.2 FACTORS INFLUENCING TOURISM SUPPLY

Tourism supply refers to the willingness and ability of firms to supply various quantities of a tourism product at various prices during any one period of time. In similar fashion to tourism demand, tourism supply is influenced by price and non-price factors. We can specify the supply function of a tourism product (Q_s), measured in physical units, as an equation:

$$Q_s = f(P_x, P_0, C, T, N, \pi, \dots) \tag{4.1}$$

Where,

P_x is the price of the product;

P_0 is the price of other products;

C is the cost of inputs;

T is the level of technology;

N is the number of suppliers;

π is the expected profit.

The dot points inside the brackets refer to other determinants of supply that are specific to the particular tourism firm and product.

The *market supply* (the sum of the quantities supplied by each individual firm at each price) shows the quantities of the product supplied in the market per unit of time at various alternative prices while holding everything else (non-price factors) constant.

4.2.1 TOURISM SUPPLY AND PRICE

Economic theory suggests that price and quantity supplied of a product have a positive relationship. The higher the price, the more firms are willing to supply and vice versa. Figure 4.1a shows the market supply curve, sloping upwards from bottom left to top right, indicating that firms are more willing to supply a greater quantity at higher prices and will supply less quantity as price falls. There are two basic reasons for this. First, higher prices generally lead to higher profits, inducing firms to supply more. Second, firms will seek higher prices to cover any increases in the marginal cost of production that might accompany increased production.

4.2.2 TOURISM SUPPLY AND NON-PRICE FACTORS

Following standard economic theory, supply should change and the supply curve shifts to the right (or left) as more (or less) of the product is supplied at each price, when changes in non-price factors affect supply (see Figure 4.1b). Such changes relate to:

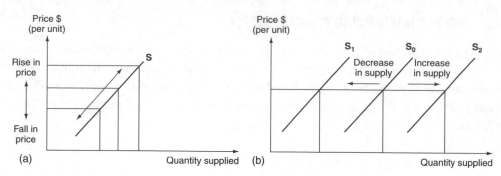

Figure 4.1 (a) Quantity supplied changes with changes in price, (b) Supply shifts with non-price factors

- *The price of inputs*. Changes in input (resource) prices are the most likely cause of changes in supply. An increase in wage rates for tour leaders, for instance, or a rise in the price of raw materials such as petrol, may cause tour operators to supply less, shifting market supply to the left. Another way to understand this is to note that, at the quantity supplied, costs are now higher, pressuring firms to raise the price of their supply. Conversely, a fall in input costs (such as fuel savings on cruise ships) will shift supply to the right (reducing costs at the quantity supplied).

- *The level of technology*. Positive technological change means that the firm can produce more output for the same amount of inputs, reducing costs per output and making supply more profitable at any given price. The market supply curve will shift to the right. The adoption of computer reservation systems by airlines and hotels, for instance, has reduced their costs of service. Better training of workers and better combining of labour and capital can raise factor productivity, increasing output at every price.

- *The number of sellers*. The supply curve will shift to the right as new firms enter the market and shift to the left as firms leave the market. The entry of new airlines, for instance, has increased the worldwide supply of air travel, even given that some airlines have quit the market.

- *The prices of other products*. Given their resources, firms could supply alternative types of products (substitutes in production). If they choose to produce one type of product, then they do not produce another type of product. This represents an opportunity cost to the firm in its choice of product to supply. As the relative prices of the different types of product change, firms may find the alternative type of product more profitable and either switch production to it or add that alternative product to their suite of products. Tour operators specialising in China tours, for instance, may shift some resources into delivering South American adventure tours to increase profits. Similarly, a resort hotel may re-allocate its resources in the aquatic activities area depending on the current demand for different types of experiences.

- *Profit expectations and future prices.* Firms may respond to expected future prices either by expanding production now and trying to sell more (if they think future prices will be lower) or by cutting back on production now in the hope of expanding future supply (if they think future prices will be higher).
- *Environmental conditions.* Bad weather can reduce supply. Hurricane Katrina devastated tourism supply in and around New Orleans in 2005. Similarly, the 2004 Boxing Day tsunami destroyed many coastal resorts bordering the affected parts of the Indian Ocean.
- *Taxes and subsidies.* Taxes imposed on tourism products will shift the supply curve leftwards indicating less amount supplied at any given price. Where government is supportive of tourism, it often subsidises supply through tax relief (e.g. hotels in India) thereby shifting the supply curve to the right.

Figure 4.1b shows shifts in the market supply curve brought about by changes in non-price factors such as the cost of inputs, the level of technology, the number of suppliers, the price of substitutes in production, supplier expectations, weather and government taxes and subsidies.

4.3 TOURISM SUPPLY AND ELASTICITY

The price elasticity of supply for a tourism product is the extent to which quantity supplied is sensitive to changes in price. It depends on both non-price factors and time:

- *The extent to which supply costs change as supply is altered.* Firms may be less willing to increase quantity supplied in the light of higher prices if their marginal costs of supply increase faster than the price of their product. In such cases, increasing supply would prove less profitable than maintaining existing supply.
- *The existence of spare capacity.* Supply will be more price elastic if the firm has spare capacity and can easily increase production and quantity supplied in response to higher prices.
- *The extent to which the firm carries inventories.* Inventories (stocks on shelves or in warehouses) act as a buffer between demand and supply. Abundant inventories may mean a firm does not have to increase production immediately in response to increased prices. This is more likely to apply to manufactured tourism products such as souvenirs or beachwear than to tourism services such as guiding.
- *The extent to which the firm can switch to substitutes in production.* As the relative prices of alternative types of product change, the firm may or may not be easily able to switch between product types or add another product type to its existing suite of products.
- *Time.* The longer the period firms have to adapt to price changes, the more elastic will be their supply. In the short run, capacity constraints or the lack of availability of scarce resource may make it difficult for tourism firms to increase supply in response to higher

prices. In the long run, the firm may be able to increase capacity or develop more resources.

Algebraically, the price elasticity of supply of any particular tourism product (ε_s) may be expressed as:

$$\varepsilon_s = \frac{\text{percentage change in the quantity supplied of the tourism product}}{\text{percentage change in the price of the tourism product}}$$

By way of example, suppose a particular boutique Paris hotel faces short-run capacity constraints and can only increase the supply of its bed nights by 4% in the face of a 10% increase in room prices throughout the hotel industry, *ceteris paribus*.

$$\varepsilon_s = \frac{\% \text{ change in quantity supplied}}{\% \text{ change in price}} = \frac{4\%}{10\%} = 0.4$$

This suggests that, in the short run, for every 1% rise in price of hotel rooms there is a 0.4% rise in supply of bed nights by the hotel, suggesting that short-run hotel room supply is fairly insensitive to changes in price. Over time, however, the hotel may be able to expand its supply of bed nights (e.g. build a new accommodation wing) and its bed supply may become more responsive to price changes.

Broadly, supply of a tourism product may be classified as

- *Inelastic* ($E_s < 1$) when tourism supply is relatively insensitive to changes in price. This may be because the firm is facing capacity constraints or the resources it requires are unavailable, for example, the boutique hotel discussed above or a tour operator that finds it cannot support planned expansion of its services because professional guides are in short supply.
- *Elastic* ($E_s > 1$) when tourism supply is relatively sensitive to changes in price. This may be because the firm has unused capacity that it can tap or the resources it requires for expansion are readily available.

Under extreme conditions, it is possible that supply may be *perfectly inelastic* (supply does not change at all in response to changes in price). Such was the case for coastal resorts immediately following the 2004 tsunami. At that time in the affected areas, hotel rooms became in short supply and there was no immediate way of increasing their number (irrespective of any demand considerations). It is also possible, at least in theory, that supply may be *perfectly elastic* (supply changes infinitely in response to a change in price), if resources were readily available to support any expansion. The alternatives are displayed in Figure 4.2.

Typically, the supply curve of a tourist product or service will be upward-sloping but the nature of the product will determine whether supply is relatively elastic or inelastic.

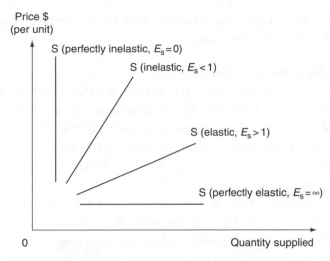

Figure 4.2 Elasticity of supply

4.4 PRODUCTION, COSTS AND SUPPLY

4.4.1 PRODUCTION

As with all goods and services, the production and supply of tourism products are based on inputs (factors of production). These inputs take three basic forms: *natural resources*, *human resources* and *human-made resources*.

Natural resources

Natural resources (sometimes referred to as *land*) include the raw materials supplied by nature: water, air, minerals, metals, oil, grasslands, forests, soil, climate and so on. In tourism supply, natural materials may either be retained in their original state, for example, wilderness areas, or, as is more usual, be worked on and modified by human and capital factors, for example, the conversion of grasslands into golf courses or the production of holiday souvenirs from metals, clays and cloth.

Human resources

The human resource input includes both *labour* and *entrepreneurship*, encompassing the physical, intellectual and entrepreneurial ability essential to tourism supply. For a travel agency, for instance, it includes front-office and back-office staff and management. Human resources cover the entire range of unskilled through to semi-skilled and skilled labour.

Human-made resources

Human-made resources (often called *capital*) include the human-made items that help to create further products, for example, the physical buildings, plant and equipment found in

143

hotels and resorts. The resources also include the built environment of destinations and their general and tourism infrastructure.

Fixed and variable factors of production

As with any industry, inputs into tourism supply are either *fixed* or *variable*. A tourism firm's variable factors are those that may be varied at short notice, for example, a restaurant may be able to hire labour (variable factor) reasonably quickly if more than the expected number of customers turn up on a particular night. Fixed factors cannot be so easily adjusted. Any physical expansion in the size of the restaurant or its kitchen (fixed factors), or relocation to bigger premises, will take time. Again, the number and size of hotel rooms and the number and configuration of seats on an aircraft are fixed factors in the short run.

Note: Labour is not always a variable factor and capital is not always a fixed factor. Firms may have trained staff with specific skills and have entered a long-term contract to employ them. If so, they represent a fixed factor and their cost would be a fixed cost.

Short-run and long-run production timeframes

The existence of fixed and variable factors gives rise to the production timeframes of *short run* and *long run*.

The *short run* is the timeframe in which at least one factor of production is fixed. For example, as the popularity of the restaurant grows, in the short run it might meet any extra demand for its services through hiring more labour (variable factor), given that the amount of capital equipment, for example, seating capacity or the size of the kitchen, cannot be altered quickly (fixed factors).

In the *long run*, however, all factors of production are able to be varied and the restaurant can expand or move to larger premises. Similarly, the hotel may add another accommodation wing and the airline can lease/purchase more aircraft.

Short-run and long-run production timeframes differ for different sectors within tourism markets. The short run for a restaurant may be as short as a few months. By that time, the restaurant will be able to vary its factors as needed. For the airline industry, though, the short run may last from 3 to 5 years for that may be the time period the airline needs to change its capital base by buying or leasing new aircraft and to have them configured to its specifications by the manufacturer.

Short-run and long-run production timeframes obviously have implications for each tourism firm's forward planning. In some destinations, natural or historical sites have fixed capacity and are not able to be varied whatever the timeframe is.

4.4.2 COSTS

Production costs in tourism depend on the quantity, price and productivity of the factors that are used in the provision of the product. Costs of production can be classified in various ways.

Explicit costs and implicit costs

Explicit costs are direct payments made by firms to outside suppliers of inputs, for example, hiring workers, buying raw materials, hiring machines and repaying loans.

Implicit costs are the opportunity costs that firms face in the use of their own resources in one task rather than in another task. For example, if a restaurant or theme park uses its retained earnings to fund expansion, it incurs the opportunity cost of not earning interest on those funds on the short-term money market. The owners of tourism firms, from sole trader to shareholders in multinationals, face opportunity costs in investing time and money in their firms since they could have received returns from investing that time and money elsewhere. Implicit costs do not involve direct payments to outsiders and can sometimes be difficult to quantify.

Fixed costs and variable costs

Fixed costs (FC) are costs of fixed factors that firms are locked into irrespective of the level of their output. The more obvious examples are rent, depreciation on plant and equipment and the repayment of bank loans.

Variable costs (VC) are costs that change with the firm's level of output and include day-to-day running costs such raw materials, labour and power.

In the 'short run', at least one factor is fixed and so some costs are fixed in this period. This is in contrast to the 'long run' where all factors are variable and so all costs are variable.

Total cost, average cost and marginal cost

Total cost (TC) is the full cost to the firm in the provision of its product (the combined cost of natural, human and human-made inputs). It is the sum of fixed and variable costs ($TC = FC + VC$).

Average cost (AC) is the product's unit cost and is measured as total cost divided by output ($AC = TC/Q$).

Average fixed cost (AFC) is measured as total fixed cost divided by output ($AFC = FC/Q$).

Average variable cost (AVC) is measured as total variable cost divided by output ($AVC = VC/Q$).

Marginal cost (MC) is the extra cost to the firm of producing an extra unit of its product and is measured as the change in total cost divided by the change in output ($MC = dTC/dQ$). The meaning of 'unit', of course, differs with the type of tourism product under study. It might refer to one extra plane load of passengers or one extra passenger or to one more container load of souvenirs or one extra souvenir. The MC curve intersects from below the AVC and AC curves at their minimum points.

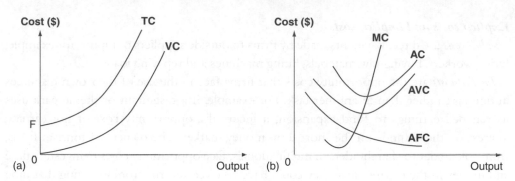

Figure 4.3 (a) Short-run FC, VC and TC, (b) Short-run AC, AVC, AFC and MC

Measuring and monitoring each type of cost are important for any tourism firm. To make rational decisions, managers need to know which types of cost their firms face and to what extent they face them since all costs add to and take from bottom line profit.

Figure 4.3a shows short-run FC, VC and TC faced by firms. Figure 4.3b shows a firm's AC, AVC, AFC and MC. The short-run rise in VC (and therefore in MC and AC) is caused by diminishing returns.

4.4.3   THE RELATIONSHIP BETWEEN PRODUCTION AND COSTS

Short run
Figure 4.4 shows typical short-run production for firms. The production function is a mathematical expression which relates the quantity of factor inputs to the quantity of outputs that result.

Total product is the total output that is generated from the factors of production employed by a business. In most manufacturing industries, it is straightforward to measure the volume of production from labour and capital inputs that are used. But in many service or knowledge-based industries such as tourism, where much of the output is 'intangible', 'output' is difficult to measure.

Average product is the total output divided by the number of units of the variable factor of production employed (e.g. output per worker employed or output per unit of capital employed).

Marginal product is the change in total product when an additional unit of the variable factor of production is employed. For example, marginal product would measure the change in output that comes from increasing the employment of labour by one person (e.g. an extra chef), or by adding one more item of capital to the production process in the short run (e.g. an extra hotplate).

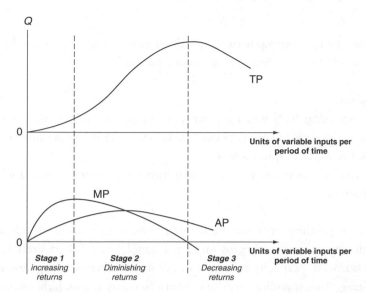

Figure 4.4 Short-run production

As depicted in Figure 4.4, in Stage 1, the total product curve increases at an increasing rate. The stage where marginal product increases when a few units of variable input are being used is called increasing returns. Increasing returns occur because additional units of the input create the synergies that come from teamwork and the division of labour, reflected in an increasing marginal product for each successive worker. However, in the short run, diminishing marginal returns will set in. This occurs at Stage 2. After a point, when a variable factor is added to a fixed factor, each successive unit of that variable factor will add to total output at a diminishing rate. For example, given a restaurant's fixed capacity, the hiring of extra chefs (variable factor) might initially bring about synergies and increase output (e.g. meals prepared) relative to inputs, but after a certain number of chefs are hired, the contribution of each successive chef will be less than that of the previous chef hired. Overall output will increase but will do so at a diminishing rate with the addition of the extra chefs. In Stage 3, total product declines with the hiring of extra workers. In our example there would be so many chefs crowding into the kitchen that total meal production would decline. When output falls as more inputs are used, the firm has reached the stage of negative returns.

The firm should produce within output Stages 1 or 2 where the marginal output of each successive worker is still positive and adds to total output. The output at which it will produce is that which maximises profits (see below).

Diminishing returns is a short-run productivity issue for tourism firms that has implications for their short-run costs. It is obvious that, if each successive worker is hired at the same wage as those who have been hired before, then, given diminishing returns, VC per unit of output will rise (see Figure 4.3a).

Long run

In the long run, the relationship between production and costs is captured by the concept of *returns to scale* (RTS) also referred to as *economies of scale*.

Economies of scale

Firms enjoy increasing RTS when a given percentage increase in all inputs leads to a larger percentage increase in the firm's output. This reduces the firm's unit costs (long-run average costs, LRAC) as output increases.

There are several reasons as to why a firm might experience *economies of scale*. Briefly, these are as follows:

- *Financial.* An expanding firm may be better placed to gain access to cheaper finance, thereby reducing its costs of borrowing. For example, established airlines typically will have more borrowing capacity at better rates of interest than start-up airlines.
- *Bulk purchasing.* An expanding firm may gain discounts on its bulk purchases and so reduce the costs of its inputs if it has monopsony (buying) power in the market. The major food retailers have monopsony power when purchasing supplies from farmers and wine growers. Larger tour operators can bulk buy cheaper seats on airlines and hotel rooms in foreign destinations and fast food restaurant chains can get large discounts on their purchases of chickens, hamburger meat and buns. Larger airlines get better discounts on their purchases of aviation fuel.
- *Managerial/specialisation.* An expanding firm can engage in division of labour and hire specialist skills, increasing labour productivity and reducing per unit costs. As tourism firms grow, their labour force will become more specialised. For example, larger hotels employ specialist financial, marketing, HR and service staff.
- *Technical.* An expanding firm is better positioned to adopt cutting-edge technologies and to learn from past experience (learning curve). Large-scale businesses can afford to invest in expensive and specialist capital machinery. For example, a national chain of fast food restaurants can invest in technology that improves stock control and helps to control costs. It would not, however, be viable or cost efficient for a small cafe to buy this technology.
- *Marketing economies of scale.* A large firm can spread its advertising and marketing budget over a large output.
- *Economies of increased dimensions.* This is linked to the cubic law where doubling the height and width of a tanker or building leads to a more-than-proportionate increase in the cubic capacity – an important scale economy in distribution and transport industries and also in travel and leisure sectors. Thus, the Airbus A380 plane can carry three times the number of passengers as a single Airbus A320 but can be purchased at less than three times the purchase price of the smaller plane, and will operate at less than three times the cost per flight.

148

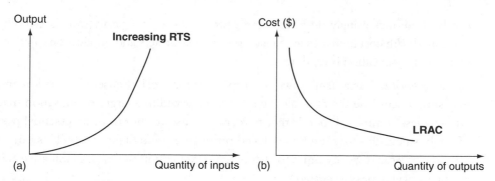

Figure 4.5 (a) Increasing RTS in production, (b) Decreasing LRAC

- *Risk bearing.* In contrast to smaller firms that often face higher rates of interest on their overdrafts and loans, larger firms are usually rated by the financial markets to be more 'credit worthy' and have access to credit facilities at more favourable rates of borrowing. A large firm is better able to spread risk and reduce exposure to market volatility. The larger airlines, for instance, routinely hedge against rising fuel prices. They are also better placed to drop or pick up routes as market conditions shift.
- *Learning by doing.* Managers and other employees learn by doing. The average costs of production decline in real terms as a result of production experience as businesses cut waste and find the most productive means of producing a larger output.

Figure 4.5a shows a firm enjoying increasing RTS with output rising faster than inputs while Figure 4.5b shows the firm's resulting economies of scale (a movement along the LRAC curve).

Diseconomies of scale

Firms suffer decreasing RTS, or diseconomies of scale, when a given percentage increase in all inputs leads to a smaller percentage increase in output. These may relate to:

Control Problems. Monitoring the productivity and the quality of output from large numbers of employees can become more expensive as the firm grows. Large firms typically experience the principal–agent problem – the isolation of decision makers from the results of their decisions. Office politics that often seem to accompany business expansion can reduce employee productivity.

Coordination Problems. The larger a firm grows, the more difficult it may be to coordinate complicated production processes across several facilities in different locations and countries. A larger organisation is harder to monitor – it is more complex and therefore coordination between different departments and divisions becomes more difficult. Growing tourism businesses, for example, can become 'top heavy' and lose touch with local markets. Maintaining efficient flows of information can become increasingly difficult in large firms. As a firm grows, this is typically associated with cost increases in managing supply contracts and duplication of effort due to communication breakdowns.

Co-operation problems. As a firm grows, its employees may feel a sense of alienation and may subsequent lose their morale. People working within a larger organisation may also feel less committed to it. If they perceive themselves not to be an essential part of the business, this may result in reduced productivity and higher costs. This can be reflected in slow response times to changing market conditions, lack of initiative and inertia (unwillingness to change).

Diseconomies of scale can also occur for reasons external to a business. For example, as a firm becomes larger it may put pressure on its supplies of raw materials and labour, raising input prices. This can occur in developing countries under rapid expansion of the tourism industry and the associated demand for labour. The growth of tourism and hospitality in particular tourist regions can result in increases in factor costs (land, labour and capital) in order to acquire the resources to support its development.

Effective management techniques and the appropriate work performance incentives can do much to reduce the onset of diseconomies of scale. Some reasons for this optimistic assessment include developments in human resource management to retain employee commitment to the firm and its performance including performance-related pay schemes. Increasingly, businesses are engaging in outsourcing of manufacturing and distribution as they seek to supply to ever more remote markets. Outsourcing is now increasingly used to reduce costs while retaining control over production. In a tourism context this includes contracting out aviation and catering service responsibilities to local firms. Although the LRAC curve may still slope upwards to the right of the minimum efficient scale (MES) (see below), it may do so at a reduced rate of growth due to these initiatives.

Figure 4.6a shows a firm experiencing decreasing RTS with output rising slower than inputs while Figure 4.6b shows the firm's resulting diseconomies of scale (a rise in the LRAC curve).

The minimum efficient scale

The MES is the scale of production where the internal economies of scale have been fully exploited. The MES corresponds to the lowest point on the LRAC curve and is also known as an output range over which a business achieves productive efficiency. The MES need not be a single output level. In reality it may comprise a range of output levels where the firm achieves constant RTS and has reached the lowest feasible cost per unit in the long run. Figure 4.7 shows long-run RTS, the resultant LRAC curve and the MES.

The size of the MES depends on the nature of costs of production in a particular industry. In a tourism sector where the ratio of fixed to variable costs is high, such as for a theme park or cruise shipping line, there is scope for reducing average cost by increasing the

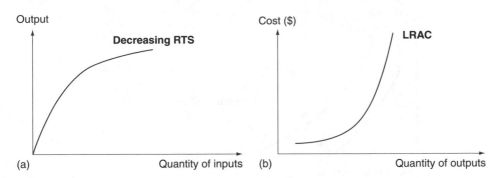

Figure 4.6 (a) Decreasing RTS, (b) Increasing LRAC

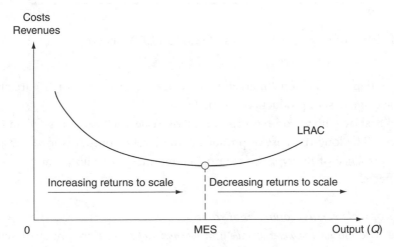

Figure 4.7 Minimum efficient scale and firm LRAC

scale of output. In contrast, there might be only limited opportunities for scale economies in areas such as cafes, day tours or boutique hotels where the MES is likely to relate to just a small share of market demand. This explains why many tourism markets are quite competitive with many suppliers able to achieve the MES.

External economies

In addition to experiencing internal economies of scale, a firm may be the beneficiary of external *economies*. These arise for groups of firms or a whole industry rather than for an individual firm. These refer to the cost-saving benefits of firms being located or organised closely together, thus reducing the cost of production for all the firms involved. Examples include: firms sharing transport links such as a railway or harbour resulting in cost savings to all, locating near locally available skilled labour, training opportunities, technological advances, shared research and development facilities or access to a network of suppliers with specialist experience and customers who can be targeted at lower cost using

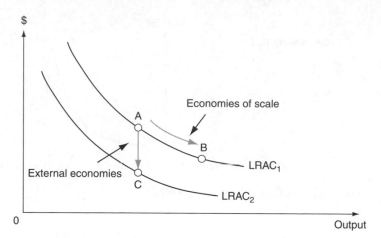

Figure 4.8 Effect of external economies of scale on LRAC curve

e-commerce than by traditional marketing activities. External economies are shown as a fall in the average cost of production for the firm.

Figure 4.8 shows how external economies of scale can lead to a fall in the entire LRAC curve. The long-run cost of producing any level of output is lower at all outputs due to the presence of the types of external economies noted above and also including learning effects.

Economies of scale versus economies of scope

It is useful to contrast *economies of scale* and *economies of scope*. Economies of scope occur where it is cheaper to produce a range of products rather than specialise in a small number of products. For example, it may be less costly for a ferry to provide a service from island X to islands Y and Z in one round trip with one ferry rather than making two separate journeys beginning at island X (one to island Y and another to island Z). A company's management structure, administration systems and marketing departments are capable of carrying out these functions for more than one product. In fast food restaurants, for example, there might be cost savings to a business from preparing several different types of hamburgers and salads rather than a more limited product offering. Expanding the product range to exploit the value of existing brands is a good way of exploiting economies of scope as Accor has done over the years with its range of different class accommodation. Additionally, a sales force selling several products can often do so more efficiently than if they are selling only one product.

4.4.4 PRIVATE COSTS AND SOCIAL COSTS IN TOURISM

The discussion above has focused only on private costs – the costs borne by individual tourism firms. Supply of tourist products, though, may generate social costs (congestion, deterioration of the environment, litter, etc.) that are borne collectively by society, not by the individual firm supplying the product. These costs are seldom taken into account by firms since they do not impact directly on their own financial situation. But they must be accounted for in an overall evaluation of the effects of tourism operations on the community. Chapters 10 and 17 provide a discussion on the difference between private costs and social costs and the importance of managing tourism's economic, social and environmental impacts.

4.5 CONSUMER SURPLUS AND PRODUCER SURPLUS

Having discussed both the concepts of demand and supply we now have the basis to understand two additional concepts which will have relevance to many of the issues to be discussed in the text to follow. These are the concepts of consumer and producer surplus.

In Figure 4.9, the market price of the product is P_0, but except for the person who purchases the last unit before equilibrium quantity Q_0 is reached, all consumers are willing to pay more than P_0 for a unit of the product. From the supplier perspective, for all units of the product short of the last unit produced at Q_0, the supplier is willing to supply each unit of the product at a lower price than P_0.

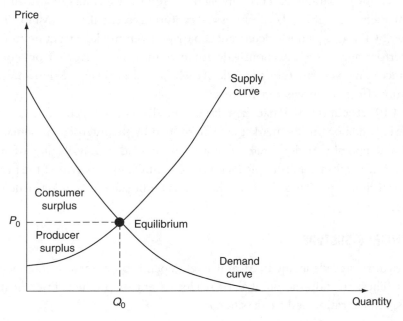

Figure 4.9 Consumer surplus and producer surplus basic conditions

Consumer surplus is the difference between what a person would be willing to pay for a good or service (the total benefit to the consumers) and what they actually pay (the price to the consumer). It is measured as the area between a demand curve and the price line. A higher market price reduces consumer surplus while a lower market price increases it.

Producer surplus is the difference between the costs of the inputs used in the production process (cost to producers) and the price received for the product sold (total benefit to producers). It is measured as the area between a supply curve and a given price for a specified quantity supplied. Basically, it is the net profit that is earned by producers. A higher market price increases producer surplus while a lower market price reduces it.

As we shall discuss below, both concepts are important for explaining firm pricing strategies (see Chapter 5) as well as for providing the basis for policy initiatives to enhance the benefits of tourism development (Chapter 10).

4.6 TOURISM MARKET STRUCTURE

4.6.1 STRUCTURE–CONDUCT–PERFORMANCE

Market structure refers to the nature of the market within which a tourism firm operates. Market structure affects the firm's *conduct* (decision-making processes), which, in turn, affects the firm's *performance* (potential to make profit, increase its market share and achieve efficiency). This linear–causal relationship is often referred to as the Structure–Conduct–Performance (SCP) paradigm. This paradigm is useful for gaining an overall picture of tourism markets, highlighting key features and capturing essential relationships (Lei, 2006).

Whether SCP is exogenously determined, moving from market structure through conduct to performance, or endogenously determined, moving in reverse from conduct and performance to market structure, or a little of each, is unclear (Davies & Downward, 2006). This will not affect our discussion, however.

Figure 4.10 sets out the SCP paradigm listing key elements of each (after Lei, 2006).

The basic conditions in the market are determined by the interplay of demand factors (elasticities, temporal variations, rate of growth in demand, the availability of substitutes and method of purchase) and supply factors (the nature and life cycle of the product and the level of technology). These basic conditions will influence the market structure at any given time.

4.6.2 MARKET STRUCTURE

Which structure prevails in any tourism market depends on numerous interlocking characteristics. These include the number of sellers, extent of product differentiation, cost structures, diversification and barriers to entry.

- *The number of sellers.* The number and relative size of firms in the market and the market concentration are important indicators of market structure. Supply by many relatively

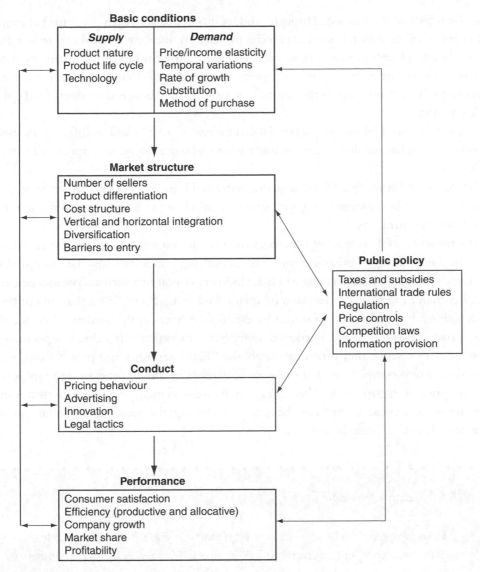

Basic conditions

Supply	*Demand*
Product nature	Price/income elasticity
Product life cycle	Temporal variations
Technology	Rate of growth
	Substitution
	Method of purchase

Market structure

Number of sellers
Product differentiation
Cost structure
Vertical and horizontal integration
Diversification
Barriers to entry

Public policy

Taxes and subsidies
International trade rules
Regulation
Price controls
Competition laws
Information provision

Conduct

Pricing behaviour
Advertising
Innovation
Legal tactics

Performance

Consumer satisfaction
Efficiency (productive and allocative)
Company growth
Market share
Profitability

Figure 4.10 Key elements of SCP
Source: Adapted from Lei, 2006

small firms suggests either perfect competition (if the product is undifferentiated) or monopolistic competition (if the product is differentiated). Supply dominated by several relatively large firms suggests oligopoly. The presence of only one firm serving the entire market indicates a monopoly market structure.

- The existence and extent of *product differentiation*. A tourism firm's product differentiation may be based on quality, packaging, type of service, brand name, trademark and the like. It may be real (better quality, better service or unique service) or perceived (existing only

155

in the minds of the buyers). Through product differentiation, each small firm attempts to carve out and maintain a tourism niche for itself: to increase its market power within an otherwise highly competitive market. The more the firm can differentiate, the more it can control its niche, set its own price and output, and control its revenues and costs. Differentiation affects the degree of substitutability between products (and entire destinations).

- The *cost structure*. If there are substantial economies of scale, it will be difficult for many firms to simultaneously compete in the market and oligopoly or monopoly will tend to develop.
- *Diversification*. Firms diversify by acquiring unrelated businesses. The acquisition of non-tourism firms by a tourism firm, for instance, may allow the firm to spread risk in times of tourism downturns.
- The presence of *barriers to entry*. Barriers to entry are hindrances to new firms starting up in competition to existing firms. The underlying conditions may be structural or strategic. Structural barriers relate to basic industry conditions such as cost and demand rather than to tactical actions taken by established firms. Strategic barriers, in contrast, are deliberately created or enhanced by established firms in the market, often for the purpose of deterring entry. Barriers to entry benefit existing firms already operating in an industry because they protect an established firm's revenues and profits from being eroded by new competitors. The presence of barriers to entry gives existing firms power to set prices at higher levels. Although generally weak in many sectors of tourism, some stronger barriers can nevertheless be generated through the presence of several types of factors. These are listed in Box 4.1.

BOX 4.1 Causes of barriers to entry

- *Capital requirements*. The existence of high start-up costs or other obstacles can prevent new competitors from gaining the finance necessary to enter an industry or area of business. Consider the substantial costs of developing an airline, cruise ship operations or major theme park. The fact that these costs might be unrecoverable if an entrant opts to leave the market acts as a further disincentive to enter the industry.
- *Presence of sunk costs*. In many industries the cost of the fixed assets is a sunk cost as far as the existing suppliers are concerned. Since established firms are likely to accept lower prices rather than reduce volumes, potential new entrants may fear that they will drive prices down too much for the market to be worth entering. Sunk costs therefore increase the risk and deter entry.

- *Low-cost production.* Lost-cost production allows tourism firms to sell at low prices, and if incumbent firms in a particular market have sustainable cost advantages, it will be difficult for other firms to enter that market. Thus the presence of a Low-Cost Carrier (LCC) on a certain route may make it difficult for subsequent entrants to gain a market share allowing adequate returns on investment.

- *Experience barriers.* Incumbent firms often have learning curve cost advantages over potential entrants. Lower costs, perhaps through experience of being in the market for some time, allow established firms to cut prices and win price wars. Further, when a good or service has a value that depends on the number of existing customers, other firms may have difficulties in entering a market where an established firm has already captured a significant customer share.

- *Product differentiation.* Successful product differentiation can allow a firm to dominate a particular market niche, making it difficult for potential competitors to enter that niche. Disneyland is an example of a product that cannot be exactly replicated by another firm.

- *Advertising barriers.* Established firms can seek to make it difficult for potential competitors by spending heavily on advertising that new firms would find expensive to match. Here, established firms' use of advertising creates a consumer-perceived difference in their brand from other brands to a degree that consumers regard the brand as a slightly different product. Developing consumer loyalty by establishing branded products can increase the costs of entry of new firms into the market. This can be important for many tourism products such as branded hotel chains or cruise shipping lines.

- *Economies of scale.* These provide effective barriers for tourism firms that work on volume trade such as international hotel chains (mass purchasing and marketing) and tour operators (operational costs, purchasing and marketing) (Evans & Stabler, 1995). Global branding, marketing and reservation systems all seek to exploit economies of scale.

- *Globalisation.* Entry of global players into local market makes entry of local players into the market difficult. Multinational firms have networks and alliances of suppliers and customers that domestically owned firms often find difficult to access.

- *Government policy.* Government regulations may make entry into an industry more difficult or even impossible. In the extreme case, a government may establish a statutory monopoly. Legal requirements for licenses and permits may raise the investment needed to enter a market, creating an effective barrier to entry. Reduced protection can reduce entry barriers, for example, de-regulation in the airline sector (see Chapter 16).

- *Access to distribution channels.* Exclusive tie-ups with providers can create effective barriers, for example, access to expert tour guides. Restrictive practices, such as air transport agreements, make it difficult for new airlines to obtain access to terminal facilities and landing slots at some airports.

- *Development and maintenance of reputation.* Reputation can be a strong barrier, especially given the intangibility and irreversibility of tourism supply and its status as an 'experience' good (Lei, 2006). Large incumbent firms may have existing customers loyal to established products. The presence of established strong brands within a market can be a barrier to entry in this case.

- *Limit pricing.* Limit pricing refers to the practice of a dominant firm lowering prices to a level that would force any new entrants to operate at a very small profits or even a loss. Established firms may not actually reduce price but may threaten a price war if another firm enters the market. The anticipated price war may itself serve as a deterrent to entry, especially if the established firm has excess capacity that could potentially be used in a price war, post-entry.

- *Vertical and horizontal integration.* The mergers and acquisition of substitute and complementary firms allow larger firms to gain and consolidate market share, thus affecting the number and size of firms within a particular market.

Broadly, economists distinguish four different market structures: perfect competition, monopolistic competition, oligopoly and monopoly.

4.6.2.1 Perfect competition

Perfect competition is characterised by several features:

- There is a very large number of buyers and sellers in the market.
- All the consumers and producers have perfect information about the market.
- The individual firms' outputs are too small to affect the market price.
- The firms sell identical products at prices set by the market.
- There are no barriers to the entry or exit of firms.

Firms are assumed to attempt to maximise profits. A profit-maximising firm will produce output up to the point where the cost of the last unit produced (marginal cost) is equal to the additional revenue it generates when it is sold (marginal revenue). Short of this output,

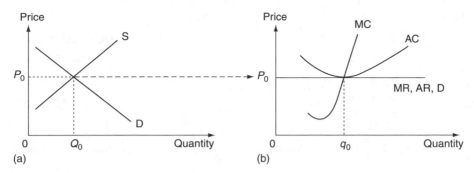

Figure 4.11 (a) Market supply and demand, (b) Individual firm in perfect competition in long run

greater profits can be earned from selling greater output. Beyond this point, an additional unit produced will cost more than the extra revenue that it will bring to the firm.

The absence of effective barriers against the entry of new competitors ensures that any profits generated are short-run only and that individual firms will only break even in the long run. Though competitive, tourism markets tend not to be perfectly competitive because of the presence of product differentiation and the characteristic of inseparability (tourists themselves contribute to production and thus no two tourism experiences are exactly alike).

Figures 4.11a and 4.11b set out the revenue and cost curves for markets and firms in perfect competition. The market price (P_0) and market quantity (Q_0) are set by the interaction of market demand (D) and market supply (S). The individual profit-maximising firm, being too small to influence the market, becomes a price taker that sells its products (q_0) at the market price. In order to maximise profits, the firm produces the amount of output where MR = MC. While the perfect competitor can make profits (or losses) in the short run, it will only break even in the long run because of a lack of effective barriers to entry. That is, firms that make profits will find that these profits attract other firms into the industry to compete for them. Those firms that make losses will exit the industry. In the long run, perfectly competitive firms make what are called 'normal profits', whereby all costs are covered including the opportunity costs of the owner's capital and labour.

In highly competitive markets (perfect competition), the profit-maximising individual *firm's supply curve* is its marginal cost curve above its minimum average variable cost (in the short run) or above its minimum average total cost (in the long run). Figures 4.12a and 4.12b show this. Assume the original equilibrium market price and quantity are P_0 and Q_0. Suppose market demand for the product increases to D_1 (due to increased incomes, for example). Since the firm now must take the new market price P_1 as given, it now faces a horizontal demand curve d_1, at this higher price. Equating MR with MC to maximise profits implies that the firm will now produce output q_1, the output where MC equals MR which equals the price taking firm's new demand curve d_1. If the market demand should rise even further (to D_2), bringing about the equilibrium market price of P_2, and

159

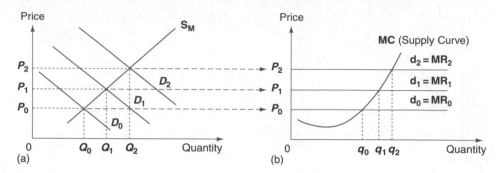

Figure 4.12 (a) Market supply and demand, (b) Individual firm's supply curve in perfect competition

equilibrium quantity Q_2, the firm now must take the new market price of P_2 as given. The firm's new demand curve is d_2. The firm will thus maximise profits where $MC = MR = d_2$, and produce output q_2. Clearly, we find that the firm's MC curve (above minimum variable cost) is effectively its supply curve. Given the price, MC determines what output the firm will produce.

In the other three market structures (monopolistic competition, oligopoly and monopoly), there is no formal supply curve.

4.6.2.2 Monopoly

Monopoly is characterised by several features:

- There is only one seller in the market.
- Consumers have imperfect information about the market.
- The firm determines the market output and price.
- There is no direct substitution for the product.
- There are very strong barriers to the entry or exit of firms.

Thus, a tourism firm will enjoy a monopoly if it supplies the entire market for that product with strong barriers that prevent new competitors from entering the market. Monopoly can be approximated when a tourist product has no close substitutes, for example, if a tour operator is the first into the market with a unique style of tour, or even if an airport terminal under construction has only one bar area for a period. Unique structures (the Pyramids of Egypt, the Great Wall of China, Angkor Wat, etc.), natural landscapes (the Grand Canyon, the Great Barrier Reef) or cultural landscapes (Prague, New York) may have the characteristics of a monopoly providing destination managers and operators with the opportunity to charge prices that will yield a profit.

Figure 4.13 sets out the revenue and cost curves for a monopoly firm. The profit-maximising firm enjoying a monopoly will produce that output where $MR = MC$,

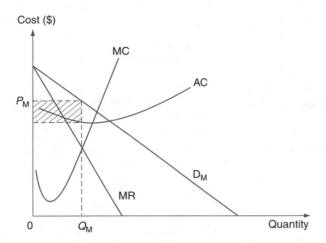

Figure 4.13 Monopoly price and output

producing Q_M at price P_M (on the market demand curve), making long-run profits (shaded area).

The standard economic case against monopoly is that, with the same cost structure, a monopoly supplier will produce at a lower output and charge a higher price than a competitive industry. Assuming that the monopolist seeks to maximise profits and it takes the whole of the market demand curve, then the price under monopoly will be higher and the output lower than the competitive market equilibrium. This leads to a net loss of economic welfare and efficiency because price is driven above marginal cost – leading to allocative inefficiency.

Figure 4.14 shows how price and output differ between a competitive and a monopolistic industry. We have assumed that the cost structure for both the competitive firm and the monopoly is the same – indeed, we have assumed that output can be supplied at a constant marginal and average cost.

Since monopoly generally implies an inefficient holding-back of production, at least in the short run, this gives rise to what is called a 'deadweight loss'. A deadweight loss (also known as excess burden or allocative inefficiency) is a loss of economic efficiency that occurs when equilibrium for a good or service is not Pareto optimal. In other words, either people who would have more marginal benefit than marginal cost are not buying the good or service or people who have more marginal cost than marginal benefit are buying the product.

The area of deadweight loss as shown in Figure 4.15 is a measure of the loss in value to society of output not produced.

4.6.2.3 Monopolistic competition

Monopolistic competition is characterised by several features:

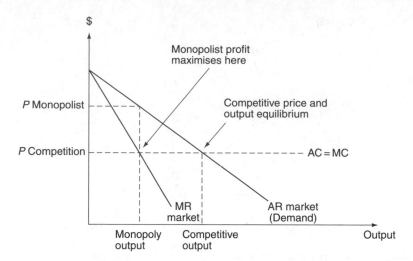

Figure 4.14 Price and output: Perfect competition versus monopoly

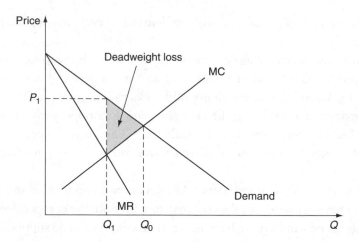

Figure 4.15 Deadweight loss from monopoly

- There is a very large number of buyers and sellers in the market, selling similar but slightly differentiated products.
- Consumers and producers have imperfect information about the market.
- Because of slight product differentiation, firms have partial control over the prices that they charge.
- There are minimal barriers to the entry or exit of firms.

Product differentiation allows firms to generate short-run profits but, with no effective barriers against the entry of new competitors or the exit of existing firms, no long-run profits are made. Small to medium enterprises (SME) are the most dominant form of business in the global tourism industry (Fletcher & Westlake, 2006). Much tourism supply

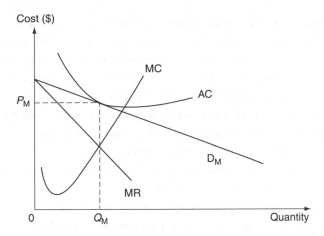

Figure 4.16 Firm in monopolistic competition in the long run

is monopolistically competitive with many destinations composed of relatively small, less powerful, but highly competitive firms that face few, if any, barriers to entry and survive purely through differentiating their product sufficiently from their competitors so as to gain and maintain a niche in the marketplace. Bed and Breakfast (B&B) accommodation, restaurants and travel agencies are examples of monopolistically competitive markets.

Product differentiation helps to generate profit in the short run. A lack of barriers to stop competitors copying the firm's differentiation and/or from entering the same niche market, though, means that, in the long run, the firm's profits will be reduced until the firm only breaks even (making 'normal profits' that just cover the costs of production). This is clearly the case with low-end hotel accommodation and restaurants. Predicting or picking trends and staying one step ahead of competitors are vital for the monopolistically competitive tourism firm.

Figure 4.16 sets out the revenue and cost curves for a firm operating under conditions of monopolistic competition. The profit-maximising firm produces at Q_M and charges a price P_M (in similar fashion to a monopolist, though with flatter demand and marginal revenue curves), but only breaks even in the long run because of a lack of effective barriers to entry.

4.6.2.4 Oligopoly

Oligopoly is characterised by several features:

- A small number of firms dominate supply in the market.
- Consumers have imperfect information about the market.
- The firms are mutually interdependent setting market output and price by reference to each other.
- There are strong barriers to the entry or exit of firms.

163

Oligopoly is characterised by a small number of relatively large firms that dominate a market. Though there are instances of product homogeneity, tourism oligopolies generally operate under strong product differentiation owing to the ease of changing service product attributes. Protected by barriers that hinder the entry of new competitors, oligopolistic tourism firms tend to be interdependent in their pricing and output decision-making.

Despite the existence of many small, highly differentiated firms, much tourism supply is clearly oligopolistic in nature with a few large firms dominating parts of the market. This applies to airlines on particular routes, cruise ships, theme parks and five star hotels in central locations. Only four large firms make up 75% of the tour operator industry in the UK, for example (Davies & Downward, 2006).

On the whole, oligopolistic tourism firms tend to compete for a profitable share of the market. However, given the risks and uncertainties involved in decision-making, the dominant firms have a tendency to try to reduce the rivalry between themselves through either integration (mergers and acquisitions) or collusion (often illegal, if explicit). This competition/collusion dilemma faced by oligopolies arises because firms find themselves *mutually interdependent* in their pricing and output decision-making. The extent of rewards (the performance returns of profit, market share, efficiency, etc.) that accrue to oligopolistic tourism firms from their pricing and output decisions (their conduct) are dependent on the output and pricing decisions of their competitors' conduct.

Table 4.1 summarises the characteristics of the four market structures and provides some tourism examples. Each market structure governs the potential profitability, market share and efficiency of the tourism firms within it, either enhancing or constraining the firms' ability to generate profits, increase market share and attain efficiency.

While tourism firms may be found within any of the four market structures, it is only within monopolistic competition and oligopoly, however, that they are found with any force. Tourism markets often exhibit elements of both these market structures and it may be that many tourism markets are predominantly oligopolistic in the main but monopolistically competitive at the edges. The UK tour operator industry, for instance, is clearly oligopolistic in that it is dominated by a relatively small group of larger companies but it nevertheless allows for the existence of a multitude of much smaller specialist companies concentrating on niche markets on the periphery in monopolistic competition (Davies & Downward, 2006). Such combined markets exhibit both product differentiation and interdependence in pricing and output.

4.6.3 CONDUCT

A firm's conduct (its pricing behaviour, advertising and production strategies, innovation and legal tactics) is largely carried out with the anticipated behaviour of its competitors in mind (Lei, 2006).

Table 4.1 Market structures and their characteristics

	Perfect competition	Monopolistic competition	Oligopoly	Monopoly
Number and size of firms	Many small firms	Many small to medium enterprises	Few relatively large firms	One firm
Degree of substitutability of products	Firms sell identical products	Firms sell similar though slightly differentiated products	Firms sell identical and/or differentiated products	Firm sells unique product (but may face substitutability from other industries)
Does the individual firm set its own price?	No. Price is set by the market	Yes. Some limited price control (through product differentiation)	Yes. Strong control (but firms are interdependent in pricing)	Yes. Strong control
Barriers to entry	None	Some, though small (through product differentiation)	Entry may be easy but cost conditions mean only a few firms can survive	Strong barriers (costs, government regulations)
Tourism examples	Street stalls	Restaurants Hotels B&Bs Travel agencies	Tour operators Airlines	Nationalised railways

- *Pricing behaviour.* Smaller, undifferentiated highly competitive tourism firms tend to be price takers, applying the market price to their products. Product differentiation will allow firms to begin to apply some premium to the price of their products. Larger oligopolistic firms will tend to avoid price wars, and may even engage in collusive pricing behaviour. Pricing within tourism markets is covered extensively in Chapter 5.
- *Advertising strategy.* Successful advertising, marketing and promotion will increase a firm's market share and make demand for its product less elastic, giving the firm some control over its pricing and output.
- *Innovation.* Innovation (which tends to accompany oligopoly markets) can give a firm an edge over its competitors, differentiating its product, allowing a price premium and increasing its market share.
- *Legal tactics.* Patents, copyright and trademarks serve a dual role acting both to protect a firm's differentiation and to create barriers to entry.

Given the importance of product differentiation and interdependence in pricing and output, product recognition and reputation become all-important, with advertising designed to differentiate the product, boost market share, raise entry barriers and lead to higher product price. The pricing behaviour of tourism firms is so important given its economic consequences that Chapter 5 is devoted to its discussion.

4.6.4 PERFORMANCE

Market performance manifests itself in the generation of consumer satisfaction, efficiency, company growth, market share and profitability.

- *Consumer satisfaction.* Given that the customer adds to the tourism experience, tourism, like all service industries, faces the problem of measuring customer satisfaction as a basis for evaluating performance.
- *Efficiency.* Smaller, undifferentiated and highly competitive firms are more likely to exhibit *productive efficiency* (by producing at minimum cost) and *allocative efficiency* (by producing at price equals marginal cost). Differentiated and larger firms can be less driven by efficiency.
- *Company growth.* Smaller, undifferentiated and highly competitive firms tend not to grow at all or else only in line with market growth. Differentiated and larger firms may be able to generate company growth beyond average market growth.
- *Market share.* Smaller, undifferentiated and highly competitive firms tend not to be able to increase their individual market share. Differentiated and larger firms may be able to do so through promotion and product differentiation.
- *Profitability.* Smaller, highly competitive firms, while enjoying the possibility of profits in the short run, tend not to be profitable (only breaking even) in the long run, due

to the absence of effective barriers to entry. Larger firm operating under conditions of oligopoly can enjoy profitability in the long run.

4.6.5 PUBLIC POLICY

Public policy (government involvement and influence in the marketplace) affects basic demand and supply conditions in the market, influencing market structure, rewarding or disparaging conduct and, ultimately, conditioning performance. The more obvious ways through which government may differentially affect tourism markets are the following:

- *Taxes and subsidies.* The differential use of taxes and subsidies by government can affect the viability and profitability of tourism markets, encouraging some markets and discouraging others. Hotels in some states of India, for instance, receive tax holidays in the hope that they can grow and prosper, while hotels in other parts of the world must pay a tax per room per night. Tourism taxes are discussed in Chapter 15.
- *Regulation.* Government imposes rules and regulation on business behaviour and, in some countries, set industry standards, for example, in accommodation, and in provision of tourism and hospitality training programmes. Regulations may also include price controls.
- *Price controls.* For socio-economic purposes, government sets either price floors (minimum prices above market equilibrium) or price ceilings (maximum prices below equilibrium). As we shall discuss in Chapter 19, the tourism industry will be affected by emissions trading schemes to mitigate global warming.
- *Competition laws.* In the drive to market forces, government has passed laws favouring competition and discouraging monopoly. Thus antitrust laws in the USA have prohibited several airline mergers.
- *Information provision.* To boost knowledge and to reduce asymmetric information, government often promotes destinations, providing websites, promotional films, advertising and brochures. Such information is provided by the majority of the Ministries of Tourism worldwide.

4.7 TOURISM SUPPLY CHAINS AND FIRM STRUCTURE

The *tourism supply chain* refers to the network of firms and activities that make up the supply of a tourism product. It encompasses the materials that flow from suppliers 'upstream', the transformation of materials into semi-finished and finished products and services, and the distribution of the finished product to customers 'downstream'.

Tourism supply chains vary between and within tourism markets and sectors and for each tourism product and firm. They involve many components, among them accommodation, transportation, restaurants, handicrafts, waste disposal, power, infrastructure and so on.

Faced with the complexity of tourism supply chains and the competitive nature of tourism markets, tourism firms seek to control and smooth their supply chains through *horizontal integration*, *vertical integration* and *strategic alliances*.

4.7.1 VERTICAL INTEGRATION

Vertical integration (VI) occurs when a firm incorporates the value chain of a supplier and/or of a distribution channel into its own value chain. This typically occurs when a firm acquires a supplier or a distributor or when it expands its operations to perform activities traditionally undertaken by suppliers or distributors, that is, a firm merges with or acquires another firm either upstream (backward integration) or downstream (forward integration) of itself in its supply chain. VI is encouraged by synergies between complementary activities, economies of scale and scope, and by potential tax savings. Vertically integrated firms thus are united through a hierarchy and share a common owner. We can distinguish two types of VI:

Backward integration occurs when a firm gains greater control of its inputs. In backward VI, a firm establishes subsidiaries that produce some of the inputs used in the production of its products. Thus, airlines perform the role of suppliers such as aircraft maintenance, training providers and in-flight catering. Similarly, a hotel chain may purchase an airline and an island resort hotel may own the ferry company that transports guests to the island. The advantages of backward integration may include assurance of the price, quality and availability of supplies, and efficiencies gained from co-ordinating production of supplies with consumer demand.

Forward integration is VI through combining a core business with its suppliers. Forward VI occurs when a firm gains greater control over its distribution channels. For example, by performing the traditional role of travel agents, airlines have achieved forward integration. Similarly, a cruise ship company may develop and own tour companies that operate at the different ports of call. The advantages of forward integration include cutting out competing suppliers, greater ability to reach final customers and better access to information about final customers.

4.7.2 HORIZONTAL INTEGRATION

Horizontal integration (HI) is the widening of a business at the same point in the supply chain. HI occurs when a firm takes over or merges with another firm in the same industry or at the same stage of the supply chain. The firms may be complementary or competitors. Example include the Air France and KLM merger; the easyJet's takeover of Go!; and the ebookers' takeover of Travelbag and Bridge The World.

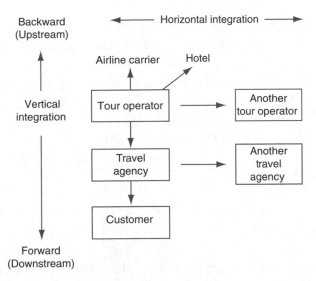

Figure 4.17 Simplified supply chain for a tour operator with horizontal and vertical integration

Vertical and horizontal integration are prevalent in the tour operator industry. The four largest UK operators all own charter airlines, accommodation and ground-handlers and travel agents (Ashley *et al.*, 2004). Figure 4.17 sets out a simplified supply chain with examples of vertical and horizontal integration within the tour operator industry. Tour operators rely on supplies that flow from firms earlier (upstream), for example, transport and accommodation providers, in order to create packaged tours that are then supplied downstream through travel agencies to the ultimate customers.

Some advantages and limitations of VI and HI are listed in Box 4.2.

BOX 4.2 Vertical and horizontal integration: Advantages and disadvantages

Advantages of VI

Vertical integration allows the firm to gain some degree of control over its supplies and outlets, allowing it to be better placed to:

• Enjoy economies of scale through increased buying power and joint marketing;
• Retain greater revenues within the firm;
• Reduce risk and uncertainty through securing suppliers and guaranteeing retail outlets (improving supply chain co-ordination);
• Reduce profit volatility and improve profit potential through control over revenues and costs;

- Enhance efficiency through improved communication and coordination;
- Reduce overcapacity;
- Raise barriers to entry that hinder the entry of potential competitors;
- Integrate packaged products along the full length of its supply chain;
- Enhance the quality of its product offering;
- Ensure markets for products (offensive/defensive).

Disadvantages of VI

- The firm will need to monitor downstream demand and ensure that its upstream operations can supply sufficient input to cater for downstream demand in peak periods and is flexible enough to survive downturns in downstream demand.
- VI may raise costs because of a lack of supplier competition and more administration.
- VI may reduce flexibility in both operations and product variety.
- VI is less attractive where the firms' core competencies are very different or there are no obvious economies of scale or scope to be enjoyed through amalgamation.

Advantages of HI

HI allows the tourism firm some control over its supply chain by allowing it to become a stronger player within that part of its supply chain. It affords the firm the potential for:

- Increased market share/domination;
- Reduced competition;
- Reaping economies of scale;
- Increased buying power;
- Cost-cutting through rationalisation of services;
- A broader customer base;
- Increased market value;
- Improved service.

Disadvantages of HI

- The expected synergies may not materialise.
- The firm grows too dominant in its market and is scrutinised under anti-monopoly laws.

4.7.3 STRATEGIC ALLIANCES

Strategic alliances are agreements, partnerships or joint ventures set up for a specific, limited purpose between otherwise competitive firms. Airlines, hotels and car rental firms, for instance, form alliances between different but complementary products. Strategic alliances are cost-effective ways for tourism firms to share risks and resources, reduce uncertainty, stabilise demand and achieve economies of scale. They offer firms the flexibility needed to deal with globalisation, increased consolidation of economic power, the high cost of keeping up with constantly changing technologies and a highly competitive business environment.

While strategic alliances can be formed within any tourism market, strategic alliances are especially prevalent within the airline industry. Strategic alliances often occur when full mergers would not be permitted. Regulation of international airlines makes it difficult for airlines to merge, and thus they have developed strategic alliances. Howarth & Kirsebom (1999) group airline alliances as *coordination* (loose marketing and sharing of information, for example, Oneworld), *sharing* (strategy coordination arrangements such as scheduling, for example, Star Alliance) and *unification* (formal arrangements via equity stakeholding). More simply, Morley (2003) classifies them as either *loose* (based on integrated marketing strategies) or *formal* (mergers, joint management) and claims that such alliances are generally either *complementary* (where airlines that do not compete on overlapping routes join forces to provide common extension routes) or *parallel* (where airlines that do compete on overlapping routes join forces to reduce costs and competition on those routes). Loose alliances, by their nature, are easier to arrange and do not carry the potential risks that attend more formal arrangements (Fletcher & Westlake, 2006). Competition authorities are more likely to approve complementary rather than parallel alliances. Parallel alliances reduce competition and overall market efficiency. Strategic alliances may also involve firms coordinating on price, if competition authorities allow. Thus, British Airways and Qantas coordinate their schedules and their pricing on the route between the UK and Australia – competition authorities allow this on condition that competition from other airlines, such as Singapore Airlines and Emirates, is strong on this route.

Strategic alliances do have drawbacks. A firm's reputation can be damaged by the activities of its strategic partners, especially in the areas of quality, safety or security. Consider the suspension by Air France of its coordination alliance with Korean Airlines over safety concerns. Strategic alliances in aviation will be discussed in more detail in Chapter 16.

All strategic alliances and partnerings are different, each with its own unique advantages and disadvantages. Box 4.3 lists some common advantages and disadvantages of strategic alliances and partnerships between firms in any industry.

171

BOX 4.3 Advantages of strategic alliances

- Improved Cash Flow
- Reduced Overhead
- Improved Access to Capital
- Obtain Capital
- Credibility
- Access to Facilities and Technology
- Access to Expertise
- Ability to Keep the Company Small
- More Products to Sell
- Innovative Products
- Access to Creative People
- Speed and Flexibility in Delivering New Products
- Ability to Hedge Own R&D Effort

- Less Costly than Buying a Company
- Cost Savings
- Product Distribution
- Diversification into New Markets
- Manufacturing Capability
- Reduced Risk
- Knowledge and Know-how
- Avoid Need to Reinvent What Has Already Been Invented
- The Shoring up of Weak Areas in the Company
- Strengthened Relationships with Key Suppliers/Customers
- Ability to Move Quickly
- Ability to Stay Focused on Core Competence
- Rationalise Marketing

Disadvantages of strategic alliances

- Sharing of Future Profits
- Foreclosure of Other Opportunities
- Barriers to Future Financing Opportunities

- Additional Distractions
- Creating a Competitor or a Potential Competitor
- Unexpected Conflicts with Partner

Source: The Corporate Partnering Institute (2009) Corporate Partnering: A How-To Handbook, An Executive's Guide to Key Partnering Practices, www.corporate-partnering.com

4.8 CONCLUSIONS AND POLICY

- The tourism 'industry' comprises outputs from a wide variety of different industry activities. In contrast to other industries, the defining element is not the type of commodity produced, but the type of consumer. Visitor consumption is not restricted to a set of predefined goods and services produced by a predefined set of industries. Whether a product or service is regarded as tourism-related is based on certain characteristics of the consumer, rather than anything inherent in the product or service.

- The nature of tourism supply makes it difficult to analyse, given issues of intangibility, irreversibility, inseparability, tourism experiences, heterogeneity, perishability, interdependence, seasonality, spatial fixity and so on.

- Though tourism is largely a service industry, standard microeconomic theory relating to production, costs and market structure still has applicability. For instance, tourism supply is affected by both price and non-price factors (among them, the price of inputs, the level of technology, the number of sellers, the prices of other products, profit expectations and future prices, weather and taxes and subsidies).

- The degree of elasticity of tourism supply depends on the extent to which supply costs change as supply is altered, the existence of spare capacity, the extent to which the firm carries inventories, the extent to which the firm can switch to substitutes in production and the time period.

- Tourism supply is also subject to issues of short-run diminishing returns and long-run economies and diseconomies of scale. The magnitude of economies of scale can be important in determining the size of firms in a tourism sector.

- Within the SCP paradigm, the market structure within which a tourism firm operates is held to affect the firm's conduct (decision-making processes), which, in turn, is held to affect the firm's performance (potential to make profit, increase its market share and achieve efficiency). This linearity may also work in reverse. The paradigm is useful for gaining an overall picture of tourism markets, highlighting key features and capturing essential relationships.

- Broadly, economists distinguish four different market structures: perfect competition, monopolistic competition, oligopoly and monopoly. Perfect competitors take the market price as given and sell all they can at this market price (price takers). In contrast, firms in the other three types of market structure can set or shape prices to maximise profits (price makers and price shapers).

- Which structure prevails in any tourism market depends on numerous interlocking characteristics, among them: number of sellers, the existence and extent of product differentiation, the cost structure, the presence of barriers to entry and the extent of vertical and horizontal integration.

- Tourism firms tend to operate within monopolistically competitive and oligopolistic markets with smaller firms trying to distinguish themselves from other firms through product differentiation while larger firms show interdependence in their pricing and output.

- The oligopolistic nature of much tourism shows that firms seek to control their supply chains through vertical and horizontal integration and through the formation of strategic alliances.

- Given the risks and uncertainties involved in pricing and output decision-making, dominant tourism firms may try to reduce the rivalry between themselves through vertical and horizontal integration, through the formation of strategic alliances or through collusion.
- Public policy (government involvement and influence in the marketplace) affects basic demand and supply conditions in the market, influencing market structure, rewarding or disparaging conduct and, ultimately, conditioning performance. Important ways through which government may differentially affect tourism markets are: taxes and subsidies, regulation, price controls, competition laws and information provision.

SELF-REVIEW QUESTIONS

1. Choose a tourism product or service and briefly explain the features that make it different from a non-tourism product.

2. Explain the difference between the short run and the long run for an airline.

3. Using a tourism example, explain (i) the relationship between diminishing returns in short-run production and increases in short-run variable costs and (ii) the relationship between increasing RTS in long-run production and the falling LRAC curve.

4. Briefly outline the SCP paradigm and its policy implications.

5. Choose one tourism market and discuss product differentiation within it.

6. Use game theory to explain interdependence in pricing and output within oligopolistic tourism markets.

7. Using the tour operator market as an example, explain the difference between vertical and horizontal integration.

8. Explain how the accommodation industry operates under aspects of both monopolistic competition and oligopoly.

9. Distinguish between integration and strategic alliances.

10. Draw a simple supply chain for the hotel accommodation industry.

ESSAY QUESTIONS

1. Standard microeconomic theory is of limited applicability to tourism supply. Argue both for and against this statement.

2. Diminishing returns is a short-run productivity issue for tourism firms. Why?

3. Using examples, discuss the relevance of both monopolistic competition and oligopoly to tourism markets.

4. Discuss the theory and practice of integration within the tour operator market.

5. Using examples, discuss the role of barriers to entry in determining the size of tourism firms.

6. Integration is better for tour operators, but strategic alliances are better for airlines and hotels. Discuss.

7. Use the SCP paradigm to analyse a selected sector of the tourism industry.

8. Discuss the competition versus collusion dilemma that confronts airlines. How do airlines resolve this dilemma?

9. The majority of tourism firms are too small to have much control over their supply chains and, as such, should not worry about it. Discuss.

CHAPTER 5

STRATEGIC PRICING IN TOURISM

LEARNING OBJECTIVES

After reading this chapter, you should be able to:

1. Appreciate that the price that is set for a tourism product is governed by the interplay of a number of factors internal and external to the firm.

2. Understand the broad competitive strategies that may be engaged in by tourism firms: cost leadership, product differentiation and segment focus.

3. Differentiate between the competitive and non-competitive pricing techniques employed by tourism firms.

4. Explain the various forms of marginal pricing and non-marginal pricing available to tourism firms, and when and how each may be used.

5. Understand the competition/collusion dichotomy faced by rival firms within tourism sectors and the different forms that such collusion may take.

6. Appreciate that hedonic price analysis provides an understanding as to the characteristics of tourism products and services that are valued by consumers, and to what extent each is valued.

5.1 INTRODUCTION

Price is not the only decision variable of importance to the tourism firm, but it is perhaps the most critical. Price is also the most adjustable of all the firm's decision variables. Price triggers buyer perception as to the quality of the tourism product and its positioning within its market segment, either attracting potential buyers or deterring them. Unlike product adjustment, distribution and promotion, which all take time to change, price can be altered quickly. Airline yield management with prices set on a daily or even hourly basis is a good example of this.

Increasingly, tourism firms differentiate their product in order to reduce its demand elasticity, and hopefully raise its price and total revenue. They divide their customers up into groups and price discriminate according to each group's willingness to pay. Pricing decisions, good and bad, have serious consequences for the firm. Given the inverse nature of the relationship between price and quantity sold, the firm must set its product prices carefully. The impacts of price changes on total revenue depend on the elasticity of demand for the product. Setting a higher price may result in fewer buyers and smaller potential total revenue if the product faces elastic demand. Setting a lower price may result in more buyers but, again, smaller potential total revenue if demand for the product is inelastic.

The price that is set is governed by the interplay of a number of factors internal and external to the firm. These include (Fyall & Garrod, 2005; Seaton & Bennett, 1999):

- The firm's objectives. Price will vary with the firm's short-, medium- and long-term objectives, for example, its target rate of return on investment, pursuit of greater market share, profit maximisation and so on.
- The firm's ownership characteristics. Price will vary with the firm's ownership structure, which is whether it is a public, private or charity/non-profit organisation.
- The market structure. While smaller firms facing strong competition may not be able to control price very effectively, monopoly suppliers can. Firms operating in an oligopoly typically exhibit interdependence in their pricing (see Chapter 4).
- The firm's position in the marketplace. Cost leaders may seek to keep prices low while firms offering highly differentiated products may be able to apply price premiums.
- The degree of competition within the market and the expected response of competitors to price cuts. Firms that fear a price war with competitors may be reluctant to lower their prices.
- The firm's cost structure and its ability to reduce costs through effective use of its value chain and supply chain.
- The seasonal nature of much tourism demand and the long lead time between pricing decision and product sales. Given increased demand, prices tend to be higher in peak seasons.
- The presence of capacity constraints, for instance, occupancy limits in hotels. The more constrained is supply relative to demand, potentially the greater is the price that can be charged.
- The price of substitute and complementary products, the strength of brand and the ease of switching to a substitute product. The higher the switching costs, the higher can be the price charged to the customer. Thus, a member of an airline frequent flier programme may be reluctant to purchase a cheaper flight on a substitute airline which does not give mileage points.
- The perishable nature of much of the tourism product. Since many tourism products are perishable, prices may fall closer to a 'use-by' date. Thus, hotel room prices might be reduced as the day progresses.

- Government involvement in the market, for example, taxation and/or the imposition of price controls.
- Classification and grading systems that affect price and positioning, for example, the star systems used to grade hotel accommodation.
- Volatility in the macro environment, especially in consumer sentiment and exchange rates, can lead to price fluctuations.

This chapter analyses the competitive and non-competitive pricing strategies employed by firms within the tourism industry. Competitive firms employ both marginal pricing and non-marginal pricing strategies. There is an incentive for non-competitive firms in oligopolies to set price in collusion. The chapter discusses each in turn.

5.2 COMPETITIVE STRATEGIES

According to Porter (1980), competitive firms pursue one or a combination of three broad competition strategies: *cost leadership*, *product differentiation* and/or *focus* (on a particular market segment). While the theory has critics, it still has application for tourism markets. The specific competitive pricing strategies discussed in Section 5.3 below follow from these three broad approaches.

Cost leadership
Pursuit of cost leadership (achieving the lowest production costs relative to competitors) is a valuable strategy when tourism markets are sensitive to changes in price. Low cost can also serve as an effective barrier to entry, making it difficult for would-be competitors to enter the market. Cost leadership can be achieved by using cheaper inputs; producing a core product (with no frills); achieving economies of scale by high volume sales; or gaining volume purchasing discounts (Evans *et al.*, 2003).

Cost leadership is common among tourism operators as they compete for market share. It is particularly common among Low-Cost Carriers (LCC) such as Ryanair in Europe and Southwest in North America, and charter airlines. Accor hotels have their budget Formule 1 brand in the accommodation sector. Successful cost leadership, the same as for any pricing strategy, requires accurate assessment and knowledge of likely competitor responses.

Product differentiation
As discussed in Chapter 4, product differentiation is achieved through better product performance or better product perception and is a common strategy among destination managers and individual operators (Fyall & Garrod, 2005). Product differentiation can create market power, reduce price elasticity of demand (enabling price rises to generate increased sales revenues) and create repeat business, especially when allied with branding, through customer loyalty. It can create effective barriers to entry and lead to higher price. It can also provide a basis for price discrimination (see the discussion below).

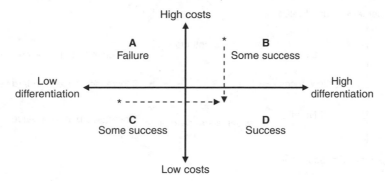

Figure 5.1 How tourism firms can use cost differentiation and product differentiation

Source: Nellis and Parker (2006) Figure 11.3, p. 238

Figure 5.1 shows how tourism firms can use cost leadership and product differentiation to achieve success through appropriate pricing. A firm (a budget airline perhaps) that is enjoying some success with a low production cost but undifferentiated product (Quadrant C) may work towards differentiating its product offering (e.g. by developing a passenger loyalty programme), and charging a higher price. A firm (a full-service airline perhaps) that is enjoying some success with a differentiated but high production cost offering (Quadrant B) may work on lowering its production costs through, say, wage cuts, and reduce the price of its services.

Focus

Firms may focus on a particular geographic area, on a particular customer segment, or on a single product or line (Drummond & Ensor, 1999). Six star hotels, for instance, focus on catering to the top end of their market, imposing *prestige pricing* (setting higher prices based on the understanding that product demand will be stronger at higher prices because of the prestige the product gives to the customer). Focus strategy may be particularly appropriate for smaller firms that pursue non-profit maximisation objectives, including boutique hotels and specialty Bed & Breakfast (B&B) operations.

It is likely, of course, that all three broad strategies exist side by side within any tourism market. Wu (2004), for example, found all three strategies operating within the Taiwanese travel industry. In most cases, the particular strategy chosen will be a reflection of the market environment in which the tourism firm finds itself.

The strategy clock (Figure 5.2) shows eight combinations that may arise for the firm from the interplay of Porter's three broad competitive strategies.

1. *No frills.* A combination of low price/low value (i.e. low cost/low product differentiation) relies on cost leadership and is usually segment-specific, for example, budget airlines.

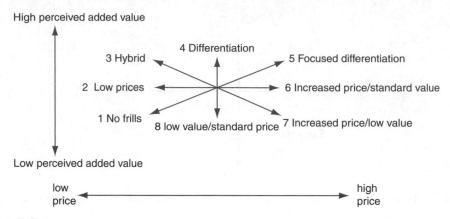

Figure 5.2 The strategy clock

Source: Fyall and Garrod (2005) (after Evans *et al.*, 2003)

2. *Low prices.* A combination of low price/standard value relies on cost leadership but tends to generate low profit margins and runs the risk of price wars, for example, roadside motels at entrances to towns.

3. *Hybrid.* A combination of low price/high value relies on low costs but needs product differentiation to be successful, for example, holiday cruises.

4. *Differentiation.* A combination of standard price/high value can increase market share and perhaps allow a price premium to be imposed, for example, five star hotels.

5. *Focused differentiation.* A combination of high price/high value encourages the imposition of a price premium, for example, six star hotels.

6. *Increased price/standard value.* A combination of high price/standard value can allow for higher margins but at the risk of losing market share, for example, full-service airlines.

7. *Increased price/low value.* A combination of high price/low value works for monopoly products only, for example, cover charge at nightclubs.

8. *Low value/standard price.* A combination of standard price/low value may lead to loss of market share, for example, restaurants in tourism precincts.

It is likely that within any given destination each of the eight strategies will be practised by different tourism operators both within a sector and across different sectors.

5.3 COMPETITIVE PRICING STRATEGIES

As discussed in Chapter 4, tourism firms largely operate under conditions of monopolistic competition and oligopoly. As such, they enjoy some limited power to set price, subject to the extent of product differentiation, segmentation of market, cost structures and barriers to entry. Here, firms set price through either *marginal pricing* or *non-marginal pricing*.

5.3.1 MARGINAL PRICING

Under marginal pricing, as indicated in Chapter 4, the tourism firm will set price under the profit maximisation rule, corresponding to the output where marginal revenue equals marginal cost (MR=MC).

The more common forms of marginal pricing include uniform pricing, price discrimination, two-part tariffs, peak load pricing, bundling, tying, price skimming and transfer pricing.

5.3.1.1 Uniform pricing

Where the tourism firm produces only one product, it often charges the same price for every unit of the product to all buyers (uniform pricing). For example, an amusement park operator might charge the same entry fee to each and every customer, regardless of age, length of stay, amount of rides taken and so on.

As Figure 5.3 shows, the profit-maximising tourism firm would produce at Q_0 (MR=MC) and charge a uniform price, P_0 to each and every customer. The firm would make a profit equal to triangle ABC (the sum of the difference between MR and MC at each level of output), less any fixed costs OC.

In practice, of course, MR is difficult to calculate. When MR is unknown, the firm can still profit maximise by applying the optimal pricing rule of thumb that we noted in Chapter 2:

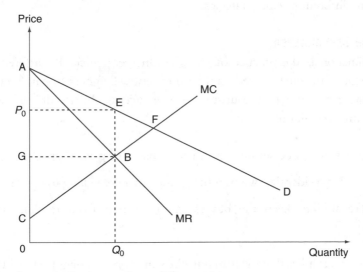

Figure 5.3 Profit maximisation under uniform pricing

$$p = \frac{MC}{(1 - 1/\varepsilon)}$$

The price may need to be determined through trial and error, especially where demand elasticity and marginal costs vary. As the formula suggests, the greater the price elasticity of demand, the lower the price, and vice versa. Profit-maximising tourism firms try to keep price down when demand for their product is elastic (faces much competition or is relatively expensive) and keep price up when demand for their product is inelastic (faces less competition or is relatively inexpensive). We considered the relationship between price elasticity of demand and the firm's total revenue in Chapter 2. To understand firms' pricing strategies we also need to understand the concepts of consumer and producer surplus as discussed in Chapter 4.

The basic shortcoming with uniform pricing from the seller's perspective is that all customers pay the same price for the same product and thus the bulk of buyers receive the product at a price below their reservation price (their willingness to pay as shown by the demand curve). That is, the marginal benefit to the buyer is greater than the price paid by the buyer. While all buyers pay the uniform price, P_0, some buyers would have been willing to pay higher prices. The difference between the buyer's reservation price and the price the buyer actually pays is termed *consumer surplus* and is shown in total as the triangle AEP_0 in Figure 5.3. We can contrast consumer surplus with *producer surplus* which is the amount that producers benefit by selling at a market price that is higher than they would be willing to accept. In Figure 5.3, the producer surplus is shown as the area P_0EBC. Note also that in this case the deadweight loss would be EFB.

Tourism firms use many pricing strategies to try to expropriate this consumer surplus and transfer it to themselves as producer surplus. To do this, rather than set uniform prices, they engage in different pricing strategies.

5.3.1.2 Price discrimination

Price discrimination is the practice of charging different prices to different buyers for the same or similar products, based on their different willingness to pay. Such differential pricing is quite common within tourism. To be a successful price discriminator, a seller must satisfy three conditions:

(1) Sellers have some price-setting power (price maker or price shaper);

(2) Sellers are able to identify two or more groups that are willing to pay different prices;

(3) Sellers are able to keep the buyers in one group from reselling the good to another group.

The first condition implies that the firm must be a monopolist, oligopolist or monopolistic competitor.

The second condition implies that the seller must be able to identify different groups of buyers, with each group having a different price elasticity of demand. The different price elasticity implies that buyers are willing and able to pay different prices for the same good. For each market segment there must be a different price elasticity of demand for the product. This allows the firm to charge a higher price to those consumers with a relatively inelastic demand and a lower price to those with a relatively elastic demand. The firm will then be able to extract more consumer surplus resulting in additional sales revenue and profit.

The third condition requires that the seller be able to segment each group of buyers into distinct markets. This means that the buyers in one market cannot resell the good to the buyers in another market. If trade among different groups of consumers is possible, price discrimination is ineffective. Firms attempt to prevent this by separating markets by geography, time or income; otherwise those buyers charged a higher price could simply purchase the good from those who purchase it at a lower price.

Tourism firms can apply one or more of three forms of price discrimination in order to capture some or the entire consumer surplus. Examples include cinemas and theatres cutting prices to attract younger and older audiences; student discounts for rail and air travel; happy hour in bars and discos; high taxi fares during the late evening; hotels offering cheap midweek breaks and off-season discounts; and lower air fares at off-peak times. Where differences in prices do not reflect the differences in costs, we have examples of price discrimination.

5.3.1.2.1 First-degree price discrimination

Firms practise perfect (pure) price discrimination (or personalised pricing) when they separate their customers into individuals and charge each individual his or her maximum willingness to pay (reservation price). First-degree price discrimination occurs when identical goods are sold at different prices to each individual consumer.

As Figure 5.4 shows, under perfect price discrimination, a tourism firm charges each customer according to that customer's willingness to pay price P_1, P_2, P_3, P_4 and so on. If every customer is charged an amount equal to their reservation price, the firm's profits will be the area AFC, equal to the total producer surplus (less fixed costs of OC). This exceeds the profits obtainable by charging a single price to all customers. In this case where every customer pays according to their reservation price, the entire consumer surplus has been captured by the firm.

Bargaining (haggling) at street stalls and in bazaars is an example of an attempt by suppliers to practise first-degree price discrimination. Street vendors often apply a price that they think the individual potential buyer facing them will pay, with the price dropping depending on how well the individual customer haggles.

If a monopolist can engage in successful price discrimination, the deadweight loss of monopoly, as discussed in Chapter 4, will be eliminated. The supplier captures the former

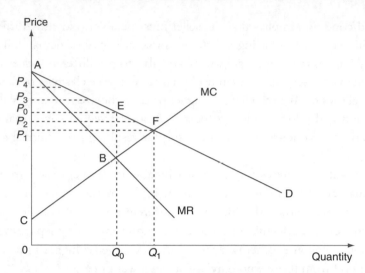

Figure 5.4 Pricing under perfect first-degree price discrimination

monopoly deadweight loss (the inefficiency caused by monopoly pricing) as well as the former consumer surplus. The monopoly, which can engage in first-degree price discrimination, can produce an output at the allocatively efficient level. Thus, first-degree price discrimination can be beneficial from a social perspective. Moreover, the consumers who were not willing to pay the previous monopoly profit-maximising price can now pay a much lower price and get the product. Some consumers will be better off, and others will be worse off as a result of the price discrimination. Economics as such cannot evaluate the desirability of these distributional effects; whether or not they are an improvement is a matter of one's value judgements.

The practical difficulty with applying pure price discrimination is that it is impossible in practice to know each and every customer's reservation price. Where each individual buyer's reservation price is unknown, the firm can simply apply a *set* of different prices, for example, P_1, and P_2 (imperfect price discrimination), in order to capture buyer willingness to pay (Figure 5.5). This approach to pricing does not capture all of the consumer surplus but it increases profits since it charges higher prices to those groups of consumers who value it the most.

5.3.1.2.2 Second-degree price discrimination

Second-degree price discrimination occurs when sellers charge lower prices per unit for higher quantities of the good supplied (quantity discounts). This type of price discrimination involves businesses selling off packages of a product with surplus capacity at lower prices than the previously published/advertised price. In second-degree price discrimination, price varies according to the quantity sold with larger quantities available at a lower unit price. This is particularly widespread in sales to tourism intermediaries where bulk

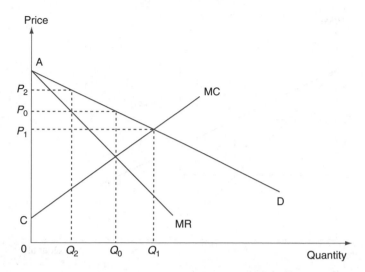

Figure 5.5 Pricing under imperfect first-degree price discrimination

buyers enjoy higher discounts. Thus tour wholesalers pre-purchase large numbers of seats on airplanes or hotel rooms in a destination. To take another example, we find that spare hotel rooms and airline seats are sold on a last-minute standby basis. In these cases, the fixed costs of production are high. At the same time the marginal or variable costs are small and predictable. Rather than be left with unsold airline tickets or hotel rooms, it is often in the firm's best interest to offload any spare capacity at discount prices, providing that the cheaper price that adds to revenue at least covers the marginal cost of each unit of supply.

Firms also transfer consumer surplus to themselves through setting differential prices based on amount. This is known as *block pricing*. The firm sets different prices for different quantities of the same product. Hotels, airlines and tour operators, for instance, routinely discount price on additional bulk purchases made by tour groups. Internet usage in hotel rooms is typically offered for purchase at a much lower rate per hour after the first hour is purchased, and the price per hour of bicycle rental may be lower after the first hour.

Not only can this strategy yield additional profits to the firm, but it can also be an effective way of securing additional market share. Firms may be quite satisfied with a smaller profit margin if it means that they can penetrate more deeply into certain consumer markets at the expense of rivals.

Figure 5.6 shows a firm that engages in second-degree price discrimination. For simplicity, marginal costs are assumed to be constant up to some capacity constraint. Suppose that the firm initially charges the profit-maximising price of P_0 producing quantity Q_0. The firm will still have a large amount of spare capacity, equal to the difference between Q_0 and full capacity where the MC curve becomes vertical. The firm will be willing to sell

185

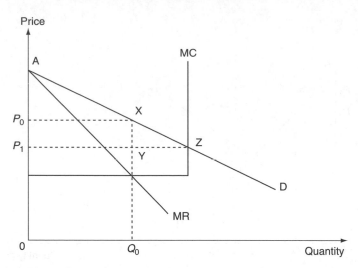

Figure 5.6 Second-degree price discrimination

this quantity for any price so long as it covers the marginal cost of production, as this will contribute to its fixed costs or profits. This will occur at the lower price of P_1 and increase total consumer surplus by XYZ.

Second-degree price discrimination may exist in any market where the aim is to eliminate excess capacity. Examples include the traditional end-of-season sale, reduced prices for air flights late at night and last-minute bargain holidays and hotel rooms. The firm will also gain as there are no revenues from having empty rooms or seats. A hotel must remain open and a plane must fly even if there are only a few paying customers. This situation also underpins the activity of yield management which is discussed below.

5.3.1.2.3 Third-degree price discrimination

Figure 5.7 shows a situation of third-degree price discrimination. It occurs when the seller is able to separate buyers based on an easily identifiable characteristic, such as age, location, gender and ethnic group. Here, rather than allowing consumers to self-select, the firm determines who pays what price based on consumer characteristics that can be identified. This also enables sellers to separate groups of consumers based on their different elasticities of demand.

The division of buyers into separate groups (third-degree price discrimination or group pricing) is the most prevalent form of price discrimination within tourism. Tourism firms regularly segment their customers and charge them differentially along whatever lines they can, for instance, geographic (local visitor/international visitor), age (adult/child/senior), gender (male/female), and timing (weekday/weekend) when there is no difference in the cost of service provision.

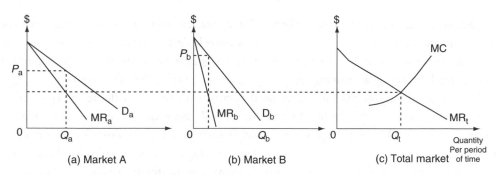

Figure 5.7 Third-degree price discrimination

Coupons (discount offers clipped from newspapers and magazines) are a common method of price discrimination and are prevalent in the tourism industry. A coupon holder may pay a lower price for the same good than a person without a coupon. By this means, suppliers try to capture the two different elasticity groups into which buyers separate themselves. Some individuals have an extremely high cost of time and are willing to pay higher prices instead of spending time to search for and acquire coupons. Others with more time available will try to reduce their expenses by devoting time to look through the coupon books and collect the coupons they need. By offering coupons, sellers are able to capture sales from both groups. In either case, sellers are not able to identify accurately the different groups of consumers. Thus, setting up a price schedule and allowing consumers to distribute themselves among these groups can be highly effective.

Figure 5.7c shows the profit-maximising price and quantity for an airline that treats all passengers equally with regard to the fare charged. Figure 5.7a shows the demand for air travel by holiday makers (Market A) while Figure 5.7b shows the demand by business travellers (Market B). While price for customers differs *between* segments, it remains uniform *within* each segment. A higher price is charged to the low-elasticity segment, and a lower price is charged to the high-elasticity segment. In order to maximise profit, the firm allocates supply between the two markets so that the marginal revenue in each market is identical. By segmenting the market, the profit-maximising firm may set price at P_a for the holiday market (where demand is fairly elastic) and P_b in the business market (where demand is fairly inelastic), thereby increasing sales and profits overall.

The main aim of price discrimination is to increase the total revenue and hopefully the profits of the seller. It helps firms to reduce excess capacity and can also be used as a technique to compete market share away from rival firms.

Examples of price discrimination abound within the tourism industry and use of its three forms is not mutually exclusive. Hotels charge business travellers and leisure travellers differently for the same room during the same time period. Theme parks and theatres differentiate entry price by age. The price of entrance to Beijing's Forbidden City is lower

187

for residents than for foreigners. Airlines offer 'restricted' and 'unrestricted' fares for the same seat on the same flight. The restrictions have little to do with costs, but they are intended to separate the different groups of passengers. This form of yield management is being made easier by advancing technology and online sales directly to buyers.

Of the price discrimination strategies used by tourism firms, first-degree price discrimination will generally yield the most profit, but it will also require the most information. Second- and third-degree price discrimination (which may involve costs such as coupon printing and the like) tend to generate less extra profit than first-degree. All three, however, are likely to generate more profit for the firm than uniform pricing, which requires the least amount of information on the willingness to pay of different types of customers.

The welfare implications of second- and third-degree price discrimination depend on a case-by-case basis. A general, though not perfect, guideline is that price discrimination improves efficiency whenever output is increased as a result. The outcome depends on whether the drop in consumer surplus relative to a one-price policy is outweighed by the gain in producer surplus. If this holds, then the price discrimination will have improved efficiency.

5.3.1.3   Two-part tariff

Within some market segments, tourism firms may be able to apply two-part tariff pricing to their product, charging customers both an upfront fee and an ongoing user fee. Amusement parks, fairs and shows, tennis clubs, golf clubs and fitness gyms, as examples, often levy an entry/membership fee and then charge customers per use of facilities.

The problem for tourism firms in their imposition of two-part tariffs is how to set both entry fee and usage fee so as to maximise overall profits. Assume that an amusement park faces demand and marginal cost curves for a single customer as depicted in Figure 5.8a. To capture the entire consumer surplus from this single customer, the firm could set its usage fee equal to marginal cost (thereby covering usage costs) and its entry fee equal to total consumer surplus (ABC). Similarly, and more realistically, the firm supplying services to more than one customer (Figure 5.8b) can divide its customers into distinct groups, say, adults (D_a) and children (D_c), and apply the same strategy, pricing usage at MC and entry

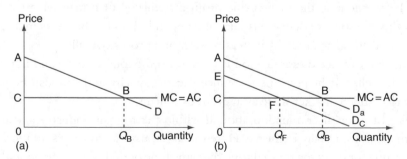

Figure 5.8 (a) Two-part tariff for a single customer (b) Two-part tariff for two groups

fee so as to capture the relevant consumer surplus (ABC for adults and EFC for children). Two-part tariffs can increase overall profits for the firm.

Interestingly, experience has taught Disneyland to charge a differential entry fee (based on age) but not to charge a usage fee for rides. One may infer that this new strategy has increased the revenues of the theme park.

5.3.1.4 Peak load pricing

Peak load pricing involves charging buyers different prices at different points of time that better reflects marginal costs of production. Peaks in demand (high seasons, weekends, etc.) lead to higher marginal costs of production or scarce capacity and therefore higher prices. Airline seasonal pricing reflects this, as do amusement park and ski lift tickets. A profit-maximising hotel, for instance, will price its rooms at P_1 during the peak season when demand is high but at P_2 during the off-peak season when demand is low (see Figure 5.9).

5.3.1.5 Bundling

The combining of two or more products into one 'package' with a single price (bundling) is a common strategy in the packaged tours and fast food industries. Tourism firms often group common products into a new, hopefully more appealing, product that will benefit both the buyer and the seller. Packaged tours (combinations of air fare, accommodation, ground transport, etc.) and 'value meals' provided by fast food outlets are obvious examples, as is the combination of skis, bindings, boots and polls into an easier-to-purchase one-priced ski package (McKercher & du Cros, 2002). Tour operators combine two or more travel services (e.g. transport, accommodation, meals, entertainment, sightseeing,

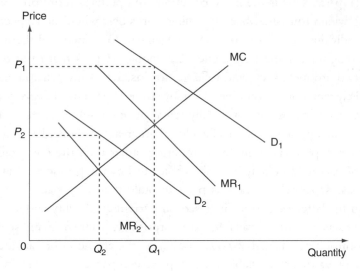

Figure 5.9 Pricing under peak load

etc.) and sell them through travel agencies or directly to final consumers as a bundled product for a single price. The components of a package tour might be pre-established, or can result from an optional purchase procedure, where tourists choose their preferred combination of services. Other obvious examples of bundling occur in the fast food industry, for example, pizza and soft drink, hamburger and french fries, and the like. Hotels occasionally offer packages so that their customers need not buy each item separately (swimming pool, gym, Internet, breakfast, etc.). Tourist destinations use this approach to evoke a destination theme and to market themselves, as for example, the packaged sale of amusement park entry tickets at a discount price.

Bundling will prove more successful for those tourism firms that enjoy economies of scale in production and/or economies of scope in distribution, that face low marginal costs of bundling but high set-up costs and that sell to customers who appreciate the convenience of a combined purchase.

There are two main types of bundling: pure bundling and mixed bundling.

Pure bundling. Here, customers are only allowed to buy the bundle and not its individual parts. Integrated resorts and cruise ships, for instance, offer all-inclusive packages on a 'take it or leave it' basis. This limits consumer choice and so tourism firms have begun to unbundle their pure bundles or at least to separate out the cost components of those bundles. Travel operators now routinely separate out various charges in order to reduce the perceived main price of their core product. This is clearly the case with 'no frills' airlines in their separate itemising of food, baggage, seat allocation and government taxes.

Mixed bundling. This allows customers the choice of buying either the bundle or its individual parts. This is the more common (and perhaps more profitable) form of bundling within tourism. Mixed bundling works best when the respective demands for the individual items are somewhat negatively correlated and the marginal costs of providing them are a little higher. Car rental agencies that offer different bundles of two products – car and mileage, for instance – give customers a choice of higher daily rental price combined with lower (perhaps zero) mileage price (favoured by sightseers, perhaps) or lower daily rental price combined with a higher mileage price (favoured by business travellers in urban areas, perhaps). Fast food customers may prefer to purchase only the hamburger rather then the complete value meal. Buyers of packaged holiday have the choice to buy the pre-determined package or to purchase separately its various parts to build their own packages (*dynamic packaging*). In the latter case, price is based on current availability and add-ons such as theatre tickets are often available. Not surprisingly, tourism firms seek to exercise some control here through *dynamic bundling* as the air, hotel or car rates offered by the tour operator are available only as part of a package or only from a specific supplier.

For their part, fast food restaurants offer customers both a la carte menus and set meals. Here, mixed bundling allows the restaurant to capture more consumer surplus. They price their a la carte menu so as to capture consumer surplus from customers who have large differences in their reservation prices for different parts of the menu (entree, main, dessert, etc.), while they price the set meals to retain those customers who have lower variations in their reservation prices for the different dishes.

Table 5.1 sets out mixed bundling by McDonald's in Hong Kong in 2004. The left-hand column lists prices for individual items sold by McDonald's. The right-hand column lists these same items bundled as meals with soda and fries, giving their unbundled price, their bundled price and the savings made by customers who buy the respective bundle.

Not all tourism sectors are moving in the direction of bundling. In the airline industry, the movement is away from bundling. Until recently, when one bought an airline ticket, the price of the ticket covered on-board food and drinks, entertainment and the ability to check in luggage. With the advent of LCC, there has been a move away from this. Initially, food and drink was not provided, but could be purchased on board. Then, airlines began to provide on-board entertainment, but at a price. While the trend was started by LCC,

Table 5.1 Mixed bundling by McDonald's Hong Kong 2004

Individual item	Price $HK	Meals	Unbundled	Bundled	Savings
		(individual item bundled with soda and fries)			
Filet-O-Fish	11.00	Filet-O-Fish	24.00	20.50	3.50
Chicken McNuggets	11.50	Chicken McNuggets	24.50	22.00	2.50
McWings	13.00	McWings	26.00	22.00	4.00
McCrispy Chicken Filet Burger	13.00	McCrispy Chicken Filet Burger	26.00	23.00	3.00
McChicken	12.50	McChicken	25.50	21.50	4.00
Big Mac	12.00	Big Mac	25.00	22.00	3.00
Double Cheeseburger	12.00	Double Cheeseburger	25.00	21.50	3.50
Soda	6.50				
Fries	6.50				

Source: Adapted from Pindyck *et al.* (2006) Table 11.6, p. 419

full-service airlines have been copying them and now many do not offer free food or drink, and some are charging for checked baggage.

5.3.1.6 Tying

When tourism firms offer a number of different products, they often try to tie the purchase of those products together. That is, customers must buy one product in order to buy or use another (e.g. airport lounges are for the use of only premium-ticketed passengers on particular airlines). Pure bundling is an obvious form of tying. Fast food franchisees are often required to buy all materials and supplies from their franchisors. Such practices are continuously under scrutiny by competition authorities, as, for example, when manufacturers of photocopy machines make their machine to work only on one type of paper (fortunately supplied only by the maker of the photocopier), or mobile phone chargers work only for a particular model of phone.

5.3.1.7 Price skimming

When a firm is the first into a new tourism market or is the first to introduce a new product, it enjoys a temporary monopoly and is able to price accordingly. The firm may initially set high prices and gain substantial profit. The first duty free shop to open within an international airport, or the first bar, for example, may be able to price skim before competitors enter. As competitors enter, the firm then reduces its price so as to cater to the next segment of the market. This process continues until the mass market is reached with prices similar to those of competitors. Skimming is a good pricing strategy when market segments are well defined, entry barriers are high, demand is inelastic, the product's life cycle is short and there are few economies of scale to be found (Doyle, 2000).

5.3.1.8 Transfer pricing

Transfer pricing involves the pricing of inputs and outputs between divisions of the same firm. As the product moves along its supply chain, it passes from one division of the firm to another. For example, a firm's airline/hotel division supplies items to the firm's tour operator division which, in turn, supplies the now value added items to the firm's travel agency division for distribution to customers. The firm prices the intermediate inputs so as to optimise overall company profits rather than to maximise profits at each stage or division. Multinational enterprises, especially, use transfer pricing to take advantage of differential tax rates across national borders. This involves the purchase and sale of inputs between firms under common ownership often at inflated prices in order to reduce the total corporate tax bill on profits.

5.3.1.9 Yield management

Yield management occurs when a firm seeks to use its price structure to make the most profitable use of the capacity it provides. Many tourism businesses operate by committing to provide a fixed capacity, and then seeking to fill this capacity in the most profitable way. Thus airlines commit to operate a schedule of flights, and each flight is operated by an aircraft with a set capacity (typically the airline has only limited scope to switch aircraft to cater for smaller or greater than expected demand). Hotels are built with a fixed number of rooms. A tour operator will have a fixed number of seats available on a coach tour. A restaurant has a fixed number of tables.

One option for these businesses is to quote a set (uniform) price to the customer and take whatever sales result. If the flight has 75% of its seats empty, or half the rooms in the hotel are empty, so be it. For many years, airlines operated like this, with set fares and no discounts – they often were content to operate only 60% to 70 % full. However, it is more profitable to use the price structure to fill the aircraft or hotel. The development of computer booking systems, and the growth of online booking, has greatly facilitated the application of yield management.

Yield management uses many of the pricing techniques discussed above. Thus it includes peak pricing – it is difficult to get a low fare on a flight which is likely to be heavily booked, such as at the beginning of the school holidays. It makes use of price discrimination – business travellers are less price sensitive than leisure travellers, and they tend to book late, particularly if the flight is under capacity. Early-bird discounts can generate extra sales. Conference convenors know this when they offer early-bird registration. Similarly, customers booking with LCC will normally find lower prices if they are prepared to commit themselves to a flight by booking early. In these cases early-bird discounting provides suppliers with information on how full their conferences or flights are likely to be as well as a source of cash-flow in the time prior to the service being provided. In the airline case, closer to the date and time of the scheduled service, the price rises, on the simple justification that consumer's demand for a flight becomes more inelastic the nearer to the time of the service. People who book late often regard travel to their intended destination as a necessity and they are therefore likely to be willing and able to pay a much higher price very close to departure. Thus airlines normally increase fares the closer to the time the flight is due to operate. However, this does not always happen, especially if demand for the flight is weaker than expected – if it is not selling the seats, the airline may lower the fares. If passengers switch their flights close to the time of the flights, it is difficult for the airline to fill its aircraft – hence it introduces non-refundability restrictions. Nearly every passenger on a flight might be paying a different fare, depending on when they booked, what restrictions they face and what other flights they are taking. This comes about because of yield management, with the airline seeking to make the most revenue it can from the flight.

Airlines were the leaders in developing yield management in the tourism industry (see Kraft et al., 1986), and today they operate the most sophisticated systems. Larger hotel chains, passenger rail networks and car hire firms also make extensive use of yield management. Simpler businesses, such as small hotels and tour bus operators, and restaurants, tend to have much simpler price structures; however, even these make some use of yield management. For example, some restaurants offer discounts to patrons who complete their meals before the busy period begins, and bars provide 'happy hour' discounts to attract patrons in off-peak times. In an era of excess capacity, the concept of yield management on a daily and hourly basis is increasingly relevant in all sectors of travel and tourism (Middleton & Clarke, 2001).

Box 5.1 discusses an investigation of some unethical pricing practices prevalent in tourism today.

BOX 5.1 The hidden costs of snapping up a bargain

The UK's competition watchdog Office of Fair Trading (OFT) is putting potentially misleading pricing practices under scrutiny to help protect consumers.

It's easy to be tempted by a Bogof (buy one, get one free) deal. But you need to look very closely at the cost as sneaky shops simply up their prices to make things seem like a bargain, when they're not. This is especially true online, where the headline deals often hide extra costs and expenses, which mean you end up paying more than you need to. That particular trick is called 'drip pricing' where the cost of an item rises as you are taken through the buying process. The worst offenders are the online ticket retailers and holiday sites where the website's various delivery charges or credit card fees can add 25 per cent to the cost of a music, theatre or sport ticket or flights. It's an infuriating practice, especially as you often don't find out about the additional costs until you reach the checkout point.

By the time you've negotiated several pages of questions and put in your address and payment details, it's often easier to sign and just accept the extra charges. But I'm glad to see that the practice could be outlawed. The OFT is finally acting against the online price tricks and is likely to crack down on the misleading tactics. As far as I'm concerned, it should be an open-and-shut case for the OFT. The online-pricing ploys either force us to pay too much, or encourage us to buy extra stuff in the hope of getting a bargain.

Other questionable tactics set to be investigated by the OFT include 'baiting sales' and 'reference pricing'. With the former, only a handful of the items advertised are available, which means the retailer can say that it offered the product at the low price (I reckon sometimes only one product is actually sold at the discount). The online shop then relies on people buying the item anyway at the higher price or spending money elsewhere on the site. In other words, it's a way to boost visitor hits. Reference pricing is when retailers use higher prices to artificially inflate the price of a product. For example, creating an attractive 50 per cent off deal when the product hasn't actually dropped that far in price. It's easy to be hoodwinked by the offer unless you actually compare prices elsewhere, which as shoppers we don't do often enough.

It's not just online that these tactics are used, so it's good that the OFT will also look at high-street selling practices. The tricks are aimed at bargain hunters. I'm particularly guilty of snapping up what seems like a good deal, only to discover that I've overpaid. It's the same kind of fever that encourages people on eBay to bid higher than the retail price for items, in the fear that they will miss on what seems like a bargain. And that's another trick the OFT is investigating: 'time-limited periods', where sales run for 24 hours or a set space of time, causing people to panic buy before the sale ends.

The OFT study will focus mainly on how the sales practices are used by online retailers and could result in sanctions against firms A range of options are available to the OFT, from giving the retailers a clean bill of health to encouraging voluntary codes of practice – or a full-blown investigation of companies suspected of breaching consumer protection laws. The OFT has also launched a separate investigation into online targeting of consumers, where prices are individually tailored using information about a potential customer's internet use.

Source: Read, S. (2009) 'The Hidden Costs of Snapping Up a Bargain', *The Independent*, Saturday, 17 October, http://www.independent.co.uk/money/spend-save/simon-read-the-hidden-costs-of-snapping-up-a-bargain-1804203.html

5.3.2 NON-MARGINAL PRICING

The discussion above has generally assumed that the firm is well informed and is able to make effective use of the information available to it. This is not always the case. While some tourism businesses, such as airlines, have extensive information about their customers and costs, others, especially smaller firms, do not. Small firms often do not have the ability or resources to analyse carefully the information they have. Firms may have to be aggressive in their pricing when they are establishing themselves, and also may have to rely on rules of thumb in pricing when established.

5.3.2.1 Penetration pricing

Penetration pricing involves setting a relatively low initial entry price, often lower than the prevailing market price, to attract new customers. The strategy is based on the expectation that customers will be attracted to or switch to the new brand because of the lower price. Penetration pricing is most commonly associated with the marketing objective of increasing market share or sales volume, rather than additional profits in the short term. While they may be foregoing profits in the short run, this strategy can lead to higher profits in the long run. It can create goodwill among the early customer segment, creating additional sales through word of mouth.

Established firms will occasionally follow a similar strategy, setting prices low in a hope to increase their market share. Penetration pricing is most commonly used and most effective when the firm has not achieved sufficient product differentiation, where demand is highly price elastic, where there are opportunities for economies of scale and the product has a long life cycle. The firm sets low prices so as to encourage people who show little brand loyalty to switch to their products. An additional consequence of penetration pricing is that it can discourage the entry of competitors, with low prices acting as a barrier to entry.

The main limitation of penetration pricing is that it establishes long-term price expectations for the product, and image preconceptions for the brand and the firm. This makes it difficult to eventually raise prices over the medium and longer term. Penetration pricing may attract only 'bargain hunters' who will switch back to their preferred products as soon as the price rises. Another potential disadvantage is that the profit margins may be insufficient for the financial viability of the firm over time. Penetration pricing can sometimes lead to predatory (destroyer) pricing when a firm initially sells a product or service at unsustainably low prices to eliminate rivalry and/or to create an additional barrier to entry for potential new competitors. As an example, when Microsoft released their web-browser Internet Explorer for free, its main competitor and then market leader, Netscape, was forced to release Netscape Navigator for free in order to remain in the market. Internet Explorer's free inclusion in Windows led to a rapid increase in its market share by computer users. In most countries, predatory pricing is illegal but often difficult to prove.

5.3.2.2 Markup (cost plus) pricing

Markup pricing is a long-established pricing practice within tourism. To determine price, the firm adds a markup (usually a percentage) to its average cost. The size of the markup is generally based on industry tradition, management experience, industry association guidelines or some rule of thumb, and changes from product to product offered by the same firm and over time as demand and cost conditions change.

Restaurants, for example, routinely apply different markup percentages *across* their range of dishes (entrees, mains and desserts) as well as *within* each type of dish (ice cream, mousse, fruit platter, etc.). A standard complaint often heard is that restaurants 'get you on the alcohol', suggesting that restaurants apply high markups to the sale and service of alcohol.

Markup pricing is a simple and easy pricing strategy that gets around the lack of detailed information and the resources to analyse it. It is good for the pricing of services that are tailored to the individual needs of customers. While markups can be arbitrary, they can reflect industry experience and be a simple and easily applicable means for small businesses to price their products to achieve maximum profits.

5.3.2.3 Non-profit goals

From time to time, firms pursue goals that are not profit driven. If the firm operates in a profitable market, such as one in which it has a monopoly or is part of an oligopoly, it has the scope to pursue some non-profit objectives. Older firms may lose their aggression, and allow costs to be higher than they need be to enjoy a 'quiet life'. Some managers are focused on growth, and pursue growth at the expense of profit (sometimes with fatal consequences). Airlines which have long been dominant in their markets may be unwilling to exit markets when they become unprofitable (perhaps because of competition from LCC).

Businesses operating in competitive markets have less scope to pursue non-profit objectives – they need to be profitable to survive. However, owner managers may operate their businesses efficiently, but they may trade off profits for other benefits, such as community image and prestige.

Some businesses may be driven by lifestyle choice, for example, B&B establishments. Skalpe (2003), for example, found that the Norwegian hospitality industry did not pursue risk-and-return strategies, but rather followed personal non-profit incentives associated with lifestyle preference. Such tourism services often attract owners who may be retired or who otherwise seek lifestyle outlets rather than business profits. This does not mean that the owners do not enjoy a comfortable living, but that achievement of profits is not of paramount importance in their business operations.

The discussion indicates that tourism firms can potentially adopt different pricing strategies according to their objectives. The pricing strategies adopted will have different implications for firm output, sales and profits.

5.4 NON-COMPETITIVE (COLLUSIVE) PRICING STRATEGIES

As discussed in Chapter 4, tourism firms operating within oligopolistic markets are mutually interdependent in their pricing decisions. Given the dictates of oligopolistic markets, firms may find it more profitable to collude than to compete, if possible. Under collusive pricing, firms set prices through either cartel arrangements or some form of price leadership.

5.4.1 CARTEL

Firms form cartels when, within the same market segment, they undertake formal agreements on price and output. Under these agreements, firms act together like a monopoly, charging a uniform price with each cartel member supplying an allocated market share. Though anti-competitive and illegal within a domestic setting, cartels nevertheless exist internationally. The International Air Transport Association (IATA) was the most obvious tourism example (see Box 5.2). The Organisation of Petroleum Exporting Countries (OPEC) is the most obvious non-tourism example. Yet, even here, OPEC cartel pricing

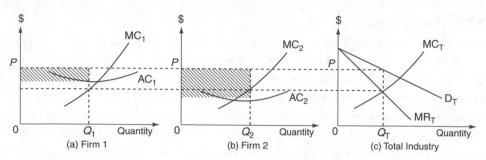

Figure 5.10 Cartel outcome within a two-firm oligopoly

of its oil affects pricing within tourism markets, as demonstrated by airline fuel surcharges on passengers.

Figure 5.10 illustrates a collusive outcome within a two-firm oligopoly. The average and marginal cost curves for firm 1 and firm 2 are shown in Figures 5.10a and 5.10b, respectively, while the total industry demand, marginal revenue and marginal cost curves are shown in Figure 5.10c. Industry output will occur where $MR_t = MC_t$ at output level Q_t and price P. Both firms will then sell at price P but will sell different quantities and will enjoy different profits, according to their respective cost structures.

Oligopolistic market structures are conducive to the formation of cartels because of their small number of large firms, product homogeneity, strong barriers to entry and similar demand and cost conditions facing members. Cartels are often inherently unstable with cheating rife and breakdowns during recession as members attempt to undercut each other to gain market share.

5.4.2 PRICE LEADERSHIP

Due to the often-illegal nature of formal collusion, tourism firms will more often avoid formal cartel arrangements though still price collusively through informal arrangements. Here, there is tacit agreement between firms either to keep prices the same or to change them by the same amount.

> *Dominant price leadership* occurs when the largest, strongest or most cost efficient firm sets the price and the others follow.
>
> *Barometric price leadership* occurs when the firm most sensitive to the market conditions sets the price and the others follow.

Figure 5.11 illustrates dominant price leadership (Keats & Young, 2009). The dominant firm profit maximises, producing at Q_d where its marginal revenue (MR_d) equals its marginal cost (MC_d) and charging price, P. The remainder of the firms do not

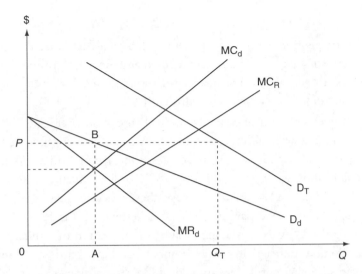

Figure 5.11 Dominant price leadership

profit-maximise. Rather, each firm adopts the price P set by the dominant firm, producing its own output for a total industry output of Q_t (on total demand curve, D_T).

Perdue (2002) found that American ski resorts operated under price leadership. One or other of the larger resorts would set capacity for the season and then apply prices under yield management to manage demand. The other resorts would then follow its lead. Similarly, Baum and Mudambi (1995) found that resorts in Bermuda avoided price-cutting wars in off-peak periods by limiting room supply and striving to differentiate their product heavily from their competitors.

BOX 5.2 International airlines and cartels

For many years, a popular example of a cartel was IATA, the International Air Transport Association. After the WWII, and until the late 1970s, international airlines, which were mainly government owned, operated price fixing through IATA. Air fares were set regularly by airlines acting together in regional tariff conferences, and in a worldwide tariff conference. These mainly met secretly, and would set fares for thousands of routes. Airlines would agree to charge IATA fares, and IATA set up compliance arrangements to ensure that airlines were not discounting. Often airlines serving a route would pool their revenues, which would lessen the incentive for them to undercut each other. Since non price competition often breaks out when price competition is not feasible, IATA also regulated other aspects of service, such as the on board entertainment offered and the quality of the food served to passengers (to ensure that the quality was not too high!). Some governments required their airlines to set their fares through IATA.

The IATA fares setting arrangements gradually broke down from 1979 onwards. In that year, airlines were allowed to join IATA as an industry association without participating in its fare setting processes. One factor leading to the break down in collusion was the growth in non IATA airlines, such as Singapore Airlines, which undercut IATA fares. In Europe there was also the growth of charter airlines which did not take part in IATA fare setting. By the late 1970s, countries including the USA were moving away from regulation of airlines, and were seeking to promote rather than hinder competition between them. Competition authorities in several countries began to prohibit their airlines from participating in IATA fare setting. With the development of yield management, fares become more complicated, making agreement on them difficult to achieve. Liberalization of the major international air routes has meant that coordinated pricing has become unsustainable.

In its heyday, the IATA fare setting mechanism resulted in air fares which were high and inflexible- few discount fares were permitted. Airlines were not highly profitable, but the high fares enabled high cost airlines to survive. While it still has some role in setting fares, especially on routes of smaller developing countries, IATA now functions primarily as an industry association, and it performs a number of coordinating functions associated with the operation of the international air transport system. For example, it operates as a clearing house for dealings between airlines associated with multiple airline trips, and it oversees the allocation of slots between airlines for using busy airports. The IATA experience illustrates how cartels can survive when they are supported by governments, and it also shows how cartels break down when competition and new entry are present.

Source: Doganis, R. (2002) *Flying Off Course*, 3rd edition, Chapter 2, London and New York: Routledge

5.5   HEDONIC MODELLING TO INFORM STRATEGIC PRICING

We have argued above that firms can compete by keeping the prices of their products low relative to those of their competitors both within and outside their destination. However, they can also improve the quality of the characteristics of goods and services. Such quality improvements often enable the products to be sold for higher prices, effectively by making the demand curve more inelastic.

The Hedonic Pricing Model (HPM), derived from Lancaster's (1966) consumer theory and Rosen's (1974) model, posits that a good possesses various attributes that combine to form bundles of utility-affecting attributes that the consumer values. A basic premise of hedonic pricing theory is that, since goods are valued for their utility-bearing characteristics, the price of a package tourism product is largely determined by the value that consumers place on its constituting characteristics or attributes. Thus, positive attributes (as evaluated by the consumer) are expected to drive up the overall price, whereas undesirable attributes will reduce the price. HPM decomposes the product offering into its constituent characteristics and obtains estimates of the contributory value of each characteristic. This requires that the composite product can be reduced to its constituent parts and that the market values those constituent parts.

HPM enables the total prices of the packages to be disaggregated such that an implicit price is attributed to each key characteristic of the package, depending on the perceived utility derived from the characteristics of the packages on offer. HPM also indicates the extent to which the provision of different tourism product characteristics can contribute to an increase in the price of the product.

The method adopted in HPM is to regard the tourism product in question as the sum of its inherent attributes or characteristics. Following Rosen (1974), the price of the tourism product is taken as an additive function of the levels of the attributes or characteristics embodied in that product.

Formally, the tourism product, Z, can be regarded as a bundle of attributes, $Z = (Z_1, Z_2, Z_3, \ldots, Z_n)$, where Z_i represents the amount of attribute i present. Because the overall price of the bundled product is assumed to be a function of its attributes, the hedonic price function is represented as $P(Z) = P(Z_1, Z_2, Z_3, \ldots, Z_n)$. Thus, in studies of package tourism,

P is the observed package price from the tour operator brochure;

Z is the vector of characteristics; and

Z_i is the individual characteristic.

The partial derivative of P with respect to the particular characteristic is the hedonic price of that individual attribute.

In the typical case, the price of, for example, a hotel room is empirically modelled as the additive function of various objective hotel attributes (e.g. type of board, distance to downtown, distance to amusement parks and presence of swimming pool, sauna, bar and restaurant) and more subjective attributes (e.g. service quality, atmosphere and hotel star rating). Usually, this model is estimated by means of ordinary least squares regression or some related technique. This method of 'unbundling' the tourism package sheds light on which attributes consumers have to pay extra for (i.e. the attributes with significant coefficients) and which attributes can be bought without a price surcharge (i.e. the attributes with zero or close to zero coefficients).

HPM has been used by tourism researchers to show how various supply-related factors explain the variation in overall accommodation and package tour prices. Sinclair *et al.* (1990) examined the determinants of UK package holiday prices to Malaga, Spain. Among their findings was that the choice of tour operator, hotel star rating and hotel facilities (i.e. hotel attributes) were important predictors of the overall package holiday price. In another study, Clewer *et al.* (1992) found that the price of inclusive tour holidays in European cities reflected attributes of the packages offered. Taylor (1995) showed how hotel star rating, type of accommodation and tour operator all were important explanatory variables for the overall price of package tours from the UK to the Mediterranean. These findings received general support from a study by Aguilo *et al.* (2001) concerning the price for German tourist packages to the island of Mallorca which also found that certain hotel attributes were important predictors of the overall package price. Papatheodorou (2002) examined the tour brochures of eight mass market UK tour operators over ten Mediterranean countries. Monty and Skidmore (2003) used HPM to evaluate willingness to pay for specific characteristics of B&B accommodations in Wisconsin, USA. More recently, Mangion *et al.* (2005) found associations between product attributes and the prices of package holiday tourism to Mediterranean resorts, while Thrane (2005) found that choice of tour operator, choice of island (i.e. destination) and choice of attributes such as breakfast, restaurant, TV and so on all had an impact on the price that Norwegian consumers pay for sun-and-beach package tours to the Canary Islands.

Hedonic price analysis provides an understanding of which characteristics of products and services are valued by consumers and to what extent. This information has implications for marketing and product development, as those characteristics of high value should be emphasised and identified for tourists during their stay. HPM enables tourism operators to identify those facilities and services which they should offer to increase sales. This information assists tourism businesses and organisations to target characteristics that contribute significantly to price increases and to attempt to increase the provision of those characteristics. That is, the results of HPM present an opportunity for tour managers to enhance their strategic pricing, through quality improvements and innovation. Tourism planners and investors can also use the findings of HPMs as an indication of which additional facilities would attract better prices and to what extent.

Box 5.3 summarises a hedonic pricing study undertaken on Spanish hotels.

BOX 5.3 The effect on prices of the attributes of holiday hotels

A study of Mediterranean package tourism investigated how the different characteristics of a holiday hotel influence its price using the hedonic pricing method. For this study the authors assumed that, due to imperfections in the market, hotel managers have monopoly power to some extent and can therefore, price discriminate; that is, charge different prices to different customers for exactly the same room or services. They therefore, take the prices from the supply side of the market. They then decompose the prices to see how each characteristic affects the price of the hotel.

In the case of accommodation, very often travellers tend to book through tour operators who set the price. However, even in this situation, the operators will still take into account the characteristics of the hotel before charging a price. The attributes of a hotel are also related to the cost or running the hotel. This implies that charging a price that is based on the relevant attributes can also be regarded as cost pricing. One way to look at this problem is to think that instead of supplying a hotel room, the manager is supplying a number of characteristics and services which altogether make up the hotel and that consumers are paying for each of these attributes which when taken together gives the prices of the hotel (room?). The hotel, therefore, can be broken down into a set of attributes as shown in the equation below:

$$H_i = (q_{i1}, q_{i2}, q_{i3} \cdots \cdots, q_{ik}, \cdots q_{im})$$

i denotes the hotel and takes the values of 1 to n. q_{ik} (where $k = 1$ to m), are each of the attributes of the hotel i. It is here assumed that the number of hotels in question is 'n' and the numbers of attributes are 'm'. For example, $\ldots q_{11}$ may refer to whether hotel 1 has a swimming pool. The prices of the hotel the can be derived as a function of the prices of each attributes. That is the price of each attributes is taken into account in order to set the price for the hotel. It is presented as:

$$P_i = P(p_{i1}, p_{i2}, p_{i3} \cdots \cdots, p_{ik}, \cdots p_{im})$$

Where P is the functional form which relates the prices of the characteristics to the price of the hotel. It is assumed to be same for all hotels and constant over time.

There are several difficulties which are encountered while formulating the above function. For example, hotel room prices are subject to seasonality. There are different price regimes a hotel can charge their guest – either on full board basis, half board or bed and breakfast. Sometimes there are special discounts given, or supplements are charged for services such as the provision of extra beds for children. The room prices were gathered from the catalogues of tour operators in Spain as these are also similar to the prices that tourist pay when they make their reservations directly.

The authors considered hotels from three different towns in Spain, namely, Lloret de Mar, Blanes and Tossa de Mar. Although the three towns are geographically quite close to one another, their characteristics were quite different. Together these three resorts offered 42,642 beds. The prices used were from the tour operator Travelmar, which dealt with most of the hotels in the region and covered 62 percent of the rooms on offer. This operator also had the longest series of data on room prices. 82,000 data points were used and this consisted of daily prices recorded from May to Oct from 1991 to 1998. The prices were in Spanish pesetas per person per day on a full board basis.

The relevant attributes were obtained by carrying out in depth interviews with managers and other professionals in the business. A total of 55 attributes were obtained from which 10 were retained for the model. These are given in Table 5.2.

Table 5.2 Hotel attributes and their descriptions

Attributes	*Descriptions*
Category	From 1 star (H1) to 4 stars (H4) as there are five stars hotel in the region
ROOMS	Number of rooms in the hotel.
EQUIP	Whether guests had access to at least a television, air conditioning, or mini bar without having to pay a surcharge.
GARDEN	Whether there is a garden or larger terrace at the hotel.
POOL	Whether there is any type of outdoor swimming pool.
SPORT	Whether sport facilities such as tennis, squash, or mini golf were offered either with or without a surcharge.
BEACH	Whether the hotel is located directly in front of the sea.
CENTRE	Whether the hotel is located close to the town centre.
RENOV	Whether the hotel has been recently renovated.
PARKING	Whether the hotel had parking spaces.

A panel estimation approach was used whereby one single model is fitted to the data set including all hotels and time points in order to obtained increased efficiency. This means that the results will provide insight as to whether the parameters obtained remain constant over across hotels, time and town, which would not be possible if single equations were fitted for each town and time. The dependent variable was the log of room prices; in addition to the variables above, a year variable was included to capture the trend over time and a month variable to capture seasonality. The model that was estimated is given below:

$$\ln(PRICE)_{ikj} = \beta_{0ik} + \beta_{1ik}H1_{ij} + \beta_{2ik}H2_{ij} + \beta_{3ik}H3_{ij} +$$
$$\beta_4(ROOMS)_{ij} + \beta_5 EQUIP_{ij} + \beta_6 GARDEN_{ij} + \beta_7 POOL_{ij} +$$
$$\beta_8 SPORT_{ij} + \beta_9 BEACH_i + \beta_{10}CENTRE_i + \beta_{11}RENOV_{ij} +$$
$$\beta_{12}(PARKING)_{ij} + \sum_{m=13}^{19} \beta_m YEAR_j + \sum_{m=20}^{24} \beta_m MONTH_j + u_{ijk}$$

Where,

> i identifies the hotel ($i = 1 \ldots 85$). k is the town ($k = 1, 2, 3$) and j is the period (May 1991, June 1991 ……. Sept 1998, Oct 1998).

u_{ijk} is the random error term.

It was found that the most important attribute in determining room prices tends to be the category of hotel. The difference between 1 and 2 stars was small but the differences tended to be very high for 4 stars. Over time, hotel room prices in general have been on the rise and there is a very strong seasonality effect with August and July being the peak months. The town in which the hotel is located matters as hotels in Tossa were priced higher than those in Blanes and Lloret de Mar.

It was found that 1 star hotels tend to price 64 percent lower than 4 star hotels, while 2 and 3 star hotels price 61 and 50 percent lower than the 4 star hotel respectively. In general, the number of rooms had an effect only on hotels with a size of 123 to 217 rooms. As the number of rooms goes up the prices tended to be lower for hotels of this size. Hotels facing the beach were priced higher. None of the other characteristics had any significant impact on prices other than PARKING. The availability of parking spaces raised the room price by 8.5 percent. Over the years, the prices went up but not in a linear fashion. The authors explained that it could have occurred due to the demand side of the market with a high demand causing prices to go up but subject to a lag. The seasonality on the prices was also captured confirming that August is the peak month followed by June.

These results are potentially very useful to hotel managers and investors in resorts. For example the location parameter can help investors decide as to what room prices they can expect based on where they are planning to invest. Furthermore, they also show how changes in some characteristics, such as providing parking facilities or increasing the number of rooms, will affect the prices. Some of the changes that investors must consider if they wish to charge higher prices are not costless. These might include an expansion of the grounds of existing hotels to provide parking space or construction of a new hotel on the beach, where prices of land are higher. Hence, decisions need to be taken by weighting the additional cost of the land against the additional expected revenues.

Source: Spinet, J.M.E., M.S. Aez, G.C. Oenders and M.F. Luvià (2003) 'Effect on Prices of the Attributes of Holiday Hotels: A Hedonic Prices Approach', *Tourism Economics*, 9(2), 165–177

5.6 CONCLUSIONS AND POLICY

- Price is a critical decision variable of importance to the tourism firm. Price is also the most adjustable of all the firm's decision variables.
- The price that a tourism firm sets for its products is governed by the interplay of a number of factors that are internal and external to the firm. These include the firm's objectives, its ownership pattern, the market structure in which it operates, the degree of competition within the market and the firm's position within the market, the firm's cost structure, seasonality, government policy, the macroeconomic environment, the price of substitute and complementary goods, capacity constraints, the degree of perishability of its products and the presence of classification and grading systems.
- Tourism firms can adopt competition strategies such as cost leadership, product differentiation and/or segment focus and set their prices by reference to one or a combination of these strategies.
- Tourism firms largely operate under conditions of monopolistic competition and oligopoly. As such, they enjoy some limited power to set price, subject to the extent of product differentiation, segmentation of market, cost structures and barriers to entry. Firms set price through either marginal pricing or non-marginal pricing.
- Competitive profit-maximising firms may choose from a variety of marginal pricing strategies. These include uniform pricing, price discrimination, two-part tariffs, peak load pricing, bundling, tying, price skimming and transfer pricing. All help in yield

management. Marginal pricing approaches work best when the firm is well informed and is able to make effective use of the information available to it.

- Non-marginal pricing strategies include penetration pricing, markup pricing and non-profit goals. Tourism firms can potentially adopt different pricing strategies according to their objectives. The pricing strategies adopted will have different implications for firm output, sales and profits.

- Given the dictates of oligopolistic markets, firms may find it more profitable to collude than to compete, if they can. Under collusive pricing, firms set prices through either cartel arrangements or some form of price leadership. As competitive pressures grow and firms become more interdependent in their pricing decisions, firms tend to adopt price leadership strategies, especially when the option of a cartel arrangement is not available to them.

- The hedonic pricing method has been used by tourism researchers to show how various supply-related factors explain the variation in overall accommodation and package tour prices, presenting tourism managers with an opportunity to enhance their strategic pricing through quality improvements and innovation. While firms can compete by keeping the prices of their products low relative to those of their competitors both within and outside their destination, they can also improve the quality of the characteristics of goods and services. Such quality improvements often enable the products to be sold for higher prices, effectively by making the demand curve more inelastic.

SELF-REVIEW QUESTIONS

1. List the generic internal and external factors that might affect the price of hotel accommodation.

2. Using tourism examples, differentiate between the three broad competition strategies: cost leadership, product differentiation and segment focus.

3. On a diagram, demonstrate how successful price discrimination may result in higher revenues to a tourism firm than uniform pricing. What conditions must be in place for price discrimination to be successful?

4. Explain each of the three forms of price discrimination that firms within tourism might seek to apply. How easy is it to apply each form?

5. Explain how a two-part tariff might be applied to some tourism products. Give practical examples.

6. Use examples from the tour operator industry to distinguish between pure bundling and mixed bundling.

7. Visit your nearest fast food outlet and explain how it bundles its products.

8. Use examples from tourism to illustrate how firms employ yield management to expand sales.

9. When and why would a tourism firm adopt a penetration pricing strategy?

10. A tourism firm that applies markup pricing cannot possibly make a loss. Comment.

11. Use tourism examples to distinguish between dominant price leadership and barometric price leadership.

12. Give examples to show how hedonic pricing may help a hotel manager provide his/her customers with better value for money.

ESSAY QUESTIONS

1. Discuss the relevance of cost leadership, product differentiation and segment focus strategies for the hotel accommodation sector.

2. It is likely that within any given tourism destination each of the eight strategies (set out in the strategy clock) will be practised by different tourism operators both within a sector and across different sectors. Discuss with examples.

3. Within tourism markets, firms may find it much easier to apply markup pricing than to follow the rules of profit maximisation. Discuss.

4. How might a hotel chain practise price discrimination to increase its total revenue? Give practical examples.

5. Tourism firms will find pure bundling more profitable and easier to apply than mixed bundling. Comment on this statement using examples.

6. Peak load pricing in tourism is a form of price discrimination that makes both customers and firms better off. Discuss.

7. It is better for tour operators to follow collusive strategies than to compete on price. Discuss.

8. Hedonic pricing presents an opportunity for tourism managers to enhance their strategic pricing through quality improvements and innovation. How so?

DISTINGUISHING THE ECONOMIC CONTRIBUTION, ECONOMIC IMPACTS AND NET BENEFITS OF TOURISM

CHAPTER 6

TOURISM'S ECONOMIC CONTRIBUTION, ECONOMIC IMPACTS AND NET BENEFITS

LEARNING OBJECTIVES

After reading this chapter, you should be able to:

1. Distinguish between tourism's economic contribution and its economic impact.

2. Appreciate that tourism makes both direct and indirect economic contributions to a destination.

3. Understand the direct, indirect and induced effects that accompany new tourism expenditure.

4. Distinguish between the costs and the benefits associated with tourism to a destination and identify their sources.

5. Recognise that distortions present in all economies can affect the extent of a nation's net benefits from inbound tourism.

6.1   INTRODUCTION

It is widely acknowledged that both domestic and international tourism make an 'economic contribution' to a destination, that tourism has positive and negative 'economic impacts' and that it brings 'benefits and costs' to a destination. Since these terms will be used throughout this book, we need to clarify them here since, to the economist, they mean different things.

The issues addressed in this chapter have substantial relevance to each of the remaining chapters of this book. Many of these issues will be discussed in greater detail below but they set out the basic approach which the authors take to economic analysis of tourism and policy formulation.

6.2   THE ECONOMIC CONTRIBUTION OF TOURISM

The economic contribution of tourism refers to tourism's economic significance – to the contribution that tourism-related spending makes to key economic variables such as Gross

Domestic (Regional) Product, household income, value added, foreign exchange earnings, employment and so on. Some key concepts are defined in Box 6.1.

BOX 6.1 Definitions of GDP and GVA

Gross Domestic Product (GDP) is a basic measure of a country's economic performance and is the total market value of all final goods and services produced in a country in a given year. GDP can be defined in three ways, all of which are conceptually identical. GDP is

(1) the total expenditures for all final goods and services produced within the country in a given year which equals

(2) the sum of the value added at every stage of production (the intermediate stages) by all the industries within a country, plus taxes less subsidies on products, in the year which equals

(3) the income generated by production in the country in the year – that is, compensation of employees, taxes on production and imports less subsidies, and gross operating surplus (or profits)

The most common approach to measuring and quantifying GDP is the expenditure method:

GDP = private consumption + gross investment + government spending + (exports − imports), or,

$$GDP = C + I + G + (X - M)$$

Gross Value Added (GVA) is the difference between output and *intermediate consumption* for any given sector/industry. It is the difference between the value of goods and services produced and the cost of raw materials and other inputs which are used up in production. GVA + taxes on products − subsidies on products = GDP

Foreign exchange earnings are proceeds from the export of goods and services of a country and the returns from its foreign investments, denominated in convertible currencies.

As we shall discuss in Chapter 7, countries are developing Tourism Satellite Accounts (TSA) to bring together basic data on the key economic variables that relate to tourism and present them in a consistent and authoritative way using internationally endorsed concepts and definitions.

The contribution of tourism to the economy in respect of the above types of variables can be direct or indirect.

The direct contribution occurs when the visitor makes purchases from suppliers of goods and services within the region. The direct contribution is solely concerned with the immediate effect of expenditure made by tourists. Such purchases may cover a variety of items such as accommodation, transport, food and beverage, shopping, touring, entertainment and so on. For example, when a tourist uses a taxi service, the direct output effect includes only the service of the taxi driver and the direct employment effect includes the proportion of the driver's employment that is spent driving tourists. Similarly, an increase in the number of tourists staying overnight in hotels directly affects sales in the accommodation sector. Applied to all tourist expenditure, the TSA enables such variables as direct tourism GVA, direct tourism GDP, direct tourism output and direct tourism employment to be estimated.

The indirect contribution occurs when firms that sell goods and services to visitors purchase inputs from other firms and these other firms (suppliers) purchase inputs from other firms (suppliers). 'Indirect effects' are the production changes resulting from various rounds of re-spending of the tourism industry's receipts on products and service inputs from other industries. For example, hotels and restaurants purchase carpets, linen, pool chemicals and computers from suppliers who purchase fuel, stationery, power, furnishings and so on from other firms that purchase their inputs from other firms and so on. Almost every industry in economy is affected to some extent by the indirect effects of the initial tourist expenditure. Application of Input–Output (I–O) modelling (see Chapter 8) allows the estimation of variables such as indirect tourism GVA, indirect tourism GDP, indirect tourism output and indirect tourism employment.

The indirect contribution of tourism is the GVA, GDP and employment that are attributable to industries which provide inputs to produce tourism output of industries characterised as 'Tourism Industries' in the satellite account. To illustrate, consider the value added associated with the production of crude oil that is subsequently used in petroleum manufacturing and then used in transport of a tourist. In a country's national accounts and other industry statistics this value added would be recorded against the mining and manufacturing industries, whereas it is really an indirect effect of tourism expenditure.

To continue the above example, Salma (2004) notes that the taxi driver during his/her shift buys fuel from a petrol station, spare parts from a car mechanic, meals and drinks during his/her shift from a cafe and so on. Service stations, car repairer workshops and food outlets all hire staff and produce the goods and services required by the taxi drivers, who in turn provide services to passengers, some of whom are tourists. The food outlet in turn engages food and drink manufacturers, newspaper and magazine publishers, electricity companies, delivery services and many other industries to provide the necessary inputs required to prepare the products it sells. Similarly, many industries are involved in supplying the necessary inputs to the gasoline stations and the car repair workshops. The chain effects on output and jobs started by the initial taxi service demand of the tourist comprise what is termed tourism's indirect effects on output, value added, GDP and employment. In this way, they reflect the value of production and employment that occurs on an economy-wide basis as a result of the demand of tourists for goods and services. Indirect effects result from redistributing the value added, GDP and employment from outside the tourism sector to the tourism sector.

The indirect effects of tourism consumption can be estimated and added to TSA estimates of tourism's direct contribution to the economy to provide an estimate of tourism's worth to the national economy. Salma (2004) has estimated that the indirect contribution of inbound tourism in Australia is greater than the direct contribution in terms of GVA, thus more than doubling the contribution of tourism reported in the Australian TSA. The indirect effects of tourism consumption can be estimated and added to TSA estimates of tourism's direct contribution to the economy to provide an estimate of tourism's worth to the national economy. The indirect economic contribution model also provides the basis for more sophisticated analyses of the impact of tourism and the comparison of alternative policy options using economic modelling (see Chapter 9).

6.3 THE ECONOMIC IMPACTS OF TOURISM

While the *economic contribution* of tourism measures the size and overall significance of the industry within an economy, e*conomic impact* refers to the *changes* in the economic contribution resulting from specific events or activities that comprise 'shocks' to the tourism system. This should not be confused with the contribution itself (Dwyer *et al.*, 2009).

There is now an extensive literature on estimating the economic impacts of tourism. This literature shows how the impacts of changes in tourism expenditure, perhaps coming about because of tourism promotion, airline de-regulation or the holding of special events (positive shocks) or the imposition of tourism taxes, or external shocks such as SARS, terrorist attacks or tsunamis (negative shocks), can be evaluated in economic terms. While different techniques are used to estimate these impacts, a major objective of such estimates has been to inform policy makers as to the appropriate allocation of resources both within the tourism sector itself and between tourism and other industry sectors. Particular attention is usually given to the estimates of the impact of tourism shocks on macroeconomic variables such as GDP, or overall economic activity, or sometimes, on aggregate consumption.

In Figure 6.1 the S curve represents the supply curve of tourism goods and services in a country and D_d represents the demand by residents for domestic tourism. The supply curve is upward-sloping reflecting increasing marginal costs of catering to and providing

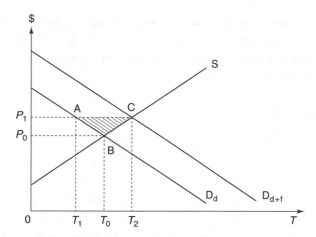

Figure 6.1 Benefits of increased inbound tourism

facilities suitable for visitor needs. The upward-sloping supply curve indicates that an expansion of tourism puts upward pressure on the prices of scarce inputs, including land, labour and capital. Of particular relevance in many destinations is land adjacent to areas of natural beauty, beaches, historic sites and so on which increase in price. In the absence of inbound tourism, the equilibrium price of tourism services is P_0 with T_0 supplied to residents. Tourism expenditure (domestic demand) is OP_0BT_0.

Assume that inbound (foreign) tourism is opened up, shifting the demand curve out from D_d to D_{d+f}. The difference between D_d and D_{d+f} is the demand for inbound tourism. The equilibrium price of tourism in the destination now rises from P_0 to P_1, with total tourism in the country rising from T_0 to T_2. However, there is some displacement of domestic tourism by inbound tourism. Residents reduce their volume of domestic tourism from T_0 to T_1, with inbound tourism now $T_2 - T_1$. Following the change, sales relating to domestic tourism expenditure are OP_1AT_1, while sales to foreign tourists are T_1ACT_2. The total change in tourism expenditure is $OP_1CT_2 - OP_0BT_0$.

This expenditure by visitors to a destination represents an injection of 'new money' into that destination. On the standard view, this new expenditure gives rise to direct, indirect and induced effects, leading to increases in economic activity at that destination.

6.3.1 DIRECT EFFECTS

The direct effects of tourist expenditure fall on the suppliers who sell goods and services directly to tourists. Some of these firms are within, and others are outside, what is taken to be 'the tourist industry'. The initial tourism expenditure thus has a direct effect on economic activity in the form of sales revenues, income to businesses for goods and services sold to tourists, salaries and wages to households for tourism-related employment and revenues to the government through tourism-related taxation and fees.

217

Direct effects give rise to both indirect effects and induced effects. These effects are captured in flow-on ('secondary' or 'ripple') effects as the initial tourist money is spent and re-spent through the economy by firms and households, stimulating income and employment throughout the economy.

6.3.2 INDIRECT EFFECTS

Indirect effects are generated by the circulation of tourism expenditures in the destination through domestic inter-business transactions. Indirect effects result from 'flow-ons' or 'upstream effects' when direct suppliers purchase inputs from other firms in the destination which, in turn, purchase inputs from other firms and so on. This indirect expenditure provides further income to other businesses, to households and to government. They, in turn, will re-spend the income received in order to buy necessary inputs and will provide income to other businesses, households and governments that, in turn, also purchase inputs thus continuing the process. Almost every industry in the economy is affected to some extent by the indirect effects of the initial tourist expenditure.

6.3.3 INDUCED EFFECTS

Induced effects arise when the recipients of the direct and indirect expenditure (owners of firms and their employees) spend their increased incomes. That is, some of the income received by households and businesses will be re-spent 'downstream' on the consumption of goods and services which are, in most cases, unrelated to the supply of tourism products. For example, wage and salary earners and firm owners will pay rent, buy groceries, theatre tickets, CDs and so on. This, in turn, sets off a process of successive rounds of purchases by intermediate firms, plus further consumption, adding to GDP and employment.

This process is displayed in Figure 6.2. Suppose a tourist buys a meal in a restaurant (new tourism expenditure). Parts of the cost of the meal will go to the purchase of inputs from other industries, such as food, electricity, the printing of menus, rent of the premises, the purchase of tablecloths and so on, and also to restaurant employee wages, owner profits and taxes. Some of these purchases will be sourced from local suppliers while others will be imported from outside the destination. The local suppliers, in turn, will buy inputs from other suppliers and so on (indirect effects). Further, owners of firms and their employees will spend their increases in disposable (after-tax) income and profits (induced effects). Once again, this expenditure sets off a process of successive rounds of purchases by supplying industries and further induced consumption. The money from the initial direct expenditure keeps circulating around the economy until it eventually leaks away.

The sum of the direct, indirect and induced effects is the *total effect*. The total effects of a specific tourism demand shock are the overall increases in output, sales, value added, GDP, household income and employment.

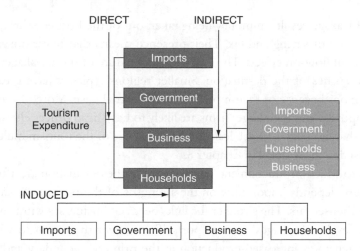

Figure 6.2 Direct, indirect and induced effects of tourism expenditure

Source: Ennew (2003)

6.3.4 LEAKAGES

At each stage of the multiplier process there are leakages that occur. The main forms of leakages from the direct and secondary effects of a change in tourist expenditure are savings, taxes and imports.

- Not all direct household income (wages and salaries) received by local residents may be spent. Rather, some of it may be saved, in which case it contributes nothing further to local economic stimulus. Some business earnings may be retained for a period to build up funds for later investment.
- Taxes, whether direct or indirect, also result in money being removed from the economy, at least in the short term. Taxes decrease the spending ability of taxpayers, both personal and corporate, and so prevent these monies from being able to contribute to further economic stimulus.
- Any import content of final goods and services associated with tourist expenditure represents a leakage out of the host economy. Import payments can take several forms, such as repatriation of profits to foreign corporations; servicing of debt to foreign lenders; remittance of incomes outside the study area, for example, by foreign workers; payment for imported consumption and capital goods; and promotion and advertising undertaken outside the destination. It should be noted that for purposes of regional economic impact analysis an 'imported' product or input need not be sourced internationally. To qualify as 'imported' it suffices that the item purchased is produced outside of the area under study. Thus, analysis of the economic impacts of tourism on the Côte d'Azur would treat wine from Provence as imported, whereas this would be regarded as sourced domestically from the perspective of tourism to France.

Each form of leakage results in money being taken out of the host economy, temporarily at least in the case of saving and tax. Their presence means that fewer dollars are left to create subsequent flow-on effects. The exact size and nature of these leakages will depend on the characteristics of the destination. Smaller regions typically have greater leakages than larger regions because of their more limited industrial base. More of their inputs are likely to be imported and their larger firms are likely to have head offices elsewhere or have non-resident shareholders. All such leakages limit the size of the tourism multiplier, which will be discussed in more detail in Chapter 8.

The extent to which production and employment in the destination are affected by visitor expenditure depends importantly on the strengths of the business linkages between tourism and other sectors. The stronger the links between businesses within a destination, the lower the level of 'leakages' from imports. The greater the extent to which tourism development generates increased production in the primary, secondary and tertiary sectors, the greater is the tourism multiplier and consequent impact of injected expenditure on GDP and employment. The issues will be discussed in detail in Chapter 8.

Estimating the economic impact of a shock to tourism demand or supply implies that the overall change in the economic contribution must take account of the extensive interactive effects which occur across the economy. For example, when inbound tourism expenditure increases, and markets are competitive, other industries are affected. Industries complementary to tourism will expand, but, on balance, economic activity elsewhere will tend to decline as tourism draws resources away from them. To assume no contraction in other industries is to assume, *inter alia*, that the tourism expansion puts no upward pressure on the exchange rate, real wages or the price of land and capital. It is possible that overall output will increase, because increased factor inputs may be used, but the increase is likely to be less than the initial expenditure injection.

In Chapters 8 and 9, we shall argue that the estimated impact of higher visitor spending is highly sensitive to the assumptions one makes about the economy. We shall emphasise that economy-wide effects must be taken into account in determining the impacts of increased tourism expenditure on a destination. An expanding tourism industry tends to 'crowd out' other sectors of economic activity. The extent of these 'crowding out' effects depends, in turn, on factor constraints, changes in the exchange rate, the workings of labour markets and the macroeconomic policy context. At this time, the following points may be noted:

- In the competition for scarce resources associated with an expanding tourism industry, increased costs reduce the competitiveness of other sectors in the economy, particularly export-oriented and import-competing industries, diminishing output and employment levels.
- Where resources are drawn away from traditional export-oriented industries, increased production costs result in these industries.

- Any increased investment associated with tourism growth places further pressure on the exchange rate, increasing the feedback effects for the period of capital inflow.
- Where tax increases or borrowing are used to finance increased government expenditure associated with tourism growth, this acts as a brake on the growth in private consumption, limiting the positive effects on income and employment.
- Where cost pressures reduce the competitiveness of a nation's tourist industry, relative to other destinations, this may also result in increased outbound tourism, implying a loss of production and employment opportunities from domestic tourism.
- The impacts of tourism growth on employment will vary according to the causes of any existing unemployment, the efficiency of the labour market in terms of real wage flexibility, the labour intensiveness of different sectors in the economy affected by tourism spending and government fiscal policy.
- Unless there is significant excess capacity in tourist-related industries, the primary effect of an economy-wide expansion in tourism is to alter the industrial structure of the economy rather than to generate a large increase in aggregate economic activity.
- Since tourism growth can impact adversely on the size of other industry sectors, we cannot consider the economic impacts of tourism in isolation from inter-industry effects.

The economic impacts of the increased expenditure must be estimated using some form of economic model. There are two main approaches to estimating the economic impacts of this change in expenditure. These are the approach using I–O multipliers and the Computable General Equilibrium (CGE) approach. We will discuss these approaches in detail in Chapters 8 and 9.

6.4   THE COSTS AND BENEFITS OF TOURISM

The benefits to a country from tourism seem obvious. The expenditure of foreign tourists, for example, by increasing business and trading opportunities for existing and new firms can create jobs, generate income, increase the nation's foreign exchange earnings, increase government revenues from taxation, stimulate investment in infrastructure, diversify industry structure and promote regional economic development. The assumed benefits become larger when multiplier effects are considered – increased tourism demand results in further expansions of economic activity to provide for additional inputs into the tourism industry. Inbound tourism can also promote certain benefits such as the preservation of valued natural environments, flora and fauna, increased variety of attractions and facilities available to residents and increased opportunities for social and cultural exchange.

The costs of inbound tourism are perhaps not so 'obvious' and must be taken into account in an overall assessment of its impact on the economy. These costs are usually taken to include such items as the cost of imported goods and services ('leakages') used to satisfy tourist needs, the costs of general price rises accompanying tourism development, the costs of increased pollution, congestion and despoliation of fragile environments and adverse socio-cultural impacts resulting from tourism growth.

Despite the common use of the labels 'benefits' and 'costs' attached to tourism expenditure and its effects, they are very often misused. The economic approach to measuring 'costs' and 'benefits' will be discussed in Chapter 10. For present purposes we discuss why it is incorrect to regard economic impacts as benefits and hence as a basis for policy making.

6.4.1 ECONOMIC IMPACTS ARE NOT BENEFITS

Contrary to what might be implied in much of the economic impacts literature, estimates of the economic impacts of different tourism growth scenarios or alternative policy prescriptions provide, in themselves, an imperfect basis for decisions about resource allocation. The problem arises from a failure to distinguish clearly between the *impacts* and the (net) *benefits* of tourism growth. The failure to make the distinction clear has resulted in the situation where tourism stakeholders generally regard 'impacts' as synonymous with 'benefits'.

Economists know that prices do not always reflect full benefits from consumption or full costs of production. Since changes in national output resulting from inbound tourist expenditure reflect unadjusted market prices, the economic impacts are an inaccurate measure of the real net benefits to a country from this activity.

Impacts on economic activity are measured by changes in GDP or similar measures as discussed above. Changes in GDP are a measure of the value of the additional economic activity which occurs as a result of changes in tourism expenditure, but this measure does not allow for the costs of achieving this extra activity. The provision of goods and services to satisfy tourist needs requires the use of scarce resources in their production and these resources must be paid for. To enable the addition to GDP, inputs are needed – additional labour must be hired, additional capital must be made available (often by borrowing from abroad, given the limitations on funds locally available in many developing countries and the global nature of capital markets), more land will be alienated and more natural resources will be used up. Thus, when additional resources are used to enable the extra activity resulting from a positive shock to tourism, the change in GDP exaggerates how much better off the country and, more precisely, its residents are. Spending $50 million to increase GDP by $100 million sounds like a good deal, even if it is not. To equate 'impacts' with 'benefits' is to regard a statement that GDP would increase by $100 million as equivalent to a statement that the community would be better off to the extent of $100 million.

Consider the following questions:

• If $10 million additional promotion increases tourism receipts by $60 million, and increases GDP by $50 million, is this worthwhile or not?

- Is a government subsidy of $5 million to a special event, which has an impact on economic activity of $50 million, a good deal?
- Is it worth sacrificing $50 million of profit to a country's international airline to gain an additional $200 million in GDP from greater tourism?

Such questions cannot be answered without distinguishing 'impacts' and 'net benefits'.

In contrast to impacts, 'net benefits' are a measure of the value of the gain in economic activity less the cost needed to enable this extra activity. Net benefits are a measure of how much better off, in economic terms, members of the community are in aggregate given some change in economic activity. A measure of the net benefit to the community as a whole can be obtained by adding up the monetary evaluation of the gains and losses experienced by all in the community. As a result of a change, individual firms, consumers and workers may be better or worse off, given changes in their own consumption, income and level of effort, as well as through how they are affected by government consumption. Firms can gain if profits are increased, consumers gain from price reductions or quality improvements and workers can gain from additional wages less any costs of additional effort. Governments may gain from a change, through increased tax receipts at existing tax rates, and they will pass these gains on to the community in a number of ways – through tax cuts, or additional expenditures which benefit the community; or they may save their gains and pass them on to future generations.

6.4.2 IMPORTANCE FOR POLICY

It is important that the net benefits from tourism (i.e. benefits less costs) be assessed accurately for policy reasons. Estimates of net benefits can help to inform such policy matters as the optimal level of tourism promotion (Dwyer & Forsyth, 1992, 1994) and the extent of government involvement in promotion and also such issues as appropriate aviation strategies, regulatory controls over the tourism industry, tourism taxes, investment incentives and formulation of a National Tourism Strategy.

The problem with the usual outputs of most economic impact models is that they are in gross terms, and this limits their use in policy making. The fact that a particular change has a positive impact, in terms of increased economic activity, does not necessarily mean that it is a desirable change – it all depends on what are the costs of achieving this extra activity. To measure the net benefits from inbound tourism, one must subtract the costs of the inputs used to produce the additional output required, since these have value in alternative uses. Changes in GDP resulting from some tourism expenditure shock are, therefore, a poor measure of net benefits. Thus, production may increase by $100 million, but if $90 million of additional factors are used, the benefit to the destination country is only $10 million. From a national viewpoint, what matters are the net returns resulting from the allocation of certain resources to satisfy tourist needs and whether greater returns could result from allocation of these resources to other uses. In addition, there can be environmental costs, which are typically not included in national accounts but which may be real costs nonetheless.

In spite of these cautions, in debates on tourism policy issues (and indeed, more widely) impacts on economic activity or GDP are often taken to be measures of the benefits of an initiative. For sound decision-making involving resource allocation, estimates of the *net* outcomes are required. This is true of private as well as of public decisions. Consider a company contemplating an advertising campaign: is one, which costs $10 million, and yields additional sales of $50 million, a good investment? It is not possible to tell with only this information, since the increase in sales does not give us the *net* improvement in the company's fortunes. To determine this, it is necessary to subtract the costs of producing the additional products for sale. If the total additional cost, including costs of goods sold, is $35 million, then the campaign will add $15 million to profit for a cost of $10 million; in short, it is worthwhile. If additional production costs were $45 million, the answer would be different. When funds are to be invested, either by private firms or by governments, it is necessary to estimate the net addition to the bottom line – to profit, in the case of the private firm, and to benefits to the community in the case of the government.

6.5   SOURCES OF COSTS AND BENEFITS

Economic theory informs us that, under certain circumstances, private markets can solve the economic problem of unlimited wants and scarce resources in an efficient or optimal manner. Market prices serve as signals or incentives to guide resources and products into their most highly valued uses. However, if there are no markets for some valuable resources and products or if markets do not function properly, the resulting resource allocation will not be optimal. This situation is known as *market failure*. Market failure occurs when market prices do not reflect the full social costs or benefits associated with a product or service.

To measure the net benefits of a tourism change, we need to identify in what ways the revenues gained from additional tourism differ from the opportunity costs of the inputs used in supplying it. Market prices often cannot be relied upon as measures of benefit or cost to the community as a whole.

Where output changes resulting from a policy initiative are significant, the valuation of benefits takes into account both the market price and any producer or consumer surplus. The changes to economic welfare that result from a proposal will comprise the total of any changes in benefits and costs or consumer and producer surplus. We discussed these concepts in Chapter 5.

We can identify some distortions which, to varying degrees, exist in all economies and which affect the net national benefits from inbound tourism. These distortions arise from the presence of terms of trade effects, market power, taxes and subsidies, government revenue effects, labour market effects, foreign exchange effects and the existence of externalities.

6.5.1 TERMS OF TRADE EFFECTS

When there is an increase in the demand for the products of an industry, and supply is less than perfectly elastic (additional supply can only be achieved at higher cost), prices will increase. Resources that are in limited supply will command a higher price. For example, a tourism boom in a city will lead to an increase in the price of land suitable for hotels. When tourism is an export industry, this can lead to a net benefit for the economy. When there are foreign tourists buying services, and the price gets bid up because of an increase in demand, the existing tourists will pay a higher price for the services they are already buying, and the owners of the facilities in short supply will gain additional profits. For example, owners of hotels preferred by tourists will gain higher profits. This is a net gain to the economy. The size of this effect depends on supply conditions; it will be larger if increases in supply can only be achieved at significantly higher cost.

Figure 6.1 shows that inbound tourism can generate benefits to the host country. As a result of inbound tourism, suppliers of tourism services for the host country obtain an increase in producer surplus equal to area $P_0 BCP_1$. Due to the price increase from P_0 to P_1, residents who use domestic tourism services experience a reduction in consumer surplus equal to area $P_0 BAP_1$.

Since the gain in producer surplus exceeds the loss in consumer surplus, there is a potential Pareto improvement equal to area ABC. In such circumstances the host country gains from inbound tourism. It is sometimes claimed that higher prices caused by foreign tourism in some areas are forcing domestic tourists out. These claims indicate that the terms of trade effect may not be negligible. Even if foreign tourism results in domestic residents being priced out of their own facilities, the nation as a whole can gain. While such gains may be reduced as a result of foreign ownership of tourism facilities (a point made by Copeland (1991)), the reduction in benefits to the host country is not as great as is commonly thought. We shall discuss the impacts of foreign direct investment in tourism in Chapter 14. Where the price increases reduce the competitiveness of a country's tourism industry compared to foreign destinations, there is likely to be some shift by domestic residents from domestic to foreign tourism.

The size of the terms of trade effect varies country to country. The size of the net gain from increased tourism depends on the impact on prices of the increase in tourist visits, the elasticities of demand for and supply of tourism services and on the proportion of foreign visitors in the total number. For many destinations the terms of trade effect is not large, though it is unambiguously positive. This is because the elasticity of supply is likely to be quite high, though less than infinite. It takes a large increase in tourism to produce a perceptible increase in overall tourism prices. It is an effect that comes about regardless of whether there are distortions present in the tourism industry, or elsewhere in the economy.

6.5.2   TAXATION, GOVERNMENT REVENUE AND SUBSIDIES

In the presence of taxes and subsidies, market prices may not be measures of the opportunity cost, or shadow prices, of inputs or outputs. When there is expenditure by a foreign tourist who pays a market price above the shadow price, there is a net benefit to the host country. Alternatively, tourist purchases or use of subsidised goods and services can impose net costs on the host economy.

Market prices of inputs to and outputs of tourism goods and services may not measure opportunity costs where taxes or subsidies are involved. Tourism, like other services, is subject to taxation, such as Goods and Services Taxes (GST) or Value Added Taxes (VAT). Some products that tourists use moderately intensively, such as fuel, are very heavily taxed. In addition, there are many other taxes which might impinge on the costs of offering tourism services, for example, payroll taxes, stamp duties and company taxes. Furthermore, some of the inputs used by the tourism industry, such as labour, are subject to taxation (e.g. income tax). Other goods and services are also subjected to these types of taxes. We shall discuss taxation issues in some detail in Chapter 15. When foreign tourists pay market prices for goods and services in excess of costs of production (opportunity costs), there is a net benefit to the economy.

Taxes cause economic agents to alter their behaviour, and produce outcomes which differ from what would occur were taxes lower or absent. In some cases, these 'distortions' benefit society, such as where high rates of taxation reduce fuel consumption and associated Greenhouse Gas (GHG) emissions. Normally, however, they are costly to society, such as where high taxes on labour cause unemployment traps, or cause employees to reduce the number of hours they are prepared to work.

Suppose some tourism service is subject to a tax. Figure 6.3 illustrates the case of a specific tax on a commercial product, for example, a bed tax. The tax raises the supply price above marginal cost. The supply curve shifts up from S to $S + t$. Suppose also that increased inbound tourism pushes the demand curve out from D_d to D_{d+f}. This results in a shift from equilibrium E_0 (price P_0, output T_0) to equilibrium E_1 (price P_1, output T_1). As before, domestic consumers lose (area $P_1AE_0P_0$), and owners of tourism resources gain producer surplus (area $P_0E_0E_1P_1$). However, there is also a gain in taxes paid, shown by the area BCE_1E_0, which equals $t \times (T_1 - T_0)$. The tourists are charged a price P_1; however, it only costs T_1C to supply them.

The additional government revenue contributed by inbound tourism through taxation, directly and indirectly, is not an effect over and above the tourist expenditure contribution to GDP. The exception is where the shadow (real) price of government revenue exceeds its nominal value. Further, the shadow price of government revenue may exceed its nominal value. Raising revenue involves imposing distorting taxes and thus the marginal cost of raising \$1 to a nation typically exceeds \$1. We shall further discuss this point in Chapter 10.

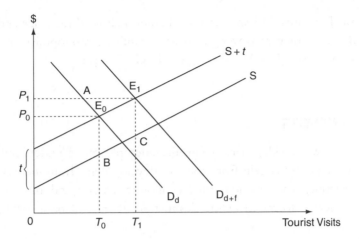

Figure 6.3 Taxation as a source of benefit to a destination

Prices may also be different from costs because of the presence of subsidies. This may be the case with the infrastructure which tourists use. Tourists may make use of facilities, such as urban centres, parks and museums, passenger rail services, freeways, which may be supplied free or on a subsidised basis. Australia's Productivity Commission has argued that since the tourism industry overlaps with a number of conventionally defined industries, a proportion of assistance to those industries can also be regarded as assistance to tourism (Dwyer & Spurr, 2009). When some of the additional tourist expenditure is used to purchase goods or services which are subsidised by the government, this will impose additional costs on the host economy, since tourists pay less than the cost of supplying the services to them.

6.5.3 MARKET POWER

It is possible that the prices paid for some tourism goods and services do not reflect their opportunity or real costs to the economy because of the presence of supplier market power. In such cases profits are higher than required to pay the cost of capital. Some suppliers may provide goods and services at prices above marginal and average costs, and thus they will profit from increased tourism expenditure. Thus, we find that some ferry services, with a monopoly of particular routes, charge high prices for passage, as do accommodation providers located close to tourist attractions.

Typically, when market power is exercised, prices will exceed shadow prices and extra expenditure by tourists will create a net benefit – tourists pay more for services than it costs the economy to supply them. In most countries, though, except for aviation, there is unlikely to be much market power at the level of individual suppliers in the tourist industry since many of the industries (accommodation, restaurants, road transport, etc.) which make up tourism are quite competitive, keeping to the minimum necessary to cover the cost of capital. Figures 4.13 and 4.16 in Chapter 4 showed the price and output that would result if the tourism firm were a profit-maximising monopolist or monopolistic competitor. In both cases, $P > MC$ at the given level of output.

6.5.4 UNDEREMPLOYMENT

In many countries worldwide, there is chronic unemployment/underemployment, and their reduction is a potential gain from tourism development. If an increase in inbound tourism, for example, leads to additional economic activity and thus to less unemployment (or underemployment) in the destination, there will be a net benefit to the economy.

Additional tourism expenditure could result in increased employment, if it occurs in a region with unemployment, or in an underemployed economy. Typically, with unemployment, owners of the resources wish to supply the resources at less than the going price. In such a case, the wage paid would exceed the supply price (or shadow wage of labour); thus, there would be a net gain to the economy. In these circumstances, the supply curve of labour lies above the marginal cost of provision of tourism services. Therefore, if unemployed individuals gain jobs, they are likely to be better off; they would be willing to work for less than the extra income they get (wage less tax less foregone unemployment benefits). With moderate tax rates and unemployment benefits, the supply price of labour could be well below the market wage, In other words, the shadow wage of labour, or its opportunity cost, would be low relative to the market wage. The situation is similar to Figure 6.2 except that taxes are not the reason for the divergence in this case.

If an increase in inbound tourism leads to additional economic activity and thus less unemployment, there will be a net benefit to the economy from this tourism. In many countries worldwide, there remains chronic unemployment. A major effect of the Global Financial Crisis (GFC) has been to increase unemployment levels in countries that previously had low unemployment. Greater existing levels of unemployment in a tourism destination can provide a basis for potentially large gains to an economy from increased tourism. These issues will be discussed in greater detail in Chapter 10.

However, as discussed in Chapter 9, we cannot be certain that an increase in tourism will necessarily lead to an increase in overall economic activity and to a decline in unemployment. This is because of the ways in which labour markets work. Increases in demand for the tourism product may lead not only to increases in demand for tourism inputs but also to increases in input prices, especially wages. Wage rises can limit or eliminate any gains in greater employment (Dwyer & Forsyth, 1998). Given that unemployment seems to remain high, even when the economy experiences boom conditions, there is evidence for this view of the labour market. As we will discuss in Chapter 9, labour market problems are often neglected in economic impact assessment, despite their crucial importance for outcomes of tourism demand shocks on economic activity.

6.5.5 FOREIGN EXCHANGE EFFECT

Additional tourism will add to foreign exchange receipts. This is not an additional benefit over and above those identified, except in so far as the destination country places a value on foreign exchange that is different from the market rate of exchange. If exchange rates are not free to vary to equilibrate demand for and supply of the currency, or where there are trade distortions such as tariffs and export subsidies, the shadow foreign exchange rate will differ from the market rate. If, for example, tariffs are in effect, additional earnings of foreign exchange will be valued in excess of their market value, since the additional imports made possible will be valued by consumers at more than the cost to buy them (the government receives the tariff revenues). In some cases, the value of the domestic currency may be so distorted that prices expressed in it are virtually useless as measures of the true value of resources to the country as a whole. This implies that foreign exchange is actually more valuable to the economy than the official rate implies. If the shadow price of foreign exchange exceeds the value represented by the market exchange rate, there will be a benefit to the economy from extra tourism expenditure. It is also possible that exchange rate appreciation will lead to a benefit through an increase in the overall terms of trade. If the shadow price of foreign exchange exceeds the value represented by the market exchange rate, there will be a benefit to the economy from extra tourism expenditure. This issue will be discussed further in Chapter 10 on Cost-Benefit Analysis (CBA).

6.5.6 EXTERNALITIES

Externalities exist when a third party receives benefits or incurs costs arising from an economic transaction in which he or she is not a direct participant. We can distinguish four main types of externalities:

External diseconomies of production: uncompensated costs imposed on some firms by the expansion of output by other firms. For example, the discharge of waste materials by restaurants located along a river affects the costs of all firms in obtaining clean water.

External economies of production: uncompensated benefits conferred on some firms by the expansion of output of other firms. For example, some hotels may train workers and these workers find employment in other firms (which benefit from employee productivity and savings in training costs).

External diseconomies of consumption: uncompensated costs imposed on some individuals by the consumption expenditures of other individuals. For example, smoking in a public place has a harmful effect on non-smokers.

External economies of consumption: uncompensated benefits conferred on some individuals by the increased consumption of a product by other individuals. For example, increased expenditures to maintain a lawn by a homeowner increase the value of neighbouring homes also, while an attendee at a theme park may derive a benefit from sharing the enjoyment of other patrons.

When externalities exist, there is a divergence between private returns – those accruing to the direct parties in an economic transaction – and social returns – those accruing to the indirect parties in such a transaction. The market fails when the social costs or social benefits that arise from the production and consumption of private goods and services are not fully reflected in market prices. There is little incentive for firms or consumers either to curb external costs (since they do directly pay for them) or to foster external benefits (since they do not directly benefit from them), and so, while costs are passed on to the public at large, benefits tend not to be.

Positive externalities

Products or services that create positive externalities are typically under-consumed (and under-produced) in the free-market economy. This means that there is a divergence between private benefit and public benefit when the good is consumed (i.e. the public benefit is greater than the private benefit). Since consumers typically take into account only the expected private benefits from consumption of any good, it is likely that such goods will be under-consumed (and so under-produced). Where the social benefits exceed the private benefits, this leads to a market equilibrium quantity lower than the social optimum. In Figure 6.4, the MPB curve shows the marginal private benefits from consumption of some product or service, while MSB curve shows the marginal social benefits from consumption. The market equilibrium resulting from individuals acting in their own self-interest

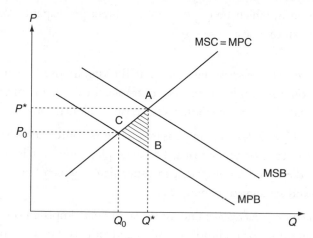

Figure 6.4 Positive externality leads to under-consumption and under-production

is output Q_0 and price P_0, whereas the socially efficient outcome (social optimum) is the output and price (Q^*, P^*) where the MSB curve cuts the demand curve. For each unit of the good that is under-consumed below Q^*, the marginal social benefits would have exceeded the costs of production. The welfare loss (social benefits foregone as a result of the reduced consumption and production) is shown as the shaded triangle ABC.

There are many examples of tourism goods generating external benefits. One example is the training of workers hired during airport or hotel construction. Any increased productivity of those workers when hired for subsequent construction activity is a social benefit. So also are the aesthetic benefits that might result to residents from demolition of derelict buildings that block scenic views. Other tourism examples include holidays which allow individuals to de-stress and to be more productive after returning to work or hospitality training programmes which lead to increased efficiencies and skills transfer. Similarly, a picturesque streetscape will be a source of pleasure to passers-by. Tourism may also foster agglomeration with increased tourism making viable more regular air services to a town, or greater variety of restaurants and entertainment facilities. Bringing about a socially optimal outcome (e.g. by means of government subsidies or regulations) can reduce the welfare loss associated with the free-market solution.

Negative externalities

Products and services that create negative externalities are typically over-consumed (and over-produced) in the free-market economy. If the production process imposes pollution costs on other firms and consumers, the social costs of supply will exceed the private costs of supply by the value of the negative externality. To determine the optimal level of output, it is the marginal social cost of supply rather than the firm's supply curve which is relevant.

Figure 6.5 shows a situation where the production of some product is associated with negative externalities. Figure 6.5 shows both the competitive market price-quantity

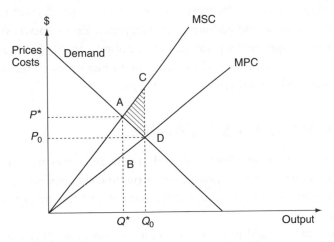

Figure 6.5 Negative externality leads to over-production and over-consumption

equilibrium and the socially optimal price-quantity combination. Q can be thought of as units of tourism services or products. The diagram distinguishes the marginal costs of supply of the product (marginal private cost, MPC), which, in a competitive market, is the sum of firms' supply curves, from the marginal social costs of its supply (MSC) curve indicating all the costs of production including the external costs. MSC is the sum of firms' marginal private costs and the marginal external costs to society that accompany extra supply of the product. At the market equilibrium outcome P_0, Q_0, there is a divergence between private marginal costs of production and the marginal social costs of production. Since suppliers typically take into account only the expected private costs of production of any good when making their output decisions, it is likely that such goods will be over-produced (and so over-consumed). Where the social costs exceed the private costs of production, this leads to a market equilibrium quantity greater than the social optimum.

As Figure 6.5 indicates, the socially efficient outcome (social optimum) would be the output and price (Q^*, P^*) where the MSC curve cuts the demand curve. For each unit of the good that is over-produced above Q^*, the marginal social costs exceed the firms' private costs of production. The loss to society from over-production to Q_0 is the shaded area ACD. This area also represents the gains to society if production by tourism firms were to be cut back from Q_0 to Q^*.

Negative externalities in tourism (external costs) arise when the environment is unable to cope with a particular level of tourism activity. Consider the individual whose property loses value because a late night disco is built in the area or the community that experiences beach pollution due to oil spills from a passenger liner. From society's (the local residents') viewpoint, the market price does not reflect the true cost of tourists visiting the area. Too much tourism is occurring and it is experienced too cheaply. The local residents incur the external costs. The firms in the industry do not consider the external costs in their willingness to supply particular quantities of tourism services at various prices. For each unit of output beyond Q^*, however, the marginal social costs of production exceed the value which consumers attach to the additional consumption. From society's (the residents') viewpoint, the market equilibrium price-quantity combination P_0, Q_0, does not reflect the true cost of tourists visiting the area. The local residents incur the external costs. Too much tourism is occurring and it is experienced too cheaply.

6.6   ECONOMY-WIDE EFFECTS ON NET BENEFITS

We have indicated that tourism growth will tend to draw resources away from other industries, inducing a contraction in their production. Structural changes in other industries have important implications for measurement of the net national benefits of the expansion in inbound tourism.

Much the same can be said in principle about the industries that contract as can be said about tourism industries. They may be taxed, or subsidised, they may possess market power and charge prices above marginal cost and they may create positive and negative externalities. They also employ labour directly and indirectly and may earn foreign exchange. Where resources are drawn away from internationally protected industries, there will tend to be a gain from a better balance of industries in the economy. And even if increased tourism numbers result in environmental effects which are, on balance, negative, contraction of other industries will result in reduced environmental impacts elsewhere. The overall environmental effects of the changing composition of industries could, on balance, be desirable or undesirable.

These considerations have important implications for the measurement of the benefits from tourism, since it is the net benefits after allowing for the contraction of other industries which is relevant. If expenditures on these other outputs create benefits, the net benefits from tourism expenditures will be correspondingly less once these have been taken into account. If the economy-wide effects are so large that there is no change in national output, then the net gains from a tourism boom will be much smaller. This is recognised by Dixon *et al.* (2002) and Blake *et al.* (2008) who introduce welfare measures into their economic modelling of demand shocks. These issues will be further discussed in Chapters 8, 9 and 10.

The issues discussed in this chapter will re-emerge at different places throughout the book. If policy makers are to make efficient decisions in respect of the resources devoted to tourism development and if policies and programmes are to be formulated to support tourism growth, the different concepts of tourism's contribution, its economic impacts and resulting net benefits must be clearly distinguished.

6.7 CONCLUSIONS AND POLICY

- Domestic and international tourism each make an economic contribution to a destination. Each has positive and negative economic impacts on that destination and each brings with it benefits and costs.
- The economic contribution of tourism is not the same thing as the economic impact of tourism. The two concepts should not be confused with each other. Tourism's total economic contribution (both direct and indirect) measures the size and overall significance of the tourism industry within an economy. It is discussed in more depth in Chapter 7.
- Tourism's economic impact refers to the changes in the economic contribution that result from specific events or activities that comprise 'shocks' to the tourism system. These changes in economic contribution (brought about by new tourism expenditure injected into a destination) generate three types of impacts or effects: direct impacts, indirect effects and induced effects. These are discussed in more depth in Chapters 8 and 9.
- Tourism to a destination brings with it costs and benefits. While the benefits may seem obvious and include such phenomena as job creation, income generation, increased

foreign exchange earnings, increased government taxation revenue, diversification of industry and promotion of regional economic development, the costs of tourism are often less obvious but relate to the leakages (cost of imported goods and services) used to satisfy tourist needs, and the costs associated with increased pollution, congestion, despoliation of fragile environments and adverse socio-cultural impacts resulting from tourism growth. The net benefits of tourism (benefits minus costs) are more fully explored in Chapter 10.

- Issues of concern in the measurement of net benefits associated with a change in tourism expenditure relate to terms of trade effects, taxation (Chapter 15); government revenue and subsidies (Chapter 11); market power; underemployment; foreign exchange effects, and externalities (Chapter 17).

- It is important that the net benefits of tourism be assessed accurately for policy reasons. Estimates of net benefits can help to determine such policy matters as the optimal level of tourism promotion, the extent of government involvement in promotion and issues such as appropriate aviation strategies, regulatory controls over the tourism industry, tourism taxes and formulation of a National Tourism Strategy.

SELF-REVIEW QUESTIONS

1. Briefly explain how tourism's economic contribution differs from its economic impacts.

2. How does tourism's direct economic contribution differ from its indirect economic contribution?

3. Use examples to explain briefly the difference in direct, indirect and induced effects that flow from new tourism expenditure.

4. Use a diagram similar to Figure 6.1 to show how, within a destination, inbound tourism may raise the price of domestic tourism, reduce the quantity of domestic tourism, but increase tourism's total expenditure.

5. Briefly discuss why tourism to a host destination carries with it costs and benefits.

6. Use a diagram to discuss the concept of the social optimum number of foreign visitors given that they generate negative externalities.

7. List the distortions, present in all economies, which can affect the extent of a nation's net benefits from inbound tourism.

ESSAY QUESTIONS

1. 'The extent to which production and employment in the destination is affected by visitor expenditure depends importantly on the strengths of the business linkages between tourism and other sectors.' Explain.

2. Tourism's economic impacts are not synonymous with its benefits. Why not?

3. Tourism benefits to a host destination are not measured in terms of either gross receipts or economic impacts. Why not?

4. Sound policy making within tourism requires a knowledge of net benefits. Discuss.

5. Explain in detail how each of the distortions present in any economy can affect the extent of the net benefits that accrue to a nation from inbound tourism.

MEASURING TOURISM'S ECONOMIC CONTRIBUTION, IMPACTS AND NET BENEFITS

CHAPTER 7

THE ECONOMIC CONTRIBUTION OF TOURISM: TOURISM SATELLITE ACCOUNTS

LEARNING OBJECTIVES

After reading this chapter, you should be able to:

1. Explain the concept of a Tourism Satellite Account (TSA).

2. Understand the important role that TSA play in estimating and understanding tourism's contribution to the economy.

3. Discuss the steps involved in compiling and updating TSA.

4. Differentiate between top-down and bottom-up approaches to designing regional TSA.

5. Evaluate TSA as a policy instrument.

6. Examine the role of TSA in helping to develop measures of tourism performance.

7.1 INTRODUCTION

Tourism has grown substantially over recent decades as an economic and social phenomenon. Unfortunately, the development of statistical concepts and frameworks for tourism has not kept pace with the changes in the nature and significance of tourism worldwide and its potential for future growth. Tourism differs from many economic activities in that it makes use of a diverse range of facilities across a large number of industrial sectors.

The problem with measuring the economic significance of tourism spending is that 'tourism' does not exist as a distinct sector in any system economic statistics or of national accounts. We raised this issue in Chapter 4. While all the products and services that are produced and consumed in meeting tourism demand are included in the core accounts, they are not readily apparent because 'tourism' is not identified as a conventional industry or product in international statistical standards (ABS, 2007). While the largest proportion of this expenditure is allocated to sectors typically associated with tourism such as accommodation, transportation, car hire, duty-free purchases, restaurants, tours and attractions, tourists also spend money in other sectors when they gamble, buy shoes, clothes, gifts, theatre tickets, ice creams, taxi hire and such like. Since it is not possible to identify tourism as a single 'industry' in the national accounts, its value to the economy is not readily revealed. Tourism activity is 'hidden' in other industry activities (accommodation, transportation, telecommunications and so on).

Several historical concerns may be identified here that highlight the need for improved statistical bases for tourism analysis and policy (IRTS, 2008; TSA, 2008):

1. Many nations typically have emphasised agriculture, mining and manufacturing as the key sectors driving economic growth, failing to appreciate the size and significance of tourism and service industries in general.

2. Tourism data tend not to be well incorporated in the complex system of official statistics, and often do not receive the full attention they deserve. Within most existing statistical systems, it has been extremely difficult if not impossible to adequately document the full scale and scope of tourism-related economic activities. This suggests that any attempt to examine the economic contribution of tourism that is focused on systems of national accounts only, and which highlights only tourism-related sectors, is likely seriously to underestimate the overall expenditure by tourists and thus its economic significance.

3. These types of problems are common to the entire service sector which historically has received far less extensive treatment in national statistical programs than primary and secondary industries. But because of this accounting issue, stakeholders in the tourism industry are concerned that governments underestimate the benefits that tourism brings to their economies – particularly so relative to other industries such as manufacturing where the outputs are easier to observe and quantify and which, for historical reasons, are more clearly reflected in governmental statistical collections.

4. Comprehensive and reliable statistics are essential for policy-makers to make effective decisions about resource allocation. Only with sufficient and adequate data that generate credible statistics is it possible to compare the performance of tourism with other industry activity. Besides measuring tourism's economic contribution to a country, tourism statistics are necessary for designing and evaluating marketing strategies, strengthening inter-institutional relations and evaluating the efficiency and effectiveness of management decisions to support tourism development.

TSA have now become the unifying framework of most of the components of the System of Tourism Statistics (UNWTO, 2008). As a consequence of the limitations of existing accounting systems, increasing number of countries have developed or are developing Tourism Satellite Accounts (TSA) consistent with the Recommended Methodological Framework (TSA-RMF). This framework has been developed by the Commission of the European Communities, the Organization for Economic Cooperation and Development (OECD), the United Nations World Tourism Organization (UNWTO) and the World Travel and Tourism Council (WTTC), and approved by the United Nations Statistical Commission (TSA RMF, 2008).

7.2 WHAT IS A TSA?

Satellite accounts allow an understanding of the size and role of activities which are not separately identified in the conventional national accounting framework. They allow an expansion of the national accounts for selected areas of interest while maintaining the concepts and structures of the core accounts.

In a TSA, all of the tourism-associated economic activity is identified in a separate but related account, that is, an account which is a satellite of the core national accounts. TSA are compiled using a combination of visitor expenditure data, industry data and supply and use relationships in the system of national accounts Supply and Use Tables (SUT). The SUT for an economy provide the framework in which data for visitor expenditure (demand) and industry output (supply) are integrated and made consistent in the TSA. The best-known STU, Input–Output (I–O) tables, capture the interdependence that exists between sectors of the economy. Through a matrix table, they describe how one sector's output becomes another sector's input, showing the I–O flows (the exchange of intermediate goods) between various sectors of the economy. As such, they are used to predict the effects of changes in one industry on output, income and employment in other industries. I–O tables will be discussed in Chapter 8.

TSA are based on the accounts for industries which are reported in the national accounts. It is argued that tourism accounts for a proportion of the outputs of a range of industries which are explicitly recorded in the accounts. The basic procedure in satellite accounting is to claim a 'share' of sales of each commodity or industry to tourism. TSA use these estimates of tourist expenditure and then allocate tourism expenditure to different industries. Thus tourism might account for 95% of sales expenditure in 'Accommodation', 90% in 'Air Transport', 30% in 'Ground Transport', and say, 15% in 'Retail Trade' and so on for other industry sectors. Thus the outputs of these industries which can be attributed to 'Tourism' are estimated and aggregated to obtain an estimate of the output of 'Tourism'. The result is a set of accounts documenting output, value added, employment and so forth for the tourism industry, consisting of the sum of the various parts of other industries which are attributable to tourism. The steps required to estimate tourism output, Tourism Gross Value Added (TGVA), Tourism Gross Domestic Product (TGDP) and tourism employment are set out in Box 7.1.

BOX 7.1 Calculating tourism GVA, tourism GDP and tourism employment

The following steps are required in the calculation of tourism gross value added:

1. Identify which products in the economy are purchased by visitors:

(i) Derive an estimate of tourism consumption for each tourism product;

(ii) Remove product taxes and subsidies, margins and imports from tourism consumption of each product at purchasers' prices to derive tourism consumption at basic prices – this represents the domestic output of tourism.

2. Determine what proportion of the domestic output of each product is consumed by visitors by dividing tourism consumption at basic prices into the total supply of each product at basic prices – this is the tourism product ratio:

(i) Identify the industries which supply each of the tourism products to visitors;

(ii) Apply the tourism product ratio to the output of each product by each industry to estimate the tourism output of each industry;

(iii) Estimate the intermediate consumption required to produce each industry's output of tourism products using relationships in the supply and use tables.

3. Calculate tourism gross value added at basic prices for each industry as tourism output less the intermediate consumption required to produce the tourism output, and sum for all industries in the economy.

4. Estimate tourism GDP by adding net taxes on tourism products (calculated using visitor expenditures as a proportion of total expenditures) to tourism gross value added at basic prices.

5. Allocate employment to tourism demand, the employment calculation using the same ratio by industry as the one used to calculate the GDP share of each industry.

Source: ABS (2007) Australian Bureau of Statistics Australian National Accounts: Tourism Satellite Accounts 2005–2006, 5249.0, para 41, May

The complete TSA provides several items of information to destination managers (TSA RMF, 2008, para. 1.15):

- TSA provide a framework of monetary flows which can be traced from the tourism consumer to the producing unit or supplier within the economy.
- TSA define and identify the various tourism 'industries' or groups of suppliers which produce or import the goods and services purchased by visitors.
- TSA thus enable the relationships between tourism and other economic activity to be explored within the national accounts framework, extracting all the tourism-related

economic activity which is included in the national accounts but not identified as tourism.

- TSA provide information as to where tourists spend, the extent to which different sectors benefit from tourist spending and the extent to which individual sectors are dependent upon tourism.
- TSA provide macroeconomic aggregates that describe the size and the economic contribution of tourism, such as tourism direct gross value added (TDGVA) and tourism direct gross domestic product (TDGDP), consistent with similar aggregates for the total economy, and for other productive economic activities;
- TSA provide detailed data on tourism consumption, a more extended concept associated with the activity of visitors as consumers, and a description on how this demand is met by domestic supply and imports, integrated within tables derived from SUT, that can be compiled both at current and constant prices;
- TSA provide detailed production accounts of the tourism industries, including data on employment, and linkages with other productive economic activities.
- TSA provide a link between economic data and non-monetary information on tourism, such as number of trips (or visits), duration of stay, purpose of trip, modes of transport and so on which are required to specify the characteristics of the economic variables.

Because TSA are derived from the overall system of national accounts structure, they enable tourism to be compared with other industries in the economy using consistent and internationally endorsed national accounting principles.

TSA should be considered from two perspectives (TSA RMF, 2008, para. 1.17):

- As a *statistical tool* that complements those concepts, definitions, aggregates and classifications, already presented in the international recommended tourism statistics (IRTS, 2008) and articulates them into analytical tables. Those tables provide elements for validly comparing estimates between regions, countries or groups of countries (if they are prepared on a consistent basis – see below). These elements are also comparable with other internationally recognised macro-economic aggregates and compilations;
- As the *framework* to guide countries in the further development of their system of tourism statistics, the main objective being the completion of the TSA, which could be viewed as a synthesis of such a system.

The document 'Tourism Satellite Account: Recommended Methodological Framework' (TSA RMF, 2008) presents 10 tables, recommending that only eight of them (Tables 1–7, 10) should be prepared at the present time in order to achieve international comparability of results. These tables are listed in Box 7.2.

BOX 7.2 Tables comprising the tourism satellite account

Table 1: Inbound tourism consumption (by products and categories of visitors)

Table 2: Domestic tourism consumption (the tourism activity of residents within their country of residence by products and categories of visitors)

Table 3: Outbound tourism consumption (by products and categories of visitors)

Table 4: Internal tourism consumption (by products and categories of visitors)

Table 5: Production accounts of tourism industries and other industries (tourism-related supply to visitors)

Table 6: Domestic supply and internal tourism consumption (by products) providing information on GDP and value added associated with tourism

Table 7: Employment in the tourism industries

Table 8: Gross fixed capital formation

Table 9: Collective consumption

Table 10: Nonmonetary indicators

Table 1
focuses on inbound tourism. It describes inbound visitor final consumption expenditure in cash, by types of products purchased.

Table 2
focuses on domestic tourism. This table presents final consumption expenditure in cash of resident visitors in the domestic economy (overnight and same day). It also shows expenditure by residents that are associated with outbound travel.

Table 3
focuses on outbound tourism. It represents visitor final consumption expenditure in cash, by products and categories of visitors by resident visitors occurring outside the economic territory of the country of reference or acquired from a non resident producer (for example, international transport).

Table 4
combines all visitor final consumption expenditure in cash associated with inbound and domestic tourism and non-monetary tourism consumption (tourism social

transfers in kind, other transactions in kind or on own account and business tourism expenses). This provides the estimate of total internal tourism consumption by product which then enters Table 6 as a separate column. This table provides data on tourism consumption which can now directly be compared with tourism supply.

Table 5

is the supply table, which, though focusing on tourism characteristic products and tourism industries, includes (in rows) all products that circulate in the selected economy as well as all industries (in columns). Table 5 presents the production accounts of tourism characteristic industries and others (that is, tourism connected industries and non specific industries), which makes possible the reconciliation with consumption.

Table 6

presents an overall reconciliation of internal tourism consumption with domestic supply. Table 6 is the core of the TSA system, where the melding between supply and internal tourism consumption takes place, and where computations of Tourism Gross Value Added (TGVA) and Tourism Gross Domestic Product (TGDP) and their components can be performed. It combines data on consumption coming from Table 4 and data on supply coming from Table 5.

Taken together, Table 5 and Table 6 include the complete classification of consumption and non-consumption products that circulate in the host economy, as well as the 12 categories of tourism industries.

Table 7:

measurement of employment is limited to the employment in the tourism industries, and the indicators to express the size will be the number of jobs and of employed persons having at least one job in these industries.

Tables 8 and 9

are included in order to gain experience in the measurement of the corresponding aggregates: tourism gross fixed capital formation and tourism collective consumption. Their estimation presents substantial conceptual and empirical challenges and at the present time they have a lower level of priority.

Table 10:

Presents selected quantitative indicators, important for the interpretation of the monetary information presented. Non-monetary indicators are very helpful to the analyst in order to understand the monetary figures included in the tables. At the same time, they provide information necessary to verify the accuracy of those data through their comparison with physical indicators, establishing ratios of daily consumption, types of accommodation, modes of transport used, number and size of establishments in the tourism industry, expenditure per visitor/day, and so on. Countries are being encouraged to develop such indicators according to their needs, using the information on characteristics of visitors and tourism industries as recommended in the 2008 IRTS (TSA RMF, 2008, para. 4.34).

Table 7.1 reproduces the basic framework of Table 5 in the Recommended Methodological Framework (IRTS, 2008). For examples of all ten tables, see United Nations (2001, Chapter 4) and the approved International Recommendations for Tourism Statistics (IRTS, 2008).

The different tables serve as a guide for presenting TSA data. Each country can decide on the most adequate format that takes into account its tourism reality and scope of available data. Table 7.2 lists 70 countries or territories known to have implemented TSA or known to be in the process of developing TSA (Libreros *et al.*, 2006).

7.3   THE IMPORTANCE OF TSA

The important contribution which TSA play in the overall task of estimating and understanding tourism's contribution to the economy can be summarised as below (Spurr, 2006):

7.3.1   TSA IDENTIFY 'TOURISM' AND 'TOURIST'

TSA concepts of 'tourism' and 'tourist' are based on the approved International Recommendations for Tourism Statistics (IRTS, 2008). For purposes of the TSA, 'tourism' is more limited than 'travel' since it refers to specific types of trips: those that take a traveller outside his/her usual environment for less than a year and for a main purpose other than to be employed by a resident entity in the place visited. Individuals when taking such trips are called visitors. Tourism is therefore a subset of travel and visitors are a subset of travellers both in an international and in a domestic context (IRTS, 2008, paras. 2.6–2.13).

In the TSA, 'tourism' is not restricted to what could be considered as *typical* tourism activities such as sightseeing, sunbathing, visiting attractions and so on. Travelling for the purpose of conducting businesses, for education and training and so on can also be part of tourism if the conditions that have been set up to define tourism are met (IRTS, 2008, para. 3.17). The TSA focuses on the economic dimension of tourism trips (IRTS, 2008, para. 2.29), mostly through expenditure by visitors or by others for their benefit.

Table 7.1 Format of Table 6 Production Accounts of Tourism Industries and other Industries (at basic prices)

PRODUCTS	TOURISM INDUSTRIES										Total Tourism Industries	Tourism Connected Industries	Non-Specific Industries	Total
	Hotels and Similar	Restaurant and Similar	Passenger Transport				Transport Equipment Rental	Travel Agents, Tour Operators, Tourism Guide	Recreation, Entertainment & Cultural Services	Retail Trade				
			Rail	Road	Water	Air								
A. Specific product														
Characteristic products														
Accomodation														
Hotel and other lodging services	24,082	2									24,084	4	26	24,114
Second homes services on own account or for free											-			-
Food and beverages serving services	3,017	118,669									121,686	129	3,302	125,117
Passenger Transport											-	-		-
Interurban railway transport services			1,553								1,553	-		1,553
road transport services				86,695							86,695	-		86,695
water transport services					29,848						29,848	-		29,848
air transport services						47,973					47,973	546	13	48,532
Travel agency, tour operator and tourist guide services								3,067			3,067	-		3,067
Transport equipment rental				1,058			2,040				3,097	-	602	3,699
Recreation, entertainment cultural services	1,647	200							53,168		55,014	-	802	55,816
Shopping										139	139	8,795	432	9,367
Connected products									8,893	17,579	26,472	2,172,439	60,192	2,259,103
B. Non specific products	2,051	2,119		36,989	152	19	266			0	41,595	6,029	5,572,940	5,620,563
TOTAL output at current producers' prices [1/]	30,796	120,990	1,553	124,741	30,000	47,992	2,305	3,067	62,061	17,718	441,224	2,187,941	5,638,309	8,267,474
1. Agriculture, forestry and fishery products	1,553	11,010			363						12,926	1,773	320,534	335,233
2. Ores and minerals	3	79									82	4,008	75,642	79,732
3. Electricity, gas and water	1,615	1,615	118	935	194	287	25	56	1,400	371	6,615	35,223	85,753	127,667
4. Manufacturing	4,977	45,167	391	44,047	8,412	13,395	644	140	2,804	394	120,370	129,798	838,675	1,088,843
5. Construction work and construction	139	6		161	169	50	25	1	148	12	710	4,768	27,156	32,635
6. Trade services, restaurants and hotel services	776	4,044	53	5,921	848	12,300	54	60	2,799	262	27,118	29,757	136,250	192,684
7. Transport, storage and communication services	510	1,046	103	1,645	2,095	1,484	39	989	693	1,126	9,729	93,520	93,520	191,820
8. Business services	1,928	693	77	2,182	3,497	6,516	235	562	2,337	1,034	19,060	118,357	122,388	259,805
9. Community, social and personal services	579	87	24	3,259	556	44	41	30	10,639	110	14,868	8,952	46,955	70,775
Total intermediate consumption (purchasers price) [2/]	12,081	63,747	765	58,151	16,133	34,075	1,063	1,837	20,819	3,309	211,480	426,156	1,746,873	2,379,195
Total gross value added of activities at basic prices	18,715	57,243	788	66,591	13,867	13,917	1,242	1,230	41,241	14,409	229,744	1,761,785	3,891,436	5,886,846
Compensation of employees	7,044	25,998	583	32,868	4,560	4,592	550	679	13,651	3,375	93,901	477,779	1,391,564	1,993,528
Other taxes less subsidies on production	1,690	4,721	13	3,674	657	890	36	59	5,330	905	17,975	113,996	185,537	315,582
Depreciation	2,531	4,333	93	13,084	1,508	4,238	113	129	2,889	832	29,749	131,707	257,492	424,517
Gross Operating surplus	7,451	22,192	98	16,965	7,642	4,197	543	363	19,371	9,298	88,119	1,038,302	2,056,843	3,153,219
Subtotal	18,715	57,243	788	66,591	14,368	13,917	1,242	1,230	41,241	14,409	229,744	1,761,785	3,891,436	5,886,846

Source: United Nations (2001: Chapter 4), p. 69

Table 7.2 Countries with TSA projects in progress as of 2006

Argentina**	Denmark**	Korea, Republic of**	Rumania*
Aruba	Dominican Republic*	Latvia**	Saint Lucia*
Australia**	Ecuador**	Lithuania**	Saudi Arabia**
Austria**	Egypt*	Malaysia*	Senegal*
Barbados*	Estonia**	Malta*	Singapore**
Belgium**	Fiji	Martinique*	Slovenia*
Belize*	Finland**	Mexico*	South Africa
Botswana*	France**	Morocco**	Spain**
Brazil*	Germany**	Mozambique*	Sweden**
Cameroon	Ghana*	Namibia*	Switzerland*
Canada**	Hong Kong, China**	Netherlands**	Thailand**
Chile**	Hungary**	New Zealand**	Trinidad / Tobago*
China*	India*	Norway**	United Kingdom**
Colombia**	Indonesia**	Panama*	Tanzania
Costa Rica*	Ireland*	Peru**	United States**
Croatia*	Israel**	Philippines**	Zambia*
Cuba*	Italy**	Poland**	
Czech Republic**	Jamaica*	Portugal**	

Source: Libreros *et al.* (2006, Table 1)

Note: The asterisks relate to completion dates

7.3.2   TSA IDENTIFY A TOURISM 'INDUSTRY'

TSA identify the sectors of the economy that comprise the tourism industry. This is a critical first step to measuring the industry and its economic contribution, and is a tool for strengthening the identity of the tourism industry. The TSA identify tourism's component products and industries through the concepts of Tourism Characteristic and Tourism

Connected products and industries (IRTS, 2008; TSA RMF, 2008). Box 7.3 identifies some important concepts.

BOX 7.3 Tourism characteristic and tourism connected products and industries

Tourism related products are the sum of the following two forms:

(i) *Tourism characteristic products* – these represent an important part of tourism consumption, or for which a significant proportion of the sales are to visitors (for example, accommodation and air transport). They are those products, that, in most countries, it is considered, would cease to exist in meaningful quantity or those for which the level of consumption would be significantly reduced in the absence of visitors.

(ii) *Tourism connected products* – the other products connected with tourism but less significant for the visitor and/or producer than the characteristics products (for example, automotive fuel retailing, and casinos). They are those that are consumed by visitors in volumes which are significant for the visitor and/or the provider but are not included in the list of tourism characteristic products. While the significance of tourism connected products within tourism analysis for the economy of reference is recognized, their link to tourism is very limited worldwide. Consequently, lists of such products will be country-specific.

Tourism related industries also take two forms:

(i) *Tourism characteristic industries* – 'industries' or 'activities' of the economy which are typical of tourism and would either cease to exist in their present form or would be significantly affected if tourism were to cease.

(ii) *Tourism connected industries* – industries other than tourism characteristic industries, for which a tourism related product is directly identifiable and where the products are consumed by visitors in volumes which are significant for the visitor and/or for the producer

All remaining products and industries are classified as 'all other goods and services' or 'all other industries'.

Source: United Nations and World Tourism Organization (2008a) *International Recommendations for Tourism Statistics* (IRTS, 2008) New York and Madrid

---

The 'tourism industry' comprises all establishments for which the principal activity is a tourism-characteristic activity. The term 'tourism industries' is equivalent to 'tourism characteristic activities' and they are used synonymously in the IRTS 2008.

Table 7.3 presents a typology of 12 tourism characteristic consumption products and activities (industries). Categories 1–10 comprise the core for international comparison, in terms of Central Product Classification (CPC) subclasses for products and International Standard Industrial Classification (ISIC) classes for activities (ITRS, 2008, Annex 3, 4). The two other categories are country-specific. Category 11 covers tourism characteristic goods and products and the corresponding retail trade activities for activities. Category 12 refers respectively to country-specific tourism characteristic services and country-specific tourism characteristic activities.

Table 7.3 Tourism characteristic consumption products and tourism characteristic activities (tourism industries)

List of categories of tourism characteristic consumption products and tourism characteristic activities (tourism industries)

Products	Activities
1. Accommodation services for visitors	1. Accommodation for visitors
2. Food and beverage serving services	2. Food and beverage serving activities
3. Railway passenger transport services	3. Railway passenger transport
4. Road passenger transport services	4. Road passenger transport
5. Water passenger transport services	5. Water passenger transport
6. Air passenger transport services	6. Air passenger transport
7. Transport equipment rental services	7. Transport equipment rental
8. Travel agencies and other reservation services	8. Travel agencies and other reservation services activities
9. Cultural services	9. Cultural activities
10. Sports and recreational services	10. Sports and recreational services
11. Country-specific tourism characteristic goods	11. Retail trade of country-specific tourism characteristic goods
12. Country-specific tourism characteristic services	12. Country-specific tourism characteristic activities

Source: IRTS (2007), para. 5.18, Table 5.1

The IRTS list of tourism characteristic products corresponds to products considered characteristic for purposes of the international comparability of results. Consequently, it is meant to serve as a proposal of how, in the future, the various international organisations could present, in a comparable way, the results of countries that have developed a TSA. The IRTS (2007) emphasises that international comparability will only be achieved on the basis of an agreed list of products and that any country or compiler wishing to develop its own list of products should select those products from the provisional list of tourism-specific products, which is contained in the first column of Table 7.3. It acknowledges that the list should be updated periodically and that broader or more detailed lists may be established by individual organisations (OECD, Eurostat and others), for appropriate

Table 7.4 Tourism characteristic industries in TSA for India, New Zealand and Canada

India TSA Tourism Characteristic Industries	*New Zealand TSA Tourism Characteristic Industries*	*Canada TSA Tourism Characteristic Industries*

• Accommodation services
• Food and beverage serving services
• Passenger transport services
  – Railway
  – Road
  – Buses
  – Other mechanised vehicles
  – Non mechanised road transport
  – Water
  – Air
• Transport equipment rental
• Travel Agencies and similar
• Other recreational and entertainment activities
	• Accommodation
	• Cafes and restaurants
	• Road, rail and water passenger transport
	• Air transport
	• Other transport, storage and transport services
	• Machinery and equipment hiring and leasing
	• Cultural and recreational services
		• Accommodation
		• Food and beverage Services
		• Railway transportation
		• Bus transportation
		• Taxicabs
		• Water transportation
		• Air transportation
		• Vehicle rental
		• Travel agencies
		• Recreation and entertainment

comparability among their member countries, provided that correspondence is maintained between these lists and the basic classifications.

In similar fashion, the list of tourism characteristic industries differs from country to country. Some examples appear in Table 7.4.

7.3.3 TSA MEASURE THE KEY ECONOMIC VARIABLES

TSA bring together basic data on the key economic variables that relate to tourism and present them in a consistent and authoritative way using internationally endorsed concepts and definitions (Frechtling, 1999). By highlighting tourism within the national accounting framework, TSA allow the tourism industry to be better included in the mainstream of economic analysis.

A country with TSA can derive estimates of many tourism-related economic variables, including the following:

– Tourism's contribution to and share of output.
– TDGDP and TDGVA.
– Tourism's share of the value added of major tourism-related industries such as accommodation, tour operators, restaurants and cafes, rental cars, air transportation and so on.
– Tourist consumption spending both by household and business tourism and by type of product.
– Consumption by overseas visitors and by residents travelling abroad.
– Tourism's contribution to employment.
– Tourism's impact on its transactions with the rest of the world.
– Tourism-generated tax and other government revenue.
– Tourist industry capital spending.
– Profits and wages of tourism-related industries.
– The productivity of the tourism supply sector.
– Changes in the above variables over time.

Box 7.4 contains definitions of some of the main headline variables of a TSA.

BOX 7.4 Definitions of key measures from TSA

Tourism expenditure
refers to the amount paid for the acquisition of consumption goods and services, as well as valuables, for own use or to give away, for and during tourism trips. It includes expenditures by visitors themselves, as well as expenses that are paid for or reimbursed by others.

Tourism consumption

Tourism consumption is the total consumption made by visitors, or on behalf of a visitor, for and during his/her trip and stay at the destination. Visitor consumption covers more than just the expenditure made by the tourist, exceeding visitor purchases on a trip Included in this definition are both actual expenditures and imputations for the consumption by visitors of certain services for which they do not make a payment- for example, the so called social transfers in kind that benefit visitors, the imputation of accommodation services provided by vacation homes to their owners, etc.

Tourism output

Output consists of those goods and services that are produced within an establishment that become available for use outside that establishment, plus any goods and services produced for own final use. Tourism output is measured at 'basic prices', that is before any taxes on tourism product are added (or any subsidies on tourism products are deducted).

Tourism Gross Value Added (TGVA)

is measured as the value of the output of tourism products by industries less the value of the inputs used in producing these tourism products. Value added is the 'value' businesses add to the goods and services they purchase (intermediate inputs) and use in the process of producing their own outputs.

TGVA is the value of wages/salaries and profits in businesses from the direct supply of goods and services to visitors. TGVA adds the parts of gross value added generated by tourism industries and other industries of the economy that serve directly visitors in responding to internal i.e. domestic, inbound international and the home part of outbound international tourism) tourism consumption. Sometimes this variable is called 'Tourism Direct GVA'. The use of the term direct in this aggregate refers to the fact that the TSA only measures that part of value added (by tourism industries and other industries) due to the consumption of visitors and leaves aside the indirect and induced effects that such consumption might generate.

Tourism Gross Domestic Product (TGDP)

enables a direct comparison with national GDP. It represents the part of GDP attributable directly to internal tourism consumption as the sum of part of gross value added (at basic prices) generated by all industries in response to internal tourism consumption plus the amount of net taxes on products and imports included within the value of this expenditure at purchasers' prices. Put otherwise, TGDP represents the total market value of domestically produced goods and services consumed by visitors after deducting the cost of goods and services used up in the process of production.

Persons employed

in tourism related industries will generally provide services to both visitors and non-visitors. Tourism employment, as meaning the employment strictly related to the goods and services acquired by visitors and produced either by tourism industries or other industries, cannot be directly observed. The OECD Employment Module (TSA RMF, 2008, Annex 8) provides a statistical framework and methodological guidelines to establish the level and some characteristics of employment in the tourism industries. Labour cannot be assigned to any particular output or part of output without the use of specific assumptions and modeling procedures.

Additional major challenges to tourism employment estimation include seasonality, high variability in the working conditions, flexibility and the lack of formality of many work contracts in many smaller firms.

Source: TSA RMF (2008)

There is disagreement as to whether some items should be included in TSA and on how they should be measured. In particular, statistical agencies in different countries continue to differ as to the treatment of travel agency services, package tours, second homes, business tourism, durable goods and tourism collective consumption in the TSA (TSA RMF, 2008, paras. 3.1–3.41). Such disagreements do not reduce the importance of the TSA as a technique for measuring and comparing tourist-related economic activity consistent with national accounting principles.

7.3.4 TSA MEASURE TOURISM'S INTERRELATIONSHIP WITH OTHER INDUSTRIES

By identifying the sources of gross value added (GVA) generated across the economy in order to satisfy visitor demand, TSA make it possible to examine the inter-relationships between tourism and other industries and to answer questions such as which industries in the economy rely most heavily on tourism and to what extent they do so.

7.3.5 TSA SUPPORT INTER-INDUSTRY COMPARISONS

TSA allow tourism activity to be compared for its importance with other major industries in terms of size, economic performance, employment and contribution to the national economy. For example, tourism's share of Gross Domestic Product (GDP) and employment, the relative importance of identified tourism components to overall tourism activity and their contribution to other non-tourism industries can all be examined. The Canadian Tourism Satellite Account (CTSA), for instance, has been linked to the future development of benchmarking tools and micro-economic tourism indicators allowing private sector operators to compare their performance with industry norms in terms of productivity, growth and earnings (Libreros *et al.*, 2006).

7.3.6 TSA SUPPORT INTERNATIONAL COMPARISONS

TSA allow for valid comparisons between regions, countries or groups of countries. In making these estimates comparable with other internationally recognised macroeconomic aggregates and compilations, TSA also facilitate comparisons of the scale, scope and performance of one country's tourist industry with those in other countries. Caution is needed in cross-country comparisons, however, because a number of variations exist in the implementation of TSA standards, including the extent of coverage of all forms of visitor consumption and tourism supply as well as differences in the interpretation and treatment of certain key concepts such as business travel, value added and gross domestic product. Presently, inconsistent definitions limit the comparability of TSA results between countries.

7.3.7 TSA GIVE 'CREDIBILITY' TO ESTIMATES OF THE ECONOMIC CONTRIBUTION OF TOURISM

As a statistical tool that is compatible with international national accounting guidelines, TSA can enhance credibility of tourism as a main economic sector. TSA can help to raise awareness of tourism and its contribution to national economies. They help tourism stakeholders to better understand the economic importance of tourism activity; and by extension its role in all the industries producing the various goods and services demanded by tourists. TSAs thus help to legitimise or give credibility to the tourism industry as a main economic sector in the minds of politicians and the general public. In doing so, they can help to solicit and justify funding for tourism development and marketing (Cockerell & Spurr, 2002).

7.3.8 TSA PROVIDE A TOOL FOR TOURISM RESEARCH AND POLICY ANALYSIS

Tourism has not been well served in statistical and information terms, precluding informed tourism policy analysis in both the public and private sectors. TSA provide policy makers with insights into tourism and its contribution to the economy providing an instrument for designing more efficient policies relating to tourism and its employment aspects (Jones *et al.*, 2003).

TSA can serve as a tool for enhanced strategic management and planning for the tourism industry. Indeed, a major purpose of the TSA is to improve the effectiveness of tourism policies and actions and to improve existing measures for evaluation of these policies in the context of a broader policy agenda (OECD, 2000).

TSAs provide the basic information required for the development of models of the economic impact of tourism. For example, analysts may use data from TSA to estimate the direct effect of changes in tourism consumption on other industries or on employment. In helping governments and businesses determine the value of tourism to the economy, TSA can also aid in the formulation of strategies for ensuring competitive advantage in this sector. Given that they allow comparisons across sectors, TSA give tourism organisations the information they need to lobby governments to ensure that tourism can compete on a level playing field.

7.4   UPDATING TSA

A complete TSA is relatively expensive to construct and requires a high level of involvement by stakeholders to maintain accuracy over time. It is not feasible to collect the detailed supply-side data required to produce a timely full-scale TSA every year. This means that they are unlikely to be fully updated every year, but rather will be updated on a rolling basis as resources and data allow.

Despite this, the key aggregates or headline outputs can be updated annually using relationships in the benchmark TSA and demand-side data that are available on a yearly basis. Several countries undertake partial updates of their TSA based upon information which is more readily available for more recent periods – typically including information on visitor consumption or business turnover, proxied, for example, by occupancy rates.

A relatively simple way to estimate the changes in tourism for more recent years is to apply tourism consumption totals to the established TSA structures for the reference year. Box 7.5 indicates the steps that can be taken in the update years. Assuming that GVA figures are available for the economy as a whole in the absence of detailed I–O tables, this method indicates the likely trends in industry growth over periods subsequent to the TSA reference year, allowing estimates of the significance of tourism within the wider economy for these years.

BOX 7.5 Steps involved in updating TSA

- Derive an estimate of tourism consumption for each tourism product.
- Remove product taxes and subsidies, margins and imports from tourism consumption of each product at purchasers' prices to derive tourism consumption at basic prices – this represents the domestic output of tourism.

- Allocate the output of each tourism product to producing industry using ratios from the benchmark TSA.
- Sum the products produced by each tourism industry to derive the output for each tourism industry.
- Allocate industry output between value added and intermediate consumption using each industry's input-output ratios taken from the benchmark TSA.
- Alter the TSA benchmark coefficients when there is strong evidence of structural change in tourism related industries or the economy more generally to reflect this.
- Sum tourism gross value added for all industries to calculate the tourism industry's gross value added. Tourism GDP is derived by adding net taxes on tourism products.
- Apply the tourism value added industry ratios from each of the benchmark years to employment estimates for each industry in subsequent years. The employment estimates between benchmark years are smoothed.

Source: Australian Bureau of Statistics (ABS) (2009) Tourism Satellite Account 2007–2008, para 41, April

However, even in a highly developed TSA, any given cell might be several years out of date. Thus, TSA will never completely reflect the 'current' context, and complementary indicators must be developed to give insights into the current economic significance of tourism to the economy. This causes significant problems for policymakers and the industry, requiring timely information to aid decision-making.

Some countries have indicators which are available quarterly, and which are very timely, enhancing the ability of the country to monitor small changes in the tourism economy. Canada, for instance, maintains a comprehensive set of National Tourism Indicators (NTI) (Meis, 1999) with time series involving over 300 variables, comprising both domestic and international tourism demand, supply and employment. The United States Bureau of Economic Analysis has a similar approach to producing timely indicators of tourism activity benchmarked to the Travel and TSA for 1996/7.

The provision of quarterly data benchmarked to the TSA brings significant policy benefits. For example, based on a study using National Tourism Industry data for a 10-year period (first quarter 1986 to fourth quarter 1996), Statistics Canada (Wilton, 1998) was able to demonstrate the following:

- Tourism is a growth industry, as tourism spending rose faster than Canada's GDP.
- Job creation in the tourism industry was higher than in the business sector as a whole.
- Tourism experiences spectacular ups and downs both cyclically and seasonally.
- Many tourism goods and services are very sensitive to cyclical fluctuations in the country's GDP, especially in the air transportation, recreation and entertainment, travel agency and food and beverage service industries.
- Cyclical variation in Canada's GDP accounts for a very small part of the variation in non-resident demand, which depends primarily on the economic situation in other countries, the value of the Canadian dollar and specific events.

The production of quarterly indicators of tourist-related activity is no small undertaking and requires significant resource investment.

7.5 REGIONAL TSA

Tourism often produces substantial economic contributions in certain regions of a national economy but with a negligible impact in others. Since tourism activity tends to be unevenly concentrated within countries, national TSA cannot help us to determine the importance of tourism to different sub-regions or provide any guidance as to its potential as a tool for regional development in particular cases (Jones *et al.*, 2003). Worldwide, regional governments are developing tourism plans to maximise the opportunities for income and employment growth resulting from an expanding tourism industry. The forms of planning implemented must depend on the estimated net benefits on local economies of different strategies. In such cases, a national level TSA may be of much less relevance to regional destination management organisations and local businesses than a regional TSA.

Not surprisingly, the extensive involvement of governments in tourism planning, infrastructure provision and marketing at a state, regional or local level, has led to a strong demand for better economic statistics to be made available at the state or regional level. Yet, only a small number of countries, in particular Canada, Spain, Norway and Australia, have attempted to develop TSA for regions (Duc Pham *et al.*, 2009; Jones & Munday, 2007).

Discussion on adapting the TSA to subnational levels is encouraged in the international guidelines. (TSA RMF, 2008, Annex 7). Reasons include the following:

- The worldwide trend towards the de-centralisation of political power and destination management, with the associated need to improved data for decision-making at the local level.

- The varied nature of tourism activities, which can potentially benefit rural areas seeking to diversify, as well as areas overlooked so far as the prevailing production model is concerned.
- The unequal geographical distribution and characteristics of tourism activity within the national territory, from the standpoint of both demand and supply, leading to additional requirements for tourism statistics at the various subnational levels.
- The growing interest of tourism-related businesses to understand the interrelation of their activity with others and its main determinants and seasonal cycles.
- The need to improve the allocation of resources in national and local economies, which can only be achieved by upgrading quantitative references and measuring economic impacts.

There are two basic approaches to constructing 'regional TSA' (Jones *et al.*, 2003):

1. The *bottom-up (regional) approach* involves the construction of a specific TSA for the region in question, with regional demand equated to regional supply for each product, enabling the derivation of a set of tourist product ratios which enable a full reporting.

The main advantage of the 'bottom-up' approach is that it treats the region for TSA purposes as a 'small nation'; treating other regions as outside the reference economy, substituting international imports with international plus interregional and so on. This means that the TSA classification and structure and the supporting data collection can be adapted to regional circumstances (Jones *et al.*, 2003).

However, the construction of regional TSA is a data intensive process on both the demand side and the supply side. Most likely it will necessitate undertaking local surveys of tourism expenditure patterns and tourism industry outputs and sales. Indeed, data requirements will often be more onerous than those for national TSA. Further, regional TSA are impossible to construct without a national TSA and a reasonably well-developed system of regional accounts.

2. The *top-down (interregional) approach* involves the regionalisation of a national account, providing a small number of 'key' results, usually by reference to indirect indicators, for example, volume of trips or supply. This involves allocating national totals for key indicators such as TVA, dependent employment and so on across regions according to indirect indicators.

The advantages of the 'top-down' approach have been discussed by Jones *et al.* (2003). These include the following:

i) Standardisation of structure across regions.
ii) Relatively low cost particularly if there are good-quality demand and supply surveys that can be regionalised.

iii) Easier integration into national series of variables, for example, TGVA, which will aid the production of up-to-date results.

iv) Expected high credibility in the eyes of politicians and officials within central government.

A major potential limitation of the 'top-down' approach, however, is that the standardisation of structure across regions can restrict adequately accounting for regional differences in tourism activities between regions and different tourism industry structures. Unless there is a full set of regional I–O tables upon which to base the TSA, it is likely that *national* ratios for important aspects such as industry production functions or imports of products (here including inter-regional imports, of course) must be adopted or adapted for regional differences (Jones *et al.*, 2003).

The final use of any fully developed regional economic accounts should determine the level of resource devoted to the project and its accounting complexity. For example, in the case of a region where tourism is an important industry (Majorca, Côte d'Azur and the like), a 'bottom-up' approach may be most appropriate. However, complete TSA which adhere to WTO and EUROSTAT guidelines can only be constructed for areas which have a set of economic accounts preferably supported by I–O tables. This, together with their costs of construction, means that TSA development is for the time being limited to nation states and those constituent regions which have well-developed regional accounts. Conversely, for regions where tourism is less important, it may be that a less rigorous and detailed approach which estimates key indicators either from a 'top-down' approach or even a one-off 'tourism impact study' may be adequate, and a better use of scarce public resources (Jones *et al.*, 2003).

For these reasons, approaches to the construction of regional tourism economic accounts will vary widely, driven by regional needs and data availability. The approach is also very costly to undertake which may be a deterrent to smaller, less wealthy regions. The challenges of implementing regional TSA are probably greater than those experienced in constructing national TSA, given differences in statistical resources and systems, in policy priorities and in technical capabilities between regions. Regions carefully need to consider the scope and nature of the account they need.

The use of the term 'satellite account' may be misleading at the regional level given that it cannot strictly conform to the national accounts. Some substantial challenges to their construction may be noted (TSA RMF, 2008, Annex 7). Nevertheless, there are benefits to estimating tourism's contribution to sub-regions of the national economy within the TSA context.

Box 7.6 displays some results following development of TSA for each of the 8 states and territories of Australia. The results highlight some of the important outcomes of constructing TSA at the regional level.

BOX 7.6 Direct, indirect and total contribution of tourism by region, Australia

Tourism plays a vital role in the life and economy of every region in Australia and is a significant contributor to the economy through employment, foreign exchange earnings and investment in businesses, communities and regional development. Directly and indirectly, tourism contributes $68 billion to the Australian economy, employs more than 848,000 Australians and is made up of more than 585,000 tourism related businesses. Tourism also drives regional and community development through investment in infrastructure, the preservation of natural and cultural resources and encouraging social development and understanding among communities.

In late 2008, Sustainable Tourism Cooperative Research Centre (STCRC), through its Centre for Economics and Policy (CEP), and in partnership with the Australian states and territories, developed a suite of state and territory specific TSAs (refer Table 7.5). These TSAs adopt internationally agreed TSA methodology and definitions and have been reconciled against the national tourism satellite account. As with the national TSAs, regional tourism satellite accounts extract data from all industry sectors to provide a direct measurement of tourism's contribution to the state and territory economies. Direct contributions are generated where there is a direct physical or economic relationship between the visitor and the producer of the goods and services, such as hotels and airlines, or when a visitor eats at a restaurant or catches a taxi.

In addition these state and territory TSAs also provide estimates on the indirect contribution of tourism. Indirect contributions arise from other industries not in direct contact with visitors but who produce services and products for the industries which have direct visitor contact. For example, a visitor takes a fully catered guided day tour, the meals provided are supplied by a catering company, the catering company purchases the raw ingredients from a food distribution company, that business sources its vegetables from a farm. This represents a series of indirect processes that link tourism to other economy sectors. The aggregation of direct and indirect effects is useful in understanding the wider flow-on effects of tourism to both the economy and employment.

The regional TSA provide valuable data to help inform policy and planning in areas including:

- infrastructure development
- education and training
- investment
- marketing
- forecasting and modeling

Table 7.5 Estimates of direct, indirect and total contribution of tourism by state and territory, 2006–07

Direct contribution	NSW	VIC	QLD	SA	WA	TAS	NT	ACT	AUS
Tourism GVA ($m)	11279.75	6905.29	7127.92	1842.97	2972.66	835.86	775.78	565.79	32306.02
Tourism net taxes on products ($m)	2057.37	1343.98	1657.27	412.52	682.06	188.43	158.14	130.26	6630.05
Tourism GSP, GDP ($m)	13337.13	8249.28	8785.19	2255.49	3654.72	1024.29	933.92	696.05	38936.06
Tourism employment ('000)	157.80	102.18	118.90	27.70	45.66	13.70	9.68	7.28	482.90
GVA ($m)	306979.75	230645.30	181638.56	62652.05	127784.47	18640.47	13369.55	20170.13	961880.26
Tourism share of GVA (%)	3.67	2.99	3.92	2.94	2.33	4.48	5.80	2.81	3.36
GSP, GDP ($m)	335144.00	247440.00	195704.00	69540.00	141368.00	21088.00	14494.00	21586.00	1046364.00
Tourism share of GSP, GDP (%)	3.98	3.33	4.49	3.24	2.59	4.86	6.44	3.22	3.72
Employment ('000)	3307.22	2548.89	2091.72	755.43	1085.53	223.16	102.46	188.01	10302.42
Tourism share of employment (%)	4.77	4.01	5.68	3.67	4.21	6.14	9.45	3.87	4.69

Indirect contribution	NSW	VIC	QLD	SA	WA	TAS	NT	ACT	AUS
Tourism GVA ($m)	8746.41	6523.68	5695.03	1885.30	3187.48	701.99	703.20	495.73	27938.82
Tourism net taxes on products ($m)	470.34	349.66	404.28	106.70	168.35	55.10	45.46	33.30	1633.19
Tourism GSP, GDP ($m)	9216.75	6873.34	6099.32	1992.00	3355.83	757.09	748.66	529.03	29572.01
Tourism employment ('000)	109.65	77.07	97.00	23.79	34.32	11.15	7.32	5.61	365.89
Total contribution	**NSW**	**VIC**	**QLD**	**SA**	**WA**	**TAS**	**NT**	**ACT**	**AUS**
Tourism GVA ($m)	20026.16	13428.98	12822.96	3728.27	6160.13	1537.84	1478.98	1061.52	60244.83
Tourism net taxes on products ($m)	2527.71	1693.64	2061.56	519.22	850.42	243.53	203.60	163.56	8263.24
Tourism GSP, GDP ($m)	22553.87	15122.61	14884.51	4247.49	7010.55	1781.37	1682.58	1225.08	68508.07
Tourism employment ('000)	267.45	179.25	215.90	51.49	79.98	24.84	17.00	12.89	848.79

Ratio of total to direct	NSW	VIC	QLD	SA	WA	TAS	NT	ACT	AUS
Tourism GVA ($m)	1.78	1.94	1.80	2.02	2.07	1.84	1.91	1.88	1.86
Tourism net taxes on products	1.23	1.26	1.24	1.26	1.25	1.29	1.29	1.26	1.25
Direct contribution	NSW	VIC	QLD	SA	WA	TAS	NT	ACT	AUS
Tourism GSP, GDP ($m)	1.69	1.83	1.69	1.88	1.92	1.74	1.80	1.76	1.76
Tourism employment ('000)	1.69	1.75	1.82	1.86	1.75	1.81	1.76	1.77	1.76
Share of Indirect in total contribution	NSW	VIC	QLD	SA	WA	TAS	NT	ACT	AUS
Tourism GVA ($m)	43.67	48.58	44.41	50.57	51.74	45.65	47.55	46.70	46.38
Tourism net taxes on products	18.61	20.65	19.61	20.55	19.80	22.63	22.33	20.36	19.76
Tourism GSP, GDP ($m)	40.87	45.45	40.98	46.90	47.87	42.50	44.49	43.18	43.17
Tourism employment ('000)	41.00	43.00	44.93	46.20	42.91	44.87	43.04	43.52	43.11

The TSAs also provide a means for each of the states and territories to make comparisons between tourism and other industries and economic activities and to measure the contribution of tourism to the economy over time. This can assist in allocating tourism expenditure across a broad cross-section of tourism related areas such as transport, water infrastructure, hotel investment and built and natural attractions.

Source: STCRC (2009) 'Tourism Within Communities: The Flow of Expenditure through Economies and Industries Sustainable', Tourism Cooperative Research Centre, Australia: Griffith University.

7.6 TSA AS A POLICY INSTRUMENT

7.6.1 DIRECT VERSUS INDIRECT ECONOMIC CONTRIBUTION OF TOURISM

TSA are mainly descriptive in nature and do not include any measurement of the indirect and induced effects of visitor consumption on the economic system as a whole. Thus direct value added does not measure the full impact of tourism on the host economy because it is limited to those businesses that have a direct relationship with tourists. That is, the additional value added generated by the industries supporting the initial 'round' of tourism spending is excluded. Additional value added results from tourism through production of the intermediate inputs used in the production of goods and services sold to tourists, although there is no direct relationship between the producer of the intermediate inputs and the tourist. This additional value added is known as indirect value added. This means that tourism's overall contribution to the economy is not fully reflected in the TSA tables and must therefore be measured and analysed using other means (Statistics New Zealand, 2008). As we shall discuss in Chapters 8 and 9, estimation of this indirect contribution requires economic modelling.

As discussed in Chapter 6, inclusion of the indirect effects of tourist expenditure acknowledges that tourism's total economic significance is greater than just the direct contribution estimated in the TSA. Additional value added is generated by the industries supporting the initial 'round' of tourism spending. Measuring indirect tourism value added involves tracing the flow-on effects of businesses' intermediate purchases that are used directly in producing tourism products and measuring the cumulative value added that these purchases generate. For example, the intermediate purchases of the accommodation and cafes and restaurants industries would include items such as carpets, furniture, electricity, tablecloths and food purchased from other industries or from imports. In turn, these other industries will have made intermediate purchases from other industries (or from imports) in order to produce the items they sell to the accommodation and cafes and restaurants industries. So the sequence continues, until all intermediate purchases can be directly accounted for, either as value added or imports. Measuring indirect tourism contribution to GVA or GDP involves summing the value added of each industry that is generated throughout this sequence (Statistics New Zealand, 2008).

These indirect effects should be understood as a method of redistributing to the tourism sector value added, GDP, employment that occurs outside the tourism sector. They reflect the value of production and employment that occur on an economy-wide basis as a result of the demand of tourists for goods and services. A comparison of the direct and indirect estimates for Australia indicates that the indirect contribution of tourism was slightly higher than the direct contribution in terms of GVA, thus more than doubling the overall contribution of tourism reported in the TSA (Salma, 2004).

7.6.2 ECONOMIC CONTRIBUTION VERSUS ECONOMIC IMPACT

TSA represent an important information base for the estimation of the economic contribution of changes in tourism demand, but TSA are not in themselves modelling tools for economic impact assessment. As previously discussed in Chapter 6, we must distinguish between 'economic contribution' and 'economic impact'.

Economic contribution measures the size and overall significance of the industry within an economy.

Economic impact refers to the *changes* in the economic contribution resulting from specific events or activities that comprise 'shocks' to the tourism system. This should not be confused with the contribution itself. Economic impact implies that the overall change in the economic contribution must take account of the extensive interactive effects which occur across the economy.

Suppose inbound tourism increases in some destination and that this generates additional tourism expenditure, output, value added and employment as the local tourism industry expands to accommodate this expenditure increase. While TSA can be employed to estimate what the direct effects of additional tourism demand might be on the contribution of the tourism industry to the economy (e.g. tourism GDP or tourism employment), they cannot be used to estimate the *economy-wide* impacts of the increased tourism since they do not contain any behavioural equations specifying how each sector responds to external shocks, including shocks normally affecting the sector directly and shocks transmitted through inter-sectoral linkages, via changes prices, wages, exchange rates and other variables. Since TSA represent a snapshot or description of the significance of direct tourism demand within an economy at a particular time, TSA do not provide a measure of net impacts on the economy of change in tourism expenditures. TSA take no account, for example, of the possible factor constraints that may present barriers to tourism growth in response to an increase in tourism demand, or the impacts that changing prices and wages might have on other (non-tourism) industries (Blake *et al.*, 2001).

Unfortunately, it is not always understood by researchers and policy makers that one cannot estimate the wider economic impacts of a change in tourism demand by using averages from TSA. Changes occur at the margin and involve inter-industry and other economy-wide effects as well, so the change on the economy as a whole will almost always be smaller than the change in TGDP and tourism employment.

To gain more comprehensive insight into the indirect and induced effects of tourism requires a further level of analysis – this is economic impact analysis, requiring the use of specific economic modelling techniques. In such an exercise, TSA provide a starting point for other more comprehensive approaches to analysing the overall economic impact of tourism. These issues will be further explored in Chapters 8 and 9.

7.7 USING TSA: DEVELOPING MEASURES OF TOURISM PERFORMANCE

TSA can provide a base to develop different measures of tourism performance. Three such measures are tourism yield, tourism productivity and tourism's carbon footprint.

7.7.1 TOURISM YIELD

A focus on 'yield' is an important aspect of both business strategy and public policy to maintain and enhance the returns from tourism in destinations world-wide. Yield is a term which refers to the gain, in financial or economic benefits which a destination achieves from attracting particular types of tourists. A growing number of destinations now empha-sise 'high yield' as a primary objective of tourism policy. Several measures of tourism yield can be developed using the data contained in TSA. Some of these are discussed below.

Expenditure measures of yield
Tourism yield can be estimated as the expenditure associated with different visitor market segments either per trip or per day. Expenditure, whether for total trip or per visitor night, is the standard measure of tourism yield.

The TSA can be very useful for estimating the contribution made by the various visitor market segments to such variables as Tourism Gross State Product (TGSP) or tourism employment.

An innovative use of TSA is to estimate the contribution made per visitor dollar spent by tourists from different origin, demographic or special interest markets. It is useful to display expenditure data in matrix form as shown in Figure 7.1. The matrix consists of four

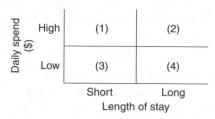

Figure 7.1 Expenditure data in matrix form

quadrants. The horizontal and vertical axes indicate average length of stay and average daily spend ($), respectively.

Quadrant 1 comprises high daily spend, short-stay travellers.

Quadrant 2 comprises the highest yielding segments and comprises high daily spend, long-stay travellers whose daily spend and length of stay lies above the average for the destination as a whole. It may be argued that segments that fall into this quadrant should carry a higher priority in terms of targeted marketing campaigns than other quadrants.

Quadrant 3 contains the least attractive markets of short stay/low spend.

Quadrant 4 comprises long stay/low spend markets.

While the matrix is drawn for expenditure, other contribution and impact data can also be displayed in this form. Thus, Dwyer *et al.* (2007) construct similar matrices to display by origin, tourists' contribution to tourism GDP, GVA and employment.

We here describe six yield measures – *expenditure per tourist, return on capital, tourism profitability, tourism GDP, tourism value added* and *tourism employment.* Each of these can be measured using TSA.

Yield as expenditure injected per tourist

Yield as expenditure per tourist may be measured rather simply

$$\text{Yield per tourist} = \frac{\text{Expenditure associated with visitor market}}{\text{Number of tourists from that market}}$$

The standard expenditure measure of yield may be criticised on several grounds.

- Gross expenditure data do not in itself provide information on what goods and services tourists purchase and so give no indication of the sectors of tourism that receive the sales revenues.
- Tourist expenditure also is not an indicator of profitability to firms since we must allow for the aggregate costs of providing the services to each visitor segment.

- Expenditure levels in themselves do not indicate the sales revenues accruing to suppliers of goods and services to tourists' net of imports.
- Expenditure is not a particularly good guide to the contribution of tourist expenditure to TGDP, TGVA and tourism employment.
- Expenditure per se does not provide information on each segment's relative spread of impacts and economic and social benefit to the wider destination.

An advantage of TSA is that they can be used to develop new and more useful measures of tourism yield which account for the contribution that additional expenditure, associated with a particular visitor market segment such as by origin, demographic market or travel motive, has on the tourism industry in respect of value added, profits and employment.

Yield as rate of return on capital

Yield as return on capital can be estimated by dividing the Gross Operating Surplus (GOS) of a tourism industry by the tourism capital in the industry:

$$\text{Yield at industry level} = \frac{\text{GOS of the industry}}{\text{Tourism capital in the industry}}$$

GOS is the surplus generated by operating activities after the labour factor input has been recompensed. It can be calculated from the value added at factor cost less the personnel costs. It is the balance available to the unit which allows it to recompense the providers of own funds and debt, to pay taxes and eventually to finance all or a part of its investment. The tourism industry can refer to all tourism industries taken together or to a particular characteristic industry (e.g. accommodation and road passenger transport).

Yield as return on capital from any niche market can be calculated as the ratio of GOS contributed by the niche market divided by tourism capital used in producing for the market segment:

Yield as return on capital from any niche market

$$\text{Yield}_{\text{niche market}} = \frac{\text{GOS due to sales to the particular tourism market}}{\text{Tourism capital used in producing the goods and services consumed by the market segment}}$$

Thus, data permitting, yield measures can be estimated for tourists from particular origin countries or particular social or demographic market segments (e.g. Japanese honeymooners, business travellers, over-55s). While GOS measures come from standard TSA, at the present time, only a small proportion of countries that have developed TSA have incorporated estimates of the amount of tourism capital, thus restricting application of this measure. Measures of capital input consistent with TSA can be developed. For example, if according to the TSA, 12% of the total output of an industry can be ascribed to tourism, then it is plausible to assume that 12% of the industry's capital stock can also be ascribed to tourism, in the absence of more explicit information.

Yield as a profitability measure

A primary objective of private sector tourism organisations is to earn a profit from their operations. The profit margin on tourism sales can be estimated using the share of GOS in tourism consumption attributable to a tourism market. GOS by industry is directly derived from industry GVA which is the value of production minus the costs of material inputs used in the production. This measure of yield can apply to the tourism industry as a whole or to particular sectors of the industry (tourism characteristic or tourism connected industries). This measure applies to the industry sector (or some part of it) associated with an additional tourist from a particular market. Where a destination has tourism expenditure data classified by origin, motivation or special interest, this enables estimates to be made of the rate of profit associated with each tourism origin or niche market.

Yield, approximated by the profit margin at industry level, is defined as follows:

$$\text{Yield}_{\text{at industry level}} = \frac{\text{GOS of the industry sector}}{\text{Tourism consumption of the goods and services produced by the industry}}$$

Yield as the profit margin for a particular niche market is defined as follows:

$$\text{Yield}_{\text{niche market}} = \frac{\text{GOS due to sales to the particular niche market}}{\text{Tourism consumption by the niche market}}$$

Yield as contribution to TGDP or TGVA

TSA can be used to estimate tourism's contribution to GVA or GDP at both the industry and niche market level. We can identify a GDP (or GVA) measure of yield at the industry level or for a niche market as follows:

$$\text{Yield}_{\text{at industry level}} = \frac{\text{Contribution of industry to GDP (GVA)}}{\text{Tourism consumption of the goods and services produced by the industry}}$$

$$\text{Yield}_{\text{niche market}} = \frac{\text{Contribution to GDP (GVA) of sales to the particular niche market}}{\text{Tourism consumption by the niche market}}$$

Yield as contribution to tourism employment

Yield can be estimated in terms of the level of employment in the tourism industry supported by the tourist expenditure. We can identify an employment measure of yield at the industry level or for a niche market:

$$\text{Yield}_{\text{at industry level}} = \frac{\text{Contribution of industry to employment}}{\text{Tourism consumption of the goods and services produced by the industry}}$$

$$\text{Yield}_{\text{niche market}} = \frac{\text{Contribution to employment of sales to the particular niche market}}{\text{Tourism consumption by the niche market}}$$

Tourism Research Australia, the national government's official tourism research agency, has recently estimated tourism yield in Australia (Collins *et al.*, 2004; Salma & Heaney,

2004). The purpose of the two studies was to illustrate how the concept of 'tourism yield' can be measured from the perspective of both tourism operators and destination managers. Both studies were based on Australia's International Visitor Survey and TSA with the first focused on the reason for visitation to Australia while the second focused on the source of visitors to Australia.

The measures of yield developed by TRA indicate how an additional tourist from a particular market contributes to the value added, or employment in the tourism industry, or how it contributes to tourism industry profits. The findings are summarised in Box 7.7.

BOX 7.7 Two Yield Studies by Tourism Research Australia using a TSA

Expenditure, profit and employment generated per visitor

Using tourist expenditure data from Australia's International Visitor Survey (Tourism Research Australia, 2002) and Tourism Satellite Accounts, Salma and Heaney estimated three yields for each of eight important Australian inbound niche markets: Gross Operating Surplus (GOS) per visitor; the rate of profit on tourism sales; and the employment generated per thousand visitors. The relevant yield rate per visitor market is found by dividing GOS for that market by the associated tourist consumption. Selected results are shown below in Table 7.6.

The study found that:

- The GOS per visit depended on expenditure in each market. Students had the highest GOS per visitor followed by backpackers and German holiday makers. New Zealand mature travellers and Malaysian first timers showed the smallest GOS per visit.
- The average yield rate (GOS per $A of tourism consumption) for the total inbound visitor market was 12.2% with five market groups above average and three (students, business and UK repeats) below.
- Students generated the highest contribution to employment per thousand visitors followed by backpackers and German holiday makers – the only three visitor markets to generate employment at or above the average for all inbound tourism to Australia (29 jobs per 1000 visitors).

Ranking of economic contribution by gross value added and employment generated by country of visitor origin

Using tourism consumption data from the TSA, Collins *et al.* (2004) estimated 'the economic contribution' made by 14 major inbound market segments and ranked

Table 7.6 Yield and employment generated by reason for visitation, Australia, 2001/02

Niche Market	Tourism consumption per visitor ($A)	Tourism GOS per visitor $A	Profit Margin per cent	Employment generated per thousand visitors number
Japanese honeymooners	3491	483	13.8	25
German holiday makers	5401	693	12.8	29
Backpackers	6158	773	12.6	54
NZ mature	1374	173	12.6	11
Malaysia first timers	1902	237	12.5	17
UK repeat	3662	432	11.8	29
Business	3020	353	11.7	23
Students	11872	1181	9.9	123
All inbound visitors	3484	427	12.2	29

Source: Salma and Heaney (2004), Table 1

them in order of their contribution to tourism gross value added and contribution to employment. Selected results appear in Table 7.7.

The study found that:

- Visitors from China, Indonesia, Korea and Thailand each consumed more than the average consumption of all visitors per trip and generated above average GVA per dollar of expenditure.
- Visitors from Japan and New Zealand each consumed less than the average consumption of all visitors per trip and generated below average GVA per dollar of expenditure.

Table 7.7 Gross value added and employment generated by country of visitor, Australia 2001/02

Origin	Visitors ('000)	Average consumption per visitor ($)	Tourism GVA per $ of consumption	Direct employment generated per $ million of consumption
Canada	88	4834	0.37	7.0
China	162	4162	0.48	8.6
Germany	132	5806	0.39	7.0
Hong Kong	134	5029	0.47	8.2
Indonesia	84	4834	0.51	8.8
Japan	614	3295	0.40	7.2
Korea	165	4043	0.46	8.5
Malaysia	136	3283	0.49	8.8
NZ	713	1664	0.38	7.4
Singapore	256	2904	0.47	8.5
Taiwan	90	3115	0.46	8.1
Thailand	72	4032	0.50	8.8
UK	590	4644	0.37	6.9
USA	397	6129	0.40	7.0
Total	4390	3891	0.41	7.5

Source: Collins *et al.* (2004), Table 1

- Visitors from Malaysia, Taiwan and Singapore, each consumed less than the average consumption per visitor but produced greater tourism GVA per dollar of tourism consumption and employment per million dollars of tourism consumption than the average for total inbound travel.
- Visitors from USA, UK, Hong Kong, Canada, and Germany, each consumed more than the average consumption per visitor but produced smaller tourism

GVA per dollar of tourism consumption and employment per million dollars of tourism consumption than the average for total inbound travel.

- Visitors from Asia generally, except Japan, generated higher than average tourism GVA per dollar of tourism consumption and employment per million dollars of tourism consumption.
- Visitors from western countries (Canada, Germany, Japan, New Zealand, UK, and USA) produced less than the average tourism GVA and employment per dollar of tourism consumption.

Source: Salma and Heany (2004); Collins *et al.* (2004)

These types of yield measures can be placed alongside other TSA outputs to provide useful information to tourism stakeholders. A major advantage of the financial measure of yield over the standard expenditure measure is that the GOS measure used in the estimates is net of cost of goods and services sold to tourists. This method of estimating yield is an improvement on some alternative measures because its profit focus (GOS) takes both revenues and costs into account and that from an industry point of view, the definition of yield is more closely related to the 'actual' rate of return earned in the industry (Collins *et al.*, 2004).

However, it must be re-emphasised that this type of analysis gives only partial equilibrium measures or the direct impacts on the tourism industry. That is, TSA-based measures do not incorporate the economy-wide effects of tourist expenditure after allowance is made for inter-industry effects of the injected expenditure resulting from changes in prices, exchange rates in the presence of factor constraints. Since the TRA studies estimate only the direct effects of tourist expenditure on GOS, GVA and employment, it would be inappropriate to draw policy conclusions from these findings alone. While the tourism industry private sector may not be particularly concerned about the effects of additional tourism numbers and expenditure on other industries, governments that are required to support destination marketing and promotion may be more interested in the net impacts of such activity, taking into account the overall effects on industry balance. It is only by taking account of indirect effects (positive and negative) that changes in industry balance can be determined. The GOS and GDP per visitor and the employment generated per visitor are likely to be substantially lower once inter-industry effects are recognised.

Proper acknowledgement of these effects requires going beyond TSA-based yield measures to undertake CGE modelling of the tourism expenditure associated with each market segment. Estimation of the inter-industry effects is essential for a complete picture. In Chapter 9, we discuss some yield estimates based on CGE modelling.

7.7.2 TOURISM PRODUCTIVITY

TSA can be used to develop valuable economic performance indicators. These include measures of productivity, prices and profitability for the tourism industry as a whole. They can also be used to explore performance in individual sectors, such as accommodation or motor vehicle hire. The measures can be used to explore the performance of individual tourism sectors or of tourism relative to that of other industries – for example, how productivity growth in tourism compares to that elsewhere.

Productivity is a core measure of performance. The simplest productivity relationship is between outputs and inputs. Productivity = Outputs / Inputs.

Productivity growth is simply the growth in output less the growth in inputs.

Productivity measures need to be compared to one another to be informative. An increase in productivity associated, for example, with the introduction of new technology and improved management practices, tax reforms, economies of scale and price changes can increase TGVA. Productivity can be measured for tourism characteristic and connected industries with benchmarking comparisons made between different regions, states and countries for each industry, including comparisons of productivity growth over time. Productivity growth rates can be very valuable in forecasting – prices or competitiveness in the future will depend on productivity growth and changes in input prices. Aggregate industry productivity changes or differences can be linked in with profitability, price and competitiveness indicators as in the study highlighted in Box 7.8.

BOX 7.8 Tourism productivity using a TSA

Study 1. Tourism performance in Australia

The authors have developed measures of tourism industry performance using Australian TSA data over a 9 year period. Value Added in tourism was used as the output measure. Since the Australian TSA only reports nominal Value Added, to develop a series on real value added, TSA parameters were applied to the real Value Added measures for component industries from the National Accounts. These are reported in Table 7.8. These data indicate that real tourism Value Added grew only slowly following the boom (Sydney Olympics) year of 2000. Employment data for tourism are also reported in this table, enabling a measure of labour productivity (Real Value Added per Employee). This measure indicates that over the whole period, productivity has changed little, though it rose during the boom years, and has fallen since.

Compensation per employee has been growing faster than output prices. With static productivity, this suggests that the tourism sector in Australia has been facing a profitability squeeze.

Table 7.8 Tourism value added, employment and productivity, 1997/98–2002/03

Year	Nominal Value Added ($m)	Real Value Added ($m)	Employment ('000)	Real VA/ Employee ($'000)
1997/98	21,855	24,800	422,500	58.7
1998/99	23,948	26,865	514,330	62.7
1999/00	25,118	28,014	526,420	63.9
2000/01	26,920	29,865	561,070	66.1
2001/02	27,428	29,767	552,500	66.6
2002/03	28,551	30,401	552,670	66.5
2003/04	29,367	30,241	530,300	67.4
2004/05	29,692	29,692	514,790	64.7
2005/06	31,291	30,815	529,660	66.3

Source: Dwyer, L., P. Forsyth and R. Spurr (2007a) 'Contrasting the Uses of TSAs and CGE Models: Measuring Tourism Yield and Productivity', *Tourism Economics*, 13(4), 537–551, December.

Study 2. Tourism performance in New Zealand

Over the period 1997–2004 in New Zealand the performance of tourism's characteristic industries (e.g. Accommodation, Transport and Recreation) as a value-creator and productive employer fell short of what was being achieved by tourism's related industries (Retail). Outputs from Tourism's characteristic industries displayed 1.2% real growth but succumbed to inflationary pressures; absorbing steadily rising costs and reducing production efficiency without adjusting prices so as to maintain value growth. This behaviour was not seen in tourism's related industries where real growth was almost 6% over the same period.

Throughout the same period New Zealand's labour productivity growth was relatively low at an annual average of 1.1% but tourism's characteristic industries fared less well – averaging negative growth, yet tourism's related industries averaged 1.7% annual growth. Tourism characteristic industry labour content rose and production efficiencies (technology, process improvement, etc) that may have occurred were masked by visitor arrival growth.

New Zealand's visitor arrival growth during this period averaged 6.55% per annum and was amongst the highest in the world. Should visitor volume growth decline, the degree to which tourism enterprises will be able to maintain their position in the labour market and invest in product leadership is questionable. The over-compensatory performance of its related industries and the good fortune of strong visitor arrivals growth from traditional markets seeking safe destinations, contributed to tourism's overall performance as a remarkable GDP contributor over the period 1999–2003.

Source: Moriarty, J. (2006) 'Enhancing Financial and Economic Yield in Tourism: Analysing New Zealand's Tourism Satellite Accounts for Measures of Sector Performance and Business Benchmarks', Tourism Recreation Research and Education Centre (TRREC) Yield Report No. 2

The use of TSA to estimate tourism productivity has been relatively neglected by researchers. Thus TSAs represent an important but little used tool for estimating tourism productivity measures for comparison between tourism industries within the country and internationally.

7.7.3 CALCULATING THE CARBON FOOTPRINT OF TOURISM

There is increasing interest in the environmental impacts of tourism, and especially its impact on greenhouse gas (GHG) emissions. We have discussed how the TSA documents the outputs and value added in the various industries which make up tourism – that is, they summarise the productive activities. It is these activities which generate GHG emissions. If the relationship between industry production and GHG emissions is known, then it is possible to calculate the emissions which are due to tourism as measured by the TSA.

A number of researchers have combined TSA estimates with data on carbon emissions from economic activity to measure the direct and indirect impact of tourism activity. Patterson and McDonald (2004) found that the tourism sector ranked fifth largest for the total amount of energy used and CO_2 emissions released within New Zealand, when internal energy use was considered. If return overseas travel by inbound tourists was included, the tourism sector then became the second highest user of energy and the highest CO_2 emitter out of the 25 sectors considered. In another study, Jones and Munday (2007) combined the Wales TSA estimates to pilot environment satellite account estimates to produce direct, indirect and induced waste and GHG emissions due to tourism demand. More recently, in Australia, Forsyth *et al.* (2008) used the TSA to estimate the carbon footprint of Australian tourism. To measure the GHG emissions directly associated with tourism production in Australia, Forsyth *et al.* (2008) used the TSA to estimate the outputs of each

Table 7.9 Economic and environmental measures of selected tourism industries, Canada 2002

| Industry | Economic measures of tourism | | Environmental measures of tourism | |
	CTSA tourism GVA[a] ($ millions) (1)	Tourism[b] shares of industries (%) (2)	Energy Use[c] (terajoules) (3)	GHG emissions[d] (Kt of CO_2-e) (4)
Air transportation	3,088	78.7%	151,572	10,595
Food and beverage services	2,898	17.3%	7,019	210

[a]Gross Value Added (GVA) is known as Gross Domestic Product in the Canadian System of National Accounts. GDP at basic prices is GDP at market prices minus taxes less subsidies on products. Canadian Tourism Satellite Account Handbook, Catalogue no. 13-604 no. 52, Statistics Canada.

[b]Also known as the tourism GVA ratio, it is calculated by taking tourism GVA and comparing it with the total GVA of the industry (i.e. Tourism GVA + Non-tourism GVA). It measures how much of the production of a certain industry is attributable to tourism. Canadian Tourism Satellite Account Handbook, Catalogue no. 13-604 no. 52, Statistics Canada.

[c]Energy use to satisfy TSA tourism demand. Calculated as energy use from the Material and Energy Flow Account (MEFA) multiplied by the tourism shares of industries.

[d]Greenhouse gas emitted while satisfying TSA tourism demand. Calculated as GHG from the MEFA multiplied by the tourism shares of industries.

of the components of the tourism industry, and then linked the output data with data on carbon emissions for the different industries.

Jackson *et al.* (2008) combined the CTSA and the Canadian System of Environmental and Resource Accounts for the year 2002. On the left-hand side of the Table 7.9, the economic measures for the air transportation and the food and beverage services industries are shown. Column 1 shows the tourism GVA while column 2 shows the 'tourism shares of industries' as calculated in the CTSA. In 2002, 79% of the output of the air transportation industry was directly attributable to tourism while 17% of that of the food and beverage services industry was due directly to tourism.

Columns 3 and 4 set out the quantitative impact on the environment of the tourism activity in the two industries. For example, in 2002, air transportation combusted 151,572 terajoules and emitted 10,595 KT of CO_2-equivalents as a direct result of the transportation of visitors, while the emissions in food and beverage services were 7019 terajoules and 210 CO_2-equivalents. They found that air transportation directly generated 1.03 tonnes of GHG emissions for every $1000 of tourism output (in nominal terms) in 2002, while food and beverage services produced almost 33 times fewer GHG emissions, for every $1000 of output. If this exercise were repeated for each industry, one could sum the amount of energy used and the related GHG emissions needed to directly serve tourists and same-day visitors. This could be used to examine the tourism share of the energy consumption and GHG emissions of each industry as well as the aggregate for the sum of all industries providing services to visitors.

The advantage of using the TSA to estimate the carbon footprint is that it ensures that the measure is comprehensive and incorporates all emissions from all industries which make up tourism. In addition, since the TSA is extensively used as a measure of the economic contribution of size of the tourism industry, this carbon footprint is an environmental measure which is consistent, in terms of definition of the industry, with the economic measure. We shall discuss tourism's carbon footprint in more detail in Chapter 19 in association with tourism's impact on climate change.

7.8 CONCLUSIONS AND POLICY

- A TSA highlights the contribution that tourism makes to each other sector of the national accounts. In doing so, they provide an internationally recognised and standardised method of assessing the scale and impact of tourism spending and its links across different sectors, allowing tourism's role in an economy to be identified and compared with other sectors.

- In helping to estimate and understand tourism's contribution to the economy, TSA help to: identify a tourism 'industry'; measure key economic variables; measure tourism's interrelationship with other industries; provide support for inter-industry comparisons;

provide support for international comparisons; give credibility to estimates of the economic contribution of tourism; and provide a tool for tourism research and policy analysis.

- TSA should be considered from two perspectives: as a statistical tool and as the framework to guide countries in the further development of their system of tourism statistics. Those countries in which TSA have been implemented are able to gain a much clearer picture of tourism's position within their economy and are thus able to evaluate more accurately the benefits tourism offers.

- Given their relative expense and high level of involvement by stakeholders, it is not feasible to produce completely up-to-date TSA every year. Key aggregates of TSA, though, can be updated annually using relationships in the benchmark TSA and demand-side data.

- TSA can be used to guide policy in that they: measure the direct contribution of tourism to the economy; distinguish economic contribution from economic impact; allow focus on tourism yield; and can be used to develop performance indicators such as tourism productivity.

- The extensive involvement of governments in tourism planning, infrastructure provision and marketing at a state, regional or local level has led to the development of regional TSA. The use of the term 'satellite account' may be misleading at the regional level given that it cannot strictly conform to the national accounts and there are some challenges to the construction of regional TSA. Nevertheless, there are benefits to estimating tourism's contribution to sub-regions of the national economy within the TSA context.

- TSA provide a starting point for other more comprehensive approaches to analysing the overall economic impact of tourism. Several measures of tourism yield can be developed using the data contained in TSA. TSA can also be used to develop valuable economic performance indicators. These include measures of productivity, prices and profitability for the tourism industry as a whole. They can also be used to explore performance in individual sectors, such as accommodation or motor vehicle hire. The measures can be used to explore the performance of individual tourism sectors or of tourism relative to that of other industries. Another use of TSA is to measure tourism's 'carbon footprint'. That is, if the relationship between industry production and GHG emissions is known, then it is possible to calculate the emissions which are due to tourism as measured by the TSA.

SELF-REVIEW QUESTIONS

1. Briefly outline the concept of the TSA.

2. What items of information do the TSA provide for destination managers?

3. List and briefly describe each of the ten standard tables that comprise the TSA.

4. Summarise the eight important contributions that TSA make in estimating and understanding tourism's contribution to the economy.

5. Why undertake regional TSA? Differentiate between the top-down and bottom-up approaches to designing regional TSA.

6. Distinguish different measures of tourism yield that can be estimated through the use of TSA.

7. Briefly explain how TSA might be used to guide policy decision making.

ESSAY QUESTIONS

1. 'Any attempt to examine the economic contribution of tourism that is focused on systems of national accounts only, and which highlights only tourism related sectors, is likely to seriously under-estimate the overall expenditure by tourists and thus its economic significance.' Discuss.

2. Adopting a top-down approach to constructing regional TSA is so much more sensible than adopting a bottom-up approach. Argue for or against this statement.

3. By highlighting tourism within the national accounting framework, TSA allow the tourism industry to be better included in the mainstream of economic analysis. How so?

4. Analyse the important contributions that TSA make to the estimation and understanding of tourism's economic contribution.

CHAPTER 8

ECONOMIC IMPACTS OF TOURISM USING INPUT–OUTPUT MODELS

LEARNING OBJECTIVES

After reading this chapter, you should be able to:

1. Define the concept of economic impact analysis and discuss its application to tourism.

2. Differentiate between the direct effects and secondary effects (indirect and induced) of changes in tourism expenditure.

3. Discuss the main forms of leakages that may accompany changes in tourism expenditure.

4. Understand the concept of the tourism multiplier and distinguish between Keynesian multipliers and multipliers based on economic modelling.

5. Understand the basic structure of an Input–Output (I–O) table.

6. Differentiate between the different types of Input–Output (I–O) multipliers and appreciate the limitations and potential misuse of tourism multipliers.

7. Distinguish between an I–O table and a Social Accounting Matrix (SAM).

8.1 INTRODUCTION

There is now an extensive literature on evaluating the economic impacts of tourism. This literature seeks to show how the impacts of changes in tourism expenditure, perhaps due to improved promotion, development of special events or external shocks such as terrorist attacks, can be evaluated in economic terms. An economic impact analysis estimates the changes that take place in an economy due to some existing or proposed project, action, event or policy. As typically employed in tourism research and policy analysis, economic impact analyses trace the flows of spending associated with tourism activity in an economy through business, households and government to identify the resulting changes in economic variables such as sales, output, government tax revenues, household income, value added and employment. A major objective of such estimates has been to inform policy makers as to the appropriate allocation of resources both within the tourism sector itself and between tourism and other industry sectors.

Economic impact analyses indicate that expenditure by tourists can potentially have significant additional effects throughout the rest of the economy, resulting in increased income and expenditure for a range of different stakeholders, many of whom are not directly connected with the tourism industry. The extent to which production, income and employment in the destination are affected by tourism expenditure depends importantly on the import content of consumption goods and inputs to production and on the strengths of the business linkages between tourism and other industry sectors. Almost every industry in the economy is affected to some extent by the indirect and induced effects of the initial tourist expenditure. These flow-on effects are called multiplier effects. The size of the multiplier effects will determine the impact of a tourism shock (positive or negative) on important economic variables such as GDP (GSP), value added, factor incomes and employment.

8.2 PURPOSE OF ECONOMIC IMPACT ANALYSIS

The most common applications of economic impact analysis to tourism are related to the evaluation of the following (cf. Stynes, 2006):

1. *The effects of changes in tourism demand.* As discussed in Chapter 2, important factors underpinning tourism demand including population changes, transportation costs, destination price competitiveness, changing exchange rates, marketing activity changing consumer tastes and preferences, and both expected and unexpected events, can alter levels of tourism numbers, expenditure and associated economic activity. An economic impact study can estimate the size and nature of impacts resulting from projected changes in tourism demand.

2. *The effects of policies and regulations* which affect tourism activity either directly or indirectly. These policies, whether they expand or contract tourism activity can be assessed for their impacts on key economic variables. Where there is uncertainty regarding the impacts of policy options, scenarios can be created to estimate a likely range of economic impacts under different assumptions.

3. *Factors beyond the direct control of the industry itself.* Tourism depends on many factors in both origin markets and destinations that are often beyond the direct control of tourism industry stakeholders. These could include natural events such as tsunamis, hurricanes or Bird Flu or human-made events such as terrorist activity or increasing crime affecting the destination directly or affecting a competitor destination. Economic impact analysis can provide useful information on the impacts of such events on tourism and hence on the wider economy. This can inform tourism stakeholders as to the potential gains from undertaking measures to mitigate such impacts in the future.

4. *Public and private investment proposals.* Economic impact studies provide information to help decision makers better understand the consequences of various investment proposals on the tourism industry as well as on other sectors of the economy. These investments may be funded by the public sector (e.g. airport construction or a convention facility) or private sector (e.g. resort hotel development or a tourism shopping complex). Changes in the supply of tourism opportunities may involve a change in *quantity*, such as the opening of new facilities, closing of existing ones or expansions and contraction in the range of tourism-related attractions in a destination. Supply changes may also involve changes in *quality*, including changes in the nature and variety of the tourism products and services that are provided in an area, environmental quality and improved access to and within the destination.

5. *Resource allocation, policy and management of tourism development strategies.* Economic impact analysis can compare the economic impacts of alternative resource allocation, policy, management or tourism development strategies. A government deciding the budget to be allocated to tourism development will have an interest in comparing the impacts of a dollar spent on tourism support development (e.g. financial support for a special event), as compared to a dollar spent on marketing activity. Economic impact analyses can be local, regional or national in scope, and the information gathered can be used in both tourism planning and policy making to enhance the economic contribution of tourism to a destination.

6. *Lobbying.* Economic impact analysis can be used as a device to lobby governments to make decisions favourable to tourism development. Tourism stakeholders, often aided by consultants, may attempt to convince decision makers to allocate more resources for tourism in their destination or to establish policies that encourage tourism, by showing that tourism has significant economic impacts. In this way, tourism's economic impacts can become an important consideration in national, state, regional and community planning and in wider economic development.

An economic impact analysis thus can allow for an objective evaluation of the economic impact of a particular action on the local economy. These impacts are typically modelled either through Input–Output (I–O) analysis or, more comprehensively, through Computable General Equilibrium (CGE) models. This chapter will focus on economic impact analysis of tourism shocks using multipliers from Input–Output (I–O) tables. Chapter 9 will focus upon economic impact analysis using CGE models.

8.3 THE TOURISM 'MULTIPLIER'

In Chapter 6, we noted that expenditure by visitors to a destination represents an injection of 'new money' into that destination. The direct effects of tourist expenditure which fall on the suppliers who sell goods and services directly to tourists give rise to both indirect effects and induced effects. These effects are captured in flow-on ('secondary' or 'ripple') effects as the initial tourist money is spent and re-spent through the economy by firms and households, stimulating income and employment throughout the economy. The sum of the direct, indirect and induced effects is the *total effect* or *economic impact*. The economic impacts of a specific tourism demand shock are the overall increases in output, sales, value added, Gross Domestic Product (GDP), household income and employment.

A multiplier is the number by which a given change in spending is multiplied in order to estimate the impact of that change on an economy's output, income, value added or employment. Multipliers measure the economic impact of an injection of spending into an economy, including any flow-on effects. They are a measure of the degree of interdependence between the industry of interest (in this case tourism) and the rest of the economy.

Algebraically, multipliers can be expressed as the ratio of total impact (on output, household income, value added or employment) to the original expenditure impact, as follows:

$$\text{Multiplier} = \text{Total Impact} / \text{Direct Expenditure}$$

At each stage of the multiplier process there are two factors that limit the size of the economic impacts of a shock to tourism expenditure – leakages and factor constraints.

Leakages

As discussed in Chapter 6, the main forms of leakages from the direct and secondary effects of a change in tourist expenditure are saving, taxes and imports. For purposes of estimating the economic impacts of tourism shocks the leakages from tourism-related imports are particularly important as a constraint on the size of the multiplier effects. It should be noted that for purposes of regional economic impact analysis an 'imported' good or input need not be sourced internationally. To qualify as 'imported' it suffices that the item is produced outside of the area under study. Thus, analysis of the economic impacts of tourism on the Côte d'Azur would treat wine from Provence as imported whereas this would be regarded as sourced domestically from the perspective of tourism to France.

Each form of leakage results in money being taken out of the host economy, temporarily at least in the case of saving and tax. All up, their presence means that fewer dollars are left to create subsequent flow-on effects. The nature and extent of these leakages will depend on the characteristics of the destination. Smaller regions typically have greater leakages than larger regions because of their more limited industrial base. More of their inputs are likely to be imported, and their larger firms are likely to have head offices elsewhere or have non-resident shareholders. All such leakages limit the size of the tourism multiplier.

Factor constraints

In reality, economies experiencing an increase in tourism expenditure, particularly developing countries will face labour, land and capital constraints. In such circumstances, tourist expenditure will result in increased prices rather than increases in output, income and employment. We will explore the influence of factor constraints below in some detail as these lead to interactive industry effects which change the industrial composition of an economy and hence the multiplier effects from any shock to tourism demand.

The economic impacts of tourist-related spending can be estimated using an economic model that identifies and quantifies the linkages between different sectors of the local economy and linkages with other regions. The relationship between expenditure and output, income and employment (direct, indirect or induced) can be described by multipliers.

The value of the 'multiplier' will depend on the type of model employed. We can distinguish two broad types of multipliers: Keynesian multipliers and multipliers based on economic modelling.

8.3.1 KEYNESIAN MULTIPLIERS

Keynesian multipliers are relatively straightforward to calculate and provide a quick and simple way of assessing the overall magnitude of a change in tourism expenditure. Macroeconomic theory informs us that any injection of new money into an economy's circular flow of income will start a multiplier effect. That is, an initial change in autonomous spending will generate a magnified effect on total spending through many rounds of spending and re-spending. One person's spending thus becomes another person's income. Each subsequent round of spending will get smaller and smaller due to leakages, but the overall effect will still be much greater than the original injection. For example, following an exogenous increase in tourism expenditure, the businesses and workers receiving the money would re-spend some fraction of that amount, generating a total amount of spending and re-spending in excess of the initial spending.

Tourism impact analysis has often relied on simple Keynesian multipliers. These are calculated based on estimates of leakages from a given economy. Factors that affect the multiplier are the size of the local economy, the propensity of tourists and residents to buy imported goods or services, as well as the propensity of residents to save rather than spend (where saving reflects money kept out of circulation, i.e. not consumed or reinvested), and the rate of tax on household consumption. In a simple Keynesian model, the multiplier (K) can be represented as follows:

$$K = 1/(1 - C + M + T)$$

Where,

 C is the marginal propensity to consume (i.e. the proportion of any increase in income spent on consumption of goods and services). Thus, $1 - C = S$, the marginal propensity to save.

 M is the marginal propensity to import (i.e. the proportion of any increase in income spent on imported goods and services).

 T is the marginal rate of income taxation.

The greater the size of the leakages, the smaller the size of the multiplier. Suppose $100 million is injected into an economy by way of increased investment expenditure. If C is 0.8, T is 0.1, and the M is 0.2, the tourism multiplier would be $2[1/(0.2 + 0.1 + 0.2) = 1/0.5 = 2]$. The initial increase in investment of $100 million would then generate $200 million in total spending.

More sophisticated Keynesian-type models can be constructed. Keynesian-type multipliers can be calculated for a country, region or community.

A major difficulty with Keynesian multipliers, especially for regional economies, is that the data required to produce estimates are not readily available and generally require further econometric modelling of tenuous assumptions. For example, such models need information sufficient to allow distinctions to be made between different categories of expenditure. This is to recognise that $100 spent in a local restaurant as opposed to, say, an admission fee paid to a foreign-owned themed attraction or $100 spent on souvenirs, may have different multiplier effects on the local economy because of the different direct, indirect and induced effects of the expenditure.

Simple Keynesian multipliers, in any case, provide only a rather limited and partial perspective on the impact of tourism on the economy. They employ simplifying assumptions about the mechanisms which determine income, employment, savings, consumption and imports when an autonomous stimulus, such as increased visitor expenditure occurs. In their focus on simple aggregates they are unable to address the nature of linkages between sectors, nor do they allow for the range of factor constraints that generate inter industry effects.

8.3.2 MULTIPLIERS BASED ON ECONOMIC MODELLING

The effects of tourist expenditure on the economy can also be estimated using economic models that identify and quantify the linkages between the different sectors of the local economy and the linkages with other regions.

For any given injection of tourism expenditure, the increment to value-added and employment in the region will vary according to several features of the economy. These include the following:

- the particular industries are the recipients of the direct expenditure;
- the structure of the model employed;
- the assumed factor constraints;
- the production and consumption relationships assumed;
- changes in the prices of inputs and outputs;
- the workings of the labour market; and
- the government fiscal policy stance.

The standard approach is to estimate the economic impacts using either an Input–Output (I–O) model or a CGE model. In this chapter, we focus on I–O multipliers as a basis for economic impact estimation. CGE modelling is discussed in Chapter 9.

8.4 MULTIPLIERS BASED ON I–O MODELS

I–O tables can provide a basis for deriving multipliers, for economic planning and analysis, forecasting and economic impact assessment. I–O multipliers can be derived from the direct requirements coefficient matrices based on I–O tables.

8.4.1 STRUCTURE OF AN I–O TABLE

I–O tables are a set of accounts relating the components of final demands to the various industrial sectors, the interaction between industrial sectors and the relationship between the industrial sectors and the primary inputs.

I–O tables show the various industries that comprise the economy and indicate how these industries interlink through their purchase and sales relationships. In simple terms they show, for each industry, which other industries it purchases from and to which other industries it sells. The financial information provided in I–O tables enables the complex interrelationships between different industries and sectors to be quantified and assessed. I–O tables enable analysis of inter-industry relationships in the flow of goods and services in an economy, through the chain of producers, suppliers and intermediaries to the final buyer. Different I–O tables contain different degrees of detail in the number of products and industries included.

I–O tables illustrate, in matrix form, how transactions flow through the economy over a given time period. The rows of the matrix show the sales of the total output by each sector to every other sector. The columns show the inputs required by every sector from other sectors. The basic structure of an I–O table is discussed in Blake (2005).

Table 8.1 sets out a typical I–O matrix, sometimes referred to as a symmetrical I–O table (ABS, 2000).

In Table 8.1 the columns report the monetary dollar values of the various industry inputs, summed down for input payments and total input purchases. The rows report the value of the industry outputs, summed across for final demand and total output sales.

Table 8.1 Input–Output table

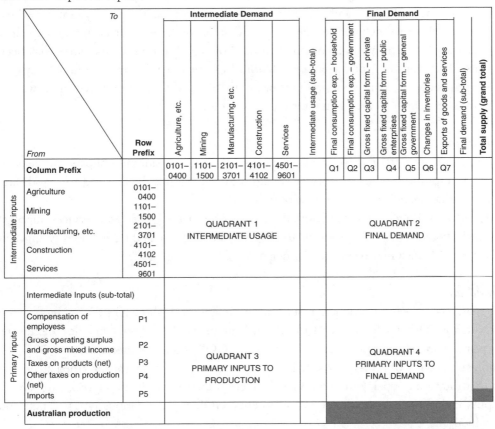

Source: ABS (2000)

The industry column total shows industry gross output, or the value of products produced by that industry. The column totals for final demand components show total expenditure. The row totals for products show total demand for each product, which also equals total supply. The value added row totals show labour earnings, Gross Operating Surplus (GOS) and the taxation of products and production. The following is based on the interpretation of each quadrant of Table 8.1 as discussed in ABS (2000).

Quadrant 1

The intermediate usage sub-matrix, or quadrant 1, measures the flows between industries. This quadrant (rows and columns 0101 to 9601) comprises inputs and outputs of domestic industries and is known as the inter-industry quadrant. Each column in this quadrant

shows the intermediate inputs into an industry in the form of goods and services produced by other industries, and each row shows those parts of an industry's output which
have been absorbed as intermediate inputs by other industries. For example, the cell at
the intersection of row i and column j shows how much output of industry i has been
absorbed by industry j for current production. In some tables, a row or column may represent a product or a group of products rather than an industry. For this reason, rows and
columns in quadrant 1 are often referred to as 'sectors'.

Quadrant 2

Comprising rows 0101 to 9601 and columns Q1 to Q7, quadrant 2 shows the disposition of output to categories of final demand. Final demand is the demand for goods and
services that are not used to produce other goods.

Quadrants 1 and 2 together show the total usage of the goods and services supplied
by each industry. Total usage equals total supply because quadrant 2 includes changes in
inventories (which may be positive or negative).

Quadrant 3

The primary inputs to production sub-matrix, quadrant 3, show all primary inputs into
production. This quadrant (rows P1 to P5 and columns 0101 to 9601) includes the returns
to primary inputs: compensation of employees; GOS and gross mixed income; imports;
and various types of taxes on production. These inputs differ from the intermediate inputs
in that they are not part of the output of current domestic production (ABS, 2000). Such
inputs include wages, salaries and supplements, GOS and the various types of taxes on
production.

Quadrants 1 and 3 together show the inputs used to produce the total supply (outputs)
of each industry. The sum of the inputs equals total supply (outputs) because the primary
inputs in quadrant 3 include GOS and gross mixed income (which may be positive or
negative).

Quadrant 4

The primary inputs to final demand sub-matrix, quadrant 4, show all primary inputs into
final demand. For example, it shows how much accommodation, air transport, food and
beverage and so on are purchased as inputs by the construction sector. Typically, these
types of final demand include private households, government, investment and exports.
Any of these items can be more detailed as required. An import row is also included in
final demand. For each of these types of final demand, the I–O table shows the value of
domestic consumption of each product, the value of taxes paid on these products and the
value of imports purchased.

I–O tables may be compiled for industries or products (or both), but they are similar
in essentials. We have displayed an industry-by-industry table, which is the type of table

published by many statistical agencies. A row in the table shows the disposition of the output of an industry and a column shows the origin of inputs into an industry. Since the output of an industry must be equal to the sum of its inputs (including GOS), the row total for an industry must be equal to the corresponding column total. They are simply two sides of an accounting identity (ABS, 2000).

In the I–O framework, the GDP, defined as the value of final goods and services produced in a given year, can be measured as net final demand, the sum of value added or primary incomes (see Box 8.1). In Table 8.1, two areas of the table have been shaded; the first (in the lighter shade) contains the components of GDP calculated by the income approach, while the second (darker shade) area contains the components of GDP calculated by the expenditure approach. In properly balanced I–O tables, both approaches to calculating GDP will yield the same value.

BOX 8.1 Estimation of GDP from an I–O table

GDP as net final demand (the expenditure approach)
On this approach, GDP is the sum of the final uses of goods and services (all uses except intermediate consumption) measured in purchasers' prices less the value of imports of goods and services. Final uses or final demand are equal to: household final expenditure + final expenditure of non-profit institutions serving households, the general government sector + gross capital formation + exports f.o.b.

This is a simple measure to compute from the I–O table, as it is the column totals for final demand minus the row total for imports. That is, GDP = C + I + G + X − M.

GDP as sum of value added (the production approach)
The production approach involves taking the value of goods and services produced by an industry (i.e. output) and deducting the cost of goods and services used up by the industry in the production process (i.e. intermediate consumption) and adding the result across all domestic industries. Gross Value Added (GVA) is defined as labour payments plus GOS plus taxation payments made by final demand.

Thus GDP = total industry output at basic prices − total industry intermediate consumption in purchasers' prices + taxes less subsidies on products.

GDP as sum of primary incomes (the income approach)

The income approach involves summing net factor incomes, consumption of fixed capital (depreciation) and taxes less subsidies on production and imports. GDP is also equal to the sum of primary incomes distributed by resident producer units. Values added at basic prices are calculated as the sum of compensation of employees, other taxes less subsidies on production, gross mixed incomes and GOS.

GDP can be calculated through the income approach, where GDP is equal to total value added – the sum of the row totals for labour, GOS and taxation.

8.4.2 THE DIRECT REQUIREMENTS MATRIX

An important application of I–O tables is in calculating inputs as a percentage of output of an industry and using these percentages for estimating the input requirements for any given output of that industry. The percentages are known as 'direct requirements coefficients' and are at the core of I–O analysis. Manipulating the direct requirements coefficients allows the derivation of measures known as Input–Output (I–O) multipliers.

Using I–O tables, multipliers can be calculated to provide a simple means of estimating the flow-on effects of a change in output in an industry on one or more of imports, income, employment or output in individual industries or in total. The multipliers can show both the 'first-round' effects and the aggregated effects once all secondary effects have flowed through the system. For example, in order to produce output from the manufacturing industry (in response, say, to increased visitor demand for retail shopping), inputs are required directly from the forestry industry (e.g. wood products). However, to supply this direct requirement, the forestry industry itself requires inputs from the construction industry which itself requires inputs from trade and transportation, manufacturing industry, mining and so on. The requirements can be traced, step by step, throughout the industrial structure, until the increments of output required indirectly from each industry become insignificant (which occurs after a few rounds).

If this operation is carried out for all industries and the direct and indirect requirements are added together, a matrix of total requirements coefficients is obtained. However, if the number of industries is large, the iterative method is too cumbersome, and so the total requirements are calculated on a computer by the method known as matrix inversion. This is why the matrix of total requirements is frequently described as the inverse matrix (or Leontief inverse matrices) and its coefficients as inverse coefficients. The procedure used for multiplier derivation is relatively complex and will not be described here. The underlying mathematics known as the Leontief inversion requires sophisticated mathematics (see United Nations Department for Economic and Social Affairs Statistics Division, 1999).

8.4.3 TYPES OF I–O MULTIPLIERS

I–O multipliers give the economic impact on a region's economy from a one-dollar change in the final demand for the output of one of the region's industries. There is no single multiplier for the whole economy. Rather, there are several different types of multipliers reflecting which secondary effects are included and which measure of economic activity is used. The five most common multipliers used in I–O analysis are sales, output, income, value added and employment.

- The *sales (transactions) multiplier* measures the total increase in business turnover generated by an extra unit of final demand.
- The *output multiplier* measures the effects generated by an extra unit of final demand on the output of industries in the economy, where output is equal to sales plus the increase in the value of stocks.
- The *income multiplier* shows the relationship between the direct and total income earned by households as generated by a unit of final demand. That is, it relates to the additional 'compensation of employees' paid to workers producing the extra output.
- The *value added multiplier* shows the value added at factor cost due to the change in output (i.e. wages, salaries and supplements earned by households plus GOS of business) as generated by an extra unit of final demand. It relates to the additional value-added, which is the sum of the compensation of employees, GOS and mixed income, and taxes less subsidies.
- The *employment multiplier* describes the ratio of direct and secondary employment to direct employment generated by an additional unit of final demand. This multiplier is usually expressed in terms of an increase of 'N' Full Time Equivalent Employees (FTEs) per million dollars of extra spending.

Sales and output multipliers have limited practical value for policy making. They measure the increase in gross turnover or output in the destination by summing all the intermediate transactions resulting directly and indirectly to satisfy a change in final demand and thus substantially exaggerate the economic activity generated by a tourism demand shock. While many studies employ income multipliers, these are somewhat narrow in scope since they measure only that proportion of gross value added that accrues to individuals within a region as wages and salaries (income earned by households), excluding GOS of businesses.

Of these different multipliers, value added multipliers, which measure the change in net economic activity at each stage of production are the preferred measure for the assessment of the contribution to the economy of some shock to final demand (Mules, 1999).

8.4.4 DISAGGREGATING I–O MULTIPLIER EFFECTS

The above multipliers can be decomposed into their various multiplier effects which are initial; first round and industrial support; and consumption-induced effects (ABS, 2000). We now define these effects with output as the selected variable.

Initial effects

The initial effect on the output of an industry is a one-dollar change in output to meet the change of one dollar in final demand. Associated with this change, there will also be initial effects on household income, employment and imports. These are determined by the industry's income, employment and imports coefficients.

First-round effects

To produce an extra unit of output to meet a one-dollar increase in final demand, an industry must increase its purchases from other industries and from itself. These additional intermediate inputs sum to the first-round effects. Thus, first-round effects indicate the amount of output required from all industries of the economy to produce the initial one dollar extra output from an industry.

Industrial support effect

Other industries in turn will need to increase their purchases of inputs to expand their output in order to meet the first-round requirement. Following this will be second, third and subsequent round requirements of indirect purchases. These indirect purchases sum to the industrial support effect.

Production-induced effect

The first-round effect can be combined with the industrial support effect to produce the production-induced effect. This indicates the amount of output required from all industries of the economy to produce the initial one dollar of extra output and all the subsequent induced output.

Consumption-induced effect

To produce the initial and production-induced output, wage and salary earners earn extra income which they spend on commodities produced by all industries in the economy. This spending induces further production by all industries. The output resulting from this further induced production is the consumption-induced effect.

Box 8.2 distinguishes between Simple and Total Multipliers (sometimes referred to as Type 1 and Type 2 multipliers).

BOX 8.2 Type 1 and Type 2 multipliers

Total multiplier:

The sum of the direct, indirect and consumption induced output effects arising from the initial one dollar stimulus to final demand.

Total Multiplier = initial effects + first round effects + industrial support effects + consumption induced effects.

Simple multiplier:

The sum of the direct and indirect output effects arising from the initial one dollar change in final demand.

Simple Multiplier = total multiplier − consumption induced effects = initial effects + production induced effects

Production induced effects = first round effects + industrial support effects.

Industrial support effects = simple multiplier − initial effects − first round effects.

These multipliers can be expressed in ratio form as follows:

$$\text{Simple (Type 1) multipliers} = \frac{\text{Direct effects} + \text{indirect effects}}{\text{Direct effects}}$$

$$= \text{initial effects} + \text{production induced / initial effects}$$

$$\text{Total (Type 2) multipliers} = \frac{\text{direct effects} + \text{indirect effects} + \text{induced effects}}{\text{direct effects}}$$

$$= \text{initial effects} + \text{production induced}$$

$$+ \text{consumption induced / initial effects}$$

Type 1 and Type 2 multipliers can each be divided into two types.

Type 1A multiplier: The ratio of the initial effect plus the first round effect, to the initial effect. In the case of an output multiplier, since the initial effect is assumed to be one, the Type-1A multiplier is equal to the initial effect plus the first round effect.

Type 1B multiplier: The ratio of the sum of the initial and the production-induced effect, to the initial effect. Since the initial effect is one, the type 1B multiplier is equal to the simple multiplier.

Type 2A multiplier: The ratio of the total multiplier to the initial effect. As the initial effect is one, the type 2A multiplier is equal to the total multiplier.

Type 2B multiplier: The ratio of the difference between the total multiplier and the initial effect, to the initial effect. Since the initial effect is equal to one, the type 2B multiplier is equal to the total multiplier minus one.

Source: ABS (1989) *Australian National Accounts, Introduction to Input-Output Multipliers* (Cat. no. 5246.0), Australian Bureau of Statistics, Canberra

Total multipliers include the full range of flow-on effects generated by an increase in economic activity. Thus, the total output multiplier is the total amount induced by the requirement from all industries to produce output to satisfy the demand for an extra dollar of output from an industry, and by the spending of the extra wage and salaries earned from producing the output by households (consumers).

It should be noted that the multiplier principle also works in reverse enabling estimates of reductions in output, income, employment and so on occasioned by reduced tourism expenditure. It is well known that natural disasters or outbreaks of war or terrorism or financial crises can initiate falls in tourism spending that in turn generate multiplied negative impacts on regional or national economy.

8.4.5 SAM MULTIPLIERS

A standard I–O table provides information on incomes to factors of production (capital and labour), but no information as to the owners of these factors. These owners include households, corporations, government (which can provide capital and levy indirect taxes) and foreign entities. As such, an I–O table misses important links on the distribution of income.

A Social Accounting Matrix (SAM) is a system of representing the economic and social structure of a country (region) at particular time, by defining its economic actors and recording their transactions. A SAM provides complementary economic indicators, which concern not only the macroeconomic aggregates of the System of National Accounts but also the socio-economic structure and distributional aspects of the economy (de Melo, 1988; Sugiyarto *et al.*, 2003).

A SAM is an expanded version of an I–O table which includes the transfer of money between industries and institutions and contains both market-based and non-market financial flows, such as inter-institutional transfers. An overriding feature of a SAM is that households and household groups are at the heart of the framework; only if there exists some detail on the distributional features of the household sector can the framework truly earn the label 'social' accounting matrix (Pyatt & Round, 1977). Entries in a SAM can be categorised into two groups, one that reflects flows across markets (i.e. representing product and factor markets) and the other that reflects nominal flows or transfer payments (Sugiyarto *et al.*, 2003; Wagner, 1997).

Several features of a SAM can be highlighted:

- A SAM represents flows of all economic transactions that take place within an economy (regional or national).
- A SAM is, at core, a matrix representation of the national accounts for a given country, but can be extended to include non-national accounting flows, and created for whole regions or area.
- Estimates provided by a SAM can be useful for calibrating a much broader class of models to do with monitoring poverty and income distribution.
- A SAM illustrates the circular process of demand leading to production leading to income, which in turn leads back to demand.
- A SAM also contains additional data on payments among owners. Payments arise from a variety of reasons: ownership of certain assets, direct taxes on corporations and households, pensions and transfers.
- The disaggregation level and choice of representative actors depend on the motivation underlying its development and the availability of data, so that there is no 'standard SAM'.
- In a balanced SAM there is an exact correspondence between rows and columns, implying that supply equals demand for all goods and factors, tax payments equals tax receipts, there are no excess profits in production, the value of each household expenditure equals the value of factor income plus transfers and the value of government tax revenue equals the value of transfers. (Rutherford & Paltsev, 1999)

A simple SAM is presented for illustration purposes in Table 8.2 (Mitra-Kahn, 2008). All institutional agents (firms, households, government and 'rest of economy' sector) are both buyers and sellers. Columns represent buyers (expenditures) and rows represent sellers (receipts). The SAM is read from column to row, so each entry in the matrix comes from its column heading, going to the row heading. Finally, columns and rows are added up, to ensure accounting consistency, and each column is added up to equal each corresponding row.

The SAM performs two functions:

First, SAM can be easily extended to include other flows in the economy, simply by adding more columns and rows, once the Standard National Account flows have been set up. Often rows for 'capital' and 'labour' are included, and the economy can be disaggregated into any number of sectors. Each extra disaggregated source of funds must have an equal and opposite recipient. So the SAM simplifies the design of the economy being modelled.

Table 8.2 An illustrative Social Accounting Matrix

	Firm	Household	Government	Rest of Economy	Net Investment	Total (Received)
Firm		C	G_F	$(X-M)_K$	I	$C + G_F + (X-M)_K + I$
Household	W		G_H	$(X-M)_C$		$W + G_H + (X-M)_C$
Government	T_F	T_H				$T_F + T_H$
Rest of Economy	$(X-M)_K$	$(X-M)_C$				$(X-M)_K + (X-M)_C$
Net Investment		S_H	S_G			$S_H + S_G$
Total (Expended)	$W + T_F + (X-M)_K$	$C + T_H + (X-M)_C + S_H$	$G_F + G_H + S_G$	$(X-M)_C + (X-M)_K$	I	

Source: Mitra-Kahn (2008), Figure 8

Abbreviations: Capital letters: Taxes, Wages, Imports, Exports, Savings, Investment, Consumption, Government Transfer.
Subscripts: Firms, Households, Government, Consumption Goods, K: Capital Goods

Second, since the SAM represents the national accounting system, it includes the institutional structure reflected in the national accounts which feed into any I–O or CGE model of the economy.

In the IMPLAN model which is used extensively for purposes of tourism regional impact analysis throughout the USA, total multipliers are referred to as 'Type SAM multipliers' where the induced effect is based on information in the SAM. Type SAM multipliers take into account the expenditures resulting from increased incomes of households as well as inter-institutional transfers resulting from the economic activity. Thus, Type SAM multipliers assume that as final demand changes, incomes increase along with inter-institutional transfers. As these people and institutions increase expenditures, this leads to increased demand from local industries and so on. In the IMPLAN model, this multiplier is flexible and can include any institutions deemed to be relevant (IMPLAN, 2000).

However, as a tool for impact analysis, tourism multipliers including Type SAM have all of the limitations of I–O multipliers in general. These limitations are displayed in Box 8.3.

It must be noted that every SAM provides a static image or 'snapshot' of an economy. Nevertheless, it can provide the statistical basis for the development of plausible models when more than a static image is required (see de Melo, 1988; Pyatt & Round, 1985; Robinson & Roland-Holst, 1988 for fuller discussions about a SAM and modelling based on a SAM).

8.4.6 STATIC VERSUS DYNAMIC I–O MODELS

Static multiplier models take no account of the length of time the multiplier effect takes to work its way through the economy. However, research indicates that different multiplier values can result from different estimates of the speed with which the resultant transactions occur in the economy. This has given rise to the development of dynamic I–O models. The essential distinction of a dynamic model is that it traces the path of the economy from a particular year to the target year, and it may be applied to calculate the requirements of a given final output not only in the current year but also in all preceding years through direct and indirect capital requirements. Dynamic models look at the future growth path of the economy year by year (Dixon & Parmenter, 1996). Since they share many of the same restrictive assumptions of the static I–O models, these models are subject to the same types of criticisms.

8.4.7 USE OF I–O MULTIPLIERS IN TOURISM ECONOMIC IMPACT STUDIES

I–O analysis has been used as the basis for estimating tourism multipliers and the effect on household income, value added and employment in several contexts:

Estimating the economic impacts of inbound tourism to a country. Examples include Antigua (Pollard, 1976); Bahamas & Bermuda (Archer, 1995, 1977); Mauritius (Archer, 1985);

Hong Kong (Lin & Sung, 1983); Korea (Song & Ahn, 1983); Puerto Rico (Ruiz, 1985); Singapore (Heng & Low, 1990; Kahn *et al.*, 1989); Ireland (Baum, 1991; Henry & Deane, 1997); India (Pavaskar, 1987); the Seychelles (Archer & Fletcher, 1996); Tanzania (Kweka *et al.*, 2001) ; and Balearic Islands (Polo & Vaile, 2008).

Estimating the economic impacts of tourism to a region within a country. Examples include Wales (Archer, 1973; Witt, 1987); Klamath River, Oregon (Johnson & Moore, 1993); Andhra Pradesh (Dwyer, 2000); and Victoria (West & Gamage, 2001).

Estimating the economic impacts of special events and festivals. Examples include Formula One Grand Prix (Burns *et al.*, 1986); Atlanta Olympic Games (Humphreys & Plummer, 1995), Washington DC (Frechtling & Horvath, 1998); Springfield Festival (Crompton *et al.*, 2001); South Pacific Games (Ryan & Lockyer, 2001); and Kaustinen Folk Music Festival Finland (Tohmo, 2005). We will consider the special problems of event evaluation in Chapter 11.

Sometimes lists of multiplier values are published for a range of countries, regions or events. In our view such comparisons are meaningless. The size of a tourism multiplier depends on the particular model employed, the specific circumstances of the destination, including the structure of the local economy and particularly the degree to which its various sectors are inter-linked in their trading patterns, and the existing factor constraints. Moreover, since tourism multipliers can be calculated in a number of different ways, care must be taken when comparing the different multiplier estimates. As we shall argue, the derivation of multipliers based on I–O models is so dependent on a range of unrealistic assumptions that they have little policy significance.

Despite their problems, multipliers based on I–O modelling have become so widely used as to have become 'standard practice' in economic impact assessment. These measures have tended to be too uncritically accepted by tourism researchers and consultants. The use of I–O multipliers implies that 'big numbers' are generated for important economic variables such as changes in GDP and employment resulting from tourism demand shocks. Some limitations of I–O-based multipliers are discussed in the following section.

8.5 LIMITATIONS OF TOURISM I–O MULTIPLIERS

Despite its continued use in economic impact assessment in tourism, I–O analysis has been rejected in other areas of economic impact evaluation (Harrison *et al.*, 2000).

I–O analysis can be criticised on several grounds. The major problem lies with the assumptions underlying the use of I–O models. These assumptions are so unrealistic that they affect the validity of the results obtained by the technique (Dwyer *et al.*, 2004). An overview of the underlying assumptions appears in Box 8.3. Some assumptions that are particularly relevant to tourism economic impact analysis will be discussed below.

8.5.1 RESTRICTIVE ASSUMPTIONS

I–O multipliers for tourism are based upon the same set of restrictive assumptions that underpin I–O modelling. Each assumption plays its part in producing exaggerated economic impact estimates of changes in tourism supply or demand. Some important assumptions are as follows (Briassoulis, 1991; Hollander, 1982a).

8.5.1.1 The proportionality assumption (fixed factor proportions assumption)

This postulates that production functions are linear. That is, for any output, each of its inputs will be a fixed proportion of the total. The constant technical coefficients used in I–O analysis also assume no changes in technology that may lead to substitution between factors. Thus, any additional production in any industry requires inputs in the same proportions as existing production – double the level of tourism activity/production and you double all of the inputs needed, double the number of jobs and so on.

The proportionality assumption effectively rules out possibilities of substitution between inputs, including imports, in response to increased tourism demand for goods and services. In reality, however, given changing relative factor prices, tourism firms are likely to make substitutions between factors used in the production of goods and services. In the face of increased demand for tourism services, resulting cost pressures can lead to substitution between labour and non-labour factors of production. An I–O model contains no price mechanism, however, and cannot capture the effects of changing factor costs within its framework. It also assumes that there are no changes in production techniques resulting from any price changes of inputs or changes in real wages. In some circumstances, if domestic demand increases it might be more efficient for industries to divert some exports to local consumption or import to some extent rather than increasing local production by the full amount. Indeed, import shares in particular can be very volatile for regional economies and this can make multipliers unstable. In tourism, seasonal conditions or natural disasters can result in the proportionality assumptions breaking down.

Over the longer term, the inputs into tourism are likely to change in form and intensity under the influence of economic, environmental, technological and socio-political factors. Particularly in a service industry such as tourism, some production processes can involve substitution between different inputs so that the same output can be produced using a different set of inputs to that specified in the I–O model (Johnson, 1999). Changes in trade patterns including import substitution and outsourcing beyond regional boundaries may be expected as economies change structurally over time.

The employment multipliers based on I–O analysis also assume a constant proportional relationship between sales turnover and the level of employment. However, different firms, according to the nature and scale of their business, will have different marginal propensities to employ labour following increased demand. In some firms, staffing levels may be relatively insensitive to changes in turnover, while other firms may seek better use of those currently employed. For these sorts of reasons, we cannot realistically assume a simple linear relationship between changes in tourism expenditure and changes in employment.

8.5.1.2 The homogeneity assumption

The homogeneity assumption postulates that each sector produces a single output, implying that all the products of the sector are perfect substitutes for one another and that there is no substitution between the products of different sectors. The homogeneity assumption is needed to allow unique sectoral disaggregation to occur in the I–O table – preventing products or their close substitutes from being assigned to more than one sector.

A consequence of this assumption is that I–O multipliers cannot take full account of the fact that tourist-related services produced by an industry may require labour, capital or material inputs that differ in composition from the industry's total inputs. Nor can the multipliers account for different outputs (defined by, say, price or service levels) produced for international and domestic tourists.

The homogeneity assumption is particularly problematic for newly emerging tourism areas. For example, the accommodation, food or shopping needs of foreign tourists may differ markedly in terms of service levels, price and profit margins from those for domestic residents or even domestic tourists. If expenditure by foreign tourists covers goods and services with more capital-intensive modes of production or with higher import content, for example, the I–O analysis would overestimate the employment impacts of additional expenditure by inbound tourists.

8.5.1.3 Consumption functions are linear and homogeneous

The assumption that consumption functions are linear implies that any increase in income to beneficiaries of tourist spending will be spent on the same items and in the same proportions as for previous consumption. That is, I–O multipliers assume that households consume additional goods and services in exact proportion to their initial budget shares. Thus, if consumers spend, on average, 30% of their incomes on food, they are assumed also to spend on food 30% of any additional incomes generated by tourism.

However, it is likely that income changes will lead to a changing structure of consumption by households and adjustments in the investment pattern by business. And given the high income elasticity of demand for tourism, greater incomes may imply that a greater proportion of income is allocated to tourism-related expenditure, and conversely.

For similar reasons, the income re-distributive effects of increased tourist expenditure may affect consumption patterns. In developing countries, in particular, the beneficiaries of tourist spending may allocate their additional expenditure to (non-tourism) goods and services which differ either in labour intensiveness or in import content from population purchasing patterns. This will affect the economic impact of the tourism-related shock.

Inbound tourism expenditure, particularly in developing countries, can alter consumption patterns via the demonstration effect (Sinclair, 1998). Since I–O multipliers cannot allow for such differences, this assumption probably leads to an overestimate of the induced effects of tourism (included in Type 2 total multipliers).

8.5.1.4 No supply constraints

The multiplier mechanism implicitly assumes that there are unused resources (land, labour, capital plant and equipment) available to meet any extra demand. I–O modelling assumes that all inputs and resources are supplied freely and no resource constraints exist. These resources are, therefore, effectively assumed to be not used elsewhere; they do not come from other industries and do not result in reductions in output elsewhere.

Economies experiencing an increase in tourism expenditure, particularly developing countries will face labour, land and capital constraints. When the economy is at or near full employment, with no spare capacity in some key sectors, increased tourism demand imposes cost pressures as the price of scarce resources are bid up. In such circumstances, tourist expenditure will result in increased prices rather than increases in output, income and employment. When additional inputs are imported due to domestic shortages this further reduces the multiplier effect.

Moreover, if other industries employ the same resources as does the tourist industry, they also face cost pressures resulting from the increased tourism demand. In the absence of offsetting productivity improvements, price increases attract resources into tourism, increasing the industry's costs and making the destination less price competitive. The size of the cost increases depend on the supply of different factors, whether these factors account for a significant proportion of the tourist industry total production costs, and how quickly extra supplies can be made available (Dwyer *et al.*, 2000).

In this competition for scarce resources, increased costs will tend to reduce the competitiveness of other sectors in the economy, particularly export-oriented and import-competing industries. Price increases may particularly affect trade exposed sectors that face world prices for their products. Firms may be unable to pass on cost increases without losing market share. Any loss of market share by domestic producers means that the net gain to the economy from further tourism will be lower.

Where cost pressures reduce the competitiveness of a nation's tourist industry, relative to other destinations, an additional result may be an increase in outbound tourism, implying a further loss of production and employment opportunities in the destination and reduced domestic tourism.

Such constraints may be quite substantial if tourist expenditure is relatively high or if the region under consideration is small. This is the main reason why Total (Type 2) multipliers (those that include consumption-induced effects) should be used with caution since they assume no resource constraints on economic activity.

Labour constraints

The effects of tourism growth on a tourism destination differ depending on the ability of the tourism sector to obtain labour without the consequence of higher wages (i.e. whether or not there is a pool of unemployed labour ready to move into the tourism industry). An expanding tourism industry will place additional pressure on the demand for labour whether skilled, semi-skilled or unskilled.

If labour shortages exist in an economy, expansion in final demand for tourism products and services will increase the demand for labour, raising wage rates and reducing the demand for labour elsewhere.

Different sectors of the tourism industry have different labour requirements, and constraints on available supplies can impede development in any sub-sector. Labour cost pressures are perhaps most evident in the case of labour which has some skills component. Skilled labour cannot be increased quickly in response to increased tourism demand. Many employees, for instance, pilots, air traffic controllers, engineers and maintenance tradespeople in the air transport industry, are skilled workers who have undertaken lengthy periods of training. Because their skills take time to acquire, wages in these occupations can be bid up in the short term as tourism faces an excess demand for labour brought about by firms competing for fixed supplies of labour inputs.

In developing countries in particular, labour supply has sometimes been quite inadequate to meet tourism's increasing needs and wages in both tourism and related industries have tended to increase. While some destinations (particularly in Europe) are able to hire workers from other countries to boost the tourism labour force in peak seasons, there is a limit to which the tourism industry can immediately meet its higher demand for skilled and semi-skilled occupations by attracting trained workers from other industries or from immigration.

Where skilled labour is difficult to acquire, either from other industries or from other countries, tourism booms can lead to upward pressure on wages for a large proportion of the workforce. If increased real wages spill over to the agriculture, mining and other industries, then they will impose a cost burden on those industries' profit margins. Unless these industries are willing to suffer reduced profitability, they also will raise their prices, thereby further raising input prices, reducing industry cost competitiveness, contracting output in non-tourist industries and constraining output growth. In this manner, an expanding tourism industry will put upward pressure on other costs and prices, feeding eventually into domestic inflation through the country's Consumer Price Index (CPI) as a result of pressure for general wage increases to maintain real wages.

The extent to which wage pressures on particular skills is translated into actual wage increases relative to other occupations depends on the wage-setting environment and government wages policy. Real wages may be fixed if there is unemployment in the economy or if there are no shortages of labour with the skills necessary to serve the increased demand for tourism goods and services. The assumption of fixed real wages, implicit in

I–O modelling, implies that the supply of labour to all industries is perfectly elastic. That is, the supply can be increased indefinitely without an increase in real wage levels. With labour prices constrained, most of the adjustment in the labour market occurs in the transfer of people from unemployment or outside the workforce to employment in the workforce. It also implies that any initial price pressure reflected in the CPI leads to an increase in money wages sufficient to maintain a constant level of real wages. In many economies, the labour market is characterised by institutional rigidities that constrain wages awarded to government employees. This limits their ability to attract additional skilled labour in the short term from other industries and in the long term through training.

Land constraints

Land is required for capital infrastructure such as roads and airports. Land for tourism development is often required near the urban and coastal fringe where it competes with retail and residential development (consider Hong Kong and Macao). Given that land prices increase according to their scarcity value, locational requirements can lead to rising land prices as the tourist industry attempts to attract land away from other uses. By way of example, land near attractive environmental resources, such as beaches or nature reserves, becomes more in demand as tourism develops, increasing land values.

Increases in land values due to tourism development will impact on the costs of other industries. These costs could include higher prices for residential or conservation purposes.

Sometimes, through zoning, governments set aside land for tourism precincts or for dedicated tourism facilities. If an increase in tourism demand leads to a greater share of desirable sites being absorbed by the tourism industry at less than market prices because of zoning laws, there will be a reduction in supply available to other uses such as fishing, mining, forestry and so on, resulting in increasing cost pressures in those industries as they must use their existing resources more intensively.

Capital constraints

Expenditure on capital in response to increased tourism expenditure is undertaken by both private and public sector stakeholders. Expansion in tourism will lead to greater use of existing capital plant and equipment such as buildings, ferries and aircraft, at least in the short run. In the medium to longer term, additional investment will result in an expansion of physical capital stock. Some new investment, for example, cafes or souvenir stalls, can expand capital stocks relatively easily. Other investment, such as aircraft and airports and cruise ships, require long lead times, suggesting that existing capital stock needs to be used more intensively in the short run, thus pushing up operating costs and thence prices for tourists through congestion and flight delays. We shall consider tourism investment in more detail in Chapter 12.

The lack of suitable infrastructure to support tourism development is one of the greatest constraints to growth in this sector in developing countries. Tourism expansion generates additional demand for water, sewerage, sanitation facilities, telecommunications and provision of energy. New resort developments located in coastal regions can lead to increased use of local roads, requiring greater expenditure on road maintenance and repair. Infrastructure issues will be addressed in more detail in Chapter 13.

Each of these types of factor constraints acts to reduce the value of the tourism multiplier in a given destination.

There are several other problems with multipliers based on I–O modelling. Two of the more important of these for the estimation of tourism multipliers relate to exchange rate changes and the government fiscal policy stance.

8.5.1.5 Exchange rate changes

The nature of the exchange rate regime is a crucial determinant of the economic impacts of foreign inbound tourism. Under the floating exchange rate system that characterises most of the world's major economies, including an increasing number of developing countries, an expansion of international tourism will strengthen a country's real exchange rate, leading to a reduction in other exports and/or an increase in demand for imports at the expense of the demand for domestic import competing commodities. If tourism expands at the expense of other tradable industries, there is a reduced multiplier effect on income and employment (although there may be a small positive impact on employment if tourism is more labour intensive than other industries which it replaces).

In many less developed countries with small open economies, the most obviously affected sectors will be the traditional export sectors such as agriculture, mining and manufacturing which suffer reduced competitiveness on world markets due to exchange rate appreciation. If increased tourism demand leads to increased investment, foreign borrowing will increase and so may foreign direct investment for a period, pushing the exchange rate even higher. This will further reduce traditional exports and increase imports.

8.5.1.6 Fiscal policy stance

The economic impact of increased tourism to a destination will also depend on the nature of current government fiscal policy. In the estimation of I–O multipliers, the Government budget sector is regarded as neutral. That is, I–O modelling does not allow for the impacts of different constraints on the Public Sector Borrowing Requirement (PSBR) which affects the levels of taxation and government spending and, hence, economic impacts from any changes in tourism expenditure. The expansion of tourism implies increased demand for airport facilities, road and rail transport, utilities, convention facilities and other infrastructure, much of which is provided by government or semi-government authorities.

If additional infrastructure spending by government is required to cater for increased tourism demand, there will be a positive effect on spending, but it must be financed through reduced expenditures on other programs, raising taxes, or by additional borrowings. Any of these compensating adjustments will act to offset the impact of the initial expansion of government expenditure.

If fiscal policy is directed towards maintaining a fixed PSBR, then taxes would have to rise to offset growth in government expenditure. This moderates the growth in private consumption leading to downward pressure on the output of consumption-oriented industries, including those that are, and those that are not, tourism related. Here, in the absence of full cost recovery on infrastructure, both short-run operating costs and the long-run costs of capital expansion will be met, at least in part, by the wider community.

Alternatively, tax revenues generated by additional tourism profits and employment may be used to reduce income and corporate tax rates. If the cause of any existing unemployment is rigid real wages that are higher than the market clearing wage, then the impact on unemployment of reduced tax rates could be large because reduced taxes imply increased private consumption, investment spending and exports depending on the type of tax. Taxation issues will be further discussed in Chapter 15.

In many economies, the increased demand for funds is met by inflows of capital from abroad enabling an increase in production as measured by GDP. However, it will lead to a deterioration in the current account via an increase in income payable abroad to the lenders of the finance, reducing the impacts of tourism growth on the income accruing to residents.

For the above reasons, the stance of government fiscal policy can help to determine the size of economic impacts from tourism growth. As other industries expand or contract, there can be a positive or negative overall impact on government revenue depending on the tax rates in different industries.

Box 8.3 summarises some of the main criticisms of the standard assumptions of I–O modelling.

BOX 8.3 Underlying assumptions and interpretation of I–O multipliers

The *basic assumptions* in I–O analysis include the following:

- There is a fixed input structure in each industry, described by fixed technological coefficients
- All products of an industry are identical or are made in fixed proportions to each other
- Each industry exhibits constant returns to scale in production

---

- Unlimited labour and capital are available at fixed prices; that is, any change in the demand for productive factors will not induce any change in their cost

Implications of the restrictive assumptions

- The I–O tables underlying multiplier analysis only take account of one form of *interdependence*, namely the sales and purchase links between industries. Other interdependencies such as collective competition for factors of production, changes in commodity prices which induce producers and consumers to alter the mix of their purchases and other constraints which operate on the economy as a whole are not generally taken into account.
- In reality, constraints such as limited skilled labour or investment funds lead to competition for resources among industries, which in turn raises the prices of these scarce factors of production and of industry output generally in the face of strong demand.
- All inputs and resources to production are supplied freely, and no resource constraints exist. In real-world economies, however, resource constraints generally are present and must be taken into account when estimating impacts of the increased visitor expenditure on economic activity.
- All price effects and financial effects are treated as being neutral when in fact there may be capacity constraints in the economy that cause prices and costs to rise in an expansion of economic activity. If the prices of inputs and wages increase due to an increase in demand, the net impact of output and jobs from the increase in demand is much less than the initial injection of spending. These price rises will limit the extent of the expansion and may even lead to contractions in economic activity in some sectors.
- There are no other constraints, such as the balance of payments or the actions of government, on the response of each industry to a stimulus. The behaviour of the government budget sector is treated as being neutral in I–O analysis. However, tax revenue will increase as a result of an economic expansion, enabling the government to increase spending, reduce other taxes, reduce borrowings from the public or some combination of these, with further effects on activity.

Exaggerated effects

- The multipliers describe *average effects, not marginal effects*, and thus do not take account of economies of scale, unused capacity or technological change. Generally, average effects are expected to be higher than the marginal effects.
- The combination of the assumptions used and the excluded interdependence means that I-O multipliers are higher than would realistically be the case. That

is, they tend to *overstate* the potential impact of final demand stimulus. The overstatement is potentially more serious when large changes in demand and production are considered.

- The multipliers also do not account for some important pre-existing conditions. This is especially true of Type 2 multipliers, in which employment generated and income earned induce further increases in demand. The implicit assumption is that those taken into employment were previously unemployed and were previously consuming nothing. In reality, however, not all 'new' employment would be drawn from the ranks of the unemployed; and to the extent that it was, those previously unemployed would presumably have consumed out of income support measures and personal savings. Employment, output and income responses are therefore overstated by the multipliers for these additional reasons.

Usefulness

- The most *appropriate interpretation* of multipliers is that they provide a relative measure (to be compared with other industries) of the interdependence between one industry and the rest of the economy which arises solely from purchases and sales of industry output based on estimates of transactions occurring over a (recent) historical period.

In principle, it is possible to introduce elements into an economic impact model that take account of the above shortcomings of I–O. Researchers have attempted to overcome these limitations either by including the effects of changes in consumption patterns associated with rising incomes (Sadler *et al.*, 1973) or by building capacity constraints into their models (Fletcher & Archer, 1991; Wanhill, 1988). Though refinements, such inclusions unfortunately still fail to address the major weaknesses inherent in I–O analysis. As we shall argue in Chapter 9, a new paradigm is required for economic impact assessment in tourism.

8.6 HOW TOURISM MULTIPLIERS ARE MISUSED

I–O multipliers have often been used too uncritically in tourism policy formulation. Unfortunately, many researchers and tourism policy makers have often tended to ignore the limitations of the multipliers that they have estimated for a particular destination.

8.6.1 USING 'INAPPROPRIATE' MULTIPLIERS

Since multipliers are often employed to estimate the economic impacts of some tourism expenditure shock, there has been a tendency for policy advisors to use those multipliers which cast tourism development in the most favourable light. Small multipliers may not be acceptable to stakeholders in both the public and private sectors who wish to use the economic analysis to underpin proposals for tourism development.

To this end, one often finds that sales, output and employment multipliers are used to estimate the economic impacts. However, sales and output multipliers both suffer from double counting (the increased output of one industry is used as an input into another industry and so can be counted more than once). As indicated, the appropriate multiplier is the value added multiplier.

Caution must be also exercised particularly in the estimation and use of employment multipliers since different firms have different marginal propensities to employ labour in response to increased sales. In many firms, staffing levels may be relatively insensitive to changes in turnover, while other firms may seek to better use those currently employed, for example, through the provision of overtime and weekend work, rather than hiring new staff. In any case, the value of the employment multiplier needs to be revised frequently because as wages rise a million dollars will fund fewer full-time jobs.

8.6.2 FAILURE TO RECOGNISE EXPENDITURE DIVERSION

A multiplier indicates that a dollar of tourist expenditure generates, say, x dollars of income or y jobs, but it is not true in general that this income or additional employment would not have been produced in the absence of tourism. Multipliers indicate the additional income, sales or employment only if the expenditure stimulus comes from outside the region (e.g. inbound or interstate tourism). Expenditure by residents should be treated merely as a transfer in I–O modelling since it does not result in additional outlays that would not have otherwise occurred should the consumer have remained at home. Thus, for a national I–O model, domestic tourism merely redistributes economic activity, possibly even from industries with higher multipliers and higher economic impact. Unfortunately, many studies of tourism's economic impacts, particularly associated with special events, have failed to distinguish between money which is injected into the region from outside the area and that which is merely transferred. For economic impact assessment, it is only the injected expenditure (new money) that is relevant for income and job creation. Chapter 11 elaborates upon this issue.

8.6.3 'INDUCED INCOME' MULTIPLIERS

Total (Type 2) multipliers are often employed to estimate the economic impacts of a change in tourism demand. As discussed above, these include the induced effects generated when recipients of direct and indirect tourism expenditure spend their increased income on additional goods and services. This type of multiplier implicitly assumes that there is excess capacity (unused resources) in the economy, and these unused resources can be brought into use to increase the production of the additional goods and services required. In the absence of excess capacity there can be no induced income generated in this way. Rather, there will be inflationary pressures on wages and prices stimulated by excess demand. There may also be a diversion of resources from other uses. Even with high unemployment and under-utilisation of capital, structural rigidities may prevent some of the potential benefits being translated into real increases in income and employment. In essence, Total multipliers provide an upper estimate of the impacts that might occur under restricted, idealised conditions.

8.6.4   MISUSE OF 'RATIO' MULTIPLIERS

As shown above, it is possible to express multipliers as the ratio of direct plus indirect effects (plus induced effects) to direct effects alone. While this can indicate the extent of inter-industry linkages, ratio multipliers cannot be compared with each other to show that expenditure in one industry is somehow more beneficial than expenditure in another. This is because 'large multipliers' are not the same as 'large multiplier impacts'. The impacts or effects depend on both the size of the multiplier and the magnitude of the 'exogenous' stimulus. The important thing to consider in an impact study is not the size of the multiplier but the size of the total impact on output, value added, income and employment. A small multiplier can correspond to a large total impact on the economy and a large multiplier to a small impact depending on the size of the initial change in final demand.

Consider hypothetically two regions, A and B. In region A, an extra dollar of tourist expenditure generates 40 cents of direct income and another 40 cents of indirect income. In region B, the direct effect is 20 cents and indirect effects are 40 cents. In region A, the ratio multiplier of total to direct income is 2 (80 / 40), while in region B it is 3 (60 / 20). Yet, the lower multiplier for region A is associated with a higher amount of income per dollar expenditure injection (80 cents) than region B (60 cents), which has the higher ratio multiplier. By itself, a ratio multiplier gives no indication of the amount of income or employment generated by tourism. It simply quantifies the extent to which the initial effects flow on to indirect beneficiaries.

Given the potential for misinterpretation or misuse of ratio multipliers, it is preferable to express multipliers in terms of the effects of a unit of expenditure on income and employment. In each case the effects can be subdivided into direct, indirect and induced effects. It is also advisable to explicitly acknowledge the assumptions of the model used to estimate multiplier values.

8.6.5   USING AN INAPPROPRIATE MODEL

A common mistake is to apply I–O multipliers estimated for a nation to calculate the economic impacts of tourism shocks to a smaller region. This ignores the fact that multipliers will vary between nations, states and regions because of the differing relative size of industries, differences in the connections between industries and because a regional or state economy will have varying degrees of interconnection with its surrounding regions. Thus, a regional economy may be highly dependent on a few activities, thereby under-representing the linkages with other parts of the economy and exaggerating the multipliers. Nationwide or Statewide multipliers tend to be larger than regional multipliers, given that they are not subject to as much leakages. The larger the defined area, the greater the opportunity for inputs to be sourced from within that area. A regional economy with modest industrial activity is likely to be unable to provide all of the inputs required by local industry to meet the additional demand for goods and services consequent upon a demand shock.

In some instances, the model used for a region may accurately describe the links between industries in the region as a whole but not for the tourist precincts where the expenditure occurs. For example, a particular tourist town or sub-region may have industries for which inter-industry links are completely different from the relationships established for the broader region. This could occur, say, in a coastal resort area where the only significant industry other than tourism is fishing but where the most disaggregated I–O tables include a larger town with a wide industrial base. This would flag the need to develop a new database to underpin model development.

Another type of 'inappropriate model' is one which is out of date in respect of some key elements of industry production and consumption interrelationships. Due to changing industry structures, relative input prices and technology change, it cannot be assumed that I–O derived coefficients and multipliers remain stable for any destination over time.

A related concern is that economic impact assessments that focus on regional tourism activity often ignore the economic effects on other regions within the wider economy. A tourism shock that is estimated to generate positive economic effects on a sub region may generate negative effects on surrounding regions. Researchers need to be mindful of the broad-ranging effects of tourism shocks that affect jurisdictions outside of the region that is the focus of analysis.

8.7 CONCLUSIONS AND POLICY

- An economic impact analysis estimates the changes to an economy that take place because of an existing or proposed project, action or policy. It traces the flows of spending associated with tourism activity to identify resulting changes in such economic variables as sales, output, government tax revenues, household income, value added and employment.
- The more common applications of economic impact analysis to tourism have centred on the evaluation of: the economic impacts of changes in tourism demand; the effects of policies and regulations which affect tourism activity either directly or indirectly; the effects on tourism demand from events beyond the direct control of the industry itself;

public and private investment proposals; resource allocation, policy and management of tourism development strategies; and aspects of lobbying.

- Expenditure by visitors to a destination represents an injection of 'new money' into that destination. This new expenditure gives rise to direct and secondary (indirect and induced) effects, leading to increases in economic activity at that destination.

- The direct effects of new tourist expenditure fall on the suppliers who sell goods and services directly to tourists. Direct effects give rise to secondary effects, both indirect and induced.

- Indirect effects result from 'upstream' effects when direct suppliers purchase inputs from other firms at the destination which, in turn, purchase inputs from other firms and so on.

- Induced effects arise when the recipients of the direct and indirect expenditure spend their increased incomes 'downstream' on the consumption of goods and services which are in most cases unrelated to the supply of tourism products.

- The relationship between new tourism expenditure and changes in economic variables such as output, income and employment can be described by multipliers. A multiplier is the number by which a given change in spending is multiplied in order to find the impact of that change on the economic variable under review.

- There are two broad types of multipliers: Keynesian multipliers and multipliers based on economic modelling (e.g. I–O multipliers).

- An I–O table illustrates, in matrix form, how transactions flow through the economy over a given time period. The rows of the matrix show the sales of the total output by each sector to every other sector. The columns show the inputs required by every sector from other sectors. The table provides a snapshot of the transactions occurring in an economy over a selected period, showing from which other industries a particular industry purchases and to which industries it sells.

- I–O multipliers (relating to sales, output, income, value added and employment) can be decomposed into multiplier effects (initial, first-round, industrial support, production-induced and consumption-induced). These multipliers can be derived from the direct requirements coefficient matrices based on I–O tables. Value added multipliers, which measure the change in net economic activity at each stage of production are the preferred measure for the assessment of the contribution to the economy of some shock to final demand.

- Multipliers can be decomposed into their various effects which are initial; first round and industrial support; and consumption-induced effects, Simple multipliers include only the direct and indirect effects of a demand shock while total multipliers include the induced effects as well.

- A SAM is a system of representing the economic and social structure of a country (region) at particular time, by defining its economic actors and recording their transactions. Although more comprehensive than I–O models in that they include inter-institutional transfers, as a tool for impact analysis, tourism multipliers including Type SAM have all of the limitations of I–O multipliers in general.

- Though widely used, I–O multipliers are based upon restrictive assumptions such as: fixed factor proportions; output homogeneity; linear, homogeneous consumption functions; and no constraints on supply. They typically ignore the effects of input price changes including changes in real wages, changes in the exchange rate and the government fiscal policy stance.

- I–O multipliers have often been used too uncritically in tourism policy formulation. Unfortunately, many researchers and tourism policy makers have often tended to ignore the limitations of the multipliers that they have estimated for a particular destination. In particular, the economic impacts of tourism shocks to a sub-regional destination may spill over (positively and negatively) into other regions.

- Multiplier analysis only tells part of the story of the impacts of tourism shocks. It has nothing to say on the costs and benefits of alternatives to tourism in generating income and employment in a particular region. It has nothing to say about the process of adjustment which must take place to respond to any changes in demand by tourists.

- Taken together, these limitations tend to invalidate the usefulness of the I–O technique for analysing the effects of an expenditure shock on the economy, particularly at the national level. I–O multipliers therefore have limited policy relevance for tourism.

SELF-REVIEW QUESTIONS

1. Briefly describe the more common applications to tourism.

2. Using examples, distinguish between direct effect, indirect effects and induced effects in new tourist spending at the London Olympics.

3. Outline the main forms of leakages that can accompany changes in tourism expenditure.

4. What is a 'tourism' multiplier? Distinguish between the various types of tourism multipliers.

5. What are the basic differences between Keynesian multipliers and multipliers based on economic modelling?

6. Draw and briefly explain the structure of an I–O table.

7. Use tourism examples to show how Type II multipliers differ from Type I multipliers.

8. How does a SAM differ from an I–O table?

9. How would a static tourism multiplier differ from a dynamic tourism multiplier?

10. Evaluate the limitations associated with the use of I–O multipliers in tourism.

11. Use tourism examples to describe how multipliers may be misused.

12. What role can multiplier analysis play in tourism policy?

ESSAY QUESTIONS

1. The extent to which production, income and employment in a host destination are affected by tourism expenditure depends on the strengths of business linkages between tourism and other industry sectors. Discuss.

2. The size of a tourism multiplier is in inverse proportion to the size of the expenditure leakages. How so?

3. The total effects of a specific tourism demand shock to a host destination are the overall increases in output, sales, value added, GDP, household income and employment. Discuss this statement in the context of the recent 2010 Commonwealth Games in India.

4. Tourism uses multipliers based on economic modelling rather than on Keynesian modelling. Why?

5. I–O tables illustrate, in matrix form, how transactions flow through the economy over a given time period. How so?

6. Multiplier analysis only tells us part of the story in tourism's economic contribution. Explain why.

7. The major limitation to the application of the I–O model to tourism is the assumptions that underlie the I–O model. Discuss.

CHAPTER 9

ECONOMIC IMPACTS OF TOURISM: CGE MODELLING

LEARNING OBJECTIVES

After reading this chapter, you should be able to:

1. Explain the difference in approach between Computable General Equilibrium (CGE) models and Input–Output (I–O) models in the assessment of the economic impacts of tourism.

2. Broadly understand the structure of a CGE model.

3. Distinguish between static and dynamic CGE models.

4. Apply CGE models to the tourism setting, demonstrating a familiarity with recent examples of economic impact assessment using CGE models.

5. Understand the strengths and weaknesses associated with CGE models.

9.1 INTRODUCTION

The weaknesses inherent in the Input–Output (I–O) model as discussed in Chapter 8 highlight the fact that any analysis of the effects of a change in tourism demand on national or regional economies must not only contain information on the links between tourism and other industries but must also be able to account for factor constraints and resulting price and cost pressures that act as a brake to future economic expansion or contraction.

Analysts need to be able to model an economy, as far as is possible, as it really is, recognising other sectors and markets and capturing feedback effects. The effects of tourism growth cannot be anticipated *a priori*. The increased output of the tourism industry may be more than offset by contractions in output elsewhere in the economy. With a comprehensive model of the economy that incorporates consumers, businesses and governments, it is possible to make explicit assumptions about government policy settings, incorporate a more realistic set of economy-wide constraints on the supply side of the economy and analyse the economy-wide impacts of changes in tourism spending, changes in subsidies or taxation, destination promotion and other policy and market changes (Ennew, 2003).

The study of the economic impacts of tourism shocks has recently undergone a 'paradigm shift' as a result of the use of Computable General Equilibrium (CGE) models in place of I–O models. CGE models are widely used by various national and international organisations (IMF, World Bank, OECD, the European Commission, etc.), the European Commission, research centres and consulting firms for economic policy analysis at the industry sector-level as well as the economy-wide level. They are now the standard tool for the quantitative analysis of policy formulation in many domains including fiscal policy, trade policy and environmental policy. For survey articles see, for example, Bandara (1991), Shoven and Whalley (1992) and Bhattacharyya (1996).

The development and application of this technique has major implications for research on the economic impacts of tourism and for the policy advice they give to decision makers in both the public and private sectors. Thus, in recent years, there has been a 'paradigm shift' in favour of CGE models for tourism analysis and policy.

9.2 THE STRUCTURE OF A CGE MODEL

CGE modelling involves a mathematical specification of key relationships within the economy (what determines levels of demand, supply and so on. A CGE model is calibrated to real data to ensure that the model provides a good representation of the economy. CGE models treat an economy as a whole, allowing for feedback effects of one sector on another. They represent the economy as a system of flows of goods and services between sectors. The goods and services include both output (produced commodities) and primary inputs (labour, land and capital). The sectors include the household sector, several industry sectors, government and the foreign sector. The flows are shown via a Social Accounting Matrix (SAM) (see Chapter 8). Sectors are represented by columns, and commodity groupings are represented by rows. Each cell of the table shows the money value of usage of the relevant commodity by the relevant sector.

The construction of a CGE model involves setting up a series of markets (for goods, services and factors of production), production sectors and demand groups (households). Each market, sector and household has its own set of economic rules that determine how it reacts to external changes. CGE models consist of a set of equations characterising the production, consumption, trade and government activities of the economy. Table 9.1 illustrates the flows in a simple CGE model. These flows include the following:

- The flow of commodities from industries to households, governments, export markets and investment.
- The flow of commodities from industries to other industries for use in current production (intermediate usage).
- The import of commodities from abroad to meet domestic demand.
- The flow of primary factor services from households to industries.

Table 9.1 Commodity flows in a simple CGE model

		Intermediate Usage Ind.1 Ind.g	Household	Government	Investment	Exports	Total Sales
Commodities	Comm. 1 Comm. H	X	X	X	X	X	Total
Indirect Taxes		X	X	X	X	X	Total
Imports		X	X	X	X	X	Total
Labour		X	0	0	0	0	Total
Capital		X	0	0	0	0	Total
Land		X	0	0	0	0	Total
Total Costs		Total	Total	Total	Total	Total	Total

Source: McDougall (1995)

There are four types of equations in the set which are solved simultaneously. The four types of equations are (McDougall, 1995):

- *Equilibrium conditions* for each market ensure that supply is equal to demand for each good, service, factor of production and for foreign exchange. Assuming flexible prices and wages, this enables factors of production, such as labour and capital, and foreign exchange markets to be modelled (although some sticky prices can be assumed such as might occur in the labour market).
- *Income-expenditure identities* ensure that the economic model is a closed system. All earnings must be accounted for through expenditure or savings. These conditions apply to all private households, the government, firms and any other economic agents that are modelled. These define various macroeconomic identities such as aggregate employment and the components of Gross Domestic Product (GDP).
- *Behavioural relationships* state how economic agents (consumers, suppliers, investors and so on) acting in their own best interests can lead to changes in price and income levels. For example, businesses will seek to maximise profits. Consumers will look for lowest prices for equivalent products. The zero-pure-profits condition for production is assumed. Resource allocation is via market forces – where markets behave imperfectly unemployment may increase. Increasing government expenditures are met either by raising taxes or by borrowing, with implications for the expenditure of other economic agents.

- *Production functions* determine how much is output is produced for any given level of factor employment. With assumptions regarding market structure, these determine what levels of labour employment, capital usage and intermediate input usage are required to satisfy a given level of output for a given set of prices. The production assumptions allow substitution between intermediate inputs and factors of production as prices and wages change.

9.2.1 THE 'NOTTINGHAM' CGE MODEL

To appreciate the structure of a CGE model, it is informative to summarise those developed by Adam Blake in a series of papers (Blake, 2000; Blake, 2004; Blake & Sinclair, 2003; Blake *et al.*, 2003a, b, c; Blake *et al.*, 2006), known as 'The Nottingham Model'. The Nottingham CGE model comprises a set of relationships governing industries, institutions and markets in the relevant economy. Industries undertake all production activities of goods and services, using labour and capital as well as intermediate inputs to produce their output. In addition to the intermediate products consumed by industries, three institutions (households, government and the Rest of the World (ROW)) consume these goods and services. The discussion below relies heavily on Blake *et al.* (2003c), since their exegesis is an excellent overview of the essential features of any CGE model.

Figure 9.1 shows the circular flow of income in an economy. Income flows counter-clockwise around the four main parts of the economy in this diagram, from industries to factor markets to institutions to commodity markets and back to industries. In addition, there are other flows from industries to commodity markets (intermediate demand), tax payments from industries (taxes on production) and commodity markets (taxes on products) to government institutions. The ROW receives income from the economy's

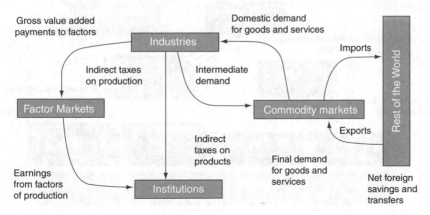

Figure 9.1 The circular flow of income

Source: Blake (2004), Figure 1

imports; the economy's commodity markets receive income from exports; and institutions pay and receive income from the ROW through foreign savings and transfers, which include payments for factor services owned abroad and for domestic factor payments that are transferred abroad.

Of course, each of the industries, institutions and markets is significantly more detailed than shown in Figure 9.1. Nor does the figure display all flows relevant to economic impact analysis. In particular, there are flows of income between and within institutions that are not shown in the figure, such as income taxation from households to government, transfers from the government to households and between-household transfers.

9.2.1.1 Industries

Any CGE model must describe how industries in a destination respond to changes in output and input prices. CGE models involve functional forms to describe the relationships that take place at the level of industries that represent the aggregate activity of large numbers of individual firms.

The structure of each industry in the Nottingham model is displayed in Figure 9.2. In order to produce output, each industry *i* uses inputs of factor services and intermediate goods. Factor services comprise labour and capital services. Intermediate demands for each commodity are divided into demand for domestically produced goods and demand for imports. Each of these demands may be taxed according to existing commodity

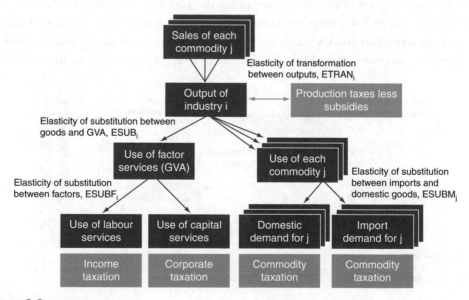

Figure 9.2 Industry output

Source: Blake *et al.* (2003c), Figure 2

320

taxation rates. Industry output may also be subject to a production tax or subsidy and may comprise the output of more than one commodity.

The responses of industries to changes in prices are governed by functions that specify the elasticity of substitution between inputs and output functions that specify the elasticity of transformation between outputs. An elasticity of substitution specifies the ease with which technological processes can enable changes in inputs in response to a change in prices or wages. For example, the elasticity of substitution between labour and capital specifies how industries' demands for labour and capital will change following a change in the price of either factor. A high elasticity implies that an increase in the wage rate of labour will have a greater effect on the demand for capital. Thus, if wage rates rise, firms will employ less labour and more capital. A lower elasticity limits the ability of industries to respond in this way to price changes. At the extreme, an elasticity of zero means that industries will not make substitutions between inputs in response to changes in prices. In this case, a change in the wage rate of labour would not change an industry's demand for capital.

In the Nottingham model, the elasticity of substitution between factors is governed by a parameter, $ESUBF_i$, that is taken from the Global Trade Analysis Project (GTAP) database (Hertel, 1997). These elasticity values are commonly used in CGE models and are based on econometric studies. The elasticity of substitution between goods and value added, $ESUB_i$, is set to zero in the short-run version of the model. This is a common value of this parameter in CGE models, reflecting the difficulty in short periods of time to implement technological change that uses different intermediate inputs. Values for the elasticity of substitution between imported and domestic goods, $ESUBM_j$, are also taken from the GTAP database. The same elasticity $ESUBM_j$ is used for each type of input in different industries, but the elasticities for different goods have different values.

The elasticity of transformation between outputs is governed by a parameter, $ETRAN_i$. In the application of the Nottingham model to Malta and Cyprus this is set at one. In the relevant simulations all industries except accommodation are assumed to produce just one product. Thus, this parameter only has an effect in the accommodation sector, where it governs how the accommodation sector responds to changes in prices in accommodation and food and drink in accommodation establishments. A value of one allows the accommodation industry to change the provision of these services in response to price changes, Blake *et al.* (2003c).

Various measures can be used to project changes to the economy resulting from different shocks to tourism demand. Different simulations can reveal the percentage change in the output of all industries, whether positive or negative. The change in employment of labour and/or capital can be used to determine how the structure of employment changes. Gross Value Added (GVA) can be used to determine how the structure of employment changes across sectors indicating which industries have the more substantial effects on earnings. GDP generated by each sector can also be used to show changes in each industry's economic contribution.

9.2.1.2 Households

The household is an important component of a CGE model, as any estimate of the economic impacts of a tourism shock will depend to a large extent on how it affects household expenditure and its provision of labour and capital (savings). The household receives the largest share of after-tax factor income, and it is the largest source of final demand expenditure. In addition to net factor incomes, households receive a net income from the ROW that comprises net transfers from abroad as well as net labour earnings from abroad. The household also receives transfers of income from the enterprise and government institutions. It spends income received on consumption goods and investment goods (domestic savings).

The functional forms used in specifying the behaviour of the household are similar to those used in the industry specifications. Figure 9.3 displays the flows of income, consumption and savings associated with households. The household does not produce goods or services, but rather it purchases goods and services in order to maximise its utility. In the

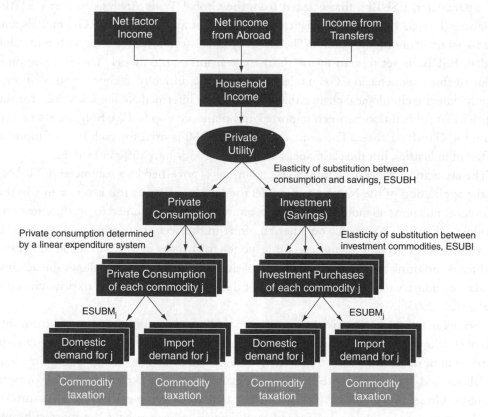

Figure 9.3 The household institution

Source: Blake *et al.* (2003c), Figure 3

322

Nottingham model, utility is created by the purchases of private consumption and investment, each of which is a product of purchases of (potentially all) commodities. Aggregate investment is a function of investment purchases of each commodity and an elasticity of substitution, ELASI, governs how investors may respond to rises in the prices of capital goods. The demand for each commodity is divided into demand for domestic and imported goods, in a similar manner to the intermediate purchases of industries.

Aggregate consumption is a function of the consumption purchases of each commodity. This function is governed by a linear expenditure system (LES) that is a more general form of the function used for private consumption expenditures. The use of the LES function means that income elasticities of demand are inputted into the model, with private consumption changing when household income changes. The consumption of each commodity is divided into demands for imported and domestically produced goods in the same manner as intermediate and investment purchases. Commodity taxation is also applied in the same manner (Blake *et al.*, 2003c).

In the Nottingham model, the elasticity values used in the household institution are either sourced from the same database as the industry elasticities (income elasticities, Hertel, 1997) or set to commonly used values (ELASI=0, ESUBH=1).

The use of a utility function with demand conditions that are consistent with it leads to a model that is micro consistent. This means that the household utility that is calculated within the model is fully consistent with the demand functions that are used. The advantage of a micro-consistent utility function is that the analyst can evaluate whether a simulation leads to the household being better or worse off than without the simulated changes. The way that government consumption is treated enables changes in household utility to be interpreted as changes in economic welfare. The Nottingham model, consistent with economic theory, measures a change in welfare by equivalent variation (EV), which indicates how much the change in welfare is worth to the economy at the pre-simulation set of prices. This measure takes the results from what may be quite complex effects of a simulation on a household and produces a single value to describe how much better (or worse) off the economy is as a result of such effects. The Nottingham estimates employ EV, along with production measures such as GVA and GDP, to assess the welfare effects of simulations on the economy. This welfare concept has been employed in various studies including projected effects of the London Olympics 2012 (Blake, 2005) and the poverty reduction potential of tourism to Brazil (Blake *et al.*, 2008). As such it is consistent with our discussion in Chapter 6 where we emphasised the importance of benefit measures for policy analysis.

9.2.1.3 Firms

The firm (enterprise) is the simplest institution in CGE models. The supply of products and demand for factors by producers are based on the objective of profit maximisation, subject to the constraints of technology. Firms receive income from capital, purchase investment goods to replace depreciated capital, receive net investment from abroad, and transfer any remaining income to the household. Investment demand is fixed in terms of the quantity of aggregate investment goods that the firm demands. With ELASI set to zero, the demand for each individual commodity is effectively fixed, as price changes do not lead to substitution between capital goods. In the long-run assumptions, ELASI is not zero, making substitution possible between different types of commodities even though the aggregate demand for investment goods by the firm is fixed to replace only depreciated assets.

9.2.1.4 Government

The government receives income from all forms of tax payments and income from abroad. Income from taxes is received from both direct and indirect taxation. Direct taxes include income tax on labour earnings and corporation tax on eligible capital earnings. Indirect taxes are (net) taxes less subsidies on production, import tariffs and taxes on consumption (Value added tax (VAT) or Goods and Services Tax and excise duties). Government spends its income on public consumption goods and transfers any income left over to the household. The fixed demand for public consumption goods is a necessary assumption in order to make welfare calculations. If government consumption were to vary, it would not be possible to calculate welfare measures such as EV because the value of the additional public consumption would need to be incorporated, and this could only be done in an *ad hoc* manner (Blake *et al.*, 2003c).

9.2.1.5 The ROW

The ROW fulfils several different functions in the CGE models. It purchases exports from the domestic economy and supplies imports. The ROW has direct interactions with the other institutions, with net transfers being paid to the household, net capital income being paid to the enterprise, and net government receipts from abroad being paid to the government. Finally, the ROW also purchases goods and services in the domestic economy to satisfy tourism demand.

9.2.1.6 Tourism demand

Tourism demand by each tourism market is split into demands for individual commodities, as shown in Figure 9.4. An elasticity of substitution between goods and services purchased by tourists, ELAST, is set to equal one, so that tourists are able to substitute between commodities, purchasing more of one commodity and less of others in response to price changes.

Given the type of function indicated in Figure 9.4, the analyst can estimate the aggregate price paid for the products purchased by each tourism market. Figure 9.5 shows the way in which aggregate tourism demand responds to prices. Aggregate tourism demand in each market is then derived as a function of that price. If, for example, car rental prices fall, this

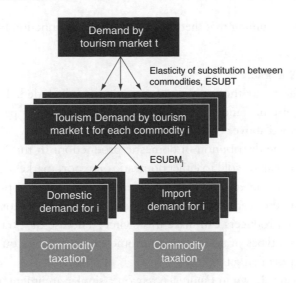

Figure 9.4 The structure of tourism demand

Source: Blake *et al.* (2003c), Figure 4

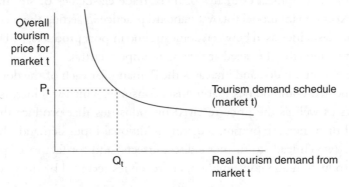

Figure 9.5 Overall tourism demand by market

Source: Blake *et al.* (2003c), Figure 5

will not only lead to tourists renting more cars as a share of their total expenditure, but will also lead to a fall in the aggregate price that tourist's face. This decrease in price will lead to an increase in the quantity demanded of tourism along the demand curve in Figure 9.5.

As Figure 9.5 indicates, increased aggregate demand will lead to increases in the demand for each individual commodity through the structure given in Figure 9.4. These effects will work through each tourism market in different degrees because the demand shares are different for different markets. A tourism market where a higher proportion of expenditures are spent on shopping would, for instance, be affected more by these changes than tourism markets where the shopping expenditure share is lower. The Nottingham model follows common practice in assuming that there is a transformation function between export and domestic markets.

9.2.1.7 Commodity markets

CGE models differ as to the number of commodities included. Both domestic and imported products are demanded by industries and institutions as part of their demand structures, as described above.

Figure 9.6 shows the distribution of domestic production. In the Nottingham model, domestic production can be sold to either domestic or export markets. A change in export or domestic prices is assumed to induce producers to change the proportion of their output that they sell to the respective markets. The elasticity of transformation, $ETRAN_i$, describes how easily producers can make this switch. The use of a transformation function assumes that the types of goods sold on domestic markets are qualitatively different to those sold on export markets.

The import markets shown in Figure 9.6 rely on a similar argument, in that imports are different products from domestically produced products (this is already incorporated into the way that domestic and import demand are differentiated in industry and institution demand above). As empirical estimates of these trade elasticities of substitution are not available, the Nottingham model follows standard practice in setting them equal to double the value of the elasticities used between domestic and import products, $ESUBM_i$. Imports from different regions may be taxed according to import tariffs.

An increase in tourism demand increases the demand for each of the domestically produced and imported commodities that tourists consume, which will increase the price of those products as well as the price received by industries that produce those products. Industries will then increase output, requiring additional input demands, both for intermediate inputs (which leads to further indirect effects) and for factors of production. At all stages of production and consumption, tax revenues received by the government may change.

9.2.1.8 Factor markets

The factor markets for labour and capital determine many of the underlying characteristics of the model. An increase in the demand for factors of production will increase the wage that they earn, and therefore increase the wages that firms in all industries must pay for

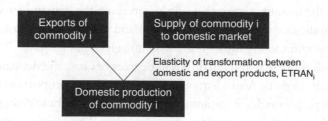

Figure 9.6 Domestic markets in the Nottingham CGE model

factor services. This has effects across the economy and depends on the way in which factor markets are modelled. A number of different aspects of factor markets are modelled in the Nottingham CGE:

- The ease with which labour and capital can move to different sectors of employment is specified, with different values according to whether short-run or long-run assumptions are being used. Factor mobility can vary from completely rigid (capital is sector-specific in the short run) to completely mobile.
- Unemployment is incorporated into the model, with a Phillips curve relationship between real wages and unemployment. This specifies that as real wages increase, unemployment will fall (and vice versa). The values for the parameter governing this function are different in short-run and long-run assumptions.
- Factor supplies are fixed in the short run, but vary in the long run in a relationship with real wages. Under the long-run assumptions, increases in real wages lead to increases in factor supply. This is because (i) households supply more labour and take less leisure time when wages are high and (ii) higher real wages increase the returns from training and education (for labour) and investment (for capital), increasing the efficiency value of factor supplies.

9.2.2 STATIC VERSUS DYNAMIC GENERAL EQUILIBRIUM MODELS

The majority of CGE models can be separated into two broad categories, *comparative static* and *recursive-dynamic*.

Static models project just how much difference a shock will make to the values of variables in a particular year. The comparative static CGE model does not contain any explicit time dimension. In reality, static models may be appropriate for much of the analysis that is undertaken on tourism policy, where inter-temporal allocation is not the major concern, for example, involving inter-country and/or inter-sectoral effects (Blake *et al.*, 2006).

For the most part, the models applied to tourism analysis have been static models. Each of the investigations that we discuss below uses a static CGE model. In the Nottingham model, the short-run assumptions are applicable to the economic adjustment that will take place over 1–2 years. The long-run assumptions are applicable to adjustment over 3–5 years or longer. This is the approximate time scale under which all economic adjustments will have been made following an external change. Long-run models generally involve higher elasticities than the short-run model, because production technologies can be replaced over a long period of time.

Dynamic general equilibrium models consist of a series of static models, referring to a sequence of years, linked by inter-temporal equations describing investment decisions and capital accumulation. The model can then be used to trace out a specific time path of the economy following the change in the policy or introduction of a supply-side or demand-side shock. Using a dynamic model, we would first project a base forecast giving the values of variables in the year(s) of interest without the shock and then project a revised forecast with the shock in place. The economic adjustment can then be determined by the difference between the two alternative time paths. The effects of the shock in any year would be calculated explicitly as the differences between values of variables in the revised and base forecasts for that year. Dynamic models can be used to forecast the structure of the economy as well as to assess the effects of policy and other shocks. A forward looking dynamic model was used by Blake (2005) to project the economic impacts of the London Olympics 2012.

Dynamic CGE models can provide a richer set of information than that available from static models, depending on the assumptions that are made about the changes that are occurring in the economy. One area where a dynamic approach is particularly useful is in modelling the effects of climate change mitigation policies. Thus, Hoque *et al.* (2009) have projected the potential economic impacts of introduction by the Australian government of its proposed Emissions Trading Scheme (ETS) to commence in 2011 to reduce Greenhouse Gas emissions (GHGs) in Australia, subject to agreement in the Australian parliament. The analysis is summarised in Chapter 19, Box 19.5.

CGE Models can be formulated at a number of spatial levels:

- Single-country models with only top-down regional disaggregation such as ORANI or MONASH.
- Stand-alone models of regional economies, for example, Meagher & Parmenter (1990).
- Multi-regional models such as MONASH-MRF. Or
- Multi-country models, for example, Hertel (1997).

Models of one or more of these types would be suitable for assessing most tourism impact issues.

9.3 ECONOMIC IMPACT ASSESSMENT USING CGE MODELS

CGE models are now increasingly used in tourism economics analysis and policy formulation. Some examples of topics addressed include the following:

- *Economic impacts of changes in inbound tourism* (Adams & Parmenter, 1995, 1999; Dwyer *et al.*, 2003; Narayan, 2004; Zhou *et al.*, 1997).
- *Economic impacts of tourism crises* (Blake *et al.*, 2003a; Dwyer *et al.*, 2006; Narayan & Prasad, 2007; Pambudi *et al.*, 2009).
- *Economic impacts of Climate Change* (Berrittellaa *et al.*, 2006; Hoque *et al.*, 2009).
- *Economic impacts of special events* (Blake, 2005; Dwyer *et al.*, 2005, 2006a,b; Madden, 2006)
- *Economic impacts on destinations of tourists from different market segments* (Dwyer & Forsyth, 2008; Dwyer *et al.*, 2007)

- *Evaluation of economic policy* (Blake, 2000; Blake & Sinclair, 2003; Mabugu, 2002; Sugiyarto *et al.*, 2003)
- *Tourism effects on income distribution and poverty reduction* (Blake *et al.*, 2008; Wattanakuljarus & Coxhead, 2008).

A good summary of the usefulness of CGE modelling in tourism analysis and policy development is provided by Blake *et al.* (2006). Perhaps, the best way to appreciate the scope and power of CGE modelling is to provide overviews of some of the studies that have been undertaken. Some recent uses of CGE modelling of tourism's economic impacts are discussed below. We have selected these studies for their interest and also to display the range of uses of CGE modelling in economic impact analysis. The use of CGE modelling to estimate the economic impacts of special events will be discussed in Chapter 11, and its use to estimate the economic impacts of climate change will be discussed in Chapter 19.

9.3.1 INCREASED TOURISM TO AUSTRALIA

Adams and Parmenter (1995) construct a 117-sector general equilibrium model for Australia using the ORANI-F database to assess the effects on the Australian economy of additional expansion of inbound tourism, relative to a base case for the period 1989–1995 in which inbound tourism was already assumed to grow strongly. To highlight the effects on the economy of the increased international tourism, Adams and Parmenter compared the base-case growth path with an amended path in which the number of tourist arrivals grows by an additional 10 percentage points per annum (from 7% to 17%). The effects of the additional tourism growth rate were reported as the differences between the amended and base-case simulations.

The effects of increased tourism demand were projected for key macroeconomic, sectoral and regional growth rates. The addition to the international tourist intake was assumed to exhibit expenditure patterns and a regional distribution identical to those of the existing intake. The results are reported as percentage point additions to the average annual growth rates of variables over the entire six-year period.

In setting up the model for the study, Adams and Parmenter made explicit assumptions about the macroeconomic environment in which the additional tourism expansion was assumed to take place. It was assumed that there is no excess capacity in tourism facilities and variables assumed to be unaffected by the additional expansion of tourism included aggregate employment, the rate of return on capital, real government consumption and the Public Sector Borrowing Requirement (PSBR).

Base-case projections
   The study's base-case projections for the Australian economy 1989–1995 are set out in column 1 of Table 9.2.

Table 9.2 Projections for 1989 to 1995 macroeconomic variables

	Variable	Base projections	Effects of 10% additional growth in tourism
1	Net foreign debt/GDP, end of period	40.52	−0.2063
2	Net foreign debt/GDP, end of penultimate year	40.24	−0.1956
3	Change in balance of trade/GDP[a]	0.54	−0.0104
4	Average annual percentage of devaluation	2.41	−0.2113
Average annual percentage growth rates			
5	Real hourly wage rate before tax	0.08	0.0625
6	Capital stock	2.61	0.0139
7	Effective labour input	2.80	0.0000
8	Employment	1.80	0.0000
9	Real GDP	2.69	0.0037
10	Real consumption (private)	2.08	−0.0017
11	Real consumption (public)	2.25	0.0000
12	Real investment	0.29	0.0838
13	Imports (volume index)	1.25	0.2537
14	Exports (volume index)	7.20	0.1613
15	Income tax rates	−1.80	0.1116
16	Consumer price index	5.00	0.0000
17	GDP deflator	4.54	0.0094
18	Capital goods price index	4.76	−0.0174
19	Price index for imports	7.48	−0.2034
20	Price index for exports	5.69	−0.1738
21	Terms of trade	−1.79	0.0296

[a]The balance of trade covers both merchandise and services trade

Note: Decimal points following zero are missing from some estimates in column two

Source: Adams and Parmenter (1995), Table 2

Macroeconomic effects of increased inbound tourism

The projections of the macroeconomic effects of the assumed increased inbound tourism to Australia appear in column 2 of Table 9.2.

- The tourism expansion stimulates capital formation (row 6) and generates an increase in the rate of growth of investment (row 12).
- Holding both employment growth and technical change at their base-case rates, there is a small increase in real GDP (row 9).
- Growth in private consumption (row 10) is reduced slightly due to an increase in income tax rates (row 15).
- To maintain a fixed PSBR, income tax rates must rise to offset rapid growth in government investment expenditure. With additional growth in aggregate real domestic absorption (consumption plus investment) exceeding additional growth in real GDP, there is an increase in the balance of trade deficit (row 3).
- The import content of the induced investment contributes directly to the deterioration in the trade balance. In addition, an appreciation of the real exchange rate (row 4) is required to make room for the increased level of domestic demand. This generates substitution towards imports (row 13) and reduces the traditional exports of mining and agricultural commodities.
- This reduced export growth explains why the terms of trade improve (row 21) and why growth in the aggregate volume of exports increases by only a very small percentage. The improvement in the terms of trade and the reduction in the activity levels of land-intensive export industries allow an increase in the real wage rate (row 5).

Output by sector

Table 9.3 contains output projections for 19 sectors aggregated from the 117 industries distinguished in the ORANI database. The base-case (column 1) is characterised by rapid growth of traded goods sectors especially export-oriented sectors, relative to the production of non-traded commodities. Particularly, poor growth prospects are projected for the investment goods sector (including construction) reflecting the sluggish growth of aggregate investment in the macroeconomic projections.

Table 9.3 illustrates that, at the sectoral level, there will be losers as well as gainers from the expansion in inbound tourism. Four groups of industries can be distinguished.

- *Service industries catering directly to international tourists* (e.g. air transport, restaurants and hotels). These are strongly stimulated by the additional expansion in tourism. This strengthens further the industries' base-case growth implied by the strong growth assumed for tourism in the base forecasts.
- *Industries indirectly supplying tourism-related activities* (e.g. aircraft maintenance and construction). These are also stimulated by the additional expansion of tourism. Except for

331

Table 9.3 Projections for 1988–1989 to 1994–1995 *percentage output growth rates* by sector

Sector	Base case	Effect of additional tourism growth
Agriculture, forestry and fishing (industries 1 to 11)	4.5263	−0.1839
Mining (12 to 17)	4.3983	−0.4616
Food, beverages and tobacco (18 to 29)	4.1601	−0.1041
Textiles, clothing and footwear (30 to 39)	3.3044	0.0411
Wood, wood products, paper and paper products (40 to 48)	2.0488	0.0301
Chemicals, petroleum and coal products (49 to 56)	3.5716	−0.0526
Non-metallic mineral products (57 to 62)	−0.7587	0.0026
Basic and fabricated metal products (63 to 67)	4.1318	−0.2309
Transport equipment other than aircraft (68 to 70)	5.3072	−0.1792
Aircraft (71)	4.2073	2.2536
Other machinery and equipment (72 to 78)	4.1967	0.0194
Miscellaneous manufacturing (79 to 83)	3.6239	−0.0041
Electricity, gas and water (84 to 86)	2.7380	−0.0327
Construction (87 and 88)	−0.6760	0.0481
Trade and repairs (89 to 92)	2.3876	0.0228
Transport other than air transport (93 to 95)	3.3314	−0.0274
Air transport (96)	4.6058	3.0753
Service industries directly catering for tourists (97, 109 to 111)	2.2808	0.1873
Other service industries (98 to 108)	2.4096	0.0014

Source: Adams and Parmenter (1995), Table 3

construction, most of them also enjoy strong prospects in the base forecasts because of base-case growth of tourism. In the base forecasts, since investment growth is weak, especially residential investment, the additional expansion of tourism eases the adjustment problems that the construction sector would otherwise have experienced.

- *Non-tourism exporters* (e.g. agriculture, mining, food and metal processing). Growth prospects in these industries are reduced by the appreciation of the real exchange rate produced by additional tourism expansion. However, the base forecasts are characterised by exchange rate depreciation, giving the export industries good prospects. The adverse effects of the additional tourism expansion should thus be easily accommodated.
- *Import-competing industries* (e.g. transport equipment, chemicals, textiles, clothing and footwear). Prospects in these industries are reduced by the tourism induced appreciation of the exchange rate.

The results demonstrate the usefulness of CGE models in providing information on the structural effects of tourism expansion. Adams and Parmenter were among the first researchers to provide empirical evidence to support Copeland's (1991) theoretical argument that some sectors benefit and some lose as the result of tourism expansion.

9.3.2 INCREASED TOURISM TO FIJI

Tourism is often regarded as a catalyst for economic growth in developing countries. Tourism is Fiji's largest industry, earning over F$500 million in foreign exchange and employing around 40,000 people. The tourism industry over the last decade has grown at an annual rate of 10%–12%. The expansion of tourism, which generates more expenditure in the economy, is likely to have implications for other industries. Using a CGE model based on the ORANI model, Narayan (2004) simulated the long-run impact of a 10% increase in visitor expenditures on Fiji's economy. His model consists of 35 domestic industries, 34 commodities and 2 occupational types. In total, there are 13 agricultural sector industries; 10 industrial sector industries; and 12 service sector industries including hotels, cafes and restaurants.

Economy-wide effects of tourism expansion

The projected long-run macroeconomic impacts of a 10% increase in inbound tourism are presented in Table 9.4.

Increasing economic activity created by tourism expansion increases real wage rates which positively impacts private disposable incomes, which increases by 1.88%. This, in turn, leads to an increase in real private consumption of 1.89%, helping to increase real GDP. Additional tourism expenditure will create more private investment – real aggregate private investment will increase by around 0.35%.

Table 9.4 also indicates that the increased economic activity due to an expansion of tourism leads to increased government revenues; VAT and income tax revenues. There is projected to be a 2.5% increase in revenue from VAT due to the additional tourist expenditure. Further, the additional economic activity reflected in the increase in exports and real investment will also generate revenue for the government from other sources: income tax revenue will increase by 2.4%, while production and company tax revenues will increase

Table 9.4 Macroeconomic effects from a 10% expansion of tourism to Fiji

Variable	% increase
Private savings	1.8846
Private consumption	1.8971
Balance of payments surplus	540.1*
Private investment expenditure	1.2939
Total government savings	860.0*
Imports	1.0952
Exports	1.6489
Consumer price index	1.1642
Investment price index	0.8245
Private disposable income	1.8846
Income tax revenue	2.3826
Company tax revenue	1.8703
Production tax revenue	1.6211
Tariff revenue	0.7923
Excise tax revenue	1.7404
VAT revenue	2.5223
Real aggregate private investment	0.3494
Real GDP	0.504
Real consumption	0.7220
Real national welfare	0.6700
Labour market	%
Net after tax rural wage rate for unskilled labour	1.8359
Net urban wage rate for unskilled labour	1.1695
Wage rate for informal sector labour	5.7882
Aggregate demand for informal unskilled labour	−2.9222

Note: * indicates value in thousands of Fiji dollars.

Source: Narayan, P.K. (2004) 'Economic Impact of Tourism on Fiji's Economy: Empirical Evidence from the Computable General Equilibrium Model', *Tourism Economics*, 10(4), 419–433.

by over 1.6%. The increase in imports will obviously generate tariff revenue – this will increase by 0.79%. All these developments will have a positive impact on real GDP. With employment growth fixed, the impact on real GDP is projected to be 0.50%. With additional growth in real GDP exceeding additional growth in aggregate domestic absorption (consumption plus investment) there is an increase in the balance of trade surplus, which is also reflected in a surplus in balance of payments of F$540,000.

Narayan's simulations indicate that wage rates for unskilled labour in rural and urban areas will increase by 1.8% and 1.2%, respectively. The informal sector labour wage rates will increase by a relatively large 5.8%. These contribute to the increase in private disposable incomes and the increase in real consumption. All these will ensure an improvement in the national welfare (defined as including GDP, net private receipts of investment income from abroad, net private unrequited transfers from abroad and net foreign aid), which will increase by around 0.67%.

Sectoral effects

Narayan's simulations indicate that some sectors gain and others lose from an expansion in tourism to Fiji. See Table 9.5.

Regarding export effects, the real outputs of the hotel industry, transportation, commerce and other private sector output are among the most positively affected. However, the real output of the various traditional export sectors decline. One of the most striking results is the fall in exports in Fiji's traditional export sectors. Among the agricultural sectors, Kava, dalo and fish exports will be the most affected, falling by around 2.5%, 2.3% and 2.0%, respectively. Processed food exports, including tinned fish, flour, biscuits, natural water and fruit and vegetables, will fall by over 8%. Other manufactures and textile and clothing exports will fall by around 2.6% and 1.7%, respectively. A reduction in the real output of these traditional export sectors will also occur (not shown here).The negative export and real output performances of traditional export sectors occur because the additional tourist expenditure induces an appreciation of the real exchange rate. There are also associated increases in the domestic prices of goods and services and in wage rates relative to foreign prices that erode the competitive advantage of traditional export sectors.

Narayan also finds that those industries closely related to the tourism industry will experience an increase in imports. Fruit and vegetable imports, for instance, will increase by about 39%, transport imports by around 5.6%, private services by around 8%, and business and property services imports will increase by around 4.3% and 3.5%, respectively. This is to be expected given the upward pressure on the Fiji dollar.

Narayan's study indicates that, for an island developing country such as Fiji, an expansion in inbound tourism can generate growth in real GDP, but effects on the real exchange rate, real wages and the CPI imply that the gains to tourism-related sectors are offset to some extent by losses in traditional export and import competing industries.

Table 9.5 Export and import effect from 10% expansion in tourism to Fiji

Exports		Imports	
Products/Services	% Change	Products/Services	%Change
Coconuts	−1.1229	Fruit and vegetables	38.828
Ginger	−0.6693	Dairy	0.6087
Dalo	−2.2710	Rice	−0.2523
Kava	−2.5474	Other crops	0.2876
Fish	−2.0406	Fish	0.7966
Gold	−0.6027	Processed food	2.1658
Sugar	−0.4061	Textile, clothing and footwear	0.9138
Processed food	−8.3215	Other manufactures	0.9316
Textile, clothing & footwear	−1.7104	Transport	5.6522
Other manufactures	−2.5963	Insurance	1.7169
Hotels	4.9543	Property services	3.5489
Transport	2.5931	Business services	4.3318
Other private services	0.3916	Other private services	8.1386
Commerce	0.2440	Beverage and tobacco	0.7057

Source: Narayan, P.K. (2004) 'Economic Impact of Tourism on Fiji's Economy: Empirical Evidence from the Computable General Equilibrium Model', *Tourism Economics*, 10(4), 419–433.

9.3.3 REDUCED TOURISM TO HAWAII

Zhou *et al.* (1997) analysed the impacts on the Hawaii State economy of a 10% projected *decrease* in visitor expenditure.

Noting that Hawaii's major sources of export income are visitor expenditure, defence expenditure, and pineapple and sugar sales, Zhou *et al.* observe that over time, the growth of tourism has gradually changed the structure of Hawaii's economy. Four transformations are evident:

- Hawaii's export industry has been transformed from commodity exports based on plantation agriculture into service-based exports.

- The growth in the service sector and the decline in agriculture have realigned employment opportunities and changed labour skill requirements.
- State and local governments acquire more tax revenues from tourism and thus can provide expanded and better public services.
- As the service sector expands and attracts more labour, construction and complementary industries also experience increases in final product demands.

The Hawaii CGE model is based on the 1982 USDA CGE model. The Hawaii economy is disaggregated into 14 sectors. There are three primary factors of production (labour, capital and land) and six institutional actors (households, enterprises, state government, federal government, capital account and the ROW), which record all transactions in the macroeconomic circular flow of income.

Similar to other CGE models, there are several operational assumptions:

The competitiveness assumption. This describes a competitive world which includes utility maximisation in consumption, cost minimisation in production, zero pure profits and market clearing.

The small country assumption for imports. This implies that Hawaii's market transactions cannot affect world prices of imported commodities because imports to Hawaii represent only a small share of the total world trade.

The Armington assumption which implies that the model incorporates imperfect substitution between import and domestic goods in demand.

The market behaviour assumption for primary inputs. This assumes two modes of behaviour for land, labour and capital. For the short-run version, capital is assumed to be sectorally fixed, and the final equilibrium will have sectorally differentiated rental rates. In the long run, all factors are mobile and average factor returns adjust to clear factor markets with full employment.

Results

The 10% decrease in tourism expenditure is projected to result in:

- A reduction in Gross State Product.
- A small reduction in the general level of prices.
- Output reductions in the industries servicing tourist needs, and in traditional exports, manufacturing, construction and services.
- A reduction in imports, particularly those associated with tourist-related industries.
- A fall in the balance of trade.
- Reduced employment in the hotel industry, restaurants and bars and transportation.

Table 9.6 Output demand effects from a 10% reduction in visitor expenditure

Variables	Base Year Value Domestic Output (US$millions)	Percentage Change from Base Year	
		CGE Model (%)	IO Model (%)
Sugarcane	230.8	−0.607	−1.15
Pineapple	94.37	−1.642	−5.4
Other Agriculture	192.77	−2.911	−7.81
Sugar Processing	383.25	−0.62	−1.1
Food Processing	728.17	−3.219	−6.97
Manufacturing	2307.59	−4.543	−10.43
Construction	1741.84	−0.776	−1.75
Transportation	1595.3	−7.254	−10.41
Communication	492.53	−5.324	−8.15
Energy	816.64	−5.362	−6.95
Total Trade	2349.09	−6.378	−8.06
Restaurant and Bars	1512.72	−8.258	−9.4
Hotels	1181.58	−9.656	−11.22
Services	9020.22	−4.286	−4.52

Source: Zhou *et al.* (1997), Table 4

An interesting aspect of the study was to compare projections based on the CGE modelling with projections based on I–O modelling. Table 9.6 shows the sectoral output results from the I–O and CGE models.

In general, the I–O model results are larger in terms of percentage reduction in domestic output. The I–O model shows larger effects for those industries closely related to tourism, namely, the hotel, transportation, and food and beverage industries. In contrast, the CGE effects are smaller because this model allows for resource reallocation. Although the external market was fixed and aggregate factor prices were not permitted to change, the CGE model still shows the price effects on the visitor expenditure scenario which the I–O model is not capable of providing.

9.3.4 EFFECTS OF FOOT AND MOUTH DISEASE ON UK TOURISM

Blake *et al.* (2003a) investigated the economy-wide effects of Foot and Mouth Disease (FMD) in the UK. They note that FMD has considerable effects not only on agricultural production and farming industries but also on the tourism sector due to the inter-sectoral linkage and effects of the ways in which the UK government handled the outbreak. The latter includes the imposition of 'restricted areas' that include historic sites and tourist attractions, closed countryside walking paths and waterways, and cancelled/postponed sports and public events. Many tourist attractions, ranging from zoos and safari parks to country houses and even Stonehenge, were also closed because of the risk to animals on their property. The closure of footpaths and inland waterways to the public, as well as the inaccessibility of businesses in exclusion zones around infected areas, had a considerable impact on rural tourism activities as well as on other rural businesses. There was also concern about decreases in the number of foreign tourists, especially Americans, who were deterred from visiting the UK by media images of burning carcasses, fears about food safety and the possibility of importing FMD into overseas countries.

The researchers used the Nottingham model to assess the economic impacts of FMD on tourism-related activities and other sectors of the economy. The model includes production relationships for 115 sectors of the economy and markets for 115 goods and services. The CGE model is linked to a micro-regional tourism simulation (MRTS) model to analyse the economy-wide impacts of FMD in the context of intersectoral and interregional linkages in the economy.

The tourism effects of FMD are quantified by inward shifts of the tourism demand curves, for (inbound) international tourism, domestic (overnight) tourism and domestic same-day visits. These reductions in demand from tourists lead to reductions in demand for goods according to the make-up of expenditures for the three categories of tourism and visitors.

The reduction in demand for goods affects the economy through similar channels as do the agricultural export reductions, although in this case it proceeds through different sectors. Additionally, any income released because of the reduction in domestic (overnight and same-day) expenditures leads to increases in expenditures on other goods and services and to savings, according to the pattern of initial expenditures and savings rates.

Overall effects on the UK economy
The main results from the model, shown in Table 9.7, display the estimated effects of FMD on the UK economy. The first column shows the reduction in tourism expenditures in the UK economy as a whole. The second column shows the resulting fall in GDP from the tourism expenditure reductions. The total effects of the FMD crisis (tourism expenditure reductions and agricultural effects) are shown in the final column.

Table 9.7 Reductions in total tourism expenditure and GDP, 2001–04

	Reduction in tourism expenditure (£ billion)	*Fall in GDP due to tourism expenditure reductions (£ billion)*	*Total fall in GDP due to the FMD crisis (£ billion)*
2001	7.7	2.0	3.6
2002	5.2	1.3	1.6
2003	1.3	0.4	0.6
2004	0.6	0.3	0.5

Source: Blake & Sinclair (2003), Table 4

In 2001, a fall of £7.7 billion in tourism expenditure reduced GDP by £2.0 billion. When agricultural effects are also included, the fall in GDP attributable to the FMD crisis is £3.6 billion. The FMD crisis, therefore, had larger adverse effects on GDP through tourism than through agriculture. The fact that the fall in GDP attributable to tourism expenditure reductions in 2001 is just over one-quarter the size of the fall in expenditures is because some primary factors previously employed in industries satisfying tourism demand are reallocated to other forms of production. As the authors note, this is the reverse effect of the more familiar 'crowding-out' argument.

Industries in the UK that rely heavily on sales to tourists (such as hotels and air transport) experienced the largest declines in output and value-added. Industries that sell some of their produce to tourists (such as entertainment and rail and road transport) can be expected to have smaller declines in output and value-added, as can industries that are heavily involved in the tourism intermediate supply chain. Other industries that sell little or none of their produce to tourists, either directly or indirectly, may well increase output and value-added because they can draw on primary factors no longer needed in the adversely affected industries. Further, their ability to export will be enhanced through a real exchange rate depreciation, and they may gain custom as demand shifts away from domestic tourism.

Table 9.8 identifies the ten production sectors in the UK that are worst affected in absolute terms in terms of real factor earnings by the full FMD crisis.

Hotels, catering and pubs constitute the worst-affected sector, with reductions in real factor earnings of £978 million in 2001, £725 million in 2002 and smaller reductions in 2003 and 2004. The 2001 reduction is a 3.9% fall in real factor earnings in this sector. The other sectors with large reductions in real factor earnings sell a large proportion of their products to tourists (e.g. road transport, recreational services and ancillary transport services), are involved in the distribution of products to tourists and tourism industries

Table 9.8 Changes in real factor earnings by sector: The 10 largest sectors

Sector	2001	2002	2003	2004	2001 % change due to FMD crisis
	£ million				
Hotels, catering and pubs	−978	−725	−274	−174	−3.9
Road transport	−412	−280	−49	−29	−2.2
Agriculture	−207	−100	−38	−11	−2.1
Retail distribution	−205	−134	−64	−44	−0.5
Wholesale distribution	−194	−98	−46	−30	−0.5
Recreational and welfare services	−142	−65	−24	−22	−0.3
Ancillary transport services	−93	−49	−9	−10	−0.5
Railway transport	−69	−40	−7	−4	−2.5
Motor vehicle retail and repair	−57	−19	−14	−12	−0.3
Owning and dealing in real estate	−54	−38	−17	−12	−0.3

Source: Blake and Sinclair (2003), Table 5

(retail and wholesale distribution) and are directly affected by the agricultural restrictions (agriculture).

Policy implications

The results from application of the Nottingham model show that FMD has much larger adverse effects on tourism in the UK than on agriculture. The policy implication is, in setting appropriate agriculture policy, to consider the roles of other sectors. Application of the CGE tourism model of the UK economy showed that the effects of the tourism decreases were to reduce GDP by more than the loss of agricultural production. The total cost of the policy was even greater, as it also included the cost of slaughter and carcass disposal, as well as compensation payments. The implication is that a policy geared towards supporting tourism would have been far less costly than the government's policy of supporting agricultural exports by means of slaughtering animals and prohibiting access to many rural areas.

It is clear that FMD has had considerable impacts not only on sectors directly related to tourism but also on other industries. The policy of maintaining FMD-free status supported meat exports, but it cost the UK tourism industry substantially. There is therefore a need to adopt a whole of industry approach to policy making relating to FMD. Blake *et al.* conclude that the 2001 crisis provides a very good opportunity for looking back and analysing the costs and benefits of the current agricultural policies that affect other sectors. It is necessary to put the role of agriculture into perspective and to take account of the roles of other sectors (especially tourism!) when formulating agricultural policies.

9.3.5   CGE MEASURES OF TOURISM YIELD

An understanding of the yield potential of different source markets and segments can underpin destination marketing by both public and private sector organisations. As discussed in Chapter 7, the standard yield measure relates to expenditure injected into a destination from different market segments. CGE modelling can be used to develop 'economy-wide' yield measures. Economy-wide yield measures indicate the bottom line for the economy when all inter-industry effects have taken place (Dwyer *et al.*, 2007).

Dwyer and Forsyth (2008) estimated three economy-wide yield measures associated with 14 of Australia's major tourism origin countries and for three regions. The yield measures are GVA, Gross Operating Surplus (GOS) and Employment, and are set out in Table 9.9. (Note: these economy-wide yield measures, based on CGE modelling of economic impacts, differ from the TSA-based yield measures as discussed in Chapter 7). The expenditure estimates in columns one and three of Table 9.9, based on the International Visitor Survey (IVS) (Tourism Australia, 2002, 2003, 2004), provide the data that were fed into the model to generate the economic impacts of the different tourist market segments. The economic impacts were then converted to yield measures by determining the economy-wide effects of an additional tourist from each market.

Table 9.9 shows real GVA and real GOS in the economy per visitor night and employment generated per $1 million tourism expenditure. The total column shows the average overall inbound markets. Regarding real GVA origins with above average contribution on this measure ($12.13) are Singapore, Hong Kong, Malaysia, Japan, USA, Indonesia, Taiwan, Korea, Thailand and China. Country origins with the lowest contributed GVA per visitor night are Other Asia, UK, Other World and Canada. The German market (0.134) has the highest proportion of GVA per dollar of expenditure, followed by Other Europe, Other countries, New Zealand, Japan, Taiwan and USA. The results indicate that the spending volume and pattern of these visitors is such as to result in a greater GVA per dollar spent in Australia than for the other origin markets. The smallest contribution to GVA per dollar spent is associated with visitors from Hong Kong, Indonesia and Singapore.

The results for GVA can be displayed in Matrix form as in Figure 9.7. The axes cross at the average value added per day for all markets ($12.13) and average real value added per visitor ($332.65). The North East Quadrant indicates above average value added per visitor (over total trip) and above average value added per visitor day. Origin markets located in

Table 9.9 Economic impacts of inbound tourism expenditure by origin (annual average period, 2001/02–2003/04, Australia)

Origin	Total injected expenditure ($m)	Real GVA per visitor $	Real GVA per visitor night ($)	Real GOS per visitor $	Real GOS/ visitor night ($)	Real GOS/ expenditure (%)	Number of jobs per $m spend
Canada	256.73	388.90	10.88	244.51	6.84	8.22	6.31
China	672.49	476.58	12.18	205.31	5.25	5.47	6.25
Germany	461.79	466.89	11.50	293.78	7.24	8.46	5.97
Hong Kong	503.57	434.25	15.49	193.19	7.84	4.88	5.32
Indonesia	324.57	506.22	13.06	202.49	5.23	5.05	6.29
Japan	1030.21	211.22	14.14	117.73	7.88	7.13	5.60
Korea	541.94	386.66	12.40	176.07	5.65	5.83	6.01
Malaysia	422.92	386.22	14.56	148.76	5.61	4.88	6.02
NZ	972.05	167.40	12.01	110.54	7.93	8.61	6.51

Singapore	627.02	339.30	17.53	157.68	8.15	5.87	6.28
Taiwan	200.52	295.66	12.93	137.15	6.00	5.39	6.11
Thailand	247.19	442.19	12.91	176.26	5.15	5.06	6.42
UK	1837.74	393.09	10.19	261.34	6.80	8.72	6.21
USA	1157.71	372.33	14.14	204.29	7.76	7.04	6.27
Other Asia	319.296	367.47	9.06	163.89	4.04	5.65	6.39
Other Europe	1,346.9	454.88	11.03	277.22	6.72	7.99	5.89
Other World	582.23	310.47	10.46	177.26	5.97	7.44	6.05
Total	11.436	332.65	12.13	184.03	6.71	7.16	6.13

Source: Authors' simulations using M2RNSW CGE model

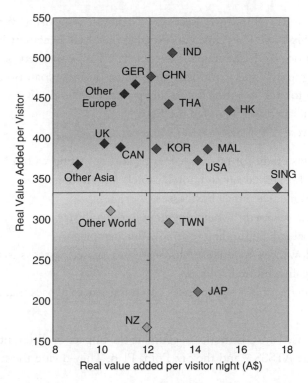

Figure 9.7 Real value added of inbound tourism expenditure by origin (annual average period, 2001/02–2003/04, Australia)

this quadrant are Singapore, Korea, Indonesia, Malaysia, Hong Kong, Thailand and USA. Other Asia and New Zealand are located in the South West Quadrant, indicating below average value added per visit and below average value added per day.

Similar matrices were constructed for the other economic impact variables of interest (Dwyer & Forsyth, 2008; Dwyer *et al.*, 2007). Yield measures based on CGE modelling can inform organisations in both the private and public sector about effective allocation of marketing resources and types of tourism development that meet operator and destination manager objectives.

9.3.6 POLICY RESPONSES TO THE IMPACT OF 9/11 ON US TOURISM

Blake and Sinclair (2003) modelled the impacts on tourism in the USA of actual and proposed policy responses of the US government following the terrorist attacks of September 11, 2001.

US Federal government response to the attacks was swift, with the Air Transportation Safety and System Stabilization Act (ATSSSA) being passed on 22 September. This act provided federal government loans and compensation to airlines, as well as other financial and safety measures. The Travel Industry Recovery Coalition, comprising 25 tourism organisations, proposed a Six-Point Plan aimed at restoring the levels of activity in the US industry to those existing prior to the September events. The Plan consisted of a series of policy measures covering tourist and workforce tax credits, business loan programs, the extension of allowances for net operating losses, and government and private sector funding for advertising to stimulate travel to and in the USA.

The six points were as follows:

- Provide a $500 tax credit for travel originating and occurring within North America on air, cruise, train, bus, rental car and hotel/motel expenditures.
- Expand loan programs to small businesses.
- Offer a workforce tax credit for employment in the industry.
- Supply substantial federal funding for marketing campaigns.
- Increase tax allowances to enable businesses to offset losses sustained because of September 11 against future earnings.
- Restore full tax deductibility for business entertainment expenses that are currently only 50% deductible.

Blake and Sinclair used a CGE model to estimate the impact of different policy responses included within the ATSSSA and the Six-Point Plan. They divide the measures into two categories:

- those designed to stimulate economic activity across the whole industry in order to offset the downturn caused by the September events; and
- those aiming to increase liquidity and to prevent firms from incurring major costs and possibly going out of business.

The CGE model was used to estimate the relative magnitudes of the first category of policy measures.

Findings

The estimated effects of September 11 with and without these crisis management responses are included in Table 9.10.

Table 9.10 indicates that the terrorist attacks had severe effects in terms of a variety of criteria, including income, government revenue, labour and capital adjustment costs, and employment and job losses. As the first column shows, the fall in tourism expenditures of $50.68 billion reduces GDP by $27.27 billion less than it would otherwise have been and worsens the government budget by $7.27 billion. Factor adjustment, the amount of capital and labour that leave their original sector of employment, is $30.93 billion. The loss of employment is high, at 383,000 full time equivalents. A total of 559,000 jobs are lost, of which 203,000 are in airlines and 174,000 in accommodation establishments.

Table 9.10 Effects of September 11 without/with ATSSSA and ATSA measures

Types of Effects	Effects of September 11, Without ATSSSA and ATSA Policy Responses	Effects of September 11, Including ATSSSA and ATSA Policy Responses
Total change in tourist spending ($bn)	−50.68	−37.47
Constant dollar GDP ($bn change from base)	−27.27	−9.34
Net effect on government budget ($bn change from base)	−7.27	−11.14
Constant dollar factor adjustment ($bn)	30.93	17.42
Relative factor adjustment (%)	0.75	0.49
Constant dollar employment ($bn)	−13.57	−3.65
FTE employment ('000)	−383	−144
FTE jobs lost ('000)	559	335
FTE jobs lost in airlines ('000)	203	93
FTE jobs lost in hotels and other accommodation establishments ('000)	174	141

Source: Blake and Sinclair (2003), Table 2

The simulations indicate that the policy responses are very effective in offsetting the adverse effects of the crisis. The fall in GDP is much lower than it would otherwise have been, at $9.34 billion compared with $27.27 billion in the 'without policy' case. The measures reduce net government revenues by the relatively large amount of around $11.14 billion, which includes $5 billion in airline compensation and $4.5 billion in security spending outlined in the ATSSSA and ATSA acts. The policies also reduce the factor adjustment costs relating to the crisis, almost halving the value of the labour and capital that leave their original sector of employment. The loss of employment is less than half of what it would otherwise have been, so that the number of people affected is 144,000 compared with 383,000 in the non-response case.

Table 9.11 shows the results of modelling several different possible policy responses to the crisis. Each of these involves a specific type of subsidy scheme, which can be interpreted as an equivalent tax reduction. The different types of crisis management responses

347

Table 9.11 Marginal effects of alternative subsidy schemes

Type of Subsidy	GDP ($m)	Net Budget Effect ($m)	Factor Adjustment Saved ($m)	Total Jobs Saved	Airline Jobs Saved	Accommodation Jobs Saved
Per $1m Production Subsidy to:						
Airlines	3.1	−0.02	1.6	27.8	20.7	0.1
Hotels	2.0	−0.4	0.6	11.9	−0.1	12.4
Other accommodation	1.8	−0.1	1.6	23.7	−1.5	24.2
Eating & drinking places	0.7	−0.8	0.7	22.8	0.2	−1.0
Other entertainment sectors	−0.1	−1.1	−0.2	0.6	−0.2	−4.0
Airlines, hotels and other accommodation	2.5	−0.2	1.1	20.2	10.2	6.5

Per $1m Consumption Subsidy on:

Business air travel trips	2.7	−0.3	0.5	7.8	1.3	0.4
All business trips	2.4	−0.3	0.4	6.7	0.8	0.3
International trips	2.0	−0.04	1.1	19.4	5.1	4.9
All air trips	1.6	−0.4	0.7	12.5	4.7	2.1
Domestic air trips	1.4	−0.6	0.5	9.0	4.5	0.7
All tourism trips	1.3	−0.6	0.4	7.7	2.2	1.6
All domestic tourism	1.1	−0.7	0.2	4.8	1.5	0.8
Domestic air travel trips	0.3	−0.9	0.5	10.2	7.4	1.0
All domestic trips	0.2	−0.9	0.1	3.7	1.9	1.0

Per $1m Employment Subsidy in:						
Airlines	3.1	−0.01	1.6	32.4	25.5	0.04
All tourism sectors	2.6	−0.2	1.2	28.4	12.9	12.5
Per $1m Subsidy to Profits in:						
Airlines	3.1	−0.1	1.6	10.1	2.3	0.2
All tourism sectors	2.3	−0.3	1.0	−2.0	0.7	−5.8
Per $1m of:						
Direct tax cuts	0.2	−0.9	−0.1	−0.5	−0.02	0.05
Military expenditure	0.2	−1.0	0.3	−2.3	−0.1	−0.1

Source: Blake and Sinclair (2003), Table 4

are divided into five main types: subsidies to production, to consumers' expenditure, to labour employment, to capital profits and more general fiscal stimulus measures.

Conclusions and policy implications

Two major findings by Blake and Sinclair are that:

- An airline production subsidy outperforms all other types in each of the criteria with the exception of the number of accommodation jobs lost. However, an airline subsidy fails to take account of job losses outside the sector that are caused by the fall in demand from tourists who would have travelled by air.
- Subsidies to accommodation establishments are reasonably effective at boosting GDP and saving jobs in this sector. These subsidies are significantly more effective than those allocated to catering and entertainment. In fact, subsidies to the latter can have the effect of worsening GDP and labour and capital adjustment, as they encourage workers to move out of the airline and accommodation sectors, thereby increasing the job losses in these sectors.

These findings suggest that government subsidies can prove effective in limiting the adverse effects of a major tourism crisis. However, the relative effectiveness of the different policy responses varies considerably. The overall conclusion is that directing subsidies to the sector that is most severely affected by the crisis is the most efficient policy response in terms of both GDP and the total number of jobs saved. Policymakers should be very careful in their decisions as to which sectors to assist, as the provision of subsidies for those relatively unaffected can even be counter-productive.

9.3.7 TOURISM AND POVERTY REDUCTION IN BRAZIL

While it is often assumed that tourism provides a means of relieving poverty, researchers have neglected to investigate this in the context of the distributional effects of tourism across entire economies. Blake *et al.* (2008) thus provide an economy-wide analysis of the distributional effects of tourism expansion to determine whether and how tourism can contribute to poverty relief.

Poverty is widespread across Brazil. The Brazilian government sees tourism as a major potential source of job creation and reduction of economic disparities, and long-term policies to improve the industry in the country have been established. The number of tourist arrivals increased from 1.1 million in 1990 to 4.1 million in 2003. The government expects that about 1.2 million jobs will be created in tourism businesses in 4 years, should the growth trend continue.

Blake *et al.* state that tourism may be expected to reduce poverty via three channels:

- The first channel is prices, by which tourism spending leads to changes in prices for goods that poor households purchase.

351

- The second channel relates to the effects that tourism spending has on the earnings of employed and self-employed labour and in returns to capital.
- The third channel is government, by which the expenditure changes government revenues and can thus affect government spending, borrowing or tax rates.

The authors use a CGE model for Brazil to quantify the effects on income distribution and poverty relief that occur via changes in prices, earnings and government revenues following an expansion of tourism. The CGE model is calibrated using a SAM that shows the payments that take place among the different industries, products, factors, households, firms, the government and the ROW. The model incorporates the earnings of different groups of workers within tourism, along with the channels by which changes in earnings, prices and the government affect the distribution of income among rich and poor households. The model has the advantage of incorporating the entire range of activities undertaken in the Brazilian economy, thereby permitting analysis of the interrelationships between tourism and other sectors.

A 10% increase in demand by foreign tourists in Brazil is assumed in order to investigate the effects of this on income distribution in the economy.

The assumed 10% expansion in inbound tourism leads to rises in the prices that tourists pay for goods and services which lead to a fall in demand that counteracts part of the original 10% increase. Blake *et al.* also note that wages in Brazil will also be sensitive to changes in demand, pointing out that average unemployment has been around 10% over the last five years, and real wages have fluctuated in accordance with economic conditions during this period. The tourism demand expansion will also lead to changes in production in all industries, changes in employment, earnings, household incomes, prices and all other variables in the model.

Results

The results from four simulations are included in Table 9.12. The differences among these simulations are in the way that the government allocates the additional tax revenues received directly and indirectly from the tourism expansion (net of falls in revenue from other activities). In each of these simulations, additional government income is transferred to households, either through increases in transfer payments or through reductions in direct tax levels, as follows:

Simulation 1 – additional revenue is transferred to households in proportion to their original receipts of government transfers.

Simulation 2 – additional revenue is transferred according to households' levels of tax payments (e.g. reducing income taxes).

Simulation 3 – additional revenue is transferred in proportion to income levels.

Simulation 4 – all additional revenue is transferred to the poorest household group.

Table 9.12 shows the effects that the tourism demand shock has on some of the key economic variables: tourism consumption, prices and expenditure, EV for Brazil as a whole, compensated EV for the four household groups and the ratio of real income in the highest-income to the lowest-income households.

The tourism and the macroeconomic results are very similar for the four simulations. The 10% rise in foreign demand leads to increases in prices of, on average, just under 0.7%, which reduces the growth in tourism consumption to around 8.5%. Expenditure increases by 9.2%. In each simulation, the resulting rise in tourism expenditure is around $0.23 billion. The authors estimate that the welfare benefit to Brazil of this additional expenditure is around $0.106 billion, implying that the country benefits by $45 for every $100 of additional tourism spending.

Simulation 1: Transferring additional government revenues to households in proportion to their original receipts of transfer income essentially maintains the current system of government payments but at a higher level.

Simulation 2: Transferring revenues in proportion to income tax payments is equivalent to the government choosing to spend the gains from tourism expansion on tax cuts. Simulations 1 and 2 have similar effects on the compensated EV of the lowest-income household ($0.018 billion) and on the ratio of income levels for the highest- and lowest-income household, which falls by 0.035%, so that the level of income inequality by this measure is reduced.

Simulation 3: Transferring revenues to households in proportion to their income levels results in a welfare gain for the lowest-income households that is slightly higher, at $0.020 billion, with a greater reduction in income inequality (0.039%). The reason for this latter effect is that the lowest-income household has a much higher share of income (8.5%) than either income tax payments (0.2%) or government transfers (0.5%).

Simulation 4: Transferring all additional government revenues to the lowest-income household results in significantly different distributional impacts from the other three scenarios, although the macroeconomic impacts are very similar, with a slightly lower welfare gain for Brazil as a whole ($0.104 billion compared to $0.106 billion). By allocating transfers to the lowest-income household, the benefit of tourism expansion to this group is doubled, and the poorest household gains around $1 for every $7 of additional foreign tourism spending in Brazil.

The results show that the total earnings effects (column 3) are often lower than the direct plus indirect earnings effects; and that for the medium- and high-income households, the

Table 9.12 Main results for tourism and welfare

Simulation Closure rule: additional government income is transferred in proportion to...	1 Original transfer receipts	2 Levels of income tax	3 Levels of income	4 Only to the poorest household
Percentage change in tourism consumption	8.484	8.484	8.484	8.484
Percentage change in tourism price	0.697	0.697	0.697	0.696
Percentage change in tourism expenditure	9.239	9.239	9.239	9.240
Change in tourism expenditure (R$bn)	0.680	0.679	0.680	0.680
Equivalent Variation ($bn)	0.106	0.106	0.106	0.104
Equivalent variation as a percentage of original income	0.025	0.025	0.025	0.025
Compensated equivalent variation ($bn)				
Lowest income household	0.018	0.018	0.020	0.037
Low income household	0.038	0.036	0.038	0.033
Medium income household	0.010	0.011	0.008	0.004
High income household	0.040	0.041	0.040	0.030
Percentage change in Highest:Lowest real income	−0.035	−0.034	−0.039	−0.092
Household equivalent variation as percentage of total equivalent variation				
Lowest income household[a]	17	17	19	35
Low income household[a]	36	34	36	32
Medium income household[a]	9	10	7	4
High income household[a]	38	39	38	29

[a] Percentages.

Source: Blake *et al.* (2008), Table 3

total earnings effects are small. Other export sectors are much more intensive in their use of factors of production – capital and skilled labour – that are owned by the richer household groups, than are tourism businesses. Therefore, the greatest burdens of the crowding out activities fall on the medium- and high-income households.

The price channel (column 4) is shown to have a moderate effect, increasing the real income of the poorest household groups but reducing the real income of the richest group. The government channel (column 5), in this simulation, acts to increase the incomes of all households except the poorest as they receive very low levels of transfers. The firms' effect (column 6) comes through the fact that establishments invest more in response to the tourism shock, and the additional holding of capital (with future earnings potential) is allocated to households in proportion to their ownership of firms.

However, there are considerable variations in the redistributive effects of the different simulations. Table 9.13 shows changes in the composition of real earnings resulting from the 10% increase in foreign tourism demand, by household.

Column 1 shows the direct earnings effects, which are the earnings by household in the sector from which foreign tourists are purchasing goods and services.

The figures in column 2 show that the indirect earnings effects are highly significant for the high-income household, which earns more through the indirect than through the direct effects.

Table 9.13 Distribution of earnings by households ($millions)

Household	1	2	3	4	5	6
	Direct effect	Direct plus indirect effects		Total effects, simulation 1		
	earnings	earnings	earnings	prices	government	firms
Lowest income household	11	15	12	1	0	5
Low income household	25	35	25	4	5	0
Medium income household	14	22	3	1	6	4
High income household	18	39	7	−6	11	29

Source: Blake *et al.* (2008), Table 5

In columns 3–6, the CGE model results from Table 9.13 are decomposed into earnings, prices, government channels as well as the effects of increased firm investment.

The results show that tourism benefits the lowest-income sections of the Brazilian population and has the potential to reduce income inequality. The lowest-income households are not, however, the main beneficiaries, as households with low (but not the lowest) income benefit more from the earnings and price-channel effects of tourism expansion.

High- and medium-income households, followed by the low-income group, benefit most from the government channel effects, with the exception of the case when government directs the revenue from tourism expansion specifically towards the lowest-income group. The latter type of revenue distribution could double the benefits for the lowest-income households, giving them around one-third of all the benefits. The implication is that policies directed specifically towards benefiting the lowest-income group are required if the poorest are to achieve the greatest gains.

The results suggest caution when generalising the effects of tourism growth on poverty within a country. In the case of Brazil, there is a strong reinforcement effect whereby the industries that reduce their output following a tourism demand increase are export industries that employ factors of production from the richer households. Therefore, the structure of earnings in non-tourism export sectors plays a significant role in determining the net poverty effects of tourism. The authors emphasise that this type of earnings structure may not apply in other countries. Hence, it would be important to apply the model to tourism expansion in other countries, in order to investigate the effects that would occur under different types of earnings structures.

9.3.8 IS AN EXPANSION OF TOURISM GOOD FOR THE POOR IN THAILAND?

It is generally believed by policy makers in developing destinations that that the growth of tourism disproportionately benefits the poor, primarily by stimulating the expansion of sectors that are assumed to be relatively labour-intensive. The promotion of tourism thus appears to generate private gains and also to advance broader societal goals; in particular, policies that promote tourism are seen as 'pro-poor' in that they are often anticipated to create disproportionately more jobs for less-skilled (and thus poorer) workers.

Tourism expansion in a destination may well create jobs for unskilled workers, and this would have a direct poverty alleviation impact. But much of the gain from tourism growth accrues to factors other than unskilled labour, so income distribution may actually worsen. In addition, low-skill jobs in other sectors may be destroyed, and returns to agricultural land, from which the poor derive a considerable share of their income, may fall as tourism expands.

Clearly, the growth of tourism can be expected to raise aggregate income as with any export boom, and in this sense the sector may indeed offer pro-poor outcomes if indeed 'a rising tide raises all boats'. But whether tourism growth reduces the *relative* deprivation of the poor is less obvious. If it does not, then government efforts to promote tourism growth may thus be inconsistent with the goal of reduced income inequality.

Wattanakuljarus and Coxhead (2008) use a CGE model for Thailand and simulate the effects of tourism growth. Their stated goal is to take account of general equilibrium adjustment mechanisms in answering the question: is tourism growth pro-poor?

Foreign tourism is by far Thailand's largest export industry. 'Visitor exports', or sales of tourism goods and services to foreign visitors, averaged US$ 10.2 billion (bn) (12% of total exports) in 1998–2005 on more than 10 million annual visitor arrivals. The next largest category of exports, computers and parts, averaged US$ 8.5 billion in the same period. On average during 1998–2005, Thai tourism directly and indirectly accounted for 13% of GDP, 10% of employment (3 million jobs) and 12% of investment. Successive Thai governments have placed great store in earnings from tourism, and have supported a range of promotional programs.

The authors assume that inbound tourism increases by 10%. Depending on the assumptions regarding factor constraints, this induces growth in real GDP of between 0.88% and 2.06%, leading households to increase consumption by between 3.81% and 4.11%. Due to increased household and tourism consumption, total domestic absorption increases by between 2.90% and 3.25%.

The authors distinguish the following categories:

LowAg the poorest 80% of households in agriculture

HighAg the richest 20% of households in agriculture

LowNag the poorest 80% of households in non-agriculture

HighNag the richest 20% of households in non-agriculture

On these definitions, pro-poor' growth is characterised by a relatively faster rate of increase in the incomes of households in the LowAg group, since that is where most poor Thai households are found.

Table 9.14 shows the additional factor income accruing to each of the four sectors following a 10% increase in tourism to Thailand. Owners of the factor that gain most from a given shock will benefit most from tourism growth. Table 9.14 indicates that a 10% tourism expansion generates an extra 75,413 Million Baht (MB) of income for owners of non agricultural labour. Of this, 2115 MB goes to LowAg, 1087 MB goes to HighAg, 21,197 MB goes to LowNag and 51,014 MB goes to HighNag. Other factor income changes can be read in the same way. The largest percentage increase in factor earnings goes to capital in non-agricultural sectors, and the largest part of this gain is earned by the HighNag group. As a result, just over 55% of the total increase in factor incomes accrues to this group.

Table 9.14 Distribution of additions to factor incomes across households (million baht)

	LabAg	LabNag	Land	CapAg	CapNag	Forest	Total (MB)	Distribution (%)
LowAg	4229	2,115	1616	2196	14,499	79	24,734	14.04
HighAg	240	1,087	1612	908	4,636	33	8,516	4.83
LowNag	717	21,197	841	125	22,435	4	45,319	25.72
HighNag	188	51,014	1162	28	45,223	1	97,616	55.41
Total (MB)	5374	75,413	5231	3257	86,792	117	176,185	100
Distribution (%)	3.05	42.80	2.97	1.85	49.26	0.07	100	

Source: Wattanakuljarus and Coxhead (2008), Table 6

The simulations indicate that capital and labour in non-agriculture are the factors that gain the most. In Thailand, corporations are the major owners of capital in non-agriculture, and corporate income accrues mainly to wealthy non-agricultural households. Similarly, since high-income non-agricultural households are the major owners of labor in non-agriculture, they are the next biggest beneficiaries. As a result, given the distribution of factor ownership across household groups, the inbound tourism expansion raises incomes across the board, but main share of the gains accrues to the non-poor.

The authors conducted sensitivity analysis with different assumptions regarding factor constraints. In every scenario, however, although tourism growth benefits all household classes, the biggest gains accrue to high-income and non-agricultural households. It is concluded that tourism growth in Thailand is not pro-poor or pro-agriculture.

The study has interesting policy implications. One is that a tourism promotion campaign leading to increased international visitation may increase the gap between rich and poor. To address this increased inequality, additional policy instruments are required to correct for the inequalities occasioning tourism growth.

9.4 STRENGTHS AND LIMITATIONS OF CGE MODELLING

The examples above indicate just some of the range of uses to which CGE modelling can be put. There are many other examples in tourism analysis. In Chapter 14, we discuss how CGE modelling can be used to estimate the economic impacts of special events; and in Chapter 19, we discuss the use of CGE modelling to estimate the impacts of carbon taxes as a response to global warming. Nonetheless, the studies highlighted should serve to convey the power of the technique in estimating the effects of tourism shocks. We summarise the strengths of CGE modelling of the economic impacts of tourism in Box 9.1.

BOX 9.1 Strengths of CGE modelling of tourism's economic impacts

- CGE models recognise that complex interactions occur in the behaviour of producers and householders as they act in their best interests. The CGE approach specifically models business and household demand for goods and services, relative price changes and substitution effects (for example, equipment for labour).
- CGE analysis is already playing an important role in improving our understanding of the limits of tourism as a catalyst for growth. By allowing factor constraints, exchange rate changes, price and wage changes and government

---

taxing and spending policies to be explicitly taken account of, the results of CGE modelling can provide substantial input into policy making.

- The initial shock in a CGE model can originate anywhere in the economy and can be literally anything that can occur in an economic framework, ranging from changes in taxes and subsidies, to technological change, population growth, shifts in demand and regulatory changes.

- CGE models can incorporate all I–O mechanisms. In fact, CGE models have I–O model embedded in them, allowing I–O calculations to be specified as a special case.

- CGE models can incorporate welfare measures to estimate the 'net benefits' of a tourism shock. The most common of these measures in the EV, which estimates the amount of money that leaves residents as well off as they would be after a change in economic activity. It is also a simple matter to adjust impacts, or measures of the change in the value of the gross output to produce measures of net benefits or welfare gain; to do so, one subtracts the cost of additional inputs used to produce the increase in activity.

- The assumptions of a CGE model can be varied and the sensitivity to them tested, providing researchers and policy makers with a mechanism for investigating the sensitivity of the results to changes in assumptions about the parameters. This can provide very useful information to policy makers in predicting the economic impacts of particular types of tourism shocks in different macroecoconomic contexts.

- CGE simulations can be undertaken using different assumptions, the realism of which can be discussed and debated. This provides a transparency to the assessment process that rarely exists in I–O modelling.

- CGE models are particularly helpful to policy makers who can use them to provide guidance about a wide variety of 'What if?' questions, arising from a wide range of domestic or international shocks or alternative policy scenarios.

- In addition to greater accuracy in estimation, CGE models can also provide a greater understanding of the nature of the impact of external shocks and policy changes to gain greater insight into sectoral links within the tourism industry and tourism's links with other sectors.

As might be expected, CGE modelling is not without its critics. We list (and respond to) some common criticisms in Box 9.2

BOX 9.2 Criticisms of CGE modelling

- CGE models are sometimes said to be too difficult to use and too data demanding.

  Response: CGE modelling techniques and software systems are now routinely available. In any case, the data should be assessed in terms of its importance for the question to be investigated, other than just in terms of the ease of data mobilisation. Results from general equilibrium models can be explained clearly in terms of straightforward economic mechanisms and properties of the data incorporated in the model. It is the responsibility of the modeller to produce such explanations for the users of the results.

- The assumption of market clearing in CGE modelling is unwarranted – although there are forces pushing economies towards equilibrium, there are also forces that prevent such equilibrium outcomes from being achieved.

  Response: As Blake *et al.* (2006) point out this type of criticism can be levelled against the great majority of economic models. However, all models provide a simplified representation of reality, and if they provide an effective means of understanding and/or predicting economic interrelationships and outcomes, they obviously serve their purpose. Since alternative functional forms can be used to take account of different types of market structure and competition, it is likely that more CGE models involving imperfect competition will be developed in the future (Blake *et al.*, 2006).

- CGE analysis tends to rely on static models, based on I–O tables that are dated.

  Response 1: Most analysis of the economic impacts of tourism is done using a static framework; in other words, using an approach which models the economy at a point of time and examines shifts from one point of time to another. When the issue addressed involves what difference a change in tourism makes to variables in the economy, this type of analysis is sufficient. In cases where economies are not changing rapidly, static models, based on I–O tables that, though dated, provide accurate representations of the ongoing structural inter-relationships between different sectors in the economy, may provide useful information and policy guidance. Such models may provide a cost- and time-effective means of policy modelling for economies for which limited data and resources are available, such as developing countries.

  Response 2: When there is an interest in the adjustment process, for example, how long it takes for a shift in tourism flows to influence other variables in the economy, then a dynamic framework is required. An increasing number of dynamic CGE models are now being developed, in line with improvements in software

361

and increasing computational power. Dynamics can be readily incorporated in CGE models, so that the development path of the economy, and changes from that path, can be investigated

- The results obtained from CGE models are particularly sensitive to some of the parameter values that are included in them. If such parameter values are inaccurate, the results obtained from the models are also likely to be inaccurate, as well as misleading for policy purposes.

Response: Sensitivity analysis can be conducted by including alternative parameter values in the model, to determine the bounds within which the model results lie, for changes in the parameter values that are deemed to be realistic.

9.5 CONCLUSIONS AND POLICY

- CGE models are now increasingly used in tourism economics analysis and in policy formulation. Based on real data and mathematically specified key relationships within the economy, they are used to assess the economic impacts of changes in tourism expenditure.
- CGE models are constructed as a series of markets (for goods, services and factors of production), production sectors and demand groups (households). Each market, sector and household has its own set of economic rules that determine how it reacts to external changes. In this way, CGE models consist of a set of equations that characterise the production, consumption, trade and government activities of the economy.
- CGE models can be separated into two broad categories: comparative static models and recursive-dynamic models. Forward looking dynamic CGE models are useful for projections of the economic impacts of different tourism shocks.
- Static models do not contain any explicit time dimension and simply project how much difference a change in tourism expenditure will make to the values of economic variables (sales, output, employment and so on) in a particular year.
- Dynamic general equilibrium models consist of a series of static models, referring to a sequence of years, linked by inter-temporal equations describing investment decisions and capital accumulation, and so can be used to trace out a specific time path of the economy following the change in tourism expenditure.
- The strengths of the CGE approach to assessing the economic impacts of changes in tourism expenditure are many and varied and include the ability: to model business and household demand for goods and services, relative price changes and substitution effects; to take account of the interrelationships between tourism, other sectors in the domestic economy and foreign producers and consumers; to incorporate endogenous

price determination mechanisms; to identify and test underlying assumptions; and to allow initial expenditure shocks to originate from anywhere in the economy.

- CGE models recognise resource constraints and consider the demand, price and income effects flowing from government policies and structural changes in the economy. They incorporate all I–O mechanisms; they incorporate mechanisms for potential crowding out of one activity by another, as well as for multiplier effects. CGE models can guide policy makers in a variety of scenarios arising from a range of domestic or international shocks or alternative policy scenarios. They can be tailored to allow for alternative conditions such as flexible or fixed prices, alternative exchange rate regimes, differences in the degree of mobility of factors of production and different types of competition.

- Criticisms of the CGE approach are rather limited and not that well founded. They include arguments to the effect that the model is too difficult and too data demanding; is based on the problematic assumption of market clearing; is reliant on static models; is based on dated I–O tables; and may be subject to factor sensitivity issues that render any results inaccurate and misleading for policy.

- CGE models are helpful to tourism policy makers who seek to use them to provide guidance about a wide variety of 'What if?' questions, arising from a wide range of domestic or international expenditure shocks or alternative policy scenarios.

- CGE models can be used to quantify the effects of actual policies, such as changes in taxation, subsidies or government borrowing, as well as predicting the effects of a range of alternative policies or exogenous expenditure shocks. They can be used to estimate the impacts of changes in tourism expenditure under a range of alternative macroeconomic scenarios; tailoring them to alternative conditions such as flexible or fixed prices, various exchange rate regimes, differences in the degree of mobility of factors of production, different government fiscal policy stances and different types of competition.

SELF-REVIEW QUESTIONS

1. Discuss the concept of a CGE model and outline its main elements.

2. List the advantages that CGE models have over I–O models.

3. Outline the basic difference between static and dynamic CGE models.

4. Describe areas in which CGE models have been used to assess tourism's economic impacts.

5. In dot-point form, list the strengths and weaknesses inherent in applying CGE modelling in tourism contexts.

ESSAY QUESTIONS

1. CGE models enjoy an advantage over I–O models in that they can make specific, more realistic assumptions about the availability of factor inputs and the behaviour of households, firms and government. Use tourism examples to show how CGE models do this.

2. Draw a CGE matrix (similar to Table 9.1). Define the headings in each column and in each row. Explain how each cell in the table is treated in a CGE model.

3. CGE tourism models are helpful to policy makers who can use them to provide guidance about a wide variety of 'What if?' questions. Discuss.

CHAPTER 10

COST-BENEFIT ANALYSIS

LEARNING OBJECTIVES

After reading this chapter, you should be able to:

1. Distinguish between financial appraisal and economic appraisal.

2. Compare and contrast Cost-Benefit Analysis (CBA) with each of Input–Output (I–O) analysis and Computable General Equilibrium analysis (CGE).

3. Understand the importance of CBA to tourism project evaluation and when it is appropriate to undertake CBA.

4. Discuss the eight main steps to be undertaken in conducting CBA of a tourism project, policy or program.

5. Know when and how to apply each of the different investment decision rules to tourism projects: Net Present Value (NPV), Internal Rate of Return (IRR) and Benefit-Cost Ratio (BCR).

6. Understand the importance of addressing the issues of shadow pricing, double counting, and income distributional effects when undertaking a CBA.

7. Appreciate the strengths and weaknesses associated with the CBA of tourism projects.

8. Differentiate between CBA and Cost-Effectiveness Analysis (CEA) in tourism.

10.1   INTRODUCTION

Tourism development requires substantial investment in public and private infrastructure. All proposed investments must be evaluated for the returns that they generate to the investor.

Financial appraisal looks at the costs and benefits of an investment project from the perspective of the economic agent (individual, firm or organisation). It attempts to determine the net financial benefit (or loss) to an entity rather than the net benefit (or loss) to the economy or society. Financial evaluations are only concerned with cash flows in and out of the organisation. In a financial evaluation, no account is taken of external costs or benefits.

In contrast, *economic appraisal*, considers the costs and benefits to society as a whole to determine whether the project will make society better or worse off. This requires estimating a wider range of costs and benefits than those included in a financial appraisal, including the estimation of values where no direct price is charged.

Suppose an adventure tour operator was considering constructing an ecotourism lodge in a wilderness area. The operator would undertake a *financial appraisal* estimating and comparing the direct costs and benefits to the business. Costs considered would include direct fixed costs (e.g. the construction of the ecolodge) and the variable costs expected in the running of the ecolodge. Environmental effects, if considered at all, might only relate to the costs of reaching and maintaining government standards. Benefits counted would include the expected revenue stream from the ecolodge plus less easily identifiable and measurable benefits such as enhanced business reputation and so on. The operator would estimate Net Present Value (NPV) using the opportunity cost of their financial capital (the market rate of interest) as the discount rate. (We shall consider issues in private investment appraisal in Chapter 12).

An *economic appraisal* would necessarily be broader in scope. It would take in all stakeholders, covering not only the direct costs and benefits to the ecolodge operator but also the external costs and benefits to the rest of society. Social costs might include estimates of environmental destruction, noise pollution, impacts on local communities and so on. Social benefits might include increased tax revenues, reduction in unemployment, preservation of wilderness and so on. It might also look at the needs of future generations. Economic appraisal also uses 'true' prices, adjusting prices where they have been distorted by market imperfections such as taxes, subsidies and exchange rate manipulation.

Of course, undertaking an economic appraisal does not remove the need for a financial appraisal. The financial appraisal will show the demands on cash flow which will result from the project – an important factor when managing government finances. It will also indicate the NPV and internal rate of return (IRR) from the project which is important information for informed decision-making by the economic agent.

In the public sector, the fundamental requirement is for an economic appraisal of projects, policies and programs. The public sector is a major user of a destination's available resources and, as such, should ensure that it makes a significant positive contribution to the economy and society. More particularly, no new proposal, program, project or policy should be adopted without first answering questions such as:

• What are the specific outcomes sought?
• Do the gains to people exceed the costs the sacrifices required?
• Are there better ways to achieve these outcomes?

- Are there better uses for these resources?
- Is this an appropriate area of responsibility for government?

The primary technique that should be used for the economic appraisal of actions or proposals in terms of economic efficiency is Cost-Benefit Analysis (CBA). CBA is the most comprehensive of the economic appraisal techniques. CBA is particularly important in the context of evaluating tourism policy, programs, regulations, projects and developments. Specific examples might include regional or local tourism plans; rezoning of land for tourism purposes; and major tourism developments such as the creation of tourism shopping precincts, airport development, resorts and hotels, nature reserves and sporting facilities. As such projects generally have relatively wide economic, environmental and social implications for a community that are not captured in the basic financial analysis undertaken by project proponents.

CBA is especially appropriate to tourism because there is often a clear trade-off between economic benefits and social costs. Tourism projects which might be economically beneficial may be rejected because of their adverse environmental and/or social impacts.

This chapter explains the what, why, how, when and where of CBA in tourism contexts, detailing the steps to be taken in conducting such an analysis, the issues to be clearly understood and the common errors to be avoided. The chapter also compares CBA with other forms of project evaluation such as Cost-Effectiveness Analysis (CEA). Throughout the chapter, the emphasis is on CBA from a societal point of view in the use of social resources, rather than from an individual firm's point of view in the use of its own private resources.

10.2 CBA

By quantifying the net benefits of projects, programs and policies in a standard manner, CBA improves the information base for public sector decision-making, thereby assisting in the assessment of relative priorities. Some features of CBA are highlighted in Box 10.1

BOX 10.1 CBA

- CBA is a systematic process for identifying and assessing all costs and benefits of a proposal (project, program, policy) in monetary terms, as they are expected to occur through the life of the project.
- CBA is concerned with measuring, the change in all sources of economic welfare, whether occurring in markets or as implicit values. Benefits are defined as increases in social welfare while costs are defined as reductions in social welfare. A CBA balances costs with benefits to show the estimated net effect of any policy or project. In CBA, welfare benefits are generally calculated by measuring

---

the additional consumer surplus and producer surplus of a given option over the 'do nothing' or 'base case'.

- All costs and benefits, including social and environmental aspects, are assigned a money value, allowing the calculation of the net benefits of different proposals as a basis for evaluating alternatives. These net benefits/costs can then be used to rank alternative proposals quantitatively.

- A CBA provides an estimate of the worth of a proposal relative to an accompanying estimate of what would happen in the absence of the proposal. Decision makers have a consistent basis for assessing proposals and can be better informed about the implications of using economic resources.

- CBA are used to capture, measure, weight and compare all expected present and future benefits of a policy with all its expected present and future costs. Future costs and benefits are discounted relative to present costs and benefits in the NPV sum. For a capital investment development, program or policy to be socially acceptable, the sum of the benefits to society (including private and social benefits) must exceed the sum of the costs to society (including private and social costs).

- In principle, a CBA enables agencies to compare the relative merit of alternative programs or projects in terms of their returns on the use of resources, public and private. CBA is primarily designed to answer the question 'does the expenditure of money on this particular project or program provide a net benefit to the economy and the public, given that these resources could be applied in an alternative use?'

10.3   WHEN TO USE CBA

CBA can be used to guide a wide range of decisions on types of tourism development, especially within the following four broad contexts.

10.3.1   ANALYSING CAPITAL EXPENDITURE

Many projects involve capital expenditure for new or replacement facilities. Such projects might include airport construction or expansion, the development of cruise shipping terminals, a resort development or highway construction. Larger capital projects, including buildings, equipment and other forms of infrastructure and productive investment, should be subjected to an analysis of their costs and benefits over their lifetime. Key questions are whether or not to undertake the investment, whether to undertake it now or later and which option to choose.

10.3.2   ANALYSING A POLICY OPTION

In principle, any proposal or policy option can be subjected to CBA. Thus, a government may wish to estimate the costs and benefits of some policy regarding requirements for tourist visas, bilateral aviation agreements, tourism and hospitality training programs or restrictions on the use of migrant labour. Policies almost always confer benefits on some parties and impose costs on others. CBA helps to uncover unanticipated costs and benefits of projects. It explicitly estimates the size of gains and losses for affected individuals and groups. This information is important in public sector decision-making and should be made explicit because it is important to identify those who stand to gain and lose from a program or project. These costs and benefits can be valued in the same way as costs and benefits arising from capital expenditures.

10.3.3   RETAINING OR DISPOSING OF AN EXISTING ASSET

CBA can be undertaken where an agency is considering the retention or disposal of an existing asset. A government agency may be considering closing a rail link to a tourist region or closing a museum, cruise terminal facilities or zoo. CBA can address issues such as whether or not to sell land, whether to relocate facilities and whether to repair an asset or to replace it. The potential benefit of an economic appraisal of assets is to improve the allocation of public sector resources to ensure Government's objectives are met to the maximum extent as are community benefits.

10.3.4   POST EVALUATION OF A PROJECT OR PROGRAM

CBA provides a means of determining whether or not a particular program or project has generated a net benefit for the community. Thus, tax concessions offered to hotel developers or tourism and hospitality training programs may be reviewed to assess the net benefits, and a government agency may investigate whether its decision to provide financial support for a special event such as a Formula One Grand Prix event or an Olympic Games generates an appropriate return on public funds.

A growing number of researchers now argue that the assessment of special events should go beyond economic impact analysis in favour of an holistic assessment that includes CBA (Jago & Dwyer, 2006). Used retrospectively instead of prospectively, the known outcome from the activity, in terms of both costs and benefits, can be compared with what would have happened in the absence of the project ('the counterfactual'). This provides transparency and accountability in reporting on how well public funds have been spent. It is also useful for technical reasons as it provides evidence on the validity and appropriateness of assumptions, forecasts and analyses used in future decision-making. Chapter 11 considers the economic evaluation of special events.

A review of the use of CBA in tourism reveals that comprehensive analyses are scarce. While various articles and reports purport to be 'cost benefit analyses' of tourism-related projects or programs, very few apply the rigorous standards of analysis that the technique requires. Perhaps the main area in which CBA has been applied to link up with tourism concerns has been in transportation facilities, such as rail links, roadworks and road safety improvements and airport construction. Box 10.2 looks at the ban on smoking for the Dutch hotel and catering industries.

BOX 10.2 A smoking ban in the Dutch hotel and catering sector, a cost-benefit analysis

The Dutch government has decided on a smoking ban for the Dutch hotel and catering industry, effective from July 1, 2008. Marlon Spreen and Esther Mot (2008) undertook a CBA of this policy. A smoking ban is compared to a less drastic alternative, improved ventilation. Using plausible assumptions the study concludes that the benefits of a smoking ban exceed by far the costs. Sensitivity analyses with a number of different assumptions, for example regarding the value of improved health, do not change this conclusion. Improved ventilation also has a positive net effect, but this effect is much smaller than that of smoke-free pubs, hotels and restaurants.

The goal of a smoking ban is a safe workplace
In the Netherlands, a smoking ban for workplaces was introduced on January 1, 2004 in order to protect employees from the dangers of passive smoking (associated with among other things a higher probability of getting lung cancer and cardiovascular diseases). The government decreed that the hotel and catering sector, previously exempted, must conform to this rule from the 1st of July 2008 on. In this analysis, this decision has been studied from an economic point of view: costs and benefits for society in the long run were determined.

The benefits of a smoking ban: mostly life years gained
The life expectancy of workers in pubs, bars, hotels and restaurants increases when they are no longer exposed to environmental tobacco smoke (ETS). Smoking men gain on average 0.5 life years and non-smoking men 0.2 life years. For women, the gains are somewhat lower.

Workers who stop smoking altogether can increase their life expectancy to a much larger extent. A small part of the smoking workers quit when a smoking ban in the workplace is introduced. A non-smoking man lives almost eight years longer than a smoking man; for women, this difference is more than six years.

Other quantifiable benefits of a smoking ban are reduced damages by fire and reduced health-care costs related to smoking and ETS. However, these benefits are much smaller. For non-smoking customers and workers, it is an important advantage that they are not bothered by smoke anymore, but this advantage could not be quantified.

The costs of a smoking ban

From the perspective of employees who smoke, it is a cost that they can no longer smoke during work. These costs are, however, not very large compared to other costs and benefits that play a role in the analysis. The decrease of excise taxes and the costs in life years gained (for public pensions and health care) are much larger. The costs related to health improvements are included.

Possibly, the turnover in pubs will decrease somewhat because of the smoking ban. For restaurants, no adverse effects are to be expected, positive effects seem more likely. Money that is no longer spent in pubs will be spent elsewhere. So, if sales go down in pubs, only short-term transition costs are to be expected for the community.

Uncertainty

Quantifying costs and benefits has a number of uncertain aspects. For example, what is the value of a healthy life year gained and how many workers in the hotel and catering sector will stop smoking? In the basic CBA, a healthy life year was valued at 100,000 euro. This value seems reasonable but the literature shows a degree of variation in this estimate. Because of this variation, sensitivity analyses were carried out with lower and higher values for a life year and with alternative assumptions for a number of other factors. In all these analyses, the calculated benefits of a smoking ban were higher than the costs.

Conclusions

It is estimated that the benefits of a smoking ban in the Dutch hotel and catering sector exceed the costs. This is mainly through the improved health of both smokers and non smokers. The costs of a smoking ban are just like the benefits related to health improvements, i.e. costs for public pensions and health care in life years gained. This is the main conclusion of the CPB report.

Costs and benefits were also studied for an alternative policy with improved ventilation. This demands much smaller adjustment from smokers, but a safe workplace can not be guaranteed. For this alternative, the benefits are also larger than the costs, but the difference is much smaller than for a smoking ban.

It is noteworthy that smoking workers in the sector turn out to be 'winners'. This is because, in the long run, the value of their life years gained is higher than the disutility of no longer being allowed to smoke during work. However, this does not mean that all individual smokers will consider themselves winners. For example, they can value the life years gained lower than society as a whole does.

Source: English summary of CPB Document 159, *Een rookverbod in deNederlandse horeca, Een kosten-batenanalyse* (A smoking ban in the Dutch hotel and catering sector, a cost-benefit analysis), Marlon Spreen and Esther Mot, Netherlands Bureau for Economic Analysis, February 2008. (Main report only in Dutch)

10.4 EIGHT MAIN STEPS IN PERFORMING CBA

There are several steps to be taken when preparing a standard economic evaluation of a proposal. Here we identify eight steps. Within each step, a number of options are available.

10.4.1 DETERMINE THE SCOPE AND OBJECTIVES OF THE ANALYSIS

The first step is to outline the nature of the problem to be addressed: its background, context and rationale. Every proposal to spend money must have an underlying objective. What is the program, project or activity trying to achieve? Thus a destination manager may enquire as to the benefits expected from an international tourism promotion campaign or the construction of a cruise shipping terminal. These objectives should be defined, initially, in terms of the possible market failure or market imperfections that could warrant government intervention. A clear statement of objectives will provide information on whose costs and benefits are being assessed.

10.4.2 CONSIDER THE ALTERNATIVES

CBA must identify and specify a set of alternatives. A basic principle of any type of project evaluation is the 'with-without' principle. In practice, this means that the forecast 'state of the world' with the proposal to be undertaken is compared with the 'state of the world' that would have existed in the absence of the project (the 'do nothing' or 'status quo' option). For example, government decision makers may assess the benefits of a tourism training program, or regulations to control 'unethical practices' of tourism operators by comparing scenarios with and without such schemes. A 'do nothing' option is generally required as a base because costs and benefits are always measured as incremental to what would have happened had the project not been undertaken.

To ensure that all alternatives for meeting the identified objectives are feasible, various constraints that may apply need to be considered, including financial, distributional, managerial, environmental or other constraints.

10.4.3 IDENTIFY THE IMPACTS

Impacts (outcomes) must be identified before they can be valued. There are likely to be substantial uncertainties attached to the data with which the analyst works. For instance, consider the case of a project to clean up river pollution from a manufacturing facility to enhance the tourist potential of an area. An industrial chemist is needed to calculate the incremental change in the amount of pollutants entering the river. A biologist is needed to determine the effect of this change on bacteria and other life forms in the river. An engineer is needed to recommend best practice technical ways of reducing emissions and cleaning up the river. A health scientist is needed to evaluate the effects of that change on the health and recreation opportunities of residents. Tourism forecasting is needed to project increases in visitor numbers. Input from other scientists will also be needed before an economist can even begin to estimate in dollars the value of the costs and benefits to the community.

In many cases, the identification and measurement of impacts is itself fraught with difficulties. This involves issues of both *delineation* (What is an impact? To what extent is it an impact? Is it a direct or indirect impact?) as well as *timing* (Is the impact immediately noticeable? Will an impact manifest itself sometime in the future? How long will an impact last?).

To the extent that the social sciences are less developed than the natural sciences, the socio-cultural impacts of tourist activities are even more difficult to determine than the physical impacts. While studies show that tourism can lead to changes in the lifestyle and social structure of local communities, it is often difficult to separate out the tourism impacts from the broader community impacts brought about by continuous changes in the community's political, social and cultural climate.

10.4.4 VALUE THE RELEVANT COSTS AND BENEFITS

The benefit that a private firm receives from a project is the extra revenue (additional costs) received less the (private) costs incurred. In contrast, the social benefits and costs from a public project are more difficult to measure.

- The social benefits from a project refer to the total amount that consumers would be willing to pay for the goods and services flowing from the project, not just the amount that they actually pay. That is, the social benefit from a project includes the consumers' surplus that it generates.
- The social costs of a project are measured in terms of opportunity costs – that is, the value of the marginal benefits foregone from the same resources in alternative uses.

All economic evaluations should be based on *incremental* costs and benefits associated with a particular proposal. These can be classified usefully into three categories:

1. Effects which can be readily identified and valued in money terms (e.g. ticket sales to residents for a special event, revenues generated from restaurant meals and costs of waste disposal).

2. Effects which can be identified and measured in physical terms but which cannot be easily valued in money terms because of the absence of market (e.g. the value of preserving a wilderness area, the cost of noise from airport or hotel construction, time savings to travellers from a new transport link or greenhouse gas emissions (GHGs) from motor coaches).

3. Effects that are known to exist but cannot be precisely identified and accurately quantified, let alone valued (e.g. crime prevention effects of police programs, outcomes of a publically funded tourism and hospitality training program, aesthetic effects of streetscape beautification programs or loss to humans from species extinction). Costs and benefits that cannot be valued in money terms are often described as 'intangibles'.

We discuss each in more detail below.

10.4.4.1 Effects which can readily be valued

Costs and benefits are typically based upon market prices as they are the easiest to identify and usually reflect implicit opportunity costs. Where competitive markets exist, prices reflect Willingness to Pay (WTP) at the margin for goods and the opportunity costs of resources.

Costs

The *explicit cost* of a proposal would include such items as the initial capital costs; costs of any buildings, equipment or facilities that need to be replaced during the life of the project; and operating and maintenance costs over the period of a program or project.

The *implicit cost* of a proposal is measured by its value in the 'next best' or most valuable alternative use and reflects the benefits foregone by society in not using these resources for an alternative purpose. Opportunity cost comprises the conceptual basis for valuing costs in CBA. This is because implementing a program or policy always requires the use of resources (or inputs) that could be used elsewhere.

Benefits

An economic benefit is any gain in the welfare of society or of the individuals comprising society. Typical benefits of a proposal would include those which can be valued in money terms, in the form of revenues, cost savings, avoided costs or residual value.

While market prices provide the starting point for measuring WTP, they sometimes do not adequately reflect the true value of a good to society. Consumers are often willing to pay more than the market price rather than go without a good they consume – for example, a person might be willing to pay much more to attend an event than the ticket price. Underlying the valuation of the benefits of a particular project or activity is the principle. WTP is the *maximum* value placed by a firm or individual on a resource or on a good or service in monetary terms. WTP provides an aggregate measure of what individuals are willing to forego in order to obtain a given benefit.

10.4.4.2 Valuing costs or benefits when there are no market values

The goods and services flowing from a project are not often sold in the marketplace in the same way that goods and services produced by private firms are sold, and hence may not have values (prices) attached to their use. Thus, there are often cases where a market does not exist or market prices are not directly observable or easy to estimate. This makes it difficult to estimate costs and benefits (or even to determine to whom the costs and benefits accrue). For example, undertaking a project may result in benefits received or costs incurred by others not associated with the activity and for which payment is neither given nor received. Such spillovers are termed 'externalities' (also referred to as social effects or third-party effects). As discussed in Chapter 6, externalities are impacts on third parties that are not the primary parties (producers or consumers) in an economic exchange and hence are not required to pay for a cost imposed or benefit received. This is particularly the case for policies and programs that generate social and/or environmental impacts.

Some oppose the monetary valuation of many externalities that they claim have 'immeasurable' intrinsic and aesthetic values. However, the attempt to value resources (however imprecisely) can suggest the worth of protecting them. And remember the adage 'what gets measured gets managed.'

Valuation of 'externalities', whether positive or negative, is often complex. Where the service is not freely traded or there is no price charged, or indeed where the benefits fall broadly on the community rather than on individual users, more indirect measures of the WTP to gain the benefits or to avoid the costs need to be used. Where benefits and costs relate to goods and services that are either not traded in markets or are traded in markets with distortions, economic values are imputed to them. Economists have developed specific economic valuation techniques to measure non-market changes in welfare. The two main general approaches to valuing externalities are the 'revealed preference' and 'stated preference' methods.

Revealed preference

Revealed preference is based on consumer behaviour in related markets, and it compares situations where people have made trade-offs between a cost and some form of benefit. This information indicates the extent to which people are prepared to pay for a given benefit. Two approaches often used in valuing tourism-related benefits and costs are the Travel Cost Method (TCM) and Hedonic Pricing Method (HPM).

Stated preference

Stated preference techniques involve asking people about their preferences to identify the trade-offs they are prepared to make as regards costs and benefits under certain hypothetical scenarios. The approach simulates a market by estimating a consumer's WTP for the good or service, or Willingness to Accept (WTA) compensation to tolerate a negative or adverse economic outcome.

The recommended approach is to consider whether or not to estimate the monetary value of externalities on a case-by-case basis. As a general rule, externalities should be valued if they can be quantified and are capable of being valued in a satisfactorily reliable way. Any assumptions utilised in arriving at this decision should be fully explained and justified.

Valuation techniques based on revealed and stated preferences are discussed in detail in Chapter 17.

10.4.4.3 Treatment of intangibles

Examples of 'intangibles' in tourism projects could include benefits from the development of special 'themed' events to improve 'destination image', 'branding' or 'community pride'. Similarly the construction of a large-scale hotel adjacent to an attractive beach might be 'aesthetically displeasing' or 'socially alienating' to local residents. Lost assets as a result of tourism development may be considered to have 'heritage value'. Effects that cannot reasonably be quantified in monetary terms should not be ignored in the CBA. If the externalities are unable to be quantified, they should at least be identified and explained to decision makers. Intangible benefits and costs can sometimes be significant in relation to the quantitative impacts and can heavily influence the final accept–reject decision. If they appear to be significant, they should be explicitly highlighted and explained in the analysis so that decision makers are aware of the values underpinning a particular option. This explanation can be quantitative, qualitative, descriptive or some combination.

As noted in Chapter 6, examples of negative spillovers abound in tourism. The construction of a golf course resort hotel that discharges residues into a nearby river will have a negative impact on people who use the river downstream of the resort. Similarly, the GHGs from aircraft affect the environment of people on the ground. Alternatively, the achievement of one outcome may have a detrimental impact on the achievement of another; as, for example, when increased tourism demand generates greater household income but also adversely affects achieving environmental objectives through increased water or energy usage (Lundie *et al.*, 2007). Where a resort hotel provides increased entertainment and leisure opportunities for residents or the increased tourism flows enhance cultural exchange between hosts and guests, the spillovers are positive.

While it is desirable to give a monetary value to as many benefits and costs as possible within the resource and time constraints, often not all benefits and costs require valuation in order to obtain relevant information from benefit-cost analysis. For instance, in some situations the valuation of only some benefits may be sufficient to indicate that benefits exceed costs.

10.4.5 DISCOUNT THE FUTURE COSTS AND BENEFITS

The costs and benefits flowing from a project will be spread over time. Initial investment costs are borne up front while benefits and operating costs may extend far into the future. It is necessary to discount costs and benefits occurring later relative to those occurring sooner since money has an opportunity cost – money received now can be invested and converted into a larger future amount. The size of the interest rate that is used in discounting analysis is of crucial importance in calculating NPV. The discounting concept will be further discussed in Chapter 12.

For purposes of CBA, the selection of a discount rate introduces some complexities not relevant to financial appraisal. Two alternative bases for estimating the discount rate are the social time preference and the opportunity cost of capital.

Social time preference rate (STPR). Resources devoted to a publically funded project will be at the expense of current consumption or private sector investment. In a growing economy with rising living standards, a dollar's consumption today will be more highly valued than a dollar's consumption at some future time for, in the latter case, the dollar will be subtracted from a higher income level. The STPR represents society's preference for present against future consumption (NSW Treasury, 2007).

Opportunity cost of capital. Undertaking a project implies giving up one or more other projects. The value given up is the social opportunity cost of capital (SOC). This reflects the rate of return on the investment elsewhere in the economy that is displaced by implementing a proposal. To justify taxing the private economy to undertake public sector investments, the government must achieve a return on investment at least equivalent to what the money would earn if left in the private sector. If the government cannot achieve this, it would be better for the community if the money is left untaxed in the private sector. Overall national welfare is reduced if residents give up a portion of their incomes in the form of higher taxes to support public undertakings which are of less social value than the uses to which their funds would otherwise be put. The way for government to assure this result is to adopt in public investment appraisal an interest rate policy which reflects the private sector opportunities foregone. There is general agreement that the government, in pursuing national economic efficiency, should undertake no expenditure which earns a smaller rate of return than the same resources would earn in an alternate use. Because the resources used by the government would be alternatively used in the private sector, the government must look to the private interest and profit rates to determine the appropriate public interest rate for discounting. This position reflects the application of the basic 'opportunity cost' principle – the cost of the resources used by the government is equal to the loss of the value which these resources would otherwise produce. The SOC is in effect the pre-tax rate of return that can be expected from private sector investments that have similar risk characteristics. The main tool used to calculate this discount rate is the capital asset pricing model (New Zealand Treasury, 2008).

In an economy with no distortions or taxation, the STPR and the opportunity cost of capital should be the same. However, for various reasons such as profits taxes and taxation of interest or dividend payments, the two may differ. In theory, a perfectly competitive capital market operating with no tax distortions will bring about equality of the investor's marginal rate of time preference, the investor's opportunity cost of capital (rate of return on the marginal project) and the market rate of interest.

While debate continues at the theoretical level, in reality analysts use the market interest rate to discount the costs and benefits associated with different projects. The essential argument is that the government must achieve a return on investment at least equivalent to what the money would earn if left in the private section to justify taxing the private economy to undertake public sector investments. If the government cannot achieve this by investing in some project, it would be better for the destination if the money is left untaxed in the private sector (Treasury Board of Canada, 1998).

10.4.6 APPLY DECISION RULES

Various investment criteria are available to assist in reaching decisions on different proposals. Standard criteria for CBA are as follows:

- Net present value.
- Internal rate of return.
- Benefit-cost ratio.

10.4.6.1 Net present value

In CBA, the net social benefit (NSB), or the excess of total benefit over total cost, is represented by the NPV of the proposal.

The present value of the stream of benefits is stated thus:

$$\sum_{t=1}^{T} \frac{B_t}{(1+r)^t} \tag{10.1}$$

Where,

$\sum$ means summation over all the years of the project life (T years);

B_t stands for the benefits expected in the tth year;

$(1 + r)^t$ represents the discounting factor by which values expected in the future are turned into today's values;

T is number of years that the benefits are produced.

The present value of the capital and future operation costs is stated:

$$K + \sum_{t=1}^{T} \frac{C_t}{(1 + r)^t} \qquad (10.2)$$

in which

K is the capital or construction costs (assumed to occur in the current year);

C_t is the operation, maintenance and repair costs expected in the tth year;

t is number of years that the costs are incurred.

NPV is the sum of the discounted project benefits minus the discounted project costs. Formally, it can be expressed as follows:

$$\text{NPV} = \sum_{t=1}^{T} \frac{B_t}{(1 + r)^t} - (K + \sum_{t=1}^{T} \frac{C_t}{(1 + r)^t}) \qquad (10.3)$$

Under this decision rule, a project is potentially worthwhile (or viable) if the NPV is greater than zero, that is, the total discounted value of benefits is greater than the total discounted costs. If projects are mutually exclusive, the project which yields the highest NPV would be chosen.

10.4.6.2 Internal rate of return

As an alternative to NPV analysis, the decision maker could determine the IRR from the project and then compare it to the social discount rate. The IRR is the annualised effective compounded return rate which can be earned on the invested capital, that is, the yield on the investment. A project should be undertaken if its IRR exceeds the rate of return that could be earned by alternate investments (investing in other projects, buying bonds, even putting the money in a bank account).

To estimate the IRR (r), we determine the value(s) of r that satisfy the following equation:

$$K = \sum_{t=1}^{T} \frac{B_t - C_t}{(1 + r)^t} \qquad (10.4)$$

For purposes of CBA, the decision maker should undertake projects as long as (and until) the internal rate of return from the project exceeds the social discount rate or the agency exhausts its investment funds. The NPV approach is superior to the IRR when choosing among mutually exclusive investments (see also the discussion in Chapter 12).

10.4.6.3 Benefit-Cost Ratio

The BCR is the ratio of the present value of benefits to the present value of costs. In algebraic terms, it can be expressed as follows:

$$\text{BCR} = \frac{\sum_{t=1}^{T} \frac{B_t - C_t}{(1+r)^t}}{K} \tag{10.5}$$

It is conventional to split costs into two types when calculating BCRs: initial capital costs and ongoing costs. Ongoing costs in each year are subtracted from benefits in that year to identify a net benefit stream, while initial capital costs are used as the denominator.

A project is potentially worthwhile if the BCR is greater than 1, that is, the present value of benefits exceeds the present value of costs. Thus:

If BCR > 1, implementation of the project is judged to be economically worthwhile.

If BCR = 1, the project adds nothing to economic welfare

If BCR < 1, the project reduces economic well being.

If projects are mutually exclusive, this rule would indicate that the project with the highest BCR should be chosen.

The BCR is a useful measure because, when there are a large number of proposals, there may not be enough resources available to undertake them all, even if they all have high NPVs. As a rule of thumb, picking the projects with the highest BCR can ensure maximum value for money in terms of contributing to outcomes, though only if all the projects have similar time patterns of benefits and costs.

10.4.6.4 The impact of discount rates on project ranking

The choice of the discount rate is important as it can have a significant impact on the ranking of options/projects and hence their choice. In general, short-lived options are favoured by higher discount rates relative to long-lived options.

As the discount rate rises:

- The more are net benefits further into the future downgraded in present value terms relative to net benefits closer to hand.
- Projects with larger initial outlays become relatively less attractive compared with projects with lower initial outlays.
- Projects with lower ongoing outlays become relatively less attractive compared with projects with higher ongoing outlays.

For these reasons, it is sometimes argued that the activity of discounting implies that the needs of future generations are given less weight than those of the current generation. The higher the interest rate, the fewer projects which will show a positive NPV. That is, the higher the rate the more difficult it is for projects whose outputs occur far into the future to generate a positive NPV. In particular, it is sometimes claimed that high discount rates unfairly devalue benefits to future generations, who have as much right to such basics as clean water, clean air and pristine natural environments as does the current generation. Inter-generational equity is fostered if the discount rate is low, and some claim that this is appropriate when environmental sustainability is an issue.

In response, it should be noted that a low discount rate can make projects seem profitable and can encourage their implementation even if they are at odds with sustainability. Assuming no irreversible environmental effects are involved, a project with a high rate of return when all of its costs and benefits are counted is better for the present generation and, through reinvestment, better for future generations as well. Only when benefits are non-renewable and consumed rather than reinvested is there conflict across generations, with one generation paying and another benefitting (Treasury Board of Canada, 1998).

It is also sometimes argued that the discount rate should be made dependent on the degree of risk associated with the project: high-risk projects would be allocated high discount rates and low-risk projects low discount rates. Such an adjustment often takes place in private sector evaluation of projects. However, this argument presupposes that risk increases over time. This is not necessarily the case – the risk may be introduced by an event which may occur in the near future or may be the same throughout the life of the project. Thus, while adding a risk premium to a discount rate is a commonly used technique, it needs to be remembered that it is an approximation and will not always be appropriate.

10.4.6.5 Choosing project size

If the decision maker can undertake as many projects or programs as are efficient, CBA can assist in choosing the optimal size project. In Figure 10.1, the total amount of benefits from a most efficiently designed project of each possible size is shown by the curve TB. The line TC indicates total cost. At project size A, total benefits of an efficiently designed project are AB, total costs are AC and the BCR is AB / AC. Similarly the BCRs of project sizes D, G and I are DE / DF, GH / GH (equals 1) and IK / IJ. For project sizes D, G and I, the BCRs are, respectively, greater than one, equal to one and less than one.

Assuming that project sizes A, D, G and I are the only possible ones, then clearly the optimal size is D, where the excess of benefits over costs is the greatest. At size D, marginal benefit equals marginal cost and total benefits less total costs are at a maximum. Given that alternative designs of project size D will yield different benefits (e.g. one project design may yield benefits of DE'), the benefit-cost comparison can help determine which design is optimal. In this case it is the design that generates benefits of DE. The maximum benefit

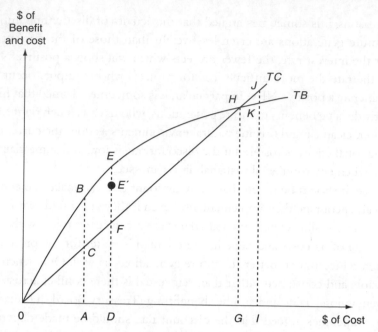

Figure 10.1 Benefit-cost ratio for different sized projects

Source: Haveman (1970), Figure 8.1

criterion can assist the decision maker to choose among alternative project designs, project sizes and discrete project with different purposes.

10.4.6.6 The investment horizon

The investment horizon is the end of the period over which costs and benefits are compared to ascertain whether an investment is acceptable. If costs and benefits can be identified over the useful life of the project and uncertainties are low, then this provides the best investment horizon. This will be a long time for some tourism infrastructure projects such as airports, highway systems and cruise shipping terminals. As a general rule, the period of analysis should extend over the useful life of the project.

Residual values are also an important component of the total value of a proposal and should be included in the assessment. The residual or terminal value of a project is its estimated value at the end of the analysis period. While, in theory, an asset's residual value at the end of its economic life should be zero, in practice it may not be so.

10.4.6.7 Treatment of inflation

Since the inflation rate over the course of a loan cannot be known with certainty, inflation represents a risk to borrowers and lenders. Thus, costs and benefits should be valued in *real prices* (constant prices) as opposed to *nominal prices* (prices at the time the goods or services were provided).

382

A real discount rate should be used to discount constant dollar or real benefits and costs. A real discount rate, eliminating the effects of expected inflation, can be approximated by subtracting expected inflation from a nominal interest rate. Benefits and costs should be expressed in real terms and adjusted for differential price effects where a specific resource price is expected to move at a rate different from the general inflation rate.

To ensure that changes in relative prices are properly identified, tables of costs and benefits should be first constructed in nominal dollars, and cash flows should be set out for each period to the investment horizon. Conversions to constant dollars or to present value dollars should wait until all costs and benefits over time are estimated in nominal dollars.

10.4.6.8 Costs excluded from CBA

A number of items that are included as costs in accounting reports or financial appraisals should not be included in an economic evaluation of an investment proposal. Among them are sunk costs, depreciation and interest payments.

- *Sunk costs.* In a project evaluation, all costs must relate to future expenditures only. The price paid in the past to build a facility is no longer relevant. It is the opportunity cost in terms of today's value (or price) which must be included. All past or sunk costs are irrelevant and should be excluded from the CBA.
- *Depreciation.* Depreciation is an accounting allowance that recognises that physical assets wear out or become obsolete by spreading purchase costs over the useful life of the assets. In CBA, the cost of the project is explicitly recognised, and thus depreciation is unnecessary.
- *Interest payments.* As future cash flows are discounted to present value terms in economic evaluations, the choice of the discount rate is based on various factors which include the rate of interest and associated finance charges. The discounting process removes the need to include finance charges in the cash flows.

10.4.7 SENSITIVITY ANALYSIS

The values of future costs and benefits on which the NPV is based cannot be known with certainty. While they should be forecast on expected values, it is important to test the NPV for 'optimistic' and 'pessimistic' scenarios. This is known as sensitivity analysis and is a critical component of any CBA.

Sensitivity analysis is a form of quantitative analysis that examines how NPVs, total cost or other outcomes vary as individual assumptions or variables are changed. The purpose of such scenario analysis is to test the sensitivity of results to changes in different variables and to provide information on the viability of the project to changes in those variables. Sensitivity analysis can help in forecasting uncertainty and in assessing and treating project risks. Risk can be incorporated into CBA by attaching probabilities to costs and benefits and deriving an expected NPV.

The simplest form of sensitivity analysis is *scenario analysis* with estimates of costs and benefits under alternative scenarios.

Scenarios can be chosen to highlight the major types of uncertainties upon which the success of a proposal depends. For instance, are there any variables (such as exchange rates, salary costs, demand drivers and project timings) that materially influence the net benefits?

Sensitivity analysis can help to highlight those factors that require especially careful assessment or management. This analysis can address key questions:

- Would the proposal still be worthwhile pursuing if some of the key assumptions do not eventuate?
- Under what circumstances does the preferred option change?
- Are there actions that can be taken to reduce the risks before accepting a particular option?

A common approach to conducting sensitivity analysis is to test three combinations of key variables: pessimistic or conservative scenario; most probable or base scenario; and optimistic scenario. The scenario analysis should then focus on asking 'what if' questions and recalculating the expected NPV for several scenarios. Sensitivity analysis is particularly useful in assessing the effects of different discount rates on NPV calculations.

A CBA of a transportation system for Los Angeles is summarised in Box 10.3

BOX 10.3 Cost-Benefit analysis of a transportation proposal for Los Angeles

Peterson (1975) critically examines a cost-benefit study undertaken for a proposed rapid transit system in the Los Angeles metropolitan area in order to illustrate some problems in method.

In 1968 the voters of the Southern California Rapid Transit District (SCRTD) rejected a $2.5 billion fixed rail transit system. The rejected proposal was an 89-mile, 66-station, 5-corridor rapid transit system. The proposed system also included the inauguration of 250 miles of express feeder bus route and 300 miles of local feeder bus service. The estimated cost was almost equal to the maximum debt limit the SCRTD could incur.

The SCRTD paid a consultant, SRI, to undertake a cost-benefit analysis of its proposed rapid transit system. Specifically, SRI was commissioned to: (1) evaluate the traveler benefits accruing to both rapid transit users and automobile travelers, (2) identify and appraise the community benefits accruing to the public, (3) compare traveler and community benefits with system costs, and (4) appraise the overall feasibility of the system.

Traveler benefits

The CBA estimated travel time savings, based on 1980 trip patterns, by comparing trip travel times both with and without rapid transit. The difference in travel time after allowances for congestion from construction was valued at $39.5 million per year. Travel time saving for airport patrons was valued at $3.05 million per year. Since no airport study was undertaken, these savings are based on the 1.4 million airport patrons required for the airport route to break even. The decrease in vehicle operating costs for motorists who switch to rapid transit and for those who continue to use the less congested street and freeway facilities was valued at $46.5 million annually.

The CBA study also emphasised that the system would also reduce required parking spaces. SRI reported that rapid transit would result in an estimated reduction of 117,770 parking spaces needed, at an annual saving of $22.7 million in the cost of providing these spaces. The cost of providing parking spaces at the transit stations was included in the systems cost.

The consultant asserted that automobiles no longer needed for commuting are a benefit assigned to the rapid transit system. This benefit is due to the availability of rapid transit, which would allow some former automobile users to sell their cars or use them for other purposes. SRI valued the decrease of 10,000 automobiles at $3.4 million per year.

Use of rapid transit was likewise expected to decrease the number of vehicle miles driven per year, which would decrease the number of automobile accidents. The decrease in accidents was valued at $4.7 million per year.

Also included under traveler benefits by the consultant was a $14.9 million yearly 'revenue surplus' used to improve bus service and to avoid fare increases. This alleged 'benefit' is, however, merely an income transfer payment because it is not generated from the investment in rapid transit. The total value of all traveler benefits estimated by SRI is $134.8 million per year. The benefits are greatly dependent on the number of passengers carried. If passenger estimates are not achieved, then these traveler benefits must likewise be reduced.

Peterson argues that several of these benefits are exaggerated. For one thing, SRI wrongly increased the estimates to allow for inflation, whereas the correct method would have been to use constant dollar estimates of both benefits and costs. Also it was estimated that 72.5 percent of the new system's rapid-transit passengers would be former automobile users. This figure is extremely high in light of the experience of other transit systems. The Yonge Street subway in Toronto and the Congress Street Rapid Transit in Chicago which were opened in the 1950s diverted less than

13 percent of their passengers from automobiles. No other rapid transit system has had the passenger diversion from autos that the SCRTD expects. Even the BART system developed in San Francisco anticipated attracting only 30.3 percent of its passengers from automobiles. The small role that public transit plays in the Los Angeles area, where over 95 percent of the daily trips are taken by automobile, is another reason Peterson offers for doubting the SCRTD's passenger estimates.

Community benefits

The second classification of benefits from the system are those that accrue to the population as a whole as a by-product or consequence of traveler benefits. The consultants identified that community benefits result from:

(1) structural and functional unemployment reductions

(2) construction unemployment reductions

(3) improved business productivity

(4) improved government productivity, and

(5) improvements in life style.

(1) SRI estimated that by 1980 rapid transit improvements to labour mobility could reduce the monthly jobless total by 4,200 through improved access to areas of labour shortage. This benefit is questionable since rapid transit alone is not expected to have a major impact on the hard-core unemployment problem in the poverty areas of Los Angeles County. Improved transportation does not by itself increase job opportunities, since the lack of public transportation may not be the major cause of unemployment in poverty areas of Los Angeles. SRI valued a permanent reduction in unemployment due to improvements in labour mobility at $30 million per year. SRI asserted that the construction of the rapid transit system would have a major impact on unemployment in the construction industry. The construction program was estimated to provide an average of 5,300 jobs for construction workers over a seven-year period, with one-half of the workers estimated to come from the ranks of the unemployed.

(2) The increased jobs in construction valued at $24 million per year may be questioned given the difficulty of predicting the level of unemployment that would exist without the project. If the employment of one-half of the workers who construct the system is counted as a benefit, one can ask why the decrease in parking space

expense, valued at $22.7 million per year, is also counted as a benefit. Even if the gain from increased construction activity due to the rapid transit were counted, other individuals would lose their jobs. For example, gas station attendants and others associated with automotive transport, including insurance claim adjusters and freeway fence repairmen. Peterson asks: why does the consultant count only the positive effect on employment and not the negative effect? To solve this difficulty, the effect on employment due to construction and operation of the system should not be counted in a CBA.

SRI also argued that millions of dollars of local expenditures for materials, machinery and services will be a further short-term aid to employment demand and a major boon to local industry. However, as Peterson points out, these items are costs, not gains, and should be treated as such.

(3) A third source of benefits to the community from the system is an increase in business productivity. This benefit, estimated at $15 million per year, results from improved labour supply, so-called environmental factors, and business profit on increased labour employment. However, if the gain to merchants located in the central district is at the expense of outlying business districts, then the system only results in an income transfer payment from merchants outside the central area to those located in the central area

(4) Another $15 million yearly benefit is estimated to result from improved government productivity. Part of this productivity improvement was derived by SRI based on a "hypothetical city structure." SRI also estimated that the efficiencies through a mass improvement in labour supply would reduce costs by 0.1 percent, to produce $3 million in savings annually

(5) SRI asserted that there are several non-monetary improvements that rapid transit will bring to many District residents to broaden their range of choice of mobility as well as residential possibilities that will enrich their 'style of urban life'. This was estimated by SRI at $25 million annually, but no sound justification was given for this estimate.

As Peterson highlights, the quantifiable community benefits, estimated at $109 million-plus per year by SRI, are reduced to only $60 million when the construction employment and 'life-style' benefits, valued at $24 million and $25 million per year, respectively, are eliminated. Peterson says these alleged benefits should be excluded because the construction employment benefit is erroneous and the 'life-style' benefit is highly subjective.

Costs

The estimated 'equivalent annual cost' of the investment is $135.7 million. Peterson argues that this estimate is inaccurate in several respects.

A cost overlooked by SRI is the increase in police costs required to provide safety for users. An indication of this cost can be gained by considering the subway system of New York, where $11 million were spent in fiscal 1964–65 policing its trains and stations.

Another cost of the system which must always be considered when a public service replaces a private one is the foregone taxes that a private undertaking would pay, not only on the land right-of-way, but also on the equipment and on all the income earned from operations.

Peterson also reminds us that the rapid transit proposal is to be financed entirely by bonds. This means that some allowance for risk should be calculated in the SCRTD's proposal, because a similar private undertaking could not be financed entirely by bonds. The riskiness of the project would require that there be some equity financing, the return on which is heavily taxed.

Conclusion

For the proposed Los Angeles rapid transit system, the consultant estimated a favourable benefit cost ratio (exceeding unity) only because:

(1) many benefits are incorrectly calculated due to such factors as inflation, anticipated unemployment reductions and expenditure decreases, along with double counting and the inclusion of non-quantifiable benefits;

(2) many costs are under-stated or omitted entirely; and

(3) the passenger estimates are overly optimistic. (This last point is particularly important since passenger estimates are crucial to a cost-benefit study of any rapid transit system).

Because of the interest in rapid transit for solving a city's transportation problems, a CBA undertaken for Los Angeles can provide valuable insight to an agency contemplating such a system for its own area. The consultants report demonstrates that the benefits are often incorrectly estimated, while some important costs may be ignored. Further investigation is also needed to estimate passenger demand, since the number of passengers greatly influences the benefits to be derived from the system. If Los Angeles, or any other city, is planning to introduce a rapid transit system, the difficulties of using CBA raised in Peterson's paper must be faced.

Source: Peterson, T. (1975) 'Cost-Benefit Analysis for Evaluating Transportation Proposals: Los Angeles Case Study', *Land Economics* 51(1), 72–79, February

10.4.8 POST-IMPLEMENTATION REVIEW

Ex post evaluations involve:

- Re-evaluation of the benefits and costs of the selected option to assess whether the anticipated benefits were realised and the forecast costs were accurate.
- Reconsideration of alternative options.
- Examination of the project design and implementation to assess the scope for improvement to the option adopted.

By re-examining these issues, *ex post* evaluations will assist in the development and evaluation of future projects. Box 10.4 demonstrates the value of the post-implementation review given the failures of megaprojects to perform according to expectations.

BOX 10.4 Megaprojects and risk

Flyvbjerg, Bruzelius and Rothengatter (2003) suggest that megaprojects, multi-billion dollar infrastructure developments, despite their actual and symbolic importance, 'have strikingly poor performance records in terms of economy, environment and public support'. They demonstrate that the studies used to justify transport megaprojects typically underestimate costs and overestimate benefits, sometimes by orders of magnitude.

The authors investigate the processes behind the approval and implementation of megaprojects. The primary focus is on transport projects such as international transport links and urban passenger rail networks. Examples include the Channel Tunnel, the new Hong Kong and Denver international airports, the Akashi Kaikyo bridge in Japan, the Sydney harbor tunnel, Thailand's Second Stage Expressway, the Great Belt link between East Denmark and Continental Europe, the Øresund link between Sweden and Denmark, the Boston 'Big Dig', freeways and railways in California.

The authors' main argument is that the typical ex ante evaluation of a large transport project is based on what the World Bank calls EGAP (Everything Going According to Plan). In practice, of course, things do not go according to plan. Occasionally, things go better than expected, as in the case of the Øresund road bridge, which experienced substantially more traffic than was expected. But, more often than not, things go worse than expected. Hence, the EGAP evaluation yields estimated benefit-cost ratios that are biased upwards.

Some examples are instructive. 'The Channel tunnel, opened in 1994 at a construction cost of £4.7 billion, was associated with several near bankruptcies caused by construction cost overruns of 80%, financing costs that are 140% higher than those forecast and revenues less than half of those projected ...'. Denver's *US$5* billion new international airport '...was close to 200% in cost overrun and passenger traffic in the opening year was only half of that projected'. The authors find that real cost overruns of between 50 and 100 percent are common, and overruns above 100 percent are not uncommon, while demand is typically overestimated, with typical overestimates between 20 and 70 percent. The tendency to overestimation is particularly severe in the case of urban rail projects.

The authors cite the lack of transparency in decision making and the weak involvement of the civil society, or what they call a 'democracy deficit' as a core factor, underlying failure to accurately assess the costs and revenues associated with megaprojects, In particular this has involved systematic failure to adequately account for risks for projects undertaken by organizations in both the private and public sectors.

Some of the conclusions are the following:

- In 9 out of 10 transport infrastructure projects, costs are underestimated, resulting in cost overrun
- For rail, actual costs are, on the average, 45% higher than estimated costs
- For fixed links (tunnels and bridges), actual costs are, on the average, 34% higher than estimated costs
- For roads, actual costs are, on the average, 20% higher than estimated costs
- For all project types, actual costs are, on the average, 28% higher than estimated costs
- Cost underestimation and overrun exist across 20 nations and five continents; it appears to be a global phenomenon
- Cost underestimation and overrun appear to be more pronounced in developing nations than in North America and Europe (data for rail only)

- Cost underestimation and overrun have not decreased over the past 70 years. No learning seems to take place
- Cost underestimation and overrun cannot be explained by error and seem to be best explained by strategic misrepresentation, namely, lying, with a view to getting projects started
- Regional development claims for megaprojects are often merely a sop to promote political acceptance, and many of them depend upon 'nonmeasurable or insignificant claims'

Features that are systematically ignored or underplayed include uncertainty about facts, high-decision stakes, and values in dispute. Risk assessment, essential to dealing with these factors, is usually absent or inadequate.

For the widespread failure to provide accurate forecasts of demand, the authors cite seven reasons: inadequate methodology, often involving applying the wrong forecasting tool; poor database; discontinuous behavior and the influence of complementary factors; unexpected changes of exogenous factors; unexpected political activity or missing realization of complementary policies; implicit appraisal bias of the consultants; and finally, appraisal bias of the project promoters.

The authors also criticize the use of environmental impact analysis, citing three generic causes of failure: a lack of accuracy in impact predictions; the narrow scope of impacts and their time horizon; and an inadequate organization scheduling and institutional integration of the environmental impact assessment process into overall decision making. In respect of environmental impact assessment itself they state that 'the main obstacles to understanding the actual environmental risks are the absence of mandatory, institutionalized requirements for post auditing and the indifference among authorities, developers and the general public to such audits'. The authors argue for more consistent attention to environmental issues beginning in the design phase and ending with ex post assessments of actual, as compared to predicted, environmental impacts.

To improve accountability in assessment of megaprojects the authors propose four instruments. These are (1) transparency; (2) performance specifications determined by stakeholders; (3) explicit formulation of a regulatory regime and identification and elimination of policy risks before decisions are taken; and (4) the involvement of risk capital as far as possible.

Source: Flyvbjerg, Bent, Nils Bruzelius and Werner Rothengatter (2003) *Megaprojects and Risk: An Anatomy of Ambition*, Cambridge, UK: Cambridge University Press.

10.5   OTHER ISSUES IN CONDUCTING A CBA

There are at least three other important issues which a CBA must address. These are as follows:

- Shadow pricing.
- Double counting.
- Income distributional effects.

10.5.1   SHADOW PRICES

As noted, the general principle in CBA is that market prices, where available, should provide the basis for the measurement of the opportunity cost of inputs or the WTP for outputs. However, market prices do not always reflect the marginal social cost or value of goods or services. When market prices exist but are distorted for some reason, we need to estimate what the prices would be in the absence of the distortions and then use these adjusted market prices. These adjusted prices are called *shadow prices* (sometimes called social prices or true prices).

The use of shadow prices rather than market prices is most commonly advocated for the following market distorting situations:

- Labour markets (when unemployment and/or underemployment exists or wages are artificially high);
- Foreign exchange market (where the value of foreign exchange is different from the market rate);
- Market power (distortion of market prices by monopoly seller or monopsony buyer);
- Government regulations, taxes and subsidies

We discussed the role of shadow pricing in Chapter 6. For present purposes, we will focus on its role in CBA.

Labour markets. To ascertain how labour should be priced, the question needs to be asked what the workers would be doing in the absence of the project. If they would otherwise be unemployed but are giving up only leisure time to participate in the project, then the shadow wage rate (the rate at which the workers are willing to work) might be low. In other words, the shadow wage of labour, or its opportunity cost, would be low relative to the market wage. From a social point of view, then, workers who would otherwise be unemployed might 'cost' only a small proportion of their market wage rate. For example, if the market wage is $25,000, and a worker is willing to work for $20,000 after tax (the shadow wage), there would be a net gain of $5000 from creating a job. The benefit from the reduction in unemployment can be calculated as the difference between the after tax wage and the shadow wage, multiplied by the change in employment.

In general, job-creation claims associated with tourism-related projects are warranted from the national point of view only when an investment can be made equally efficiently in two regions that have markedly different unemployment rates. In this situation, it may be appropriate to estimate a lower-than-market cost of labour in the area that has severe unemployment. The underlying reason is that part of the labour force would otherwise be unemployed, and therefore it has a low opportunity cost from the point of view of the economy as a whole. In such circumstances, tourism development in a region with unemployment may have substantial benefits.

As a general rule, we should assume that resources used in the project would otherwise be fully employed. This is most likely to be realistic of skilled labour which is relatively mobile. If special circumstances are deemed to warrant the assignment of shadow prices to the use of otherwise-unemployed resources, the rationale for making such adjustments must be carefully outlined and defended.

Foreign exchange market. If exchange rates are not free to vary so as to equilibrate the demand for and supply of the currency, or where there are trade distortions such as tariffs and export subsidies, the shadow foreign exchange rate will differ from the market rate. If, for example, tariffs exist the additional earnings of foreign exchange will be valued in excess of their market value, since the government receives the tariff revenues from the additional imports made possible. If so, there can be a benefit to the economy from a tourism development that brings in valuable foreign exchange (Dwyer & Forsyth, 1993). The shadow price of foreign exchange will depend on the level of the trade distortions, the relevant demand and supply elasticities and the uses to which revenues are put (Fane, 1991). Jenkins and Kuo (1985) estimated that the shadow exchange rate for Canada exceeded the market rate by about 6.5%. Thus, for most developed countries, a gain in foreign exchange resulting from increased inbound tourism is unlikely to provide substantial benefits over and above the market price, though this need not be so for developing countries with exchange rate and trade distortions.

Market power. The distortion of market prices by monopoly seller or monopsony buyer can result in a deadweight loss to society. The loss of producer and consumer surplus comprises the deadweight loss. As indicated in Chapter 6, this is not likely to be a significant source of distortion for the tourism industry in many countries since many of the industries (accommodation, restaurants, road transport, etc.) which make up tourism are quite competitive, and thus margins are kept to the minimum necessary to cover the cost of capital.

Taxation. The shadow price of government revenue may exceed its nominal value. Raising revenue involves imposing distorting taxes, and thus the marginal cost to a nation of raising $1 typically exceeds $1. The marginal cost of raising funds of $1 from income taxation in Australia, for example, has been estimated to range from A$1.23 to A$1.65 (Campbell & Bond, 1997). If tourism results in increased net revenues to government, it will be possible for governments to reduce tax rates or increase expenditure elsewhere. In a study using a general equilibrium model of the US economy, Ballard *et al.* (1985) examined the combined welfare cost of all taxes in the US revenue system. It was found that the welfare losses caused by distortionary taxation can be very large, both on average and at the margin. The marginal welfare loss to consumers from raising an additional dollar of revenue is in the range of 34¢–48¢, depending on certain elasticities. This has very important implications for CBA. If a public project must be financed by distortionary taxes which cause dead-weight loss, this excess burden must be taken into account in the decision whether or not to undertake the project.

It is appropriate to adjust market prices for the effects of taxes and subsidies where they may make a material difference to the decision on the preferred project. In practice, though, it is relatively rare to make adjustments for taxation, because similar tax regimes usually prevail across the range of alternative projects. However, where tax regimes applying to different alternatives vary substantially, adjustment is necessary to avoid distorting the option choice. It is not correct, except in special circumstances, simply to use market prices less tax as a measure of shadow price (Boadway, 1975).

While theoretically interesting, the above types of distortions may not have much effect on the CBA estimates. In many cases given the potentially small changes that result to the net benefit calculation, it may not be worthwhile for the analyst to confront the difficult measurement problems associated with shadow pricing.

10.5.2 DOUBLE COUNTING

The double counting of costs or benefits must be avoided. Often external costs and benefits are no more than transfers of internal costs and benefits. An example is the development of a new railway linking two towns. The increase in value of houses in close proximity to the two railway stations may be accepted as a measure of the expected benefits of the railway. If this measure is used, it is important not to also include benefits such as reduced travel times, better access to shopping and other amenities and expanded job opportunities, since these benefits would have been capitalised into the increased value of house prices. To count them again separately, would be double counting.

Again, suppose a new sewage treatment plant is installed in a tourist destination. Consequently, the recreation value of the river improves, land values in the neighbourhood increase and health problems decrease. However, if all these effects are counted as benefits there is likely to be some double counting. The increase in land values is a measure of the combined benefits, not an additional benefit.

The thing to remember here is that often factors that could give rise to externalities are built into market prices and are therefore already accounted for. Decisions need to be made case by case.

10.5.3   INCOME DISTRIBUTIONAL EFFECTS

CBA often aggregates costs and benefits across individuals, without regard to the distribution of those costs and benefits between individuals. Thus, the technique is sometimes criticised for ignoring social equity. However, there is no reason why a CBA cannot make explicit allowance for distribution.

To illustrate, a CBA of a new highway that bypasses a country town will compare, primarily, the costs of constructing the new road with the benefits in terms of travel time savings and reduced accidents (involving both travellers and local residents). However, building the road is likely to bring about gainers and losers; for example, established shops in the town may be adversely affected while new retailing opportunities, such as service stations, restaurants and motels, may open up along the new highway. Similarly, the development of new origin-destination routes by a low-cost airline may lead to a modal shift from car to air and may thus adversely affect retailers in towns en route that depend on passing traffic flows for their incomes.

In reality, it is highly likely that a change in resource allocation, such as the introduction of a new tourism resort or new tourism policy or program, will increase the welfare or well being of some people but reduce the welfare of others. One approach to recognising this in a CBA is to identify the gainers and losers, and measure the extent of their gains and losses in monetary terms. This information is then provided to the decision maker, who then must make the distributional value judgements. Alternatively, others (Ray, 1984) have suggested that distributional weights be assigned to the benefits and costs experienced by different groups in society (e.g. with higher weights being given to benefits and costs to poorer groups than benefits and costs to richer groups). These weights would be provided by the government. The criterion for proceeding with the project then depends on whether weighted benefits exceed weighted costs. While analytically this approach has its attractions, the problem of finding the appropriate weights makes it difficult to implement in practice.

Box 10.5 summarises a CBA of expanding capacity at Heathrow airport

---

BOX 10.5 Expanding capacity at Heathrow airport

Heathrow airport plays a vital role in the economy of London, the South East, and the UK as a whole. Heathrow employs around 100,000 people directly and indirectly, and is part of a sector that employs over 200,000 people directly in the UK, contributing over £11 billion a year to the economy. As the UK's major hub airport, Heathrow should be able to support a wider range of direct flight destinations and frequencies than would be possible without transfer passengers. This

---

brings benefits for business passengers, those visiting friends and relatives, as well as leisure passengers.

Heathrow has experienced strong growth over recent decades, currently handling 68 million passengers and 477,000 flights a year compared to around 48 million passengers and 427,000 flights a year in 1996. In the absence of any increase in runway capacity, this growth has resulted in Heathrow's runways operating at around 99% capacity compared to its main European competitors which operate at around 75% capacity, leading to increased delays, lower resilience and fewer destinations served.

Airport delay imposes costs on society in terms of increased costs for airlines, passengers and the wider community. The airlines bear additional costs on the fleet, as well as on flying and ground personnel, since delays prevent them from operating at optimum conditions. Delay-related costs for users are mostly airline passengers' opportunity costs, measured by the value of their time.

Three possible sequencing options on how the airport operator might provide more capacity at Heathrow airport have been identified, which are assessed against the 'base case'. The base case assumes that no changes are made to the airport between 2010 and 2080 and the existing operating procedures and the current annual air transport movements (ATMs) limit of 480,000 per annum remains. Briefly the sequencing options are:

Option 1 – Third runway with new terminal around 2020

Option 2 – Mixed mode within existing capacity around 2010 and third runway with new terminal around 2020

Option 3 – Mixed mode within existing capacity around 2010, mixed mode with additional capacity around 2015 and third runway with new terminal around 2020.

The introduction of mixed mode within existing capacity would lead to additional resilience benefits, relative to the base case. Mixed mode within capacity would bring much needed operational resilience in times of severe disruption, as the flexibility of using both runways for landing and take off may allow the airport to operate more flights compared to the current segregate mode system.

Additional capacity under each of the three options would allow an increase of capacity to 605,000 ATMs in 2020, rising to a maximum of 702,000 ATMs by 2030. The relaxation of the capacity constraint results in a higher forecast of passengers travelling through Heathrow compared to the base case (maximum use of existing capacity).

The Table presents a summary of the quantified costs and benefits, assuming 'central case' assumptions. The net economic benefits range from £5.5bn to £6.2bn depending on the nature of the sequencing option and the surface access requirements.

Table NPV of three options to expand heathrow capacity, central case scenario

		Option 1 – Heathrow third runway 2020	Option 2 – Mixed mode at 480,000 ATMs around 2010, third runway in 2020	Option 3 – Mixed mode at 480,000 ATMs around 2010, mixed mode at 540,000 ATMs by 2015, third runway around 2020
Benefits	User and Producer Benefits	19.2	19.2	19.2
	Delay Reduction Benefits	–	0.9	1.0
Costs	Infrastructure	7.8	8.0	8.1
	Noise	0.3	0.4	0.4
	Air Quality	0.1	0.1	0.1
	GHG Emissions*	5.4	5.4	5.5
Net Present Value		**5.5**	**6.2**	**6.1**

Each option would generate significant *monetised benefits* to society. The transport user and producer benefits were estimated using the concepts of consumer and producer surplus (see Chapter 4). These benefits include greater ability to travel, reductions in travel costs for passengers, additional producer surplus and benefits from additional freight movements. By expanding the airport, the operator will gain additional revenues through levying airport charges on more aircraft. Air

Passenger Duty (APD) is levied on airlines for each UK departing passenger that they carry excluding transfers at hubs. The change in APD revenue that additional capacity brings through additional non-transfer passengers. This revenue accrues to government, but it is a benefit to society, to be passed on through lower taxation or increased spending on other sectors.

There are important additional benefits from increased runway capacity that are harder to quantify. In general all the options would lead to significant *non-monetised impacts*. These include potential benefits to airlines and passengers from reduced delays in the early years of opening, increased efficiencies of freight operations, wider economic impacts and greater resilience of the airport in times of severe disruption, for example in times of severe weather. The wider economic benefits include indirect benefits of additional capacity in the form of reduced costs to the economy, including additional local employment, lower business costs, increased FDI and productivity benefits to the UK economy as a whole. The increased resilience recognizes that additional capacity may lead to fewer cancelled flights as the flexibility of three runways would allow the airport to operate more flights per hour compared to a two-runway system.

Each option would entail significant *monetized* infrastructure costs to the airport operator. Significant capital, refurbishment and operating costs would be associated with the new runway, new terminal, and surface access infrastructure, which would ultimately fall on users. The social costs include additional carbon dioxide emissions, air quality and aircraft noise costs, increased accident risks (increased flights increase the risks of accidents at Heathrow). These are costs not borne by the airport operator, but by society in general.

The *non monetized costs* relate to impacts on landscape, townscape and historic environment (including loss of the village of Sipson), as well as potential for additional impacts from subsequent road congestion (e.g. road noise) and possible loss of biodiversity.

In so far as Option 3 delivers additional capacity earlier than all other options, it is expected that some of the non-infrastructure related impacts to be more severe compared to other options.

All three options are expected to deliver impacts under these headings, with Option 3 perhaps delivering more benefits due to early delivery of capacity. However, Option 2 also brings significant early resilience and improved performance.

As of October 2009 the UK government had not made a decision as to which option will be pursued.

Source: Department for Transport (2009)

Box 10.6 summarises some of the strengths and limitations of CBA.

BOX 10.6 Strengths and limitations of CBA

CBA has a number of strengths and caveats.

Strengths
- CBA is a systematic and consistent evaluation method that facilitates comparisons between different options.
- It has a well-developed theoretical foundation – neoclassical welfare economics – which is based on the individual being the best judge of their own welfare and the welfare of society being the sum of the welfare of individuals.
- Its use promotes the efficient use of resources.
- It makes proponents consider costs and benefits that are external to the proponent.
- It forces the decision-maker to think in a rational way about the costs and benefits of alternative actions.
- It can provide a clear focus on net benefits of a proposal without regard to who wins and who loses from projects and programs.
- It encourages clear consideration of the true *value added* from a proposal by focusing on incremental net benefits.
- Its emphasis on the quantification of costs and benefits on a comparable basis can provide a useful 'hard edge' to an evaluation strategy.

Caveats
- CBA is inexact. It can yield dramatically different numbers, especially as different methodologies for assigning economic values to non-economic benefits can vary significantly.
- CBA often includes subjective assumptions regarding non-economic values. While the analysis usually highlights the various qualitative costs and benefits, assessing the actual quantitative values can be quite contentious.
- Exponents of CBA should endeavour to value whatever can be quantified and valued reliably within the resource constraints of the situation. The remaining intangible effects should be listed and described as fully as possible, and some consideration given to the impact of the intangible component of the CBA on the results.
- It is sometimes suggested that some non-market effects cannot be valued or have infinite values. However, finite values for non-market effects are routinely

explicit in government decisions and the behaviour of consumers. For difficult to quantify values, it is therefore important that analysts make their assumptions clear and that margins for error be identified or sensitivity testing be undertaken.

- CBA has been criticized for being complex and too onerous in its information requirements. However, in some situations this may simply reflect the complexity of public decisions and, in most cases, unnecessary complexity should and can be avoided. Even simple applications of the technique can yield valuable information for proponents and decision-makers.
- Distributional information can be supplied as an adjunct to CBA. It is then up to decision-makers and the political process to identify the appropriate trade-off between equity and efficiency.

Source: Commonwealth Department of Finance (1992)

One area of tourism in which CBA is expected to play an increasingly important role is in the assessment of special events. The success or contribution of a particular event should not be measured only by its direct financial contribution but needs to consider the wider economic, social and environmental impacts that are invariably associated with it. There is a growing awareness among researchers that event assessment which focuses only on economic impacts is too narrow in scope to provide sufficient information to policy makers and government funding agencies and that, where practical, a more comprehensive approach should be employed to embrace the importance of social and environmental impacts in addition to economic impacts. These critics highlight the potential importance of CBA in event evaluation. These issues will be explored in some detail in Chapter 11.

10.6   COST-EFFECTIVENESS ANALYSIS

Cost-effectiveness analysis (CEA) compares the costs of different options for achieving the same or similar outputs or performance criteria. It is often used to find the option that meets a predefined objective at a minimum cost.

CEA measures the benefits in physical units rather than in monetary terms, for instance, through measuring cost per passenger transported or meal served. It offers a priority ranking of programs or activities on the basis of a comparative 'cost per unit of effectiveness', or alternatively, of comparative 'units of effectiveness per dollar'. Thus:

$$CE = \frac{C}{E} \tag{10.6}$$

Where,

CE is the cost-effectiveness of the proposal;

C is the cost (measured in dollars);

E represents the effectiveness (i.e. the benefit measured in physical units).

Under C/E ranking, projects with the lowest ratio are the most effective – their average 'cost per unit of effectiveness' is at a minimum. Decision-making in such cases is straightforward. For example, given a desired effectiveness goal, the decision to proceed or not is based on a simple cost-minimisation exercise subject to the constraint that the project's effectiveness meets or exceeds its set goal.

Alternatively, under an (inverted) E/C ranking, projects with the highest ratio are the most effective – their average 'effectiveness per unit of cost' is maximised. Again, decision-making is simple. Where a particular cost constraint is imposed, the decision is based on maximising the project's effectiveness subject to the cost of the program not exceeding its set cost.

For example, regarding tourism promotion, CEA could be used to assess the relative outcomes of alternative marketing campaigns in terms of relative cost for given projected increases in tourism numbers or expenditure. Thus Kulendran and Dwyer (2009) have estimated the injected expenditure return to Australia of tourism marketing in different countries, using a dynamic modelling approach and CEA. The study found that the return per dollar investment is 17:1 for Asia, 8:1 for Japan, 36:1 for New Zealand, 3:1 for the UK and 7:1 for the USA. That is, for Japanese visitors to Australia, \$1 of additional expenditure on tourism promotion in Japan is estimated to generate \$8 additional expenditure in Australia by Japanese visitors. The results have implications for targeting the highest yield markets to increase the economic returns to Australia from its destination marketing activity. The cost-effectiveness approach is a useful tool for destination managers to ensure the effectiveness of their marketing expenditure. Of course, as discussed, the injected tourism expenditure in this case is not to be equated with tourism 'benefits' as it excludes the wider economic, social and environmental impacts of the expenditure.

Destination managers may, however, be more interested in determining whether a new (proposed) program is preferable to maintaining a current program. If so, the incremental cost-effectiveness ratio (ICER) could be used, as follows:

$$ICER = \frac{(C_n - C_c)}{(E_n - E_c)}$$

Or

$$ICER = \frac{\Delta Costs}{\Delta Effectiveness}$$

Where,

C_n is the cost of the new proposal;

C_c is the cost of maintaining the current program;

E_n is the effectiveness of the new proposal;

E_c is the effectiveness of continuing with the current program.

Here, the smaller the ratio, the higher is the cost-effectiveness. A cost-effectiveness ratio can be determined for each alternative (or option). Once this is done, each alternative can be ranked from the most cost-effective (lowest ratio) to the least cost-effective (highest ratio).

CEA differs from CBA in several respects. In the case of CEA:

- The benefits are not expressed in money units, and hence it does not provide an absolute measure of the benefit to the economy of the project.
- The alternatives being assessed must be similar in nature.
- The discounting procedure is often applied only to the cost side of the analysis.

Whether CBA or CEA is the more appropriate assessment technique depends on the objectives of the project. For projects that seek to maximise the net benefits to the community a CBA is preferred. For projects that have a less ambitious but clearly defined goal, CEA may be preferred.

10.7 POLICY AND CONCLUSIONS

- Decision-makers need a consistent basis for assessing competing proposals and to be fully informed about the implications of using economic resources. CBA is a systematic process for identifying and assessing all costs and benefits of a policy, project or program in monetary terms, including those costs and benefits not usually represented by dollar values, and then subtracting the costs from the benefits to show the estimated net effect of that activity.
- CBA captures, measures, weights and compares all expected present and future benefits of a tourism policy or project with all its expected present and future costs. Future costs and benefits are discounted relative to present costs and benefits in an NPV sum. The policy or project is deemed to be socially acceptable if the sum of the benefits to society (including private and social benefits) exceeds the sum of the costs to society (including private and social costs).
- There are eight main steps in undertaking CBA. These involve: the determination of the scope and objectives of the analysis; a consideration of the alternatives; the identification of the impacts; the valuation of the relevant costs and benefits; the discounting of the

future costs and benefits; the application of the decision rules; a sensitivity analysis; and the post implementation review. When undertaking CBA, it is necessary to be mindful of four important issues: shadow pricing; double counting; deadweight losses; and income distributional effects.

- CBA is different from CEA. CEA measures the benefits in physical units rather than in monetary terms. It ranks programs on the basis of a comparative 'cost per unit of effectiveness', or alternatively, of comparative 'units of effectiveness per dollar'. Projects with the lowest ratio are the most effective since their average 'cost per unit of effectiveness' is at a minimum. Under an inverted E/C ranking, projects with the highest ratio are the most effective since their average 'effectiveness per unit of cost' is maximised.

- CBA is not without its problems: costs and benefits can be difficult to quantify; double counting is common; and income distributional effects tend to be ignored. But, as an overall accounting technique, it can be used by government to determine the worth of a project based on true (social) values.

- CBA is also particularly useful in situations where there are likely to be significant impacts on areas which lie traditionally outside the economic accounting framework. While it cannot ensure that a particular policy is implemented, it can improve the political process by uncovering gains and losses which might otherwise be neglected in the bargaining process between different stakeholders of some project, program or policy.

SELF-REVIEW QUESTIONS

1. Use tourism examples to explain the difference between financial appraisal and economic appraisal.

2. Why is CBA appropriate for use in tourism project evaluation?

3. Discuss contexts within which CBA can be used to guide tourism decision-making.

4. Outline the eight main steps needed in performing CBA on a tourism project.

5. What types of costs are excluded from CBA, and why?

6. How does CEA differ from CBA?

7. When and why are shadow prices rather than market prices used in CBA?

8. How does CBA differ from each of I–O analysis and CGE analysis?

ESSAY QUESTIONS

1. Financial appraisals look at the costs and benefits to an individual stakeholder while economic appraisals consider the costs and benefits to society as a whole. Discuss, using examples from tourism.

2. Using examples, discuss why the choice of the discount rate can have a significant impact on the ranking of tourism projects and hence their choice.

3. The activity of discounting in tourism CBA implies that the needs of future generations are given less weight than those of the current generation. Discuss.

4. In principle, CBA enables tourism agencies to compare the relative merit of alternative programs or projects in terms of their returns on the use of public resources. Explain.

5. In the presence of taxes and subsidies, market prices may not fully measure the opportunity cost, or shadow prices, of inputs or outputs in tourism sectors. Explain why this might be the case.

CHAPTER 11

ECONOMIC EVALUATION OF SPECIAL EVENTS

LEARNING OBJECTIVES

After reading this chapter, students should be able to:

1. Assess the rationale underlying government support for special events.

2. Discuss the steps involved in the economic evaluation of a special event.

3. Evaluate the use of each of Input–Output (I–O) analysis and Computable General Equilibrium (CGE) analysis in the economic evaluation of special events, and be able to compare each with Cost-Benefit Analysis (CBA).

4. Understand the challenges to best practice in the economic impact assessment of special events.

5. Appreciate the wider positive and negative effects and intangibles associated with the holding of special events requiring cost benefit analysis.

6. Understand how event evaluation can be improved

11.1 INTRODUCTION

Special events provide important recreational opportunities for local residents. In many destinations, they form a fundamental component of the destination's tourism development strategy. There are many types of special events and it is quite difficult to find an all-embracing definition. For present purposes, special events are defined as 'one-time or infrequently occurring events of limited duration that provide consumers with leisure and social opportunities beyond their everyday experience' (Jago & Shaw, 1998: 29).

Special events of one kind or another have played an important role in the economic and social development of communities internationally for many years. In recent years there has been a substantial increase in the number and type of special events. This growth is largely due to the emphasis being placed on regional economic development and destination marketing by many governments and tourism marketing organisations. Special events increase the opportunities for new expenditure within a host region by attracting visitors to the region. They have the capacity to stimulate business activity, creating income and jobs in the short term and generating increased visitation and related investment in the longer term.

The success or contribution of a particular event should not be measured only by its direct financial contribution. It is recognised that there may be other perceived benefits from events, such as enhancing the image of a city or region, facilitating business networking and civic pride. Events can also result in associated social and cultural benefits to a destination, providing forums for continuing education and training, facilitating technology transfer and the like. Sponsorship by governments of special events, even when they are run at a financial loss, is often justified by the claim that the events produce economic benefits for the region, and country, in which they are hosted. Event organisers may emphasise the developmental benefits of targeted infrastructural investments in deprived areas and the long-term 'legacy' benefits that the increased exposure to the international media brings through increased tourist arrivals and tourism receipts in the years after (and before) a special event. The Olympic Games and World Cup Football are probably the best current example of events with expected large flow-on benefits. Others such as ethnic festivals or events for disadvantaged groups may help to address social/cultural issues in the community.

On the negative side, events are recognised to generate adverse environmental impacts such as various forms of pollution and adverse social impacts such as disruption to local business and community backlash. Venice, for instance, cited adverse tourism environmental impacts as its reason to withdraw its bid to host the 2000 Expo.

Governments are often asked to provide financial support for special events including the allocation of large expenditure to construct or upgrade the required facilities and will therefore require credible forecasts of the event impacts and net benefits (as we shall see below, impacts and benefits are not the same thing). In recent years, a growing number of researchers have been critical of the approach taken to assessing the economic impacts of special events. Three main types of criticism have been advanced:

(1) The economic impacts of events are often exaggerated. Critics (e.g. Crompton, 2006; Matheson, 2002; Matheson & Baade, 2003a, b; Porter, 1999) have highlighted some inappropriate practices in event assessment (e.g. inclusion of residents expenditure as 'new money', exaggerating visitor numbers and expenditure, abuse of multipliers, inclusion of time switchers and casuals), as well as the tendency to ignore the various costs associated with special events such as opportunity costs, costs borne by the local community and displacement costs.

(2) Other researchers have argued that the entire approach to event assessment needs a re-examination. At issue is the relevance of Input–output (I–O) modelling which, for two decades, has been the standard technique for converting event expenditure data into

economic impacts. These critics argue that the economic assessment models used for estimating the economic impacts of major events should reflect contemporary developments in economic analysis, particularly regarding the use of Computable General Equilibrium (CGE) modelling. They argue that in most cases I–O modelling does not provide an accurate picture of the economic impacts of events and is thus incapable of informing event-funding agencies or governments of the 'return on investment' to be expected from event funding. These arguments, by and large, are based on the types of arguments that were highlighted in Chapter 9 (Blake, 2005; Dwyer *et al.*, 2005, 2006a, b; Madden, 2006).

(3) A third group of researchers, containing many advocates of CGE modelling, argues that event assessment which focuses only on economic impacts is too narrow in scope to provide sufficient information to policy makers and government funding agencies and that, where practical, a more comprehensive approach should be employed to embrace the importance of social and environmental impacts in addition to economic impacts. These critics highlight the potential importance of Cost-Benefit Analysis (CBA) in event evaluation.

11.2 THE LOGIC OF GOVERNMENT SUPPORT FOR SPECIAL EVENTS

There are sometimes good economic and non-economic reasons why a government may provide support for a special event. Much of the public justification of events funding seems to centre on their expected positive economic impacts.

The basis for commissioning economic impact studies is illustrated in Figure 11.1 (adapted from Crompton, 2006). It shows that *residents* and *visitors* in a community provide funds to local, state and national governments in the form of rates and taxes. Governments use a proportion of these funds to subsidise *tourism programs, promotions, activities* or *facilities*, which attract *visitors* who spend *money* in the destination location. This new money from outside the community creates *income* and *jobs* for *residents*. Taxes and rates paid by community residents, aided by visitors' bed and sales taxes, provide the initial funds, and thence receive a return on their investment in the form of additional sales revenues, employment and household income. It is the income accruing to residents that provides the justification for a community to bear the costs which are associated with the holding of special events.

Since special events typically do not make financial profits, without government funding they would tend to be provided at a level below that which is optimum or desirable. In Figure 11.2 the 'market forces' outcome can be depicted as an equilibrium, E, where the demand and supply curves refer to special events (Mules & Dwyer, 2005). Consumer demand for attending such events is a decreasing function of the admission price and is represented by the demand curve D. (In actual fact, the 'price' to consumers includes travel costs, purchase of food and merchandise at the event, etc.) The number of such events that would be financially viable, given consumer demand, is the equilibrium quantity Q_c.

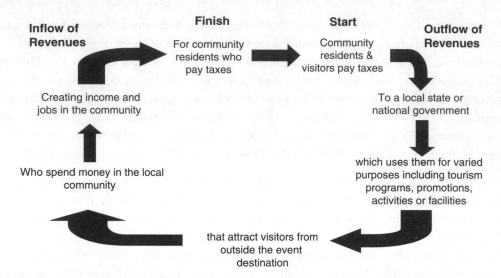

Figure 11.1 Rationale for public support of special events

Source: Adapted from Crompton (2006)

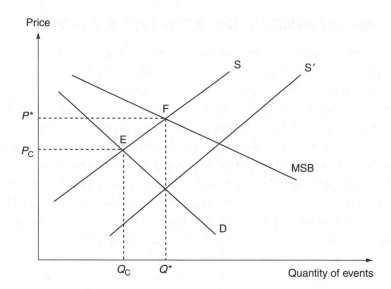

Figure 11.2 Supply and demand curves for a special event

Public spending could be justified if the benefits to the host community are greater than the costs. However, because individual firms (transport companies, hotels, restaurants, tour operators and so on) that will provide services to event attendees are unable to capture all of the benefits of funding the special event, they will be unwilling or unable to fund the event individually. Free riding will occur as the very firms that will benefit from the event seek to avoid the funding of it. If a large enough number of firms attempt to 'free ride', the event will not be held and the benefits of staging the events will be lost to all stakeholders.

The demand curve shows the price that consumers would be willing to pay for each different quantity of events, and it indicates the private benefits that consumers expect to receive from attending such events. However, since there are benefits that accrue to the community beyond the direct consumers of the event, this gives rise to the marginal social benefits curve (MSB in Figure 11.2), and the socially optimum level of events would be Q^*. This is the number of events which would maximise social welfare. The Government subsidy of events will shift the supply curve from S to S′. Ideally, the Government should provide the level of subsidy such that S′ cuts the demand curve D at the same quantity of events as Q^*. In other words, welfare is maximised if events are subsidised up to the point where the total number of events which are viable is Q^* rather than Q_c. In practical terms this indicates how many events should get Government financial aid or which events qualify for a subsidy and which events do not (Mules & Dwyer, 2005).

Figures 11.1 and 11.2 indicate why government support for special events may be appropriate. The main problem facing any government, for any given event is: what degree of support, if any, is warranted? The answer to this question varies according to the perceived benefits and costs associated with the event. An event may incur a financial loss to organisers but produce net benefits to the community.

11.3 ESTIMATING EVENT-RELATED 'NEW' EXPENDITURE

The theoretical basis of economic impact assessment of special events is to be found in the pioneering work of Burns *et al.* (1986) in their study of the Adelaide Grand Prix. Since then, contributions have been made by several authors (including Crompton, 1995; Crompton & McKay, 1994; Delpy & Li, 1998; Dwyer *et al.*, 2000; Getz, 1994; Mules, 1999). The approach involves estimating the additional expenditure generated by the event, and then using some form of economic model to estimate how this expenditure translates into increased income and employment in the destination.

There are several steps involved in the economic evaluation of a special event. These are as follows:

- Determine the boundaries of the 'host region' for the event.
- Estimate 'new' expenditure associated with the event.
- Estimate the economic impacts of the new expenditure.
- Estimate the net benefits to the destination associated with the new expenditure.

11.3.1 SETTING THE BOUNDARIES OF THE HOST REGION FOR THE EVENT

Prior to assessing the economic impact or net benefit of a special event, it is essential that the geographical boundary of the host region for the event be clearly defined. This boundary will determine whether the estimated expenditure is new to the host region or are sourced from within. An event may take place within a major centre of economic activity (a Grand Prix in a city) or in a remote location (a small town distant from a major city). An events may be held in more than one state of a country (World Cup Rugby in Australia 2005) or even in more than one country (World Cup Football 2006 in Japan and Korea; World Cup Rugby 2007 in France and England).

Three main levels of jurisdiction of an event may be identified: local area, state or broader region, and nation. Thus we note:

- A *local authority* will be interested primarily in the economic activity and jobs created within its local area.
- The *state (regional, provincial) government* primarily will be interested in the impact on the state and also, perhaps, on the local area (especially if it is a depressed area).
- The *national government* will be interested in the impact of large-scale events on the national economy as a whole, but it also may be interested in the state and local impacts for regional policy reasons.

In evaluating the economic impact of the Monaco Formula One Grand Prix, for example, there may be interest in assessing its impact on both the Principality of Monaco and the wider Côte d'Azur region. For the first part of the study the region would be defined by the geographical boundaries of Monaco, and for the second part the region would be defined as the Côte d'Azur. The scope of analysis can also be expanded to include the impacts on the economy of France.

Once set, the geographical boundaries of an event provide the basis for distinguishing between local residents and visitors to the event. These boundaries also determine whether income received and expenditure made by event organisers and sponsors come from within the region or outside. Clearly, the smaller is the host region, the greater is the number of attendees that will be defined as *visitors* to the region. The size of the study area not only determines who is regarded as a visitor and who is not (affecting the measure of new (injected) expenditure), but also influences the size of the multipliers that are applied to the injected expenditure. In our Monaco Grand Prix example, for the first part of the study, an attendee from Cannes, a city on the Côte d'Azur, would be classed as a *visitor* to Monaco. However, for the second part of the study, the same person would be classed as a *local* when the impact of the event on the Côte d'Azur is being assessed. If the event organiser purchased some equipment for the event from a supplier in Antibes, also on the Côte d'Azur, this expenditure would be classified as a *leakage* from the region for the first part of the study but included within the region for the second stage. If the focus is national, then only injections and leakages of expenditure into and from France are relevant.

11.3.2 'NEW' EXPENDITURE

The fundamental ingredient needed to conduct an economic impact assessment of an event is an estimate of the 'new injected expenditure' or 'inscope expenditure' that is generated by the event. This expenditure covers the event-induced expenditure made by visitors, participants, competitors/entrants, team managers/support staff, officials, media, VIPs, event organisers, corporate incentive groups, friends/family of those connected to the event and spectators. This refers to expenditure that would not have occurred in the host region had the event not taken place. Only that proportion of expenditure which represents an injection of 'new money' into an area is relevant to the calculation of the economic impacts.

New expenditure can be de-composed in several ways:

- *By spending group*: delegates, accompanying visitors, participants, sponsors, exhibitors, organisers, and so on.
- *By industry allocation*: allocation of expenditure to major industry categories such as accommodation, transport, shopping, food and beverage, entertainment and so on.
- *By geographic source of expenditure*: from within region, from elsewhere in the state, nation or internationally.
- *By timing*: expenditure can be injected into the destination before, during and after an event.

Expenditure injections are estimated via surveys of the relevant spenders. Expenditure volume and patterns may differ according to type of event. Visitors to special events are likely to have different purchasing patterns to other visitors to a destination. Fundamental to the estimation of new expenditure of event attendees, therefore, is the issue of sampling and crowd estimation which bring forth issues of sampling methods, data collection methods, response rates, sampling precision, validity of measurement and reliability of measurement (see Jago & Dwyer, 2006: Ch. 3).

In estimating 'new' expenditure associated with an event, we need to make several different types of adjustments. These relate to:

- Expenditure of local residents (transferred expenditure).
- Expenditure by 'casuals'.
- Expenditure by 'time switchers'.
- Retained expenditure.
- Expenditure diversion.
- Direct imports.

11.3.2.1 Expenditure of local residents (transferred expenditure)

The expenditure made by locals at an event cannot be considered as new money to the region. Such expenditure is usually referred to as 'transferred expenditure' and is ignored

411

for purposes of economic impact assessment of an event. It is assumed that residents of a host city, or a state, who attend a special event would, in its absence, have spent the same amount on other goods and services within the host region if the event was not staged. That is, it is assumed that expenditure by residents attending the event represents a transfer of expenditure either from one location to another (e.g. purchases of food at the event site instead of elsewhere in the region) or from one expenditure category to another (e.g. purchase of food at the event site instead of clothing items within the region). If the event was not held, the expenditure would still be undertaken on other goods and services and local businesses would still experience the demand. The distribution of the impact may be different, but the aggregate size would be much the same.

Similarly, sponsorship of the event from local sources or from within the specified destination must be regarded simply as transferred expenditure unless there are reasons to believe that an additional injection of funds results from the event sponsorship. If local sponsorship of an event was not forthcoming, it is likely that the funds would have been used to sponsor an alternative event or have been allocated within the destination in some other way. Similarly, expenditure by an organising committee will only be counted as relevant to event impact assessment when it represents additional or new money in the host location.

11.3.2.2 Expenditure by 'casuals'

Some persons may attend an event but have other reasons for being in the event location during the event period. The expenditure of event attendees who reside outside the host region but were coming to the region anyway cannot be counted as new expenditure. As these visitors would have visited the region anyway, it is assumed that their expenditure would have been made on other goods and services within the region had the event not been staged. These visitors are referred to as 'casuals'.

The exception to this is where, because of a special event, a 'casual' spends more time and or money in the destination than he or she otherwise would have spent. Such visitors are referred to as 'extenders'. Thus, if an event attendee was coming to the host destination anyway but extended the length of their trip to attend the event, the expenditure made on these additional days is 'new money' to the region and is included as new expenditure for purposes of the economic impact assessment. Estimates of this additional expenditure can be obtained via a visitor expenditure survey, but it is difficult to obtain accurate data about what people would have spent in the absence of an event.

11.3.2.3 Expenditure by 'time switchers'

In estimating the level of injected expenditure into a destination it is necessary to allow for 'time switching' by visitors or sponsors.

Sometimes, event attendees would have visited the region in which the event was staged, irrespective of the event, and simply adjust the timing of their visit to coincide with the staging of the event. In such cases, this expenditure should not be attributed to the event.

For example, suppose a businessman living in Paris has to visit Nice sometime during the year and sets the time for his visit in early July so that he can attend a sailing regatta. The expenditure of the businessman during his visit to Nice should not be attributed to the sailing regatta as he would have visited Nice anyway during the year. The regatta has affected the timing of his visit but it did not generate the visit. Given that this person was coming to Nice in any case, it is assumed that the money that he spent at the regatta would have been spent on other entertainment activities while in Nice if he came at a time when the event was not being staged. Similarly, if a visitor from a foreign country had planned to visit New York in any case but brought the visit forward to coincide with the New York Marathon, there is no incremental expenditure resulting from the event. It may be assumed that the same amount would have been spent by the person in that year in New York, albeit at a different time.

The same principle applies to the expenditure of government and sponsors where it is often the case that expenditure attributed to an event would have occurred in any case (e.g. out of a fixed sponsorship budget), but the timing was such that it was shifted to coincide with an event. If such expenditure was shifted to coincide with an event, it cannot be attributed to that event and should not be included in the new expenditure.

The extent of 'time switching' may be expected to vary according to the tourism attractiveness of a destination. For the 1998 Gold Coast Wintersun Festival, the percentage the visitor time switching expenditure for the Australian State of Queensland was estimated at 24.2% (Fredline *et al.*, 1999). Similarly, time switchers at the Australian Motor Cycle Grand Prix at Phillip Island have been estimated at 15% of interstate visitors and 35% of overseas visitors (NIEIR, 1989), with an overall weighted average of 16%, a figure comparable with estimates of time switching associated with the Adelaide Grand Prix in 1985 and 1988 (17% and 13%, respectively) (Price Waterhouse, 1989).

11.3.2.4 Retained expenditure

Some event assessments have included the expenditure of residents and organisations located within the host region where the expenditure would have occurred outside the region had the event been staged elsewhere. Such assessments, for instance, would include expenditure by avid football fans who can stay in their local region and not have to travel elsewhere when the World Cup is held in their country.

Some researchers (see, e.g. Getz, 1994) question whether it is appropriate to include retained expenditure for purposes of economic impact assessment of events on the grounds that it does not represent an injection of 'new money' into a destination. Noting this concern, if the analyst decides to include 'retained earnings' as equivalent to an expenditure injection, it is perhaps best to include it only when the event held in some destination was selected from a competitive bidding situation or chosen from a particular set of destinations. In such circumstances, the alternative event location is known and the retained expenditure can be estimated on the basis of estimated losses of expenditure by residents who would otherwise have travelled to the successful host destination for the same event.

Another major problem with retained expenditure, however, is in actually estimating its size. It is very difficult to obtain reliable information about what locals would have done in the absence of an event.

Including retained expenditure for the purposes of event assessment is very weak on conceptual grounds. In our view, retained expenditure should be ignored in the estimation of new expenditure. Since in most cases, retained expenditure is not expected to be substantial, leaving it out of the calculations leads to a more conservative result.

11.3.2.5   Expenditure diversion

In estimating the net injected expenditure associated with an event, it is also important to account for expenditure leakages that occur when event-related expenditure displaces or 'crowds out' expenditure that would otherwise have occurred in the destination. There are three components that must be considered in this context:

(i) *Some potential visitors are deterred from visiting a destination because of an event.* When a large special event is held, some potential visitors may be deterred from travelling to that destination at that time. When the Olympic Games was held in Athens in 2004, it is likely that some international visitors elected not to visit Greece that year due to concerns regarding congestion, terrorist fears and increased prices. It has been suggested that continuous reporting by the mass media implying exorbitant pricing by hotels and potential congestion at the World Cup site, may have negatively affected potential tourists to Korea during the event period. Lee and Taylor (2005) highlight the situation in the 2002 World Cup Football where Japanese tourists who traditionally account for more than 40% of the Korean inbound market fell by almost 50% during the period of the event, staying in their own country to watch the event because they co-hosted it. If such potential visitors did not simply change the timing of their trip, but instead visited another destination, then the expenditure that they would have made in the host destination is lost as a result of the event.

(ii) *Local residents may leave the host region during the event.* Local residents may be prompted to leave the host region due to the staging of an event. If this results in extra trips out of the region, the foregone expenditure of these locals must be counted as a loss due to the event. An example of this is where local residents of Monaco leave the region during the Monaco Grand Prix due to their concerns regarding noise, congestion and access to their residences and recreation areas. They take with them funds that would otherwise be spent on entertainment and the like within the host region.

Tour operators often provide incentives for resident exodus. For example, international airlines, faced with the prospect of returning from event locations with empty seats offer large discounts on outbound travel thus providing additional incentives for resident exodus during the period of the event. Travel agents reported an upsurge in Sydney residents who took advantage of cheap flights out of Sydney during the 2000 Sydney Olympic Games and during the Asia Pacific Economic Community 2007 event featuring world leaders when, for security reasons, Sydney was effectively in lockdown mode. For the Los Angeles Olympics, displacement costs were estimated to be US$163 million of out-of-region tourist expenditures which would have occurred if the Olympics had not been held (Crompton, 1999: 33).

(iii) *Local residents may spend less in the destination because of the event.* This type of displacement – an expenditure diversion effect – occurs because consumers may change their activity and spending patterns during the event. During the period of the event, residents may spend less on purchases of goods and services than they otherwise would have. For example, they may be less inclined to dine out because of perceived 'crowding' of restaurants and night clubs and anticipated traffic problems and security concerns. Crowding out and price increases by input suppliers in response to increased demand for goods and services and the tendency of suppliers to lower prices to stimulate sales when demand is weak reduce the net new economic activity due to the event.

In the build up to the Sydney and Athens Olympics, construction activity made access to many shops difficult causing local businesses to suffer large declines in their sales. Blake (2005) has observed that significant expenditure switching by residents occurs during the Olympics, partly because of the congestion and higher prices because of Olympic visitors and partly because local residents tend to watch the Olympic events on television rather than engage in their normal evening entertainments such as eating meals in restaurants.

To take account of this type of expenditure diversion effect, in his assessment of the economic impacts expected from the London Olympics in 2012, Blake (2005) assumed that the expenditure of residents will fall by 10% in London and 2% nationally during the two-week period of the Olympics. Investment that would have taken place in London in industries not directly affected by the Games is assumed also to be put on hold because of higher prices, particularly the prices of construction services during the construction phase of the Games.

However, while some businesses will lose sales as residents reduce their expenditure, unless these residents increase their savings, which is unlikely, residents will spend the money saved during the event on other types of purchases once the event is completed. These purchases may include patronage of those businesses that they avoided during the event, but may also include patronage of other local businesses. Unless the money saved by residents during the event due to their reduced expenditure is spent on goods and services with a higher import content (such as outbound travel), the net result is that some businesses gain and others lose because of the event but the overall sales to residents remains fairly stable. The exception is the loss of expenditure due to the resident exodus effect.

These components result in a loss of expenditure that would otherwise be spent within the region and thus must be seen as a cost of the event. As it is virtually impossible to measure these costs in a convenient and reliable fashion, they are generally left out of the calculation of new expenditure. This does not imply that switches in expenditure by residents are unimportant. Rather, these switches are income distributional effects rather than efficiency effects. In any case, as Blake points out, a CGE model automatically handles many of the displacement effects that arise from expenditure associated with special events. The fact that households are modelled as facing an income constraint implies that (before considering any income effects) households attending a special event must substitute the extra expenditure they make on this activity for expenditure on other commodities.

11.3.2.6   Direct imports

Event assessment has often ignored the issue of whether the money spent at an event stays in the local economy. To some extent, the economic model used will allow for the import content of outputs of goods and services and inputs into production. However, much of the money spent by visitors on hotel rooms, rental cars and restaurants goes to national chains, and the profits earned by these businesses do not increase the welfare of citizens in the local economy but, rather, accrue to stakeholders located outside the area. Similarly, revenue from ticket sales may be paid to a league or the event association's ruling body instead of local organisers. Matheson and Baade (2003b) give the example of a touring circus of foreigners who entertain in a host city. If the circus is entirely self-supporting requiring no local labour or local purchases to permit its operations, it has an effective multiplier of zero. Thus, any local spending on the circus will actually reduce local income as residents substitute their regular spending on local goods for spending on the circus.

Delpy and Li (1998) highlight a form of leakage which they refer to as 'VIP switching'. This refers to the proportion of entertainment dollars distributed to catering and special event companies, rather than to local eating and drinking establishments. As the event profile increases, so does the demand for corporate hospitality and entertainment services. These tend to be sourced from larger urban, rather than regional areas, and thus may increase the size of the leakage from regional events.

Direct imports of goods and services (i.e. purchases of event-related products that are sourced from outside the destination) represent a leakage out of the host economy. In general, sub-regions of an economy have a higher overall propensity to import than a region as a whole since they tend to be less self-sufficient in producing goods and services for visitor needs. Direct imports should be subtracted from new expenditure prior to economic impact assessment of a special event.

The volume of direct imports will depend upon how freely goods and services flow from one region (state or province) to another in response to an increase in demand associated with a special event. The extent to which goods and services flow between states in the short and long run will affect the economic impact of the new expenditure. Will the additional expenditure be met by increased production by industries within the state or flows of imports from interstate and abroad? This depends on the nature of the goods (whether heavy or perishable) and how readily traded they are. Some services can be supplied readily from outside regional borders (e.g. call-centre services), while others cannot (skilled carpenters). If goods and services markets are highly integrated, a demand increase

Table 11.1 Summary of new expenditure inclusions and exclusions

	New Expenditure	*Considerations*
Expenditure of visitors	✓	Classified as an injection of new expenditure – if the special event was the primary reason to visit. Only the injection of 'new money' is relevant.
Switched expenditure	✗	Not classified as new expenditure – unless there is additional expenditure due to the special event.
Expenditure by casuals	✗	Not classified as new expenditure – unless the casual visitor spends more in the destination due to the event.
Retained expenditure	✗	Not classified as new expenditure – unless the expenditure can be identified that would have occurred outside the region had the event been staged elsewhere. This is very difficult to estimate and thus it is usually ignored.
Organisers and sponsors	✓	Classified as an injection of new expenditure – if the money would not otherwise have been spent in the destination.
Diversionary expenditure	✓	Difficult to estimate but are relevant to estimation of the economic impact of the event.
Direct imports	✓	Classified as a leakage from new expenditure. Event-related goods and services that are sourced outside the destination are subtracted directly from new expenditure.

stimulated by an event will be less likely to stimulate local economic activity because the goods and services will tend to be imported from interstate and abroad.

As was discussed in Chapter 8, the greater the import content of tourism-related expenditure, the smaller will be any multiplier effects on total income, value added and employment. If the net injected expenditure is exaggerated, this error will be compounded in estimating the indirect and induced effects through standard multiplier analysis. Correct multiplier analysis (whatever the economic model used) includes all 'leakages' from the circular flow of payments and uses multipliers that are appropriate to the event industry.

Table 11.1 contains a summary of new expenditure inclusions and exclusions.

11.4   THE ECONOMIC IMPACT OF AN EVENT

The total new expenditure that occurs as a result of an event is used as the input to an economic model to determine the economic impacts on the destination. The inscope expenditure of visitors and organisers/sponsors stimulates economic activity and creates additional business turnover, employment, value added, household income and government revenue in the host community. See Figure 11.3.

The economic impacts of the new expenditure associated with a special event can be estimated using an economic model that identifies and quantifies the linkages between different sectors of the local economy and linkages with other regions. The injection of new money has *direct, indirect and induced* effects on the local economy. As discussed in Chapter 8, the relationship between expenditure and output, income, value added and employment (direct, indirect or induced) can be described by multipliers. As indicated there, the size of the multipliers will depend upon the type of model used to estimate the impacts.

Unfortunately, it is in the area of event assessment that multipliers often are employed in a most uncritical way. A major reason for this has been the use of I–O models to estimate the economic impacts of special events. As discussed in Chapters 8 and 9, I–O models typically make extreme assumptions about the behaviour of economic agents which tend to exaggerate the multiplier effects of shocks to tourism demand. The result has been that tourism researchers and consultants have very often failed to produce estimates of

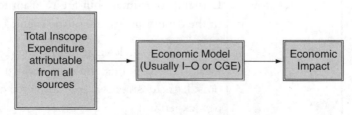

Figure 11.3 The economic impact of an event

the economic impacts of events that are realistic and that can provide accurate input into government policy formulation.

In recent years, the literature on event assessment has moved away from the use of I–O models to provide the multiplier effects of the new expenditure, and toward the use of CGE models (Blake, 2005; Dwyer *et al.*, 2005, 2006a, b; Industry Commission, 1996; Madden, 2006; Victoria Auditor General, 2007). CGE modelling possesses the same types of advantages in respect of event assessment that it does in economic impact analysis generally. In other words, the same types of arguments advanced in Chapter 9 on behalf of using CGE models instead of I–O models also support its use in the special events area.

Except for some isolated sceptics, claims of very large economic impacts or benefits from events have tended to be uncritically accepted in the tourism literature. Best practice event assessment requires that the relevance of a number of issues be understood and be taken into account in the analysis of results. These issues are addressed below.

11.5 CHALLENGES TO BEST PRACTICE EVENT ASSESSMENT

Some important failures in event assessment include failure to correctly estimate 'new' expenditure; uncritical use of I–O multipliers to estimate the economic impacts of events; failure to use an appropriate model to estimate an event's economic impacts; the use of inappropriate multipliers; failure to recognise expenditure diversion; failure to recognise the relevance of the labour market; failure to recognise the relevance of the jurisdiction; failure to correctly treat construction expenditure; and failure to correctly account for taxes and subsidies. We now discuss each issue in turn.

11.5.1 FAILURE TO CORRECTLY ESTIMATE 'NEW' EVENT-RELATED EXPENDITURE

Multipliers enable the estimation of the additional income, sales or employment only if the expenditure stimulus comes from outside the region. Expenditure by residents is merely a transfer for the purposes of modelling the economic impacts since it does not result in additional outlays that would not have otherwise occurred should the consumer have remained at home. Event participation by local residents merely redistributes economic activity, possibly even from industries with higher multipliers and higher economic impact. Unfortunately, many studies of the economic impacts of special events, have failed to distinguish between money which is injected into the region from outside the area and money which is merely transferred. For economic impact assessment, it is only the injected expenditure (new money) that is relevant for income and job creation.

Unfortunately, in many studies of event impact assessment, the expenditure of 'time switchers' and 'casuals' has also been included. This exaggerates the expenditure associated with a special event and, regardless of the model used to estimate the multipliers, exaggerates the economic impacts of the event. The expenditure associated with an event also sometimes includes 'retained expenditure' in circumstances where this attribution is quite inappropriate. Thus an economic impact analysis of the Qantas Formula One Grand Prix 2005 held in Melbourne includes an estimate of 'retained expenditure' based on what sales could have been lost to the state of Victoria if the Grand Prix had been held instead in the city of Adelaide in the state of South Australia. This is despite the fact that the event had been shifted to Melbourne over 15 years earlier. Moreover, at $17.7 million, when added to the other estimated expenditure items, the retained expenditure estimate was a substantial 16.5% of the total net injected expenditure (NIEIR, 2005)

Another item that is often ignored in event impact assessment is the expenditure diversions that might occur. Many studies of special events fail to allow for reduced expenditure associated with potential (non event) visitors who would otherwise have visited the event location, but are deterred from their visit because they perceive the destination will, at the time of the event, be full, disrupted, congested or overpriced (perhaps all of these). In many cases the additional numbers of event visitors projected are simply added to existing visitor numbers even though the numbers in total would exceed the capacity of the location to meet visitor needs.

The earlier discussion noted that direct imports need to be deducted from the 'gross' new expenditure estimates. Studies sometimes fail to address the amount of 'injected' expenditure that immediately leaks out of the destination due to direct imports and which does not stay or circulate in the local economy. Much of the money spent by visitors to a region goes towards hotel rooms, rental cars, and restaurants, which typically are owned by national (or sometimes international) chains.

11.5.2 UNCRITICAL USE OF I–O MODELS TO ESTIMATE ECONOMIC IMPACTS OF EVENTS

The type of model employed in an impact assessment will determine the size of multipliers that underpin the estimates of changes in output, value added and employment resulting from the staging of a special event. These multipliers can be based on either an I–O model, or a CGE model.

The use of I–O modelling has meant that event impact assessments have often ignored crowding out effects. Many special events are staged in communities that are already popular tourist destinations. If hotels, restaurants and other attractions in a host city normally tend to be at or near capacity throughout the event period during, event-related expenditure may simply replace rather than add to regular visitor expenditure. In the absence of excess capacity, however, there can be no induced income generated in this way. Rather, there will be inflationary pressures on wages and prices stimulated by excess demand.

Adam Blake has expressed some concerns regarding some common assumptions underlying economic impact studies of Olympic Games (Blake, 2005: 20). Blake's concerns, which hold for any large special event, are highlighted in Box 11.1.

BOX 11.1 Issues neglected in studies of economic impacts of large events

- The common perception of the Olympic Games since 1984 (Los Angeles) of being commercial successes can be called into question when host cities' debts are taken into account.

- Since the costs of infrastructure projects are borne by the host city, there is an issue as to whether those infrastructure projects would have proceeded without the Olympic Games. If so, they bring no additional benefits to the host city, implying that the event diverts public investment from other worthwhile investment projects, such as health or education.

- Economic impact studies estimate indirect and induced effects but ignore the full costs of holding the Games, such as the time costs of public servants, security and policing costs, and the costs of transporting, accommodating and entertaining IOC officials and members of the international press.

- Assumptions that employment will increase without any wage or price effects are unrealistic. In particular, the common assumptions of I-O models that the additional economic activity occurs using previously unemployed resources is unrealistic for a 17-day event, a period which is generally considered to be too short a time period to expect employers to hire and train new employees.

- The distributional impact of the Games is often ignored. Real estate developers, hotel owners, broadcasters and the IOC benefit from the staging of the Games, but little is known as to who gains and who loses both within and outside the event location.

- Tax revenues are needed to finance the Games, which means that those required to pay higher tax rates or new taxes may lose out. In the UK, lottery funding is likely to be displaced from other 'good causes' and household expenditure is diverted away from other goods and services.

- Displacement effects are often ignored in economic impact assessments, particularly those relying on I-O techniques. Other economic activities are displaced as a consequence of the Games, as businesses that are positively affected by the Games are able to pay higher wages and take workers away from other economic activities.

- Tourists who would normally visit the host city during the Games period may be discouraged because of the perception of high prices and congestion caused by the hosting of the Games, and for the similar reasons, residents may leave the host city for the duration of the Games.

- In many cases, we find over optimistic pre-Games evaluations, whether of the numbers of visitors that are expected because of the Games, their average spending, an over optimistic assessment of the proportion of ticket sales purchased by non-residents, or because the construction impacts are exaggerated.

- Environmental costs of the Games are often underestimated. The most common types of environmental costs are congestion, local pollution (due to increased emissions from cars, buses, and other transport in city areas where emissions are already high) and global pollution, where the Games will increase the emission of greenhouse gases because of the increased use of air transport and other emission-intensive transport activities.

Source: Based on Blake (2005)

Actual economies comprise a complex pattern of feedback effects and resource constraints which are not captured by I–O analysis. We have discussed the advantages of CGE modelling of economic impacts of tourism in Chapter 9. CGE modelling also has substantial advantages over I–O modelling in event impact assessment. The main advantages in the context of event assessment are reproduced in Box 11.2.

BOX 11.2 Advantage of CGE models for event economic impact assessment

- The events sector will need to expand output to meet additional demand by employing additional land, labour, capital plant and equipment. CGE models can allow for the resource constraints on land, labour and capital that are generally present in an economy and that can limit changes in economic activity due to an event-related increase in the final demand for goods and services. The constraints are perhaps most evident, in the case of labour which has some skills component and may be in limited supply, for example, particular labour skills or workers for particular shifts or locations.
- CGE models include more general specifications of the behaviour of consumers, producers and investors, than those allowed for in I–O models, thus permitting specific models to be calibrated to actual conditions for a particular event in a particular economy.
- CGE models recognise that relative prices of land, labour and capital may change due to an event, causing businesses to change the composition of their inputs. When there are capacity constraints, the prices of

inputs and wages will increase in the face of an increase in demand. These price rises, including (for some destinations) any upward pressure on the exchange rate due to increased foreign expenditure associated with an event, will limit the extent of economic expansion associated with the event and may even lead to contractions in economic activity in some sectors.

- CGE models recognise the behaviour of the Government budget sector as relevant to the estimated economic impacts of a special event. For example, if additional infrastructure spending by government is required to support a special event, such as expenditure on stadia, roads and airport landing facilities, there will be a positive effect on spending but it must be financed. This may moderate the growth in private consumption associated with the event, leading to downward pressure on the output of consumption-oriented industries.

- CGE models can recognise that the net impact on economic activity within the state, in the rest of the economy, and the national economy will differ according to the source of the additional spending. An increase in spending as a result of interstate visitors to an event will not affect a country's exchange rate. However, an increase in spending as a result of additional visitors from abroad will, pushing it up, with adverse effects on other export- and import-competing industries. Thus, while I–O analysis relies only on the total of injected expenditure, regardless of its source, and thus is incapable of estimating the differential effects due to exchange rate movements, CGE models, which explicitly allow for the exchange market, will capture these effects. For many countries, this is an essential input to the assessment of large events.

- The assumptions of a CGE model can be varied and the sensitivity to them tested to assess the economic impacts of an event. These include assumptions about factor constraints, workings of the labour market, changes in real wage rates and prices, and government taxing and spending policies. The fact that CGE simulations can be undertaken using different assumptions, the realism of which can be discussed and debated, provides a transparency to the event assessment process that rarely exists in I–O modelling. This can provide very useful information in predicting the economic impacts of particular types of events in different macroeconomic contexts.

Shaffer *et al.* (2003) have criticised what they argue to be the exaggerated projections of economic impacts of the Vancouver 2010 Winter Olympics estimated by government commissioned consultants. The I–O model used assumed no capacity constraints and consequently no impact on wages or prices.

Shaffer *et al.* make two main types of responses to the government commissioned economic impact study.

First, they point out how uncertain the economic effects are when the event destination already has high demand. Unemployment rates in the cities of Whistler and Vancouver are relatively low compared to other areas in the Province of British Columbia (BC), and it is unlikely that a large percentage of the local workers hired as a result of the Games would otherwise be unemployed or underemployed. The more likely effect will be that the Olympic Games will lead to wage increases that will attract local workers from other activities or possibly unemployed and underemployed people from other regions within BC and from elsewhere in Canada. Thus, even if unemployment exists in a host region, an event will not reduce unemployment by much because labour will flow from other states to take up the jobs.

Second, Whistler tourism facilities are not under-utilised in peak periods. Expanding capacity for a relatively short impact period, however, is not generally financially worthwhile. Unless capacity was to expand to meet the increased demand for goods and service, prices would likely rise given the limited supply. Therefore, some increase in prices (including, e.g. reductions or the elimination of promotional rates) is likely to occur.

As this example makes clear, many of the failures of 'good practice' event assessment and the confusions of many analysts are due to their thinking within the restrictive box of I–O modelling. However, it is completely unrealistic to use models to estimate the economic impacts of events which assume no capacity constraints and consequently no impact of the event on wages or prices. The assumption of constant prices alone makes these models unsuitable for event assessment, particularly for larger-scale events.

11.5.3 UNCRITICAL USE OF SALES (OUTPUT AND TRANSACTIONS) MULTIPLIERS

Since multipliers are often employed to estimate the economic impacts of a special event, there has been a tendency for consultants to use those multipliers which cast special events in the most favourable light. Small multipliers may not be acceptable to stakeholders in both the public and private sectors who wish to use the economic analysis to underpin proposals for event funding support. Thus, we find that sales multipliers based on I–O modelling have often been used to estimate the economic impacts of events. These provide a measure of the effects of an exogenous change in final demand on the sales output of industries in the economy. However, sales and output multipliers both suffer from double counting (the increased output of one industry can be used as an input into another industry and so can be counted more than once). Since they involve the multiple counting of economic activity at the various stages of production of a final good or service, sales multipliers have limited practical value for policy making. Not surprisingly, they have often been employed by event organisers interested in claiming the maximum economic contribution possible from the staging of an event (Crompton, 2006). As we argued in

Chapter 8, the preferred multipliers are value added and income multipliers, which avoid the multiple counting of the indirect effects.

11.5.4 RELEVANCE OF THE LABOUR MARKET

The workings of the labour market are particularly relevant to event economic impact assessment. Particular caution needs to be exercised in use of employment multipliers in event impact assessment, since they tend to exaggerate the amount of employment generated by an event. In many firms, staffing levels may be relatively insensitive to changes in turnover, while other firms may better utilise their current staff (for example, provision of overtime, weekend work). Volunteers provide services for many events. The relatively short duration of events means that any employment effects, if they occur at all, may be small and are likely to be brief.

If the demand for labour increases and there is unemployment in the economy, the real wage stays constant, unemployment will be reduced and economic activity will increase significantly. On the contrary, if the response to an increase in demand for labour is a wage increase (which can take place even though there is considerable unemployment), the impact on unemployment will be much less, as will be the impact on overall economic activity.

What situation prevails depends importantly on whether (1) there exists a separate local or regional labour market, or else a wider national labour market, and (2) whether there is unemployment in the event region.

(1) In an integrated national economy, as a consequence of an event, labour will flow to the region that is experiencing increased demand for resources. If a national labour market exists, labour will flow from other states to meet this demand. Interstate differences in wages and in unemployment rates will be eliminated. Thus, if resource markets are highly integrated, the event will lead to greater impact on economic activity in the host state or region than if they are not.

(2) On the other hand, if a region operates as a moderately separate economy the economic impact of an event taking place within its borders will be smaller than if the state is part of a seamlessly integrated national economy. With statewide labour markets, an increase in labour demand that comes about because of an event will lead to some combination of reduction in unemployment within the state and increase in wage rates in the state. The increased prices and wages choke off some of the potential increase in economic activity.

It is an empirical matter as to how well integrated are the state or regional labour markets in a particular country. The degree of integration, particularly in the short run, will depend on how far separated the states are and on cultural factors such as the willingness of workers to move out of their home state to seek employment. The long-term persistence of regional unemployment in many industrial countries of Europe and in Australia suggests that labour markets are often far from perfectly integrated.

11.5.5 RELEVANCE OF THE JURISDICTION

The role of government has been largely neglected in special event assessment. To make informed decisions about events policy, governments may need to know the answers to questions such as: how much will the event add to economic activity and jobs after accounting for inter-industry effects? To what extent do the impacts and benefits of the event in the host region come at a cost to other regions?

A local council might undertake an economic impact study to determine whether to support a festival in the town. If the perspective of the local government is taken, it is only the local effects of the event that are relevant.

A state or federal government contemplating financial support for an event will be interested not just in the impact in the local area, but also the impacts on the state and/or nation. Local impact studies will not provide public sector decision-makers with sufficient guidance as to whether they should support local events financially or otherwise, since they will also need to know the overall state-wide impacts. An event may increase economic activity substantially within a local area but its net impact on the economic activity within the state will normally be much less, and conceivably negative. The impact on national output will be even less again. Blake's results for the London Olympics show that while London gains from the 2012 Olympics it implies reduced Gross Domestic Product (GDP) and employment for the rest of the UK.

For these reasons, the perspectives on an event from the local, state and national levels will be quite different. An event may be highly attractive to a rural city, though only of marginal or negative benefit to a state. Even so, a state or national government may be prepared to subsidise the event, even though it is basically shifting, rather than creating, economic activity and jobs. This could be so if a region is depressed, and the central government wishes to provide a stimulus for the local economy. For this to be worthwhile, the event must be assessed in comparison with other forms of stimulus – there may be ways in which the same funds could generate a greater impact on local economic activity, or a similar impact without as large a negative impact on other parts of the economy. If so, it would be more effective to subsidise these alternatives rather than the event. Such decisions should be taken in full awareness of who will be the winners and losers within the state, both in regional and industry terms. The losers might well be other depressed regions, or industries, within the wider economy.

11.5.6 TREATMENT OF CONSTRUCTION EXPENDITURE

Special events, particularly those scheduled for a dedicated venue, often generate investment in direct infrastructure (e.g. facilities for the event) and indirect infrastructure (e.g. roadways, increased sewage facilities). Following the event, expenditure may be required to re-adapt or to dismantle facilities. Additional investment in tourism/recreation infrastructure can increase the attractions available in an area for use by locals as well as visitors. The Sydney Olympics generated around A\$5 billion worth of stadia and sporting infrastructure, as well as investment in road, rail and transport interchange systems, all of which benefit residents of, and visitors to, Sydney into the future. The main stadium for the Sydney 2000 Olympics has subsequently hosted large crowds at football matches of various codes, including the Rugby World Cup in 2003 but still does not return a financial profit. Similarly, many of the stadia constructed for the Athens Olympics continue to lie in a disused state years after the event.

Facility construction associated with events can be a source of economic and urban development, and bid documents for cities wishing to host an Olympic Games emphasise this. While the investment generated by events, privately or publicly sourced, has multiplier effects on income, value added and employment, so also would alternative forms of investment that it replaces. For purposes of assessing the economic impacts of special events, it is only investment that would not have been generated except for the special event, and which represents the injection of 'new money' into the destination, that is relevant. If the construction would have proceeded with or without the event, then it does not count as associated with the event and thus is not counted in economic impact assessment. The question must be asked: was the money redirected from another project (public capital switching), and, if so, was that project within the impact area or outside? If a central government reallocated funds originally earmarked for hospital construction in one region to build an event facility in another, this switching would be a net gain to the second region and a net loss to the first. The issues here are not straightforward since they involve hypothetical issues of what would have occurred had the particular type of investment not taken place.

In the case of public sector investment, taxation revenue used to fund facilities construction reduces the net disposable income of residents and hence their consumption of goods and services and thus does not represent a net gain of expenditure within the destination. Funding may well have been allocated to other infrastructure projects had it not been allocated to support an event. In this case, the expenditure can be regarded as 'switched' from one type of investment to another. An important exception to this is where the investment expenditure is based on a special grant from an external source, for example, a federal government grant to a State, or an internationally sourced grant to a developing country for a specific purpose. In the case of new investment from the private sector, there are two alternatives – no new investment would have been undertaken, or else it would have been investment of another type. Only in the first case will the investment be considered to have economic impacts resulting from the injection of new money into the destination. For the second case, the issue arises as to the opportunity cost of the investment alternative foregone.

Researchers and consultants, using I–O modelling to generate event impact multipliers, sometimes mistakenly regard construction expenditures as always having a positive effect on the economy. However, the economic resources required to stage the event are correctly modelled as a cost (Blake, 2005; Madden, 2006). From a national or state government perspective, investment expenditure on event facilities must be funded by a reduction in some other component of domestic demand (domestic savings) or an increase in external liabilities (foreign savings). CGE models require income–expenditure conditions to be met, implying that the construction spending must be paid for. Since government spending on construction is usually financed from taxation, the net effect of the construction projects may be negative. Researchers have examined the relationship between building new facilities and economic growth in urban areas. Matheson (2002) points out that independent work on the economic impact of stadia and arenas has found that, taking opportunity costs into account, there is no statistically significant positive correlation between sports facility construction and economic development.

As Blake (2005) has indicated, a dynamic CGE model that takes into account the time dimension should also include the effects of the availability of infrastructure following the event. This is to recognise that capital stocks should increase in the relevant industries, with income from this infrastructure accruing to whoever owns the capital (for example, the government that financed the construction), which might lease out the built infrastructure or receive income from its sale. If the value of constructed capital exactly meets the construction costs, there may be an initial net zero effect on GDP. As Blake (2005) emphasises, certain distortions may be introduced into the economy by the holding of the event since investors would not have chosen the same industry in which to put their investments; construction costs may be increased during the construction phase because of the increased demand for construction services; and the value of the capital may fall because of increased supply of capital in the relevant sector. For these reasons, the net effects of construction projects are therefore likely to be small, and also negative (Blake, 2005: 13).

11.5.7 TREATMENT OF TAXES

The hosting of a special event will have implications for government revenues and outlays. Possible revenue sources for the state or national government include taxes or fees imposed on visitor expenditure, taxes on business expenditure; income taxes; and ticket sales on state-owned public transport and admission fees to publically owned attractions.

Changes in the patterns of expenditure brought about by an event give rise to increases and decreases in tax revenues from different sectors because different aspects of economic activity are taxed differently. While tourism-related industries may gain from the special event, other industries may experience reduced output and sales revenues and thus pay less taxation. The net effect on government tax revenue cannot be known prior to the modelling exercise. Furthermore, changes in tax revenues lead to changes in government spending and tax rates that in turn influence economic activity. I–O models cannot be used to estimate the net effects of the event on tax revenue since they do not estimate the negative impacts on expenditure and activity. These effects are captured in CGE models. CGE models also pose the question of what the government does if increased economic activity leads to increased tax receipts. The government could add the tax receipts to its budget surplus (or subtract them from its deficit), or it could increase spending or lower taxes. The different options will have different effects on economic activity.

11.5.8 EVENT SUBSIDIES

Events often are subsidised by governments. In addition to direct subsidisation, including tax concessions, this can take various indirect forms, for example, public expenditure on construction of facilities and supporting infrastructure such as road works, provision of additional police, ambulance officers and so on. These subsidies must be financed from government revenue or reductions in other government spending, with consequent effects on economic activity.

When the event stimulates economic activity, it generates an increase in tax receipts. In a federal system, some of these will accrue to the host-region government and some to the national government. When the event increases economic activity, the net cost to the government will be less than the subsidy to the event. Indeed, it is possible that an event that receives only a limited subsidy relative to the revenue effects could be revenue positive for the government. Where there is a net cost to the government, however, this cost must be funded. The government has several funding options. It could cut expenditure in other areas, leading to reduced economic activity. Alternatively, it may increase taxes. For example, it might raise taxes on doing business in the destination. This could have a significant negative impact on economic activity in the region because it would make the region less competitive and economic activity would shift to other regions.

Whichever way subsidies are funded, they can be incorporated into a CGE model, and the negative impacts on the host region from expenditure cuts or tax increases can be estimated. These will reduce the overall impact of the event on economic activity. It is possible that the overall net impact on economic activity of an event that relies very heavily on subsidies could be negative. Mules and Faulkner (1996) point out that, as most large sporting events run at a loss with taxpayer revenues failing to cover taxpayer contributions, it difficult to avoid the conclusion that the taxpayer is generally the loser in hosting major sporting events.

Using a CGE model, the researcher can set up model simulations, in which governments neutralise the effects of the event on their own budgetary positions, and, in the case of a national government, on the country's external debt. As Blake (2005) notes, this feature is particularly important in a weighing up negative fiscal effects in relation to an estimated stimulus to economic activity. As we shall discuss in more detail in Chapter 15, welfare losses caused by distortionary taxation can be very large, both on average and at the margin.

The issues highlighted above are unfortunately often ignored in event assessment. This indicates that considerable caution must be employed before the results of any economic impact assessment of an event may be accepted. The issues addressed certainly need to be better understood by the research community, but importantly they need to be better understood by industry stakeholders since it is their hired consultants who often flaunt 'best practice' in their objective to provide the client with large numbers and optimistic economic impact assessments of events. A recent example of a government commissioned study which failed to appreciate the abovementioned issues is the projected economic impacts of the Vancouver 2010 Winter Olympic Games. The inaccurate economic analysis did not of course prevent industry stakeholders from lauding the study as 'confirming' the substantial expected economic contribution of the event to the economies of Canada and BC (see Shaffer *et al.*, 2003).

11.6 ESTIMATING THE ECONOMIC IMPACTS OF EVENTS USING CGE MODELS

Adam Blake has used a dynamic CGE model of the UK and London economies to forecast the economic impacts of the London 2012 Olympics (Blake, 2005). The results of Blake's study indicate that a mega event, even of the size of the summer Olympics, is unlikely to provide any substantial boost to either the national or host-region economy.

Box 11.3 summarises some of the main findings.

BOX 11.3 CGE analysis of economic impacts of London Olympics 2012

Adam Blake divides the event impacts of the London Olympics 2012 into three categories: pre-Games, during-Games and post-Games.

Pre-Games impact
The pre-Games impact includes the impacts of the construction phase of the project, other pre-Games costs, as well as increases in visitor arrivals that occur because of London's increased profile in the run-up to staging the Games.

During-Games impact
The during-Games impact relates to revenues from staging the Games; the impact of visitors during the Games; and its costs of operation.

Post-Games impact

The impact of the Olympics after the Games is often referred to as the 'Legacy' effect. This includes a higher profile of London and the consequent increased future visitation to London because of this profile. In addition, the stadia and transport infrastructure developed for the Games will provide experiences to residents for many years after the Games, and the 'legacy' effect of these infrastructural improvements should be included.

Blake emphasises that the timescales of the economic impacts generate very different effects in the pre-, during- and post- Games periods. He notes that much of the literature has not identified these effects separately. Static (one period) models can only treat the three effects separately at best, although the literature studies almost all look at a single period of impact, with no attempt to sum the effects. He therefore employs a dynamic CGE model to take account of the time element by including all three periods in a single modelling process, with effects calculated for individual years and summed (and discounted) to estimate the Present Value of hosting the Games.

The modeling for this study was undertaken at three levels – the UK, London, and for five sub-regions within London.

Blake undertakes a systematic sensitivity analysis of the effects of the Games around a central case. The sensitivity analysis indicates that there is a great deal of uncertainty about just what a London 2012 Olympics would mean for the economy.

The main findings, as set out in Table 11.2, are that the London 2012 Olympics will have an overall positive effect on the UK and London economies, with an increase in GDP between 2005–2016 of £1,936 million and an additional 8,164 full-time equivalent jobs created for the UK. The impacts are concentrated in 2012 (£1,067 million GDP and 3,261 FTE jobs) and in the post-Games period 2013–2016 (£622 million GDP and 1,948 additional FTE jobs). These figures represent the difference in GDP and employment between the 'without Games' and the 'with Games' scenarios. In London, there will be a larger impact on GDP, with £925 million extra GDP in the Games year, £3,362 million in the years leading up to the Games and £1,613 million after the Games.

Blake takes the Equivalent Variation (the nominal income the consumer needs at one set of prices in order to be as well off at an alternative set of prices) as a measure of economic welfare. He employs this as a monetary measure of the welfare effects of different policy scenarios. The value of all the future changes attributable to the hosting of the Games in 2012 is £736 million. This is the change in welfare,

Table 11.2 Projected impacts of the London 2012 Olympics

	UK		London	
	£million or no. of jobs	%	£million or no. of jobs	%
Change in welfare (equivalent variation)	736	0.004	4,003	0.193
Discounted value of all future GDP	1,559	0.006	5,647	0.135
GDP 2005–2011	248	0.002	3,362	0.147
GDP 2012	1,067	0.066	925	0.258
GDP 2013–2016	622	0.009	1,613	0.106
Total GDP change 2005–2016	1,936	0.010	5,900	0.143
FTE Jobs 2005–2011	2,955	0.002	25,824	0.104
FTE Jobs 2012	3,261	0.015	3,724	0.105
FTE Jobs 2013–2016	1,948	0.002	9,327	0.066
FTE Jobs Total	8,164	0.002	38,875	0.092

measured in terms of the equivalent amount of money that could be given to the UK in 2005 that would have the same benefit as hosting the Games. The change in welfare for London is significantly larger, at £4,003 million.

While the overall impacts on GDP and employment in the UK are positive, the simulations reveal that there is a loss of GDP and employment in the areas outside London. Reasons for this include: spending in London by UK residents from outside London visiting the Games; movement of workers, whether migrants, commuter or temporary migrants, into London because of higher wages in the capital; and the provision of Lottery funding, which in effect transfers money to London.

The study also shows that the impact of the Games will vary significantly across different sectors of the UK economy. Sectors that expand include construction, passenger land transport, business services, hotels and restaurants. Sectors that are not directly related to the Games may contract in size indirectly as a result of hosting the Games. These include manufacturing, agriculture, fishing and other services. However, these results are relative to the 'No Games' scenario in which a substantial amount of growth takes place in all sectors of the economy. Thus, while no sector is predicted to contract in the time span modeled, some will grow less because of the impact of hosting the Olympics.

The simulations indicate that any changes to the UK economy associated with the Olympics 2012 will be comparatively small. Even in the Olympic year, the total economy-wide effect for the UK is only 0.066% of total UK GDP at 2004 prices.

Source: Blake, A. (2005) 'The Economic Impact of the London 2012 Olympics', Research Report 2005/5, Christel DeHaan Tourism and Travel Research Institute, Nottingham University

11.6.1   DO EVENT SIZE AND LOCATION MATTER?

It is not the size of the event *per se* that determines the appropriate model for analysing the impacts. Strictly, any size event will have interactive effects that must be accounted for. Small changes can be analysed using CGE analysis just as readily and correctly as large changes. With a large event, such as the Olympics, the negative impacts on other parts of the regional and national economies may be obvious – accommodation prices are bid up, as is the price of skilled labour. When the event is small these effects still exist, though they are not so obvious. The negative impacts on economic activity elsewhere will be small, though they still will be significant relative to the positive effects of the event on activity, and thus, it is necessary to take them into account. The degree of accuracy required in the assessment may not of course always warrant the undertaking of a CGE analysis and this is a judgement for the analyst to make. But whatever the approach adopted the underlying assumptions must be clearly stated.

Does the choice of model depend on the location of the event? It might be claimed that CGE analysis is inappropriate to evaluate small, local events, and that I–O analysis is sufficient for this purpose. To explore this claim, we need to distinguish between an event held in a regional or remote area and one held in an urban area.

Regional and remote events

Some researchers have claimed that there is a case for using I–O models to estimate local impacts of events in areas that are separate from the main centre of the economy (for example, rural towns and cities). CGE models are rarely available at this level of detail, but, more to the point, they claim that the assumption which I–O analysis makes – that all inputs are in elastic supply to the area – may be approximately met (Burgan & Mules, 2000; Mules, 1999).

It is true that that, since an event in a rural location will draw many of its required resources (labour, services, goods) from outside the area, resource constraints may not overly restrict the expansion of economic activity. The event will draw on resources from the rest of the region and nation and thus economic activity, and jobs, will rise, temporarily, in the local area. While general equilibrium effects will still exist, it is sometimes claimed that the assumptions of free supply of inputs, made by I–O analysis, may be approximated. At least two qualifications must be made to this view, however.

First, even in this context, the assumptions of I–O analysis may not be met – some key inputs cannot be expanded readily if at all. In a relatively remote local area, such as a rural town, the displacement effects are likely to be greater than in the main centre of economic activity. Consider accommodation: an event will increase accommodation demand, but the local accommodation supply may be tightly constrained. With the increased demand associated with the event, prices will increase, and other potential visitors may go elsewhere. I–O analysis will not pick up these effects and will overestimate the size of the economic impact unless the resource constraints are allowed for by making downward adjustments to the estimated impacts.

Second, while economic activity within the area may increase, some of this will have only a peripheral impact on the local economy. During the event, labour and services from outside the region will be hired in. This will count as increased economic activity within the area, though it will not have any real impact on it, since the incomes earned will be mainly spent outside it (e.g. VIP leakages as noted above).

Urban events

The concept of a 'local event' has a clear meaning if an event is taking place in a rural city, some distance from the capital city or main centre of economic activity. Here there is a distinct local economy. However, when the area under consideration is a suburb of the main city, or close to the main city, there is really no 'local' economy. Suburbs of large cities do not have their own local economies, separate from the urban, and indeed, state economy. Thus, if only the local effects were of interest, it may suffice to use the simpler I–O approach (taking note of the above considerations). However, for an event in a large city, or in a supra-metropolitan region like the Costa del Sol or Côte d'Azur, there are likely to be feedback effects on a significant scale within the local economy which require CGE analysis. I–O analysis is not appropriate to estimate the local effects of an event which takes place within a major centre of economic activity, such as a large city. If the event is held in a major centre of activity, the resource constraints will be critical.

11.6.2 A PRACTICAL SOLUTION: FOCUS ON INSCOPE EXPENDITURE

It may not always be practical to employ a CGE model. CGE models are not generally available for regions below state level. In some event evaluations, the budget available to undertake the assessment may not be sufficient to cover the cost of constructing or purchasing a CGE model. Despite this, however, there is increasingly the expectation that some form of economic assessment should be undertaken. On the other hand, as has been noted, there has been substantial abuse of multipliers in the past that has led to the gross overstatement of economic impact. As a practical response to the situation where economic models are unavailable, it has been recommended that *direct inscope expenditure* be used as the basis to measure economic performance of the event to the host region (Jago & Dwyer, 2006). In similar vein Porter (1999) and Matheson and Baade (2003a, b) employ the concept of taxable sales as a proxy for economic impacts. While this approach does not measure the actual economic impact of the event it has some advantages:

- Direct inscope expenditure measures the level of new funds that are attracted to the region as a result of the event, and which provide the injection for subsequent flow-on impacts in the local economy.
- Direct inscope expenditure can be used to compare quite simply the economic performance of one event with another and thus underpin government decisions as to which events to support as higher priorities.
- A further benefit of this approach is that economic impact analysis can be done subsequently if required, given that a direct inscope expenditure figure is the fundamental starting point for any economic impact study irrespective of which economic impact model is used.
- As long as it is understood to be *indicative* of the economic significance of the event, the new or inscope expenditure estimate can be a very informative key performance measure.

Destination managers allocate budgets to support the development of special events. Once a decision is made to provide a pool of funds to the event sector, the key issue is then to decide which particular events to support and to what level. This is where direct inscope expenditure can be used to compare quite simply the economic performance of one event with another and thus underpin government decisions as to which events to support as higher priorities. When the economic impacts of events are compared, it is often more a function of a comparison between the workings of the host economies rather than of the events themselves. Using direct inscope expenditure as the basis to compare events overcomes this problem.

11.7 CBA OF EVENTS

Although the focus of this chapter thus far has been on the economic evaluation of events, the importance of assessing the more holistic impacts of events rather than simply relying on economic dimensions should be emphasised.

Some important potential effects of events that are often not captured in standard economic impact analysis are set out in Box 11.4.

BOX 11.4 Wider effects of events

Wider economic effects

Positive

- increased tourism flows associated with event-related promotion and publicity – an event may enhance the image of an area with longer-term positive effects on tourism visitation expenditure and tourism investment.
- The hosting of events can lead to growth of existing businesses, the establishment of new ones and the development of a more skilled workforce.
- Stimulation of business activity within and between nations helps forge stronger business links and additional trade and business development between firms, providing opportunities to promote both the national interest and international cooperation.
- The hosting of successful events can be associated with increased business confidence (the business counterpart to increased civic pride), inducing greater business activity including increased business investment, and induced construction and development expenditure.
- The hosting of special events can provide valuable national and international exposure for a host destination among the business, scientific and educational communities, including development of new export markets.
- The global marketing opportunity created by major events can be instrumental in attracting inward investment. Successful events can be effective marketing tools for attracting new business and visitors to an area, offering businesses an effective means of promoting their products and services to a targeted audience.
- Increased convention business is often generated by major events.
- Businesses and Government use corporate entertainment facilities at events that can serve as networking opportunities to result in new sales/trade and new investment.

Negative

- Destination image and reputation can be harmed if event-related facilities and services are regarded as inadequate.
- The holding of a special event may cause some residents of a destination to travel out of the area for all or part of its duration (a 'repulsion effect' or 'resident exodus'). The event destination thus suffers a loss of sales revenue which would otherwise have accrued to local businesses.
- The perception that events cause the destination to be crowded, with inflated prices, may deter potential visitors either during or after the event.
- A common legacy of many past events worldwide has been a huge debt and much under-utilised infrastructure. Operating losses subsequently incurred by facilities constructed for a specific event, combined with interest repayments on debt, are economic costs over the longer run. To the extent that these losses are met from tax revenues, residents subsidise the events sector.

Social and environmental effects

Positive

- For many communities, playing host to a special event instils a sense of pride in their city or region. Residents often feel a sense of excitement about an event held locally.
- An important benefit of staging an event might involve some form of sports, artistic or cultural development impact which could encourage more people to take up the activity showcased.
- The benefits of an event may also include such emergent values as increased community interest in the issues comprising the event 'theme'.
- Events provide opportunities for access to new technology and exchange of ideas, help establish and maintain valuable business and professional contacts, and are a source of continuing education and other favourable socio-cultural impacts.
- Events can be used as a demonstration of good environmental practice such as recycling and site clean-up. They can also play an important role in helping to educate attendees of the importance of environmental protection.

Negative

- An event may disrupt resident lifestyles. Examples include: traffic congestion, road accidents, crime, litter, noise, crowds, property damage, environmental degradation, police and fire protection, and vandalism.

- Events are associated with increased energy consumption and water use, and waste generation, which can put strain on the limited resources of some locations.
- Increasingly, events are also recognised to be associated with a relatively large carbon footprint resulting in substantial emissions of greenhouse gases.

Once these wider effects of events are acknowledged, we can appreciate why estimation of the economic impacts of events is only part of the evaluation story. For government assistance to be provided, it is necessary that the cost of these funds be compared to the wider costs and benefits from the event. Clearly, there are many potential effects of events that are often not accounted for in a standard economic impact analysis. In order for the government to be more comprehensively apprised, event assessments need to be broadened to take, where practicable, a more comprehensive approach embracing not only economic but also social and environmental factors.

The standard economic method of estimation of net economic benefits of these types of effects is CBA a topic that was discussed in Chapter 10.

11.7.1 THE ECONOMIC IMPACTS OF AN EVENT ARE NOT ITS 'BENEFITS'

Very often in academic publications and in the media, the impacts of an event (on GDP or employment) are quoted as the 'benefits' of the event to the destination. This loose talk can give a very misleading impression about the value of an event to the destination. In Chapter 6, we argued that the economic impacts of an event are not the same thing as the economic benefits which arise. Economic impact studies can only estimate the effect on economic variables such as GDP, employment and so on. The impact on GDP is a *gross* measure of the change in value of output as a result of an event. This addition to output normally requires additional inputs, of land, labour and capital, to enable it to be produced. As argued in Chapter 6, these inputs have a cost, and this cost must be deducted from the change in value of gross output if a measure of the net economic gain is to be made.

With information about the net economic benefits from the event, the government or agency is in a position to make an informed decision about the event. If the net benefits are positive, it can give its approval to the event, if that is required. If benefits exceed costs, it can judge how much subsidy would be justifiable, if the event will only go ahead with a subsidy or with tax concessions. In CBA, 'value' or 'benefit' is measured by willingness to pay – what people are willing to pay (or give up) to get what a project provides. Economic costs are measured by 'opportunity cost' – what people or a society give up by investing capital and employing workers in one project or activity as opposed to any other.

The relevant question is: what are the implications to a region of holding an event as compared to what could be expected without it and what costs and benefits do they entail? A prerequisite for this is an understanding of the main types of effects that must be valued.

The CBA framework discussed in Chapter 10 can be applied in a straightforward manner to special events. In this context, CBA attempts to incorporate all of the costs incurred and the benefits received by the community as a result of the holding of an event. If the benefits exceed costs, there is a positive net social benefit and the event should be supported. Conversely, if costs exceed benefits, there is a negative net social benefit and the event should be modified or not supported. The main problem, of course, involves identifying and valuing the event associated costs and benefits as comprehensively as is feasible.

While economic impact assessments of events emphasise the injected expenditure associated with events as the basis for further analysis, a CBA recognises that the consumer surpluses of residents will be important to event evaluation. As indicated above, the expenditures of residents is regarded as transferred expenditure for economic impact assessment purposes, but the consumer surpluses they receive due to the holding of the event is a primary component of benefit assessment in a CBA of the event.

On the basis of a CBA, it is possible for the decision maker to make a judgement of whether the economic benefits of the event are greater than the costs, and to also judge whether the event would represent the best use of the funds, when funds are limited and alternative calls on funds exist.

11.7.2 CBA OF SPECIAL EVENTS: THREE CASE STUDIES

To illustrate the role that CBA can play in event evaluation, we present three Case Studies.

11.7.2.1 Case Study 1 V8 Car Race

The major costs and benefits identified in the V8 Car Race study are displayed in Box 11.5.

BOX 11.5 CBA of a V8 car race event

The ACT Auditor General conducted a CBA of the V8 Car Races held in Canberra (ACT Auditor General 2002). The relevant cost and benefit items are summarised thus:

- *Net direct financial costs*. The net direct financial cost is the sum of the expenses (current and capital) met by CTEC, less revenue received by Capital Tourism Event Corporation (CTEC) from sources other than Government. The Government subsidy to CTEC is funded by taxpayers and thus is not revenue generated by the event. The (current) costs of conducting the races are opportunity

---

costs – what has been paid to attract resources away from their next best alternative use. Capital costs are treated as expenses in the year in which they are incurred. The residual value of the capital stock at the end of the project is counted as a benefit.

• *Revenues*. The price consumers pay for a good reflects their marginal willingness to pay. Therefore, ticket revenue received by CTEC reflects the value of the race to paying spectators. The Goods and Services tax (GST) revenue raised on ticket sales is not included as a benefit because it accrues to the Federal Government.

• *Other direct and indirect net benefits*. Benefits are generated from (i) 'new' tourist expenditure (ii), consumer surplus, and (iii) intangibles such as civic pride and publicity value.

i) 'New' tourist expenditure. A CBA estimates the benefits to the destination from additional visitor spending and not just the gross expenditure of visitors. The actual benefit from a dollar of visitor spending is difficult to determine. It has been estimated that, in the ACT, a dollar of interstate visitor spending translates into an increase of 71 cents in GSP. This represents the benefit of the additional dollar spending only if it is assumed that the resources used to produce the goods and services purchased have no alternative use. Since this is unrealistic, the 71-cent estimate is an upper bound to the benefits accrued per dollar of additional visitor spending.

ii) Consumer surplus. Consumer surplus measures the gain to local residents who attend the event. It is the difference between the amount residents would be willing to pay for a ticket and what they actually pay. A consumer survey was undertaken to estimate the price responsiveness of demand and to construct a simple linear demand curve and consumer surplus measure. With many events, what patrons are willing to pay to attend the event exceeds what they are required to pay to attend: there is a net gain to the patrons from attending the event. In short, the monetary value of the benefits exceeds the revenues that the organisers are able to collect from the patrons, even with quite sophisticated pricing structures. This will be especially so when prices are held down intentionally to enable a wide cross-section of the community to attend, not just the well off. When tickets are in short supply and are rationed, this indicates that the benefits to patrons exceed the revenues collected from them by some margin.

iii) Intangible Benefits. The two main intangible benefits for the car race are considered to be publicity for the destination (ACT), and enhanced civic pride in their city by the community.

Publicity. Media coverage of the race may result in a general increase in tourism in the future. Additional tourism increases economic activity, and this can lead to additional economic benefits. Given the difficulty of quantifying this, the Audit estimated how many tourists would need to be attracted to justify the net cost of the race (that is, the financial cost less direct and indirect benefits). Several estimates were made, based on different assumptions regarding the additional tourism and benefits to the local community resulting from the additional expenditure. It was concluded that large numbers of future tourists additional to those who come for the race must be attracted for the race to break-even on economic grounds. As a result of raising the profile of a city or region, special events may generate tourism flows for some years on. These effects are difficult to measure.

Civic pride. This is sometimes referred to as 'psychic income'. For many communities, playing host to a special event instils a sense of pride in their city or region. Residents often feel a sense of excitement about an event held locally. Home hosting opportunities, providing social and cross cultural interaction, are often explored. The Audit considered that that a race car event was unlikely to enhance civic pride or provide 'warm glow' benefits to all residents. Indeed, many residents oppose such events on various grounds. The conclusion was that the net overall effect on civic pride is likely to be very small and will not outweigh the costs of the race to the ACT resident community.

iv) Intangible costs. The main intangible costs comprise road congestion and noise costs.

Road congestion. Estimation of the time lost due to road works to set up the V8 Supercar race circuit requires information on the extent of traffic delays, the number of people affected, the duration of the disruption. To estimate the costs of road congestion, the cost of travellers' time must also be imputed, together with an estimation of the extra running costs of cars and additional pollution while in traffic jams. The Audit concluded that such costs were small compared to the direct expenses associated with the event.

Noise. Estimating the cost of additional noise nuisance generated by the event is also difficult. The cost of noise can be estimated from how much people are willing to pay to avoid it and economic techniques are available to estimate this. The Audit concluded that noise cost associated with the race is likely to be small. The standard economic method of valuing impacts such as noise effects or crowding is to determine the willingness to pay of the people to avoid them. Time lost due to *congestion* can be estimated and priced at average wage rates. The increased incidence of *crime* associated with an event can be estimated from statistics for previous events, as can *property damage* and *vandalism*. Costs of cleanups of *litter* can also be estimated.

Other costs are also difficult to estimate. These would include the value of time of CTEC and other public service staff who work on the project but not full time. Also omitted are the additional costs generated by taxes to meet the financial cots of the race. These include administrative costs incurred by government in assessing and collecting the taxes and compliance costs incurred by taxpayers. As the Audit notes, taxes impose economic costs, or 'excess burden' because the induce individuals to consume a less desirable bundle of goods and services than they otherwise would purchase. The more the tax changes behaviour, the greater the excess burden.

With this information, it is possible for the decision-maker to judge whether the economic benefits of the event are greater than the costs, and to judge whether the event would represent the best use of the funds when funds are limited and alternatives exist. As a result of the CBA, the ACT Auditor General concluded that the V8 supercar races created net costs for the ACT in both 2000 and 2001. This was despite the estimation of positive economic impacts on the region using traditional I-O analysis.

Source: ACT Auditor General (2002) *ACT Auditor General's Office Performance Audit Report V8 Car Races in Canberra – Costs and Benefits*, Canberra, ACT

11.7.2.2 Case Study 2 Winter Olympics Vancouver 2010

In the province of BC, Canada, which hosted the Vancouver 2010 Winter Olympics, a 'multiple account evaluation' framework is used to evaluate public projects. Multiple account evaluation frameworks attempt to capture all of the factors that should be considered in a social benefit-cost analysis. The results are presented in several distinct evaluation accounts, to indicate clearly the different types of consequences and trade-offs an investment or project can have. These accounts are Government financial account, Resident 'consumer' account, Environmental account, Economic development account and Social account. In their *ex ante* study of the main costs and benefits associated with the Olympic Games, Shaffer *et al.* (2003) used this framework to present the main items of relevance. The results are presented in Box 11.6. Although it does not comprise a formal CBA, the discussion is very useful to a better understanding of the types of costs and benefits relevant to event evaluation. This section relies heavily on the study by Shaffer *et al.* (2003) which is instructive for the framework it provides for purposes of a CBA of a major event.

BOX 11.6 Costs and benefits of Vancouver 2010 Winter Olympic and Paralympic Games

The Winter Olympic Games is projected to have a wide range of effects on residents of British Columbia (BC). Shaffer *et al.*(2003) highlight some of the more prominent effects using five evaluation accounts:

Government financial account
This account indicates the net financial effect of all of the investments and activities required for or resulting from the Games on government – in effect the net return or cost to taxpayers.

- The net financial cost of the Games to British Columbians is $1.23 billion. This figure incorporates a provision for unbudgeted costs, the opportunity cost of federal funding, incremental taxes, and the benefit of undertaking Sea-to-Sky upgrades that would otherwise be done at a later date.
- The costs may be substantially higher, and are subject to numerous risks. The Provincial government, as the sole guarantor of the Games, is assuming all the financial burden of what is, clearly, a risky business venture.
- The 2010 Games will not 'pay for themselves'. There is a marginal welfare cost of taxation that must be accounted for in the CBA (see Chapter 15).

Resident 'consumer' account
This account indicates the value that BC residents place on the facilities and services the Games provide and the costs of the adverse impacts it may entail. This equates to the net benefit to British Columbians as consumers of what is provided to host the Games.

- The positive impacts for BC residents or consumers include the pride and enjoyment from hosting the Games; the opportunity to attend Games events; and the use of new sports, housing and transportation facilities.

- Negative impacts include disruption/congestion during construction and the Games themselves, and displacement of existing activities from some facilities.
- While there would be user benefits from advancing improvements on the Sea-to-Sky highway, they are lower per dollar spent than improvements on widely recognized higher-priority projects in the Lower Mainland and elsewhere.
- On balance, in terms of the resident/consumer account, one could expect that there would be a net benefit to BC residents – particularly for those who would attend events and use the facilities. The economic question is what *value* do British Columbians place on these benefits – how much are they willing to pay in higher taxes, increased public debt, or displaced government spending on other investments. Shaffer *et al.* (2003) emphasise that this question is fundamental to the economic evaluation of the Games, but had yet to be clearly put to the public.

Environmental account

This account indicates the environmental impacts of the construction and operation of Games-related facilities.

- The Bid Corporation and its member partners have made extensive environmental commitments. If those commitments are kept, environmental impacts may be minimized. However, little detail is provided about what specific measures would be taken, what they would cost, and whether those costs have been fully budgeted for.
- The negative environmental impacts of the development and expansion of facilities and increased accessibility to new sites such as the Callaghan Valley will be difficult to effectively mitigate.
- The urgency of meeting the 2010 deadline may reduce the opportunity to delay, alter or abandon any Olympic project because of environmental concerns.

Economic development account

This account indicates the magnitude and economic significance of the income and employment effects of the investments and activities required for or resulting from the Games.

- Shaffer et al. (2003) state that claims by some proponents that the Games will generate over $10 billion in provincial GDP and more than 200,000 jobs grossly exaggerate the likely impacts. They point out that these estimates include the benefits of an expanded Vancouver Trade and Convention Centre, even though the convention centre is not part of the Bid, has not been included in the estimate of Games-related costs, and will proceed with or without the Games. In addition, the employment estimates incorrectly assume that Games-related projects would only hire British Columbians who would otherwise be un- or underemployed.

- The extent to which the Games will result in increased economic activity (referred to as 'incremental effects') is inherently uncertain, depending not simply on the success of the Games and complementary marketing efforts, but also on what would or could have occurred without them.
- The incremental employment generated by the Games is estimated to range between the equivalent of 1,500 and 5,600 full-time, continuing jobs over the seven years the Games are estimated to have an impact.
- Based on a net cost of $1.2 billion dollars for hosting the Games, Shaffer et al. estimate that the effective public subsidy would be $220,000 per job, and possibly as high as $820,000 per job.
- The Games would concentrate economic benefits in the Lower Mainland and Whistler, where economic help is less needed than elsewhere in the province.

Social account

This account indicates the nature and significance of the community impacts of the investments and activities required for or resulting from the Games.

- The Games pose social risks, such as the displacement of low-income tenants and rising housing costs.
- The Bid Corporation and its member partners have committed to minimizing negative social and community impacts associated with the Games, while maximizing opportunities for British Columbians, and in particular, low-income individuals.
- While some funding has been committed to and accounted for in the budget, additional funding is needed to ensure that the commitments are fully realized. It is unclear whether the required additional funding will be made available.
- Some proponents argue that the Games are needed in order to leverage provincial and federal support for much-needed social infrastructure, such as social housing and public transit. This view is questionable. Positive social ventures have merit and are worth pursuing with or without the Games. Both social housing (after a concerted national campaign) and public transit seem now to be firmly on the public agenda, with or without the 2010 Winter Games.

Table 11.3 Multiple account evaluation summary

Government Financial	2010 NPV
Net Financial Cost to BC	($1.228 billion)
• Minimum/Lower Bound Estimate	($860 million)
• Potential Net Cost with advancement of Richmond Vancouver Rapid Transit	($2 billion) or more
Financial Risk: Unanticipated costs/ inflation/revenue decline	Not estimated
Resident "Consumer"	
• community Pride	
• attendance at Games	
• use of facilities	
• disruption/congestion during construction and Games	
Environment	
• extensive commitments to limit impacts (details unclear, mitigation may increase financial cost)	
• impacts of development of new areas and expansion of tourism in Whistler may be difficult to mitigate effectively	
Economic Development	
• direct impacts estimated at $1.2 billion to $2.7 billion in GDP and 31,000 to 71,000 person years of employment	
• considerable uncertainty over magnitude, effect and net benefit of impacts	
• employment impact (medium visits scenario) equivalent to 5,600 continuing jobs over 7-year impact period; other estimates much lower	
• effective subsidy is $220,000 per continuing job, possibly as high as $820,000 per equivalent job	
Social	
• extensive commitment to mitigate negative social impacts and create positive benefits, particularly for low-income individuals (follow-up required by OCOG and government to realize commitments; additional funding also required)	

As summarized in Table 11.3, the Games will entail a significant net cost to BC taxpayers. The minimum net financial cost estimated in this study is $860 million (2010 NPV). It is more likely to be over $1.2 billion and could reach or exceed $2 billion if the Richmond/Airport-Vancouver rapid transit line is advanced for the

Games. Moreover, the Games face numerous risks, any of which could significantly increase the costs of hosting the Games.

Source: Shaffer, M., A. Greer and C. Mauboules (2003) 'Olympic Costs and Benefits', *Canadian Centre for Policy Alternatives Publication*, February

11.7.2.3 Case study 3 Eurovision Song Contest

The Eurovision Song Contest (ESC) is screened live to over 100 million viewers. Hosting the ESC demands a significant injection of public funds in order to provide the suitable facility and broadcasting infrastructure demanded by the European Broadcasting Union (EBU). While some support for staging the contest is provided by the parent organisation, the balance has to be found by the broadcasting authority of the host nation who is ultimately responsible for producing the event. The Israeli Broadcasting Authority (IBA) allocated nearly $3 million from its annual budget in order to host the competition in 1999. The ESC is an annual, one-evening, competitive event, held in an enclosed arena or concert hall and not generally open to the public. It can be hosted without any of the large infrastructure investments that go with sporting events such as the Olympics and has little of the substantial visitor expenditure that provides much of the economic injection that accompanies festivals and cultural events.

A CBA of the ESC held in Israel in 1999 is summarised in Box 11.7

BOX 11.7 Cost benefit analysis of Eurovision song contest held in Israel

Fleischer and Felsenstein (2002) present a cost-benefit analysis of the ESC to ascertain the social justification for the Eurovision Song Contest. This is undertaken from the perspective of Israel focusing on the benefits accruing to the Israeli population from the public spending that accompanies staging such an event, while acknowledging the opportunity cost of diverting public resources from other areas.

The ESC generates benefits in three types of economic surplus: producer, consumer and government surplus. The authors define these as follows:

Producer surplus is approximated by private sector incremental profits to local producers. This surplus is not identical to profit but relates instead to the broader concept of economic rents associated with the event which accrue to other input suppliers beyond firm owners. The authors claim that the use of a profit measure for producer surplus yields a measurable indicator and is conceptually justified given the relatively small size of the event.

Consumer surplus is measured as the incremental willingness of residents to pay for an event staged at home. The consumer benefits derived from the ESC result from the wide television coverage that the contest generates and its popularity amongst viewers. In contrast to most other events, the utility derived from the ESC is not observable, even imperfectly, through the price structure as tickets are not sold for the live performance. Assuming viewers are willing to pay for the utility derived from the Eurovision broadcast and assuming that Israeli viewers received additional utility from the fact that the contest was broadcast from Israel, then this economic benefit needs to be identified and included in the analysis.

Government surplus is an implicit national benefit, measured by the authors as promotional advertising cost savings. The massive television coverage of the event offers exposure for the host country through short image clips screened between the songs. The benefits of this exposure are much more indirect and are realized through increased visitors and total tourism receipts to the host country in the medium to long term.

The authors construct a 'Balance of Payments Account' and a Cost Benefit Account for the ESC.

The balance of payments account. The event can be regarded as a 'net export' of entertainment services. This calculation, while additional to the main CBA, illustrates a benefit often overlooked in studies of televised events.

Receipts from staging the ESC as a televised event ('export' of entertainment services) include

(a) a transfer payment from the EBU to the Israeli Broadcasting Authority for staging the event ($3.026m)

(b) the expenditures of the foreign delegations within Israel. Daily expenditure per foreign visitor arriving for the purpose of conducting business or participating in a conference is estimated at $121. Thus the 1,100 visitors are estimated to generate over $0.8m in direct revenues.

(c) Additional 'receipts' relate to the alternative cost of promotion and marketing activity. The net social benefit is taken to be the saving in public sector promotional and marketing expenditure that would have occurred in the absence of the Eurovision-generated exposure. The authors estimated the alternative cost of prime-time promotional broadcasting on European TV in order to estimate this savings. The authors emphasise that these are not actual receipts but can be considered as payment in kind, since the national tourism authorities do not actually spend these sums in advertising and promotion and since the exposure effect of the ESC is not via direct advertising but rather a by-product of staging the event. Due to the range of advertising rates in the different countries, the authors produce a maximum and minimum estimate of $0.17m and $1.14m respectively.

Table 11.4 Balance of payment account for the ESC

Receipts	$ Th.	Costs	$ Th.
Transfer from the European Broadcasting Union (EBU)[a]	3,026	Rental of technical equipment from abroad[a]	1,173
Expenditures of the delegations in Israel[b]	800	The import component (25%) in ESC costs[c]	1,481
Alternative cost of promotion:		The import component (25%) in expenditures of ESC delegations	200
1. Minimum	170		
2. Maximum	1,140		
Total: Using min. estimate	3,996	Total	2,854
Using max. estimate	4,966		
Net gain:			
Min. estimate	1,142		
Max. estimate	2,112		

On the cost side, the total budget for the ESC in 1999 was $7.1m. Of this, $1.173m was used to purchase technical equipment from abroad and the rest ($5.93m) was used to purchase goods and services within Israel. Assuming a 25% import content from local spending the imported component of the ESC operational costs is estimated to be $1.481m and $0.2m for the import content of delegation expenditures.

As Table 11.4 shows, the net gain in foreign currency to the local economy is estimated at between $1.1m and $2.1m (depending on the level of promotional benefits).

Cost benefit account for the ESC. Table 11.5 shows the cost benefit account for the ESC 1999. Total benefits range between $2.58m and $3.75m.

Benefits to producers, governments and consumers

Producer benefits are taken to come from two sources: the marginal profits to Israeli suppliers of goods and services to the ESC and profits arising from the expenditures of foreign delegates to the ESC.

The revenue to suppliers of goods and services to the ESC is $5.9m. The profit margin or return to capital in the sectors servicing the ESC is around 10%, which comes to $0.59 m.

Most of the revenues accruing from the expenditure of the delegations (estimated to be $0.8m) are in the hotel and restaurants sectors. Here the authors assume a highly competitive market and use a conservative profit margin of 15% for firms in this sector.

Table 11.5 Cost-benefit account for the ESC

	Maximum estimates	Minimum estimates
Benefits ($ m)		
Profits to suppliers of goods and services to the ESC	0.59	0.59
Profits from delegation expenditures	0.12	0.12
Government surplus	1.14	0.17
Consumer surplus	5.0	4.5
Total	6.85	5.38
Costs ($ m)		
The alternative cost of broadcasting the ESC from Israel	3.1	2.9
Net gain ($ m)	3.75	2.58

Total benefits from delegations expenditures are thus $0.71m (first two rows in Table 11.5).

The government surplus, as indicated, is represented by the cost saving in promotional advertising, considered as a transfer in kind, estimated at minimum and maximum levels.

Analyzing the consumer surplus derived from the ESC means estimating the benefits of the event as the utility derived from staging the contest plus the extra utility derived from staging it in Israel. Measuring the consumer benefits from the televised production of the ESC means eliciting willingness-to-pay responses from viewers using the Contingent Valuation Method. The method is grounded in consumer price theory where willingness-to-pay (WTP) for a good equates the value of additional utility one receives from the use or the existence of the good (see Chapter 17).The cost in this instance is the foregone utility that could have been derived from an alternative televised event produced with the same level of public support. The authors' assume that in the absence of the ESC, the IBA would have allocated funds to alternative programming that would have elicited benefits no greater than those derived from the broadcasting of the ESC from a foreign county. On this assumption the net utility derived from the ESC is the marginal benefit derived from staging the event in Israel. Residents were presented with a hypothetical case of the IBA demanding payment for the costs incurred in staging the Eurovision Song Contest (through an increase in the television license tax). Respondents were requested to indicate how much they would be willing to pay in increased licensing fees in order to receive the ESC broadcast in Israel and how much more they were willing to pay in order to have Israel host the contest.

The average WTP value is calculated by taking the midpoints of the different ranges. Total WTP is estimated by multiplying the average by 1.9 million, the relevant adult population of Israel.

With respect to the economic benefits of the promotional effect of the ESC on Israel, the authors acknowledge that the most direct way of capturing this impact would be a survey of foreign tourists with a view to ascertaining whether ESC-generated exposure played a part in their decision to visit Israel. However, the costs, accuracy and representativeness of such a survey are likely to call this approach into question. The authors thus estimated the cost of promoting Israel on prime time on the major national television networks in those countries to which the ESC was broadcast. This cost represents the savings to the national tourism authorities in advertising fees as a result of ESC-generated exposure of the destination.

Conclusions

These estimates should be considered as representing minimum benefits. They do not account for the future stream of benefits likely to accrue to producers as a result of the promotional effects of the ESC and the increased visitor levels that might ensue. On the other hand, the study has assumed some slack in the economy. Under full employment, increased surplus realized by the ESC would just result in a decrease somewhere else. The economic surpluses estimated here imply that the ESC generated an increase in productive capacity in the economy that would not have occurred in its absence.

The results show moderate social justification for public support of this high profile televised spectacle and suggest that a CBA approach to cultural events can have wider applications.

Source: Fleischer, A. and D. Felsenstein (2002) 'Cost-benefit Analysis using Economic Surpluses: A Case Study of a Televised Event', *Journal of Cultural Economics*, 26(2), 139–156, May

11.8   IMPROVING EVENT EVALUATION

A rational events strategy for government involves funding events at a level which is appropriate given the benefits they create, and which reflects the benefits which could be obtained by using the funds elsewhere. It also involves allocating the funds available to the events which create the greatest net benefits. Achieving this requires at least two things to happen. *First*, there needs to be rigorous economic evaluation of events, implying a move away from the current practice of exaggerating economic impacts using I–O models in an uncritical way. *Second*, there needs to be an institutional framework under which there is the incentive for this to happen.

(1) *Good economic evaluation of events* is a precondition for efficient allocation of resources in this sector. The best practice approach to measuring the impact on economic activity, and in particular, on output (GSP or GDP) and employment is to use a CGE approach. Estimation of the economic impacts is only part of the evaluation story. If funds are to be provided to assist an event, it is necessary that the cost of these funds be compared to the benefits from the event. The event should be subjected to a CBA. Auditor General Departments in Australia at least are strongly recommending that CBA be conducted for all major events requiring government support.

The minimum requirement is that the jurisdiction considering attracting the event should undertake these calculations to determine whether the event is in its own interest.

However, as has been noted, the economic impacts and benefits on other jurisdictions, and on the nation as a whole, will differ from the impacts on the host jurisdiction. Typically, some of the benefits of an event in one area will be at the expense of costs in other areas, and the gain to the state or nation as a whole will be less than the gain to the host area. A rational approach to event strategy will require that benefits and costs to all affected jurisdictions be evaluated, particularly when government support is sought.

(2) *Institutional Framework for Event Assessment.* Many of the institutions responsible for developing events appear to have too great an incentive to oversell events, and to be seen as 'winning' events, and too little an incentive to evaluate events rigorously to determine if support is warranted. An institutional structure which sets up events corporations which have events promotion and subsidising as their sole or main objective creates poor incentives for rigorous event evaluation. What is needed is for events funding to be decided by a body which has an acute realisation of the value of the alternative uses of the funds. There is an important role for central agencies, such as treasuries and auditors-general to put pressure on operational agencies to improve the evaluation of events projects. Post-event evaluations should be upgraded and broadened to cover the increasingly important social and environmental impacts, the degree to which risks have been effectively managed and the potential for continuous improvement. By outlining criteria and providing guidelines for evaluation, and by reviewing events and their assessment by the relevant agencies, these can put strong pressure on for events evaluation to be improved.

11.9 CONCLUSIONS AND POLICY

- Special events play an important role in the economic and social development of communities internationally. They have the potential to attract visitors, stimulate business activity, generate income and job opportunities in the short term and garner investment in the longer term.
- The success or contribution of a particular event should not be measured only by its direct financial contribution. There may be other perceived benefits from events, such as enhancing the image of a city or region, facilitating business networking and civic pride. Events can also result in associated social and cultural benefits to a destination, providing forums for continuing education and training, facilitating technology transfer and so on.
- On the other hand, events are recognised to generate adverse environmental impacts such as various forms of pollution and adverse social impacts such as disruption to local business and community backlash.
- The fundamental ingredient needed to conduct an economic impact assessment or CBA of an event is an estimate of the 'new injected expenditure' or 'inscope expenditure' that is generated by the event. This refers to expenditure that would not have occurred in the host region had the event not taken place.

- In estimating 'new' expenditure associated with an event, we must be mindful of and possibly make allowances for: expenditure of local residents (transferred expenditure); expenditure by 'casuals'; expenditure by 'time switchers'; retained expenditure; expenditure diversion; and direct imports.

- The total new expenditure associated with an event is used as the input to an economic model to determine the economic impacts on the destination. Estimates of impacts will depend both on the type of model used and on the particular assumptions that underlie that model.

- The limitations of I–O modelling apply also to its use in event economic impact assessment – in particular, the use of I–O multipliers in event assessment results in exaggerated impact estimates. Critics of this standard approach argue that, where possible, the economic assessment of special events should use CGE models (rather than I–O models) since they better reflect contemporary developments in economic analysis.

- Some important failures in event assessment include failure to correctly estimate 'new' expenditure; uncritical use of I–O multipliers to estimate the economic impacts of events; failure to use an appropriate model to estimate an event's economic impacts; the use of inappropriate multiplier; failure to recognise expenditure diversion; failure to recognise the relevance of the labour market; failure to recognise the relevance of the jurisdiction; failure to correctly treat construction expenditure; and failure to correctly account for taxes and subsidies.

- Although CGE modelling is the recommended approach to assessing the economic impact of special events, it will not always be practical to employ a CGE model. As a practical response to the situation where economic models are unavailable, it has been recommended that *new expenditure* be used as the basis to measure economic performance of the event to the host region. As long as it is understood to be *indicative* of the economic significance of the event, the new or inscope expenditure estimate can be an informative key performance measure.

- The economic impacts of an event are not the same thing as the economic benefits which arise. Economic impact studies can only estimate the effect on economic variables such as GDP, employment and the like. The impact on GDP is a *gross* measure of the change in value of output as a result of an event. This addition to output normally requires additional inputs, of land, labour and capital, to enable it to be produced. These inputs have a cost, and this cost must be deducted from the change in value of gross output if a measure of the net economic gain is to be made.

- There are many potential effects of events that are often not accounted for in a standard economic impact analysis. Event assessments need to be broadened to take, where practicable, a more comprehensive approach embracing not only economic but also social and environmental factors. The standard tool of measurement of such effects in order to undertake a holistic or comprehensive evaluation of an event is CBA. Where public funds are to be provided to assist an event, it is necessary that the cost of these funds be compared to the benefits from the event via a CBA.

- Given that governments have alternative uses for funds, it should be expected that any request would demonstrate the nature and extent of the benefits to justify the request for funds. On the basis of a CBA, it is possible for the decision maker to make a judgement of whether the economic benefits of the event are greater than the costs, and to also judge whether the event would represent the best use of the funds, when funds are limited and alternative calls on funds exist.

- There is common ground between CBA and economic impact analysis of special events, since the two techniques focus on different aspects of the evaluation problem. CBA is the established technique for assessing the wider benefits and costs of a project, and as such, it is an appropriate framework for classification and measurement of the projected outcomes of an event. While CBA would emphasise consumer surplus as a primary source of gains from an event, in the case of larger special events, however, their outcomes are not aimed specifically at providing benefits to local consumers, but rather at attracting tourists and their expenditure from outside the region. It would seem then that economic impact analysis can provide important information on what is essentially a major source of benefit of a special event.

- A rational events strategy for government involves funding events at a level which is appropriate given the benefits they create, and which reflects the benefits which could be obtained by using the funds elsewhere. It also involves allocating the funds available to the events which create the greatest net benefits.

SELF-REVIEW QUESTIONS

1. List valid economic and non-economic reasons as to why a government may provide support for a special event.

2. Outline the conceptual rationale for commissioning economic impact studies.

3. Outline the steps involved in the economic evaluation of a special event.

4. It is essential that the geographical boundary of the host region for the event be clearly defined. Why?

5. List the major determinants of event generated 'new' expenditure.

6. What is meant by the term 'transferred expenditure' and why is it not considered as 'new' money into a destination?

7. What is meant by the term 'time switching' in event tourism? Why is it necessary to allow for time switching in estimating the level of injected expenditure into a destination?

8. What is meant by the term 'expenditure diversion' in event tourism? Briefly describe the three ways in which expenditure diversion may occur because of the holding of a special event.

9. Briefly compare the use of I–O analysis and CGE analysis to estimate the multipliers associated with a particular event.

10. State the role of CBA in the economic evaluation of special events.

ESSAY QUESTIONS

1. 'Event assessment which focuses only on economic impacts is too narrow in scope to provide sufficient information to policy makers and government funding agencies'. Discuss.

2. 'Only that proportion of expenditure which represents an injection of "new money" into an area is relevant to the calculation of the economic impacts of a special event'. Do you agree? How is new money defined? In event tourism, what is included as new money and what is excluded?

3. 'A rational events strategy for government involves funding events at a level which is appropriate given the benefits they create, and which reflects the benefits which could be obtained by using the funds elsewhere.' What does this mean and how can it be done?

4. Governments and destination managers should broaden the post-event assessment focus beyond the economic to embrace social and environmental impacts. Explain the rationale for this and discuss how this may be done.

5. Compare and contrast the evaluation of a special event by means of an economic impact assessment and a CBA.

TOURISM INVESTMENT

CHAPTER 12

INVESTMENT BY TOURISM FIRMS

LEARNING OBJECTIVES

After reading this chapter, you should be able to:

1. Distinguish between capital and financial tourism investment, between private and public tourism investment and between domestic and foreign tourism investment.

2. Discuss the reasons for capital investment in tourism and the various sources for its financing.

3. Describe the steps involved in the selection of capital tourism investment projects.

4. Discuss the factors that underlie the accept–reject decision in tourism investment.

5. Be aware of the main pitfalls that must be avoided in capital budgeting.

6. Appreciate the challenges facing tourism investment.

12.1 INTRODUCTION

Investment refers to the spending on capital and financial assets undertaken by private firms and governments in the expectation of realising future returns. Tourism investment underlies and supports tourism development. It is vital both to the individual firm, ensuring its future productive viability, and to the destination, adding strongly to the economy's overall capacity to satisfy tourism demand.

This chapter discusses the importance of tourism investment in its many forms, distinguishing capital investment from financial investment, private investment from public investment and domestic investment from foreign investment. It also discusses the elements of risk and uncertainty that accompany tourism investment decision-making generally and reviews the various techniques used to assess return on tourism investment. The focus is on investment in physical assets rather than investment in human capital (education, training, etc.).

Tourism investment takes the form of spending on both capital and financial assets. It is undertaken by both private firms and the public sector. It occurs both domestically and internationally. Whatever its form, source or reason, tourism investment underpins the tourism supply by providing the funds necessary for the developing and upgrading of tourism projects. It also influences tourism demand by enhancing a destination's range of facilities and attractions and enticing more tourists to it.

Strong, continuing tourism investment is vital to a strong, successful tourism industry. Apart from the increase in capacity and profits that accrue to individual firms and the tourism sector in general from successful investment, the perceived national and regional benefits that come from a more favourable tourism investment climate include (Australian Government, 2007):

- Economic growth.
- Job creation.
- Utilisation of domestic resources, particularly renewable resources.
- Skills acquisition.
- Expansion of exports.
- Development of remote areas of the country.
- Facilitation of increased ownership of investment by the nation's citizens.

The importance of tourism investment became particularly evident during the recent Global Financial Crisis. Declining asset values impacted on the ability of firms to fund debt or invest and many capital projects (including fleet expansion, hotel projects, attractions, etc.) were shelved due to financing difficulties. Credit availability and de-risking of bank balance sheets stifle the volume of tourism investment needed to support tourism growth over time with its attendant economic effects.

12.2 CATEGORIES OF TOURISM INVESTMENT

Investment related to tourism can be categorised along three broad lines: *capital* versus *financial*; *private* versus *public*; and *domestic* versus *foreign*. We discuss the first two distinctions in this chapter and foreign investment in the following chapter.

Capital investment versus financial investment
Both capital investment (spending on long-term capital goods) and financial investment (short-term money loans) are essential to the development of tourism projects and infrastructure.

Capital investment refers to spending that is specifically designed to generate further long-term output, for example, spending on capital goods such as factories, machines, and plant and equipment which in turn helps produce more goods and services. *Financial investment* refers to the placement of funds on financial markets in order to earn interest or dividend payments on monies presently not earmarked for capital investment.

Private capital investment in the tourism industry takes two forms: investment in *fixed capital* and investment in *working capital*.

Fixed capital investment involves direct spending on physical assets such as buildings, plant, equipment and so on that a firm or organisation needs in order to help it to produce services for tourists. It is undertaken in the expectation of longer-term increased output and future profits. Fixed capital investment includes buildings (hotels, casinos, airports, theme parks, leisure centres, guesthouses, resorts, tour offices, etc.); the modes of tourist transportation (airlines, cruise ships, tour buses and the like); and the associated developments (golf courses, playing parks, viewing platforms, air walks, etc.).

The amount of fixed capital investment undertaken by any tourism firm depends on many interlocking factors, amongst them:

- The cost of the fixed capital (the volume of investment required).
- The interest rate.
- The duration of the project.
- The market conditions (pricing, degree of competition, expanding market, etc.).
- Political stability.
- Expectations (re-expected tourist number, sales revenues, political stability, transport access, etc.).
- Sensitivity to random shocks (e.g. winning the rights to hold the Olympics or a tourism downturn due to terrorism).

Fixed capital tourism investment is particularly sensitive to the changing state of the tourism market and to the broader economy in general. Rather than flowing smoothly and predictably, capital investment tends to be reactive and volatile, moving rapidly with slight changes in the economy. While a stable economic environment and positive economic growth will tend to stimulate tourism investment, especially longer-term investment, uncertainty and economic contraction will tend to constrain it.

When tourism demand is relatively stable, much of the investment in fixed capital is in the form of replacing worn-out buildings, machinery and equipment. However, if tourism demand rises (or expected to rise), and there is no spare capacity, investment in fixed capital will increase significantly to include new capital as well as replacement capital. Conversely, if tourism demand falls, firms, faced with over-capacity, will reduce fixed capital stock by not replacing worn out capital.

Working capital refers to investment spending tied up in the stocks of raw materials, semi-manufactured goods and manufactured goods (inventories) that have not yet been sold. Examples of fixed and working capital investment abound in the tourism industry. Working capital investment includes the tourism merchandise and souvenirs that appear on shelves and in warehouses that are produced but not yet sold (e.g. luggage items, snow skis, snorkelling gear, swim costumes, cameras, etc.).

We may usefully distinguish *gross investment* (total spending on such physical assets) and *net investment* (gross investment minus *depreciation*, the replacement investment that becomes necessary when old capital becomes worn out). In simple terms, when:

- Gross investment is more than depreciation, then net investment is positive, tourism firms will expand their capital base, and their productive capacity rises.
- Gross investment is less than depreciation, then net investment is negative, capital is wearing out faster than it is being replaced, and productive capacity falls.
- Gross investment is equal to depreciation, then net investment is zero, worn out capital is just being replaced and productive capacity remains the same.

Private investment versus public investment

Capital and financial investment are each undertaken by both the private sector and the public sector.

Private investment is undertaken by private firms in the expectation of greater output and future profit. This is the focus of this chapter.

Public investment is undertaken by government collectively on behalf of the community, and usually takes the form of infrastructure works, subsidies and grants. Public investment in tourism will be discussed in Chapter 13.

Domestic investment versus foreign investment

While private firms and governments typically spend the bulk of their investment monies within their own country (*domestic investment*), *foreign investment* (the placement of investment money in other countries) is becoming more common and more important to individual firms and governments competing in today's global economic and financial environment. Issues concerning Foreign Direct Investment (FDI) in tourism will be discussed in Chapter 14.

12.3 SOURCES OF CAPITAL INVESTMENT FINANCING

The source of capital financing is an important issue in tourism investment decision-making, since it can substantially affect a tourism project's overall costs. Broadly, capital investment can be financed in any of the following five ways:

- *Profits.* Firms can use their retained earnings (unused profits) to fund their investment projects. Retained earnings are often placed at call on financial markets, and so can easily be converted into capital investment. The use of retained earnings for expansion and development does, however, present the firm with opportunity costs, namely, the loss of the potential interest the funds would have earned if left in financial markets or the non-payment of dividends to shareholders.

- *Debt.* To fund investment projects, firms can borrow the money rather than use their retained earnings. Borrowing takes two forms: commercial borrowing and bond issuing. Commercial borrowing involves taking out either bank loans (at commercial rates of interest) or development loans (often at interest below commercial rates). As an alternative to taking out a loan, larger firms, under strict conditions, may issue bonds (promissory notes) on which they pay interest. Either way, incurring debt results in the pay back of principal and interest by the borrowing firm.
- *Equity.* Under certain conditions, listed companies are allowed to raise finance through the issue of new shares. New share issues, however, tend to dilute ownership in the company.
- *Securitisation.* More recently, large corporations have turned to asset-backed and lease-backed securitisation in order to fund large investment projects. Here, the firm does not have to use its retained earnings, or borrow funds or sell shares. Through the use of a special entity set up for the purpose, the firm assigns the cash flows that derive from the investment project to the investors who put up the money with which to develop that project.
- *Grants and subsidies.* Where deemed appropriate or necessary, government and industry groups make grants or subsidies aimed at seed funding private development.

Typically, the sources of finance that firms access will comprise some combination of debt and equity. Financing a project through debt implies that the firm incurs a liability that must be serviced, with implications for cash flow. Equity financing implies lower risks regarding cash-flow commitments but dilutes ownership and can result in reduced earnings. The cost of equity is also typically higher than the cost of debt which may offset any reduction in cash-flow risk.

Various theories of the basis of firms financing decisions have been proposed in the literature. The *Pecking Order Theory* argues that firms that have access to internal financing avoid external financing and avoid new equity financing if they can undertake new debt financing at reasonably low interest rates (Fama & French, 2002). In contrast, the *Trade-Off Theory* in which firms are assumed to trade-off the tax benefits of debt with the bankruptcy costs of debt when making their decisions (Frank & Goyal, 2008). An emerging area in finance theory is *right-financing* whereby investment banks and corporations can enhance investment return and company value over time by determining the right investment objectives, policy framework, institutional structure, source of financing (debt or equity) and expenditure framework within a given economy and under given market conditions. Many researchers accept the *Market timing hypothesis* which states that firms look for the cheaper type of financing regardless of their current levels of internal resources, debt and equity (Baker & Wurgler, 2002). There is insufficient space to elaborate on these views in this text (see Block & Hirt, 2008).

12.4   GENERATING CAPITAL INVESTMENT PROPOSALS

Ideas for new capital investments can come from many sources both inside and outside the firm. We may usefully classify investment projects into the following categories:

Replacement. Investments to replace equipment that is worn out in the production process. For example, a restaurant manager may buy new tables and chairs to replace old stock.

Cost reduction. Investments to replace working but obsolete equipment with new and more efficient equipment, expenditures for training programs aimed at reducing labour costs and expenditures to move production facilities to areas where labour and other inputs are cheaper. Tourism examples include the purchases of more efficient airplanes, development of in-house hospitality training programs to enhance staff efficiency and location of aircraft offices at secondary airports.

Output expansion of traditional products and markets. Investments to expand production facilities in response to increased demand for the firms traditional products in traditional or existing markets. Thus a resort hotel may add a new accommodation wing or a rental car company may expand its fleet.

Expansion into new products and/or new markets. Investments to develop, produce, and sell new products and/or enter new markets. Thus a cruise shipping line may either add new ports of call to its schedules or open offices in new destinations.

Government regulation. Investments made to comply with government regulations. These include investment projects required to meet government health and safety regulations, pollution control and to satisfy other legal requirements. Tourism firms will be required to comply with the various mitigation and adaptation policies to combat climate change.

Other. All investments not categorised as above.

12.5   THE OPTIMAL LEVEL OF INVESTMENT

A financial appraisal essentially views investment decisions from the perspective of the organisation undertaking the investment.

The generation of ideas and proposals for new investment projects is crucial to the future profitability of the firm and its very survival over time. Capital budgeting refers to the process of planning expenditures that give rise to revenues or returns over a number of years. It is essentially an application of the general principle that a firm should produce the output or undertake an activity until the marginal revenue from the output or activity is equal to its marginal cost. In a capital budgeting framework, this implies that the firm should undertake additional investment projects until the marginal return from the investment is equal to its marginal cost.

The schedule of the various investment projects open to the firm, arranged from the one with the highest to the lowest return, represents the firms demand for capital. The marginal cost of capital schedule gives the cost that the firm faces in obtaining additional amounts of capital for investment purposes. The intersection of the demand and marginal cost curves for capital that the firm faces determine how much the firm will invest.

In Figure 12.1a, the horizontal axis measures the dollars of investment during a year; the vertical axis shows both the percentage cost of capital and the rate of return on projects. The boxes denote projects: project A, for example, calls for an outlay of $3 million and promises a 17% rate of return. Project B requires $1 million and yields about 16% and so on. The last investment, project E, simply involves buying 8% government bonds. The investment opportunity schedule measures the yield or rate of return on each project. The rates of return of Projects A through D exceed the marginal cost of capital, and they should be accepted. However, Project E should be rejected because its marginal cost of capital is greater than its Internal Rate of Return (IRR).

Figure 12.1b generalises the concept to show a smoothed investment opportunity schedule, the curve labelled IRR (the yield on a project is generally calculated as the IRR. The process of calculating the IRR is explained below.

In Figure 12.1b, the curve MCC designates the marginal cost of capital or the cost of each additional dollar acquired to make capital expenditures. As drawn, the marginal cost of capital is constant over a certain range after which it begins to rise. The smoothed generalised curves in Figure 12.1b indicate that the firm should invest I^* dollars. I^* is the optimal investment level at which the marginal cost of capital equals the marginal return on the last project accepted. At this investment level, the marginal cost of capital, the cost of the last dollar raised, is 12%, the same as the return on the last project accepted by the firm, and the optimal level of investment is $11 million.

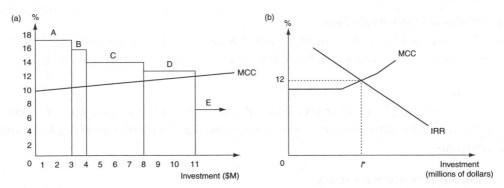

Figure 12.1 (a) Discrete investment projects, (b) Smooth investment opportunity schedule

Application of the capital budgeting process in reality is much more complex than the above example suggests. Projects just do not appear. A continuous stream of good investment projects result from hard thinking, careful planning and often, large outlays for R&D. In addition, difficult measurement problems are involved. The revenues and costs associated with particular projects must be estimated, often for many years into the future. Finally, conceptual and empirical problems arise over the methods of calculating rates of return and the cost of capital.

12.5.1 THE RATE OF INTEREST

While we sometimes talk about 'the' rate of interest, the rate of interest varies at different times and in different markets. Thus at a given point in time and in a given capital market, there is a large number of interest rates depending on relative risk, term structure, administration costs and tax treatment.

Risk

The risk of the loan is often the major reason for differences in rates of interest at a given time and place. In general, the greater the risk the higher the rate of interest. Two types of risks can be identified. *Default risk* refers to the possibility that the loan will not be repaid. Loans unsecured by collateral (such as instalment credit) usually charge higher rates of interest than loans secured by collateral (such as home mortgages). *Variability risk* refers to the possibility that the yield or return on an investment such as a stock may vary considerably above or below the average. Given the usual aversion to risk, investors generally demand a premium or higher yield for investments with more uncertain returns.

Duration of loan

Loans for longer periods usually require higher rates of interest because the lender has less flexibility or liquidity during this period.

Costs of administering the loan

Smaller loans and loans requiring frequent repayments (such as instalment loans) usually imply greater service costs per dollar of loan and thus result in a higher interest charge.

Tax treatment

Since investors emphasise after-tax returns, the tax treatment of interest and investment income can lead to differences in rates of interest among otherwise comparable loans and investments.

Nominal versus real interest rates

During the period of the loan, the general price level may rise so that the loan is repaid with dollars of lower purchasing power than the dollars borrowed. In everyday usage of the term, the interest rate refers to the nominal or money rate of interest. The nominal rate of interest (r') refers to the premium on a unit of a monetary claim made today compared to a monetary claim in the future. In contrast, we distinguish the real rate of interest (r), which refers to the premium on a unit of a commodity or real consumption income today compared to a unit of the commodity or real consumption income in the future. However, the nominal rate of interest is affected by the rate of inflation (i), while the real rate of interest is not. Thus, the nominal rate of interest equals the real rate of interest plus the expected rate of price inflation. That is,

$$r' = r + i$$

Anyone who borrows money now and repays in money in the future must expect to pay an additional monetary amount to cover any expected increase in the monetary price of real claims by the time of repayment. Only if expected inflation is zero will $r' = r$. Since the nominal rate of interest must be sufficiently high for a lender to cover any increase in the price level (or the price of real claims) during the loan period, it is the real rate of interest which is shown on the vertical axis of Figures 12.1a and 12.1b.

12.6   SELECTING CAPITAL INVESTMENT PROJECTS

The process of selecting capital investment projects consists of several important steps:

1. Estimate all cash inflows and outflows associated with the project

2. Measure all future cash inflows and outflows in terms of today's dollars

3. Evaluate and choose, from the alternatives available, those investment projects to implement

4. Review the investment projects after they have been implemented

12.6.1   ESTIMATING CASH FLOWS FOR THE PROJECT PROPOSALS

One of the most important and difficult aspects of capital budgeting is the estimation of the *net cash flow from a project*. This is the difference between cash receipts and cash expenditures over the life of a project. Since cash receipts and expenditures occur in the future a great deal of uncertainty is involved in their estimation. One need only think of the substantial lead times involved in purchasing new aircraft or commissioning work on the construction of a cruise ship to appreciate the difficulties of estimating cash flows accurately.

Estimating cash flows requires *demand forecasts* and *cost forecasts*.

Future *revenues* depend on the demand for the service, and relatedly, the prices that are charged as well as on diverse issues such as competitor actions, government policy, taxes, regulations, consumer and business expectations, and random events. Chapter 3 highlighted the difficulties of making accurate tourism forecasts of tourism demand.

The future *costs* of tourism investments are equally unpredictable and may rise with unexpected increases in wages and materials (e.g. the rapid rise in the price of aviation fuel in recent years), unforeseen technical difficulties, specification changes due to mandated safety requirements and legal disputes. Even when known, net operating cash flow is not necessarily smooth and stable, changing over the duration of the project as revenues and costs change.

Some general guidelines must be followed in estimating net cash flows:

- Cash flows should be measured on an incremental basis. That is, the cash flow from a given project should be measured by the difference between the stream of the firm's cash flows with and without the investment project.
- Care must be taken to include *all* incremental cash flows, including revenue and cost changes for other activities of the firm that a particular capital investment would affect (e.g. a new products effect on the sales revenue of an existing product).
- Cash flows must be estimated on an after-tax basis using the firm's marginal tax rate.
- As a noncash expense, depreciation affects the firm's cash flow only through its effects on taxes. However, the scrap value of assets must be accounted for by including a residual cash flow. This captures the residual or resale value when the firm sells the capital at the end of the capital's life. This may amount only to scrap value for amusement park equipment, but may be substantial for a cruise ship or airplanes.

12.6.2 DISCOUNTING

It is standard practice to measure all future cash inflows and outflows in terms of *today's dollars*. If receiving $1 of income is deferred, its present value is less than $1. Conversely, if you have $1 today, you can turn it into more than $1 in the future, by loaning it at some rate of interest. For example, if the interest rate is 10%, you can turn the dollar into $1.10 a year from today. However if you expect to receive $1.10 a year from today, the present value of that $1.10 is only $1.

Typically, for tourism investment projects, the large outflow of funds associated with the supply price of capital occurs upfront at the start of the project (year 0) while the net operating cash flow begins in, and continues over, later periods (see Figure 12.2). Operating outflows may exceed inflows in the project's early life, suggesting that it may take some time for the investment project firstly to break even and then to turn a profit for the firm.

Since cash flows are discounted at a cumulative rate, their impact is felt more towards the beginning of the investment project's life and less towards the end of the project's life.

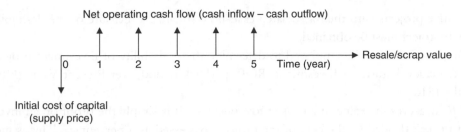

Net operating cash flow (cash inflow – cash outflow)

0   1   2   3   4   5   Time (year)   → Resale/scrap value

Initial cost of capital
(supply price)

Figure 12.2 Investment cash flows over time

Source: Modified from Keat and Young (2006)

Cash flows over time are affected by the time value of money, in that future earnings and future costs have a lower dollar value than current earnings and current costs.

The basic problem in measuring and comparing the desirability of investment projects is assessing the cash flows that occur at different points in time. To put cash flows originating at different times (year 1, year 2, year 3 and so on) onto an equal basis, a discount rate is applied to each flow so that all become expressed in terms of the same point in time, usually year 0. Since $1 paid or received next year is worth less than $1 paid or received today, discounting is used to properly evaluate and compare different investment proposals.

To assess and compare the estimated after-tax cash flows of a project and its options, all cashflow streams should be discounted either by the weighted average cost of capital (WACC) or by the opportunity cost of capital. Determining the firm's cost of capital to set the appropriate discount rate is an essential part of the capital budgeting process (see below).

Once the discount rate is selected, calculating present values from future values and vice versa is straightforward. The formula is

$$PV = FV/(1 + k)^n \qquad (12.1)$$

Where,

PV is the present value at t_0;

FV is the future value at t_n;

k is the discount rate (%);

n is the number of periods between t_0 and t_n.

12.6.3 THE ACCEPT–REJECT DECISION

Once a capital expenditure project has been identified and the cash flows have been estimated, a decision to accept or reject the project is required. To compare and choose among alternative projects with their associated cash-flow streams, a measure of the desirability of each project must be obtained.

Various criteria can be employed to determine the desirability of investment projects. These include Return on Investment (ROI), payback period, Net Present Value (NPV) and the IRR.

ROI measures the value of a project to a business. It is simply the profit on an investment project divided by the cost of the project, expressed as a percentage. This is most useful when all costs are known and easily quantifiable. It is less useful where risks are significant and where costs are uncertain.

Payback Period refers to how long an investment takes to 'pay for itself'. It is estimated by dividing the initial project investment cost by the annual cash inflows. Although this tool is simple and easy to understand, it ignores the time value of money. It also ignores revenues received or costs incurred after the payback period.

This section focuses on three widely used discounted cash-flow methods: NPV, the IRR and Profitability Index (PI) methods.

12.6.3.1 NPV

The NPV of a project is equal to the present value of the expected stream of net cash flows from the project, discounted at the firm's cost of capital minus the initial cost of the project. NPV is the sum of the discounted project benefits less discounted project costs. Formally it can be expressed as follows:

$$\text{NPV} = C_0 + \sum_{t=1}^{N} \frac{R_t}{(1 + r)^t} \qquad (12.2)$$

Where,

C_0 is the initial cost of the investment;

t is the time of the cash flow;

N is the total time of the project;

r is the real discount rate (the rate of return that could be earned on an investment in the financial markets with similar risk);

R_t is the net cash flow (the amount of cash) at time t.

The decision rule for NPV is straightforward: the project is deemed acceptable if its NPV is greater than or equal to zero. A zero amount means that the future income from the project measured in today's dollars is equal to the present outlay measured in today's dollars, assuming that the discount rate is equal to the borrowing interest rate. A positive amount means that the project brings in a positive dollar return, after allowing for the cost of debt. The project is deemed unacceptable and should not proceed if NPV is less than zero. If projects are mutually exclusive, the project which yields the highest positive NPV would be chosen.

12.6.3.2 IRR

The IRR is the discount rate at which the NPV of a project is equal to zero, that is, discounted benefits equal discounted costs. It is a commonly used measure of investment efficiency. In algebraic terms, the IRR is the value of r which solves the equation:

$$\text{NPV} = C_0 + \sum_{t=1}^{N} \frac{R_t}{(1 + r)^t} = 0 \tag{12.3}$$

The firm should undertake the project if the IRR on the project exceeds or is equal to the marginal cost of capital or risk-adjusted discount rate (r) that the firm uses and it should not undertake the project if the IRR is smaller than the marginal cost of capital. When comparing capital investment projects, those with the highest IRR should be selected.

A problem with the IRR is that it assumes that interim positive cash flows are reinvested at the same rates of return of the project that generated them. This is unrealistic. It is more likely that the funds will be reinvested at a rate closer to the firm's cost of capital. The IRR therefore often gives an overly optimistic measure of the returns to investment.

A second problem of the IRR relates to projects that have irregular cash flows alternating between positive and negative values. Several IRRs can be identified for such projects potentially leading to confusion and the wrong investment decisions being made.

12.6.3.3 Comparison of NPV and IRR

In most circumstances, the NPV and the IRR methods result in identical decisions to either accept or reject individual projects.

If NPV > 0, IRR > discount rate;

If NPV = 0, IRR = discount rate; and

If NPV < 0, IRR < discount rate.

In other words, the NPV is greater than (less than) zero if and only if the IRR is greater than (less than) the required rate of return r.

However, in the case of mutually exclusive projects – that is, projects where the acceptance of one alternative precludes the acceptance of one or more other alternatives – the two methods may yield inconsistent results; one project may have a *higher* IRR than another, but a *lower* NPV.

The outcome depends on what assumptions the decision maker chooses to make about the implied reinvestment rate for the net cash flows generated from each project. The NPV method assumes that cash flows are reinvested at the firms cost of capital, whereas the

IRR method assumes that these cash flows are reinvested at the estimated IRR. Generally, the cost of capital is considered to be a more realistic reinvestment rate than the estimated IRR because this is the rate the next (marginal) investment project can be assumed to earn. Thus the NPV approach is superior to the IRR when choosing among mutually exclusive investments.

Despite the conceptual superiority of NPV, business executives often prefer IRR over NPV. Managers often find it easier to compare investments of different sizes in terms of percentage rates of return than by dollars of NPV. IRR, as a measure of investment efficiency, may also give better insights in capital constrained situations. Nevertheless, NPV remains the 'more accurate' reflection of value to the business. For comparison of mutually exclusive projects, NPV is the appropriate measure.

12.6.3.4 Profitability Index

A variant of NPV analysis that is often used in complex capital budgeting situations is the PI, sometimes (misleadingly in our view) called the benefit/cost ratio. The PI shows the relative profitability of any project, or the present value of benefits per dollar of cost.

$$PI = \frac{\sum_{t=1}^{n} R_t}{C_0} \tag{12.4}$$

In PI analysis, a project with PI > 1 should be accepted and a project with PI < 1 should be rejected. This means that projects will be accepted provided they return more than a dollar of discounted benefits for each dollar of cost. Thus the PI and NPV methods always indicate the same accept–reject decisions for independent projects, since PI > 1 implies NPV > 0 and PI < 1 implies NPV < 0. However, as shown in Table 12.1 for alternative projects of unequal size, PI and NPV criteria can give inconsistent rankings when mutually exclusive projects are being evaluated.

Table 12.1 Comparison of NPV and PI rankings of projects with unequal costs

	Project X	*Project Y*	*Project Z*
Present value of net cash flows $\sum_{t=1}^{n} R_t$	$2,500,000	$1,300,000	$1,300,000
Initial cost of project C_0	$2,000,000	$1,000,000	$1,000,000
NPV	$500,000	$300,000	$300,000
PI	1.25	1.3	1.3

The data in Table 12.1 show that Project X has a higher NPV than either Project Y or Z and would thus be the only project undertaken according to the NPV rule if the firm could invest only 2 million. However, the PI for projects Y and Z are each greater than for project X. Thus the firm should undertake both of these projects instead of project X. Where investment funds are limited, precluding the undertaking of all projects with a positive NPV, the investor should rank projects according to their PI, rather than those with the highest NPVs. That is, jointly, projects Y and Z increase the value of the firm by more than project X ($600,000 as compared to $500,000), but they would not be undertaken if the firm followed the NPV rule and could invest only $2 million. The example shows that, with capital rationing, the PI or relative NPV rule may lead to a different ranking or order in which projects are to be undertaken.

For a firm with substantial investment resources and a goal of maximising shareholder wealth, the NPV method is superior. If the proposed project and its alternatives are of a similar financial scale, the highest NPV identifies the best option among those considered. If the alternatives considered are not of a comparable financial scale, the best measure of the value of the proposed project is the NPV per dollar of capital invested.

For a firm with limited resources, however, the PI approach allocates scarce resources to the projects with the greatest relative effect on value. Using the PI method, projects are evaluated on the basis of their NPV per dollar of investment, avoiding a possible bias towards larger projects. In some cases, this leads to a better combination of investment projects and higher firm value. The PI approach has also proved to be a useful tool in public sector decision-making, where allocating scarce public resources among competing projects is a typical problem.

Table 12.2 summarises the advantages and limitations of the three investment appraisal techniques.

12.6.4 REVIEWING INVESTMENT PROJECTS AFTER IMPLEMENTATION

An important but neglected step in the selection process is the review of investment projects *after* they have been implemented. A post-audit review involves comparing the actual cash flow and return from a project with the expected or predicted cash flow and return on the project, as well as an explanation of the observed differences between predicted and actual results. One important purpose of the post-audit is to improve forecasts. When decision makers systematically compare their projections to actual outcomes, estimates tend to improve. Conscious or subconscious biases are observed and eliminated and new forecasting methods will be sought as their need becomes apparent. The purpose of the review is to provide information on the effectiveness of the selection process. The actual cash inflows and outflows from a completed project are compared with the estimated cash flows at the time the project was proposed. The

Table 12.2 Strengths and weaknesses of discounted cash-flow methods

Criterion	Project Acceptance Decision Rule	Advantages	Limitations
NPV	Accept project if project has a positive or zero NPV; that is, if the present value of net cash flows, evaluated at the firm's cost of capital, equals or exceeds the net investment required.	Considers the timing of cash flows. Provides an objective, return-based criterion for acceptance or rejection. Most conceptually accurate approach.	Difficulty in interpreting the meaning of the NPV computation.
IRR	Accept project if IRR equals of exceeds the firm's cost of capital.	Easy to interpret the meaning of IRR. Considers the timing of cash flows. Provides an objective, return-based criterion for acceptance or rejection.	Sometimes gives decision that conflicts with NPV. Multiple rates of return problem.
PI	Accept project if PI exceeds one.	Easy to interpret meaning of PI. Considers timing of cash flows. Provides an objective, return-based criterion for acceptance or rejection. PI and NPV methods indicate the same accept–reject decisions for independent projects.	PI and NPV can give inconsistent rankings when mutually exclusive projects are being evaluated.

analysis should emphasise checking for discrepancies in the cash-flow estimates. Some discrepancies are inevitable in view of the uncertainties surrounding future cash flows especially when entirely unforeseen events occur which are beyond the firm's control. Such analysis will enable decision makers to make better evaluations of future investment proposals.

12.6.5 COMMON PITFALLS FOR TOURISM FIRMS TO AVOID IN CAPITAL BUDGETING

We can distinguish five main pitfalls that need to be avoided in capital budgeting:

1. Firms frequently overestimate their cost of capital. The firms cost of capital is an important input in the capital budgeting analysis. Firms may use an estimate of the cost of capital that is too high in the mistaken belief that it is a good idea to screen out all but the most profitable projects. This is bad strategy because so long as a project's rate of return exceeds the firms true cost of capital, its acceptance will increase the firm's value.

2. Firms frequently assume that if they do not invest in new equipment their profits won't be affected. As indicated above, the cash flows used in capital budgeting are incremental, reflecting the difference between what will occur if the project is undertaken and what will happen if it is rejected. In some cases, if the project is not undertaken, the firms' earnings will drop if the firm experiences reduced competitiveness.

3. Firms frequently omit the effects on cash flows of factors that cannot be quantified. Many costs and benefits associated with, for example, improved staff training, computer technology, worker and customer satisfaction or dissatisfaction are often regarded as intangibles which are not explicitly accounted for in the accept/reject decision.

4. Firms frequently create biases favouring small-scale incremental projects and discouraging more ambitious ones. When faced with pressures for change, managers often look for strategies, which are familiar to them. This may involve improving the ways in which they operate, but only piecemeal. This can lead to a phenomenon known as 'strategic drift'. However, managers may not perceive the need for major strategic changes but rather adapt the current ways of operating, and this may lead to a situation of strategic drift. It has been argued that tourism organisations are particularly vulnerable to suffer strategic drift (Dwyer & Edwards, 2009). In many firms, investments are tailored to department budgets, leading to smaller projects than may be required for the firm to maintain competitive advantage.

5. Firms sometimes do not estimate the average weighted cost of capital. The theory and measurement of a firm's cost of capital, which is essential in setting the appropriate discount rate, is a complex topic that is more appropriately dealt with in financial management texts. Only a brief overview is offered here.

In general, a firm is likely to raise capital from undistributed profits, by borrowing and by the sale of stocks, and so the marginal cost of capital to the firm is a weighted average of the cost of raising the various types of capital. The cost of using *internal funds* is the opportunity cost or foregone return on these funds outside the firm. The cost of *external funds* is the lowest rate of return that lenders and stockholders require to lend to or invest their funds in the firm. The cost of each of the various component sources of capital is an important input in the calculation of a firm's overall cost of capital.

The WACC represents the expected rate of return that investors would require in order to supply debt and equity capital for investment in a similar asset. The WACC reflects the returns that could have been earned in the market with this capital, and therefore represents the *opportunity cost* of this capital.

The proper set of weights to be employed in computing the WACC is determined by the optimal financing structure of the firm.

The composite cost of capital to the firm (K_c) is the weighted average of the cost of debt capital (K_d) and equity capital (K_e) as given by

$$K_c = w_d K_d + w_e K_e$$

Where:

w_d is the proportion of debt capital in the firm's capital structure.

w_e is the proportion of equity capital in the firm's capital structure.

For example, if the (after-tax) cost of debt is 7.5%, the cost of equity capital is 15%, and the firm wants to maintain a debt/equity ratio of 40:60, the composite or weighted marginal cost of capital to the firm is

$$K_c = (0.40)(7.5\%) + (0.60)(15\%) = 12\%$$

This is the composite marginal cost of capital that we have used to evaluate all the proposed investment projects that the firm faced in Figures 12.1a and 12.1b. That is, the proportion of debt to equity that the firm seeks to achieve or maintain in the long run is not usually defined for individual projects but for all the investment projects that the firm is considering. Note that the marginal cost of capital eventually rises as the firm raises additional amounts of capital by borrowing and selling stocks because of the higher risk that lenders and investors face as the firm's debt/equity ratio rises.

12.7 CHALLENGES FACING TOURISM INVESTMENT

Despite the tourism industry's impressive growth internationally, it continues to face challenges in attracting private sector investment. A number of critical issues and areas of focus need to be addressed if tourism investment is to be appropriately harnessed to not only maintain our current position in the market but more critically to meet growth forecasts. Box 12.1 summarises some impediments that have been identified as the main factors inhibiting new investment in the tourism accommodation sector.

BOX 12.1 Impediments to new investment in tourism accommodation in Australia

1. *Trading Volatility:* Hotel cash flows are volatile because they are subject to daily tenanting, demand seasonality, property cycles and external shocks such a labour strikes or financial crises. This volatility is exacerbated by the use of management agreements as opposed to leases, which are commonly used in other business relationships.

2. *Poor past performance:* Hotel investments have a history of over- promising and under- delivering; Hotel profits have been constrained by minimal real average daily rate (ADR) growth, high labour costs and periods of oversupply. Since 1997, hotel capital values have decreased.

3. *Return not commensurate with risk:* Hotel investments are seen as riskier than other property due to their business element. Despite this inherent risk profile, hotels have traded at initial yields on par with office yields.

4. *Operator and owner alignment of objectives:* The interests of operators and owners are not completely aligned. While the operator's future business depends on the quality and state of repair of the property, the owner's concern is to maximize investment returns and minimize outgoings. Operators generally have more power in the relationship because they control hotel operations and are experienced with hotels, while owners tend to be fragmented and distanced from hotel operations.

5. *Lack of understanding and need for education:* Institutional investors generally lack experience in hotel investments. This inexperience increases the level of perceived risk and deters investment in the sector. The sector's poor performance and limited size has given institutional investors little incentive to increase their understanding of the sector.

6. *Overpriced and overvalued:* Potential investors believe that investors have paid too much for hotels in the past and that business risk is not sufficiently priced into hotel purchases.

7. *Lack of information:* Although the availability and reliability of market and hotel information has improved in recent years, there is still room for further improvement, particularly relating to operating margins and profit and loss accounts.

8. *Liquidity and exit strategy:* A flexible exit strategy is critical for investors. The relative illiquidity of the hotel market is therefore a major concern. An increase in investment interest and an expansion of the investor base would improve the liquidity of the market.

9. *Size:* The hotel market's small size limits the choice of assets and adversely affects its liquidity, investors' interest and desire to gain knowledge about the sector.

10. *Alignment of industry:* The success of a hotel investment is extremely dependent on other sectors such as airlines, tour operators, tourism marketing bodies, destination attractions etc.

11. *Capital intensive:* Hotels are expensive to establish and maintain. Investors are deterred by the capital intensive nature of hotels.

12. *Government distortions:* Investors believe governments should promote a fair market environment where all types of accommodation are developed to meet demand. At present, investors believe hotels are adversely affected by incentives given to strata titled development.

13. *Fund manager and investor alignment:* Asset consultants need to be convinced that the interests of the fund manager and investors are aligned through attractive structures and fees.

14. *Low barriers to entry:* Investors are wary of the risk of over supply as a result of low barriers to entry, which can adversely affect profitability and investment returns.

15. *Unrealistic investor expectations.* In the past, investors have had negative experiences due to unrealistic expectations and overly optimistic promises. Investors need to understand the risks involved and the level of return they should reasonably expect given these risks.

Source: Property Council of Australia (2003) 'New Investment Frontiers: An Industry Action Plan For Reshaping Hotel Investment', Sydney: PCA

Box 12.2 summarises a study of the factors influencing hotel investment decision-making.

BOX 12.2 Factors influencing hotel investment decision making

Newell and Seabrook conducted a survey of the major hotel investors and hotel owners/operators in Australia to assess the importance of 30 financial, location, economic, diversification and relationship factors in influencing hotel investment decision making. A total of 30 leading hotel investors/owners/operators in Australia were invited to participate, with 15 responding, giving a survey response rate of 50 %. The respondents comprised: hotel investors (47 %), hotel owners/operators (53 %); and publicly listed hotel investors (60 %), private hotel investors (40 %).

An initial content analysis of previous research and the authors' knowledge of the hotel investment sector identified seven factors and 63 sub-factors potentially influencing hotel investment decision making. A first-stage survey of the 15 participants over January–April 2004 rated these factors/sub-factors to achieve a consensus on the most important of these. Those factors/sub-factors, with an average rating of importance of at least 4.5 out of 7 were included in the second-stage survey.

A total of 25 sub-factors in five categories (factors) were subsequently set up in the categories of:

(1) location: six sub-factors;

(2) economic: six sub-factors;

(3) financial: six sub-factors;

(4) diversification: four sub-factors; and

(5) relationship: three sub-factors.

The relative weights of importance assigned to each of these hotel investment decision-making factors and sub-factors were assessed using the multi-criteria decision-making procedure of analytic hierarchy process (AHP). An overall AHP analysis was performed, with separate AHP analyses done to assess. hotel investors versus hotel owners/operators.

Table 12.3 presents the weightings for the five hotel investment decision-making factors based on the AHP analysis for the 15 hotel investment stakeholders, The average consistency ratio of .092 and respondent consistency ratio range of 0.050–0.170 confirms the reliability of these factor weights. The factors in order of importance were financial (37.0 %), location (29.9 %), economic (14.5 %), diversification (12.0 %) and relationship (6.6 %). These AHP results indicate three levels of importance:

(1) level 1: financial, location;

(2) level 2: economic, diversification; and

(3) level 3: relationships.

The financial and location factor weights accounting for over 66 per cent of the total factor weights.

Financial factors (37.0 %) had the highest weight, given hotel investments are prioritized based on underlying financial performance (e.g. forecast ROI, gross operating profit, RevPAR), which is strongly influenced by local market conditions via the location factors (e.g. site attributes, hotel supply and demand); hence the strong link between the financial factor (37.0 %) and the location factor (29.9 %). The relationships factor (e.g. stakeholder alignment, asset management) (6.6 %) was least important.

Table 12.3 also presents the AHP sub-factor weights for the 25 hotel investment decision-making factors. The average consistency ratio of 0.086 and respondent consistency ratio range of 0.024–0.144 confirms the reliability of these factor weights. Forecast ROI (12.5 per cent), site attributes (7.4 per cent), gross operating profit (6.4 per cent) and current hotel supply (6.4 per cent) were the highest weighted sub-factors, with the top ten sub-factors accounting for 63.1 per cent of the sub-factor weights.

Among the 25 sub-factors, the financial sub-factors were most important (ranked 1st, 3rd, 6th, 7th, 11th and 13th) compared to the location sub-factors (ranked 2nd, 4th, 5th, 9th, 15th and 17th), accounting for eight of the top ten sub-factors. Amongst the other factors, only two sub-factors were ranked in the top ten; namely for the diversification factor (segment diversification (8th) and for the relationships factor (alignment with stakeholders (10th). No economic sub-factors were ranked in the top ten sub-factors. Within the financial sub-factors, hotel investors placed greatest emphasis on short to medium return on investment (five-year forecast ROI) as well as gross operating profit and historic rate of return. While RevPAR is consistently presented as an important barometer of hotel trends it was only ranked 7th amongst the hotel investment decision-making sub-factors, with a weighting of 5.1 %.

Table 12.3 AHP weightings for hotel investment decision making

Factors	Factor weight (%)	Sub-factors	Sub-factor weight (%)	Sub-factor rank
Financial	37.0	Forecast ROI (five years)	12.5	1
		Gross operating profit	6.4	3
		Historical rates of return	6.2	6
		RevPAR as a return measure	5.1	7
		Unsystematic risk	3.5	11
		Economies of scale advantages	3.2	13
Location	29.9	Site attributes	7.4	2
		Current hotel supply	6.4	4
		Volatility of demand	6.3	5
		Number of domestic visitors	4.5	9
		Number of international visitors	2.8	15
		Age of target hotel	2.6	17
Economic	14.5	Business spending patterns	3.5	12
		Interest rates	2.7	16
		Extent market is emerging	2.3	18
		Tourist spending patterns	2.2	19
		Extent market is mature	2.1	21
		Employment growth (office)	1.8	24
Diversification	12.0	Segment diversification	4.8	8
		Geographic diversification	3.0	14
		Link to target property	2.2	20
		Brand diversification	2.0	23
Relationships	6.6	Alignment with stakeholders	3.5	10
		Independent asset management	2.1	22
		Regulatory influence	0.9	25
Total	100		100	

The authors note that location sub-factors are seen to be more important than the economic sub-factors. Hotel investors place greater emphasis on location attributes that they can specifically identify, rather than macroeconomic impacts such as business and tourist spending patterns and growth patterns in employment. In particular, site attributes were seen as the second most important sub-factor, with site attributes including hotel visibility, proximity to infrastructure including transportation, attractions, convention facilities and other demand generating facilities.

None of the economic sub-factors were in the top ten sub-factors or had sub-factor weights exceeding 3.5 %. Whilst many of the economic sub-factors influence financial performance and investment returns, they were not considered major influences when evaluating hotel investments, but tending to influence the location and financial sub-factors indirectly. The authors suggest that hotel investment issues appear to be micro or localized rather than being broader macroeconomic influences.

Amongst the diversification sub-factors, segment diversification (4.8 %; ranked 8th) to reduce property-specific occupancy risk was seen to be more important than geographic diversification (ranked 14th) and brand diversification (ranked 23rd). The relationships sub-factors did not figure prominently, with only alignment with stakeholders (3.5 %; ranked 10th) being seen as important. The lesser importance given to independent asset management (ranked 22nd) reflects the fact that a number of the respondents were hotel owners/operators or hotel investors with in-house asset management teams.

Newell and Seabrook also assessed whether there were differences between the hotel investors and hotel owners/operators. Table 12.4 presents the respective factor weights for these two groups.

Whilst the two group's factor weights were highly correlated (rank correlation = 0.90), there were significant differences in their factor priorities. In particular, hotel owners/operators placed a higher weight on location factors (37.1 %) than did hotel investors (21.7 %), while hotel investors placed the highest weight on financial factors (40.2 percent). This reflects hotel owners/operators greater familiarity with the key drivers of operational performance when evaluating hotel investments, as well as greater awareness of the business aspects of hotel investment compared to hotel investors. Hotel investors emphasized financial factors (40.2 %), reflecting their focus on financial performance outcomes such as forecast ROI, historic returns and gross operating profit, while hotel owners/operators placed greater emphasis on the process or factors influencing the outcome.

Table 12.4 AHP Weightings: Hotel Investors Vs Hotel owners/operators

	Weights				Significance*
	Hotel investors (%)	Factor/ sub-factor rank	Hotel owners/ operators (%)	Factor/ sub-factor rank	
Factors					
Location	21.7	2	37.1	1	Yes
Economic	17.4	3	15.9	3	No
Financial	40.2	1	34.1	2	No
Diversification	14.1	4	10.2	4	No
Relationships	6.5	5	6.6	5	No
Sub-factors					
Volatility of demand	5.1	6	7.3	3	*No*
number of international visitors	2.8	15	2.8	14	No
number of domestic visitors	3.8	10	5.0	7	No
Site attributes	3.2	14	11.0	2	Yes
Age of target hotel	1.4	24	3.7	9	Yes
Current hotel supply	5.4	5	7.3	5	No
Interest rates	4.2	9	1.4	23	No
Tourist spending patterns	2.1	22	2.3	17	No
Business spending patterns	3.7	12	3.3	12	No
Employment growth (office)	2.5	19	1.2	24	No
Extent market is mature	2.2	20	2.0	19	No

Extent market is emerging	2.9	16	1.8	21 ·	No
Forecast ROI (five years)	12.3	1	12.6	1	No
Historical rates of return	8.9	2	3.9	8	No
Unsystematic risk	4.8	8	2.4	16	Yes
RevPAR as a return measure	4.9	7	5.2	6	No
Gross operating profit	5.5	4	7.3	4	No
Economies of scale advantages	3.8	11	2.7	15	No
Geographic diversification	2.5	18	3.5	11	No
Brand diversification	2.1	21	1.9	20	No
Segment diversification	6.7	3	3.1	13	No
Link to target property	2.8	17	1.7	22	No
Regulatory influence	1.0	25	0.9	25	No
Independent asset management	2.0	23	2.2	18	No
Alignment with stakeholders	3.6	13	3.5	10	*No*

Notes: *Significance represents significant difference between hotel investor and hotel owner/operator factor/sub-factor weights ($p < 5$ per cent)

The authors conclude that their study should assist hotel investors' prioritize the key factors and sub-factors in their hotel investment decision making.

Source: Newell, G. and R. Seabrook (2006) 'Factors Influencing Hotel Investment Decision Making', *Journal of Property Investment and Finance*, 24(4), 279–294

In late 2009, as this chapter is being written, the global financial crisis (GFC) is affecting tourism worldwide. The world economy is in, or going into, recession. Financial, business and consumer confidence are at almost record low levels. Asset prices and wealth have been declined substantially. International trade volumes have been adversely affected, with further declines likely. Unemployment is rising sharply, consumer spending is falling and businesses are collapsing, with investment reduced or cancelled. Inflation is slowing rapidly, commodity prices have collapsed, with deflation a real possibility in some countries. Currency values in many destinations have declined to historically low levels. Initially at least, attempts to halt the economic slide by policy stimuli are, at most, slowing the decline, not reversing it.

Broad solutions to restore conditions for growth all have serious consequences for tourism. Individuals and businesses need to reduce debt ('de-leverage'). Asset prices need to fall to more sustainable levels (to prices reflecting capitalised sustainable investment yields). In short, collectively we need to save more, consume less and accept wealth reductions as asset prices fall. In mid-2009 depressed consumer and business confidence were delivering all three (Carmody, 2009).

It is not only tourism flows and associated expenditure that are being affected by the GFC. Declining asset values impact on the ability of firms to fund debt or invest, and many capital projects (including fleet expansion, hotel projects, attractions, etc.) are being shelved due to financing difficulties. Credit availability and de-risking of bank balance sheets stifle tourism investment.

Despite its immediate effects on tourism investment, the GFC presents opportunities for both tourism operators and destination managers to undertake actions to enhance competitive advantage over the longer term. Thus tourism firms can undertake various actions that will better position them to access higher yield visitors when GFC ends. They can, for example:

- identify distortions that increase the costs of doing business, thereby reducing destination price competitiveness;
- assess areas for productivity improvement including staff training;
- carry out internal structural reforms which facilitate technological and organisational innovations;
- assess existing and future markets in light of changing consumer values and needs, including competitor analysis;
- identify demand-creating strategies, specifically those that *add value* rather than those that give price cuts to customers to maintain or improve market share;
- maintain or improve the quality of existing capacity to move up the yield curve to provide the basis for competitive advantage after GFC ends.

To undertake any of these strategies, a sound knowledge of the rationales for tourism investment, methods of financing as well as an understanding of techniques of evaluating such investments are required.

12.8 CONCLUSIONS AND POLICY

- Tourism investment refers to the spending on capital and financial assets that is undertaken by private tourism firms and governments in the expectation of future returns. It underlies and supports tourism development and is vital both to the individual firm and to the destination.
- Successful investment by a tourism firm increases that firm's capacity and profits and aids the tourism sector generally.
- The broader national and regional benefits that come from a more favourable tourism investment climate include economic growth; job creation; utilisation of domestic resources, particularly renewable resources; skills acquisition; expansion of exports; development of remote areas of the country; and facilitation of increased ownership of investment by the nation's citizens.
- Tourism investment is analysed under three pairings: (1) capital tourism investment (fixed and working capital spending that is specifically designed to generate further long-term output) versus financial tourism investment (the placement of funds on financial markets in order to earn interest, or dividend payments on monies presently not earmarked for capital investment); (2) private tourism investment (undertaken by private firms) versus public investment (undertaken by government collectively on behalf of the community); and (3) domestic investment (undertaken within a country) versus foreign investment (undertaken within other countries).
- Capital investment may be financed in any of five ways: profits, debt, equity, securitisation, and grants and subsidies. It may be generated by the need to: replace capital assets, reduce production costs, expand output, or expand into new product lines or markets, or by government regulation.
- Capital budgeting is the name given to the process of planning the capital investment expenditures. Successful capital budgeting depends on several steps: the accurate estimation of all future cash inflows and outflows (measured in terms of today's dollars) for each potential alternative capital investment project; the evaluation of these alternative projects; the choice of one or more of them for implementation; and the review after the investment projects have all been implemented.
- Following the principles of marginal analysis, a tourism firm should undertake additional investment projects until the marginal return from the investment is equal to its marginal cost. The firm's actual decision as to whether to accept or reject any particular investment project will depend on its accept–reject criteria.
- At a given point in time and in a given capital market, there is a large number of interest rates depending on relative risk, term structure, administration costs and tax treatment.

- Common accept–reject criteria include ROI, payback period, NPV, the IRR and the PI.
- Pitfalls for firms to avoid in capital budgeting include over estimating the cost of capital; assuming that profits will be unaffected by new investment; omitting the effects on cash flows of factors that cannot be quantified; creating biases favouring small-scale incremental projects and discouraging more ambitious ones; and failing to estimate the average weighted cost of capital.
- Despite the tourism industry's impressive growth internationally, it continues to face challenges in attracting private sector investment. Impediments to new capital investment include trading volatility in some tourism sectors; poor past performance; misalignment of risk and return; misalignment of owner and management objectives; misalignment of investors and fund managers; misalignment of different sectors within the tourism industry; the illiquidity and capital-intensive nature of some tourism sectors; low barriers to entry within much of the tourism industry; lack of information on and understanding of tourism investment; the small size of some tourism sectors; and government distortions.

SELF-REVIEW QUESTIONS

1. Briefly distinguish between the following types of tourism investment:

(i) Capital tourism investment and financial tourism investment.
(ii) Private tourism investment and public tourism investment.
(iii) Domestic tourism investment and foreign tourism investment.

2. Use tourism examples to explain the relationship between gross investment, net investment and depreciation.

3. What might generate the need for a tourism firm to undertake capital investment, and from what sources might the firm obtain its finances?

4. Define the term capital budgeting.

5. Outline the steps that need to be taken in the selection of a capital tourism investment project.

6. Explain both the reason for and the practical use of discounting in the measurement of future cash flows emanating from a tourism project.

7. What is your understanding of the difference between NPV, IRR and PI?

8. Briefly examine the five pitfalls that need to be avoided in capital budgeting.

9. The WACC represents the opportunity of that capital. How so?

ESSAY QUESTIONS

1. In a capital budgeting framework the tourism firm should undertake additional investment projects until the marginal return from the investment is equal to its marginal cost. Explain why.

2. Explain how, at any one time and in any given capital market, there may be a large number of interest rates depending on relative risk, term structure, administration costs and tax treatment.

3. One of the most important and difficult aspects of capital budgeting is the estimation of the net cash flow from a project. Why is this so?

4. Compare and contrast the use of NPV and IRR in the selection or rejection of a tourism project.

5. For a selected tourism sector, discuss the types of challenges that might affect the appropriate level of investment.

6. Explain the various ways that the GFC adversely impacted upon levels of tourism investment.

CHAPTER 13

INVESTING IN TOURISM INFRASTRUCTURE

LEARNING OBJECTIVES

After reading this chapter, you should be able to:

1. Explain the meaning of tourism infrastructure and argue the importance of investment in tourism infrastructure.

2. Distinguish between private tourism infrastructure and public tourism infrastructure and appreciate the move from the public provision of public tourism infrastructure towards the private provision of tourism infrastructure.

3. Discuss the reasons for the increasing emphasis on 'user pays' and the rise in the use of public–private partnerships (PPPs) in the provision of tourism infrastructure and the benefits that such partnerships can generate.

4. Appreciate the congestion problem that may accompany the use of tourism infrastructure.

5. Argue for and against the regulation of monopoly tourism infrastructure and discuss the broad approaches that authorities may take to its regulation.

6. Appreciate the environmental issues surrounding the development of tourism infrastructure.

7. Appreciate the particular problems that developing countries face in ensuring that their infrastructure helps their tourism development.

13.1   INTRODUCTION

Infrastructure refers to the basic physical and organisational structures needed for the operation of a society or the services and facilities necessary for an economy to function. The term typically refers to the technical structures and assets that support a society, such as networks, air services, airports, water supply, waste disposal systems, energy and power generation, post and telecommunications, recreational assets and so forth. Infrastructure facilitates the production of goods and services; for example, roads enable the transport of raw materials to a factory, and also for the distribution of finished products to markets, while power supply enables many of the economic activities associated with tourism. Infrastructure may also include basic social services such as education and health care.

In this chapter, infrastructure is used in the sense of technical structures or physical networks that support society (Gramlich, 1994). The operation of tourism facilities, services and amenities is heavily dependent on the available quantity and quality of public infrastructure. In addition to the provision of public infrastructure, the success of any tourism destination is dependent to a large degree on the nature of the facilities and services infrastructure that are available to the tourist. While the infrastructure does not in itself generate tourism flows, they do enable or facilitate visitation, by adding value to the tourism experience, and can act as a deterrent to tourism if perceived to be inadequate in quantity or quality. We can usefully divide these facilities into three groups

Primary tourist facilities and services (accommodation/hotels, restaurants, fast food outlets, taverns/bars, travel and tour services, car rental companies, etc.);

Secondary tourist facilities and services (shopping facilities, convention facilities, recreational assets, entertainment and visitor information services);

Tertiary tourist facilities and services (health services and care, emergency and safety services, financial services and personal services, police force, legal system, etc).

These facilities and service infrastructure provide complementary experiences that contribute to the overall attractiveness of a tourism destination.

In their Travel and Tourism Competitiveness Index, the World Economic Forum (WEF, 2009) distinguishes four main types of indicators of infrastructure as important for destination competitiveness. These are as follows:

Air transport infrastructure: Quality of air transport infrastructure; Available seat kilometres; Departures per 1000 population; Airport density; Number of operating airlines; International air transport network.

Ground transport infrastructure: Quality of roads; Quality of railroad infrastructure; Quality of port infrastructure; Quality of domestic transport network; Road density.

Tourism infrastructure: Hotel rooms; Presence of major car rental companies; ATMs accepting Visa cards.

Information Communications Technology (ICT) infrastructure: Extent of business Internet use; Internet users; Telephone lines.

The developed countries tend to rank highly in respect of the quantity and quality of the different types of infrastructure, highlighting the inherent competitive advantages of developed economies across their industrial sectors. These basic infrastructure differences between developed and developing destinations will take many years to overcome.

A visitor's experience depends on all these forms of infrastructure. Poor infrastructure provision will result in a less enjoyable trip, and in the longer term will discourage tourism visits. Poor transport infrastructure, for example, makes it difficult for the tourist to enjoy a visit – the tourist is held up in airport delays, experiences long waits in passport and customs controls when entering the country, faces traffic jams in travelling to the hotel and faces inconvenience in travelling around the destination. Good infrastructure facilitates tourism development in a region or country, and in turn, enables the destination to maximise its economic and other benefits from tourism. If infrastructure is good, it is hardly noticed by the tourists, who can concentrate on experiencing the benefits of the trip.

Investment in tourism infrastructure is important for a number of reasons:

- Infrastructure is required for the development and growth of tourism capacity so that supply can match a growing demand.
- The creation of tourism infrastructure creates jobs – both during the construction stage and in operations.
- Public sector investment in 'tourism and community infrastructure' may have both counter-cyclical and longer-term merits, provided the social return justifies the use of taxpayer funds involved.
- Infrastructure increases the efficiency of privately producing and distributing tourism services and makes possible the supply of tourism services.
- The provision of tourism infrastructure is of particular importance for long term tourism growth. Expanded facilities are needed to serve the needs of visitors and to maintain relatively uninterrupted service levels.
- The infrastructure on which a country's tourism industry relies, such as its roads, railways, airports, terminals, accommodation facilities, shopping, entertainment, restaurants, currency exchange facilities, telecommunications and so on are major determinants of its overall destination competitiveness including destination 'experience' and perceived trip value (WEF, 2009).

There are few infrastructure investments that can be regarded as purely tourism infrastructure. Just as tourism is not a single well-defined industry, but rather a sector which draws, to a greater or lesser degree, on several other industries, so too there is no clearly defined 'tourism' infrastructure. Some infrastructure facilities are largely tourism oriented – airports, and some long-distance rail systems, are primarily oriented to serving tourists, though even these serve other markets (e.g. an airport also handles freight). Airport rail links, roads to tourism destinations and cruise terminals are also primarily oriented to tourism. In addition, tourists also make extensive use of general infrastructure, even though they account for only a small proportion of total demand. Thus tourists use a city's public transport system, urban and rural roads, the hospital system and telecommunications facilities.

Getting tourism infrastructure 'right' is easier said than done. Infrastructure industries are often complex ones which pose a number of public policy problems which need to be addressed – for example, they are often monopolies, and governments will wish to limit the use of their market power. Infrastructure projects, which often involve large, capital-intensive investments, often have a large environmental impact, which means that obtaining approval for them is a drawn out process.

In this chapter, we cover some of the main economic problems associated with ensuring the supply of tourism infrastructure. The issues addressed are as follows:

- the changes that have been taking place in the institutional structure of infrastructure – the move from public to private provision;
- the congestion problem which impedes the efficiency of infrastructure provision;
- problems in government regulation of tourism infrastructure;
- the effects of environmental constraints on infrastructure;
- how provision of good infrastructure can stimulate tourism;
- the particular problems that developing countries face in ensuring that their infrastructure helps their tourism development.

13.2 PUBLIC INFRASTRUCTURE INVESTMENT FOR ECONOMIC DEVELOPMENT

Public investment in tourism infrastructure may occur to promote a more balanced economic development or for competitive positioning reasons. In the case of developing countries, capital markets are also undeveloped, and governments assume a larger role in the provision of infrastructure.

Public infrastructure investment, and other forms of government intervention in providing infrastructure, is supported by new theories of economic growth (Sakai, 2006). These suggest that economic growth arises not only from physical equipment capital but also from public infrastructure and human capital. In this expanded definition of capital, airport and roadway infrastructure would clearly support tourism-driven economic growth, shifting the country's comparative advantage towards a targeted tourism sector and moving the economy to a higher growth path by producing a product with a higher income elasticity of demand (Sinclair & Stabler, 1997: 149–150).

The benefits that come from the provision of additional capacity can be illustrated by means of an example. Recently, a study was undertaken of the costs and benefits of additional capacity at Heathrow airport (Department for Transport, 2009). We referred to this study in Chapter 10. For present purposes, we can highlight how overcoming capacity constraints brings benefits to a destination. In Figure 13.1, consumer surplus is the difference between what a passenger would have been willing to pay for a flight and the actual fare,

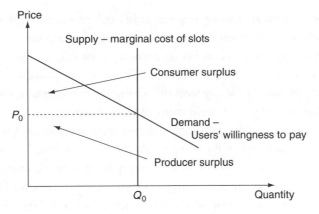

Figure 13.1 Producer and consumer surplus with supply constraint

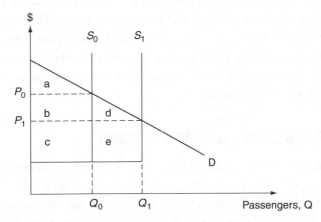

Figure 13.2 Effects on consumer and producer surplus of increased capacity

Source: Adapted from Department of Transport (2009), Annex C, Figure C2

aggregated over all passengers. Producer surplus measures the difference between the cost of each additional flight and the actual charge for those flights. The vertical supply curve reflects the capacity of the airport to service flights thus limiting passenger movements.

Additional capacity may generate benefits for users as shown in Figure 13.2. The change in supply of airport capacity is shown in the change from S_0 to S_1, while the demand for flights is represented by D. As additional capacity becomes available, price will fall by the amount $(P_0 - P_1)$, as the equilibrium moves from the initial situation of capacity S_0 to a new equilibrium with additional capacity S_1. This means that the number of passengers increases by $(Q_1 - Q_0)$ as a result of the reduction in costs.

The move from capacity S_0 to S_1 affects the volume of consumer and producer surplus. Before the capacity increase, the consumer surplus was area a. Areas b and c were producer surplus, similar to Figure 13.1 above. As capacity increases out to S_1, additional consumer surplus of the area d is created while area e is additional producer surplus (airport expansion allows operators to gain additional revenues through levying airport charges on more aircraft). Another change also occurs because when prices fall, the area b which was previously captured by producers is now captured by consumers. However, because this area is not created through additional capacity, this change is considered a *transfer* of benefits, and thus, is not counted as a net benefit from additional capacity.

Government participation in providing tourism infrastructure is likely to be high if tourism plays a significant role in the economy or its development. This implies that government support for tourism infrastructure development is not confined to developing countries. In North America and increasingly in Europe, rejuvenation of urban core areas is being supported by public infrastructure investment. As Sakai (2006) notes, destination cities are discovering the economic potential of developing the city as a recreational centre, linking existing cultural attractions and building new ones to create tourist precincts. Among the growing examples of infrastructure for this vision of the city are convention centres, stadia or other sporting venues, and festival malls. Baade (1997) has noted the links that are being increasingly developed between airport, highway, convention centre and stadia financing. Typically, they are integrated into a single economic package designed to attract visitors to the destination city.

13.3 INFRASTRUCTURE PROVISION: THE NEW MODEL

Infrastructure may be provided by the public sector or the private sector, and the outcome is often determined by domestic economic, social and political policies. Infrastructure generally, and in particularly the infrastructure which is used by tourists, has experienced a major shift in its patterns of provision. Two or so decades ago, most tourism infrastructure outside North America was provided by the public sector. Airports, roads, railways, urban transport and terminal facilities were predominantly publicly owned. Governments often set up public enterprises or authorities to operate them.

While this remains the model for some forms of infrastructure in some countries, the emphasis has shifted to private infrastructure, albeit usually still government regulated. The trend to privatisation has been strong in the UK, Australia and New Zealand, and it has been present, though to a lesser degree in many Asian countries and in European countries such as Germany and Poland. There has not been much of a shift in North America however – infrastructure which was publicly owned (airports) has remained so, and private infrastructure (railways) has also remained relatively unchanged.

There are several economic and political rationales for this shift towards privatisation. These include the following:

- Dissatisfaction with the poor performance of many publicly owned enterprises.
- High operating costs.

- Low-quality service.
- Unreliable service.
- Enterprises unresponsive to customer needs.
- Inadequate investment in new capacity due to government restrictions on capital raising.

Regarding the concern over excessive investment, sometimes the problems were the reverse of this – public enterprises would be pressured into making extravagant investments by their government owners, Thus airports were expected to build lavish terminals to be regarded as icons, and railway stations were seen as expressions of a city's identity. Sometimes taxpayers paid for these, but in a world moving towards 'user pays' it was often the traveller who paid by way of higher fares.

Moves to privatisation have been expected to result in improved performance of infrastructure generally, including tourism-oriented infrastructure. Anticipated benefits are the reverse of the above concerns. It is expected that private owners would have a strong incentive to keep costs (though not prices) down. They would be more responsive to their customer's needs, and would provide services of a quality that the customers were prepared to pay for. They would have a strong incentive to ensure that capacity was adequate to meet demand – they cannot make profits out of potential customers that cannot be served. Equally, private owners would have an interest in more efficient investment decision-making.

The problem with private ownership is that the owners also have a strong incentive to make use of their market power and raise prices to increase profits. Many forms of tourism-oriented infrastructure possess market power. Thus an airport may be a monopoly in a particular city, a railway may have a monopoly of fast surface transport in a region, and there is likely to be only one cruise terminal in a city. Recognising this, when governments have privatised, they have also tended to introduce price controls. Thus the London airports are subjected to limits on the prices they can charge. The rail track monopoly in the UK was price regulated (until it was re-nationalised), and private toll roads have price restrictions written into their contracts. However, while regulation handles the problem of private infrastructure suppliers abusing their monopoly power, it does this by creating a number of other difficulties. The problems in designing regulation to ensure adequate and efficient infrastructure are discussed below.

The move to privatisation has been associated with more than just sale of government-owned enterprises. Two recent trends may be highlighted. These are the establishment of Public–Private Partnerships (PPPs), and an increasing emphasis on 'user pays'.

13.3.1 PUBLIC–PRIVATE PARTNERSHIPS

A PPP or P[3] describe a government service or private business venture which is funded and operated through a partnership of government and one or more private sector companies. In some types of P[3], the government uses tax revenue to provide capital for investment, with operations run jointly with the private sector or under contract. In other types, capital investment is undertaken by the private sector under contract with government to provide agreed services. Government contributions to a P^3 may also be in kind (notably the transfer of existing assets for use by the partnership). The government may also provide a capital subsidy in the form of a one-time grant, so as to make the partnership more attractive to the private investors. In some other cases, the government may support the project by providing revenue subsidies, including tax concessions or by providing guaranteed annual revenues for a fixed period.

Partnerships between the public sector and the private sector for the purposes of designing, planning, financing, constructing and/or operating projects represent an important trend in many countries. In Canada, P^3 include the 407 ETR toll road north of Toronto, the Confederation Bridge construction in Prince Edward Island and Canada Line automated rapid transit service in Greater Vancouver. In the USA, P^3 include New York City's Central Park and the Las Vegas Monorail and the redevelopment of downtown Chattanooga, Tennessee from the mid-1980s to the present. Australian examples include: Sydney Airport Link, the Sydney Harbour Tunnel, and the Southern Cross Station redevelopment in Melbourne. Traditionally, such projects would have been regarded as falling under the exclusive responsibility of the public sector.

P^3 can yield three main types of benefits

- P^3 can increase the volume of investments that can be delivered during a given period of time;
- P^3 can drive the restructuring and privatisation of incumbent companies, leading to reduced government subsidies and greater transparency;
- Substantial efficiency and quality gains may result from giving more responsibilities to the private sector. The basis of all P^3 is the provision of private sector capital. Within a P^3 framework, this can enhance the effectiveness of government support for infrastructure development through transferring risks to the private sector (in cases where the latter is presumed to be better able to assess the risks) and creating powerful private sector incentives for the long-term delivery of reliable public services.

However, ensuring that P^3 are successful requires the structuring of the P^3 in consultation with the private sector, together with regulatory bodies or a public sector dedicated to industry development and competitiveness.

In P^3, the government will set the terms of the contract, and may become the ultimate owner, but the private sector builds, and perhaps operates, the facility. Thus a private developer may rebuild a railway station for the government owner, or may build and operate a toll road to government specifications. While P^3 are a new institutional format, many of the issues they pose are similar to those with regulated private infrastructure. It is expected that more P^3 will be prominent in tourism infrastructure development in the future.

13.3.2 USER PAYS

Another trend over recent decades has been towards 'user pays' to access infrastructure. Previously, governments were willing to subsidise key infrastructure quite heavily – airports and railways were not expected to cover costs, and most roads were provided free of charge to users. Nowadays, private suppliers of infrastructure expect to make a profit from their investments, and public enterprises are expected to at least cover their costs. Users, including tourists, are expected to pay the cost of the services they use.

As Sakai (2006) notes, if private benefits are large and if direct users are easily identified and charged for their use of infrastructure, government may assess user charges or benefit taxes to finance that portion of the infrastructure investment associated with private benefits (Fisher, 1996). These user charges provide a signal to users of the opportunity costs of the resources used. User charges are often used to recover the costs of operation and to bring about efficient pricing in the presence of congestion externalities. User charges may be earmarked or deposited into special funds that support specific infrastructure spending, such as highway or aviation funds. Although earmarking of general tax revenues create budget inflexibility and inefficiency in allocation (see Chapter 15), this is less so with user charges, particularly when the amount of user charge reflects marginal costs and benefits. Overall, user charges or benefit taxes are attractive as an efficient and equitable method of paying for the private benefits derived from infrastructure.

Given that public infrastructure tends to exhibit increasing returns to scale and that tourism infrastructure users are easy to identify, Sakai (2006) claims it is no surprise that roads, water systems and waste systems, and parks are managed as quasi-public enterprises, funded by special taxes earmarked to the enterprise fund; and that new roles for a larger private share of infrastructure investment are emerging as important methods of financing airports, seaports, stadia and sporting venues, and convention centres.

13.4 THE CONGESTION PROBLEM IN TOURISM INFRASTRUCTURE

One important feature of much of tourism infrastructure is that it becomes congested as demand presses up against capacity. Much infrastructure does not have an absolute capacity limit. More and more people can be processed through an airport terminal – the problem is that as this happens, the quality of the service declines, as spaces become crowded, and queue lengths and delays grow. Thus, as more cars use a tourist road, traffic congestion increases and journeys become slower. As more tourists attempt to use a train, it becomes uncomfortably crowded, and as more aircraft attempt to use an airport, flights are stacked and aircraft have to wait longer on the ground for permission to take off.

At its simplest, increased congestion of a facility such as an airport, road or railway implies that the quality of the service declines. Congestion comes about when more and more users try to use a facility of limited size. As additional users come, they experience delays or crowding. However, their very act of adding to the numbers makes the situation

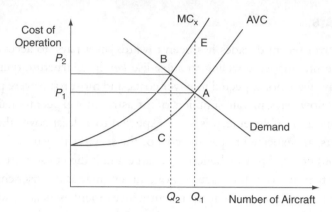

Figure 13.3 Congestion and aircraft cost curves

Source: Adapted from Poole and Dachis (2007)

worse for the others. If you join a queue, you have to wait, but you also make the wait longer for others who join the queue after you do. Thus there is an external cost associated with the use of the facility. When this is the case, and users face only the costs that they themselves bear, but not the extra costs they impose on others, there will be excessive use of the facility.

This is shown in Figure 13.3, which is the traditional congestion diagram. As the use of the facility increases, the Average Variable Cost (AVC) also increases. Figure 13.3 shows that AVC curve of a single plane departing an airport. Each individual plane has an AVC that, due to density of aircraft, increases as it spends more time waiting in the departure queue. With a demand curve D, the equilibrium will be one where the effective 'price' of use is P_1 and amount of use is Q_1.

The external marginal cost is represented by the curve MC_x. These external marginal costs would include the time costs to travellers checking in to an airport resulting from delays at the check-in, and the cost of delays to other airlines and their passengers when queues develop to take off and land at a busy airport. The overall cost imposed by a marginal user is above AVC, because of the effect that each user has in making delays worse for other users. However, airlines consider only their internal costs of delays and schedule flights up to the point Q_1. This is despite the fact that an additional user at Q_1 would impose a cost equal to Q_1E, reflecting an externality cost of EA. To ensure more efficient use of this facility, it is necessary to internalise the externality – for example, by imposing a charge on it.

If a congestion tax equal to BC were levied on users, they would reduce their use to Q_2. A congestion charge equal to BC will bring internal airline costs in line with the external costs imposed on the travelling public and other departing aircraft and will reduce the demand for departures at a given time period, not necessarily overall, to the level Q_2.

While fewer users use the facility, overall congestion costs would fall considerably, and overall, better utilisation of the facility would be achieved. The effects of taxes on tourism will be discussed in detail in Chapter 15. Further treatment of externalities in tourism will be addressed in Chapter 17.

The thrust of this argument is that much infrastructure, and especially that which is used by tourism, can become overused. Congestion can be lessened by increasing the capacity of the facility, but this can be very expensive, and it is not always feasible (it is very difficult to expand capacity at many airports). Thus there is a major problem in ensuring that limited facilities be used as effectively as is possible.

An example of this is the London road system. For some years, there has been a congestion charge for driving on central London roads (and some cities, such as Singapore have had congestion charges for much longer than this). While fewer cars use the London roads, traffic congestion has been much reduced, and journeys are quicker.

A less obvious example occurs with airports. The airports of North America and Europe are subject to heavy demand, and capacity is often inadequate. In the USA, long queues develop to use the busier airports. By contrast, in Europe, the problem is recognised, and use of airports is limited. To use a busy airport at a busy time, an airline must have a 'slot' – and only a limited number of slots, corresponding to the number of flights that can be handled with low delay, are issued. Since they are in limited supply, slots to use popular airports can be very valuable – a daily slot pair at London Heathrow airport can command £10 million. In Figure 13.3, this would correspond to the airport issuing an amount Q_2 of slots. The result is that while there are still delays at European airports, these are small compared to those at US airports, even for the busiest European airports.

Thus it is not just a matter of providing enough infrastructure capacity – one of the big issues with tourism infrastructure is one of ensuring that whatever capacity is provided is utilised most effectively. This can become a real issue for regulators. Box 13.1 discusses some issues in pricing congestion at New York airports.

BOX 13.1 Congestion pricing at New York airports

Congestion, caused by demand for flights in excess of airport capacity, with its effects on air traffic control systems, has placed a heavy burden on travellers and airlines. Delayed flights, long waits for takeoff, in-air holds for landing, and long taxi-in delays have made air travel much less convenient and have imposed substantial costs on airlines. The problem is particularly severe in New York, where congestion has reached unacceptable levels at Kennedy, LaGuardia, and Newark. Consequently, the Department of Transportation is proposing to introduce congestion charges at New York's LaGuardia and Kennedy airports.

Levine (2007) agrees that this seems a good idea since it has long been recognized that airport congestion can best be relieved by levying airport takeoff and landing fees based on the economic costs of imposed delays on other airport users rather than based on aircraft weight. Levying airport charges that reflect the scarcity of the chosen landing or takeoff time would force all operators, airline and general aviation alike, to consider whether they value use of the runway at that time enough to pay for the costs they impose on others. The principle should be the same for air traffic control. Congestion in the terminal area calls out for a system of charges that makes the aircraft operator ask 'How much do I value this trip at this time? Would saving money by rescheduling it make sense? Is this trip necessary?' As Levine emphasises, imposing congestion charges would both assign existing capacity to use by those who value it most and signal that additional capacity is needed. Such a scheme not only constitutes a means of valuing capacity expansion, but also of providing the necessary funding.

Economic theory supports the imposition of congestion charges to promote economic efficiency. Theatres, movie exhibitors, hoteliers, restaurants, telephone companies, parking lots, and many other businesses implement peak/off peak pricing (a form of congestion charges) every day. Congestion charges will direct valuable and limited capacity to its highest-valued use and improve social welfare. However, Levine cautions us that under the particular conditions of New York, there are reasons to be concerned that the proposal will not just fail and do economic damage, but will develop a political constituency that would make it very hard to undo. He argues that the institutions and legislation that are already in place will create perverse incentives that could worsen the congestion problem. Instead, such prices would become just another tax – an inefficient source of politically useful funds.

Levine argues that the impediments to successful congestion charges that exist at important airports around the country, and particularly at airports with extensive aircraft operations by foreign airlines and general aviation, must be eliminated before congestion charges are implemented. Noting that legislated public monopolies control all air-carrier airports (or, in cases like New York, all such airports capable of supporting long-haul operations) in the most important aviation markets in the country. While in most places the effects of these monopoly city departments or public authorities are constrained by legislation and regulations that limit charges and the uses to which airport revenues can be put, that is not universally the case. For these reasons this can cause problems of the following sort:

- Some monopolies – including the Port Authority of New York and New Jersey, have 'grandfathered' exemptions from many of those restrictions.
- In addition, the FAA and the Department of State have interpreted American obligations under international bilateral aviation agreements as requiring them to exempt foreign carriers from congestion-relieving airport measures that might impede foreign carrier exercise of their bilateral rights at particular airports, even if the regulations apply non-discriminatorily to US carriers.
- Political and congressional advocates for general aviation and for service to smaller communities have carved out exceptions to previous congestion limiting measures, designed to mitigate their impact on those constituencies and concentrate the impact on other US airlines.

In this context, to make congestion pricing work in a way that promotes rather than impedes economic efficiency, several key problems must be addressed.

There must be no exemptions. Levine argues that exemptions for foreign carriers to accommodate bilateral concerns, or for general aviation aircraft, or for service to small communities will be both inefficient and discriminatory. It cannot be assumed that the exempted operations value the use of the runway more than those who are charged, so exempting them creates economic inefficiency. Also, if the exempted users are free to increase aircraft operations while those who are charged reduce theirs, that this backfilling by those exempted this may simply reestablish the congestion problem while raising the congestion prices to US airlines. This could result in a situation wherein US airline operations, which presumably are at least as valuable as those exempted, have been minimized and replaced by less valuable uses. This discrimination against US airlines would also imply a waste of scarce and valuable airport capacity.

Airport monopolies must be addressed. Most metropolitan areas, including New York, have only one operator for all of their air-carrier airports, thus creating a monopoly even if there is more than one such airport. The most obvious exception is San Francisco/Oakland/San Jose, where inter-airport competition has contributed greatly to cost control and efficiency. Where there is an airport monopoly and the monopolist benefits financially from congestion charges, there is a financial incentive to maintain congestion, especially if runway capacity expansion is politically unpopular. Acknowledging that the monopolies have proved virtually impossible to regulate from the outside from both a political and monitoring standpoint,

Levine argues that a mechanism must be found to link funds raised from congestion charges to expanding runway capacity or to provide substitutes that some identified users will choose. Without such a mechanism, the incentives for most airport operators are all wrong, including incentives to encourage development contrary to environmental objections, restrict output and create scarcity, thereby gaining revenue and reducing costs at the expense of the traveling public and the economy.

To accomplish the goal of no exemptions and especially to remove monopoly incentives, Levine argues that legislative changes are necessary before pricing is adopted. He agrees that these changes would be very difficult to make – they would involve the drastic modification of the statutory (grandfathered) exemptions that allow operators of airports in New York and several other metropolitan markets to divert airport revenue for non-aviation uses.

Create a congestion-charge fund for capacity expansion. To ensure that the result of congestion pricing is to expand, not restrict, capacity, it will be necessary to create a congestion charge fund that can be used only to relieve airport congestion by expanding runway capacity. This would prevent the airport operator from using the funds from the congestion charge to invest in other facilities (terminals, parking lots etc). Levine regards off-airport expenditures that make capacity expansion possible, such as soundproofing homes or even to support schools and playgrounds as permissible, but any off-airport expenditures would need to be linked directly to aircraft acceptance capacity expansion. He emphasises that if runway congestion revenues can be used for other 'worthwhile' and politically-popular public expenditures unrelated to relieving the limitations that generate them, then they are not 'user charges', don't reflect congestion costs, and don't promote economic efficiency. Congestion charges would just become another economically inefficient output-distorting excise tax of a kind that economists criticise.

Levine concludes that incentive problems from monopoly and the exemption from pricing of users like foreign carriers, general aviation, and services to small communities are so serious that a pricing system with such exemptions is unlikely to maximize the economic value of airport use. In addition, there is great danger that the creation of a fund of money that can be expanded by increasing scarcity and be diverted to other uses will create vested interests in maintaining congestion, so as to fund other public sector projects. These interests will make it very difficult to reverse the policy if it provides poor outcomes. In imposing congestion pricing at Kennedy and LaGuardia without addressing the points above, the perverse incentives and results that are economically and politically distorted will discredit the concept of congestion pricing in aviation and in many other valuable uses.

Levine concludes that congestion pricing works best in the context of transparent and equitable pricing and efficient use of the funds generated. Until this can be assured at Kennedy and LaGuardia, congestion pricing will not be effective as a congestion-relief measure and may be counterproductive.

Source: Levine, Michael E. (2007) 'Congestion Pricing at New York Airports: Right Idea, But Can We Really Start Here and Now?' Policy Brief No. 66, Los Angeles: Reason Foundation, November, www.reason.org/pb66_nycongestion.pdf

13.5   REGULATING TOURISM INFRASTRUCTURE

While, at first glance, regulation of a monopoly's price or output would seem to be a straightforward exercise, in reality this is far from the case. By attending to one problem, such as keeping prices low, the regulator sets in train behaviour by the firm which can make other problems worse, such as that of ensuring adequate quality of service. Regulation is by its nature a compromise, and getting the balance right is difficult. Tourism industries worldwide (e.g. airlines, rail services, public transport) display the problems associated with regulated infrastructure such as inadequate investment, excessive investment, poor service quality, excessive service quality, high-cost operation and ineffective use of available capacity. These problems also appear with tourism infrastructure. The positive side is that in many destinations the problems are being diagnosed, and regulation is being better designed to take account of the problems that have developed.

There are two broad approaches to monopoly regulation. These are cost-plus regulation and price-cap or incentive regulation.

Cost-plus regulation

Until the wave of privatisation starting in the 1980s, most regulated firms, especially those in North America, were subjected to cost-plus forms of regulation. Under a common form of cost-plus regulation, rate of return regulation, monopolies were permitted to earn a specified rate of return on capital. This had the effect of keeping prices down to the level of average cost. However, this type of regulation sets up perverse incentives. The firm could earn more profits if it had more capital invested – thus it had an incentive to overcapitalise. In addition, the firm had little incentive to keep costs down – if managers succeeded in lowering costs, the regulator would lower the price which the firm was allowed to charge. Cost-plus regulated firms would provide a good quality of service, but costs would be high. National airlines of countries are a good example of this.

Price caps

The problems which were experienced with cost-plus regulation led to the development of alternative approaches to regulation. 'Incentive' regulation sought to regulate in ways which provided the firm with incentives to perform well, especially in respect of keeping costs down. In the UK, 'RPI-X' regulation, or price caps, were imposed on regulated firms from the mid-1980s on. Price caps set a maximum allowable price for the firm for a period, such as five years. If the firm is able to lower costs, it can keep the profits. At the end of the regulation period, allowable prices would be revised, to a degree influenced by the firms recent cost levels. Thus the firm has a clear incentive to keep costs down. Incentive regulation is now used extensively in the Anglo Saxon countries and in some parts of Europe.

For some time, price caps seemed to work very well, but over time, problems emerged. Two particular problems affecting tourism organisations were those of quality and of investment in capacity.

Quality. With price caps the firm is required to charge a set price for its output. Thus regulated, the firm has an incentive to downgrade quality. Often firms can lower costs by lowering the quality of service – thus an airport can lower costs by employing fewer staff and allowing queues for service to grow. Quality of service has become a controversial issue in some regulated infrastructure firms – especially airports. The quality of service at the London airports, especially Heathrow is widely regarded as poor. Terminals are crowded (partly because it has been difficult for the owner, BAA, to obtain permission to expand them), queues at essential services such as security are long, and when problems such as strikes develop, the airport descends into chaos. Poor service quality is no surprise – it is to be expected given the way the airports have been regulated. It is possible to address the problem to some extent by giving the firm rewards for better quality – this is now happening with the London airports, though it does not appear that the rewards are high enough. A further difficulty is that some aspects of quality are easy to measure, while others are not.

Investment in capacity. To some extent, investment and quality are linked – service quality will improve when the firm invests in additional capacity and avoids overcrowding. However the regulator needs to ensure that the infrastructure provider has an incentive to expand capacity when needed and can cover the costs of the extra capacity. Expanding infrastructure can be very costly (e.g. building new runways at airports or adding to rail track in a confined area), and the firm will not be able to cover the costs if it continues to be regulated at current prices. The regulator needs to offer higher prices to induce the firm to invest. While it can do this, it is difficult for the regulator to get things right. The regulated firm has an interest in exaggerating the need for extra capacity and expenditure (and thus the price it is allowed), and the regulator needs to know a good deal about the detailed operations and plans of the firm. Recently, some regulators have sought to encourage investment by allowing higher prices conditional on the firm actually making the investments. Thus, in the case of London Heathrow airport, the regulator has been allowing it to charge more in aircraft landing and departure fees as long as it delivers on increasing terminal capacity (construction of Terminal 5) (Czerny *et al.*, 2008).

Granted these difficulties, it is not unexpected that the infrastructure sector remains one of the less well-performing aspects of the supply side of tourism. It is difficult to get things just right. Some facilities are crowded and inadequate, which others are built to an excessively high standard and are necessarily expensive to use. Service quality is variable – even matters which are essentially simple, such as security checking at transport terminals, are often handled very poorly. When regulation is implemented to restrain the use of market power by the firm, getting the balance of controls right is extremely complex.

13.6 ENVIRONMENTAL CONSTRAINTS AND TRADE-OFFS

Often the problem of inadequate tourism infrastructure is not so much a matter of regulatory failure or poor performance by the infrastructure companies – rather it is a matter of environmental constraints. This is especially the case in Europe and North America, where expanding infrastructure can lead to serious environmental problems. Thus expanding an airport can lead to increased noise, greenhouse gas emissions (GHGs) and road traffic congestion. New or expanded rail links have environmental impacts and impacts on existing communities. Expanding a tourist road into a sensitive area could have adverse ecological impacts. Dredging a harbour to allow larger cruise ships will disrupt the seawater ecology. These adverse environmental effects can be real and costly – as a result, expansion of infrastructure will be difficult. Local communities will oppose expansion, governments will institute planning restrictions which may ban or severely limit development, and even when permission for expansion is granted, planning processes may delay projects for a very long time (decades, in the case of airports).

The consequences of this is that tourism infrastructure capacity is often much lower than would otherwise be warranted. This raises two issues for consideration:

- while environmental costs are genuine and should be taken into account, is this happening in the most efficient and effective manner? Sometimes all development at a site is banned, because of community pressure, which means that development is shifted to another, possibly more environmentally damaging, site. Sometimes it may be feasible to redesign the developments at the original site to substantially lessen adverse environmental impacts, thereby enabling expansion at least environmental cost. Chapter 17 discusses this issue in more detail.
- if capacity is limited because of environmental constraints, then there is a premium on ensuring that the capacity which is available is utilised as efficiently as is possible. Indeed, environmental considerations may not only limit the amount of capacity but also the extent of its use. Thus some airports, such as London Gatwick and Sydney, are not

permitted to expand their runway capacity, nor are they permitted to use their capacity all the time – during the night, curfews are imposed on flights. Ensuring effective use of capacity involves both recognising the congestion processes which may develop as well as addressing them. As noted before, some infrastructure providers simply allow congestion to get out of hand, and make poor use of the capacity which they have at their disposal.

13.7   INFRASTRUCTURE AND TOURISM GROWTH: NECESSARY BUT NOT SUFFICIENT

If you build it, will they come? Many cities are keen to encourage tourism, and they see provision of good infrastructure as a way to achieve this. Adequate infrastructure is generally regarded as a necessary condition for tourism growth (though some destinations are so attractive that they can survive with poor infrastructure). However, simply providing excellent infrastructure is not a sufficient condition for tourism to boom – destinations need to be attractive to tourists. Few travellers through London Stansted airport go there to admire the terminal, even though it was designed by Lord Foster. On the other hand, poor infrastructure will discourage tourism, especially if a destination faces competitors with a similar product (e.g. a beach destination which is competing with other beach destinations with superior facilities). Thus infrastructure can be a constraint on tourism growth, though it is not necessarily a catalyst for such growth. Some destinations do prefer to build ahead of time, to ensure that infrastructure does not limit tourism growth. An example is Singapore, which is very successful as a stopover destination ensuring that its airport capacity is always sufficient for growth in the short to medium term.

Infrastructure can be a competitive weapon when destinations are seeking to attract traffic. A good example of this arises with secondary airports in Europe which seek to attract Low-Cost Carriers (LCC). If LCC such as Ryanair or Air Berlin fly to a city, that city's tourism industry will receive a boost. As a result, many regional and city governments are willing to provide airport facilities on attractive terms to potential LCC operators. Some, like Carcassonne in France, have been very successful – LCC flights have put these cities on the tourist map – even though they were originally thought of as indirect routes to reach the main destination (Toulouse in the case of Carcassonne). Some cities with LCC services have become destinations in their own right. Not all these airports have succeeded in stimulating tourism in their hinterlands – in many cases, tourists step from the airport to a bus to take them directly to their main destination.

While infrastructure is critical in winning this business, it is important to recognise the importance of provision of infrastructure of the right quality level and at the right price. In the case of LCC traffic, what is wanted is a basic level of quality, no more, and a price which is kept to a minimum. Typically, large investments are not required – in fact they are counter-productive if the owners try to recover the costs of infrastructure through the airport charges which are then passed on to customers.

As noted earlier, airport capacity tends to be undersupplied in Europe – demand has been pressing against capacity, but it is difficult to obtain permission to expand capacity. The emergence of secondary airports, especially in the UK and Germany, has had a useful function in relieving pressure on the main airports. Their presence has meant that one segment of the market, the LCC market, has been able to expand rapidly even though there has been little expansion of airport capacity overall.

13.8 TOURISM INFRASTRUCTURE IN DEVELOPING COUNTRIES

Provision of adequate infrastructure can be a particular problem for developing countries, especially the poorer ones. Often, this requires the removal of institutional and financial obstacles that make such investment difficult and, at times, counter-productive. In addition to all of the problems we have noted, developing countries face additional difficulties, particularly in accessing funds to invest in infrastructure. To finance the full range of tourism infrastructure needs, several strategies and different sources of finance may be tapped. Among these sources are domestic private investment, foreign private investment sources and foreign aid.

While adequate infrastructure is a necessary precondition of tourism growth, infrastructure investments are often seen as the key to tourism development. Countries are often under pressure to build costly and excessive tourism infrastructure. International aid donors often wish to see the results of their aid in concrete – thus they are willing to finance infrastructure projects, even if they are excessively large. The running costs of large facilities are also high, but aid donors do not provide for these. Home country governments may also be keen to invest in prestige projects. While these excessive investments might generate some extra tourism, when high running costs must be recovered from the users the country will be making itself less competitive in tourism markets.

Maintenance is often a problem with infrastructure in developing countries. Donor countries provide aid to build infrastructure, but they rarely assist in maintaining it. Thus, particularly in the poorer countries, infrastructure crises develop, with systems breaking down and facilities becoming unworkable.

While the infrastructure which is primarily oriented to tourism (and tourism from richer countries) can be provided at a quality level adequate for the market, general infrastructure which is provided for the population at large will have a quality level which is deemed to be suitable for this population. Thus, the service quality may be much lower than that which tourists from the richer countries expect. While backpackers may not object to crowded trains, other tourists will. Ways round this problem often exist – tourists who do not want to use public transport can hire taxis. However, if roads are very congested, they will still face poorer service qualities than they would be willing to pay for. Low quality general infrastructure makes poorer countries less competitive in tourism markets.

A final difficulty is that the investment climate in many developing countries is quite risky. The legal protections that investors enjoy in developed countries may not exist. While the private sector may be willing and able to invest to ensure that the infrastructure for tourism is in place at an adequate standard, the investment may still not happen. Investors will hold off investing if the legal framework for investment is uncertain and if they risk losing their investments.

13.9 CONCLUSIONS AND POLICY

- Infrastructure refers to the basic physical and organisational structures needed for the operation of a society.
- The operation of tourism facilities and services at a destination depends heavily on the quantity and quality of infrastructure at that destination.
- Infrastructure may be provided by either the public sector or the private sector with the relative degree of provision between them dependent on prevailing domestic economic, social and political policies. Recent years have seen a growth in the West in the private provision of infrastructure, especially in airports, terminals, road links and rail. There has also been a proliferation of P^3 in which the government sets the terms of the contract and may become the ultimate owner but the private sector builds, and perhaps operates, the facility.
- Whether public or private, or both, investment in tourism infrastructure aids the development and growth of tourism capacity, helps create jobs, supports long-term tourism growth and adds to a destination's overall competitiveness.
- Like all infrastructure, tourism infrastructure faces issues of capacity and efficiency. It may become congested as demand presses up against an absolute capacity limit. Alternatively, where such a limit is not reached, the quality of the service may decline as spaces become crowded, queues lengthen and delays grow. To ensure more efficient use of the infrastructure, it may be necessary to internalise the externality, perhaps by imposing a charge on it.
- Where tourism infrastructure exhibits monopoly power, it may be necessary to regulate it. The two broad approaches to monopoly regulation are cost-plus regulation (under which monopolies are permitted to earn a specified rate of return on capital) and price-cap or incentive regulation (under which monopolies face maximum prices for their services, giving them an incentive to keep their costs down). The resulting regulated service, however, may be poor and investment inadequate.
- By its nature, tourism infrastructure may face environmental constraints. The consequence of this is that tourism infrastructure capacity is often much lower than would otherwise be warranted, or is opposed or delayed.
- Infrastructure may be a competitive weapon when destinations are seeking to attract tourists. Certainly, adequate infrastructure is a necessary precondition of tourism growth

but so is the provision of the right type and quality of infrastructure at the right price. Provision of such infrastructure and its maintenance, however, may be a particular problem for developing countries given lack of local investment, limitations on local legal systems and pressure from donor countries.

SELF-REVIEW QUESTIONS

1. Explain the meaning of tourism infrastructure. Why is it important within an economy?

2. Distinguish between primary tourist facilities and services, secondary tourist facilities and services and tertiary tourist facilities and services.

3. What types of infrastructure does the World Economic Forum believe are important for destination competitiveness?

4. Distinguish between private tourism infrastructure and public tourism infrastructure. Why has there been a move in recent years away from the public provision of public tourism infrastructure towards the private provision of tourism infrastructure?

5. Use tourism examples to define the concept of P^3. Why have P^3 become popular?

6. Use both a diagram and examples to analyse the congestion problem that may accompany the use of tourism infrastructure.

7. Distinguish between the cost-plus and price-cap approaches in the regulation of monopoly tourism infrastructure.

8. Briefly describe how environmental issues may affect both the efficiency of existing tourism infrastructure and the provision of new tourism infrastructure.

ESSAY QUESTIONS

1. Since there is no clearly defined tourism infrastructure, it does not need separate discussion to that of general infrastructure. Comment.

2. Getting tourism infrastructure 'right' is easier said than done. Comment.

3. Infrastructure may be provided by the public sector or the private sector, and the outcome is often determined by domestic economic, social and political policies. Discuss.

4. While adequate infrastructure is a necessary precondition of tourism growth, infrastructure investments are often seen as the key to tourism development. Discuss.

5. It is not just a matter of providing enough infrastructure capacity. Rather, it is a matter of ensuring its most efficient use. Discuss.

6. Choose a PPP in tourism infrastructure. Analyse its structure and discuss its advantages and limitations.

7. Compare and contrast the different issues that may be faced during the development of tourism infrastructure in Addis Ababa and London.

8. Discuss impediments to the provision of tourism infrastructure in developing countries.

CHAPTER 14

FOREIGN DIRECT INVESTMENT

LEARNING OBJECTIVES

After reading this chapter, you should be able to:

1. Distinguish between foreign direct investment and foreign portfolio investment in tourism.

2. Understand the motives that drive foreign direct investment in tourism.

3. Analyse the potential benefits and costs for host destinations that accompany foreign direct investment in tourism.

4. Evaluate the arguments for and against domestic versus foreign ownership of tourism operations.

5. Recognise the implications for policy that accompany tourism foreign direct investment into a host country.

14.1 INTRODUCTION

Foreign Direct Investment (FDI) occurs when an investor resident in one country (the source country) acquires ownership in and a significant influence over the management of an enterprise or productive asset in another country (the host). This may involve creating a new enterprise (greenfield investment) or changing the ownership of an existing enterprise (via a merger and/or acquisition) (UNCTAD, 2008a: 8). FDI can be important to any economy, especially to developing nations. In particular, it is considered to be critical to the fast-expanding services sector.

It is widely held that FDI in any industry has the potential to

- Contribute to growth and development.
- Create jobs.
- Build exports.
- Provide additional sources of finance for commercial expansion.
- Facilitate technology transfer and innovation.
- Increase opportunities for global networking.

511

The need for FDI in different countries depends on several factors including political orientation, general economic and tourism development and the type and scale of tourism development required.

Since some tourism activities are relatively capital intensive (e.g. air transportation, construction of cruise shipping facilities and high-standard hotels), it can be expected that many developing countries that lack capital, entrepreneurship and access to international brands, expertise and marketing networks need FDI to offset their disadvantages in tourism.

Some see FDI as disadvantageous to a country, resulting in a loss of profits that could have been kept at home, and also a reduction in local sourcing of inputs. Potential costs of FDI to the host country include its potential to crowd out domestic investment, increased leakages from tourist expenditure, reduced employment opportunities for locals, loss of equity and control of the tourism industry and inappropriate form and scale of development.

In reality, FDI is associated with both benefits and costs to the host destination. The question that any destination must ask is: do these benefits exceed the costs? This chapter reviews the patterns of FDI in tourism, its motives and the potential costs and benefits to host destinations. This chapter also discusses the issue of the effects of domestic ownership versus foreign ownership.

14.2 PATTERNS OF FDI IN TOURISM

Foreign investment refers to investment money flowing into one country from another. It can be private investment money or public investment money.

Foreign investment takes two forms: *foreign portfolio investment* (part ownership/no control) and *foreign direct investment* (ownership/control).

Foreign portfolio investment

Portfolio investment is the category of international investment that covers investment in equity and debt securities, excluding any such instruments that are classified as direct investment or reserve assets. Foreign portfolio investment reflects investment by persons who are not interested in taking an active part in the management of a company. It represents passive holdings of securities such as foreign stocks, bonds or other financial assets, none of which entails active management or control of the securities' issuer by the investor. Portfolio investment includes purchase of shares in a foreign company, purchase of bonds issued by a foreign government and acquisition of assets in a foreign country. Factors affecting international portfolio investment include the following:

- Tax rates on interest or dividends (investors will normally prefer countries where the tax rates are relatively low).

- Interest rates (money tends to flow to countries with high interest rates) and dividend yields.
- Exchange rates (foreign investors may be attracted if the local currency is expected to appreciate).

Foreign direct investment

Foreign direct investment is investment by foreigners that enables them to manage and control assets in other countries. Firms invest to derive the maximum expected return. They exploit their competitive advantages, often in the form of brand equity, technology or other proprietary know-how, by utilising them in another country. What is unique about FDI in tourism is the separation of ownership and control that frequently occurs (Brown *et al.*, 2003).

FDI flows comprise

- Equity capital (i.e. a foreign direct investor's purchase of shares of an enterprise in a host economy).
- Reinvested earnings (i.e. the foreign investor's share of earnings not distributed by dividends or earnings not remitted to the foreign investor).
- Intra-company loans.

FDI stock is the sum of

- The value of capital and reserves (including retained profits); and
- The net indebtedness of foreign affiliates.

Accurate data on the volume of FDI in the global tourism economy are lacking (Endo, 2006; UNCTAD, 2008a, b). There are three main reasons for this:

- Tourism comprises a large number of diverse and interlinking activities, making the compilation of standardised FDI statistics in tourism at international level almost impossible.
- Many countries do not distinguish between domestic and foreign investors.
- The frequent use of managerial contracts or franchising operations (whereby multinational corporations can still retain significant control over an operation without having committed equity capital) implies that there is a gap between the official FDI data and the activities of firms in practice.

Developed countries are estimated to receive about two-thirds of tourism FDI inflows, a share roughly equivalent to their share of total FDI inflows. A number of developing countries, though, have experienced extremely rapid increases in tourism FDI, often from very low base levels. Developing countries were the target of 21% of world tourism-related mergers and acquisitions during the years 2002–2005 and hosted 70% of all tourism-related 'greenfield' investments (Barrowclough, 2007). FDI is mainly concentrated in hotels and accommodation. However, its impact can be substantial, especially when the definition of FDI is widened to include non-equity forms of Multinational Enterprise (MNE) involvement, such as management contracts which are much more prevalent.

14.3 MOTIVES FOR FDI IN TOURISM

The ability of a tourism destination to attract investment in tourism infrastructure is influenced by a complex number of characteristics (ESCAP, 2001). These include the following:

- the economic growth rate of the country;
- the productivity and performance of the tourism industry, including the profitability of tourism-related enterprises;
- access to sources of financing and the availability of sufficient information and data needed to make investment decisions;
- government regulations, procedures and incentives (attractiveness of the taxation policies regarding local and foreign investment and imports);
- the resources and conveniences offered (e.g. attractions, transportation, access, hospitality, medical and other services, pricing, etc.);
- market characteristics (visitor tastes and preferences, disposable income, propensity to travel, proximity to destination, etc.);
- political stability;
- the ability of the destination to market and promote itself effectively.

Only if these factors combine to allow investors to earn an adequate return on their investment will they make the necessary long-term commitment to allocate funds to a host destination.

The various motives for foreign investment in tourism can be explained in large part using the widely accepted 'eclectic paradigm' of international production (Dunning, 2001; Dwyer & Forsyth, 1993, 1994b). The eclectic paradigm asserts that the extent, pattern and growth of value-adding activities undertaken by MNEs outside their home countries are dependent on the value of and interaction between three main variables. These are *ownership advantages*, *location advantages* and *market internalisation advantages*.

14.3.1 OWNERSHIP ADVANTAGES

Ownership advantages include the competitive advantages which firms of one nationality possess over those of another nationality in supplying any particular market or set of markets. These advantages may arise from firms' privileged ownership of, or access to, specific technological, managerial, financial or marketing assets. Ownership advantages may be of a structural or a behavioural nature. For the tourism industry, they might include the following:

- The size of the company and its ability to obtain economies of scale.
- Proprietary competitive advantages including strong brand name or established reputation in providing tourism services that would allow the firm to increase market penetration.
- Greater availability of equity finance of the type appropriate to the tourism industry.
- Better knowledge of, and favoured access to, international tourism markets.
- Better-trained personnel.
- Better management, and reservation systems.
- Better organisational and IT capabilities to successfully integrate separate value-adding activities.

14.3.2 LOCATION-SPECIFIC ADVANTAGES

The advantages of location are the benefits of value-adding activities that combine ownership-specific advantages with immediate factor endowments in a foreign country. Factors that make a destination attractive to international investors include

- Size, growth and stage of development of the overall tourism market in the host country.
- Existing tourism facilities in the host country including type of attractions (existing tourism infrastructure, appealing environmental features, etc.).
- Destination market potential in the context of global and regional tourism trends.
- Policy of the host government towards FDI in the country including investment incentives.
- Political, social and economic stability of the host destination.
- Quality of general infrastructure in destination (e.g. transport, telecommunications, water, power, etc.).
- Input prices, quality and productivity.
- Lack of entrepreneurship in the host country, reflected in an unwillingness to take risks as owner/manager of a tourism facility.
- Deficiencies in the host country's capital market as it affects tourism, with associated barriers to local investors.
- Taxation differences between the host destination and overseas countries.
- Compatibility with the firm's strategy to diversify operations for the purpose of reducing risks geographically.

Location-specific advantages do not in themselves explain the incidence of foreign ownership relative to domestic ownership of tourism in any particular destination. Instead, they are a motive for investment in that destination by foreigners rather than elsewhere, especially when involvements in different locations may be mutually exclusive.

14.3.3 MARKET INTERNALISATION ADVANTAGES

Market internalisation advantages refer to the advantages of controlling and coordinating ownership and location-specific advantages with a MNE hierarchy rather than selling the right to use those advantages to domestic firms in the host country. In tourism, these advantages might include

- Easier control by a firm over the character of the tourism product, including security of supply, price and quality.
- Better planning.
- Better coordination.
- Greater opportunities to increase profits.

The utilisation of these advantages depends primarily on the relative costs of equity and non-equity forms of managing interrelated economic activities. The benefits to the firm of the FDI must be weighed against communication and control difficulties (Buckley, 1987). Thus, on the one hand, 'arm's length transactions' can be costly for firms. If they try to control product quality when independent firms produce the inputs (e.g. transport and accommodation), they incur costs of negotiation, quality monitoring and risks of inappropriate price and quality levels.

On the other hand, minority joint ventures or non-equity agreements may sometimes be preferred. In the accommodation sector, for example, international hotel chains exact rigid management standards over the hotels that bear their names regardless of their ownership. Contract-based control, as opposed to equity-based control, is prevalent in the hotel sector internationally because of the coincidence of interests of management and owners.

The eclectic paradigm is useful for explaining the extent, pattern and growth of value-added activities undertaken by multinational firms outside their national boundaries. The interrelations of these ownership, location and internalisation advantages, and the response to them by firms, vary according to industry, countries of origin and destination of investment and firm-specific characteristics. They also vary over time as changes in technology and the entrepreneurial and economic environment affect the competitive position of firms and the location of their value-adding activities (United Nations, 1989). These advantages must suffice to compensate for the costs of setting up and operating a foreign value-adding operation in addition to those faced by the domestic firms.

14.4 EFFECTS OF FDI ON HOST DESTINATION

Effects of FDI on the host destination may be positive or negative, as shown in Figure 14.1.

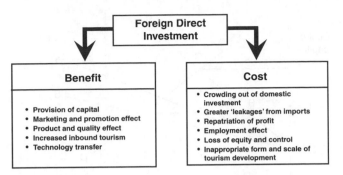

Figure 14.1 Potential benefits and costs of FDI on host destination

14.5 POTENTIAL BENEFITS OF FDI TO HOST DESTINATION

Several positive effects may result for the host destination. These include additional provision of capital in the tourism industry, additional marketing and promotion of the destination and raising the profile of the destination in world tourism markets, broadening the economic base and creating jobs, increased competitiveness, access to global distribution networks, enhanced product quality and technology transfer (Barrowclough, 2007; Kusluvan & Karamustafa, 2001).

14.5.1 PROVISION OF CAPITAL

FDI can add to the existing stock of capital (or may simply crowd out domestic investment as we discuss below). In some destinations there appears to be a relative shortage of the longer-term capital appropriate for development of major tourism facilities. Tourism developments often require long-term equity, which may not be in adequate supply in a destination, particularly in a developing country. Developing countries are unlikely to be able to provide from domestic resources the savings and finance to invest in the land improvements, infrastructure development and construction of facilities that are required in order to host international tourism. Given shortages of long-term equity for investment in tourism, destinations can gain if foreign investors are prepared to supply it. FDI helps to unlock capital constraints particularly in lesser developed economies where financial markets are narrow and poorly developed. Effectively, the host country 'imports' a service (long-term equity holding) from a more readily available source in another country.

In Figure 14.2, it is assumed that foreign investment results in an increased supply of equity capital, leading to increased total investment in the tourism industry. Without foreign investment, the supply of equity funds is shown as S_d and the demand for them is D (for simplicity we assume no loan funds are used). Equilibrium is at C. The cost of capital is r_1, and investment equals X_1.

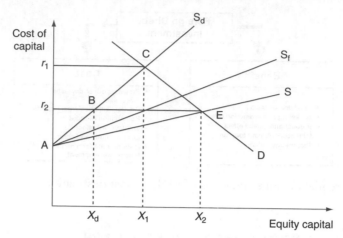

Figure 14.2 Tourism equity capital: Supply and demand

The foreign supply of equity funds is shown as S_f. When foreign investment is present, the overall supply of funds shifts outwards to S. The new equilibrium is E, with a lower cost of capital r_2 and greater level of investment, X_2.

Local suppliers of equity will lose. That is, producer surplus will fall from ACr_1 to ABr_2. Local investors will be crowded out by foreign investors, and reduce their investment from X_1 to X_d.

Consumers will gain since prices will be sufficient to yield returns on capital of r_2, not r_1.

Owners of the resources used by the tourism industry (land, labour and capital) will gain from the higher prices for these resources occasioned by the expansion of tourism. If all tourists are foreign, and if the original owners of the resources used in tourism are foreign, the country as a whole would lose from the foreign investment.

Domestic owners of facilities will, of course, suffer through lower prices and hence lower rates of return on investment, while residents who holiday domestically will gain. The extent of the gains and losses will depend on supply and demand elasticities. For countries with substantial domestic use of their tourism industries (such as France or the USA), the losses faced by resident investors are likely to be made up by gains enjoyed by domestic tourists. However, for small countries that rely heavily on foreign tourism and have limited supplies of local equity, foreign investment could impose a net cost, especially if a high proportion of the resources used in tourism (e.g. land near beaches) is foreign-owned. This needs to be compared to the other gains achieved from increased tourism expenditure.

FDI will increase visitor numbers to a destination (e.g. through lower prices made possible by the lower cost of capital, or if it somehow increases the awareness or the attractiveness of the tourism product). In Europe, in the context of mass market tourism, intense competition has reduced profit margins of suppliers of tourism services and consumers have benefited from lower prices. In respect of the accommodation sector, for example, there is some evidence that the growing size of international hotel chains has enabled economies of scale associated with spreading fixed costs over a greater number of hotel guests, and resulted in them being able to obtain finance and purchase inputs on the most favourable terms, enabling greater functional specialisation of staff (McQueen, 1989).

On the financing side, if foreign investors are prepared to accept a lower expected rate of return for a given profile of returns and level of risk, they force prices down in those sectors of the industry that are competitive. As compared to a situation where there is no foreign investment, there will be a greater expansion of capacity and, to fill it, rates will fall, and tourist numbers are likely to rise. This applies in both the short term and the long term. In the former, foreign investors may have more liquidity and be more willing than local investors to incur losses through the operation of facilities during a slump. Over the longer term, the greater expansion of tourism facilities, resulting from the foreign investment added to domestic investment, can generate lower yields and prices for tourism services.

For investment in a less developed country, one which, perhaps, is just building up its tourism industry, the impact that comes through the capital market side is likely to be greater than for a developed country. The local capital market is likely to be thin, and the availability of equity capital for tourism will be very limited. This will imply a large drop in the effective cost of capital, which will mean a greater drop in returns for the few local investors. The impact on tourism prices, and availability of facilities, will be large, and so will be the effect on the flows of tourists and their expenditures. Foreign investment may be essential for the industry to develop in a competitive way.

14.5.2   MARKETING AND DESTINATION PROMOTION EFFECTS

Foreign investment may result in greater or superior promotional effort in the home country of the investor, leading to higher visitor numbers from that country. Both domestic and foreign owners of higher-standard facilities seek to market those facilities in countries that generate tourists. Compared to resident investors, the foreign investor may have better knowledge of their home country's travel market and be better placed to market the destination more effectively in that market. Multinational hotel companies, in particular, provide market connections including marketing ties through computer reservation systems with a variety of firms within a destination including tour operators, car rental agencies, attractions and airlines. These types of market connections related to global marketing and access to global distribution networks can generate greater flows of tourists from the main tourist origin countries to those countries that host FDI or MNEs involved in the tourist industry.

The role of well-known hotel brands with a global marketing reach may be particularly important for developing countries that have limited resources or abilities to promote their destinations, or that have not yet developed their own 'brand identity'. Overall, the involvement of MNEs in marketing and promotion activity can increase destination awareness and inbound numbers. Barrowclough (2007) presents examples of this happening in Bhutan and the Dominican Republic but also points out that the effect diminishes over time.

14.5.3 PRODUCT AND QUALITY EFFECTS

Control of the flow of transactions enables tourism multinationals to monitor and control the quality of the services they provide. For example, tour operators can give quality guarantees to the tourist, thereby reducing the perceived risks of default, unsatisfactory service or other transactional uncertainties.

Small, domestically owned and operated businesses, particularly in developing countries, may have little knowledge of tourist expectations regarding service standards and may find it difficult to compete internationally. Accommodation is an 'experience' as opposed to an 'inspection' product (United Nations, 1989). An experience product is one whose attributes cannot adequately be determined prior to use. Because most holidays are bought 'sight unseen', the information that home-familiar hotels of assured quality are available internationally may provide additional security to potential travellers. The brand name can act to reduce the information search costs of potential tourists (Buckley, 1987), especially in choosing to holiday in developing countries about which little is known internationally. A study by UNCTAD (Barrowclough, 2007) notes that foreign brand names tended to enhance destination image among business tourists in all the countries which she studied.

14.5.4 INCREASED INBOUND TOURISM CREATING INCOME AND JOBS

Several of the above 'positive' impacts of FDI imply an increase in inbound tourism numbers to the host destination. Increased tourism numbers, in turn, imply increased injected tourism expenditure with its 'multiplier' effects on output, income and employment, and increased government revenues. As discussed in Chapter 6, these can, though do not necessarily, lead to benefits for the economy. In this way, FDI in tourism can have positive effects beyond the tourism industry itself and on the wider economy. There is evidence that FDI in China has resulted in increased tourism flows (Tang *et al.*, 2007). The economy can generally gain as a result of increased expenditure by larger numbers of tourists which is likely, on balance, to produce positive economic impacts in the destination. These effects are the production- and consumption-induced effects as discussed in Chapter 8.

There also is evidence of a positive and significant relationship between tourism and subsequent new FDI. Sanford and Dong (2000) suggest that increasing tourism can improve a country's attractiveness to foreign investors. The study suggests that tourism stimulates direct investment in a wide variety of industries, and subsequently gives rise to economic development. While their study focuses on the USA, it implies that national efforts to stimulate tourism (including marketing, developing tourism attractions and creating a social and political environment that encourages tourism) will generate increased tourism investment.

14.5.5 TECHNOLOGY TRANSFER

One of the main reasons for (and benefits from) foreign investment is the transfer of (soft) technology including managerial expertise. Foreign firms may show the locals how to do things better involving also a 'demonstration effect' on local entrepreneurs. Destinations, particularly in developing areas, need to know business management principles and practice. International hotel chains, for example, have substantial in-house training programmes emphasising systems of accounting, procedures and management, and their operations have resulted in a substantial increase in skills levels within the hospitality industry worldwide. However, to the extent that this happens, it is more likely that the expertise is being transferred by the operators of the facilities, not by the owners. In developing destinations, in particular, increased skills levels of management have been essential in catering to the demands of foreign tourists and in maintaining the international competitiveness of the local product (ESCAP, 1994). Industry training programmes conducted by foreign-owned firms may be regarded as a form of 'technology transfer', creating spillover benefits to domestic firms wishing access to a more skilled pool of labour within the tourism sector.

14.6 POTENTIAL COSTS OF FDI TO HOST DESTINATION

Potential costs of FDI on the host destination include its potential to crowd out domestic investment; increased leakages from imports, repatriated profits, management and franchise fees; reduced employment opportunities for locals; loss of equity and control of the tourism industry; and inappropriate form and scale of development (Kusluvan & Karamustafa, 2001).

14.6.1 CROWDING OUT OF DOMESTIC INVESTMENT

To an extent, foreign investment can crowd out domestic investment which is deterred by lower expected returns. Thus, the effect of allowing foreign investment is to increase the total amount of investment, but by an amount well short of the actual foreign investment which takes place. It may also force down prices and lead to a greater flow of tourism within, and to, the host country. Foreign investment could be disadvantageous for the host country if local investment in the industry contracts in the face of foreign investment. In Figure 14.2, we saw that FDI resulted in a reduction of domestic investment from X_1 to X_d. This is particularly likely to occur where the local investment pool is small.

Barrowclough (2007) notes that when both foreign and local investors were eligible for Tunisian government subsidised loans, local investors were crowded out. However, she claims that 'crowding out' is not a problem in general. In the accommodation sector, foreign and local hotels often act as complements, providing different kinds of services to tourists.

14.6.2 GREATER 'LEAKAGES' FROM TOURISM IMPORTS

It is sometimes claimed that FDI is associated with higher use of imported goods, materials and foreign expertise according to the standards and tastes of developed countries and that this reduces the net foreign exchange earnings that might have accrued in the case of local ownership.

The size of the additional leakages overseas depends importantly on how foreign-owned facilities source their inputs (land, labour and capital) as compared to domestically owned facilities. The source of inputs (whether domestically produced or imported) and the size of the resulting leakages will help to determine the income-generating effect of the investment itself and tourism expenditure associated with its operation.

Determination of any additional outflows due to foreign investment in tourism facilities is not straightforward. In determining incremental foreign exchange outflows resulting from foreign investment in the tourist industry, one needs to be specific as to what would have happened if this investment did not take place. Unfortunately, the question cannot be answered unambiguously for any given project, let alone foreign investment in tourism generally. The extent of any differences in leakages depends on whether the foreign investment:

- Replaces *similar* domestic investment;
- Replaces *different* domestic investment; or
- *Adds* to overall investment in the tourist industry.

Foreign investment does not, in itself, imply greater use of foreign-sourced inputs. While the high import content of goods used to satisfy tourist needs generally is recognised for lesser developed economies, it is the country's profile of production, rather than ownership of tourism facilities, which determines the degree of import penetration. Barrowclough (2007) found that ownership of hotels *per se* did not make a great deal of difference, because hotel managers, including food and beverage managers, and so on, all had similar objectives: to secure high-quality inputs with reliable and consistent delivery at a competitive price.

To appreciate the relevant issues it is useful to distinguish between the construction or development stage and the operation stage of tourism facilities.

Construction stage

Tourism facilities are diverse in their source of inputs into their capital stock. Hotels, restaurants, shops and attractions require land, concrete, bricks, glass, timber and steel, for example. These inputs can be produced domestically or imported.

A foreign investor may acquire an existing asset or else develop one from scratch. In the former case, foreign investors often purchase established businesses. Unless such businesses are expressly developed for on-sale, and intentionally incorporate different inputs, the source of the inputs used in construction will typically be the same as for domestically owned facilities. In the latter case, obviously there is scope to use imported inputs in the construction stage of tourism development. Thus, the investor in a resort hotel development may employ foreign architects, consultants or engineers and prefer imported to domestically manufactured furnishings, fittings and carpets. The extent to which foreign, rather than domestically sourced, inputs are employed depends on their relative costs, quality differences and local availability.

The size of additional leakages at the development stage of a tourism facility is likely to depend primarily on the sophistication of the nation's construction industry and its manufacturing base. In a developed economy, there are unlikely to be major differences between domestic and foreign-owned tourism developments in respect of most inputs into facilities. When a hotel is constructed, for example, most of the materials and labour comes from local sources, regardless of the nationality of the developers. While some inputs are imported, any differences in import leakages between domestically sourced investment and FDI at the construction stage of tourist developments are likely to be relatively small. Accordingly, so also are any additional foreign exchange leakages because of foreign rather than domestic ownership of tourism development projects.

Operating stage

In most destinations there appears to be little or no difference in the types of intermediate goods and services purchased by foreign-owned firms compared to domestically owned firms to cater for visitor needs. Indeed, Barrowclough (2007) found that in many developing countries, MNEs often make more effort than domestically owned firms to link with local suppliers.

Foreign ownership *per se* does not imply greater use of foreign-sourced inputs into production. Both foreign-owned and domestically owned hotels stock imported products in their bar areas, gift shop and so on, but this choice in large measure reflects visitor preferences. While the purchases of international hotels may have a higher import content than hotels catering for the domestic travel market, this relates to the nature of tourism demand rather than ownership of facilities. It can be noted also that the host nation gains tariff revenue from imported products, partly offsetting any additional leakages overseas.

An exception to the above argument is the incidence of tourism resort 'enclaves'. As Wilkinson (1989: 169) argues, 'enclave resorts result in minimal economic benefit for the host country because of their dependence on international charter operations, expatriate employees and imported food and other equipment. The overall result is an extremely high leakage rate.'

Even if a higher leakage rate of enclave resorts be conceded, the important issue is whether the construction and operation of the resort makes a positive contribution to the destination. This issue needs to be addressed on a case-by-case basis and, in any case, does not preclude policy measures to forge greater links between the resort and local suppliers in order that the latter can capture more of the potential tourism value chain. Local procurement may also offer wider benefits in terms of a country's ability to market itself. The more it can offer a high-value, authentic experience, the more it is able to differentiate its tourism product, and develop a competitive advantage over other destinations.

In sum, claims that the benefits from tourism 'leak away' from a destination if facilities are foreign-owned neglect the fact that, regardless of ownership, the bulk of expenses incurred by tourism operations accrue as revenue to local producers of goods and services.

In any case, it is the impact of foreign ownership on leakages for the tourism sector as a whole which matters. Thus, even if foreign ownership of a facility leads to a more direct input-sourcing from overseas, the economy might gain more than it otherwise would from tourism (income, jobs) and the expanded size of the tourism industry may also lead to more reliance on domestic sources of inputs by competing facilities. That is to say, the leakages issue must be analysed in the context of the potential for tourism development to generate greater income and employment in the host destination.

14.6.3 REPATRIATION OF PROFITS

It is sometimes pointed out that management fees and profits associated with FDI flow out of the host country reducing the economic contribution from tourism expenditure. This criticism views repatriated profits as a 'leakage' from the host economy because of the foreign investment and is usually associated with a claim that the net benefits to the nation from tourism are correspondingly reduced.

This view rests on a misconception, however. While it is agreed that when a tourism facility is foreign-owned, a proportion of its sales will go towards profits which will be repatriated to the owners, the profits are not 'lost' to the host destination in any meaningful sense, since there would be no profits to repatriate had the investor not first brought the capital to invest.

Foreign investment may either *replace* or *add to* domestic investment. Consider the former situation. Suppose a foreign firm purchases an existing facility from a local owner. The purchase price will reflect the present value of the expected future profits from the facility, and the rights to these profits are transferred to the new owner. The domestic seller does not lose, nor does the nation. The capital received from the sale of the facility can be invested elsewhere in the destination or overseas and will generate at least as large a stream of profits (if not, then presumably the sale would not have taken place). Alternatively, the money from the sale can be used to repay debts, thereby reducing the host nation's borrowings from abroad, and reducing interest repayments on its foreign debt.

Consider now the case where foreign investment *adds* to total investment in a country. In circumstances where the foreign investor develops a facility rather than purchasing an existing asset, the investor must pay suppliers (mainly domestic suppliers) for all of the inputs used in the development. That is to say, the investor must pay for the profits. Further, there is a saving in capital outlay by domestic investors who can invest funds elsewhere or use them to reduce debt. If profits paid overseas are regarded as a 'leakage' from the economy, then the initial payment for the facility should be regarded as an 'injection' that would not have occurred except for the foreign investment. Over the longer term, there is no overall leakage.

Assuming that total investment does increase, additional profits will be paid overseas from the tourism industry. However, such profits cannot be considered as 'lost' to the host economy since, in the absence of the foreign investment, they would not exist. Nor would the additional revenue accruing to suppliers of goods and services to the foreign investors, or the increased company tax revenue to the government, exist if the foreign investment had not taken place.

14.6.4 EMPLOYMENT EFFECTS

It is sometimes argued that employment opportunities, especially in managerial positions for locals, may be limited owing to the use of the expatriate labour with limited opportunities for career advancement of local employees. In particular, in order to maintain firm-specific advantages, it is claimed that key management positions may be held by expatriates, and that only lower-level personnel requiring low skills are trained for reasons of service quality and performance.

However, the implications of any poor training received by some staff should be weighed against the revenues earned which would not have occurred in the absence of the FDI.

Several issues are relevant here:

- The preference of owners to have their own employees or representatives manage the operations of facilities in which they have invested is perfectly understandable, given the large sums of money involved and the desire for suitable returns. Such personnel can hardly be regarded as taking jobs from locals since many of the jobs would very likely not exist but for the foreign investment.
- Even in cases where some employees are foreign citizens, they will pay local income tax out of their wages and will meet their living expenses within the destination, injecting expenditure into the economy with positive economic effects.

- Those cases where a foreigner takes a job that would otherwise have gone to a resident will generally be much less than the total number of foreigners employed in the industry, although differences might exist in the proportion of foreign citizens in managerial positions. The UNCTAD study found that, typically, the number of expatriate employees was rather low, especially in countries with some history of international tourism (Barrowclough, 2007).
- The major reason for imported labour is to maintain quality in the provision of tourism services. Where imported labour serves to enhance the quality of the tourism experience, including managerial expertise, there are wider benefits to the country by way of tourism's contribution to Gross Domestic Product (GDP) and foreign exchange earnings. Regarding customer service, in the duty free sector for example, it is important for sales to Japanese tourists that shop staff speak Japanese. Where imported labour serves to generate revenues and to enhance the quality of the destination's tourism products, including customer service, there may be wider benefits to the country not readily apparent from the examination of figures relating to percentages of foreign employment in the industry.
- MNEs often provide a systematic training programme to staff, directed at international markets, in addition to international placements within a firm's different locations. This has the attendant 'technology transfer' benefits to the host economy as discussed.
- Destinations can, of course, address this issue directly through the provision of programmes aimed at developing an indigenous labour force with skills required by the tourism industry. Destination managers have a wide range of policy options that can be enacted.

14.6.5 LOSS OF EQUITY AND CONTROL

Foreign ownership of tourist facilities implies that a host nation loses some equity in its tourism industry and that the conduct of firms in the tourism industry is more subject to decisions made outside the host nation. A related concern is that developing countries can become over-dependent on multinationals for the development of their tourism industry given the market connections enjoyed by international tour operators, hotel companies and airlines. The concern is that tourism-receiving countries may be placed in a dependent, vulnerable situation because international tourism demand is determined by the actions of people in wealthier countries.

While foreign-owned firms obviously do exercise their power in the international marketplace, the issue comes down to the economic contribution that FDI makes to the host destination as compared with its absence. Presumably, foreign-owned firms will wish to ensure that the local industry grows, as their own interests are related to this. The FDI implies that residents are bearing fewer of the risks associated with the industry, fewer of the gains and fewer of the losses. When performance of the industry is good (a boom when profits are high), the local share of the gain is smaller. The converse is true when performance is poor. To the extent of foreign ownership, the gain to the host nation in expanding times will be less than if all tourism facilities were domestically owned, while in lean times foreign investors will share part of the losses.

Domination of local tourism by vertically integrated MNE is considered by some seriously to reduce tourisms' potential for growth as well as the net financial advantages that the industry brings to developing countries (Brohman, 1996: 54). As discussed above, the issue involves the overall benefits to the destination with and without FDI, and this can only be determined on a case-by-case basis.

Another concern is that Multinational Corporations (MNCs) can be fickle, exiting the market abruptly when conditions are adverse. However, MNCs may have 'deeper pockets' than locally owned firms and thus may be better able to operate during some tourism downturn maintaining the provision of facilities to visitors. There is some evidence that MNCs bring market stability and confidence to a host tourism industry. The UNCTAD study (Barrowclough, 2007) suggests that MNCs in Tanzania and Kenya were more robust than many local firms during downturns. Similarly, in Sri Lanka the internationally owned hotels in the tsunami-afflicted areas were the first to recover and return to operations. Barrowclough also suggests that noted brand names help bring confidence to destinations in conflict (Fiji military coup) or experiencing a natural disaster (Sri Lanka tsunami response).

14.6.6 INAPPROPRIATE FORM AND SCALE OF TOURISM DEVELOPMENT

Sometimes the concern is raised that foreign-owned tourism facilities are usually of greater scale than domestically owned facilities. The characteristics of mass tourism tend to favour the development of large-scale integrated facilities and this may be inappropriate for smaller, less developed destinations (Brohman, 1996). For example, multinational hotel companies may affect the scale (size) and type (class) of hotels constructed, thus affecting the general scale of tourism development.

Large-scale foreign-owned enclave-type facilities have, of course, destroyed valued environments and have alienated local populations. But so also have domestically owned facilities. The problem seems not to lie so much in the 'foreignness' of the ownership but in the nature of the planning and zoning laws that permit such constructions. Good environmental management by local communities is important for all forms of tourism development. The UNCTAD study (Barrowclough, 2007) notes that MNEs generally appeared to be more aware of the need to construct and operate facilities that conformed to international and local environmental standards than were domestically owned firms, but the larger size of foreign-owned facilities tended to increase the demand for resources such as power and water. Alternatively, if a destination wants to develop alternative small-scale locally owned, managed and integrated tourism in some regions because of the small size of the country and fragile environmental or socio-cultural concerns, it should carefully evaluate what role, if any, MNEs can play in that type of development (McNulty & Wafer, 1990).

BOX 14.1 Tourism investment in the South Pacific

Economic performance in the Pacific island countries has stagnated during the last decade, placing more importance on the development of a dynamic regional tourism industry to underpin long term sustainable economic growth and export diversification. If the tourism sectors in South Pacific nations are to expand in a way that achieves competitive advantage, this will require additional investment in tourism plant and infrastructure. The perceived benefits include: economic growth; job creation; utilisation of domestic resources, particularly renewable resources; skills acquisition; expansion of exports; development of remote areas of the country; facilitation of increased ownership of investment by citizens. The basic sources of investment available to Pacific countries include domestic private capital, foreign private capital, foreign aid (bilateral and multilateral assistance) and government finance (which may be from any or all of the above). Each is constrained, with consequent impediments to tourism development in the region.

Barriers to investment

Inadequate product development. Investment in accommodation, facility development, and refurbishment and general expansion of tourism plant has been inadequate. South Pacific island economies are characterised by relative fragmentation of the accommodation sector into small, marginal and unviable units, coupled with a sub standard quality. The combined effect is to prevent Pacific Island countries tapping major markets and attracting higher yield customers. The lack of good tourism shopping facilities and developed visitor attractions, gives rise to the perception that there isn't enough to do in the region. Underperforming units, which often are heavily discounted to attract customers, tend also to dilute national average occupancy rates achieved by industry thus reducing projected rates of return on investment. Low revenues from accommodation, rendered even lower with the practice of imposing withholding taxes on management fees and incentives, also serve to restrict the required refurbishment and upgrading of facilities. Investors tend to view hotel investments in the South Pacific as low return, high risk, ventures.

Low market awareness and lack of marketing and promotion. The region has been unable to mount a sustained marketing campaign in major potential long haul markets in

---

which awareness of region as a tourism destination is very low. Individual countries lack resources to market themselves effectively to main tourism generating countries as specific destinations in their own right, making it more difficult to achieve a balanced market mix and wider geographic spread of tourism traffic.

Insufficient trained manpower. Much of the region lack adequate expertise in both the public and private sector. Maintaining service quality is an important constraint to tourism development. The problem of inadequately skilled labour is exacerbated by restrictions on the employment of foreign workers. In most countries, except for Tonga which 'prefers' locals to be employed ahead of foreigners, work permits are only given to foreigners in circumstances where 'suitably skilled local employees are unavailable'. This rule often results in local labour being hired in preference to foreigners who are more likely to posses the skills needed for provision of quality service and sound business management.

Difficult and costly access. Air access in the region is costly, with long distances from major tourism generating markets and infrequent interregional flight schedules. The development of larger, longer range, more fuel-efficient, planes has resulted in a steady reduction of stopover services to South Pacific countries.

Inadequate capital base. Some commentators say that there is a need to provide a range of financial, fiscal and other incentives that give investors a comparative advantage over other countries in terms of inducing foreign investment in the tourism sector. However, since financial incentives must inevitably be paid for by local taxpayers, increased incentives offered to foreign investors can result in lower gains to individual countries in the region. Given the lack of domestic savings, for most South Pacific countries, foreign aid continues to play a vital role in meeting government budgetary and development needs as well as the provision of foreign exchange.

Weak institutional frameworks. South Pacific economies are characterised by: generally weak and under resourced NTO's; lack of tourism policy formulation and detailed sectoral development planning, including appropriate legislative measures; lack of a field marketing organisation to promote the region in long haul markets; inadequate market research information and poor general statistical data on tourism which could facilitate tourism development planning and marketing to cultivate the growth potential of niche markets in tourism generating countries.

Land tenure and government regulations. The land tenure system relating to the customary ownership of land limits the potential for long term investment in the region. The necessity for foreign investors to negotiate with local landowners combined with government bureaucracies in many cases constitutes an ongoing barrier to tourism development. Some countries place additional barriers in the way of foreign investment such as exchange controls and regulations hindering the repatriation of capital, profits and dividends.

Strategic response

New product development. There is a need to develop an improved range of accommodation facilities, ancillary services (restaurants, bars, entertainment, shopping and transport); Support services (travel brokering, visitor advice and professional services); and tourism enterprises (diving, snorkeling, fishing, sailing and visits to historical sites). Product development of tourism related facilities and services must match international market expectations and competition.

Need for balanced market development. There is a need to measure the effectiveness of marketing activities to optimise the allocation of the regions marketing and promotion resources, coupled with a need for specifically focused market research to provide information for more effective product design and marketing planning and facilitate private sector operations. There is a need to develop potential long haul markets of Japan, China, India, Europe, and North America to supplement traditional markets, with an increased uptake and use of new technologies- particularly information and communication technologies.

Need for integrated tourism development planning. There are excellent opportunities for the greater participation of the indigenous communities through the development of tourism activities, using their inherited natural and cultural resources and traditions. Often, investment is sought without any consideration as to how it can best be utilised. It is desirable to attempt to integrate tourism development within an overall national development strategy. The commitment of indigenous communities is vital. Local participation in the tourism sector must be encouraged, either through investment, joint ventures, land for equity swaps, employment or the transfer of technical skills and expertise.

Need for tourism research and statistics. Reliable and internationally compatible data on tourism in the South Pacific have been scarce. A sound research and statistical base is critical to maintaining and improving the tourism sectors competitiveness and to making informed public policy decisions affecting tourism. Efforts are being made to standardise basic tourism statistics. The quality, timeliness and relevance of information on tourism activity are also important to investment decisions.

Need for manpower development. The development of a skilled workforce is critical to tourism growth and investment. Investors must be assured that there is a reliable source of trained personnel in all aspects of tourism activity. Historically, tourism education and training in the South Pacific has been deficient in terms of scope, level and continuity of provision. Excellence in service provision is important to ensure satisfied customers and repeat visitation. A long term aim should be establishment of a network of regional and sub regional permanent training facilities as a part of an ongoing strategy for manpower development.

Conclusions

Barriers to tourism investment in the South Pacific cannot be resolved quickly. There is an urgent need for governments and agencies at all levels to create a climate for investment that ensures equitable distribution of benefits, and clear and transparent decision-making. Foreign investment, in its catalytic role, can be 'managed' cooperatively by the investment sources and the host government so as to: achieve critical mass, integrate enclaves of development, optimise infrastructure services, create a balanced structure of tourism activity operate within aggregate and compatible carrying capacity thresholds achieve the coordination in location, scale, quality of tourism facilities, strengthen the image of the tourism destination/region, maintain the momentum of progress through the development life cycle.

Source: Dwyer, L. (2005) 'Tourism Investment in the South Pacific: Barriers and Opportunities' in C. Cooper and M. Hall (eds) *Oceania: A Tourism Handbook*, UK: Channel View Publications

14.7   DOMESTIC OWNERSHIP VERSUS FOREIGN OWNERSHIP

Given that FDI has both positive and negative effects on a host destination, determination of the net benefits (costs) for any country is an empirical matter. Two questions need to be answered. First, could the host nation do even better if its tourism operations were domestic-owned rather than foreign-owned? Second, if so, should governments encourage and support domestic private tourism investment?

14.7.1   IS IT BETTER FOR TOURISM PROJECTS TO BE DOMESTICALLY OWNED RATHER THAN FOREIGN OWNED?

There is no simple 'yes' or 'no' answer to this question. The best way to discuss it is to assume a tourism boom and see whether changes in tourism demand are *expected* or *unexpected*, by both domestic and foreign investors.

Expected changes in tourism demand

Expected demand changes usually accompany stable economic environments. Under this circumstance, change is anticipated by both domestic and foreign investors and can be factored into forecasts.

If tourism demand is expected to increase, there is little difference in the benefits that a host nation would gain if investment projects were domestically owned as opposed to foreign owned. Conversely, if tourism demand is expected to decrease, there is little difference in the benefits that a host nation would lose if investment projects were domestically owned as opposed to foreign owned.

The impact of tourism spending on the inputs into tourism services would be much the same in both cases. The effects on foreign exchange earnings would be the same, once allowance had been made for reinvestment of the capital sums gained by domestic investors from selling tourism assets to foreigners. Any profits from operating these assets would, of course, accrue to the foreign investors, but they would have paid in full for the right to earn these profits. This might only affect the timing of the profits from the tourism assets, and the returns from the alternative investments that the sellers could make.

Thus, when change in tourism demand can be anticipated, there is little in the way of different benefits gained (losses made) by the host nation whether or not tourism facilities are domestic-owned or foreign-owned.

Unexpected changes in tourism demand

Unexpected changes may take the form of sudden shifts in consumer behaviour or unforeseen changes in government policy. If an increase in tourism demand is unexpected by both domestic and foreign investors, then the host nation would gain less from the increase if the investment projects are foreign owned than if domestically owned. Alternatively, if a decrease in tourism demand is unexpected, then the host nation would lose less from the decrease if the investment projects are foreign owned than if domestically owned.

However, a share of the 'terms of trade' gain will accrue to foreign owners. Profits will be higher (lower) than expected and foreign owners will share these profits. Foreign owners will gain their share of the excess (shortfall) of the unexpected profits over the expected profits and they will have paid for the latter. On balance, when changes in tourism demand are unanticipated, it is equally likely that tourism changes will be greater (or less) than the expected level, so the likelihood of gains is equal to the likelihood of losses.

When there is a high level of foreign ownership in the nation's tourism industry (or if the facilities are likely to be used by foreign tourists), the benefits or costs that accrue to the host nations will be correspondingly reduced, as compared to the case where there is a low level of foreign ownership. Yet, even if there were 100% foreign ownership, all that would mean is that direct terms of trade benefits/costs would be lost overseas. The other sources of benefits or costs from tourism would remain unchanged by ownership.

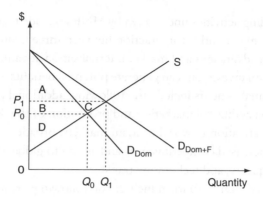

Figure 14.3 Changes in producer surplus as a result of increased tourism

This last issue has relevance for policy decisions that the government might make. This is shown in Figure 14.3 where the greater the outward shift of the demand curve, the greater will be the increase in producer surplus. The original producer surplus is measured as area D (the triangle above the supply line but below the price). This represents the difference between what producers are willing to sell their service for and what they do sell it for. With an increase in demand, producer surplus is now equal to the area $D+B+C$.

The higher the proportion of foreign ownership in tourism, the more the increase in producer surplus will accrue to foreigners rather than domestically owned firms. If these foreigners paid prices for tourism assets that reflected a lower expected demand for tourism services, they will benefit at the expense of the domestic sellers, and vice versa, where the future tourism demand is less than expected. It is unrealistic to assume that tourism asset sale prices always reflect perfect foresight as to tourism's potential.

14.8 CONCLUSIONS AND POLICY IMPLICATIONS

- Foreign tourism investment refers to private and public investment money flowing into one country from another either as foreign direct tourism investment (ownership/control) or as foreign portfolio tourism investment (part ownership/no control).
- Foreign direct tourism investment consists of flows and stocks of investment expenditure.
- Accurate data on the volume of foreign direct tourism investment in the global tourism economy are lacking because tourism's diverse and interlinking activities make the compilation of tourism statistics almost impossible. Many countries do not distinguish between domestic and foreign investors, and the frequent use of managerial contracts or franchising operations suggests that there is a difference between official FDI data and the activities of firms in practice.
- The various motives for foreign direct tourism investment can be explained through the eclectic paradigm of international production which asserts that the extent, pattern and

growth of value-adding activities undertaken by MNEs outside their home countries are dependent on the value of and the interaction between three main variables: ownership advantages, location advantages and market internalisation advantages.

- Foreign direct tourism investment can generate potential benefits and costs for host destinations. The potential benefits include the following: additional provision of capital in the tourism industry; additional marketing and promotion of the destination and raising the profile of the destination in world tourism markets; broadening the economic base and creating jobs; increased competitiveness and access to global distribution networks; enhanced product quality; and technology transfer.

- The potential costs of FDI in tourism include the following: crowding out of domestic investment; increased leakages from imports, repatriation of profits, management and franchise fees; reduced employment opportunities for locals; loss of equity and control of the tourism industry; and inappropriate form and scale of tourism development.

- The extent of costs and benefits will vary considerably from case to case. On balance, though, unless distortions generate net costs or increased market power, the net contribution of foreign investment is likely to be positive for host destinations, generating increased tourism flows and tourist expenditure.

- Determination of the net benefits (costs) for any country is an empirical matter and two questions need to be answered: Could the host nation do even better if its tourism operations were domestic-owned rather than foreign-owned? If so, should governments encourage and support domestic private tourism investment? Either way, foreign direct tourism investment is best seen as complementary to rather than as a substitute for domestic tourism investment.

- Foreign direct tourism investment has the potential to help address some of the challenges facing developing countries in an increasingly interdependent, globalised world. Developing countries that seek to access foreign direct tourism investment as part of their overall economic development need to design and implement proper policy frameworks that will make themselves more attractive to tourists and improve the bargaining position of their tourism service suppliers. When using incentives or subsidies to attract foreign direct tourism investment, socio-economic costs and benefits should be examined carefully within the framework of overall development strategies.

SELF-REVIEW QUESTIONS

1. Use tourism examples to distinguish between foreign portfolio investment and foreign direct investment.

2. What reasons are cited for the acceptance of FDI in a host country?

3. Using examples from tourism, distinguish between the flow and the stock associated with FDI.

4. Why is there a lack of accurate data on the volume of FDI in the global tourism economy?

5. How does the eclectic paradigm in industrial production provide motives for FDI in tourism?

6. Draw up a list of potential costs and potential benefits to firms and host countries that might accrue from foreign direct tourism investment.

7. Give tourism examples to show how leakages associated with foreign direct tourism investment differ in the construction stage from the operating stage.

8. Distinguish between expected change and unexpected change in tourism demand. How does each type of change relate to the question of whether tourism operations should be domestically or foreign owned?

ESSAY QUESTIONS

1. Foreign direct investment in tourism is of more concern than foreign portfolio investment to host destinations. Why?

2. 'It is better for tourism projects to be domestically owned rather than foreign-owned.' Do you agree? Why or why not?

3. 'Concerns about the effects of foreign direct tourism investment on host destinations are overstated.' Comment.

4. Given that foreign direct tourism investment has both positive and negative effects on a host destination, determination of the net benefits for any country is simply an empirical matter. Discuss.

5. The answer as to whether tourism projects should be foreign owned or domestically owned depends in large part on whether changes in tourism demand are expected or unexpected. Discuss this in the light of a global economic downturn.

TAXATION AND TOURISM

CHAPTER 15

TOURISM TAXATION

LEARNING OBJECTIVES

After reading this chapter, you should be able to:

1. Evaluate the arguments for and against taxing tourism.

2. Distinguish between specific taxes and *ad valorem* taxes and between taxes and user charges levied on tourists.

3. Demonstrate that the incidence of a sales tax on a tourism product differs with the elasticities of demand and supply for the product.

4. Understand the principles of efficient taxation.

15.1 INTRODUCTION

When tourists travel, they encounter a large array of taxes. They may have to pay an entry tax when they visit another country or an exit tax when they leave. During their stay, they encounter more taxes levied on their purchases ranging from hotel rooms, restaurant meals, gifts and souvenirs, car rentals, admissions to visitor attractions and so on. These taxes are not 'discriminatory' because residents of these destinations must also pay them when they make the same purchases. But for some items, most of the purchases at the local businesses are made by tourists (e.g. hotel rooms and car rentals), while other purchases (generally) are largely made by residents (such as fuel and restaurant meals). Likewise, 'tourist businesses' such as hotels, travel agencies and car rental companies must pay local business and property taxes that are also levied on non-tourist businesses.

A 'tourist tax' is one that largely falls on tourists (e.g. hotel room tax). There are other commodity taxes – such as a general tax, or a consumption tax – that are also paid by tourists (and local residents) but we wouldn't call them a 'tourist tax'. In reality, while there are some taxes that only tourists pay (e.g. air passenger duty), most of the taxes that tourists pay are also levied on the resident population of the destinations that tourists visit (e.g. taxes on automobile fuel use). Nevertheless, many of the taxes that are levied within destinations do have important consequences for tourists.

The World Travel and Tourism Council (WTTC) forecasts that tourism taxes, which account for US$164,352 billion in 2010 (9.7% of all taxes on travel and tourism), will account for 10.7 % of global taxation revenues by 2020 (WTTC, 2009).

The consequences of taxes on tourism vary according to the type of tax and the system of taxation that are in operation within the destination. The primary goal of a national tax system is to generate revenues to pay for the expenditures of government at all levels. Most government expenditure must be paid for through the taxation system and this is widely viewed as the principle function of taxation. Yet there are several other objectives of taxation. These include the role of taxation as a means of

- Income redistribution – to alter the distribution of income and/or wealth.
- Resource allocation – to discourage the consumption of goods and services with high social costs or demerit goods (e.g. taxes on cigarettes and alcohol, higher taxes on leaded than on unleaded petrol, taxes on imported goods and carbon taxes on transportation services).
- Economic stabilisation – to influence the level of aggregate demand to stabilise the economy.

There are likely to be conflicts among these three objectives. For example, resource allocation might require changes in the level or composition (or both) of taxes, but those changes might bear heavily on low-income families – thus conflicting with redistributive goals. As another example, taxes that are highly redistributive may conflict with the efficient allocation of resources.

The extent to which tourism taxation meets the aforementioned objectives differs between destinations. Over the past decade, there has been growing evidence that taxes on travellers and travel companies have been increasing as governments have viewed the expanding industry as a ready source of revenue. Arguably, travel and tourism is one of the few taxed export industries, and its customers are amongst the few taxed non-voters. Although the revenue gained from tourism taxation can be used to benefit residents through increased provision of public services, it may also reduce demand for tourism services and the economic gains from meeting this demand. Thus, the net benefit from tourism development depends critically on how a destination designs its public finance/revenue system to tax travel and tourism.

This chapter examines the economics of taxing travel and tourism. It addresses the following questions:

- What are the types of tourist taxes?
- What are the effects of tourism taxation?
- What are the characteristics of a 'good' taxation system?
- What are the economic reasons for taxing travel and tourism?
- What are the arguments against tourism taxation?

15.2 TYPES OF TOURISM TAXATION

The UNWTO (1998) has identified 45 different types of taxes imposed on the tourists in developed and developing countries. These can be divided into five broad areas:

- taxes on airlines and airports;
- hotels and other accommodation;
- road transportation;
- food and beverages;
- providers of tourism services.

In practice, the tourism sector can be taxed either by taxing the businesses in the tourism sector or by taxing the tourists directly. Both tax systems can be implemented via the general tax system or through the specific tourism taxes. These are shown in the tourism tax typology in Table 15.1. Of the 45 types of taxes, 30 are directly payable by the tourists and 15 are levied on tourism businesses. These taxes can be levied either as an ad-valorem tax, which is a percentage on the price or value of the good or service being taxed, or as a specific tax, which is a fixed amount of money per unit sold.

Taxes may be direct or indirect. A direct tax is collected directly by government from the persons (legal or natural) on whom it is imposed. Income taxes or corporate taxes are good examples of direct taxation. In contrast, an indirect tax (such as sales tax, Value Added Tax (VAT), Goods and Services Tax (GST) or import duty) is a tax collected by an intermediary (such as a retail store or transport provider) from the person who bears the ultimate economic burden of the tax (such as the customer). The intermediary later files a tax return and forwards the tax proceeds to government with the return. It is sometimes said that a direct tax is one that cannot be shifted by the taxpayer to someone else, whereas an indirect tax can be.

It is important to distinguish between *taxes* and *user charges*. User charges are prices charged by governments to users to pay for specific public services or for the privilege to engage in certain activities. Some of the taxes listed above are better described as user charges, while others are pure taxes which raise net revenues for the government. Airport facilities and security charges, port charges and admissions to public beaches, pools, parks and nature reserves are examples of user charges in tourism. User charges are most appropriately used to finance public services when most or all of the benefits go to identifiable users, and those who do not pay can be denied use at a reasonable cost.

15.3 EFFECTS OF TAXATION

15.3.1 EXCESS BURDEN

In addition to providing revenues to governments, taxes have the effect of decreasing the quantity demanded of a product by increasing its effective price. Taxes act as a wedge

541

Table 15.1 Types of tourism taxes

Sector	Name of Tax	Payable By
Entry/Exit Taxes	Resident departure tax/Foreign travel tax	Customer
	Visa/travel permit	Customer
Air Travel	Air passenger duty	Customer
	Air ticket tax	Customer
	Airline fuel tax	Business
Airports/Sea Ports/Road Borders	Departure tax	Customer
	Passenger service tax	Customer
	Airport security tax	Customer
	Airport parking tax	Customer
	Transit taxes	Customer
	Trekking/mountaineering fees	Customer
Borders Hotels/Accommodation	Bednight tax	Customer
	Bed tax	Customer
	Occupancy tax	Customer
	Differential VAT rate	Customer
	Surtax	Customer
	Sales tax	Customer
	Service tax	Customer
	Turnover tax	Business
	Hotel and restaurant tax	Customer
	Temporary lodging tax	Customer
	Hotel accommodation tax	Customer

	Lodging tax	Customer
	Fringe benefit tax	Business
	Payroll tax	Business
	Customs and excise	Business
Restaurants	Sales tax/VAT	Customer
	Liquor taxes/duties	Business
Road Taxes	Toll charges	Customer
	Fuel taxes/duties	Business
Car Rental	Municipal/local tax	Customer
	Purchase duty	Business
	Petrol/diesel duty	Customer
Coaches	Purchase duty	Customer
	Specific additional tax	Business
	Tourist transport tax	Customer
Tourism Attractions	Visitor attractions tax	Customer
	VAT and sales tax	Customer
Training	Industry training tax	Business
	Catering tax	Business
Environment	Eco-tourism tax	Business
	Carbon tax	Business
	Landfill tax	Business
Gambling	Betting tax	Business
	Casino tax	Customer

Source: Gooroochurn and Sinclair (2005), Adapted from UNWTO (1998)

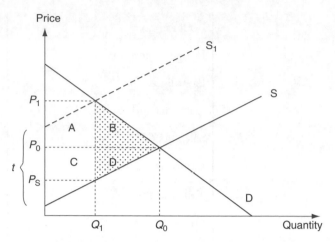

Figure 15.1 Imposition of a sales tax

between the price paid by consumers and the price received by suppliers. In Figure 15.1 the initial market conditions are shown by D and S, respectively. The market is in equilibrium at price P_0 and quantity demanded Q_0. The imposition of a tax at a rate of 't' shifts the supply curve to S_1 leading to a rise in the price to P_1, a fall in consumer surplus of A + B and reduction in producer surplus of C + D. Government collects a revenue of rectangles A + C which is equal to ($t \times Q_1$).

Taxes also have an efficiency effect, which (except lump-sum tax) change relative prices and cause distortions in the economy. Thus, consumers change consumption patterns, producers change product mix and factor allocation and workers alter the amount of leisure taken. The deadweight loss from taxation, also known as the distortionary cost or excess burden of taxation, is the economic loss that society suffers as the result of a tax, over and above the revenue that is collected (Hines, 2007). Distortions occur because people or firms alter their behaviour in order to reduce the amount of tax they must pay. The deadweight loss represents lost value to consumers and producers because of the reduction in the sales of the good. In Figure 15.1, the deadweight loss is measured as the area B + D. That is, the sum of the reduced consumer surplus B and the reduced producer surplus D. The size of the excess burden depends upon two things. The *first* is the elasticities of demand and supply of the good being taxed: the more elastic the demand or supply, the greater the deadweight loss. The *second* factor is the size of the tax. Thus, the excess burden of taxation is commonly measured by the area of the associated 'Harberger triangle' (Hines, 1999). The base of the triangle is the amount by which economic behaviour changes as a result of price distortions introduced by the tax, and the height of the triangle is the magnitude of the tax burden per unit of economic activity. As a general rule, the excess burden of a tax increases with the square of the tax rate (Hines, 1999).

The cost of a distortion is usually measured as the amount that would have to be paid to the people affected by it, in order to make them indifferent to its presence. If the price of a bus ticket is $5.00 and the train fare is $5.00, a consumer might prefer to travel by bus. If the government levies a tax of $1.00 per bus ticket, the consumer might choose train travel. The excess burden of taxation is the loss of utility to the consumer for travelling by train instead of by bus, since everything else remains unchanged.

15.3.2 TAX INCIDENCE

Tax incidence is an indicator of who bears the ultimate burden of a tax. Who pays most of the tax depends on the supply and demand elasticities for the particular tourism product or service.

Effects of different demand elasticities on sales tax incidence

Suppose that the government decides to levy a tax on ferry services. Figure 15.2 illustrates the imposition of a $5 sales tax on ferry tickets The tax shifts the supply curve vertically from S to S_t. In panel (a) with less elastic demand, the market price of the journey rises from $20 to $24, and the number of tickets sold falls from 10,000 to 9000. Government revenue from the tax is $450,000 ($5 × 9000). In this case, the supplier pays $1 of the tax per trip and consumers pay $4 tax per trip.

In panel (b) with more elastic demand, the same sales tax leads to an increase in price from $20 to $22 and the quantity of tickets demanded and supplied falls from 10,000 to 7000. In this case, the supplier pays $3 of the tax per trip while consumers pay $2. The more elastic the demand, the more the tax is paid by suppliers in the form of a lower price net of taxes. Government revenue from the tax is $350,000.

Effects of different supply elasticities on sales tax incidence

Figure 15.3 illustrates the imposition of a $5 sales tax on ferry tickets. The tax shifts both the more elastic supply curve in panel (a) and the less elastic curve in panel (b) vertically by $5.

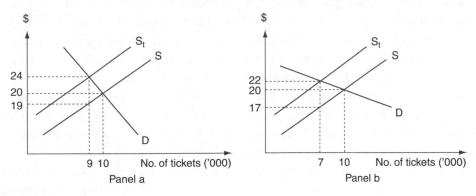

Figure 15.2 (a, b) Effects of different demand elasticities on tax incidence

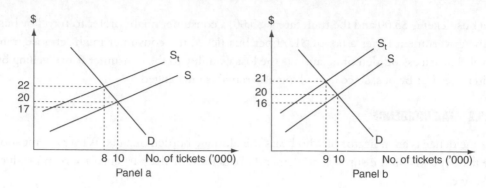

Figure 15.3 Effects of different supply elasticities on tax incidence

In panel (a) with a fairly elastic supply curve the market price rises from $20 a ticket to $22. Ticket sales decline from 10,000 to 8000. Government revenue from the tax is $400,000. In this case, the supplier pays $3 of the tax per trip while consumers pay $2.

In panel (b) with a less elastic supply curve the price rises to $21 a ticket following imposition of the tax. The more inelastic the supply, the less the tax is paid for by consumers. In this case, the consumers pay $1 of the tax and suppliers pay $4. Ticket sales decline from 10,000 to 9000. Government revenue from the tax is $450,000.

Thus, we make three observations. Other things equal,

- The more elastic the demand, the less the tax will be passed on to the consumers in the form of higher prices, and the more the tax will be absorbed by the supplier.
- The more elastic the supply, the more suppliers pass taxes on to consumers in the form of higher prices.
- The greater (smaller) the elasticity of supply relative to the elasticity of demand, the larger (smaller) the portion of the tax passed on to the consumers as a higher price.

If consumers are relatively price sensitive, suppliers will be forced to absorb more of the cost of any new tax into their cost structure. However, if suppliers are relatively more price sensitive, more of the tax will be passed onto consumers. The ratio of the price increase to tourists and the reduction in the net price received by suppliers is (approximately) equal to the ratio of the supply and demand elasticities for the good or service.

If managers have information on elasticities of supply and demand, they will be able to anticipate the effects of changes in tax policies and plan accordingly. Although precise estimates of elasticities are not always available, best judgements can help managers in making pricing decisions in response to changes in taxes.

Many sectors of the tourism industry globally have cost or supply conditions such that there are no significant economies or diseconomies of scale. Thus, if the industry expands or contracts, its unit costs do not change very much – at least in the long run. It is also the case that many sectors within tourism industries tend to be quite competitive; there are a number of competing firms, none of which dominates the market (Dwyer & Forsyth, 1993b). Under these circumstances the effects of taxes will differ between the short run and the long run.

Typically, short-run supply elasticities will be lower than long-run elasticities, since firms are unable to increase or decrease their capital stock. Thus firms will typically bear some of the burden of a tax in the short run.

In the long run, taxes levied on the output of the industry will be passed on to consumers, more or less in full. In the long run, the industry itself will not lose from a tax being levied on it, since it will be earning the minimum return to attract capital, both before and after the imposition of the tax. Thus, as a general rule, taxation of the tourism industry ultimately means taxation of the tourists.

Two additional points may be noted.

(1) While full pass-through of a tax will take place in the long run, the long run can be a considerable period of time. Essentially, the long run is the period needed for supply to adjust fully. For some parts of the tourism industry, it takes a long time for supply to adjust, perhaps several years. Supply may be constrained by the level of fixed investment, such as in hotels, and, in the short run, it may be difficult to adjust supply to the level appropriate given a change in circumstances such as a new tax.

Suppose a tax is levied on accommodation. In the short run, there will be a fixed amount of capacity available. Accommodation providers will try to pass on the tax to tourists, but this will lead to a reduction in amount demanded, and hence (net) revenues (Hiemstra & Ismail, 1993; Spengler & Uysal, 1989). Accommodation providers will compete among themselves for the custom and drop their rates. If capacity is reduced or, with a growing market, subsequent growth in demand brings demand back into line with capacity, the normal rates will be re-established. This process could take several years, and in the meantime the firms in the taxed sector will face reduced profits. Ultimately it will be the tourists who pay the tax, but in the intervening period some of the burden will have fallen on the industry. It has been argued that this occurred with an accommodation tax levied in Sydney to help fund the Olympic Games (Dwyer & Forsyth, 1999). Box 15.1 summarises some of the concerns voiced against the imposition of the Sydney Bed Tax, which was rescinded by the State government only a few months after it was first imposed.

(2) Another point concerns sectors of the industry that do not face constant costs of supply. Some tourism outputs are not capable of being expanded at constant unit cost of supply – if they can be expanded at all. Those that possess a degree of uniqueness are in this category. Operators might be in a very specific attractive location, and expansion of supply may be costly. Thus, expansion of a resort in a national park might be difficult, for environmental reasons, or accommodation on a small island might be restricted. Some tourism attractions are unique, and there are no close substitutes for them (the Pyramids

of Egypt, the Taj Mahal). Expansion of capacity at a beach location may be possible, but additional hotels might be further from the beach, and less attractively located. If a tax is levied on visiting these destinations, it is unlikely to be passed on in full.

It is important not to make simplistic assumptions about the incidence of a tax on tourism. While in the long run taxes will be passed on to the tourist, in the short run suppliers will have to pay some of the tax. For sectors such as accommodation, capacity, and thus supply, is fixed in the short to medium term, and since suppliers cannot reduce supply, they are unable to pass on a tax increase. Even a relatively low rate of tax can be very large relative to their profit margins and for a time suppliers may be adversely affected. Tourism is not like other industries, such as the petroleum industry, which can reduce the amount of the product supplied immediately.

The issue of who ultimately bears the burden of a tax depends on who can most readily make adjustments (i.e. buy some other non-taxed good; go to some other place; shift investment into non-taxed goods) in response to the tax. The person who bears the lion's share of the tax is the person who can least make the adjustment.

When considering tax policy, governments seldom have ready access to accurate information about demand and supply such as that depicted in Figure 15.1. As a consequence, their taxing decisions do not always produce the results intended.

BOX 15.1 Taxing the hotel sector to pay for the Sydney Olympics

In 1997, the State Government of New South Wales announced it would levy a 10% bed tax on hotels in the central area of Sydney. Sydney is Australia's largest city, its major tourism gateway, and is one of the most popular destinations in Australia for international and domestic tourists. Despite criticism from the industry, the Government was not been prepared to enter the debate about the levy other than to talk in generalities about the hotels contributing to the cost of the Olympics 2000 and repaying some of the profits they would make from this 16 day event. The State Treasurer described the Bed Tax as a 'tourism boom dividend'. To many in the industry, the levy was tantamount to a tax on exports, discriminating against tourism as compared to other economic sectors. Dwyer and Forsyth (1999) investigated the effects of the tax on Gross State Product, employment, investment in tourism facilities and government revenue.

Impact on gross state product.
The economic impact of the Bed Tax on the State is associated with the amount of visitor expenditure that will now be lost to the State. While there will be some

substitutions of expenditure from the region subject to the tax to other regions in Sydney, the overall impact on the State was estimated to be negative. This lost spending arises from:

- Visitation (and associated expenditure) to New South Wales that is cancelled because of the Bed Tax.
- Shortened lengths of visitor stay in New South Wales due to the tax.
- Reduced visitor expenditure on other items due to the additional accommodation tax burden, resulting in less total expenditure during a visit to Sydney.

The extent to which revenue will fall depends on the elasticity of demand for tourism in respect of the ground content. Visitors react differently to price increases depending on the purpose of their visit, the origin market, and other factors. Estimation of the overall likely effect on demand, resulting from the Bed Tax, requires estimating the price elasticities of demand from each of the identified market segments. It was estimated that the Bed Tax would result in a total decrease in Gross State Product (GSP) per annum, in 1997 dollars, of $166.5 million in a stabilized year (defined as a year in which all hotels can choose whether to absorb the tax or pass it on to guests). This estimated excludes any reductions in investment resulting from the tax impost.

Impact on employment.
It was estimated that Sydney CBD hotel revenues would fall by $59.7 million, a reduction of 8.5%. Based on studies of the price elasticity of hotel accommodation which suggest a range between $-.33$ and $-.50$ it was estimated that the 8.5% revenue reduction will cause a 2.6% reduction in employment in Sydney hotels, equal to 243 full time equivalent jobs. The loss of jobs elsewhere in New South Wales is estimated to be 939 full time equivalent jobs, giving a total loss of 1182 full time equivalent jobs. The number of people affected will be greater than this number, given the high incidence of casual and part time work in tourism generally. In addition, any reduction of hotel investment resulting from the tax will imply further job losses in facility construction and operations, unless alternative job creating investments take place.

Effect on investment.
Results of a survey of developers with proposals to develop hotels or serviced apartments within the tax affected Sydney central business district (CBD),

indicated that investments totaling $825 million, involving 3200 rooms were being reconsidered, and projects amounting to $210 million were terminated as a result of the tax impost. Beyond its impact on existing proposals, the bed tax lead to downward revisions of expected returns on investment in tourism and hospitality generally. The tax is also impacted on the profit projections of listed hotel companies with Sydney investments. The Bed Tax was expected to exacerbate an ongoing problem of inadequate support by domestic financial institutions for tourism developments in obtaining finance. Any reduction in the growth of accommodation supply puts further upward pressure on accommodation prices, thus adversely impacting on Sydney's price competitiveness as a tourist destination.

Impact on government revenue.

It was estimated that the tax yielded $64.4 million per year (in 1997 dollars) from existing hotels This figure does not allow for any expansion of available accommodation or increase in occupancy rates or room rates in the relevant areas. This figure does not include administration costs, nor was an estimate made of the net effect of the tax on the Government's budgetary position, after all inter-industry effects are allowed for. A CGE analysis would be required to determine this.

The incidence of the tax.

Two extreme industry reactions to the Bed Tax are possible:

- Accommodation providers fully absorb the tax with no price increases to customers;
- Accommodation providers fully pass on the tax by way of higher rates to customers.

It is generally agreed that the incidence of tax will be shared between the hotels and their customers. Two key factors which will determine who pays the tax are: (1) Contracts between hotels and their customers, which may be entered over periods up to three years; and (2) The demand and supply conditions in the sector.

(1) Where hotels have contracts to supply rooms to tour companies at a set price, there is little scope for renegotiation of prices, requiring the hotel to pay the tax. Interviews with accommodation providers in the tax affected area suggest that, in a stable year (one in which all contracts are open to free market negotiations), 80% of the tax will be borne by the guest, and 20% will be absorbed by the hotel. Hotels

will be less affected in the longer term. When contracts mature and are negotiated, hotels will be able to pass on the tax to guests.

(2) Supply/demand conditions are also likely to be of critical importance. Even if a hotel is not at all constrained by contracts, and it is able to alter its rates at will, supply/demand conditions will result in it bearing most of the burden of the tax in the short run. For the most part, the accommodation sector will not be able to pass on tax increases because it will be limited by demand relative to their capacity. With demand unchanged, the hotels will not, as a group, be able to raise the tax inclusive price to guests. Prices may rise temporarily, but with fewer guests occupancy rates will fall. Hotels will seek to gain customers from their competitors and discounting will break out. The net result will be "tax inclusive" final prices at much the same level as would have been the case if the tax had not been levied. Even though guests seem to be paying the tax, effectively it will be the hotels which do so. In the longer term, sectors in the tourism industry such as hotels have a high elasticity of supply. The long term adjustment to a tax will involve more or less fully passing on the tax (which will be necessary to achieve profitability) and a lower level of output of the sector.

Since the Sydney Bed tax was only levied on hotels in the city centre and immediate surrounds, over time, as more and more of the tax is passed on to higher room rates in the centre, customers will switch to hotels outside the centre. This increase in demand will enable hotels elsewhere in Sydney to increase their rates. The gains of the hotels in the non central areas will, however, be whittled away by increased investment, and thus more supply. In the long term, there will be higher room rates, lower occupancy rates and little or no gain in profit to the hotels just outside the taxed area. The imposition of the tax in only part of Sydney will encourage a wasteful pattern of investment.

Conclusion.

The proposed 10% tax on some Sydney accommodation was not good public policy. It could not be justified in terms of the gainers from the Olympics paying their contribution. The tax would have fallen almost entirely on part of the accommodation sector of Sydney for the first few years, after which it would have fallen almost entirely on domestic and foreign tourists. None of these groups is a primary beneficiary of the tourism boom which it is hoped the Olympics will generate. Of all sectors in the tourism industry, the accommodation sector is the one least well placed to profit from the boom, since the long lead time, strong competition and high supply elasticity all mean that any increased profits from the boom will be competed away. The Sydney Bed Tax was removed by the State government after a short period of operation.

Source: Dwyer, L. and P. Forsyth (1999) 'Should Accommodation Providers Pay for the Olympics? A Critique of the Sydney Bed Tax', *Tourism and Hospitality Research: The Surrey Quarterly Review*, 1(3), 253–264.

15.4   PRINCIPLES OF GOOD TAXATION

The usual criteria for good taxation are that it should be equitable (fair), efficient and administratively simple (Raghbendra, 1998).

15.4.1   EQUITY (FAIRNESS)

Economists consider two principles of equity to determine whether the burden of a tax is distributed fairly: the ability-to-pay principle and the benefits principle.

The *ability-to-pay principle* holds that people's taxes should be based upon their ability to pay, usually as measured by income or wealth. One implication of this principle is *horizontal equity*, which states that people with equal ability to pay should pay the same amount of tax. A second requirement of the ability-to-pay principle is *vertical equity,* the idea that a tax system should distribute the burden fairly across people with different abilities to pay. This idea implies that a person with higher income should pay more in taxes than one with less income. Vertical equity is usually measured by the ratio of taxes paid to income – that is, it measures the "progressivity" of taxes, meaning the degree to which people with higher incomes pay a higher proportion of their wealth in taxes. If the ratio rises with income, the tax is described as progressive; if the ratio falls with income, the tax is called regressive.

The *benefits principle* of taxation affirms that an equitable system is one in which each taxpayer contributes to the benefits which he/she receives from public services. The benefits principle regards public services as similar to private goods and regards taxes as the price people must pay for these services. Since most government services are consumed by the community as a whole, the practical application of the benefits principle is extremely limited. For example, one cannot estimate the benefit received by a particular individual for general public services such as national defence and local police protection. A fuel tax with proceeds devoted to road repair is perhaps the tax closest to the benefit principle.

15.4.2 EFFICIENCY

In addition to being equitable, a good tax system should be efficient, wasting as little money and resources as possible. It is widely agreed that tax policy should generally refrain from interfering with the market's allocation of economic resources. That is, taxation should entail a minimum of interference with individual decisions and hence minimum distortion as compared to the untaxed situation. Efficient taxes raise revenue without negative distortions such as reducing work-incentives for individuals, or unduly affecting the economic decisions of households or investment incentives for businesses. The larger the excess burden of a tax, the worse it is for efficiency.

Taxes on products and services should result in minimum change in patterns of consumption from the untaxed patterns. An optimal tax is one that minimises the deadweight loss to the society, resulting in minimum distortion from the untaxed situation (Hines, 1999). Optimal tax theory pioneered by Ramsey (Auerbach, 1985) advocates the uses of differential rates on products based on their elasticity. Goods with low demand elasticities such as cigarettes, alcohol and motor vehicle fuel are less likely to entail high adjustments in the quantity consumed resulting from increases in price, as compared to commodities with higher elasticities of demand. Thus, a tax structure which imposes a higher tax rate on goods with inelastic demand and lower taxes on other goods is more efficient as the relative impact in consumption will be lower.

Using a general equilibrium model of the US economy, Ballard *et al.* (1985) examined the combined welfare cost of all taxes in the US revenue system. It was found that the welfare losses caused by distortionary taxation can be very large, both on average and at the margin. The marginal welfare loss to consumers from raising an additional dollar of revenue is in the range of 34 cents to 48 cents, depending on certain elasticities. It was estimated that the marginal deadweight loss is between one-third and one-half of marginal revenues. In a more recent study, Gooroochurn and Sinclair (2005) thus employ a Computable General Equilibrium (CGE) model to estimate the economy-wide effects of raising tourism taxes in Mauritius. Their study is summarised in Box 15.2.

Optimal taxation theory does not offer easily applied prescriptions for policy, beyond the important insight that distortions do less damage where supply and demand are not highly sensitive to changes in taxes. Attempts have also been made to incorporate distributional considerations into this theory. They face the difficulty that there is no objectively 'ideal' distribution of income. Two propositions are widely agreed upon, however:

- On efficiency grounds, it is better to tax goods and services which are in price-inelastic demand or supply than those for which demand and supply are price elastic. Taxing products and services that are the most price-inelastic in demand and supply will minimise the excess burden. Thus, on efficiency grounds, it makes sense to tax products such as petrol, cigarettes and alcohol rather than products with high price elasticity.

- On efficiency grounds, it is desirable to spread a tax as widely as possible, and to set it at as low a rate as is consistent with the revenue requirement. A 5% tax over twice the size of tax base will raise more revenue than a 10% tax. That is, it is better to apply a tax to a broad tax base than to a narrow tax base. Thus, to minimise the efficiency cost of taxation, it is appropriate to spread the burden as widely as possible; a small addition to tax across the board is less distortionary than a larger addition on a narrow base. It is clearly the case that the more goods or services a tax applies to, the less possibility there will be of consumers switching to substitute products.

Estimates of the marginal cost of taxation associated with tax-caused distortions to economic choices have important implications for policy decisions about appropriate levels of aggregate government expenditure and about taxation system design. In order to reduce the welfare costs of taxation, tax design should aim in part for a mix of tax bases and tax rates to fall more heavily on those decisions with relatively low marginal costs of taxation.

15.4.3   EFFECTIVE ADMINISTRATION

Complicated taxing schemes reduce net revenues because of their higher administrative costs. The overall goal of effective tax administration is to minimise the costs incurred by taxpayers and government agencies to collect taxes. General requirements for the efficient administration of taxation include clarity, stability (or continuity), cost-effectiveness and convenience (Musgrave & Musgrave, 1989). Collection systems should provide taxpayers with clear and timely guidance by making sure that state and local taxes are understandable, simple and cost effective to administer. More complex taxing schemes incur greater administrative costs for both collecting agencies and the taxpayer. Unfortunately, the costs of administering taxes are seldom explicitly measured.

The principles of good taxation often conflict. Taxes with the objective of promoting efficiencies or a more equitable distribution of income may be administratively costly. Fairness and efficiency often conflict: fairness comes at the cost of efficiency. Each society must find the best trade-off between fairness and efficiency, given the ethical beliefs and values of its citizens.

BOX 15.2 Modelling tourism taxation in Mauritius

Gooroochurn and Sinclair (2005) used a CGE for Mauritius to show that raising the tourism taxes will have an adverse effect on the Mauritian economy through a rise in prices and a fall in the island's GDP.

The data for the Mauritian CGE model consist of a social accounting matrix for the year 1997. The production activities are decomposed into 17 sectors. Five sectors are related to tourism: hotels and restaurants (95.4%), transport and communications (61.4%), retail and wholesale trade (2.7%), other manufacturing (12.1%), and other services (12.3%). The tourism ratio, measured as tourism demand as a proportion of total demand, is given in brackets. The model includes 10 main categories of taxes, namely corporate, labor, sales, production, property, hotel and restaurant, gambling, import tariff, export, and income. All are treated as *ad valorem* (percentage) taxes.

Efficiency and equity effects.

The authors investigate the efficiency of taxes using the concept of marginal excess burden (MEB) per additional dollar of tax revenue. MEB is often used to quantify deadweight loss and measures the incremental cost, in terms of the change in domestic welfare (measured using the Hicksian equivalent variation), of raising extra revenues from an already existing distortionary tax, while holding other taxes constant. Welfare consists of the indirect utility function of domestic households and accounts for consumption, factor income, transfer income, and savings.

The MEB per dollar of additional revenue is formulated as:

$$\text{MEB} = \lambda_i = \frac{\text{Change in Welfare} - \text{Change in Tax Revenue}}{\text{Change in Tax Revenue}}$$

The authors investigate the relative efficiency of taxing the tourism industry by applying a small increase (of 0.1%) in the sales tax rate to each of the 17 sectors, one at a time, keeping the other tax rates constant. The associated MEB for each is calculated. The MEB can be positive or negative, representing either a higher increase or a lower reduction in welfare. The two main tourism sectors (restaurants/hotels and transport/communications) have the highest MEB, resulting from the monopoly power associated with the differentiated tourism products. The results indicate that taxing tourism-related activities is relatively efficient since a high proportion of the welfare loss is borne by international tourists and is not included in domestic welfare calculations. In this respect, an optimal tax, that maximizes domestic welfare, would be targeted entirely on international tourists and might be designed to incorporate, for example, differential pricing for international tourists and domestic residents.

Following this, the authors examine the equity effect of taxation by increasing the sales tax rate by 10% for each sector at a time. The corresponding percentage change for each of the income distribution measures is then calculated to indicate whether the distributional effects of changes in the rate on tourism-related sectors are more equitable than changes in the rate on other sectors. The authors conclude that increasing the sales tax rate for each sector in turn improves income distribution. This outcome depends importantly on the assumption that government redistributes a higher proportion of increase in revenue to the poorer household groups. Gooroochurn and Sinclair (2005) conclude that taxing tourism improves the income distribution by more than would result from taxing most other sectors. The main driver is the high proportion of domestic consumption from the richer household group for these sectors. Careful consideration of the tax design, by such means as dual pricing for international tourists and domestic residents, would assist the achievement of an optimal tax.

Macroeconomic effects.
The authors also investigated the macroeconomic effects of taxation first assuming a narrow policy where the hotel and restaurant tax rate is increased and thence a broad policy where the sales tax rate of all five sectors involved in tourism is increased at the same time.

Both policies reduce real GDP. The narrow policy (increasing hotel and restaurant taxes) is more contractionary than the broad because it entails a much higher increase (nearly four times more) in the tax rate for only one sector. This is likely to cause more distortions than increasing the rate by a small amount in each of the four sectors, resulting in a greater fall in GDP. The consumer price index also increases, showing the inflationary effect of taxation. Arrivals and consumption would be reduced by both policies, but is significantly more pronounced in the narrow policy than the broad policy. This is mainly because tourists bear a large proportion of the tax and the hotels and restaurants sector represents more than 45% of tourist consumption. With a higher increase in the tax rate (31.8%), there will be a significant reduction in tourism arrivals and consumption.

If tourism tax exportability is defined as the proportion shifted on to tourists, then the higher the degree of tax exportability, the more efficient is the policy. In this case, the tax exportability for the narrow policy is 105% while for the broad policy it is 19%. Hence if the main purpose of the government's tax on the sector is to extract revenue from international tourists, then the narrow policy is more appropriate. The proportion of the increased tax revenue contributed by the tourists is higher for the narrow policy. The narrow policy appears more efficient since it entails a higher welfare increase than the broad policy.

Conclusions.

The authors conclude that different types of policies have different effects on international tourists, domestic residents, and sectors within the economy. Although the imposition of relatively heavy taxes on tourism sectors appears to be an attractive option in terms of revenue generation, it may also be contractionary in terms of lowering GDP and the numbers of inbound arrivals.

A policy of taxing the two main tourism sectors in Mauritius is efficient relative to taxing other sectors such as primary goods production or manufacturing, in that there are relatively small effects on the welfare of domestic residents. Thus, if the government requires additional revenue, taxes on international tourism provide an efficient source. However, taxation has adverse effects in that it decreases GDP and raises the rate of inflation, particularly in the narrow policy case where the tax rate is increased for the hotels and restaurants sector alone. In the broad policy case, the increase in rates results in an increase in tax revenue from hotels and restaurants but a decrease in consumption by international tourists and a decrease in sales tax revenue from tourists. If sales tax is levied on all tourism sectors (broad policy), there is an increase in sales tax revenue from tourists but a decrease in tax revenue from hotels and restaurants.

Gooroochurn and Sinclair conclude that proposed policies for taxing tourism should be subject to considerable scrutiny before being approved or implemented. Competitiveness in the international arena is reduced by higher taxes, which may prejudice the ongoing development and growth of the tourism industry. As in the case of Mauritius, there may be a trade-off between such adverse effects and the increases in equity and efficiency that tourism taxation can bring about.

Source: Gooroochurn, N. and T. Sinclair (2005) 'The Economics of Tourism Taxation: Evidence from Mauritius', *Annals of Tourism Research*, 32(2), 478–498

15.5 ARGUMENTS FOR TAXING TOURISM

There are several main arguments for taxing tourism. Tourism taxes can

- Help to finance investment in public infrastructure.
- Expand and diversify the tax base.
- Prevent tax base erosion.
- Help to shift the tax burden to non-residents.
- Help communities to share in high business profits.
- Correct for market failure.

15.5.1 PROVISION OF PUBLIC INVESTMENT

The tourism sector relies on the natural amenities in the destination and also on publically provided infrastructure and public goods. Tourism development is not a free good. Like residents, tourists and their suppliers demand public services which have to be paid for through taxes and user charges. As tourism continues to grow in many countries, the infrastructure of these countries is becoming increasingly overburdened. Unless efforts are made to fund travel and tourism infrastructure, destinations will not be able to attract or maintain global market share.

In economics, a public good has the attributes of non-rivalry and non-excludability This means, respectively, that consumption of the good by one individual does not reduce availability of the good for consumption by others and that no one can be effectively excluded from using the good. The concept of a public good will be discussed in more detail in Chapter 17. For present purposes we note that the distinctive characteristics of public goods make it difficult to provide them via the private sector because of the difficulty of recovering costs from users. They are typically provided only by the government, which uses its right to tax to generate the resources necessary to supply them.

Domestic taxpayers usually finance the provision of publicly provided goods and services. Increased tourism numbers impose an extra cost on the government relating to the provision of infrastructure and items such as greater security and a cleaner environment. Since they are non-residents, tourists do not pay to finance these extra costs. A tax on tourism will, therefore, impose a burden on those responsible for creating the need for government to increase its expenditure on facilities and services. While user charges can be established for some attractions, such as national parks, nature reserves and highways, enforcing payment is difficult for publicly provided services such as street lighting, waste disposal, policing and security. In such circumstances, taxing may be the only way of 'charging' tourists for the public goods they consume.

Convention centre financing is a good example of the under-provision of infrastructure that is often corrected through appropriate taxation. As stand-alone facilities, convention centres are not constructed for financial profitability and indeed often operate at a financial loss. As Mak (2006) notes, the case for building convention centres is based on the expected additional economic activity, income, employment and tax revenues that conventions will generate in the community. Since private for-profit developers cannot capture those benefits, they would not be interested in building and operating a convention centre unless there were direct subsidies to cover annual operating losses and debt service. Thus, convention centres are typically built by local governments and funded through special taxes levied on tourism. In the USA, convention centres are typically financed by using hotel room tax revenues supplemented by excise/sales taxes (Mak, 2006).

15.5.2   EXPANSION AND DIVERSIFICATION OF THE TAX BASE

Taxation is often levied for revenue generation and diversification, which can be used for income redistribution and may increase domestic welfare by financing improvements in public services.

Higher government revenue from taxing tourism can increase domestic welfare, depending on the types of public services that are delivered using the revenues generated from the taxes. Furthermore, specific taxes on tourism may help to reduce the burden of income taxation on domestic residents and may also form part of a strategy for countries attempting to reduce their dependency on other taxes, including tariffs.

Many industrialised nations face growing fiscal deficits at the national level. The Global Financial Crisis (GFC) has further exacerbated this problem. Germany, Japan and the USA have responded with major tax reform initiatives in an effort to reduce their deficits. Taxing tourism seems to be an attractive option for governments facing budgetary constraints and pressures to decrease reliance on a variety of taxes.

The effects of these initiatives have been twofold. First, in the search for potential revenue sources, governments have increasingly focused on taxing tourism. Second, local governments have received less revenue-sharing funds from the national level and have focused on taxing tourism to compensate for these losses.

As noted above, the broader the tax base the better, since this will give rise to less distortion of consumption patterns. On such grounds, tourism services should be part of the tax base like other products and services, and there are no reasons why tourism *per se* should be treated differently from other commodities.

15.5.3   TAX BASE EROSION

Tax base erosion occurs when traditional components of the tax base no longer represent the expenditure patterns of the economy at large. This may result from such things as demographic changes, changing consumer tastes and values, relative changes in the structure of production, stagnation or inflationary effects, along with other shifts in the structure and character of an economy. As the relative tax shares of other sectors decline, policy makers often target tourism to make up the loss.

As we discussed in Chapter 2, the demand for many tourism products and services is likely to be income elastic. This implies that tourism (and its potential tax base) may well be growing faster than the world's income. By taxing travel and tourism, destinations are able to build in greater revenue elasticity into their own fiscal systems. Not surprisingly, tourism has become, and will likely continue to be, an increasingly important source of public revenues for travel destinations.

15.5.4   EXPORTING TAXES TO NON-RESIDENTS

It's often said that the best tax is one that someone else pays. Taxes imposed by one jurisdiction are sometimes paid by people who live elsewhere. When this happens, the tax is said to be exported. For example, gaming taxes in Nevada are largely exported, because most people who pay them are out-of-state tourists. Hotel/motel taxes are mostly passed on to customers who live outside the community.

Tax exporting is the shifting of a tax burden to non-residents of a given jurisdiction, such as a state or country. Government will normally seek to maximise the welfare of residents and will seek to introduce or raise taxes, which impose a low excess burden to the local resident. Hence, the increasing tendency of governments to the use of tourism taxation whereby the burden is shifted to non-residents (international tourists). Because of the limited possibility of retaliation, from the host country's point of view such taxes are optimal as little distortion is created with respect to the domestic consumers.

Tax exporting takes place for two main reasons. First, collecting taxation from non-residents is attractive because of the perception that the bulk of the tax burden falls upon non-constituents. By taxing visitors rather than residents, governments can avoid the unpopularity that generally accompanies an increase in taxes. Second, non-residents, or visitors, may be major beneficiaries from certain services provided by a local or state government. However, increased tourism numbers are likely to impose extra public costs relating to the provision and maintenance of some amenities. As non-residents, tourists do not pay to finance these extra costs. A tax may redress the balance, so that the burden falls on those who are responsible for increasing the costs of provision. In such cases, the interests of an efficient allocation of resources to those public services can be furthered by the use of taxes that, by virtue of their exportability, make it possible to collect an appropriate share of the costs of those services from the non-resident beneficiaries. Successful tax exporting requires two conditions to be satisfied: (1) the tax must be passed on to the consumer and (2) the consumer must be someone who does not live in the jurisdiction. In general, tax exporting can be achieved directly by imposing taxes on non-residents. Thus, hotel room taxes, car rental taxes and surcharges appeal to policy makers because of the fact that they are paid predominantly by non-residents.

In their study of tourism taxation in Mauritius, Gooroochurn and Sinclair (2005) confirm that taxing tourism-related activities is relatively efficient since a high proportion of the welfare loss is borne by international tourists and is not included in domestic welfare calculations. Thus, as the discussion in Box 15.2 indicates, unlike most other cases, tourism taxes can lead to an increase in domestic welfare, thereby rendering them more efficient than other sources. Tisdell (1983) had earlier demonstrated that, unlike the traditional outcome of a deadweight loss associated with higher taxes, increasing taxes on international tourism can improve welfare for residents of a destination. He also argued that the higher the proportion of tourism demand in total demand, and the more inelastic tourism demand is relative to domestic demand, the higher will be the welfare gain. Tisdell shows that since the burden of a tax on the tourism sector falls on both domestic residents and foreigners (tourists), the resulting deadweight loss combines the excess burden of an export tax and a domestic tax. Tisdell shows that, in the presence of tourists, the excess burden associated with commodity taxation is reduced and can even be negative (welfare gain). The welfare gain will be greater the more inelastic is inbound tourism demand relative to domestic demand. Welfare also increases more, the greater the share of tourism demand relative to total demand. In the case of variable prices, the value of the supply elasticity is also relevant.

The implication of the discussion is that, before introducing or changing tourism taxes, policy makers should pay explicit attention to the associated welfare effects. Increases in taxes can result in adverse welfare effects if the demand for tourism from non-residents is price elastic relative to domestic demand and/or if supply is inelastic. Another implication is that if policy makers wish to increase tourism taxes, they should also consider the longer-term strategy of attempting to make tourism demand by non-residents more price inelastic, for example, by increasing the quality of the tourism product and/or differentiating the product to enhance its market power. In other words, making the home destination more attractive to domestic tourists can result in both greater gains from domestic tourism and greater gains from taxes levied on foreign tourists.

A caveat

From the individual country's viewpoint, it is efficient to levy higher than normal taxes on tourism services. To the extent that it is possible to tax different services differently, the greater the proportion of sales accounted for by foreign tourists the greater would be the tax. Thus high-standard accommodation, which in a developing country is likely be used mainly by non-residents, might be taxed heavily, while internal public transport, likely to be used more by residents than by non-residents, should be taxed at a lower rate. The higher the tax on local residents, the greater will be the efficiency loss from distorting prices that they pay. Specific taxes on tourism services are very attractive for a country or region since they are among the very few that can be successfully passed on to non-residents. They represent a rare example of the practical application of an optimal tariff.

From the standpoint of an individual country, it makes sense to exploit its market power and to levy taxes that others will pay. This will result in rates of taxation on tourism that are high relative to rates on other goods and services. Once these are in place, it will be in each country's interest to maintain the taxes even though from the perspective of the world as a whole lower taxation would be preferable. In other words, what is rational for an individual country is inefficient for the world as a whole. Excessive taxation of international tourism will be the result, and this taxation will be very difficult to negotiate away implying that tourism is likely to suffer relative to other sectors in the global economy (Forsyth & Dwyer, 2002).

15.5.5 TAXES TO CORRECT FOR ENVIRONMENTAL EXTERNALITIES

As discussed in Chapters 6 and 17, market failure occurs when the market mechanism does not produce the optimal level of output. In other words, the market fails to allocate resources efficiently. In the presence of externalities, for example, production is normally not optimum since the social cost incurred during the production of a certain level of the commodity or service is not taken into account in the production decision. As shown in Figure 6.5, this gives rise to over-production and hence creates a level of negative externality which is costly to the host country.

Taxation can be used to address externalities, which include increased congestion on roads and additional environmental degradation. It is most efficient to correct distortions at their source and this can take the form of a consumption tax. The scheme would also apply to tourists to correct the distortion. The basic method is to use a Pigouvian tax (i.e. a tax on output), where the rate is set to eliminate the gap between the market price and the marginal social cost. Such charges can be applied to all users if they are generating externalities, and they should be directed to the goods and services that generate the unpriced adverse effects. The application of a tax on output helps reduce the difference between the private cost and the social cost of production of the tourism product, as shown in Figure 15.4. A similar figure was employed in Chapter 13 to illustrate the benefits of congestion pricing (Figure 13.3).

In Figure 15.4, the optimum level of activity for the profit-maximising private firm is Q_0, where its MPC_1 is equal to the Marginal Private Benefit (MPB) or Willingness to Pay (WTP) for the activity at the market price of P_0. However, the production of output generates externality costs, which, when combined with the private costs, result in social costs as indicated by the Marginal Social Cost curve MSC. At the output Q_0 the level of negative externalities is AC. From the society's point of view, an optimum is reached, where the MSC coincides with MPB at the point Q^* with the corresponding price being P^*. This results in a welfare gain to society (comprising consumer and producer surplus) equal to the shaded area ABC. If the output of the industry is competitively determined,

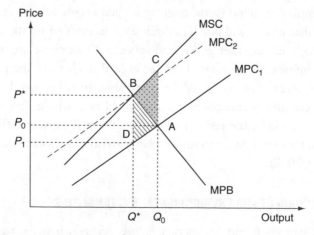

Figure 15.4 A tax on output to correct for market failure

it can be reduced from Q_0 to Q^* by the imposition of a tax per unit of output. The tax helps to 'internalise' the externality by causing a parallel upward shift in the industry supply curve (which is the lateral sum of firms' marginal private cost (MPC) curves). If the tax is set at a level equal to BD, the value of the external costs of pollution at the optimal level of output (Q^*), then the new industry supply curve MPC_2 (following the imposition of the tax) will intersect the demand curve at P^* and Q^*, the social optimal price and output. Part of the tax levied will be borne by consumers ($P^* - P_0$) and the rest ($P_0 - P_1$) will be paid for by the producers. Government will end up collecting tax revenue amounting to the area represented by the rectangle $P_1 P^* BD$ ($= OQ^*$ times BD).

While the theoretical considerations are sound, imposition of a tax which brings about the social optimum price and output is not always feasible. The above diagram presupposes that the MSC and the MSB are known, and that the setting of an optimal price is possible. Moreover, an underlying assumption is that the opportunity cost for using public resources is quantifiable. We discuss these issues further in Chapters 17 and 18.

There are many examples of this kind in the tourism industry; its relationship to the natural environment leads to many possible impacts, both positive and negative. Taxes or subsidies on the various industries that make up tourism may be the best way of controlling its impacts. This said, it is always desirable to levy taxes as directly as possible. For example, if visitors to a national park impose environmental damage and costs on its management, it is better to control for these impacts through charges for the use of the park, if feasible, rather than through some more indirect means, such as taxes on accommodation near the park, since local residents can do damage to the park just as tourists can do, even though they do not use the accommodation (Clarke & Ng, 1993).

Tourism gives rise to many environmental problems, and taxes levied to correct for the negative environmental externalities stemming from tourism have become more prevalent. Taxation can generate the necessary resources to address these problems. While there is no general argument for earmarking tax revenues, use of revenues from correcting tourism externalities can help to reduce and combat the associated degradation of the environment.

15.5.6   TAXES TO PROMOTE TOURISM DESTINATIONS

Governments fund (entirely or partially) destination tourism promotion. As a result of successful promotion, a destination may experience increased visitation with its associated positive economic impacts and additional taxes generated. Destination tourism promotion has all the properties of a public good. It is both non-rivalrous and non-excludable. Once money is spent to promote a destination, all destination businesses benefit, whether or not they helped to fund it. However, even if every business owner agrees that more money should be spent on promotion, each has an incentive to be a free-rider. Indeed, if many choose to free-ride, not enough money will be available to be spent on promotion. Not surprisingly, tourist bureaux chronically complain about the shortage of funds. Free-riding results in the misallocation of economic resources because, by under-funding promotion, the destination is unable to achieve its tourism potential.

The arguments put forward by tourism stakeholders for government support for tourism promotion are typically based on the standard economic justifications of government support for private sector activity in circumstances of market failure, that is externalities/non-appropriability of benefits, risk and uncertainty, and indivisibilities (Dwyer & Forsyth, 1992, 1993a, 1994a).

The *externalities/non-appropriability* argument recognises that private firms undertake promotional activity when they are confident that they can appropriate sufficient revenues to earn an adequate return on their investment. A major cause of under-promotion is that although the overall community benefits may exceed the costs, the individual operator often cannot appropriate enough of the benefits from tourism promotion to make it a profitable undertaking.

The *risk and uncertainty* argument recognises that commercial uncertainty and inability to predict the commercial results may lead to under-promotion of tourism products. Additionally, long lead times between expenditure on tourism promotion and subsequent tourism flows may contribute to the under-promotion of tourism by the private sector, particularly if there are differences in time preferences between the private sector and society as a whole.

The *indivisibility* problem occurs when the minimum outlay required to undertake an effective promotion campaign is beyond the resources of individual firms particularly within a highly fragmented industry. There may well be a threshold level below which it is not possible to conduct an effective promotion campaign.

The efficient solution to free-riding is for the government to fund the promotion, and it may choose to tax the tourist industry to pay for destination promotion. The most frequently employed tax to fund tourism promotion is a dedicated or earmarked hotel room tax. Despite the industry's general opposition to tourism taxes, the industry has often strongly supported legislation to levy lodging taxes to fund tourism promotion. However, many destinations still use general revenue funds rather than special taxes on tourism to pay for promotion.

15.6   ARGUMENTS AGAINST TOURISM TAXATION

A range of arguments has been levelled against tourism taxation (Hughes, 1981; WTTC, 2001). The key arguments can be discussed under two headings.

• Taxes can lead to a contraction of economic activity.
• Taxes lead to retaliation by other destinations.

15.6.1 CONTRACTION OF ECONOMIC ACTIVITY

Taxes make destinations more expensive, resulting in reduced price competitiveness, and associated reductions in tourist numbers and expenditure. This, in turn, can lead to reductions in production and output, and reductions in income and employment across the full range of tourism characteristic and connected industries. High taxes in one destination may also induce travellers to switch to alternative destinations.

While reduced destination price competiveness may well lead to a loss of income and jobs, the issue is not as clear-cut as it seems. As discussed in Chapter 9, a reduction in tourism may, depending on industry structure in the destination, lead to increased growth of traditional export- and import-competing industries.

In many destinations throughout the world, however, tax policies have been adopted which restrict both the revenue-generating capacity of tourism and the employment-creating opportunity of tourism. In some cities, such as New York, the failure of policy makers to consider thoroughly the implications of increasing hotel room tax rates has actually resulted in a net loss of tax proceeds and jobs to the city and state (WTTC, 2001). Similarly, Aguilo *et al.* (2005) estimated that a hotel tax in the Balearic Islands would result in a considerable fall in the number of visits. Some results of studies of the effects of tourism taxes on accommodation are displayed in Box 15.3.

BOX 15.3 Effects of tourism taxation

- Bird (1992) argues that although there is a strong economic case in many countries for taxing tourism more than at present, the nature of the industry and administrative difficulties severely limit what can be done in practice. He concludes that more attention should be paid to introducing adequate 'charging' policies where possible; that special taxes on hotel accommodation are generally the key to tourist taxation; and there is little reason to provide special incentives for investment in the tourist industry.
- In 1990, the imposition of a 5% tax in New York on hotel rooms of $100 or more per night increased combined State and City room taxes to 19.25% plus $2 per night (as compared with around 12% in the top 50 US cities in the mid-1990s). The result was a fall in tourism to New York. The tax was rescinded in 1994. New York State lost $962 million in taxes on visitor spending to collect $463.2 million from the 5% room tax (WTTC, 2001). The effect of a tax on government revenue depends on how high existing taxes are (WTTC Tax Policy Centre, www.traveltax.msu.edu).

- Fujii *et al.* (1985), Sakai (1985) and Hiemstra and Ismael (1992) found the demand for accommodation to be price inelastic. The responsiveness of demand to changes in tax rates can differ across different types of tourists, and Sakai (1988) found that business demand is more inelastic than that for leisure. Fujii *et al.* (1985) calculated its relative incidence on tourists and businesses as the ratio of the supply and demand elasticities for accommodation. Their results suggested that one-third of the hotel room tax was borne by the businesses themselves and the rest by tourists. They also showed that it was more readily exported (being paid mainly by international tourists) than similar taxes levied on meals, drinks and entertainment, and the general sales tax. Hence the exportability of tourism taxes is liable to vary between different components of the product. The results also suggest that taxes imposed on tourist spending have a moderately large negative output effect on the visitor industry.

- Much research that has examined the effects of a room tax has been carried out *ex ante*, that is, before the tax is actually levied. These studies have suggested that demand for lodging is generally price *inelastic* while supply of lodging is price *elastic*, implying that hotel room taxes would be largely passed on to hotel guests as higher prices. Bonham *et al.* (1992), in their *ex-post* study of the impact of a newly imposed 5% hotel room tax in Hawaii, supported this view. They found that the new tax had no statistically significant negative impact on hotel room rental revenues in Hawaii, suggesting that hotels fully passed on the room tax to their guests. They added a caveat, however, arguing that, since a 5% increase in lodging expenditures represented less than 1.5% of the total cost of a typical vacation in Hawaii, the findings may not be true for other destinations and that it was important to perform similar analyses for other destinations.

- Fish (1982) showed that the competitive nature of beach holidays in West Africa, and the elastic demand for them, means that the increase in price resulting from a tax on hotel bed nights would fail to cover the higher costs resulting from it. Hoteliers cannot raise prices further because of strong competition from other beach destinations and are forced to absorb the tax by lowering costs or by leaving the industry. In the case of a lump-sum tax on land, the tax burden would fall entirely on producers. Fish's analysis highlights the role of the elasticities of supply and demand in determining the distribution of the burden, showing that when tourism demand is elastic with respect to a change in price, a large proportion of the burden falls on local producers and little is borne by tourists.

- An increase in taxation on one sector of tourism can result in lower expenditure on another, owing to the complementary nature of many of its composite sectors. If tourists plan before their trip the amount that they wish to spend on other items such as shopping (so that demand is inelastic) and the government increases tax on them, a higher proportion of their expenditure will accrue to the government in the form of revenue. Cooperation among hoteliers in the region might allow them to bargain collectively with tour operators, so that demand would become more price inelastic and the tax incidence on them would be lower. A policy of regional uniformity in taxation would preclude intra-regional price competition via tax reductions (Gooroochurn & Sinclair, 2005).

- Mak (1988) used tax incidence analysis to illustrate the extent to which hotel operators in Hawaii can pass on a hotel room tax. Mak's finding is that tourists are more price-sensitive than previously believed. The suggestion is made that earmarking the tax funds to develop the tourist industry may help overcome negative effects.

- Bonham *et al.* (1992) and Bonham and Gangnes (1996) found that a room tax on hotel receipts in Hawaii resulted in an insignificant change in hotel revenue, implying an inelastic demand for accommodation Similarly, Combs and Elledge (1979) found that a small *ad valorem* room tax on motels and other accommodation in the USA would have little impact on the industry and would generate substantial revenue for the government.

- Hiemstra and Ismail (1993) explore the tax incidence or the ultimate sharing of the burden of room taxes assessed on the US lodging industry between guests and the lodging industry. The elasticity of supply is measured at 2.86, in comparison with -0.44 elasticity of demand for lodging services. This results in a tax incidence of 6.2, which means that about $6 out of $7 of the tax is ultimately paid by the guests and $1 is paid indirectly by the lodging industry.

- Im and Sakai (1996) employ comparative static analysis to derive a general expression for the effect of an increase in the *ad valorem* tax rate on a good on the net revenue of firms. The size of this effect is expressed as a function of the initial levels of the tax rate and net revenue of taxed firms as well as the elasticities of supply and demand for the good. The results suggest caution in relying heavily on revenues derived from hotel room taxes as they may have large negative effects on the financial viability of the industry.

- A tax proposed by the Government of the Balearic Islands of €1 per capita per day, payable in the hotels, was estimated to lead to 117,113 fewer German, British, French and Dutch tourists, a figure that represents 1.44% of the tourist arrivals for the four nationalities in the year 2000 (Aguilo *et al.*, 2005).

> - The elasticity of demand tends to be much greater in respect of the cost of getting to the destination than the prices of vacation goods at the destination. Hence, consumers may be price-sensitive to the price of air fares but much less so to the price of lodging accommodations once they get to the destination (Crouch, 1995).

In estimating the effects of tourism taxes on the economy it needs to be acknowledged that if the government needs revenues and does not tax tourism, or some other industry, it will have to raise the tax somewhere else – and it will incur the similar negative effects on activity and employment. Alternatively, the government may not raise the tax revenue and may cut expenditure, but this too will have a negative impact on activity and employment. The same is true if it reduces expenditure through greater efficiencies in government services, since these will lead to employment losses.

A tax that directly affects tourism flows will have impacts across the entire economy as the reduced demand impedes employment growth in tourism and related industries. The empirical studies outlined in Box 15.3 are predominantly based on partial equilibrium analysis of specific sectors of the economy. As we have emphasised throughout this text, to understand the full implications of any tourism shock it is necessary to move beyond partial equilibrium analysis to consider the general equilibrium (economy-wide) effects. A tax on tourism will lower employment in the tourism industry and related industries, but not necessarily overall. To show that employment overall was lower than under an alternative revenue-raising policy, it would be necessary to show that taxes on tourism were more harmful to employment, directly and indirectly, than the alternative policy. There is no general reason why this should be the case, even if tourism is a labour-intensive industry, in terms of its direct labour inputs. It would be necessary to use CGE models of the economy, with all direct and indirect linkages between sectors, to explore this issue. Claims that specific taxes, such as taxes on tourism services, will adversely affect employment may be superficially convincing, but they are based on incomplete and misleading analysis and must be treated with caution.

15.6.2 RETALIATION

Taxation generates revenue but, as in the case of export taxes (e.g. on inbound tourism), it invites retaliation by other countries if other governments regard the taxing destination as unfairly treating their citizens. For example, Kenya and Tanzania introduced visa charges for UK citizens in retaliation for visa fees imposed on their own citizens by the UK. Retaliation is always possible and it can reduce welfare for both countries. Tisdell (1983) has shown how retaliation in the case of tourism taxes can lead to a lower economic surplus for both countries because the consumer surplus that the tourists from the leader country were enjoying in the retaliating country will disappear after the tax.

The possibility of retaliation is an important consideration if a government is considering imposing a tax that will be paid by non-residents. In the case of most tourism taxes, retaliation is difficult. Countries sell tourism services to a wide range of countries and, in turn, purchase tourism services from a range of countries, not necessarily the same ones. If one country imposes tourism taxes (e.g. New Zealand), those which lose out (e.g. Japan) have little scope to be able to impose a 'tit-for-tat' tax in retaliation, since relatively few tourists from the offending country may visit. It is possible that an affected country may be able to retaliate by applying pressure on unrelated matters, for example, by limiting beef imports from a country which taxes heavily. However, few countries are likely to be so badly affected by another country's tourism taxing policies to make these an issue for trade negotiations. Furthermore, the countries adversely affected by tourism taxes will often not have much trade leverage over the offending country (Forsyth & Dwyer, 2002).

The UK Government has recently increased taxation on outbound travel. The tax is very controversial with many critics. Some issues raised are set out in Box 15.4, indicating the important interrelationship between the price of travel and tourism flows.

BOX 15.4 Air passenger duty on UK outbound travel

The Air Passenger Duty (APD) is an excise duty levied by the UK Government and collected from airlines by UK Revenue and Customs. The APD is levied on passengers flying from a UK airport. As part of the 2008 Pre-Budget Report, the Chancellor announced that the APD was to be restructured, with a dramatic increase in the rates with the new charges being based on the distance travelled.

The government and environmental groups believe that aviation is an industry that is under-taxed with no value added tax on tickets or duty on aviation fuel and that the polluter-pays principle should apply when it comes to raising the air passenger duty. The government regards the tax as an invaluable source of revenue during dire financial times – a tax on a luxury product and a way to cut carbon emissions. For tourism stakeholders it is regarded as a tax on tourism, pushing the costs of travel ever higher and acting as a disincentive to travel.

The government claims APD will cut carbon emissions by around 750,000 tonnes annually by 2010/11 – raising £2.7 billion for government coffers each year. But this is without taking full account of a fall in demand for air travel as a result of the increased cost and the economic downturn which has hit long-haul premium class travel worse than leisure economy. Nor does it allow for the losses that arise from cuts in routes and jobs by airlines operating at UK airports straining under other pressures from the economic downturn, or from outbound travellers hopping to other European hubs such as Amsterdam for long-haul flights.

What passengers will have to pay in air passenger duty.

The new levies will be implemented in two phases – the first takes effect in November 2009; the second a year later. The increased fees are based on distance travelled and cabin class. APD will now fall into four bands – with passengers being charged according to how far they fly. The duty on short-haul flights (under 2000 miles) will rise by just £2 over the next 18 months. Thus, for economy passengers travelling from the U.K to points in Europe, the increases will be relatively minor – from £10 today to £11 in November and £12 in 2010. The increases will hit medium- and long-haul travellers hardest. A family of four flying to the Caribbean, South Africa, Kenya or Thailand in 2010 will pay £300 in APD, while those families planning trips to Singapore, Malaysia, Indonesia or Australasia will pay £340 – more than double the current rate of £40 per passenger. However, Egypt – a popular summer destination – lies just beyond the 2000-mile limit (calculated as the distance between London and the destination's capital city). This means that a family of four flying to Egypt in economy class will pay £240 in APD – £80 more than the current figure. For those going to the USA in business or first class, the current departure tax of £80 ($122) jumps to £90 ($137) in November 2009 and £120 ($183) in November 2010. The fee for economy class flyers to the USA goes from the current £40 ($61) to £45 later this year ($69) and £60 next year ($92). For travel to long-haul destinations such as Australia, the Far East and South America the taxes are even higher. A business class passenger currently pays a steep £80 departure tax from the UK, but that is due to rise to £110 in November 2009 and £170 in November 2010.

A poorly timed tax on an industry that is already hurting.

Travel operators, airlines and industry associations have criticised the Government for applying tax rises during a time of financial downturn and falling passenger numbers. The industry regards the APD as an economic barrier to investment, trade, tourism and travel in and out of the UK. It has pointed out that the aviation industry is one of the many tourism sectors that are struggling in the Global Financial Crisis and with high fuel prices. The aviation sector already has substantial excess capacity which will worsen as a result of the APD. The APD will mean less passengers and lower sales revenues for airlines, many of which are projecting losses over the medium term. Struggling families are finding it increasingly difficult to afford holidays abroad while businesses are already trying to save money by restricting travel. Between 30 March 2008 and 24 October 2009, as many as 969 weekly direct flights were axed at ten leading UK airports, representing a total of nearly 131,000 seats. There is concern that the APD will simply hasten this decline.

There are fears that London will lose its gateway to Europe status. Scheduled tours used to start and finish in London now more and more start and finish on the continent. It used to be the automatic entry point and it is now becoming an optional extra. The general concern is that the APD will damage the UK's position as a global hub as more passengers start to use European airports where there is no tax.

At a time where Low Cost Carriers have been attracting increasing numbers of passengers, industry sources also regard the APD as a regressive tax which hits the poorest, most price-sensitive passengers. It is also feared that LCC such as Ryanair and Easyjet will switch their growth to other EU countries where low-cost airports are growing and where governments are welcoming tourists rather than taxing them. A general fear is that airlines will simply focus their efforts on more cost effective European destinations rather than invest in the UK. This will see consumers suffer from a reduction of choice and competition, with prices also likely to rise further.

The tax does not take into account the fact that aircraft on short-haul routes burn far more fuel per passenger because of the limited time at cruise than those on long-haul trips. Take-offs and landings are the most damaging parts of the flight, when engines are at their least efficient. The departure and climb phase of a Boeing 737 causes much the same harm whether a plane is flying 201 or 2001 miles. To reflect this, a fairly high tax should be applied to every flight, with marginal increases according to distance. In fact, the Government has done the opposite with a very low 'entry-level' tax.

There is no accounting for any advantage an airline may gain by routing passengers through a hub close to London via a partner carrier. For example, a passenger who flies out of London to Frankfurt on British Airways to connect with a Qantas flight to Australia via Singapore will pay only £24 whereas that same passenger will pay £170 if flying direct from London via Singapore on BA or a BA code-share partner. Thus, rather than taking the most direct routes which are inevitably more emissions efficient, savings of hundreds of pounds for families flying would lead them to take in-direct flights via continental Europe.

European airlines are also set to benefit. Both the Netherlands and Belgium, for example, have removed APD, making long-haul departures comparatively cost effective. This means airlines – such as Air France-KLM and Lufthansa – are set to gain passengers from the UK – especially those from outside London – who book short-haul departures to Europe in order to board long-haul flights. The changes are also likely to have an impact on tourism to Britain, with foreign visitors forced to pay APD on the return leg of their journey. The cost of ADP, when added to other government charges such as visa fees, makes the UK an expensive destination for the start and end of group tours to Europe. With the UK standing outside the Schengen Agreement on a common visa for travel to Europe, the country is looking increasingly like an optional add-on than a key element of a visit to Europe for many in-bound long-haul travellers. Many argue that if any tax must be applied, it should be far heavier where a rail option is available, such as London–Paris or Brussels.

The tourism trade states also that the APD could hinder efforts to ease poverty in developing countries since the increases will hurt developing regions such as the Caribbean and Africa which rely on the airline industry to bring tourists, and enable residents of the UK to visit family and friends in these destinations. The future of several regional airports in the UK are also in doubt, due to a dramatic fall in passengers numbers and number of routes being cut over the last 12 months..

Not really a 'green tax'.
The APD is supposed to correct for negative externalities, by making people pay the social cost of flying. It has been touted as a 'green' tax, but this is not the case. Private-jet users will continue to enjoy their tax-free status, even though the harm generated per person carried is disproportionately high. Freight operators also escape taxation.

The APD has not been earmarked to directly contribute to any environmental projects or budgets. Critics claim that the APD is functioning not as a green tax but as another means to raise revenue under the guise of environmental protection. Critics also claim that taxes on flights are higher than necessary to compensate for the environmental harm created by aircrafts' emissions. As it stands, the income from APD more than covers the full cost of offsetting emissions attributed to aviation. This includes an allowance for the non-carbon effects of flying. It is estimated that the APD will raise around £2.9 billion in 2010. Based on the Emissions Cost Assessment, aviation's environmental externalities in 2010 will cost some £1.9 billion. As a result, there will be an almost £1 billion overpayment in terms of aviation's fair environmental costs. At the same time, environmentalists have criticised the tax for encouraging air passengers to believe that they are doing their bit for the environment, making them less likely to contribute to carbon offsetting schemes. Further, as noted above, the initiative is likely to fail to the extent that long-haul travellers will simply take a short flight to Europe and depart from there to avoid the tax, in turn increasing carbon emissions.

Environmentalists also point out that any carbon tax should be a per flight tax rather than a per passenger tax. It is argued that the APD should reflect the damage caused by aviation, by applying it to every seat whether or not it is occupied. Airlines would then have increased incentive to fill their planes, and flights which regularly flew with lots of empty seats would be grounded. At present, the passenger pays the same tax regardless of the carbon efficiency of the airline. The APD distorts competition and fails to create any incentive for airlines to become more carbon efficient.

Source: Various articles Google search 'APD on UK Outbound Travel'

15.7 EARMARKING OF SPECIFIC TOURISM TAXES

While the provision of public infrastructure, public goods and tourism promotion is desirable and assists the tourism industry, should it be financed from specific taxes levied on the tourism industry or from general taxation revenue? Earmarking may appear reasonable, but it can lead to inefficient uses of funds.

Suppose that there is a good case for government expenditure on an industry, for example, that there are gains for the economy as a whole from promotion of tourism or financing a convention centre. Because these gains are external to the firms that make up the industry, the firms will not spend enough on promotion or convention centre development. Hence, it is desirable on efficiency grounds for the government to undertake some promotion (Dwyer & Forsyth, 1993a, 1994a). It is also desirable for it to enact the most efficient means of funding this expenditure; it can either use general taxation or impose a specific levy on the industry. It may seem fair and efficient that the latter option be chosen, though this is not obvious. To minimise the efficiency cost of taxation, it is appropriate to spread the burden as widely as possible; a small addition to tax across the board is less distortionary than a larger addition on a narrow base, even if this base is closely related to the industry being assisted.

In practice, earmarking takes place quite frequently, as in the case of bed taxes to fund promotion. It appears equitable, and it might actually be so, and if tax rates are not high the efficiency cost may not be large. It may be the case that earmarking is the price of getting something to happen; a government may be unwilling to fund expenditure on behalf of a specific industry out of general taxation, though it may be willing to undertake the expenditure if the industry is willing to be levied to provide the funds. While the levy may not be the most efficient means of funding the expenditure, it may be more efficient to fund it in this way rather than not have the expenditure at all. When earmarked, taxes are considered to be essentially a price for the use of facilities that are warranted; there is little objection to them. However, they can go beyond this and result in costs to tourists that produce little offsetting benefits to either tourists or the industry. This happens when uneconomic prestige projects, or promotional wars between competing jurisdictions, are funded. Requiring funds raised from tourism taxes to be used for tourism-related uses, while superficially appealing, may in fact compound the problem, if it generates the funding of inefficient projects.

If there is no requirement for earmarking, the local tourist industry is likely to oppose specific tourism taxes more strongly, and even if the taxes are levied, there will be less pressure for them to be directed towards dubious projects. Box 15.5 summarises the effects of a tax on cruise tourism earmarked to defray the cost of public services allocated to cruise tourism in Alaska.

BOX 15.5 Alaska's head tax on cruise ship passengers

In 2006, Alaskans voted to levy a head tax on every visiting cruise ship passenger of large ships (250+ passengers) per voyage. The tax takes the form of a US$46 flat tax levied on every passenger per voyage. Another US$4 tax is levied on the cruise ship for each *berth* to pay for the on-board pollution monitoring Ocean Ranger programme. Money collected from the head tax is to be appropriated by the legislature to municipalities to defray their cost of providing public services to cruise tourism. City ordinance Chapter 69.20.005 states the purpose of the Marine Passenger Fee (MPF) as follows:

'It is the purpose of the fee imposed to address the costs to the City and Borough for services and infrastructure usage by cruise ship passengers visiting Juneau, including emergency services, transportation impacts and recreation infrastructure use, and to mitigate impacts of increased utilization of City and Borough services by cruise ship passengers.'

James Mak (2008) has developed a simple model which treats the cruise ship passenger tax as a lump-sum tax and analyses how this tourist tax might influence consumer behaviour, and the likely effects on the tourist industry, state and local governments and the residents of Alaska.

Economic effects of the head tax: Analytical framework.

Mak considers a consumer planning to purchase a cruise to Alaska, assumed to be an all-inclusive package tour (with all incidentals included in a single, pre-paid price), with only one standard quality tour offered.

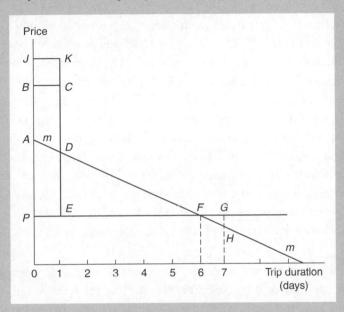

Figure 15.5 Impact of the head tax on consumer behaviour

In Mak's Figure 15.5, mm represents a passenger's demand curve for a cruise (measured in days) as a function of the price (dollars per day). Other things equal, the higher the price per day for the cruise, the shorter the cruise purchased. However, cruise companies do not offer cruises of every desired trip duration. A popular cruise to Alaska is a 7-day, roundtrip cruise travelling through the Inside Passage along the south-east Alaska coast. In Figure 15.5, the price of this all-inclusive cruise is P. At that price, the tourist wishes to purchase a cruise of 6 days but since a 6-day cruise is unavailable, she must purchase the 7-day cruise or not go at all. If the tourist could purchase a 6-day cruise, she would pay 0PF6 for the cruise package. Her consumer surplus is represented by the triangle, PAF. If she has to purchase a 7-day cruise, she would spend 0PG7 for the cruise but her consumer surplus would be reduced by the triangle, FGH.

Cruises do not usually depart from the home towns of their passengers. Thus, in addition to paying the price of the cruise, Mak notes that cruise passengers must pay the cost of travel to the port from which their ship departs. He assumes that tourists derive no consumption value (i.e. pleasure) from travel to the city of departure. Thus, we can consider the round-trip transportation cost to the departure city and back home as like a lump-sum tax. In Figure 15.1, the round trip transportation cost is stated as multiple units of the 1-day price of the cruise. It is represented by the rectangle, PBCE. The transportation cost is seen as reducing the buyer's consumer surplus from taking the cruise. In Figure 15.1, as long as EDF is greater than ABCD + FGH, the individual will take the cruise, prior to the tax. Mak now assumes that the new head tax is imposed. This is depicted by the area, BJKC. The consumer will still purchase the cruise after the tax is levied, as long as EDF is greater than AJKD + FGH. Since the head tax further reduces the consumer surplus derived from the cruise, some consumers will now be deterred from purchasing the cruise. The consumer who still purchases the cruise will pay 0PG7 for the all-inclusive cruise vacation, but her total trip cost (including round-trip transportation to and from the port of departure plus the new tax) now has increased by the addition of the head tax. Hence, the passenger is now worse off after paying the head tax. Obviously, if the head tax results in fewer cruise passengers, cruise operators and other suppliers are also potentially worse off.

Alaska's new head tax will generate additional tax revenue to the state government but, if fewer cruise ship passengers visit Alaska, less revenue will be collected from existing state and local taxes and fees that fall on tourists. On the other hand, fewer cruise ship passengers also means less demand for local government services. If the objective of levying the head tax is to maximize (net) tax revenues from cruise tourism (as opposed to economic impacts), destination managers who decide how high to set the tax must take into account how it will affect collections from existing taxes and fees and the cost to the state and local governments of providing public services to tourists.

The number of cruise ship visitors to Juneau has continued to rise, despite the imposition of the passenger fee. Mak concludes that Alaska's cruise industry need not be harmed by the new tax, especially if the proceeds from the tax are spent to support and develop the industry. The tax potentially can benefit both tourists and residents of Alaska. Juneau's experience in managing the proceeds demonstrates that the money from the head tax can be used in substantial compliance with federal law to support marine transportation and travel and tourism, and hence potentially benefit both cruise operators and their passengers. In the absence of the fee, the residents of Juneau might not have been willing to use their own tax revenues to finance all of these expenditures. To the extent that the residents also benefit from services funded by these expenditures, the fee potentially benefits both tourism and the residents of Juneau.

The model developed by Mak can be adapted easily for use in other tourist destinations where destination managers decide the merits of levying head taxes on tourists. Some conclusions are:

- the head tax need not harm the state's cruise industry. To the extent that money collected from the tax is used to support and develop the industry, the industry and its customers can actually benefit from the tax revenues.
- local residents potentially benefit from the head tax in two ways: (a) they may benefit from the provision of services funded by proceeds from the tax, and (b) proceeds from the head tax can be employed to substitute for some of the local funds previously used to support the cruise industry, allowing the local funds to be redirected to other public uses that benefit residents.
- a government that considers only the impact on its budgetary position in setting the optimum head is too narrowly focused. If the head tax reduces the number of tourist visits, the destination might lose profits, wages and employment, but might gain from having to tolerate less of tourism's negative economic, environmental, social and cultural impacts. While these are very difficult to measure it might be more appropriate for the government to focus on a larger objective, that is, to maximise the net benefit from cruise tourism to the entire destination.

Mak also notes that in the case of cruise ship visitors, the head tax (considered as an entry tax) may be the only practical way to maximize gains from tourism as cruise ship passengers generally spend little time ashore. If the consumer surplus derived from cruise tourism (described in Figure 15.1 above) is not captured by destination residents through the use of head taxes, some of it is likely to be captured by the cruise lines via discriminatory pricing strategies.

Source: Mak, J. (2008) 'Taxing Cruise Tourism: Alaska's Head Tax on Cruise Ship Passengers', *Tourism Economics*, 14(3), 599–614

15.8 CONCLUSIONS AND POLICY

- A 'tourist tax' is one that largely falls on tourists (e.g. hotel room tax). In reality, while there are some taxes that only tourists pay (e.g. air passenger duty), most of the taxes that tourists pay are also levied on the resident population of the destinations that tourists visit (e.g. taxes on automobile fuel use). Nevertheless, many of the taxes that are levied within destinations do have important consequences for tourists.

- Taxes have the effect of decreasing the quantity demanded of a product by increasing its effective price. Taxes act as a wedge between the price paid by consumers and the price received by suppliers. Taxes thus have an efficiency effect, which (except lump-sum tax) change relative prices and cause distortions in the economy. Thus, consumers change consumption patterns, producers change product mix and factor allocation and workers alter the amount of leisure taken.

- The usual criteria for good taxation are that it should be efficient, equitable and administratively simple. Policy makers should be mindful of these criteria when formulating taxes affecting the tourism industry.

- Tax incidence is an indicator of who bears the ultimate burden of a tax. Who pays most of the tax depends on the supply and demand elasticities for the particular tourism product or service.

- There are sound economic reasons for taxing tourism beyond simply collecting revenues to provide public services to tourists and their suppliers. A well-designed system of tourist taxation can benefit the residents of a destination by helping to finance investment in public infrastructure; expand and diversify the tax base; prevent tax base erosion; shift the tax burden to non-residents; correct for market failure; and support the provision of public goods. Taxes also help the community to share high business profits.

- Tourism taxes can impose costs on a destination, resulting in a contraction of economic activity; a deadweight loss to society; and retaliation by other destinations. The reduced price competitiveness of a tourism destination following the imposition of general or specific taxes may be such as to reduce the economic contribution of tourism to the wider economy. Excessive taxation of international tourism may cause tourism to suffer relative to other sectors in the global economy.

- Countries (and destinations within them) possess market power over their tourism attractions. It is in a country's individual interest to exercise this market power; it is efficient for them to do so if they are maximising their own, national, welfare – it is better to get foreigners to pay the taxes than domestic residents.

- There is concern that international tourism is regarded by a growing number of countries as a 'tax revenue cash cow', resulting in a decline in tourism worldwide relative to other industries. Taxes are levied on both tourists and tourism businesses at rates that vary considerably from country to country. These taxes tend to have been introduced in an *ad hoc* fashion, without serious consideration of their economic and social effects.

- Most countries have some market power or the ability to raise prices to foreign tourists. Many destinations use their market power to levy taxes on foreign tourists. The result is inefficiently high tourism taxes that may well be rational from the viewpoint of the individual country or jurisdiction, but too high from a more general, worldwide welfare perspective.

- Earmarking may appear reasonable, but it can lead to inefficient uses of funds. To minimise the efficiency cost of taxation, it is appropriate to spread the burden as widely as possible; a small addition to tax across the board is less distortionary than a larger addition on a narrow base, even if this base is closely related to the industry being assisted.
- Given the increasing importance of tourism taxation in both developed and developing countries, greater understanding of the economic underpinnings of tourism taxation and its effects is necessary, so that modelling of tourism taxation can be undertaken and appropriate policies for tourism taxation can be formulated.

SELF-REVIEW QUESTIONS

1. Use tourism examples to distinguish between a specific tax and an *ad valorem* tax.

2. In what ways are taxes on tourism products different from user charges?

3. Use a diagram to explain the changes in consumer and producer surplus and the deadweight loss that can occur when a tourism product such as hotel accommodation is taxed.

4. Briefly discuss the main arguments for and against taxing tourism.

5. In respect of the fairness principle of taxation, differentiate between the benefit principle of taxation and the ability-to-pay principle.

6. Who ultimately bears the burden of tourist taxes?

ESSAY QUESTIONS

1. Discuss the implications that arise for tourism since tourism is the only taxed export and its customers are the only taxed non-voters.

2. 'There are sound economic reasons for taxing tourism beyond simply collecting revenues to provide public services to tourists and their suppliers.' Discuss.

3. On the whole, the arguments for taxing tourism outweigh the arguments against taxing tourism. Evaluate this statement from the viewpoint of a host destination and from the viewpoint of world tourism.

4. If consumers are relatively price sensitive, suppliers will be forced to factor the cost of any new tax into their cost structure. However, if suppliers are relatively more price sensitive, the tax will be passed onto consumers. Discuss.

5. It is individually rational for countries to tax tourism services but inefficient for the world as a whole to do so. Discuss.

TOURISM AND AVIATION

CHAPTER 16

AVIATION AND TOURISM

LEARNING OBJECTIVES

After reading this chapter, you should be able to:

1. Appreciate the importance of aviation for both domestic and international tourism.

2. Explain both the complementary nature and the conflict of interest exhibited by the aviation and tourism industries and appreciate the dilemma that these pose for policy makers in their attempts to support or regulate each industry.

3. Discuss recent aviation de-regulation and privatisation and appreciate the accompanying growth in domestic and international tourism.

4. Understand recent advances in aviation technology and assess their effects on cost structures and price competitiveness within the aviation industry.

5. Discuss government taxation of and subsidisation of aviation.

6. Understand how aviation and tourism are linked on both the demand side and the supply side of the tourism industry.

7. Understand the development and importance of alliances within the aviation sector.

16.1 INTRODUCTION

Aviation and tourism are closely linked – for many tourists, especially international tourists, air transport is the preferred or only effective means of transport. The importance of air transport for tourism is easy to see. For most medium- and long-haul trips, tourists use air transport for at least part of their trip. For short trips, such as day trips from the city to the country, tourists rely mainly on surface modes – car, bus and train. For long-haul trips, air transport is the only effective mode, with sea travel now being used almost exclusively for cruising rather than as a means of transport.

For medium-haul transport, for example, for travel between 500 km and 2000 km, air travel competes with surface modes. Business travellers will tend to fly unless there are very good surface alternatives, such as fast trains (as there are now between Paris and London). For leisure travel, surface modes may or may not be competitive with air. For a family beach holiday, a car might be used, but for a city weekend break for a couple, air will tend to be preferred nowadays. In Europe, surface travel is a good alternative for short- to medium-haul trips – roads are good, rail is convenient and reliable and high-speed trains on some routes are just as fast, door to door, as air. Few countries elsewhere have surface transport as good as that in Europe (Japan is an exception). In the USA, Canada and Australia, roads are good, but rail is slow and inconvenient. The same is true for many parts of Asia. Where sea crossings are required, surface transport tends to be slow. Thus air transport can be very competitive for medium-haul trips, and even some short-haul trips, especially outside Europe.

The growth of tourism in the past 50 years has been greatly stimulated by developments in aviation. There are conflicts of interest between tourism and aviation sectors – lower air fares stimulate tourism but put pressure on airline profits. The restrictive regulation of earlier years ensured the profitability and stability of the aviation sector, but it discouraged tourism. Over time, however, governments have chosen to implement less restrictive regulation of air transport, and this has led to more competition, lower fares and greater travel.

Improvements in aviation technology have also impacted on tourism, notably by lowering costs, and they have also impacted on patterns of tourism. Changes in aviation technology have had a major impact on tourism, most obviously through lower costs and fares stimulating tourism. However, they have also had important impacts on patterns of tourism flows; for example, the changing strength of the economies of market density which are present in aviation has had implications for primary and secondary destinations, and increasing aircraft ranges have had implications for stopover destinations.

In spite of the links, there is not much by way of integration at the firm level between aviation and tourism, though there are some exceptions to this including tour companies which operate charter airlines, and airlines which invest in travel agents.

There are underlying policy conflicts between the two industries: what is positive for the aviation sector is often negative for tourism. We discuss the nature of this conflict in the next section.

16.2 AVIATION AND TOURISM – THE POLICY CONFLICTS

The regulatory framework governing international air services is complex. The underlying framework for the regulation of international aviation is contained in the 1944 Convention on International Civil Aviation, which is commonly referred to as the Chicago Convention. International aviation is governed by a series of government-to-government bilateral treaties determining levels of market access for countries' respective airlines. Bilateral air services agreements set out the number of weekly flights that airlines of the two countries can operate, cities they can serve in the other country and rights to operate via or beyond to third countries. The agreements typically also include provisions ranging over airline ownership and control, competition law, safety and security. The outcomes of bilateral air services negotiations often represent compromises balancing the needs of both parties, with each side seeking to maximise the benefits for their respective countries. Box 16.1 outlines the types of air service rights established under the Chicago Convention, commonly referred to as the 'freedoms of the air', which form the basis of bilateral agreements.

BOX 16.1 Freedoms of the air

First Freedom of the Air – the right or privilege, in respect of scheduled international air services, granted by one State to another State or States to fly across its territory without landing.

Second Freedom of the Air – the right or privilege, in respect of scheduled international air services, granted by one State to another State or States to land in its territory for non-traffic purposes e.g. refueling. For example an SAS flight from Stockholm to Rio de Janeiro could stop in Bermuda to refuel but no passenger is allowed to get on or off.

Third Freedom of the Air – the right or privilege, in respect of scheduled international air services, granted by one State to another State to put down, in the territory of the first State, traffic coming from the home State of the carrier. An example would be rights of Air France to fly from Paris and set down passengers in New York.

Fourth Freedom of the Air – the right or privilege, in respect of scheduled international air services, granted by one State to another State to take on, in the territory of the first State, traffic destined for the home State of the carrier. An example would be the right of South African Airways to transport passengers from London to Cape Town.

Fifth Freedom of the Air – the right or privilege, in respect of scheduled international air services, granted by one State to another State to put down and to take on, in the territory of the first State, traffic coming from or destined to a third State. An example would be a flight by American Airlines from the USA to the UK that is going on to Italy. Traffic could be picked up in the UK and taken to Italy.

ICAO characterizes all 'freedoms' beyond the Fifth as 'so-called' because only the first five 'freedoms' have been officially recognized as such by international treaty.

Sixth Freedom of the Air – the right or privilege, in respect of scheduled international air services, of transporting, via the home State of the carrier, traffic moving between two other States. Thus, Icelandair transports passengers between Europe and North America via Iceland. Singapore Airlines, Cathay Pacific Airways, Malaysia Airlines and other Asian airlines use this right to fly passengers between Europe and Australasia.

Seventh Freedom of the Air – the right or privilege, in respect of scheduled international air services, granted by one State to another State, of transporting traffic between the territory of the granting State and any third State with no requirement to include on such operation any point in the territory of the recipient State, i.e. the service need not connect to or be an extension of any service to/from the home State of the carrier. An example would be traffic from Spain going to Canada on a UK airline flight that does not stop in the UK on the way.

Eighth Freedom of the Air – the right or privilege, in respect of scheduled international air services, of transporting cabotage traffic between two points in the territory of the granting State on a service which originates or terminates in the home country of the foreign carrier or (in connection with the so-called Seventh Freedom of the Air) outside the territory of the granting State (also known as 'consecutive cabotage'). A prominent example of this right is the European Union, which has granted such rights between all its member states. Another example of this would be an airline like Virgin Atlantic Airways operating onward flights between Washington and Denver.

Ninth Freedom of the Air – the right or privilege of transporting cabotage traffic of the granting State on a service performed entirely within the territory of the granting State without continuing service to or from one's own country (also known as '*stand alone*' *cabotage*). An example would be a European based airline allowed to operate between cities within the USA.

Source: ICAO (2009) 'Manual on the Regulation of International Air Transport (Doc 9626, Part 4)', www.icao.int/icao/en/trivia/freedoms_air.htm

Aviation and tourism are complementary industries. For air-based trips, the tourist needs to make use of the services of both industries to enjoy access to the product. This being so, it is in the interest of each of the industries that the prices, and perhaps profits, of the other be low. Lower air fares bring more tourists as customers of the tourism industry, and lower ground costs induce more tourists to use the services of the airlines. From the home tourism industry's perspective, higher air fares were undesirable because they reduced the demand for its product. However, there was a partly offsetting advantage – higher air fares also discouraged outbound tourism, and to the extent that outbound tourists switched their spending to the domestic industry, the home tourism industry would gain.

Over time, policy makers have recognised and attempted to address this underlying conflict of interest between the two industries. Those countries which recognised the potential for tourism development, but which were highly dependent on air travel to bring the tourists, revised their approach to airline regulation. Spain realised the potential for visitors from Northern Europe, who would be unlikely to travel on surface modes. Singapore, and other island destinations, saw potential for stopover tourism. Australia and New Zealand realised that they would only become major tourism destinations if the long-haul air fares to them become affordable. Other countries did not see themselves as tourism destinations, or did not see air travel as essential in bringing tourists, and were content to maintain restrictive aviation regulation – a good example is Japan (Yamauchi, 1997). The dominant trend over the past four decades, however, has been one of increasing liberalisation, and this has been a critical factor in the expansion of international tourism.

Over the past decade or so, there has been a growing recognition of tourism benefits when aviation policies are assessed. Aviation policies in several countries have been subjected to a much more explicit cost-benefit framework, in which costs and benefits are evaluated and compared, than was the case before. Proposals for liberalisation or strategic alliances have been analysed using this framework (BTCE, 1993; Department of Transport and Communications, 1988; Gillen *et al.*, 1996; Gillen *et al.*, 2001; Productivity Commission, 1998). In several of these, the relevance of tourism benefits is explicitly recognised, though benefits were not quantified. Recently, however, there have been attempts to measure tourism economic benefits in the context of aviation policy analysis (Air New Zealand and Qantas Airways Limited, 2002; Australian Competition and Consumer Commission, 2003; New Zealand Commerce Commission, 2003). While tourism benefits from aviation changes are not likely to be as large as the benefits and costs to travellers and airlines, they can be significant. Box 16.4 provides an example of this approach.

Aviation regulatory policy today represents a balance between the conflicting interests of the airlines, the home country travellers and the tourism industry. While some tentative steps have been undertaken, the global application of free trade principles to international aviation remains a longer-term goal. Liberalisation within the bilateral system is likely to remain the only way to open up aviation markets for the foreseeable future (Australian Government National Aviation Policy, 2008).

By noting this critical conflict of interest between the aviation and tourism industries, it is not intended to suggest that there are no common interests. Both industries benefit from tourism promotion – hotels gain if airlines promote a destination, and airlines gain more demand if the tourism industry promotes itself. Both have an interest in lower taxes – airlines lose if hotels are taxed and there are fewer airline passengers. This said, however, many of the developments in aviation and tourism policy over recent decades can be seen in terms of this conflict.

Tourism, and especially international tourism, has grown rapidly because air travel has continued to get much cheaper. There are two main reasons for this – technological progress and airline liberalisation.

16.3 AVIATION TECHNOLOGY AND ITS ECONOMIC CONSEQUENCES

To understand how aviation and tourism fit together, it is helpful to have an understanding of the economics of aviation. Aviation is a network industry, which has particular features which condition the nature of the products it offers. For example, some tourism destinations have good air services, while others have poor services – this happens because of the interaction of features of destinations and airline economics.

Given that air transport is a key determinant of tourism flows, the technology of aviation will have an important impact on tourism. Technology determines costs, and thus it determines which destinations are price competitive and which are not. Several issues in airline economics are associated with new technology. We herein discuss:

- cost structures
- utilisation and pricing
- booking systems
- new aircraft types
- the Low-Cost Carrier (LCC) phenomenon

16.3.1 COST STRUCTURES

The unit costs of travelling by air are falling, and they can be expected to continue to do so for the next couple of decades at least. Lower unit costs lead to lower fares, and lower fares lead to increased tourism.

One important feature of airline costs is that it costs less, per passenger, to fly in large aircraft such as the Boeing 747 jumbo, or the Airbus A380, than it does in smaller aircraft such as the Boeing 737 or Airbus A320. This relationship covers the whole of the aircraft range from small 20-seater aircraft to the very largest aircraft. The size of the aircraft an airline chooses to use will depend on the market it is serving. The airline must choose the frequency of services and the aircraft size on a particular city pair. Thus, on a busy city pair, an airline might schedule moderately large aircraft, such as the Boeing 767, whereas for a small market, it will choose small aircraft to maintain an adequate frequency.

This gives rise to what is known as the *economies of density* – as a route market becomes larger, with more passengers, the airline is able to schedule more flights, leading to increased convenience, and larger aircraft, leading to lower costs. Hence it is cheaper to fly between London and Frankfurt than it is between London and Inverness.

Larger aircraft, such as the Boeing 747, Boeing 777 and Airbus A340, are used to fly on longer routes – this is because frequency is less important than on short-haul routes. On long-haul routes it is more important to keep fares down than frequency up.

Economies of density are distinct from economies of scale. As discussed in Chapter 4, economies of scale refer to the size of the overall plant or firm. There is not much evidence of economies of scale in airlines. It is possible to operate an airline with few aircraft and few routes at just as low a cost per passenger as for a large airline, with many aircraft and many routes. Large and small aircraft operate side by side and are equally viable and competitive.

The impact of economies of density changes over time, as aviation technology changes. When the Boeing 747 was introduced in the 1970s, it increased economies of density, since the per seat kilometre costs which it offered were much lower than on smaller aircraft then in service. This gave a boost to the dense markets able to support services with 747s. It meant that all but the largest cities in most countries would have to have indirect long-haul services through the main gateways. Over time, the cost advantages of the Boeing 747 were eroded, with aircraft such as the Boeing 767, the Boeing 777 and the Airbus A340 entering long-haul markets. With these smaller aircraft offering relatively low per seat kilometre costs, airlines began to offer direct services to the secondary cities, such as London to Tampa or Baltimore, rather than just London to New York. These newer aircraft have made secondary destinations easier and quicker to get to than they had been before and thus encouraged tourism to them.

Economies of density do not only exist in long-haul traffic – they also exist at the short-haul end. Costs per seat kilometre are lower using Boeing 737 and Airbus A320 aircraft than they are using smaller regional jet and turboprop aircraft. This means that fares on dense city pairs are lower than on less busy routes. This provides a challenge for the development of regional tourism. The larger cities and resort areas are always easier and cheaper for tourists to access than the smaller ones. Many promising smaller resort areas lament that they are unable to attract direct air services, and when they do obtain these services, they tend to be relatively expensive. The introduction of regional jets has made some difference, and it is possible that the next generation of regional jets will tilt the balance further and lessen the impact of economies of density, making secondary destinations easier to access and more price competitive.

Some other aspects of airline costs are worth noting. Roughly half an airline's costs are the direct costs of flying. Direct costs include the costs of fuel and of cockpit and cabin staff as well as some maintenance costs. Other indirect costs include head office costs and marketing costs. Capital costs, including the costs of aircraft ownership, or of leasing, are also important. In addition, airlines face costs of purchasing other goods and services, and these can be quite substantial, if they contract out a range of services such as maintenance or IT, which often happens if the airline is relatively small. The proportions of the different costs will vary from airline to airline – some airlines do much of their maintenance and other tasks in-house and incur relatively large labour costs, while others contract out many services and thus have quite low labour costs. For many airlines the rising cost of fuel has made this an increasingly large cost item. Partially offsetting this is the fact that fuel use is becoming more efficient, leading to cost savings, and extending the range of aircraft.

16.3.2 UTILISATION AND PRICING

Fares on routes with low traffic volumes are typically higher than fares on routes with high traffic volumes of the same length. Since smaller origins and destinations tend to be able to support only low traffic volumes, they will inevitably have high fares. Hence, smaller, secondary destinations will be less price competitive than large destinations, even when they obtain direct air services (and often smaller destinations can only be accessed indirectly through larger gateways).

An airline decides whether it can earn profits on a route, and how many flights should offer on it. Once it has decided to operate a route, it has to determine the schedule and allocate the aircraft. It sets its fares, so as to achieve this aim. This is the process of yield management which was raised in Chapter 5. There are several aspects to this.

Some flights at popular times tend to fill up more quickly than others. An airline can set higher fares for these flights – this is similar to peak/off-peak differences in prices in other parts of the tourism industry such as hotels. Airlines also try to charge more to passengers with low elasticity of demand, such as business travellers, than those with highly elasticity of demand, such as leisure travellers. In earlier years, airlines used to offer lower-round trip fares to passengers who stayed over a Saturday night than to other passengers – this was a device to exclude business travellers, who would not be prepared to stay over the weekend. Nowadays, they set lower fares for flights some time in advance, and as the time of the flight becomes closer, they increase the price. Travellers who book close to the time of the flight are more likely to be business travellers, or leisure travellers with low demand elasticity, than travellers who book well in advance. Airlines adjust fares, as the flight fills up – they will raise them, if the flight is filling up quickly, or they will lower fares if the flight is not filling up, as expected.

Airlines charge higher fares for more flexibility in tickets. It is costly for airlines to provide travellers with flexibility, because they have to operate to a schedule, and seats which are not filled at the time of the flight can never be sold. Passengers with non-refundable tickets are cheaper to accommodate than passengers with flexible tickets, who can change their bookings at the last minute, leaving seats empty. Thus there can be a large difference between a full economy fare, which is flexible, and a non-refundable discount economy fare.

In earlier years, airlines used other ways of filling their aircraft. Charter airlines, which dominated leisure markets in Europe until the boom in Low-Cost Carriers (LCC), were able to achieve high load factors, and low fares. Passengers would book in advance, often for the whole holiday package, usually on a non-refundable basis. With the growth of LCC, which offer low fares and more flexibility than the charter airlines, the latter have been losing market share.

16.3.3 BOOKING SYSTEMS

In years gone by, booking systems were a significant cost for the airlines; airlines needed to take bookings and ensure that seats were available on the flights that the passengers chose. For a multi-sector journey, this was quite complex. Airlines relied heavily on travel agents to develop itineraries and handle the booking.

By the 1970s, Computer Reservation Systems (CRS) had become established as the critical tool in handling airline bookings and in the management of capacity – allocation of passengers to flights, provision of information about loadings and in setting prices. They also provided the airline's links to travel agents. Initially, each airline had its own simple CRS, but as their complexity grew, CRS became more expensive to develop and expand. By the early 1980s, smaller airlines were attaching themselves to the CRS of larger airlines, and there was a growing belief that CRS were something of a natural monopoly (Bailey *et al.*, 1985). Ownership of a major CRS gave an airline a strong competitive advantage in the market place. For example, when listing flights on the travel agents' screen, the airline could ensure that its own flights were listed first, even if more convenient or cheaper flights were available from its rivals. It was considered that CRS might result in concentration of the airline industry – while economies of scale, *per se*, were not important, if an airline had a major CRS, it could dominate the market. In the USA, airlines with major CRS such as United and American strengthened their position in the late 1980s. Governments began regulating the use of the CRS in an attempt to ensure that the owners did not gain an anti-competitive advantage from their CRS. The period was one of consolidation in the liberalised markets, and it seemed possible that competition in the industry would falter.

Over time, technology has changed further with the development of internet booking systems. Passengers no longer need to go to travel agents or airlines with specialised equipment to make their bookings – rather, they make their own bookings by accessing the airline's website. This leads to significant reductions in the cost of handling the bookings. Internet booking was pioneered by the LCC, but they are now used extensively by all airlines including the full-service (legacy) airlines. Developments in information technology (IT) and yield management, along with de-regulation of fare setting, have contributed to making it possible to fill the large aircraft, and achieve low per unit costs. Of all tourism industries, airlines have perhaps made the most effective use of the internet. The new technology has made it much easier for the new-entrant LCC to survive and grow, and it has resulted in an industry which is significantly more competitive.

16.3.4 NEW AIRCRAFT TYPES

Another aspect of change in aviation technology, which is having an impact on patterns of tourism, is the development of longer-haul aircraft. Over time, the range of aircraft is increasing. This means that they need to make fewer stops for refuelling, and can make long, direct flights. This has meant that destinations which used to prosper as stopover destinations are now being bypassed. In the early days of jets, flights from the USA across the South Pacific had to stop in Hawaii and Fiji. With the development of longer-range aircraft, first Fiji, then Hawaii, was bypassed. The range of aircraft is continuing to increase – with the introduction of the Airbus A340 and Boeing 777, it is no longer necessary for flights to stop en route from South East Asia to Los Angeles, and flights from Australia to the Middle East need not stop at Singapore. The era of stopover tourism may be ending.

Two new aircraft have the chance to change the shape of their travel. These are the Airbus A380, which is the largest passenger aircraft in service, and the Boeing 787.

When it entered service in the early 1970s, the Boeing 747 changed travel patterns dramatically. It was much larger than the other aircraft flying, much cheaper to operate. As airlines switched from smaller aircraft to the Boeing 747, they had to concentrate on more dense markets. After the introduction of the Boeing 747, there was greater emphasis on flying through hubs rather than directly. The same may happen with the Airbus A380. This plane is about one-third larger than the Boeing 747. A380s are very suited to flying on busy routes, such as London to New York, or Singapore to Paris, with very high passenger densities – with around 600 seats. As more A380s come into service, they could bring fares down substantially.

The Boeing 787 is a different type of aircraft – wide-bodied with two aisles, but with a load of about 200 to 300 passengers. However, unlike most medium-sized aircraft, it will be able to fly very long distances. It embodies new technology, such as the use of composites, which reduce weight, fuel use and thus costs. It will also have a larger windows and higher cabin pressures, which are likely to change the passengers' experience. The Boeing 787 is likely to shift passengers away from the major hubs, and on to direct flights. With low costs, long range and medium passenger loads, it will be economic on direct services on medium-density routes. Thus Virgin Atlantic non-stop between London and Perth, a route not served directly before. Many medium-sized markets, such as between European and US cities, are expected to attract increasing custom in the future. Although the Global Financial Crisis (GFC) is affecting new orders, the 787 is selling extremely well, and a long waiting list is developing for them.

16.3.5 THE LCC PHENOMENON

LCC are the new boom segment in air transport and they are having a major impact on tourism. LCC, low-cost airline, no-frills carrier or discount carrier are all different names for the same occurrence: an airline that generally offers low fares in exchange for eliminating many traditional passenger services. Thus, the LCC sector can be distinguished from the traditional full-service sector, which is primary based upon the quality of the service.

LCC are not new – Southwest, in the USA, has been operating since the early 1970s. In the early days of US de-regulation, many LCC entered, and soon failed (Gudmundsson,

1998). Since the mid-1990s, LCC have been enjoying a resurgence in markets across the world. They are currently more profitable than the established carriers. It is possible that current LCC have learned the lessons from the 1980s and many can be expected to survive for some time (Calder, 2002; Lawton, 2002; Williams, 2002).

As their name suggests, LCC seek to keep costs at a minimum. They operate simple point-to-point networks and try to avoid costly connecting traffic. They obtain high utilisation from aircraft and crews and often pay their staff lower salaries than that of the established airlines. Most are 'no-frills' airlines and do not provide much in terms of flight service, lounges or frequent flyer programmes. The products which they are offering are new. Instead of cheap inclusive tour packages, or low-return fares subject to restrictive conditions, they offer one-way low fares with minimum restrictions, though also with limited refundability. Sometimes they contract out tour packages but sell them on their websites. They often travel to secondary airports. Sometimes these airports are alternative gateways to major destinations (as Lubeck is for Hamburg, as Senai in Malaysia is for Singapore and as Charleroi is for Brussels). Sometimes these are smaller destinations in their own right (e.g. Carcassonne in South West France) and sometimes these are both (Treviso in Italy which is near Venice but is also the gateway to the Veneto region). The LCC are flying to these destinations partly because airports are cheaper to use, partly because airports are less congested and quick turnarounds are possible and partly because they are not entering direct, head-to-head competition with strong established airlines. So far, they have been successful in keeping costs down, especially as compared with the costs of the established airlines.

There are three main differences between LCC and traditional airlines: service savings, operational savings and overhead savings. Some of the characteristic features of LCC are summarised in Box 16.2.

BOX 16.2 Characteristics of LCC

- Low cost airlines tend to focus on short haul routes (generally less than 1,500 km). To achieve low operating costs per passenger, carriers need to have as many seats on its aircraft as possible, to fill them as much as possible, and to fly the aircraft as often as possible.
- High aircraft utilisation means fixed costs can be spread over more flying hours and more passengers.
- Unreserved seating encourages passengers to board early and quickly supporting faster turnaround times.

- LCC typically have a single passenger class, facilitating simple fare structures, such as charging one-way tickets half that of round-trips. Typically fares increase as the plane fills up, which rewards early reservations.

- Greater aircraft productivity resulting from a combination of using uncongested secondary airports simplified routes, emphasizing point-to-point transit instead of transfers at hubs enhancing aircraft use and eliminating disruption due to delayed passengers or luggage missing connecting flights.

- Use of secondary airports by LCC have two main advantages over larger airports: there are lower airport charges and, as they are less busy, delays due to congestion are less.

- LCC typically operate a single type fleet, facilitating discounts for fleet acquisition. By having only one aircraft type, pilots and cabin crew can operate on any aircraft in the fleet with reduced training and maintenance costs.

- Flights to cheaper, less congested secondary airports and flying early in the morning or late in the evening avoid air traffic delays and take advantage of lower landing fees.

- LCC make substantial cost savings by direct sales to customers via the Internet and call centres and by using electronic ticketing. By de-emphasizing sales via travel agents, low cost airlines avoid travel agency commissions and also avoid computer reservation system fees.

- LCC discourage Special Service (high maintenance) passengers, for instance by placing a higher age limit on unaccompanied minors than full service carriers

- Cost savings in the on-board service. All inbound services (meals, drinks, videos, commission based products) must be paid for by passengers, creating additional revenues for the LCC.

- Employees work in multiple roles, for instance flight attendants also clean the aircraft or work as gate agents, thereby reducing personnel costs.

- LCC tend to have simple management and overhead structure with a lean decision-making process

Source: O'Connell and Williams (2005) 'Passengers' Perceptions of Low Cost Airlines and Full Service Carriers: A Case Study Involving Ryanair, Aer Lingus, Air Asia and Malaysia Airlines', *Journal of Air Transport Management*, 11, 259–272

LCC are making an impact in markets across the world. In the USA, Southwest continues to grow, and new LCC such as Jetblue have entered. In Canada and Australia LCC provide the main competition for the dominant national airline. LCC are gaining a foothold in

Asia, especially in domestic markets such as those of Malaysia, where AirAsia has been successful, and Indonesia. Further expansion of them will depend on their gaining access to international routes. However, it is in Europe where the growth of LCC has been most spectacular. The intra-European aviation market only became extensively liberalised in the mid-1990s, and since then, the LCC have been the main form of new competition. Several of the airlines, such as Ryanair, easyJet and Air Berlin, are now quite large airlines, with very large orders for more aircraft.

Competition from the LCC is creating problems for the major airlines, many of which are making losses and which find it difficult to match the fares of the LCC. Furthermore, the new breed of LCC appears to be more financially secure than their predecessors. Some incumbent airlines, such as Lufthansa, have sought to compete aggressively against them (and encountered problems from competition authorities). Several major airlines have set up their own LCC, such as British Airway's Go and KLM's Buzz, only to sell them off later on (Cassani & Kemp, 2003). There seems to be a new-wave set-ups by major airlines, with United's Ted in the USA, Singapore Airlines' Tiger and Qantas' Jetstar in Australia.

The LCC are important because they are having significant impacts on tourism. Most of them are oriented to leisure travellers, though some, like easyJet, also seek out the price-sensitive business traveller. The most obvious impact is on the overall size of the market – lower fares mean more travel (though some of this is at the expense of surface modes). Furthermore, the products they are offering are changing tourism markets. The ready availability of low fares makes trips of short duration possible. Thus a Londoner can easily afford a weekend in Dublin visiting the pubs, and it is now practical for a Berliner to have a holiday house in the South of France. Neither of these markets would have been well served by the expensive scheduled airlines or the restrictive charter airlines. On top of this, the low fares are growing the overall market for traditional destinations.

LCC are also affecting the development of secondary destinations. Holiday travellers are discovering the attractions of places which are less well known, and sometimes less crowded. These destinations in turn have realised the importance of LCC in bringing tourists, and they have been offering financial inducements to the LCC to operate services (within Europe their ability to do this may be constrained by recent limits on subsidies imposed by the European Commission – see European Commission, 2004). LCC are thus both growing and changing tourism markets. Box 16.5 addresses airport subsidies in Europe.

It is likely that these impacts on tourism will be permanent, and that further impacts will come about. LCC have brought about a major change in airline markets. Their expansion plans are bold, and new entrants continue to arrive. Some LCC are now developing long-haul routes, for example, Jetstar and Air Asia X. It is quite possible that there will be a shakeout, and that many will not survive. Nevertheless, it currently does not seem as though the major airlines will be able to force them out of the market as they nearly did in the 1980s. Quite possibly, airline markets will be characterised by traditional airlines, with a smaller market share, operating alongside LCC in a larger overall market.

16.4   AIRLINE LIBERALISATION AND TOURISM GROWTH

Countries are often faced with a choice between aviation and tourism interests. Restrictive aviation policies keep air fares high, and hamper tourism, while liberal policies encourage tourism, both inbound and outbound. At various times, countries have been called upon to make a choice between assisting their airports and stimulating their tourism industries. Some examples are highlighted in Box 16.3.

Liberalisation has meant that aviation markets are more competitive, resulting in airlines being forced to keep their fares low, and to keep costs down. Liberalisation has also meant that a wider range of airlines is able to serve a given market – for instance, UK tourists can fly to France on an Irish airline. They are no longer limited, as they were, to only UK or French airlines.

It is possible to distinguish distinct phases of liberalisation:

- the development of the charter market, especially in Europe;
- domestic de-regulation, notably in the USA;
- the liberalisation of international markets;
- the boom in LCC.

16.4.1   THE CHARTER MARKET

The first major move away from regulation came with the development of the charter market. This got under way in great fashion in the 1960s in Europe, especially with travel from the UK and Germany to the sun destinations of Southern Europe, such as the Costa del Sol. Fares on scheduled airlines in Europe were too high for mass tourism. Charter airlines offered a way around this. They were operated on a low cost basis, and seats were sold in conjunction with a tour package. The limited flexibility enabled the airlines to achieve very high load factors, and thus low costs per passenger. Charter airlines were often owned by tour companies or the major scheduled airlines. The market was very competitive, and fares were much lower than those on scheduled airlines. Charter airlines were less tightly regulated than the scheduled airlines – for example, they were often, though not always, permitted to offer as many flights as they wished. However, they were regulated as to where they could fly, and they could only offer air travel as part of a tour package (Doganis, 1986, 2001).

The significance of charters is that they offered a way around the regulatory dilemma by segmenting the market. Most countries were unwilling to open up air transport markets to more competition and put their (state-owned) airlines at risk. Charters offered a way of serving tourism demands while not impacting too strongly on the scheduled airlines. Because of the restrictions put on charters, and the destinations they travelled to, direct competition between charters and scheduled airlines was limited. Charter airlines did pose a policy problem for countries with tourism potential, such as Spain. Should these countries insist on their airlines gaining an equal share of traffic to and from them, as was usual with air transport arrangements, or should they let airlines of the origin countries dominate the market? Spain did not have many charter airlines, but it allowed access to the charter airlines of Northern Europe, which soon dominated traffic into Spain. While Spain thus only had a minor share of air traffic, its tourism industries boomed. See Box 16.3.

Charter airlines enabled the growth of holiday tourism in Europe. They enabled tourists to travel internationally to holiday and cultural destinations of about 1 or 2 hours flying time away from their origin, for holidays of about 1 or 2 weeks duration. People switched from domestic holidays, made by surface transport, to international holidays around Europe.

Charter airlines have long been mainly a European phenomenon. They have generally become less important given the growth of LCC. Charter operations have existed in the USA, on trans-Atlantic routes, and even some long-haul charters, such as from the UK to Australia, have existed. However, the reliance on charters has not been nearly as great in other markets as in the European market. This is primarily because of the ways other markets have been regulated.

BOX 16.3 Four aviation case studies

Spain and the Charter Airline Boom

In the 1950s and 1960s, Spain realised that its tourism industry would prosper if it could access the leisure markets of Northern Europe, especially the UK and Germany. The beaches of Spain were a long way away by surface transport from these countries, but only about 2 hours by air. However, as with the rest of Europe, air fares were high, and this limited the development of the market. At this stage the tour companies were developing the charter airline concept, which involved flying passengers on inclusive tours, using pre-booking to ensure that load factors were very high and thus costs per passenger were low. By operating on a no-frills basis, with high seat density and load factors, charter airlines were able to offer low-priced services, making inclusive tours very competitive. Being less protected, charter airlines were also forced to be more cost efficient than the established scheduled airlines.

However, the charter airlines were competitors for the Spanish and other legacy airlines. To a degree, they were not directly competitive, since the conditions for charter travel (early booking, only being available as part of an inclusive tour) were much more restrictive than those of the legacy airlines. This made them less attractive to business travellers and travellers who valued flexibility. In addition, most of the charter airlines were owned by the Northern European countries. Thus if

Spain were to permit charter airlines to operate (and most countries at the time did not permit them), it would only have a small share of the overall aviation market, and its own airline could suffer. Spain chose to allow charter airlines, and as a result, travel to Spain boomed. This represents an early example of a country putting tourism interests before aviation interests.

Australia and the South East Asian Airlines

By the late 1970s, many of the economies in South East Asia were well into their 'economic miracle'. These countries still had quite low wage rates, but their industries, including their airlines, were becoming very productive, and very competitive in international markets. The markets from these countries were then quite small, with few residents earning high enough incomes to support international travel, and so their airlines began to seek out other markets. Several of these countries, such as Singapore and Thailand, were strategically located between Australia and Europe, and were in an ideal position to carry passengers between them. Airlines such as Singapore Airlines, Thai International and MAS of Malaysia had low costs, and they could be very competitive with Australian and European-owned airlines. These airlines sought to fly passengers on the Australia–Europe route.

This posed a dilemma for the Australian Government. Much of the growth in market share of these airlines would come at the expense of the (then government-owned) national airline, Qantas. Qantas would have difficulty in matching South East Asian airlines' costs, and it might be forced into losses on its most remunerative route. Low air fares, however, would be very popular with Australian travellers wishing to travel to Europe. In addition, low air fares held out the promise of making Australia a more practical destination for European travellers.

While the South East Asian airlines would not be permitted to operate direct flights between Australia and Europe, no such flights existed. Airlines had to stop to refuel in countries such as Singapore (as they still do). The South East Asian airlines were permitted, under the then existing regulations, to carry passengers between the UK and Singapore and between Singapore and Australia, though they were capacity-controlled. This combination of rights, to carry passengers on two stages of a journey, became known as 'sixth freedom' – this is a more informal right, since it has not been negotiated by the countries at the ends of the route. Thus, even if it wished to, Australia could not prevent a Singaporean airline from carrying passengers from Australia to the UK via Singapore.

At first, Australia tried to protect its airline by restricting passengers carried by other airlines on the route. While it could not control the number of seats offered between Australia via Singapore and, say, the UK, it could control the capacity from Australia to Singapore. It tried to limit this capacity to the level of the expected Singapore–Australia origin destination traffic only, leaving little scope for the Singapore airline to also offer seats to the UK. In this indirect way it tried to restrict these airlines' access to the Australia–UK market. It did not take long for these arrangements to break down, and the Australian Government decided to liberalise capacity between Australia and the South East Asian countries, enabling them to compete for Australia–Europe traffic. This decision amounted to one of promoting tourism interests over airline interests. In recent years, the airlines from the Middle East, such as Emirates and Etihad, have been following the lead of the South East Asian airlines, by becoming 'sixth freedom' operators between Australia and Europe. The Australian Government has again tried to slow their growth by not permitting them as much capacity as they have requested, though it has been more liberal since 2007. The Australian airline Qantas still continues to compete on the Europe–Australia route, though all the airlines from European countries other than the UK have stopped flying to Australia, being unable to compete with the 'sixth freedom' airlines.

European Airline Liberalisation

The formation of a single aviation market within Europe is a change which is having major implications for tourism in Europe. International flights were tightly regulated, and air fares in Europe were very high as compared to those for similar distances within more liberalised aviation markets such as in the USA, Canada and Australia. During the 1990s, the countries of the EC, along with Switzerland and Norway, removed most of the regulation of international aviation (though some domestic restrictions remain). Significantly, controls on capacity, and on the entry of new airlines, were lifted. Thus, an airline from Ireland, Ryanair, is able to offer services between the UK and Italy.

Interestingly, this move to liberalise was not a matter of the member countries agreeing on a new aviation policy. Rather it was the consequence of a ruling by the European Court of Justice that by acceding to the Treaty of Rome, countries had agreed to open up markets between themselves, and this included aviation markets. European liberalisation is so far the only substantial example of several countries in a region agreeing to open skies in that region. Other international or regional agreements have been very limited in scope. It is unlikely that all the European countries would have negotiated to implement such far-reaching de-regulation. The next big test case involves the ASEAN countries, which are seeking to negotiate and implement open skies in the ASEAN region. Not surprisingly, progress has been slow.

The initial years of opening up the European market saw useful, but not dramatic, change, as some air routes become more competitive. It was the arrival of the LCC, pioneered by Ryanair and easyJet and Air Berlin, which transformed the market. The LCC offered services to new and old destinations, offered a simpler product and offered much lower fares. They stimulated travel to the destinations they served, and forced the legacy airlines to respond with competitive fares. Tourism within Europe was stimulated overall, and the new airlines changed the patterns of tourism.

Europe–USA Open Skies

In late 2006, after protracted negotiations, Europe and the USA agreed on opening up air travel markets between them. The agreement was less far-reaching than had been hoped for, but significant nonetheless. Until this time, international aviation between the USA and European countries was subject to bilateral regulation imposed by the USA and each of its European partners. While some elements of bilateralism still exist, Europe is treated as a whole for Europe–US aviation purposes. Previously, a UK airline would only be permitted to fly to the USA from the UK – now a UK airline can fly from other countries, such as France, to the USA, and a French airline can fly from London to the USA. Apart from this, the new agreement also liberalised aviation markets, since capacity limits and restrictions on the number of airlines were removed. Some very detailed restrictions, such as on the number (two) of US airlines which were permitted to fly into London's largest airport, Heathrow, were removed. Some restrictions remain, especially on who may own airlines – US airlines must remain majority owned and controlled by US interests.

Thus far, the impact of the new agreement has been limited. The legacy airlines serving the markets have been changing their routes and networks and there is more competition on some routes. Airlines are beginning to fly to the USA from countries other than their home country – for example, a subsidiary of British Airways is now flying from Paris to the USA. A big unknown is whether LCC will enter the market in a significant way. Some small LCC have tried, and some of the major LCC are considering entering. Until recently, LCC have specialised in short-haul markets, such as within Europe or within North America. If LCC are able to access this market successfully, they could make a large impact, though whether it would be as large as the impact on intra-US and intra-Europe travel is difficult to predict.

Trans-Atlantic liberalisation should lead to lower fares, though to what extent this happens is yet to be determined. Lower fares will stimulate US–Europe travel. Europe will gain more visitors as US travellers switch from other destinations to Europe, and vice versa. Other destinations will lose out. Airlines may alter their networks, possibly routing more of their traffic through the popular hubs, such as Paris or London. Thus the new agreement could change patterns of tourism in the USA and in Europe as the convenience of travel from different origins and destinations changes. The US–Europe agreement was not one which was primarily motivated by tourism concerns, but it could have a substantial impact on tourism flows between and in the two regions.

16.4.2 DOMESTIC DE-REGULATION

Prior to the late 1970s, most countries with significant domestic air transport markets, such as the USA, Canada, Australia and Brazil, regulated their markets very tightly. As a result, air travel was oriented to business, with high fares and high convenience. The breakthrough came with domestic de-regulation in the USA, which took place over the late 1970s and early 1980s (Bailey *et al.*, 1985). Other countries followed the US example later.

De-regulation in the USA led to a much more competitive airline industry which was interested in serving low-fare markets. Initially, there was rush of new entrants, mainly operating on a low-cost basis, and offering simple, low fares. Then the established airlines fought back, with low-fare offerings of their own – ultimately most of the new entrants were forced out, and the older airlines re-established their dominance. This too was made possible by effective market segmentation. The airlines worked out ways to offer low fares to price-sensitive leisure travellers while keeping the high-yield business travellers. These included minimum stay restrictions on return tickets, and requirements that travellers stay at their destination over Saturday night – a restriction which would not appeal to business travellers. The result was that low fares did become readily available, and the range of fares became quite wide. A similar pattern emerged in the other deregulated domestic markets, such as those of Canada (Oum *et al.*, 1991) and Australia (Forsyth, 1991).

Airline de-regulation led to major changes in the pattern of tourism within the countries which deregulated. Holidaymakers switched from surface transport to air transport and made longer journeys. It also meant that these countries became more competitive as destinations for foreign tourists. For example, it became moderately cheap to fly to the USA and fly to a number of destinations within the USA during a short holiday – this made the USA more attractive as a holiday destination for European and Japanese travellers.

16.4.3 LIBERALISATION ON LONG-HAUL MARKETS

The liberalisation of long-haul international markets came about at around the same time as domestic de-regulation (though some countries, such as Australia, opened up their international markets before their domestic markets). Having deregulated its domestic market, the USA sought to conclude liberal 'Open Skies' agreements with its international partners (Kasper, 1988). Typically, these agreements allowed for several airlines, not just one from each country, to serve on a route, and they avoided fare and capacity restrictions. They opened up routes to new entry and competition (Doganis, 2001). Other countries allowed airlines from third countries to serve routes between them and origin/destination countries. For example, Australia and the UK ceased to reserve the route between them for Australian and UK airlines, and they permitted airlines from countries between them, such as Thailand and Singapore, to serve the route (Findlay, 1985). These intermediate countries could serve the Australia–UK market by combining their traffic rights to Australia and the UK; however, they could still be restricted in terms of the capacity which they were permitted to schedule on each of the sectors they flew. This substantially added to competition, and because some of these countries' airlines had very low costs, this put considerable pressure on fares.

Liberalisation on international, long-haul markets has been gradual and incomplete. Some markets, such as the North Atlantic, are very competitive, while others, such as the trans-Pacific, are much less so. Air transport markets within Asia present a mixed picture, with some very open markets and other very restricted markets (Oum & Yu, 2000). Japan and Hong Kong have been very slow to open up their markets. South America has also been slow to liberalise.

The consequence of liberalisation has been the development of a mass long-haul tourism market over the last two decades. This has been especially important for countries which are relatively remote, such as Australia, New Zealand and South Africa. Prior to liberalisation, international tourism to these countries was modest, limited to business travel and niche markets for VFR and well-off tourists. Nowadays, these countries are very much competitors for mass holiday tourism. Interestingly, areas which have been slow to liberalise, such as South America, have not developed as their tourism potential would suggest.

Some countries have taken a pragmatic perspective to aviation negotiations, making careful assessments of liberalisation proposals. In 2007, when Australia considered allowing airlines from the Middle East, such as Emirates, Etihad and Qatar Airways, more flights into Australia, it assessed:

- benefits to Australian travellers from lower fares and more convenient services;
- cost in terms of lower profits to Australian airlines such as Qantas;
- benefits from increased tourism to Australia.

The Australian Government concluded that the benefits exceeded the costs, and it allowed the airlines to operate several more flights. In other situations, the Australian Government has assessed that the benefits will lessen the costs, and has refused to liberalise. Thus, it refused an application by Singapore airlines to fly between Australia and the USA. Countries are becoming more rigorous in evaluating benefits and costs of liberalisation, and they are paying more attention to evaluating the benefits from increased tourism. See Box 16.4 for discussion of the benefits and costs that are relevant to assess liberalisation of the trans-Pacific route.

BOX 16.4 Benefits of competition in trans-Pacific aviation

There are few airlines flying on the trans-Pacific route between Australia and the USA. The route is dominated by Qantas, with over 50% of the market, and United Airlines. In addition, since mid-2004 Hawaiian Airlines has entered the route in a small way and now provides around 6% of total seat capacity. There is also some indirect competition from Air New Zealand and Air Canada. Competition between the airlines is not strong, and fares are high. Qantas enjoys high profits on the route.

The airlines in the USA which have the equipment and expertise to serve the route from continental USA are cash constrained and are avoiding risks, while those which have the funds, such as Southwest, are focused on short haul domestic US routes. Thus the most obvious way of increasing competition would be to permit airlines of third countries, such as Singapore Airlines or Emirates, to enter the route. Singapore Airlines has expressed a strong interest in serving the route. Australian tourism interests would like to see this happen.

The Australian Government's international aviation policy has the objective of providing the greatest available net national benefit. Two main options are considered:

- Entry on to the route by a major airline from a third country, such as Singapore Airlines or Emirates.
- Entry on to the route by an Australian-based and 50% owned subsidiary of a third country airline or company, such as a subsidiary of Singapore Airlines or of the Virgin group.

Forsyth (2005a,b) identifies three main sources of benefits and costs to a country when air services are liberalised. These are:

- Benefits to host country travellers
- Costs of reduced profits accruing to host country stakeholders
- Benefits and costs from changes in tourism expenditure

Competitive Scenarios
Were a new foreign airline to enter the trans-Pacific route, there are several possible competitive outcomes:

- No price fall – the Australian airline loses market share, and there are no benefits to home travellers or from tourism;
- Moderate to large price falls – Australian travellers and tourists gain, and the home country airline Qantas loses some profit and market share; and
- Qantas replaced – the new airlines have such low costs that fares fall so much that Qantas exits. Qantas profits on the route are eliminated, but Australian travellers and tourists gain.

The third of these is a highly unlikely outcome given the strong marketing advantages of Qantas and its cost competitiveness. Whether Australia gains or loses depends on the size of the price fall, and the parameters identified above.

Costs and Benefits of Liberalisation of Trans-Pacific Route
Forsyth (2005) made some estimates of the likely size of the costs and benefits of promoting competition in trans-Pacific aviation.

- *Benefits to Australian Travellers.* There is a benefit when home travellers gain from the fare reductions (and possibly service improvements such as increased frequency). These benefits depend on the Australian share of travel on the route, and the size of the fare reduction. The cost of an additional $1 outbound tourism expenditure is estimated to be $0.05. The gain per passenger in total on the trans-Pacific route is $135, or $108 million in total.

Costs of Reduced Profits Accruing to Australian Stakeholders
When fares are reduced, there is a cost in terms of pressure put on the home country airline's profits and market shares. These will come about from lower selling prices of products, moderated by possible cost reductions. In addition, there may be a loss of market share, which will lead to a further loss of profit if the route remains profitable. The Australian share of this loss of profit will be less than 100% – it will depend on the company tax rate, and on the percentage of shares of

the home country airline, in this case Qantas, held in Australia. Forsyth estimates the total cost in terms of reduced profits to Qantas at $120.4 per passenger or $96.3 million.

Benefits and Costs from Changes in Tourism Expenditure

These depend on how fare reductions impact on inbound tourism expenditure (i.e. demand elasticities) and on the scale of the benefits to Australia of additional tourism expenditure. The economic benefit to Australia from an additional $1 of tourism expenditure is estimated to be $0.1.

Outbound tourism will also be stimulated and the costs of this depend on the expenditure elasticity, along with the relationship of the costs of reduced expenditure at home to the size of that expenditure. Forsyth estimates that the air fare reduction leads to an additional $900 tourism expenditure in Australia per visitor. The economic benefits of the air fare reduction are $49.5 per total passenger or, in total, $39.6 million. The reduction in airfares also leads to an additional outbound expenditure of $6.8 per passenger or $5.4 million in total.

There are some asymmetries in the sizes of inbound and outbound benefits and costs. The benefits of an additional $1 inbound tourism expenditure are greater than the cost of an additional $1 outbound expenditure because some outbound expenditure is spent at home (e.g. on airlines, travel agents). More importantly, there is a difference in the size of the impacts. A lower fare stimulates more tourism from the other country to Australia, partly because of the effect of the lower fare on total travel from the foreign country, but largely because of the substitution effect – tourists' switch to Australia from other routes. Lower fares stimulate outbound travel from Australia, but the increase in travel on the route comes partly from switching travel from other outbound routes. In terms of the impact on domestic expenditure in Australia this latter effect does not matter, since the travellers would have spent outside Australia anyway.

Net Benefit to Australia

The net tourism benefit from air fare reductions is $57.4 per passenger or $45.9 million across the economy per annum. In comparison with other potential international aviation policy changes this represents a comparatively strong net benefit result for Australia. In this scenario, tourism benefits expressed as a welfare gain to Australia are somewhat less than the benefits to Australian travellers, and the cost to Australian shareholders of profit reductions – as would be expected. However, it is a significant sum, and it essentially determines the balance between benefits and costs. These calculations suggest a clear economic gain to Australia from allowing Singapore Airlines or Emirates (or both) on to the trans-Pacific route

	Base Case, Passenger ($)	Base Case, Total ($m)	High Tourism Benefits Case, Per Passenger ($)	High Tourism Benefits Case, Total ($m)
Home Traveller Benefits	135	108	135	108
Inbound Tourism Benefits	49.5	39.6	302	241.6
Australian Share of Airline Profits	−120.4	−96.3	−120.4	−96.3
Outbound Tourism Costs	−6.7	−5.4	−41.1	−32.9
Net Benefit to Austrlia	57.4	45.9	275.5	220.4

In practice, it is expected that the major national benefits arise with the inclusion of the first additional carrier with smaller gains expected with the inclusion of any second or third carrier from outside Australia and the USA. In choosing which new carrier to provide first access to this market it might be expected that the Australian Government will consider other issues such as international political and trade relationships as well as the potential new entrants' operational issues and strategic potential as a core participant in Australian aviation.

The Foreign Subsidiary Option
One option would be to only permit an Australian based subsidiary of a foreign airline to serve the route. This has been suggested by Qantas, which has argued that if Singapore wishes to access international routes from Australia, it should have to do what Qantas did with Jetstar Asia, namely, set up a subsidiary with local interests. Singapore airlines could own nearly 50% of the subsidiary. Alternatively, a subsidiary of the Virgin group with a near 50% overseas shareholding could enter

the route. If this happened, 70% of the pre-tax profits of the new entrant would accrue to Australia, rather than none of the profits, if a fully foreign-owned airline enters. In this case, there would be no reduction in profits accruing to Australian interests due to a reduced market share being won by Australian airlines. The market share to Australian airlines would remain the same – in fact, it could increase, if the new entrant won market share from non-Australian carriers. None of the reduction in profits to Qantas from its reduced market share would now accrue to Australian interests. This would be $42 per total passenger. The total benefit to Australia would become $99.4 per passenger or $79.5 million in total.

Minimal Impact of Competition on Fares

One possible, though unlikely, scenario would be one in which the new entrant managed to gain market share but fares on the route did not fall, or fell imperceptibly. If this were the case, there would be no benefits to the home travellers, and there would be no tourism benefits or costs. The only source of benefits and costs would be a reduction in the profits from the route which the Australian carrier enjoys. In this scenario, opening up the route would be unambiguously negative for Australia. It is not likely that a foreign carrier would be able to gain a significant market share at the same time as not having any effect on fares or overall traffic. Most likely the two are linked, and a significant gain in market share would only be obtained if there were vigorous competition and fares fell substantially.

This study shows how it is possible to assess whether it is in Australia's economic interest to permit carriers such as Singapore Airlines or Emirates on to the trans-Pacific route. The conclusion is that Qantas shareholders are clearly a major loser, while Australian travellers to the USA and the inbound tourism industry are clear winners. The framework can be applied to other aviation contexts.

Source: Forsyth, P. (2005a) 'Promoting Competition in Trans-Pacific Tourism', unpublished. Since this paper was written, Virgin Blue's long-haul carrier V Pacific has entered the trans-Pacific route between USA and Australia, increasing capacity on this route

16.5   AIRPORT CAPACITY AND PATTERNS OF TOURISM

The presence of air transport services enables tourism in a region to develop. When these services are constrained, tourism growth is hampered. Airline services are quite flexible and are not likely to be a constraint except when they are regulated. Air transport infrastructure, especially airports, but also including air traffic control, is much more likely to be a brake on tourism growth.

Airport capacity is a constraint on tourism development in the major cities of Europe, North America and Japan (Graham, 2003). Airport developments have a long lead time, and they tend to be controversial. This is primarily because of their environmental impacts on noise and air quality. Thus, in many cities, further expansion of airport capacity is strongly resisted, and as a result, capacity has fallen well short of demand. The excess demand is handled in two ways – congestion and slot restrictions.

Congestion

In the USA, when there is excess demand for an airport, congestion, in the form of delays to flights, is allowed to build up. Congestion acts as a rationing device, and fewer flights are scheduled into the congested airport. Traffic is discouraged, and there is less tourism from, and to, the city (Brueckner, 2002). We discussed congestion caused by insufficient infrastructure in Chapter 13, where Box 13.1 addressed issues of congestion pricing at New York airports.

Slot controls

In Europe and elsewhere, the favoured approach to handling excess demand is through slot controls (Boyfield, 2003). Airport capacity is declared in terms of a number of slots, and slots are usually allocated to the airlines which have been using the airport before it became congested. To use the airport, an airline must have a slot for the time it wishes to land or take off. For some airports, slots are scarce and difficult to obtain – this is so for the London and Tokyo airports. A slot pair (to land and take off daily) at London Heathrow airport recently sold for £10 million stg. While slot control systems lessen congestion, they reduce the number of flights into the city and make them more expensive, thus discouraging tourism. At various stages in the past, airport capacity limitations have been a major restriction of the growth of tourism into and out of Japan. Airport capacity constraints are likely to become more of a brake on tourism growth in these countries over the future, notwithstanding the increasing use by LCC of secondary airports. The region with least problems of airport capacity appears to be Asia outside Japan. While air transport has been growing rapidly in recent years, there have been significant increases in airport capacity in cities such as Hong Kong, Kuala Lumpur and Shanghai.

Gainers and losers from airport development

At the other end of scale, lack of airport capacity can prove a barrier to tourism development in smaller cities, the regions and in remote locations. Some developing countries may have tourism potential, but their airport facilities may be inadequate, and they may not have the resources to upgrade them. Smaller cities and regions may possess airports, but they can have operational restrictions (because of runway length or strength) which prevent the use of cost-effective aircraft. As a result, tourism is hampered because air fares are higher than they might be, and frequencies are low. Usually in these circumstances the barriers to expanding capacity are not as strong as they are with the environmentally constrained major cities of North America and Europe. For these reasons expansion of regional airports is often subsidised. Some of the effects of subsidies are discussed in Box 16.5.

BOX 16.5 Estimating the costs and benefits of regional airport subsidies

Subsidies to airports have become a controversial issue, especially in Europe since liberalisation of air transport. The objectives of airport subsidies are to increase economic activity in a region. They can do this in several ways. First, regional airports tend to be less expensive than non-subsidised airports, resulting in more economic activity at the airport, with more passengers and flights to service, more maintenance activity and other aviation-related activity. Second, there may be additional freight throughput, which also generates additional economic activity. Many secondary airports cater for LCC, which typically do not carry much freight, but some have positioned themselves as freight hubs. Third, there will be more tourism through the region with its associated expenditure, and the region can gain from this.

It is recognised, however, that subsidies reduce efficiency by distorting choices, and they artificially assist one competitor over another. Thus subsidies to regional airports will distort the choices of airlines as to which airports to fly to, by inducing some to use airports they would not be willing to pay the full cost of use. Subsidies are also expensive in that they need to be funded from taxation, which is itself distortionary.

If the regions that pay for the subsidies are willing to do so, should they be stopped from doing so? The issue is not so simple, since some or perhaps all of this change in economic activity will be at the expense of reduced economic activity in other parts of the national economy. Where there is a shift of domestic or international tourism to the subsidising region, other regions will experience reduced economic activity with the result that the nation as a whole may not experience an overall increase in activity. The fact that subsidies are likely to shift, rather than stimulate overall economic activity, poses a difficult problem for governments in respect of formulating policies towards subsidies offered to regional airports. Should the region be allowed to make its own choices in funding subsidies, or should the federal government override a region the actions of which lower the welfare of the nation as a whole?

Forsyth uses a CGE model to estimate both the regional and the national impacts on economic activity of airport subsidies. He concludes that it is possible for a region to enjoy economic gains as a result of an airport subsidy, even though the nation as a whole is likely to lose, since economic activity is shifted, and not necessarily increased overall.

The Welfare Cost of Subsidies

When a region subsidises an airport, it may well be the case that the gain to consumers is less than the cost of the subsidy. Subsidies, *ceteris paribus*, are likely to reduce welfare overall. This is shown in Figure 16.1. The demand curve for the airport is shown and the initial average and marginal cost curve is shown as $AC = MC = P_1 C$. Initially the price for use is set at P_1. Following the grant of a subsidy of s per unit, price falls to P_2. The gain to the initial consumers is shown as s per unit, at $P_1 P_2 AD$, and the gain to new consumers averages ABD. The total gain is $P_2 ABDP_1$, but the cost of the subsidy is $P_2 BCP_1$.

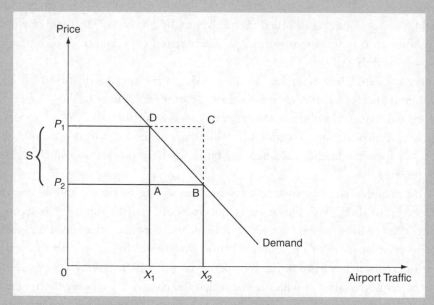

Figure 16.1 Subsidy of an airport

Additionally, subsidies must be financed. The regional government must finance the subsidy from additional tax or reduced expenditure. Typically, it will need to rely on distortionary taxation, which implies that the cost of raising a €1 in revenue will exceed €1. Thus the cost of the subsidy will be greater than its face value to the extent that the marginal cost of raising €1 exceeds €1.

In addition to this, increased taxation in the region will discourage economic activity. If subsidies generate economic activity, taxes will reduce activity, though not necessarily to the same extent. In evaluating the subsidy, it will be essential to assess the negative as well as the positive impacts on economic activity in the region, and the associated loss in benefits that it engenders. Of further concern is the issue of who enjoys the benefits of the subsidy. These typically will accrue to other regions or nations. If the subsidy results in lower air fares paid by tourists from other regions of the nation, the benefits of the subsidy will accrue to the nation. If the lower fares are paid by foreign tourists, the nation will not gain.

The Benefits of Subsidies

Additional economic activity in a region is not the same as economic benefits to that region. Typically, as argued in Chapters 6 and 10, the change in output will be greater than the change in welfare of the region or nation – it is necessary to determine how changes in activity affect economic benefits. The value of the changes in regional or national output will be typically measured by changes in Gross Regional Product (GRP) and Regional Value Added or Gross Domestic Output. These are not a measure of the welfare gain to the region or nation, or the net economic benefit which they enjoy. Where additional capital and labour are used to produce the additional output, the costs of these must to be deducted to measure the net gain to the community. As discussed in Chapter 9, CGE models can be adapted to provide measures of changes in welfare, by deducting the cost of additional inputs used from measures of the value of additional output. In addition to the welfare measures as estimated in the simulations, it is necessary to deduct the cost of the subsidy to obtain a measure of the net change in welfare as a result of the policy.

Welfare and Jurisdictions

There are several levels of jurisdictions from whose perspective welfare can be evaluated. At the *regional level*, the subsidy will lead to increased economic activity, from which there will be a gain. Against this must be set the cost of the subsidy to taxpayers who will reduce their expenditure on a range of goods and services. The region may gain or lose accordingly. At the *national level*, while the subsidising region will gain economic activity, other regions will lose. If regions are similar, there will be a net loss from subsidisation since economic activity will be transferred, rather than substantially increased. If the subsidising region is a depressed region, relative to other regions, there could be a gain from shifting economic activity even if national economic activity does not increase on balance. Further, if there is unemployment in the nation as a whole, there may be a gain from increased overall economic activity, though the size of this gain will be moderated by increases in the exchange rate induced by the inflow of tourism expenditure. At the *world level*, foreign tourists will gain from the subsidy, though nations other than the nation imposing the subsidy will lose economic activity.

The Model and Simulations

The author's approach involves three main steps:

- Projecting the effects of the subsidy, on airport traffic, visitor flows and changes in expenditure, in the region, in competitor regions and the national economy;
- Using these expenditure changes to estimate impacts on economic activity by making use of a multi-regional CGE model which can embody alternative assumptions about the ways key markets, such as the labour market, work, along with assumptions about the policy stances of governments;
- Determining what impacts these changes in the value of aggregate output have on economic welfare in the region and nation. This involves estimating the costs of any additional factors used. Forsyth considers a range of different scenarios resulting from a region subsidising an airport.

It is assumed that a regional government subsidises the local airport to the extent of $1.5 million. This is financed through local taxes, which negatively impact upon economic activity within the region. If the subsidy is passed on to airlines which use the airport, and they in turn lower ticket prices then travellers are the ultimate recipients of the subsidy (alternatively, the subsidy could be assumed to stay with the airlines, which may be foreign- or home country-owned). The subsidies to the airport are sufficient to attract LCC to switch operations from major airports which are located in other regions.

Forsyth assumes flexible employment in both regions (host region and rest of economy), and a fixed national real wage. It is also assumed that the regional government keeps its budget deficit constant – that is, it funds the subsidy from taxation (as ultimately, it will have to in the long run).

LCC are assumed to be responsive to the lower charges offered by the regional airport. A subsidy of $1.5 million is associated with additional tourism expenditure in the region of $7.5 million, diverted from other regions. Forsyth undertakes simulations using different assumptions about the effects of the subsidy on tourism flows and assumptions about the regional and national labour markets.

Results

Some results of the simulations are summarised in Table 16.1. The effects are divided into the tax effect, the tourism stimulation effect and the total effect. When the host region imposes a tax to provide for the subsidy, it has a depressing effect on the region, as measured by GRP. There is a slight positive effect on other regions – the host region becomes a little less competitive as a place to do business as a result of its extra taxes. The tourism effect is positive, and, in an economy with unemployment, the stimulatory effect is large. There is also a depressing effect in other regions as a result of the loss of tourism expenditure. The nation as a whole loses as a result of subsidisation of a regional airport.

Table 16.1 Tax, tourism and total effects on product and welfare (in million dollars)

GDP/GRP	Region	Other Regions	Nation
Tax Effect	−3.27	+0.24	−3.03
Tourism Effect	+6.35	−6.58	−0.23
Total GDP/GRP Effect	+3.08	−6.34	−3.26
Tax Effect	−1.07	+0.07	−1.00
Tourism Effect	+2.47	−2.57	−0.09
Total Effect on Real Welfare	+1.41	−2.50	−1.09

The effects on real welfare have a similar pattern to the effects on GDP or GRP. The host region makes a net gain of $1.41 million – not quite as large, in this situation, as the cost of the subsidy. Other regions unambiguously lose as a result of the subsidy, mainly because of the loss of benefits from tourism. The nation as a whole experiences a loss in welfare as a result of the subsidisation of a regional airport.

Conclusions

This research illustrates how the costs and benefits of airport subsidies can be estimated, and the overall cost/benefit balance for a specific case can be measured. The results vary with assumptions about how key markets, such as the labour market, work and with different assumptions about the impacts of the subsidies on visitor flows and their expenditure. Forsyth makes some gener-alisations which provide a basis for further research in different destinations:

- It can be in the economic interest of a region to offer airport subsidies to attract economic activity;
- It is quite likely that the economic impacts in regions other than the host region will be negative, even when they are not directly affected by the subsidies;
- The balance for the nation as a whole can be either positive or negative; and
- The impacts on the regions and nation depend importantly on the workings of the labour market. In particular, regional airport subsidies could be positive for the nation as a whole if the region offering the subsidies is relatively depressed and other regions are not.

Source: Forsyth, P. (2006) 'Estimating the Costs and Benefits of Regional Airport Subsidies: A Computable General Equilibrium Approach'. Presented at German Aviation Research Society Workshop, Amsterdam, June–July

While inadequate capacity can be a brake on tourism, excessive capacity can also have the same effect. Excessive investment often takes place in airports. Airports are often government-owned, or government-regulated, and they can usually pass on higher costs through higher charges. These are initially paid by airlines, but ultimately paid by the pas-sengers. A city or country may see an airport as a prestige project, and build a large and lavishly appointed facility. However, tourists do not come to a city or region just because there is a large airport – rather they will be discouraged by the higher air fares they have to pay so that the airport can be funded. Tourism is best served when airport investments are of a size and quality matched to the demand.

When investment to expand capacity at international airports takes place, a high pro-portion of the benefits accrue to airlines and passengers. Airlines and passengers both gain from reduced congestion, from additional flights and from operational economies enabled by better airport facilities. Many of the airlines and passengers who gain from airport investment will be foreign – this will be especially true in the case of airports in developing countries which serve mainly incoming tourists, not the local population, few of whom are well off enough to fly. From the perspective of the country doing the invest-ing, most of the costs will fall on residents, but many of the benefits will be enjoyed directly at least, by foreigners.

This poses a problem for evaluation. If these investments in airport capacity are to be justified from the perspective of the home country, this must be done in terms of the tourism and other economic benefits which flow from the extra capacity. Additional tourism will bring economic benefits to a country or region, through tax payments, terms of trade effects, additional profits, possible positive impacts on employments and general stimulation of economic activity. As argued in Chapters 6 and 10, there can be real economic benefits, especially when the stimulation of the economy takes place where there are unemployed resources.

16.6 TAXING TOURISM AND AVIATION

While regulation is one of the main arms of policy, especially in respect of aviation, taxation is the other. Governments will need to treat aviation and tourism together to ensure that they impose the right mix of taxes given their objectives. Tourism taxation and regulatory policy for aviation thus need to be determined jointly.

By taxing aviation, for example, with a passenger levy, all tourists, both inbound and outbound, will be affected with both positive and negative effects on the home tourism industry. In many countries it may not be practical to tax tourism directly. In developing countries, much of tourism may be supplied by the informal sector, for example, household businesses, which may be very difficult to include in the tax system. Taxes at the aviation level, collected from only a few firms or directly from passengers, may be much simpler to collect. Thus countries with less extensive tax systems may prefer aviation taxes. Even developed countries may use aviation as a 'tourism tax'. Box 15.5 in Chapter 15, which concerned a passenger levy for the UK, serves to reinforce the interrelationship between aviation policy and tourism flows and expenditure.

Some countries, and, more particularly, regions, also seek to encourage tourism through subsidising aviation, or more likely, aviation infrastructure. Thus several regions in Europe have sought to increase tourism by subsidising airport use of low-cost airlines, as discussed in Box 16.5.

Few countries make a systematic assessment of the extent to which they want to encourage or tax tourism and aviation, and it is quite possible that tourism development and tax policies work at cross purposes. Some countries seem keen to encourage tourism, yet they are also imposing more taxes on tourism and aviation, especially the latter. In recent years there is evidence of a growth in taxes levied on aviation – air travel is easy to tax, and its growth makes it an attractive source of revenue. To an extent, current taxes may be more transparent than the implicit taxes raised on aviation through regulation, which have been declining, though tourism industry groups have expressed concern about the trend towards them.

While levies on airports and their passengers have been growing, not all of these are true taxes. In some cases these represent a charge for services. For example, security levies have been increasing, and these pay for the additional security now implemented at airports. There is some debate about who should pay for these services. While passengers and airlines gain from safer skies, much of the benefit of tighter security is enjoyed by the community at large – thus it is suggested that these should be provided by the government, not at the expense of passengers. Environmental charges at airports are also growing in terms of coverage and levels – these cover the noise and emissions externalities created by air transport at airports. To some extent these are used to compensate persons adversely affected (through sound insulation grants for houses around airports), though not all revenues collected are spent in this way. These levies may be present to correct an externality, though they do add to the already high taxation of air travel, and do have the effect of discouraging tourism.

16.7 AVIATION AND TOURISM: SUPPLY-SIDE INTEGRATION

Aviation and tourism services are clearly linked on the demand side. To consume tourism, the tourist must purchase a range of related products, such as accommodation, meals, local travel and long-distance travel, such as air travel. These are sometimes sold jointly as a package. The question then arises of how integrated the supply of these products might be.

By and large, with some important exceptions, the links between aviation and tourism on the supply side are not particularly significant. Airlines and other tourism operators tend to be owned and operated independently of one another. This suggests that there are few strong economies to be gained from integration, and that there are managerial advantages in specialisation in one part of the industry. Perhaps the most important exception to the general rule occurs with inclusive tour companies. Tour companies, especially in Europe, such as TUI and Thomas Cook, operate their own airlines. With the development of inclusive tours, relying on charter airlines, tour companies set up their own airlines. To provide package tours competitively, the various parts of the chain need to be integrated closely – for example, available supplies of accommodation and air capacity need to be matched closely to the demand, so that high utilisation can be achieved. Tour companies found that they could do this when they owned and operated their own airlines, and the load factors of the tour-company airlines are very high. It will be interesting to see if these links persist, as market conditions change. The development of the LCC has meant that the advantages of inclusive tours and charter airlines have been eroded, as travellers are willing to pay a little extra for the additional flexibility that the LCC provide. Some tour companies have set up LCC of their own. This may be a defensive move, as they see their market share as slipping. It has yet to be seen whether there are any economies to be reaped from integration of tours and LCC, and whether this is a likely pattern for the future.

Another exception of some significance is airline ownership of travel agents. This may reflect economies of integration on the production side – travel agents are intensive users of the CRS which the airlines develop and own. Airlines may also have considered that ownership of a travel agent would give them marketing advantages, as the agent would be a direct link with their customers. However, another major reason for ownership of travel agents was probably to create an entry barrier. If all or most of the travel agents are owned by the incumbent airlines, it is difficult for new entrant airlines to sell their product. Airline ownership of agents is often identified as a barrier to entry into the airline industry. This barrier has been considerably weakened by the development of internet booking, which bypasses the travel agent. The new-entrant LCC have been particularly effective users of the internet, and the older airlines are well behind them in their internet use. In the light of this, it may well be that the major airlines no longer see ownership of travel agencies as being as strong a competitive weapon as it was, and they may divest themselves of these businesses.

Beyond these examples, there are few significant cases of cross ownership between tourism and aviation businesses. For a time, the major international airlines owned or operated hotels (e.g. Pan Am with Intercontinental and Air France with Meridien). However, they were quick to divest themselves of these when they encountered cash crises in the 1980s and 1990s. Some of the new LCC have invested in car rental and similar firms, but this is probably the result of opportunistic investments rather than to reap economies of integration at the production level (they have also been investing in mobile phone companies and credit cards). Within the tourism industry, specialisation probably pays – it is probably better to concentrate on providing airline services, hotel services or local bus tours well than to develop unwieldy conglomerates which do not excel in any of the products they sell.

16.8 AVIATION ALLIANCES

While regulation and its liberalisation constitute the most important means by which aviation policy affects tourism, they are not the only way. An important development over the last decade or so has been the development of airline alliances. Airline alliances consist of groups of independent airlines. The objective of an alliance is to be able to achieve what individual airlines are not able to achieve by themselves. Alliances can take many forms. Some alliances are very casual, with one airline agreeing to take passengers of another. In some cases, airlines invest in each other. Some alliances are motivated by an attempt to achieve cost savings: for example, airlines might share spare parts. Other alliances may be marketing-based. A key feature of airline alliances is that they attempt to create a wider network and services than individual airlines can provide. The idea is that one airline links its network with networks of other airlines and, thereby, is able to offer a product to its passengers, which is much broader than that simply offered its own network.

Airline mergers and strategic alliances can impact on tourism in several ways. Anti-competitive mergers and alliances can raise fares and discourage tourism. On the other hand, those mergers which result in improved networks and more convenient travel will encourage tourism. Competition authorities are now paying more attention to tourism implications of airline mergers and alliances. Box 16.6 indicates the airlines comprising the three major strategic alliances as of June 2008. Each of these airlines in an alliance has a strong route network in a particular region. Thus, in the OneWorld Alliance, British

Airways is strong in Europe, and across the North Atlantic; Cathay Pacific is very strong in Asia; American Airlines in the USA and Qantas in the South-east Asia and JAL in the Asia-Pacific region. By combining their networks, airlines in an alliance are able to offer the passenger a whole range of new services. A British Airways passenger can be offered the service from Bournemouth to a small city in the USA by flying on British Airways to one of its US gateways, and then on American Airlines to the destination city. Neither British Airways nor American Airlines would be able to offer this service on their own. Thus, alliances are able to offer an airline's passengers an increased number of city pairs services.

BOX 16.6 Airline alliances: Advantages and limitations

International airline alliances are an important and growing feature of the airline industry. Airlines in alliances expect to gain from lower costs, improved market access, productivity growth, reducing competition and higher barriers to entry. Tourists expect to see better service and reduced fares as a consequence.

Importance of Airline Alliances

Alliances amongst international airlines, involving high levels of cooperation and coordination of services and operations, have become a prominent feature of the airline industry in recent times. Alliances can affect both the demand and supply sides of tourism.

In strategy terms, international airline alliances are predominantly horizontal alliances (amongst peers and rivals in the same industry) rather than vertical alliances with suppliers or customers (up or down the value chain).

In the airline industry case it has been found important to distinguish between two forms of horizontal alliance.

Complementary alliances involve two (or more) airlines with non-overlapping routes linked through a common destination that coordinate schedules etc. in an attempt to realise operational economies of scope and scale. *Parallel alliances* are between airlines formerly competing on a route who agree to cooperate on the route, thereby potentially reducing competition. Most such alliances take the form of code-sharing of services by two airlines, in which one airline agrees to buy a block of seats on a flight service of another airline and then sells these seats under its own brand (the flight typically appears with both airlines' codes). But some involve greater degrees of cooperation such as recognition of each other's frequent flyer schemes, sharing of lounges and terminals, joint marketing and integration of booking systems.

The table shows the three major strategic alliances between airlines in June 2008.

Star Alliance Passengers per year: 455 million Market share: 25.1%	Skyteam Passengers per year: 428 million Market share: 20.8%	Oneworld Passengers per year: 320 million Market share 14.9%
Adria Airways	Aeroflot	American Airlines
Air Canada	Aeroméxico	British Airways
Air China	Air Europa	Cathay Pacific
Air New Zealand	Air France	Finnair
ANA	Alitalia	Iberia
Asiana Airlines	China Southern	Japan Airlines
Austrian Airlines	Continental	LAN
Blue1	Copa Airlines	Malév
BMI	Czech Airlines	Qantas
Croatia Airlines	Delta	Royal Jordanian
LOT Polish Airlines	Kenya Airways	
Lufthansa	KLM	
SAS	Korean Air	
Shanghai Airlines	Northwest	
Singapore Airlines		
South African Airways		
Spanair		
Swiss International Air Lines		
TAP Portugal		
Thai Airways International		
Turkish Airlines		
United Airlines		
US Airways		

In addition to the major alliances there are many hundreds of smaller and one-to-one arrangements and alliances. Some large and important airlines remain outside these major alliances, such as Emirates Airlines. Others such as Southwest Airlines, easyJet and Ryanair have successfully remained independent of the major alliances with strategies of low cost and concentration on high traffic routes.

Advantages of Alliances

- The most developed and general economic theory of airline alliances is that of Oum *et al.* (2001). Using an oligopolistic framework, these authors show that complementary alliances can be expected to decrease fares, increase partners' traffic and increase consumer welfare, while a parallel alliance essentially reduces competition and hence leads to increased fares and reduced consumer welfare. The authors also provide further theoretical discussion and evidence in support of the effects of alliances such as the benefits to airlines in traffic increases from linking networks, reduced delays between connections and fewer flight services.

- Airlines enter into alliances in pursuit of both economic benefits, such as productivity gains, and a stronger competitive position from improved customer service. Some airlines follow the strategy of others to minimise any advantages that competitors may gain.

  Airlines are generally believed to benefit from lower costs, improved market access, coordination of services with partners improving productivity and reducing competition, and higher barriers to entry.

- Alliances give their member airlines the potential to collaborate to some extent, depending on the regulatory environment (e.g. granting of anti-trust immunity) on trips involving more than one stage and airline. The impact on services and the fares paid by tourists could be marked.

- Allied airlines feed passengers into their partners' routes, as alliances entail the link up of airlines' networks. An allied airline can offer prospective passengers service to more destinations at greater frequency. Coordination of schedules to minimise passengers' waiting time between connecting flights and the ease of making connections (via closeness of gates, through booking of luggage and reducing check-in requirements) can add to the appeal of this expanded service, making the allied airline more attractive to travellers and increasing the airline's load factors.

- Airline alliances offer potential for operating cost reductions, through shared and more efficient use of ground facilities (lounges, terminals, etc.); risk-sharing, through the booking of block space on each other's flights and code-sharing; more efficient use of staff (e.g. coordinating and sharing flight crew); flight and route efficiencies, garnered through code-sharing services; and sharing the expenses of marketing and promotion.

- In the long term there are strong economic benefits to be garnered by airlines in an alliance from merging their frequent flyer programmes. These benefits come from greater purchasing power over their suppliers, cost savings from combining call centres and other back office operations and stronger, more coherent marketing. The resulting larger frequent flyer programme is likely to be more attractive to travellers.
- Alliances provide a means to gain market access and growth where they might otherwise be restricted by government regulation. In an industry constrained by low and variable profits that limit internal funding for capital investment, alliances provide a means to grow and offer a global service.
- There is no reason to expect the future to be any less challenging and volatile than the past. Alliances are one way of responding to future uncertainty, in an effort to reduce risk by sharing it with partners and by gaining some of the advantages of size in such an environment.
- Productivity is boosted by alliances, as combined operations enable economies of scale and scope to be realised, and access to resources and learning from partners is facilitated. Profitability will therefore be enhanced by such productivity gains (improved efficiency) and a stronger competitive position deriving from market power. Productivity gains offer the potential for fare reductions, generating increased market share.

Limitations of Alliances

- Potential negative impacts on brand and customer relationships from partner's actions (or lack thereof), loss of ability to take up opportunities due to being tied into the alliance and the need for trust in partners across national cultural differences.
- Costs of rescheduling to link in with alliance partner member flight schedules
- Alliances between formerly competing airlines on a route can reduce competition to the disadvantage of travelers.
- Reduced competition can result in fewer flight services and higher fares;
- Since most alliances involve a varying mix of overlapping markets (e.g. intercontinental routes) and complementary markets (for example, linking the networks

in two different continents), the overall effects of an alliance on competition must be evaluated carefully on a case-by-case basis.

Effects on Tourism

Tourism is likely to feel the impacts of alliances (particularly complementary alliances) through tourists experiencing key service improvements. As discussed, these include fare decreases; total travel time reductions; easier connections; more marketing of locations as a tourist destination; and, possibly, more convenient scheduling of services.

Travellers may benefit from the better service aspects and reduced fares consequent to reduced costs for the airlines. The balance of outcomes for tourists of improved efficiency of airlines versus a lessening of competitive forces needs to be determined empirically. Tourism demand could conceivably be greatly affected by the changes in the airline industry and airline operations that result from airline alliances.

The difference between economy air fares and discount air fares is important for tourism. Travelers on full economy fares can be expected to gain from alliances through fare reductions. The most price-sensitive tourists will seek out discount fares, which are already very competitive and on which alliances will probably have no significant impact. Other service considerations are less important for budget travelers. Tourists who are sufficiently price sensitive to seek out discount economy class fares, with all their associated restrictions and limitations, are likely to be less influenced by the non-fare, service improvements cited as benefits of alliances. This may limit the perceived gains for these tourists from alliances, dampening any impact on tourism flows.

Further change in the industry, especially greater liberalisation of the regulatory structure, may encourage new strategic responses by airlines, such as moving from code-sharing alliances to mergers and acquisitions. Airlines are likely to be encouraged in this direction, by the potential economies of scale and scope, and by the anticipation that they will be able to learn from and overcome the difficulties experienced in cross-national mergers in other industries.

Source: Morley, C.L. (2003) 'Impacts of International Airline Alliances on Tourism', *Tourism Economics*, 9, 31–51; Morley, C.L. (2006) 'Airline Alliances and Tourism' in L. Dwyer and P. Forsyth (eds) *International Handbook on the Economics of Tourism*, Chapter 9, Cheltenham: Edward Elgar Publishing

When airlines integrate their networks, there are some costs. Each airline must arrange schedules so as to link in with its partner airlines' schedules. This means that it is not able to operate its ideal schedule, if it did not have to connect with other airlines. An airline must make sure that the flight into a city arrives in time to catch its partner airlines' flight out of the city. In theory, switching from one airline to the other is meant to be a seamless transfer, though in practice it is not as easy as this. Connecting flights do, however, impose some costs on the airline, which must arrange for the passenger to transfer in a terminal from one flight to another and must transfer the passenger's baggage. The airline will have to ensure that the first flight arrives in time for the passenger to catch the second flight. Connecting flights make airline operations more complex, and costs rise with the complexity.

There are various ways in which the airlines try to make the transfer process as simple as possible. They try to make sure that the flights operate from the same terminal and that the arriving gates are close to the departing gates. They transfer the baggage from one flight to the other. Very often they are involved in code-sharing. This involves giving a flight of one airline the flight code of the other airline. If an airline from one country is not permitted to fly within another country, it will need to form an alliance with another so that the various component parts of the flight can be developed. Thus, an American Airlines flight from New York to a small US city may be given a British Airways code. British Airways will then be able to offer flights from London to New York, and then onto the other city using British Airways flight numbers. This makes that list the appearance of a much more integrated product to the passenger.

As summarised in Box 16.6, there are other reasons for forming international alliances. The advantages and limitations depend on the way that airlines are regulated at the international level.

16.9 CONCLUSIONS AND POLICY

- Aviation and tourism are complementary industries. Aviation depends on tourist travel and tourists depend on air transport. Yet, the two industries also exhibit a conflict of interest in that it is in the interests of each industry that the prices, and perhaps profits, of the other industry be low. This provides a policy dilemma for governments in their regulation and/or support of both industries.
- Up till the 1970s, the aviation industry was tightly regulated and its products were primarily targeted at the business market or charters. Aviation between different countries tended to be regulated in detail by the partner countries, and this regulation allowed little scope for competition and innovation. Over time, these regulations have been eased, allowing for the introduction of lower fares and new products, such as LCC airlines. The result has been a rapid growth in long-haul tourism alongside a growing market share of air transport in medium- and even short-haul travel.
- Changes in aviation have had profound implications for tourism. The availability of low fares has made air travel affordable for leisure tourism and has greatly stimulated

international tourism. Aviation shapes tourism – changes in aviation prices, technology and constraints have determined where tourists go to, have helped to create destinations and have bypassed them.

- Ongoing advances in aviation technology have helped shape airline cost structures and price competitiveness and placed focus on the economics that underlie the aviation industry, especially in respect of economies of density, yield management, booking systems and new aircraft types. Aviation advances have given rise to the LCC phenomenon with its focus on low price and no frills.

- Competition from the LCC is creating problems for the major airlines, many of which are loss-making, and which find it difficult to match the fares of the LCC. The chief difference between LCC and traditional airlines fall into three groups: service savings, operational savings and overhead savings.

- While aviation can help tourism to develop within a region by bringing in tourists, inadequate aviation infrastructure, such as limited airport capacity, can constrain tourism development. When limited airport capacity exists, usually for environmental reasons or simply through poor planning, the excess demand that can build up at the airport is handled through either air congestion or slot restriction. Here, government policy (taxation, subsidisation and regulation) need to be determined together.

- Aviation and tourism are obviously linked through demand – tourists obviously demand air travel. However, they are also linked through supply with economies of integration between airlines and travel agencies.

- Another aspect of the aviation – tourism connection – concerns aviation and tourism taxes. Does a country wish to encourage tourism, and maximise economic benefits of tourism, by keeping taxes, on both aviation and ground tourism, low? Or does it wish to make use of its market power, and use foreign tourists as a source of revenue? Whichever of these options it chooses, it will need to determine at which level – aviation or ground tourism – such taxes are best levied.

- The development of alliances between ostensibly independent airlines has allowed those airlines to create a wider network and services than they might otherwise be able to provide. Depending on the how and the where, such alliances can either encourage tourism through cheaper fares and improved networks or constrain it through raised fares and anti-competitive behaviour. There are costs to the individual airlines in forming alliances, usually centring on ensuring connecting flights and baggage handling, but in general the benefits appear to outweigh any costs involved.

SELF-REVIEW QUESTIONS

1. How are the aviation industry and the tourism industry linked?

2. In what ways are aviation and tourism complementary industries? In what ways do they exhibit a conflict of interest?

624

3. Briefly outline the four distinct phases of aviation liberalisation.

4. In what ways have advances in aviation technology reduced costs and enhanced price competitiveness within the aviation industry?

5. Draw up a list of direct costs and indirect costs that an airline might typically face.

6. Distinguish between economics of density and economies of scale when applied within the aviation industry.

7. Show how successful yield management by an airline relies on a working knowledge of demand elasticity.

8. How do LCC airlines differ from traditional airline carriers?

9. Distinguish between air traffic congestion and slot controls as rationing devices for flights into a city.

10. In what ways does government typically both tax and subsidise the aviation industry?

11. Why do airlines form alliances? What type of alliances can they form?

ESSAY QUESTIONS

1. Aviation and tourism are complementary industries but they also exhibit conflicts of interest. How so? What does this mean for policy?

2. De-regulation of the domestic airline industry is OK, but the international airline industry should not be liberalised. Argue for or against this proposition.

3. Using examples, explain how the presence of economies of density can influence the schedules that an airline might fly.

4. 'The chief differences between LCC and traditional airlines fall into three groups: service savings, operational savings and overhead savings.' Discuss.

5. Define yield management in the context of aviation and explain some of the issues that an airline must consider in striving to maximise its yield.

6. Choose a city and explore how that city's airport capacity may be a constraint on the development of its tourism sector.

7. Aviation and tourism are linked on both the demand side and the supply side. How so?

8. Discuss the move by airlines towards alliances in recent years. What implications do such alliances have for airline cost structures and price competitiveness? What implications do they have for airline travellers?

TOURISM AND THE ENVIRONMENT

CHAPTER 17

VALUING THE ENVIRONMENTAL IMPACTS OF TOURISM

LEARNING OBJECTIVES

After reading this chapter, you should be able to:

1. Understand how the relationship between environmental quality and tourist development is modelled.

2. Explain the concept of market failure and discuss how it can apply in a tourism context.

3. Understand tourism's potential for both positive and negative impacts on the environment.

4. Appreciate the debate between environmental preservation and tourism development.

5. Value the impacts of tourism on the environment through both direct and indirect techniques.

17.1   INTRODUCTION

The environment is important in attracting tourism flows with their attendant economic effects. Conservation of valued environmental features can help in maintaining tourism visitation and tourism's contribution to the economy. Tourists, however, can also 'love the environment to death', impairing the very thing that attracts them and bringing about its deterioration and destruction. Satisfactorily resolving this problem is important to the tourist industry, especially given a limited (and dwindling) supply of pristine environments and with tourism demand expected to grow into the future.

This chapter explores the broad positive and negative environmental impacts of tourism and examines the techniques by which these environmental effects are measured. Tourism impacts on the environment are both direct and indirect, and they often are not easily observable. Identifying and measuring environmental costs and benefits can be very difficult. Chapter 18 assesses the effectiveness of the economic instruments that have been developed to reduce tourism's negative impacts of tourism on the environment. Chapter 19 discusses tourism and climate change, where climate change, perhaps the most pressing ongoing issue of our time, will substantially affect tourism.

17.2 THE POTENTIAL IMPACTS OF TOURISM ON THE ENVIRONMENT

Tourism affects the environment through its interplay with *natural, human* and *built resources.* It is a two-edged sword, however, with the potential for both positive and negative impacts on these resources.

Natural resources include such diverse aspects as wilderness areas; wildlife habitats; the oceans, rivers and lakes; coastal landscapes; coral reefs; desert ecosystems; flora and fauna; and the like.

Human resources include the resident population and their associations, values, identities and cultural activities. Impacts arise from differences in attitudes, perceptions, values and expectations between tourists and local residents, with tourism having the power to change local value systems, collective lifestyles and family and societal relationships for better or for worse.

Built resources include ancient ruins, historic towns, monuments, streetscapes, shopping complexes, theme parks, transportation facilities, museums, recreational and sporting complexes and so on.

Tourism development and tourist activity can have adverse environmental effects on all three types of resources, including damage to ecosystems. Conversely, the range and quality of such resources can influence tourism flows. Just as tourism can impact on the environment, so too does the environment affect tourism attractiveness. The environmental threats to tourism are many and varied. In many mountain regions, small islands, coastal areas and other ecologically fragile places visited by tourists, there is an increasing concern that the negative impact of tourism on the natural environment adversely affects the tourism industry itself. Indeed, many tourism destinations are becoming overdeveloped up to the point where the damage caused by environmental degradation – and the eventual loss of revenues arising from a collapse in tourism arrivals – becomes irreversible. As we shall discuss in more detail in Chapter 19, tourism in many destinations is being threatened by external environmental shocks, notably the potential threat of global warming and sea-level rise.

Environmental attributes can increase the demand for tourism. As a rule, tourism demand is comprised of both *market* and *non-market attributes.* The demand for hotel accommodation, for instance, is made up of both market attributes (components that can readily be priced in the marketplace such as room size, extent of amenities provided, hotel location where it adds to supply costs and so on), and non-marketable attributes such as access to hotel, access to public beaches or access to wilderness areas. These non-market attributes add to the demand curve shifting it out beyond where it would be if it reflected only the market attributes. Because of the existence of non-market attributes, the firm's producer surplus rises by the shaded area $P_0 P_1 \text{FE}$ (Figure 17.1). The implications are that the attention to environmental features of the tourism experience can result in an outward shift of tourism demand, thereby increasing producer surplus.

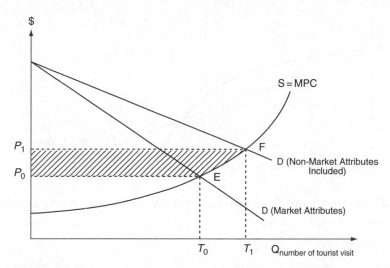

Figure 17.1 The non-market components of tourism demand lead firms to increase output and charge higher prices

Source: Tisdell (2001), p. 21

In contrast to a simple shift outward of the demand curve as illustrated in Figure 17.1, tourism demand may be subject to social influences such as bandwagon effects and snob effects (Tisdell, 1987).

Figure 17.2 illustrates the effects of these social influences on the individual tourism demand curve. The individual demand curve for tourism visits to an area, ignoring social influences, is shown by D. Where tourists positively enjoy the presence of other tourists in the area (higher tourism densities), a bandwagon effect may arise as displayed by the more

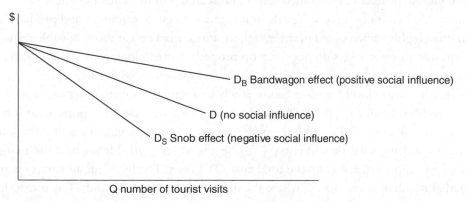

Figure 17.2 Tourism demand is influenced by tourism density

Source: From Tisdell (1987), Figure 3, p. 21

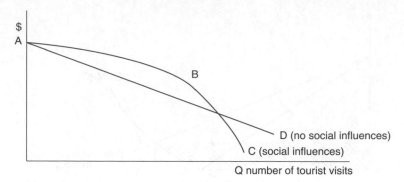

Figure 17.3 The curved tourism demand curve showing both the positive and negative social influences of tourism densities

Source: From Tisdell (1987), Figure 4, p. 21

elastic demand curve, D_B. Where tourists view increased tourist densities as negative, a snob effect may arise and the demand curve will be less elastic, D_S.

In practice, the tourism demand curve may be curved, a combination of the above positive and negative social influences.

Figure 17.3 shows that, at low visitor levels, a bandwagon effect may occur with tourists enjoying small numbers of other visitors (AB), but that the demand curve turns less elastic when visitor numbers are considered to be too large (BC). This analysis suggests that social influences should be considered in tourism policy, planning and development.

17.3 MARKET FAILURE

Economic theory informs us that, under certain circumstances, private markets can solve the economic problem of unlimited wants and scarce resources in an efficient or optimal manner. Market prices serve as signals or incentives to guide resources and products into their most highly valued uses. However, if there are no markets for some valuable resources and products or if markets do not function properly, the resulting resource allocation will not be optimal. This situation, called *market failure*, was discussed in Chapter 6.

A simple illustration of market failure is where a natural tourist attraction experiences overcrowding. Lindberg (1991) illustrates the case of overuse of a popular attraction. As shown in Figure 17.4, as visitor numbers increase, the marginal benefit of visitation decreases and the total benefit curve (TB) begins to level off. Meanwhile, the marginal cost of visitation increases and the total cost (TC) rises. The net value to society is maximised at number of visitors N_1 where the difference between TB and TC is greatest. N_1 thus represents the optimal level of visitation to this nature-based attraction.

For any number of visitors greater than N_1, the marginal benefit of each individual visit is less than the additional cost of such a visit given adverse environmental and congestion

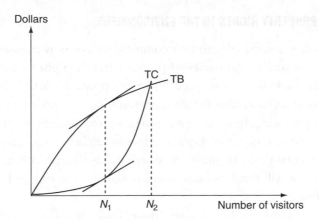

Figure 17.4 Optimal level of visitation to a natural area

Source: From Lindberg (1991)

impacts. Beyond N_1, continued use still generates gains for society (producer and consumer surpluses) since average returns exceed average costs. Under such circumstances, visitation is likely to expand to N_2 at which point the resource becomes over-exploited from the viewpoint of society's total welfare. Any level visitation beyond N_1 numbers represents a case of market failure.

As discussed in Chapter 6, market failure occurs when market prices do not reflect the full social costs or benefits associated with a product or service. More tourism may lead to environmental costs from overuse of sensitive areas or a lower quality of experience from overused attractions, extra costs through effects such as airport and road noise, Greenhouse Gas (GHG) emissions and worsening air quality. Additional tourism can place excessive demands on existing infrastructure such as roads, public transport, water and electricity supply. Congestion leads to loss of amenity, loss of leisure time, increased accidents, increased fuel consumption and greater pollution. To take another example, much production activity in tourism as well as in other industries involves the emission of GHGs, resulting in temperature increases. The climatic changes that result impose costs (and some benefits) on society. However, since the full costs of GHG emissions are not borne by the emitters, they have faced little or no economic incentive to reduce emissions. For example, commercial airfares, guided by private market forces of demand and supply, do not fully cover the true costs of flying which include noise pollution as well as the effects of the GHGs emitted by the aircraft. Similarly, a museum entry fee may not reflect the social benefits of museum visitation.

There are three major sources of market failure that are relevant to the environmental impacts associated with tourism. These are situations associated with lack of property rights to environmental resources, public goods and externalities.

17.3.1 LACK OF PROPERTY RIGHTS TO THE ENVIRONMENT

Market failure is often associated with an incomplete and/or non-transparent distribution of property rights in society. An owner of property has the right to consume, sell, rent, mortgage, transfer, exclude and exchange his or her property. A well-defined system of property rights provides incentives for efficient resource use and investments in sustainable management practices. However, in situations where it is unclear who has the right to use an environmental resource, it is also unclear whose rights can be restricted in order to promote environmental goals. In situations where this is the case, often environmentally destructive behaviour will result because there is no one that can be held liable for the environmental costs.

A lack of clear and enforceable property rights leads to the most pronounced forms of environmental degradation in cases of open-access resources. The environment is the modern equivalent of 'the commons'. Because no one owns environmental resources (e.g. air, lakes and the oceans), no prices are attached to using them. As a consequence, private economic decision makers (producers and consumers) are not receiving the correct signals concerning the full range of costs and benefits associated with use of these resources. Since their production and consumption decisions are based on the private benefits and private costs of alternative actions rather than any social benefits or social costs, the inevitable result is overuse, abuse, congestion and quality degradation of increasingly scarce environmental resources.

A lack of property rights to environmental resources characterises many contexts of tourism growth and development. It helps to explain why tourism activity can result in the environmental degradation of marine life, limestone caverns, wilderness areas and animal habitats.

17.3.2 THE PUBLIC GOOD ASPECT OF ENVIRONMENTAL RESOURCES

Underpinning the lack of a well-defined and enforceable system of property rights is the public good aspect of many environmental services.

In the case of a private good:

- its increased consumption by one individual reduces the amount available for others; and
- it is usually possible to exclude other individuals from consuming it if they do not purchase it.

In the case of a public good:

- the quantity of the commodity is not reduced by its consumption by any individual (non-exclusivity); and
- it is impossible to exclude everyone from enjoying the whole supply (non-rivalry).

Public goods tend not to be profitable for private sector provision because of these two characteristics. Market failure implies that the profits of businesses are inadequate as an indicator of the socially optimal use and development of resources.

Non-exclusivity

Non-exclusivity means that the ownership of the good or service cannot be established and thus cannot be sold. Public goods are *non-exclusive* in that they cannot be confined to just those who pay for them. It is physically impossible or economically inefficient to exclude non-payers from consuming them, for example, the attractive views of a city, road signage, radio broadcasts, national defence or even the light of streetlamps. This non-exclusivity allows some users to be *free riders*, using the good or service for free while others pay for the service. If it is costly or impossible to withhold a public good from people who can avoid paying for it, then the market system breaks down because everyone has the incentive to avoid paying for the good. When many attempt to free ride, however, the good will not be produced by private firms because there is no profit in it.

The classic example of a non-exclusivity is that of the lighthouse where any ship at sea can be guided by its light. Tourism abounds in examples of free riding and public goods. Tourists use local beaches, parks, roads, signage and street lighting without ostensibly paying for their provision or upkeep. They enjoy the free use of communal goods and services set up and paid for by the local community.

Non-rivalry

Public goods are also *non-rivalrous* in that they can be consumed 'jointly' by many people and one person's enjoyment of the good or service does not lessen another person's enjoyment of it. Regarding the lighthouse, not only can one not exclude people in the area from consuming its service but there is also no extra cost involved in the provision of that service for an extra person. Just as several ships can benefit from the lighthouse beam simultaneously, a person's enjoyment of looking at the Grand Canyon or a skydiving display does not preclude another person's view or lessen his/her enjoyment in looking at it. Since consumers are not rivals in consumption, marginal cost is zero and the price should therefore be zero.

The above considerations of property rights and public goods lead to an appreciation of the dual pressures resulting in and sustaining environmental misuse. On the one hand, because of the absence of private property rights in many environmental resources, consumers and producers lack incentive to take account of the full (private plus external) costs of their behaviour, leading to overuse of these resources. On the other hand, the public goods nature of some environmental aspects results in incentives to 'free ride' on the efforts of others, leading to an under-allocation of resources to these activities. The upshot is that public goods will not be provided in the right amounts by the market mechanism.

Goods which are either non-excludable or non-rivalrous but not both are referred to as 'semi' or 'quasi' public. An example of a non-excludable but rival good is a congested motorway. An example of a non-rival but excludable good would be a coded TV broadcast. For these types of goods the cost of providing the good increases less than proportionately to the number who benefit from it and, additionally, there are some difficulties in excluding those who do not pay from the benefit of the good. These two conditions are relative. Some quasi-public goods will come nearer the public end of the spectrum, in that costs increase much less proportionately than the number of beneficiaries and there are substantial difficulties in excluding non-payers. Other quasi-public goods are closer to the purely private end of the spectrum, in that costs increase almost in proportion to the number of beneficiaries and there is only minor difficulty in excluding non-payers. The closer is the good to the public end of the spectrum, the greater is its 'degree of publicness'. To illustrate in a tourism context, a good may be considered to be a quasi-public good if, at a certain level of use, one's enjoyment of it is diminished by another's use, for example, if the area for observing the fireworks display becomes crowded out or a street becomes crowded. Similarly, wilderness areas, national parks, highways and bridges may be considered quasi-public goods if people pay a fee to enter or a camping fee to stay or toll to cross.

17.3.3 OPTIMAL QUANTITY OF A PUBLIC GOOD

If resources are to be allocated efficiently, how much should be produced of a public good? Suppose for simplicity that there are only two groups of consumers, Gen X and Gen Y. Suppose that D_x is Gen X's demand curve for a good and D_y is Gen Y's demand curve for the same good.

Assuming that the good is a *private good* produced under perfect competition, the demand curves (marginal private benefits) are summed horizontally to obtain the market demand

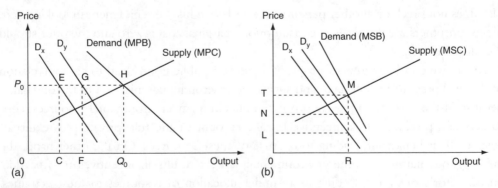

Figure 17.5 (a) Estimating aggregate demand for a private good (b) Estimating aggregate demand for a public good

curve. In Figure 17.5a the optimal output is Q_0, where this market demand curve intersects the market supply curve S the aggregate of marginal private costs. At this output, the marginal benefit each consumer would obtain from an extra unit of the good (measured by willingness to pay (WTP)) equals its marginal cost. Equilibrium price is P_0 with quantity Q_0. Since CE = FG = Q_0H, it follows that the marginal benefit to each consumer equals the marginal cost of provision of the good.

If, however, the good is a *public good*, such as the amount of street lighting or road signage, or environmental conservation measure, the optimal amount is shown by Figure 17.5b. In this case, the market demand curve is obtained by summing the Gen X and Gen Y demand curves *vertically*. This is because both consumer groups consume the same total amount of the good. The combined price paid by the two groups is the sum of the prices paid by each one. The supply curve is the marginal social cost curve and the demand curve is the marginal social benefits curve. The total price (the sum of the prices paid by Gen X and Gen Y) is OT.

The optimal output, OR, is that where marginal social benefit equals marginal social cost. The marginal social benefit from an extra unit of output of a public good is obtained by adding vertically the distance under every consumer's demand curve. This is because all consumers share entirely in the consumption of whatever quantity of the good is available and because the marginal social benefit is the sum of the marginal benefits to each consumer. The optimal output OR is where marginal social benefit (OT) equals the marginal social cost (RM).

Consider the provision of a public good that is either provided in a discrete amount or not provided at all (Tisdell, 1982: 407). Suppose, for instance, that it is a public garden for recreation in an urban area which is used by members of both Gen X and Gen Y. Suppose that the annual upkeep of the garden is $100,000. Four possibilities exist:

Case 1. Gens X and Y together value the garden at less than $100,000;

Case 2. Gens X and Y together value the garden at more than $100,000 annually and the valuation of each is less than $100,000;

Case 3. The valuation of one is greater than $100,000 annually and that of the other is less than $100,000; or

Case 4. The valuation of each is in excess of $100,000 annually.

In Case 1, it is inefficient to supply the garden, but in the other three cases Paretian efficiency requires that the garden be supplied since the sum of the valuations exceed the cost of its supply. In Case 2, neither Gen X nor Gen Y can gain by supplying the garden, although they would benefit collectively. In the absence of collective or public action, the garden will not be supplied in this case. In Case 3, the only group able to gain by supplying the garden is likely to supply it since the other group has no incentive to provide it independently, even though it gains if the facility is provided. In Case 4, Gen X and Gen Y can each gain individually by supplying the garden. However, each group has an incentive to free ride when its gains are higher if another party provides the facility and there is a chance that the other party might provide it. However, if each waits for the other to supply the facility, it is not supplied and the outcome is Pareto inefficient. In Case 4, government or collective action is required to ensure Pareto efficiency. In Case 3, government intervention might be justified on equity grounds.

The example indicates that in the absence of government intervention, the supply of public goods will be less than optimal. There are two related reasons for this:

(1) *The Free Rider Problem.* Since the public good is (by definition) non-exclusive, implying that individuals not paying for it cannot be excluded from consuming it, as indicated above there is a tendency for each individual to be a free rider. The free rider problem arises because each consumer believes that the public good will be provided anyway, whether or not he or she contributes to its payment. Since many individuals will withhold their financial support from provision of the good, a less than optimal amount of the good will is provided. In general, the greater the size of the group, the more acute is the free rider problem. Such goods will be underprovided by the private sector since suppliers are unlikely to be able to recover the full costs of their provision. This problem is most often overcome by the government taxing the general public to pay for the supply of the public good.

(2) *Disincentive to Reveal WTP.* Individuals have little or no incentive to accurately reveal their preferences or demand for public goods. Thus it is practically impossible for the government to determine exactly what the optimal amount of the public good is that it should provide or induce the private sector to provide. The problem does not arise with private goods since the market provides signals to producers as to how much of a good needs to be produced. Since the market will not provide adequate signals of how much of a public good the government should supply, Cost-Benefit Analysis (CBA) is often used (see Chapter 10). As we shall discuss below, survey techniques can elicit individual WTP for the provision of public goods.

It must be emphasised that not all goods supplied by the public sector are 'public goods'. Sometimes governments supply goods to avoid monopolies in decreasing cost industries, to maintain competition, to provide 'merit' goods or to influence the distribution of income. As discussed, a 'public good' is defined as one which has the characteristics of non-exclusivity and non-rivalry.

17.3.4 EXTERNALITIES

Where market forces and signals do not reflect the full range of costs and benefits associated with production and consumption, the goods and services traded are said to generate *externalities* (sometimes called spillover or neighbourhood effects). Externalities exist when a third party receives benefits or incurs costs arising from an economic transaction in which he or she is not a direct participant. Externalities were discussed in Chapter 6 and also in Chapter 10.

A useful classification of externalities, regardless of whether they appear as external costs or as external benefits, is set out in Table 17.1. This table also indicates how resource misallocation can occur when externalities from consumption or production are ignored. Because private sector production and consumption decisions are based on private costs and private benefits rather than on social costs and social benefits, producers and consumers do not take into account the full range of costs and benefits of their behaviour.

When externalities exist there is a divergence between private returns – those accruing to the direct parties in an economic transaction – and social returns – those accruing to the indirect parties in such a transaction. We remind the reader of the distinction between private and social costs and private and social benefits. As we have seen, the market fails when the social costs or social benefits that arise from the production and consumption of private goods and services are not fully reflected in market prices. There is little incentive for firms or consumers either to curb external costs (since they do directly pay for them) or to foster external benefits (since they do not directly benefit from them), and so, while costs are passed on to the public at large, benefits are not.

The impact of external costs associated with tourism can be illustrated through a diagram. Suppose that tourism development in a coastal town imposes costs on others (households, firms in other industries) by way of air, noise, rowdy behaviour, water and waste pollution.

Figure 17.6 shows both the competitive market price-quantity equilibrium and the socially optimal price-quantity combination. Q can be thought of as units of tourism services or products, the curve S (= MPC) is the industry supply curve, reflecting private production costs of tourism firms. The *marginal external cost* (MXC) is the vertical difference between the MSC and the MPC. It measures the amount of the negative externality (i.e. MSC = MPC + MXC). The competitive market equilibrium is at point C (P_0, Q_0), where demand by visitors to the area (MPB) is matched by the supply of tourist facilities and services (MPC). Society's equilibrium, which includes the external cost of negative impacts associated with the tourism, is at point A (Q^*, P^*).

From society's (the local residents') viewpoint, the market price does not reflect the true cost of tourists visiting the area. Too much tourism is occurring and it is experienced too cheaply. The local residents incur the external costs. The firms in the industry do not consider the external costs in their willingness to supply particular quantities of tourism services at various prices. For each unit of output beyond Q^*, however, the marginal social costs of production exceed the value which consumers attach to the additional

Table 17.1 Classification of externalities

Type of Externality	Definition	Example of Positive Externality	Example of Negative Externality
Production on consumption	when industrial activity affects the community	Busking activity in popular tourist precincts lends added ambience to the area for the enjoyment of residents	Construction and roadwork activity associated with large sporting events can lead to traffic problems for residents
Production on production	when one industry (or firm) affects another industry or firm	Regulated trucking hours results in less motorway congestion for tourist coaches	Noise and congestion associated with the construction of major sporting facilities in an area drive customers away from local businesses
Consumption on consumption	when consumers of some good or service affect the well being of other consumers	The presence of other screaming passengers on the roller coaster can enhance the thrill experienced by all	The congregation of large numbers of tourists in an area can lead to loss of enjoyment of that area by non-tourist locals
Consumption on production	when consumers of some product affect an industry or firm	Tourist visits to Angkor Wat foster better restaurant, accommodation and transportation services in Siem Reap	Tourist visits to Angkor Wat generate litter which is cleared at the expense of the local community

consumption. The loss to society from over-production to Q_0 is the area ABC. This area also represents the gains to society if production by tourism firms were to be cut back from Q_0 to Q^*.

In Chapter 18, we will consider different types of policies that can be implemented to policy makers to bring about a socially optimal level of industry output.

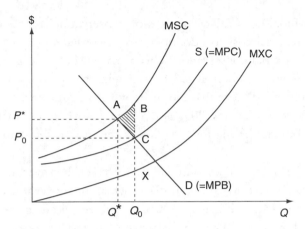

Figure 17.6 Tourism development and negative externalities

17.4   ENVIRONMENTAL PRESERVATION VERSUS DEVELOPMENT

Where there is potential for considerable externalities to arise, such as associated with development within national parks, government is often a key decision maker regarding the extent of any such development. Political decisions, however, may result in either too much conservation or too little conservation. In Figure 17.7, MBC (marginal

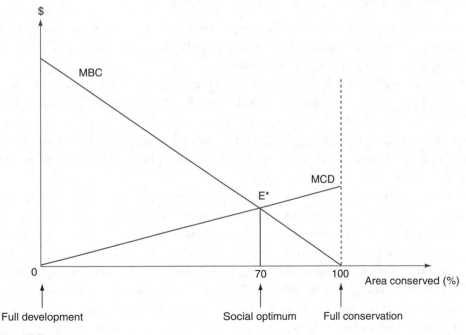

Figure 17.7 Social optimum a majority decision rule is applied

641

benefit to conservationists) is the willingness of conservationists to pay to conserve an area, and MCD (marginal cost to developers from conservation) is the willingness of developers to pay to avoid conservation. Given that an outcome is more efficient if a Pareto optimal outcome can be reached by arranging some compensation from those that are made better off to those that are made worse off, the social optimum is where 70% of the area is conserved and 30% is developed – where the marginal benefits to conservationists from conserving the area equals the marginal cost to developers from conservation.

Depending on the political decision-making processes, however, the social optimum may not be realised. If majority rule is in place (where the government is influenced by majority opinion), then the area may be 100% conserved – leading to too much conservation from a social optimum viewpoint. Alternately, if developers exert power, 100% of the area may be developed – leading to too little conservation from a social optimum viewpoint. This analysis suggests that, from an economic point of view, a compromise is optimal, but may not occur. In view of the influence that natural areas proximate to tourism businesses may have in influencing the demand curve (see Figure 17.1), it is understandable that the tourist industry may lobby governments for greater preservation of natural areas within a destination.

17.5 VALUING THE IMPACTS OF TOURISM ON THE ENVIRONMENT: TOTAL ECONOMIC VALUE

In order to assess the impacts of tourism on the environment, economists attempt to apply dollar values to those impacts, making price the yardstick by which impacts can be valued and compared, and economic decisions made.

Valuing the impact of tourism on the environment presents some difficulties. For one, the natural resources used for tourism tend to be mixed goods that hold value for many different purposes (Tisdell, 2001). Secondly, it is often hard to separate present and future environmental concerns. Thirdly, while some external costs and benefits can be valued *directly* through their obvious price effect in the marketplace, others have to be valued *indirectly* through the use of proxy prices.

It is important to try to value tourism impacts on the environment. Tourism development often involves a trade-off between positive and negative impacts. Continually, we need to decide on issues such as whether or not to allow tourist access to delicate ecosystems or whether or not to build a profitable resort that will have adverse environmental impacts. Increasingly, governments are formulating policies to address GHG emissions from aviation. To make such decisions, effectively and efficiently, we must be able to measure and compare the relative values of good and bad impacts. The diagrams above highlight ideal solutions where the marginal social costs and social benefits associated with tourism's environmental effects can be

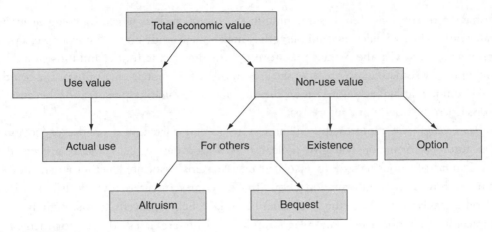

Figure 17.8 Total economic value

measured. We now discuss methods which economists use to value these environmental effects.

The standard approach to assessing tourism impacts is to estimate the Total Economic Value of an environmental attribute. As displayed in Figure 17.8, the total economic value is the sum of the amenity's total use and total non-use values, such that

$$\text{Total Economic Value} = \text{Total Use Value} + \text{Total Non-use Value}$$

17.5.1 USE VALUE

Actual use value is the direct value to humans in their use of some environmental amenity. It is reflected in the actual market price of that amenity. The market price is considered a fair measure of the relative 'value' of the amenity to the user. It reflects the maximum amount that a person is willing to give up to get more of something. For example, the fee of US$20 per person per day for a tourist to enter the Angkor Wat world heritage complex shows the minimum direct use value that each visitor attaches to a visit to the site.

17.5.2 NON-USE VALUE

Since many environmental amenities are not traded in markets and are not closely related to any marketed goods and services, people cannot 'reveal' what they are willing to pay for them through direct market purchase prices. An amenity may be valued for its non-marketed attributes such as beauty, charm and pleasure.

Option value measures the value of delaying the use of some environmental aspect until later, for example, preserving a wilderness area or urban streetscape now for future possible use, respectively, as a National Park or tourist precinct. It is the value that people place

643

on having the option to enjoy something in the future, such as whale watching or white water rafting in the wilderness, although they may not currently do so. For example, a person may hope to visit the Brazilian rainforests sometime in the future, and thus would be willing to pay something to preserve the area in order to maintain that option. If a tourist site is unique, individuals not visiting the site may still value its preservation because it keeps open the option of a future visit.

Quasi-option value captures the willingness to forego current use on the expectation that future information will give a clearer view of what its uses are. It reflects the extra value of choosing not to take irreversible steps associated with tourism development now if new information about the outcomes of alternative decisions might become available in the future. An example might be to prevent tourist activity in a tropical area abundant in exotic plants until the plants are assessed fully for medicinal purposes.

Existence value is the 'price' people place on an environmental amenity in order to preserve it. It captures the intrinsic value of an environmental aspect in its own right, independent of human use. It is an expression of willingness to forego current use to retain the amenity irrespective of any future use. For instance, people may place value on the continued existence on a wilderness area containing animals in their natural habitat, with no intention of ever visiting it, but simply to maintain its existence. Similarly, one may view a world in which whales swim the oceans as better than one without whales. This reflects a respect for nature and acknowledges human responsibilities towards preserving it.

Bequest value measures the value that the present generation places on preserving an environmental amenity for the benefit of future generations. It reflects the value that people place on knowing that future generations will have the option to enjoy something. Thus, bequest value is measured by peoples' WTP to preserve the natural environment for future generations. For example, a person may be willing to pay to protect Arizona's Grand Canyon so that future generations, including future tourists, will have the opportunity to enjoy it. An imputation of bequest value helps to ensure a legacy of endowing natural environments undamaged by human activity to future generations.

Altruism or vicarious value measures the value that people attach to the knowledge that others are enjoying use of the natural environment passively or actively. It reflects the value that people place on knowing that other people enjoy features of natural environments. Thus, altruism is measured by peoples' WTP to preserve the natural environment for the present generation to experience and enjoy.

For some natural amenities the non-use (indirect) option, existence, bequest and altruism values, when summed together, can outweigh the direct use value of that amenity (see Bandara & Tisdell, 2003).

Box 17.1 describes the measurement of Total Economic Value.

BOX 17.1 Estimating total economic value

Figure 17.9 shows on the vertical axis the monetary value (costs/benefits) associated with some environmental amenity and on the horizontal axis the number of tourist visits per period.

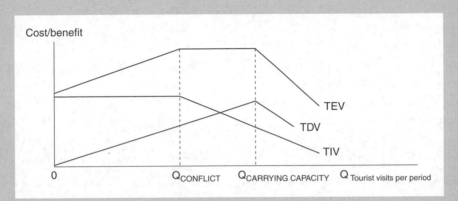

Figure 17.9 Total economic value per visitor numbers per period

Source: Modified from Tisdell (2006)

The total direct use value (TDV) curve is assumed to rise with the number of tourist visits (indicating increasing benefits from use of the amenity) until the amenity's carrying capacity is reached $Q_{\text{CARRYING CAPACITY}}$, after which it declines with increasing tourist visits. Carrying capacity represents the maximum number of tourists using the environmental amenity beyond which their satisfaction from the environment amenity begins to suffer.

The total indirect (non-use) value (TIV) curve is the sum of the amenity's non-use option, existence, bequest and vicarious values. Up to a certain level of visitation TIV may be expected to remain constant irrespective of the number of tourist visits (i.e. its value is considered to be independent of tourist visits). After the conflict level is reached (Q_{CONFLICT}), the value of TIV would be expected to decline with increasing tourist use. The conflict level represents the level at which tourism begins to impact adversely on the environment.

The total economic value (TEV) curve is the vertical sum of the total direct use value and total non-use value curves. The TEV curve rises in line with TDV until Q_{CONFLICT}, after which it levels off as the falling TIV curve crosses the still rising TDV curve, then begins to decline after $Q_{\text{CARRYING CAPACITY}}$ as both TDV and TIV fall. The seemingly even trade-off between the TDV and TIV curves between Q_{CONFLICT} and $Q_{\text{CARRYING CAPACITY}}$ (hence the constant peak of the TEV curve) is arbitrary. In practice, TEV will continue to rise between Q_{CONFLICT} and $Q_{\text{CARRYING CAPACITY}}$ if the rise in TDV outweighs the fall in TIV. Similarly, TEV will fall between Q_{CONFLICT} and $Q_{\text{CARRYING CAPACITY}}$ if the fall in TIV outweighs the rise in TDV.

The diagram above is merely illustrative. In reality, Q_{CONFLICT} and $Q_{\text{CARRYING CAPACITY}}$ may be more to the left or right. The points may also be closer to each other or further apart, depending on the amenity under consideration. Tourism to the Antarctic, for instance, may have conflict and capacity levels much closer to zero than tourism to a beach.

Figure 17.9 can be used to guide policy. It suggests that any particular tourist activity will have positive, but no negative, impacts on the environment until the number of visits per period reaches Q_{CONFLICT}. For visitor levels above that, however, the trade-off between TDV and TIV needs to be carefully monitored.

17.6   ESTIMATING THE NON-USE VALUE OF ENVIRONMENTAL AMENITIES

There are three generally accepted practical methods for measuring the non-use value of an environmental amenity:

* *stated preference* – value is determined through a survey of peoples' preferences in hypothetical market situations in which people state what they would do in a given situation(s);
* *revealed preference* – value is determined through peoples' observed behaviour in related markets;
* *imputed valuation* – value is determined through the actual costs that people undertake either to avoid loss of an amenity or to store a lost amenity.

17.6.1   STATED PREFERENCE

Stated preference techniques (direct valuation) attempt to elicit preferences in a direct way by use of survey or questionnaire. This enables economic values to be estimated for a wide range of commodities which are not traded in real markets.

The two basic stated preference approaches that use surveys to elicit value through peoples' responses to given hypothetical situations are *contingent valuation* and *contingent choice*.

17.6.1.1   Contingent valuation method

The Contingent Valuation Method (CVM) is the most widely used method for estimating non-use value. The basic principle of CVM is that people have preferences in relation to all goods including goods that are not available in any existing market. CVM attempts to reveal these hidden preferences by means of questionnaires. People are asked the maximum amount of money they are willing to pay (or willing to accept as compensation) for a hypothetical change in the quantity or quality of a good. It is assumed that this professed WTP would equate to actual willingness if a real market for the good did exist. The method is called 'contingent' valuation because people are asked to state their willingness to pay (accept), contingent on a specific hypothetical scenario and description of the environmental amenity. As we have stated earlier,

- *Willingness to Pay* (WTP) reflects how much of all other goods and services a person is willing to give up either to gain or retain that amenity.
- *Willingness to Accept* (WTA) assumes that the amenity already belongs to the people and so measures the monetary compensation that people are willing to accept for loss of that amenity.

A typical CVM survey consists of four parts (Nunes & Nijkamp, 2009).

The first part describes the environmental change that will occur if the policy is implemented. Ideally, this means describing the availability (or quality) of the environmental commodity in both its present state (the *status quo*) and 'projected state' (after enacting the policy).

The second part describes the contingent market. Since all monetary transactions occur in a social context, it is essential to define the contingent market. This involves informing the respondent about the rules specifying the conditions that would lead to policy implementation as well as how mode of payment that would apply to the respondent's household.

In the third part the respondent is asked to state his/her monetary valuation for the described policy formulation. This part is the core of the survey. The major objective of this section is to obtain a monetary measure of the maximum WTP of respondents for the described environmental policy action.

The fourth part of the CVM instrument is a set of questions that collect socio-demographic information about the respondents. The answers to these questions help to better characterise the respondent's profile and are used to understand the respondent's stated WTP responses. This part can be extended with follow-up questions.

CVM can be used to put dollar values on non-market values of the environment, including everything from the basic life support functions associated with ecosystem health or biodiversity, to the enjoyment of a scenic vista or a wilderness experience, to appreciating the option to go hiking, fishing or rafting in the future or the right to bequest those options to one's grandchildren. It also includes the value people place on simply knowing that giant apes, whales and rainforests exist. CVM studies have been published on wildlife and the environment (Chase *et al.*, 1998; Giraud *et al.*, 2002; Nunes & Nijkamp, 2009), and various outdoor recreation and ecotourism settings (Bhat, 2003; Dharmaratne *et al.*, 2000; Lee, 1997; Lee *et al.*, 1998; Lockwood & Tracy, 1995; Solomon *et al.*, 2004). CVM has also been applied to valuing cultural heritage (Beltran & Rojas, 1996; Bille Hansen, 1997; Chambers *et al.*, 1998; Lockwood *et al.*, 1996; Pollicino & Maddison, 2001; Salazar & Marques, 2005).

Advantages of CVM

- CVM is very flexible in that it can be used to estimate the economic value of virtually anything.
- CVM allows the estimation of an amenity's total value rather than just its individual attributes.
- It uses open-ended survey techniques that can determine maximum WTP and WTA.
- CVM is particularly useful in approximating passive use values such as option, existence, bequest and vicarious values.
- CVM covers residents and visitors evaluations alike.
- CVM is compatible with the concepts of democracy and community values. It is an accepted tenet of tourism planning that developments must have general community support if they are to be sustainable over the longer term.
- The constructed nature of CVM enables the valuation of environmental changes that have not yet occurred. CVM thus offers a greater potential scope and flexibility than the revealed preference methods since it is possible to specify different states of nature (policy scenarios) that may even lie outside the current institutional arrangements or levels of provision. Thus CVM can be a useful advisory tool for policy decision-making (Nunes & Nijkamp, 2009).

Limitations of CVM

- CVM assumes that people understand the amenity in question and will reveal their preferences in the contingent market just as they would in a real market. Most people, however, are unfamiliar with placing dollar values on environmental amenities and therefore may not have an adequate incentive for stating their true value (Rahim, 2008).
- The choices of the rich, who have more ability to pay, carry more weight than those of the poor.
- Because it is based on 'buying', CVM reflects only the minimum value people put on the environmental resource.
- Peoples' stated values may not be the same as what they would actually to willing to pay (accept). Respondents may act 'strategically'. Thus, response values may be unrealistically high if people believe they will not have to pay for the amenity and that their answer may influence the resulting supply of the good. Conversely, response values may be

unrealistically low if people believe they will actually have to pay. It may be that WTP would be much lower if the respondent were made to pay at the time of the survey.

- Respondents may give different WTP amounts, depending on the specific mode of payment. For example, some payment modes, such as taxes, may lead to protest responses from people who do not want increased taxes. Other payment methods, such as contributions or donations, may lead people to answer in terms of how much they think their 'fair share' contribution is, rather than expressing their actual value for the particular good.

- It has been argued that people derive greater benefit ('warm glow') from saying that they would contribute to a good cause than through greater consumption. For this reason, Kahneman and Knetsch (1992) regard CVM to be more a reflection of WTP for moral satisfaction than a valid means of assigning monetary value to a natural resource.

- As the difference between WTP and actual behaviour, or hypothetical bias, has come under scrutiny, the idea of 'cheap talk' was introduced. The cheap talk design includes an actual discussion of hypothetical bias in the survey in an attempt to make it an integral part of the survey instrument (Cummings & Taylor, 1999; Nunes & Schokkaert, 2003).

Box 17.2 summarises a study of the value of forests for tourism in Sweden, using CVM.

BOX 17.2 The value of forests for tourism in Sweden

Approximately 60% of Sweden is forested and is an important attraction for tourism. The Right of Common Access means that visitors can enter and enjoy forests without having to pay for them. They must of course pay for goods and services such as lodging, fishing, and use of various facilities. What the individual tourist experiences is thus a composite good, which includes market-priced as well as non-market-priced components.

In their study of the value of forests for tourism in Sweden, Bostedt and Mattsson (1995) address two questions:

(1) *what do forest characteristics mean for Swedish tourism in economic terms?* That is, how much do tourists value the forest as an environment for activities such as hiking, walking, fishing, camping, and the like? In this context, the authors emphasise that the concept 'forest characteristics' comprises not only the trees, but all attributes of the forest that form its value to tourists. Since these forest attributes result to a large extent from forest management practices,

(2) *how should Swedish forestry be modified in order to increase the value of forest nature to tourists?* The authors apply the contingent valuation method (CVM) to elicit the visitor's maximum willingness-to-pay (WTP) for a trip to a forested area. The question was 'What is the maximum amount you would be willing to pay for a trip such as the one you have made up to now?' The aim was to assess the value of the nonmarket-priced components of the tourists' experience, in addition to the market priced components. This means that a value was estimated for the tourists' experience that equals the price it would have fetched if market imperfections had not existed – i.e. if all components had been market-priced.

Method

Empirical data from two tourist areas were used. These areas were chosen as being 'nature tourism areas' representative of Southern Sweden and Northern Sweden, respectively. The two areas are Harasjijmala in the south and Arjeplog in the north. Two hundred thirty-six questionnaires were distributed in Harasjbmala, and 240 in Arjeplog.

Some questions concerned the travel distance between residence and the tourist area, the time spent in the area, and the time away from home (up to the departure from the area), household size, household income, and the actual cost for the tourist trip (up to the departure area). Questions were also asked to obtain data to estimate how much of the WTP value of the trip was attributable to the actual tourist area, and how much of the area's value was assignable to the experience of the forest characteristics. The first of these questions involved marking a point on a graphic scale from 0 % to 100 %, while the second question involved distributing a sum of 100 'points' to six different 'power of attraction' categories (including an open alternative) – one of them being forest characteristics.

To obtain information on the tourists' preferences regarding forest attributes, a question was asked about what would have made the experience in the area more positive (if the respondent was not totally satisfied with the situation as it was). The respondent was requested to mark one of two alternatives associated with five different forest attributes – 'My experience would have been more positive if the forest': 'had been more dense/more open'; 'had more/less broad leaved trees'; 'had more clearcuts but each of them smaller/had fewer clearcuts but each of them bigger'; 'had more/fewer old trees'; and 'had been more accessible and visited by more people/had been less accessible and visited by fewer people' (i.e., accessibility in a physical sense, via roads etc., not in a legal sense). Another question asked 'If forest characteristics in the area had been in total accordance with your preferences – how much higher would your valuation of the tourist trip have been?' The aim of these two questions was to obtain data which, in combination with data from the CVM question, could provide information on how the value of forests to tourists might be enhanced by changing forest management practices.

In the regression analyses undertaken to determine the value of forest characteristics, the increase in WTP value of the tourist trip was the dependent variable, with preferences regarding forest attributes as explanatory variables. In this question, the respondent was asked to mark one of the many 10 %-intervals presented as answer alternatives, thereby denoting the value increase if the forest nature had been in complete accordance with his/her preferences (or the 0% alternative if the respondent was already totally satisfied). The interval midpoints were used as proxies for obtaining the dependent variable.

Results

Some important measures are summarized in Table 17.2. Given the long travel distance for many tourists visiting the northern area, their average cost for the trip (see A in the table) is higher than that for the southern tourists (though the average cost on site may be higher for the southern tourists since they stay for a longer time). Moreover, the mean value of the trip (B in the table), as well as the 'consumer surplus' (the value of the trip minus the actual cost for it – i.e., B minus A), is higher for tourists visiting the northern area than for those visiting the southern area.

Table 17.2 also shows that the mean value of the visit in the area (C in the table) is lower for the southern tourists than for the northern tourists. However, the

Table 17.2 Magnitudes of Cost and Values in SEK' for the Southern (Harasjiimila) and the northern (Arjeplog) Tourists (mean figures per household and visit)

Cost and value	The Southern tourists	The Northern tourists
A: Actual cost for the tourist trip	2325	4401
B: Value (WTP) of the tourist trip	3089	6868
C: Value of the visit in the area	2367	3052
D: Value of the forest nature in the area	386	418

* A SEK is approximately USD 0.12

area's share of the value of the tourist trip (i.e. C/B) is much larger for the average southern tourist than for the northern tourist. For the value of the forest nature in the area (D in the table), the figure for the average southern is slightly lower than that for the northern tourist, though the forest nature's share of the value of the visit in the area (i.e. D/C) is somewhat larger for the southern than for the northern tourist.

With respect to the issue of how should Swedish forestry be modified in order to increase the value of forest nature to tourists, the results may be summarised thus:

- For the southern tourists the value of the trip would be higher if the forest were more open (had less stand density, than at present, while such an indication is not found for the northern area.
- For the southern area, more broad leaved trees in the forest would obviously have a positive effect on the value. This is also the case for the northern area, where a comparison between the coefficient for this forest attribute and the coefficients for the other attributes suggests that an increase of broad leaved trees would be the most effective way to increase the value.
- With respect to clearcuts, a decrease in the size and increase in the number would positively affect the value of the forests in both areas.
- Increased accessibility to the forest-which to a considerable extent corresponds to the road network (e.g. wood truck roads) would positively affect its value for the northern tourists. In this sense, the area is still a 'relative wilderness'. The figures for the southern tourists suggest that the 'balance' between the accessibility of the forest and the concentration of tourists is appropriate.

The study indicate that for the two areas investigated, a considerable portion of the value to tourists is attributable to forest characteristics, and thus the value of forest nature can be increased by modifying forest management practices.

Source: Bostedt, G. and L. Mattsson (1995) 'The Value of Forests for Tourism in Sweden', *Annals of Tourism Research*, 22(3), 671–680

17.6.1.2 Contingent choice method

The Contingent Choice Method (CCM) asks respondents to state a preference between one group of environmental attributes, at a given price or cost to the individual, and another group of environmental attributes at a different price or cost. Willingness to pay (accept) can then be inferred from the hypothetical choices that include cost as an attribute (Hanley *et al.*, 2001; Louvier *et al.*, 2000).

Contingent choice, also referred to as *conjoint analysis*, measures preferences for different attributes of a multi-attribute choice. CCM is similar to CVM, in that it can be used to estimate economic values for many environmental services, but differs in that it does not directly ask individuals to state their values. Instead, values are inferred from the hypothetical choices or trade-offs that people make between sets of attributes.

Because it focuses on trade-offs among scenarios with different characteristics, CCM is especially suited to policy decisions where a set of possible actions might result in different impacts on natural resources or environmental services (Rahim, 2008).

There are a variety of different survey-based formats for applying contingent choice methods (Rahim, 2008), including:

- *Contingent Ranking* – respondents are asked to compare and rank alternate programme outcomes with various attributes, including costs. For instance, people might be asked to compare and then rank in order of preference several mutually exclusive environmental improvement programmes under consideration for a beach reserve, each of which has different outcomes and different costs.
- *Discrete Choice* – respondents are simultaneously shown two or more different alternatives and their attributes and asked to identify the most preferred alternative in the choice.
- *Paired Rating* – a variation on the discrete choice format, respondents are asked to compare two alternative situations and rate them in terms of strength of preference. For example, persons might be asked to compare the environmental outcomes of two different development options for a tourism destination, and to state which option is preferred, and whether it is strongly, moderately or slightly preferred to the alternative.

Whichever format is selected, the choices that respondents make are statistically analysed using discrete choice statistical techniques, to determine the relative values for the different attributes. If one of the attributes is a monetary price, then it is possible to compute the respondent's WTP for the other attributes. In order to collect useful data and provide meaningful results, contingent choice surveys must be properly designed, pre-tested and implemented (Rahim, 2008).

Advantages of CCM
- CCM can be used to value the outcomes of an action as a whole (e.g. an integrated tourism development strategy) as well as the individual attributes or effects of the action (e.g. the effect on a particular beach of a project to reduce sand erosion).
- Respondents may be able to give more meaningful answers to questions about their behaviour (preference for one alternative over another) rather than to questions that

ask them directly about the dollar value of a good or service or the value of the environmental changes associated with different tourism development options.

- By de-emphasising price as simply another attribute, respondents are generally more comfortable providing qualitative rankings or ratings of attribute bundles that include prices, rather than dollar valuation of the same bundles without prices.
- CCM uses close-ended questioning techniques that allow respondents to make choices. This is better for estimating relative values than absolute values. Thus, even if the absolute dollar values estimated are not precise, the relative values or priorities elicited by CCM are likely to be useful for policy decisions.
- CCM minimises many of the biases that can arise in open-ended contingent valuation studies where respondents are presented with the unfamiliar and often unrealistic task of putting prices on non-market amenities (Rahim, 2008).
- The method has the potential to reduce problems such as expressions of respondents acting 'strategically', and some of the other sources of potential bias associated with CVM.
- The major advantage of the CCM approach is that it can be applied to any valuation problem.

Limitations of CCM

- Respondents may find some trade-offs difficult to evaluate, due to unfamiliarity with the issues;
- There may be no incentive for respondents to tell the truth or to consider their answers carefully;
- Respondent behaviour underlying the results of a contingent choice study is not well understood. Respondents may adopt simplified decision rules if the choices are too complicated, thereby biasing the results of the statistical analysis;
- By providing only a limited number of options, CCM may force respondents to make choices that they would not voluntarily make;
- Translating the answers into dollar values may lead to greater uncertainty as to the actual value that is placed on the good or service of interest (Rahim, 2008).

CVM and CCM have different strengths. CVM seems best suited to value the overall policy package, whereas CCM better values those individual characteristics that constitute actual or hypothetical goods, policies, projects or proposals. Therefore, there is scope to use both techniques in tourism research given their complementarity.

17.6.2 REVEALED PREFERENCE

Revealed preference techniques are based on preferences from actual, observed and market-based information. These preferences for environmental goods and services are revealed indirectly when individuals purchase marketed goods which are related to the environmental good in some way. Revealed preference techniques infer an environmental amenity's value from the actual choices that people make in related markets, rather than from their 'stated' preferences. For example, there are markets for certain goods to which environmental commodities are related, as either substitutes or complements to the goods in question. In this way people's purchasing behaviour in actual markets reflect, to a certain extent, their preferences for environmental assets. Thus, people often pay a higher price for a hotel room with a view of the ocean, or will take the time to travel to a special spot for swimming or bird watching. These kinds of expenditures can be used to place a lower bound on the value of the view or the recreational experience.

Two well-known revealed preference approaches are the *Hedonic Pricing Method* (HPM) and the *Travel Cost method* (TCM).

17.6.2.1 Hedonic pricing method

Hedonic pricing uses the different characteristics of a traded good to estimate the value of an attribute. The HPM assumes that people value the attributes of a good, or the services it provides, rather than the good itself. The price that a person pays will reflect the value of the set of attributes that he/she considers important when purchasing the good. On this assumption, we can value any individual attribute of any good by looking at how the price people are willing to pay for it changes when that attribute changes. In Chapter 2 we discussed the use of the hedonic pricing technique to value the attributes that people attach to the various elements of a holiday package. So also, a particular environmental aspect, say, a wilderness area, is typically composed of many separate attributes: location, ease of access, sense of freedom, beauty, quiet aspect, attractive views, closeness to beach and so on. We can infer the value we put on a particular attribute by the change in price we pay as that attribute changes in the package.

Hedonic pricing uses regression analysis to determine the values that consumers place on these separate attributes in so far as they enter into prices. For example, the value of a hotel room with beachfront view could be estimated by comparing the price of hotel rooms with and without such views. Similarly, the cost of aircraft noise disturbance on the community can be estimated by comparing house prices in noise-affected areas with prices of comparable houses in similar areas but which are not subject to aircraft noise. Provided the houses in the two areas are otherwise comparable, the aggregate difference in price approximates the value the community places on the noise nuisance. In valuing environmental attributes tourism researchers have used HPM to estimate the value of aircraft noise (Espey & Lopez, 2000; Rahmatian & Cockerill, 2004), scenic views (Monty & Skidmore, 2003), urban wetlands (Mahan *et al.*, 2000), recreational and aesthetic value of water (Lansford & Jones, 1995) and clean air (Harrison & Rubinfeld, 1978).

Use of HPM in estimating the costs of airport noise is discussed in Box 17.3.

BOX 17.3 The effects of airport noise on resident property values

Both amenity and disamenity values become capitalized in the value of houses. Espey and Lopez use the hedonic pricing technique in the year 2000 to determine the impact that airport noise and proximity to the airport have on residential property values in Reno and Sparks, Nevada. While past studies have calculated a noise discount for residential properties, most have ignored the effect of the distance between the property and the airport.

The Reno-Sparks (Nevada) metropolitan area has been one of the fastest growing areas in the United States for more than the past decade. Population growth has been associated with Reno's growing popularity as a vacation site, leading to a rapid increase in the number of flights at the Reno-Tahoe International Airport. While growth slowed during 1999, the number·of passengers increased by nearly thirty-five percent between 1995 and 1998 compared to national growth of about seven percent for these years. In addition, freight traffic increased by over two hundred percent between 1996 and 1998 and airport officials anticipate a new terminal will be needed by 2002. While the increase in flights has coincided with economic growth in the area, plans for further airport expansion have created controversy in neighbourhoods affected by airport noise and physical expansion of the airport.

The hedonic pricing technique, as applied to housing, is based on the idea that the value of a house is a function of the value of the individual attributes that comprise the house such as square footage, number of bedrooms or bathrooms, and proximity to school or parks. Espey and Lopez state that the price of a house (P_H) can be written as:

$$P_H = f(S_{i1}, \ldots, S_{ij}, N_{i1}, \ldots, N_{ik}, Q_{i1}, \ldots, Q_{im}).$$

Where, S_j, N_k, and Q_m indicate vectors of structural, neighborhood and environmental variables, respectively. This equation represents the hedonic (implicit price) function of housing. The implicit price of any characteristics, for example, N_k, a neighborhood variable, can be estimated as:

$$\frac{\delta P_h}{\delta P_k} = P_{Nk}(N_k)$$

This partial derivative gives the change in expenditures on housing that is required to obtain a house with one more unit of N_k, ceteris paribus. If the value of the partial derivative is positive then the attribute is an amenity, if the value is negative then the attribute is a disamenity such as air pollution or airport noise.

The authors collect the data for this study from individual sales data available for Washoe County. A random sample of single-family, owner occupied houses was drawn from eleven different census tracts near the airport. The majority of these census tracts lie within the city of Reno. Parcels with housing values less than $50,000 were determined to be uninhabitable and excluded. The total sample consists of 1,417 homes with 109 observations from 1991 sales, 253 from 1992, 348 from 1993, 378 from 1994, and 329 from 1995.

The data for each observation consist of the housing sales price, the quality of the house, the year the structure was built, the size of the lot in square feet, the size of the house in square feet, the garage type associated with the house, the number of bedrooms in the house, the number of bathrooms in the house, the existence of fireplaces in the house, whether or not the parcel is within the noise contour, distance from the airport, and the year in which the house was purchased.

The authors include dummy variables for the census tract within which the property is located in the hedonic regression in order to capture neighbourhood characteristics that influence property values.

The data on noise used in the study is from the Noise Exposure Maps furnished by the Washoe County Airport Authority for each year, These maps show the noise contours for the 65, 70, and 75 L_{dn} areas. The areas that fall into these contours are where airplanes are the dominant source of noise. Individual properties used in this analysis were coded with a noise decibel level according to the noise exposure contour into which they fell on the noise exposure map that corresponded to the year the property was purchased.

The effect on housing value of proximity to the airport was also considered by Espey and Lopez, with houses coded as falling within one of nine concentric circles every half mile from the main airport terminal. Because the noise contours are elongated, with take-offs and landings occurring either to the north or the south, the correlation between 'Noise' and 'Distance' is smaller than one might expect at 0.09. Hence distance should be picking up effects of proximity other than noise, such as visual, safety, or traffic impact.

Model and Empirical Results

The hedonic price of housing is estimated as:

$$P = \beta_0 + \beta_N \text{ Noise} + \beta_D \text{ Distance} + \sum_{i=1}^{n} \beta_1 X_i + u$$

Where, P is the price of the house, β_0 is the constant term, Noise is one if the house is within the $65L_{dn}$ noise contour, Distance is distance from the airport in miles, X_i is the ith non-noise variable, and u is a stochastic error term.

Several different functional forms (log-linear, semi-log, linear, and Box-Cox) have been estimated in previous studies of the airport noise-property value relationship. Arguing that not all of these forms are directly comparable and there is no theoretical justification for favouring one form over the other, the authors estimate the coefficients using the log-linear, semi-log, and linear functional forms as well as the Box-Cox model. One model is estimated using the Box-Cox transformation on the dependent variable only (where $y^{(\lambda)} = (y^\lambda - 1)/\lambda$), and another using the same Box-Cox transformation on the dependent variable and the quantitative independent variables. The log-linear, semi-log, and linear models were corrected for heteroscedasticity using the White estimator (1980). Results are shown in Table 17.3. For ease of comparison, only the noise and distance terms and the impact of each at the means are shown here. All of the variables had the expected sign.

Table 17.3 Results from hedonic price regressions

Coefficient	Box-Cox All	Box-Cox Price only	Semi-log	Linear	Double-log
Distance	3.611	4.186	0.025	2854.1	0.052
	(3.24)	(2.78)	(2.48)	(2.30)	(3.48)
Noise	− 2.074	− 3.532	− 0.02	− 2565.3	− 0.014
	(−2.08)	(−1.96)	(−1.80)	(−2.11)	(−1.25)
Lambda	0.39	0.44			
Log Likelihood	− 15099.6	− 15115.0	− 15145.3	− 15165.7	− 15122.6
Adjusted R^2	0.869	0.867	0.852	0.875	0.857
Distance Elasticity	0.053	0.056	0.056	0.057	0.052
Noise impact at mean	−$2505	−$2371	−$2225	−$2565	−$1567

(*T-statistics are in parentheses*)

The consistency of the values across models for the impact of noise and distance illustrates the robustness of the results. The only model in which noise is not statistically significant is the double-log model and distance is statistically significant on all of the models. The results indicate that houses in the noisier zones have a value of about $2400 less than the equivalent houses in the $60L_{dm}$ zone. Note that this value does not necessarily represent homeowners' willingness to pay to avoid airport noise, but reflects the average impact on the market value of a property.

The elasticity of price with respect to distance ranges from 0.052 to 0.057, with a mean value of 0.055. This suggests that, at the means, a house located one mile from the airport would have a market value about $5500 less than the equivalent home located two miles from the airport. The authors state that some of this negative value of proximity probably relates to closeness to an industrial area and increased traffic. It is also possible that houses closer to the airport have a lower value because of the perception that the airport noise would have a large impact, even when that is not always the case.

Conclusions

The study by Espey and Lopez indicates that property values in noisier zones are about 2.4 percent less than in quieter zones. Empirical results suggest there is a statistically significant negative relationship between airport noise and residential property values, with the average home in areas where noise levels are 65 decibels or high selling for about $2400 less than equivalent homes in quieter areas.

The authors suggest that airport expansion would have a negative impact on property values. Any change in property values would also impact property tax revenues collected by the city and country. Knowledge of the size of the impact on housing values could be used to calculate the impact on revenues if an accurate projection could also be made of the number of houses placed in closer proximity to the airport due to expansion, the number of houses impacted by a change in noise level, and what the new noise contours would be. Such information could also motivate increased noise abatement regulations in an effort to minimize the tax revenue impacts.

Source: Espey, M. and H. Lopez (2000) 'The Impact of Airport Noise and Proximity on Residential Property Values', *Growth and Change*, 31(3), 408–419, Summer

Advantages of HPM

- An important advantage of HPM is that it can be used to estimate values based on actual choices, whether these choices involve features of package tours, cabins on cruise ships or hotel rooms with ocean or mountain views, or purchasing the family home in a context of airport noise.
- The type of data that is used in HPM such as property values and characteristics of accommodation, hotel facilities, room prices and so on are readily available through many sources and can be related to other secondary data sources to obtain descriptive variables required for the analysis.
- The method is versatile and can be adapted to consider various possible interactions between market goods and environmental quality.

Limitations of HPM

- The validity of the technique for tourism–environment interactions depends on the extent to which the price of the tourism product is determined by the attributes of the natural environment. HPM captures only the benefits from environmental attributes that actually manifest themselves in market prices, resulting in potential undervaluation of main features of the environment. Thus, for many visitors, a hotel's overall location may be more important than having a room with a view.
- HPM assumes consumers have perfect information regarding prices and environmental attributes and hence can make the necessary trade-offs between environmental and other values.
- HPM will only capture people's WTP for *perceived* differences in environmental attributes, and their direct consequences. Thus, if individuals are unaware of the linkages between the environmental attribute and benefits to them, the value of the environmental features will not be reflected in the purchase price.
- The results depend heavily on model specification. To the extent that the demand function for any particular estimation does not contain all relevant factors affecting consumer choice in any given context, the results will be flawed. This limitation, of course, is not unique to the HPM but is equally true of all statistical methods, including stated preference methods.
- HPM is not suitable for measuring option, existence, bequest or vicarious values which are important determinants of many of the environmental attributes associated with tourism.

The limitations are not regarded as of sufficient weight as to overcome the advantages of the technique. Consequently, the HPM has found increasing acceptance by researchers concerned to value environmental attributes.

Tourist WTP for aesthetic quality is discussed in Box 17.4.

BOX 17.4 Are tourists willing to pay for aesthetic quality?

Tourism can have a negative effect on the environment of the destinations in several ways. The detrimental effect on the environmental occurs because either the tourists are willingly free riding and do not care about the environment; or because they are not aware that their consumption and behaviour affect the local environment. There are several ways, which can be used to assess whether the tourists value the environmental quality of their destinations. One of these is willingness-to-pay (WTP).

Since the provision of high quality environmentally friendly products entails extensive investment in equipment, such investment will only take place if a higher price can be charged for the services provided. The operator who is willing to incur the additional cost will seek a premium for offering higher quality products. This is more likely to work when the demand is inelastic due to lower level of competition in the market. However, as the degree of competition in the market rises, the premium will be eroded since demand will become more elastic. The question which then arises is whether consumers are willing to pay a higher price for environmentally certified resorts. If this is not the case or if the premium that the customers are willing to pay is not adequate, the operator will have no incentive to provide environmentally friendly products in the short run.

In Thailand, tourism receipts seem to have had positive implications for employment at a national and regional level. The areas of Thailand where tourism has been developed include the impoverished Northern uplands and the Southern coasts. Prior to the development of the tourism industry, the main economic activity were small-scale primary industries. Untapped resources were readily available and were exploitable by the tourism industry. It is argued that rapid tourism development has not taken sufficient account of the biophysical and socio-cultural environment. In Ko Samui, for example, a sudden influx of more affluent tourists has encouraged the construction of up market accommodation facilities without any planning controls. Building restrictions have been ignored. This is now posing a threat to marine biodiversity and the natural environment has undergone irreversible changes. It is also argued that local communities have not benefited from the growth of the tourism industry.

Baddeley argues that if visitors to Thailand are more environmentally conscious, this will be reflected in their demand for the Thai tourism product and will motivate the suppliers to these to be pay more attention to the environment when supplying there products. Further development in other part of Thailand can be carried out with a minimum of impact to the environment.

A survey of local tourism operators was carried out in Krabi Province of Thailand to investigate whether the visitors valued the aesthetic quality of the area and were willing pay a premium to stay in higher quality resorts. The author estimated a tourism demand model. She regressed the room prices of resorts against a number of variables associated with quality variables. The following model was developed:

$$\ln R_i = a + b_1 \ln Q_i + b_2 \ln \text{LI}_i + d_1 O_i + d_2 \text{LS} + d_3 \text{CI} + d_4 A_i$$
$$+ d_5 E_i + d_6 S_i + d_7 X_i + d_8 \text{HS}_i + Sd_r \text{Area}_{ri} + e_i$$

R is room rent; Q is environmental quality variable; LI is labour intensity (rooms per employee); O, origin of tourists; LS, use of seasonal labour force; Dummy Variables: C, class of room; A, air-conditioning; E, ensuite facilities; S, suite accommodation; X, other extra facilities; HS is the high season; 'Area' is the vector of dummy variables used to capture variations in room rents in Phi Phi, Ao Nang or Railay relative to Krabi Town (the reference category); e_i is the error term.

The aim of the study was to identify the determinants of the rental rate of the rooms. Some of the factors included were to reflect the quality of the services provided. These were accounted for by variables such as class of the hotel, the number of employees per room the uses of seasonal staff versus skilled staff, the use of seasonal versus skilled labour, and the provision of facilities like air conditioning, en-suite facilities and others. Baddeley also controlled for the fact that non-Asian travellers were often willing to pay more for their rooms and that rates were higher during peak seasons.

To capture the environmental value, each type of room was assigned an aesthetic environmental quality ranking by scaling the immediate area according to three facets of the environmental experiences namely; aesthetic pollution, congestion or noise pollution.

- Proximity to the resort centre (*5 = more than 15 minutes walk to the centre; 1 in the centre*)
- Proximity to roads (*5 = vehicular access prohibited, 1 = network of roads*)
- Proximity to unimpeded views (*5 = no buildings visible, 1 = surround by other buildings*)

With the exception of the environmental variables, all other were positively correlated with room prices. Labour intensity was an important determinant implying expansion of the tourism industry was likely to create employment. The quality of the services provided were the crucial determinant of room rates. To some extent the origins of the tourist were also important, with non Asian tourists more willing to pay higher room rates. This entails that an increase in demand from developed countries were likely to be inflationary.

The environmental quality variable did not play a significant role in the determination of the price charged for rooms and was, surprisingly, negative. This implies that the tourist does not value the environment. For example, the tourist will rather stay in a hotel, which is closer to the amenities, valuing convenience over the aesthetic environmental value. Baddeley suggests that remote resorts are more likely to suffer from underinvestment in sewage treatment and in clean water supplies.

The other possibility is that the tourist did not have sufficient information to be able to form an accurate idea of the environmental quality of the place they have chosen to stay especially when holiday brochures do not provide the relevant information.

The implications were that tourists are willing to pay for higher quality services but not for higher environmental quality. Either they did not place a high value on the environmental quality when deciding where to stay or they value it but do not have sufficient information to judge the room properly before they go on holiday. The consequence could be serious for the environment in Krabi. It means that in order to fill in the hotels, the suppliers need not consider environmental quality as a marketing tool and there will therefore, be little incentive for them to incorporate the environmental aspect in their development plans.

Source: Baddeley, M.C. (2004) 'Are Tourist Willing to Pay for Aesthetic Quality? An Empirical Assessment from Krabi Province, Thailand', *Tourism Economics*, 10(1), 45–61

17.6.2.2 Travel cost method

Travel cost analysis uses the value of traded goods and services which tourists incur to estimate the value of non-traded goods (Ward & Beal, 2000). The TCM estimates the economic values associated with environmental attributes or sites that are used for recreation. Thus, peoples' WTP to visit the site can be estimated based on the number of trips that they make given different travel costs. This is analogous to estimating peoples' WTP for a marketed good based on the quantity demanded at different prices. Expenditure on travel costs defines a *minimum* value for the good. Whatever the true value of the experience itself, it cannot be less than what the recreationist actually pays to participate. Outfitting costs (at home or on site), equipment rentals, access fees, the value of travel time and so on may be included as well. The higher these costs, the greater are the presumed benefits derived from the environmental experience.

A basic assumption is that the time and travel cost expenses that people incur to visit a site represent the 'price' of access to the site. The cost of travel is considered to be a proxy for WTP and is used in many studies of visits to areas of high scenic value. The method assumes that the recreational benefits at a specific site can be derived from the demand function that relates observed users' behaviour (i.e. the number of trips to the site) to the cost of a visit. The TCM assumes that changes in the costs of access to a recreational site have the same effect as a change in price. That is, the number of visits to a site decreases as the cost per visit increases. Under this assumption, the demand function for visits to the recreational site can be estimated using the number of annual visits as long as it is possible to observe different costs per visit.

There are two basic approaches to the TCM: the Zonal approach and the Individual approach (Rosato, 2008). The two approaches share the same theoretical premises, but differ from the operational point of view.

(1) The *zonal travel cost method* estimates the visitation rate to a given point of interest of persons coming from different zones. The information from a sample of visitors is then grouped according to distance travelled from the point of origin to the site. The dependent variable is the rate of visits per capita for each zone. Earlier studies have used concentric zones (see Figure 17.10), though in later studies it was observed that by defining zones according to areas of population or other geographic units, official census figures could be used to obtain more precise calculations.

By calculating the average cost of the trip and the percentage of visits for each zone, as many value pairs may be obtained as there are zones. A graphic representation of the two variables gives a downward-sloping curve called the basic demand curve. A final demand curve representing the variation in the number of visits as the cost of travel goes up is then constructed. This may be done by simply making a linear interpolation of the increased costs on the basic demand curve. Once the final demand curve is constructed, the area

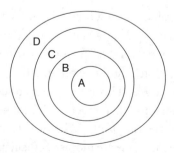

Figure 17.10 Concentric zones as used in TCM

under the curve gives the consumer surplus, which we intend to calculate as an aggregate value of consumption (Bedate *et al.*, 2004).

(2) *Individual TCM.* By contrast, the individual approach estimates the consumer surplus by analysing the individual visitors' behaviour and the cost sustained for the recreational activity. Developed subsequently to the zonal travel cost method outlined above, the individual TCM is based on individual visits to a site. This approach attempts to estimate the demand for recreational goods for each individual at a given site. In this case, the dependent variable is the number of visits made to the site by each individual, implying that the cost of travel may vary from one person to another even where the point of origin is the same. These are used to estimate the relationship between the number of individual visits in a given time period, usually a year, the cost per visit and other relevant socio-economic variables. By aggregating the individual demand functions, an aggregate demand function may be derived. The individual approach can be considered a refinement or a generalisation of the zonal approach (Ward & Beal, 2000).

Figure 17.11 depicts the expected relationship between the number of visits and cost per visit, *ceteris paribus*, showing that the number of visits decreases as the cost per visit increases. If we assume that all users have the same preferences and the same income, the number of visits is a function of the cost per visit.

The TCM has been applied to demand estimation in various tourism contexts including hiking and biking (Hesseln *et al.*, 2003); fishing (Morey *et al.*, 2006); snorkeling (Park *et al.*, 2002), visits to islands (Chen *et al.*, 2004), national parks (Liston-Heyes & Heyes, 1999), beach resorts (Bell *et al.*, 1990) and coral reefs (Carr & Mendelsohn, 2003).

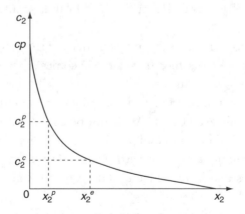

Figure 17.11 Estimating the demand curve using TCM

Source: From Rosato (2008)

Advantages of TCM

- TCM is well suited to estimating the economic costs and benefits resulting from changes in access costs for a recreational site, elimination of an existing site or the addition of a new site as well as changes in environmental quality at a recreational site.
- The method is relatively inexpensive to apply.
- The results are relatively easy to interpret and explain.
- On-site surveys provide opportunities for large sample sizes and, hence, more accurate estimates of travel cost for different visitor segments.

Limitations of TCM

- The demand to visit a given site depends not only on the distance from the point of origin but also on budget and time constraints related to travellers' employment conditions.
- The TCM assumes that people perceive and respond to changes in travel costs in the same way that they would respond to changes in admission price.
- The most basic models assume that individuals take a trip for a single purpose – to visit a specific recreational site. Because it can be difficult to apportion the travel costs among the various purposes, TCM is difficult to apply when tourists make multi-purpose and multi-destination trips. If a trip has more than one purpose, however, the value of the site may be overestimated. It is difficult to determine what part of the estimated cost of travel should be assigned to any particular site.
- TCM works best when the majority of visitors live a large distance from the site, and so need to spend money to reach the site. Some travellers such as walkers, bicyclists and hitch-hikers, however, may incur no travel costs and thus bias the results.
- In its less sophisticated forms, TCM does not measure the value of *travel time*. Because the time spent travelling could have been used in other ways, it has an 'opportunity cost'. The value of the site will be underestimated unless the time spent is estimated in the total travel cost.
- TCM ignores any personal benefits that might be derived from the act of travelling itself. If people enjoy the travel *per se*, then travel time becomes a benefit, not a cost, and the value of the site will be overestimated.
- Application of TCM is limited to certain use values of the environment, particularly in relation to site-specific activities. TCM cannot be used to measure non-use (option, existence, bequest or vicarious) values. Indeed, a major limitation of the method is that it provides no information about non-participants and the value that they may attach to the site. Thus, sites that have unique qualities that are valued by non-users will be undervalued.
- As in all statistical methods, the choice of the functional form used to estimate the demand curve, the choice of the estimating method and the choice of the variables to include in the model can each affect the findings.

Box 17.5 summarises a study of the economic value of a recreation island in China which employs the TCM.

BOX 17.5 Recreation demand and economic value of Xiamen Island

The development of the southeastern area of Xiamen Island in the People's Republic of China has been proceeding at a rapid pace. Although the local government has identified tourism and recreation as dominant functions of the region, there has been a tendency for business and policymakers to place more weight on short-term direct economic benefits of development over the longer term benefits that are associated with recreational use. Chen *et al.* (2004) employ the travel cost method to evaluate the recreational benefits of a beach along the eastern coast of Xiamen Island in China. In 1999, the total number of the visitors to the beach was approximated to be 3.168 million, according to on-site observation and some statistical information.

Method

The authors adopt the zonal travel cost method. An on-site survey on the beach along the eastern shore of Xiamen Island was conducted during the summer months of 1999, and was performed using a semi-interview questionnaire. Questions regarding the visitor's zone of origin, travel costs, travel time, educational background, wage, and opinions on six of Xiamen Island's main tourist destinations were used in an attempt to gather travel and socioeconomic details. Visitors were approached at random, and a total of 560 effective questionnaires were collected, representing approximately 9800 visitors.

The visitors' zones of origin were divided with respect to local government administrative districts. The researchers identified a total of 34 zones of origin. The visitation rate to the beach from each zone of origin is defined as the estimated number of visitors from a given region divided by the region's population. Travel costs contain the opportunity cost of travel time, and this was assumed to be a value equal to one third of the daily wage rate.

The authors acknowledge the fact that there are several scenic spots on Xiamen Island. The beach along the eastern coast of Xiamen Island is just one of them. Since visitors are likely to visit multiple sites on any one trip, it was assumed that visiting the beach was not the sole purpose of an individual's journey from their zone of origin, except for the local people of Xiamen Island. Total travel costs were therefore prorated amongst the six main scenic spots of Xiamen. The prorating was based on the tourists' opinions given on the questionnaire. This prorating allowed the researchers to establish the average travel costs of a round trip (for the purpose of a visit to the beach) between the visitor's zone of origin and Xiamen Island. This cost is denoted as TC_{pro}. The average travel costs of a round trip from the visitor's residence or lodging on Xiamen Island to the beach itself, including on-site expenditures and the value of on-site time, is denoted TC_{beach}. The estimation of the value of on-site time was the same as that of travel time.

The sum of TC_{pro} and TC_{beach} is equal to the average total travel costs for an individual from their zone of origin to the beach on the eastern shore of Xiamen Island. This sum is denoted as TC_{total}.

The authors develop two trip-generating functions as follows:

$$\log(v_i/p_i) = \alpha + \beta_1 TC_{total i} + \beta_2 TD_i + \beta_3 ED_i \tag{1a}$$

and

$$\log(v_i/p_i) = \alpha + \beta_1 TC_{total i} + \beta_2 TD_i + \beta_3 I_i \tag{1b}$$

Where,

v_i is the total number of visits to the public beach along the eastern coast of Xiamen Island by individuals from region i.

$TC_{total i}$ is the travel costs by visitors from a given region.

P_i is the population of the i regions.

ED_i is the percentage of the zone of origin who have higher education levels.

TD_i denotes a travel dummy equal to unity when travel has originated on Xiamen Island.

I_i denotes the per capita net income of a given zone of origin.

Results

The regression results are given in Table 17.4a and 17.4b, respectively. The authors separate the inclusion of the education and income variables due to their collinearity. The adjusted R_2 value and the F statistic indicate the overall significance of the independent variables. The coefficient for total travel costs, TC_{total}, is negative and significant at the 1% level in both regressions, implying that as

Table 17.4 Regression results

Regression results		
Variable	**Est. coefficient**	**t Statistic**
(a) Dependent variable: $\log(v_i/p_i)$ (education variable included)		
Constant	4.780	7.77
Total transportation cost	−0.060	−7.98
Transportation dummy	2.821	2.48
Income	0.003	2.24
Adjusted $R^2 = 0.77$		
Standard error = 0.96		
F statistic = 37.89		
(b) Dependent variable: $\log(v_i/p_i)$ (income variable included)		
Constant	5.425	15.74
Total transportation cost	−0.073	−10.78
Transportation dummy	2.550	2.85
Education	0.268	4.59
Adjusted $R^2 = 0.84$		
Standard error = 0.79		
F statistic = 59.86		

travel cost increases, the visitation rate decreases. The results also indicate that income, education, and residing in Xiamen Island are also significant indicators of beach visitation. For all of these variables, the estimated coefficient is positive and significant.

To estimate the relationship between the number of visitors and the total cost of the trip, the estimated coefficients from the regression in Table 17.4 is used to calculate visitation rates from each zone of origin as total travel costs are increased in six-dollar increments.

Specifically we have

$$\log(v_i/p_i) = 5.43 + 0.268\text{ED}_i + 2.55\text{TD}_i - 0.073\text{TC}_{\text{total},i} \qquad (2)$$

For each of the 34 regions the visitation rate and total costs are estimated first by assuming an entrance fee of zero. Thence a demand curve for each origin is estimated by increasing the entrance fee in six-dollar increments until the estimated number of visits is less than 0.1. Finally, the total number of visitors from all zones of origin is summed according to the entrance fee. With the entrance fee and visitation rate data in hand, our next step was to obtain a functional form for the relationship between estimated visits total costs. Using commercially available software, the authors approximated the relationship between entrance fee and number of visitors with the following function:

$$p_{\text{fee}} = 860.7 - 102.8\ln(Q_{\text{v}}) \qquad (3)$$

where P_{fee} denotes the price of entry and Q_{v} is number of visitors. The aggregate recreational benefits from the beach along the eastern coast of Xiamen Island is estimated by measuring the area under our quasi-demand curve given in Eq. (3). To find the estimate for aggregate recreational benefits, the authors calculated the definite integral for Eq. (3) from 0 to 1100. Their estimate for the aggregate recreational benefits from the beach in 1999 was US$53.5 million. This equates to a per visitor consumer surplus of approximately US$16.9.

Conclusions

The aggregate recreational benefits from the beach along the eastern shore of Xiamen Island are estimated to be approximately RBM$ 53.5 million per year. The findings demonstrate that the beach, as a nonmarket good, has its own economic value and considerable economic benefits. The authors conclude that the decision to declare 'tourism and recreation' as the dominant function of the area, recently made by the government, seems to be a reasonable one.

The authors caution, however, that the maintenance of such benefits depends on the effective management and protection of the coastal environment and the beach itself. The degradation of coastal environment and beach quality could lead to substantial loss in value, which eventually would be reflected in the reduced number of visitors and shortened visits. This implies that the loss of significant economic benefits has to be considered in the decision to develop such regions.

This result can be used to generate valuable economic information for local government policymakers. Due to the expense of maintaining the coastal beach area, the authors point out that policymakers may wish to consider the implementation of a user access fee. For example, if 5% of the benefits from the beach are recovered through the implementation of a user fee for the beach (such as a beach pass), more than $2.675 million in annual revenue could be generated. For the individual visitor, this works out to approximately US$0.84 per visitor, per visit. Considering the cost of many competing entrance fees, both scenic and otherwise, the authors conclude that the possible implementation of a small user fee could prove useful to the institutional management and protection of the coastal environment and natural resources in the area.

Source: Chen *et al.* (2004) 'Recreation Demand and Economic Value: An Application of Travel Cost Method for Xiamen Island', *China Economic Review*, 15, 398–406

17.6.3 IMPUTED VALUATION

Imputed valuation (direct cost) methods assume that the value of an environmental amenity can be determined through the actual costs that people pay either to avoid degradation of the amenity or to repair or replace that amenity if it becomes degraded. Imputed valuation methods do not provide strict measures of economic values, which are based on people's WTP for a product or service. Rather, they assume that the costs of avoiding damages or replacing ecosystems or their services provide useful estimates of the value of these ecosystems or services. This assumes that, if people incur costs to avoid damages caused by lost ecosystem services, or to replace the services of ecosystems, then those services must be worth at least what people paid to avoid the damage or replace the services. Thus, imputed valuation methods are most appropriately applied in cases where damage avoidance or replacement expenditures have actually been made, or will be made. The more commonly used direct cost methods include *Replacement Cost, Damage Cost Avoided* and *Production Factor Method*.

17.6.3.1 Replacement cost

The Replacement Cost method values the negative environmental impacts of an activity by measuring the cost of replacing a lost asset or restoring a damaged asset to its original state. The method estimates the cost of specific measures designed to restore or compensate for deterioration in or loss of nature and environment. Thus the cost of restoring a park following devastation by a tsunami is taken to be its (minimum) value as an environmental feature.

A variant of the replacement cost method is the substitute cost method which estimates the costs of providing substitute services. An example would involve valuing the loss of habitat from tourism development by the costs of establishing similar habitat elsewhere.

17.6.3.2 Damage cost avoided

The Damage Cost Avoided (also known as the prevention cost or mitigation behaviour method) measures the cost of defensive spending to prevent the environmental amenity from declining in value. It is based on the prevention expenditure incurred by households, companies or governments to mitigate or avoid particular environmental risks or effects. Since people will only incur this prevention expenditure if the expected usefulness of the expenditure is greater than the expected inconvenience created by the environment effect, willingness to incur this expenditure is an indication of the minimum cost of the effect or of the minimum benefit of mitigation of the effect. Examples of avoidance costs are the costs of constructing paths so impacts of visitors to a rainforest are minimised, or the costs of eliminating pollution in a recreation site by installing and operating filters. The use of wooden walkways to control tourists movements through parts of the temples in the Angkor Wat world heritage precinct and Stonehenge are typical examples of damage cost avoidance measures, as is the construction of dikes to prevent flooding. Further, the cost of airport noise can be estimated as the cost of installing noise barriers or sound proofing in nearby homes and offices.

17.6.3.3 Production factor method

Also known as the dose response method, the Production Factor approach values changes in the productivity of natural or human-made systems as a result of a change in the environment. The method values negative impacts as the value of resources needed to treat the effects of the externality. An example is the reduction in fish catch as a result of deterioration in water quality caused by hotels and restaurants not cleaning their wastewater sufficiently before discharging it into a river. If the relationship between the water quality (dose) and the fish catch (response) is known, the value of deterioration in water quality can be calculated. The changes to the financial return of production (the fish catch) can be translated through the dose/response relationship into a corresponding value for the environmental effect (change in water quality). Similarly, a reduction in tourism-related expenditure attributed to declining environmental quality in a destination can be estimated (Persson, 2008). Further, the cost of restoring polluted water discharged from a hotel to its former unpolluted state, or the medical expenses that must be incurred to keep people healthy, is a measure of the environmental cost of such pollution as are the values of the carbon trade-offs made to reduce GHG emissions from aviation.

17.6.3.4 Advantages and limitations of imputed valuation methods

Advantages
- Imputed valuation methods provide surrogate measures of value that are as consistent as possible with the economic concept of use value for services which may be difficult to value by other means.

- The methods provide a rough indicator of economic value, depending on the degree of similarity or substitutability between related goods.
- It is often easier to measure the costs of producing benefits than to measure the benefits themselves, when goods, services and actual benefits are non-marketed. Thus, these approaches tend to be less data- and resource-intensive than the stated and revealed preference approaches.

Limitations
- Imputed valuation methods assume that expenditures to repair damages or to replace environmental services are an accurate measure of the benefits.
- The replacement cost method requires information on the degree of substitution between the market good and the natural resource. Few environmental resources, however, have such direct or indirect substitutes. Substitute goods are unlikely to provide the same types of benefits as the natural resource, for example, tourists may not value elephants in a zoo as highly as they do elephants in the wild.
- A major drawback of the production factor method is the uncertainty that involves the specification of the dose-response function, which is crucial to its accuracy. The described approach can be used whenever the physical and ecological relationships between a pollutant and its impact are known.
- The attributes being replaced may represent only a portion of the full range of services provided by the environmental amenity. Thus, the benefits of an action to protect or restore the resource would be understated.

Given data limitations it may be appropriate to use a combination of techniques to measure the various environmental consequences that are associated with some tourist activity. This will be required, for example, if one is trying to measure both ecological and commercial losses associated with a resource, such as the loss to a fishery of wastewater pollution from the hospitality industry. In such cases, care must be taken to avoid counting the same loss more than once.

17.7   CONCLUSIONS AND POLICY

- Tourism affects the environment through its interplay with *natural, human* and *built resources*. Tourism impacts on the environment are both direct and indirect, and often are not easily observable.
- Conversely, the range and quality of such resources can influence tourism flows. Thus, attention to environmental features of the tourism experience can result in an outward shift of tourism demand, thereby increasing producer surplus.
- Market prices serve as signals or incentives to guide resources and products into their most highly valued uses. If there are no markets for some valuable resources and

products or if markets do not function properly, the resulting resource allocation will not be optimal.

- There are three major sources of market failure that are relevant to the environmental impacts associated with tourism. These are situations associated with lack of property rights to environmental resources, public goods and externalities. The inevitable result is overuse, abuse, congestion and quality degradation of increasingly scarce environmental resources.

- The 'public good' aspect of many environmental resources leads to their under-provision. Private markets will fail to allocate sufficient resources to the production of so-called public goods, including environmental quality, resulting in a misalloca-tion of resources. Collective action is needed to provide such goods in sufficient quantities.

- The environmental impacts of tourism activity may be measured either directly (through their obvious price effects in the marketplace) or indirectly (through the construction of proxy prices).

- The total economic value of a tourism environmental amenity is composed of its use value (actual use value) and non-use value. Components of non-use value are option, quasi-option, existence, bequest and vicarious value.

- The techniques available to measure the non-use of an environmental amenity include stated preferences (e.g. contingent valuation and contingent choice), revealed prefer-ences (e.g. hedonic pricing and travel cost) and imputed valuation (e.g. replacement cost, damage cost avoided and production factor method).

- Revealed preference methods tend to be the more reliable, but stated preferences can be applied in more situations and can generate more data. Imputed valuation tech-niques are particularly useful when people actually spend money to prevent loss of an environmental amenity.

- Non-direct use valuation techniques allow for planning and better management of environmental resources by imputing non-market values to them.

SELF-REVIEW QUESTIONS

1. Use an example to differentiate market attributes from non-market attributes in demand for a tourism product. How might the presence of environmental attributes increase the demand for tourism development?

2. What is meant by the term 'market failure'? Outline the three major sources of market failure that are relevant to the debate on the potential for tourism activity to impact the environment.

3. Why will many public goods associated with tourism be under-allocated in the absence of government funding and support?

4. List potential positive and negative environmental effects that might flow from tourism in the Grand Canyon National Park.

5. Use a tourism example to differentiate between the use value and the non-use value of an environmental amenity.

6. Outline the three generally accepted practical methods for measuring the non-use value of an environmental amenity.

7. In the tourism context, distinguish between the following sets of valuation methods:

(i) CVM and CCM.
(ii) HPM and TCM.
(iii) Replacement cost, damage cost avoided and production factor method.

8. In the context of a national park, how would valuation by WTP differ from valuation by WTA?

9. How is the total economic value of an environment amenity measured?

ESSAY QUESTIONS

1. 'Tourism is a two-edged sword, with the potential for both positive and negative impacts.' Discuss using examples.

2. 'Different types of tourists, who tend to undertake different patterns of activities, will obviously have different types and levels of impact on a destination.' Discuss this statement in respect of visitors to (1) the Pyramids at Giza and (2) Bangkok City.

3. Considerations of property rights and public goods can lead to an appreciation of the dual pressures resulting in and sustaining environmental misuse. How so?

4. Tourism development may proceed even though it is against the general interest. Why?

5. 'Valuing the impact of tourism on the environment is neither easy nor straightforward.' Discuss.

6. Converting environmental impacts into monetary values is always problematic. How so?

7. Use the potential impacts of increased tourism within a wilderness area to explain the difference between use and non-use techniques in valuing that wilderness area.

8. Use a diagram to explain the potential changes in consumer and producer surplus and the deadweight loss to society that is likely to accompany any negative externalities in the development of tourism facilities.

CHAPTER 18

ECONOMIC INSTRUMENTS AND ENVIRONMENTAL PROTECTION IN TOURISM

LEARNING OBJECTIVES

After reading this chapter, you should be able to:

1. Appreciate the use of economic instruments in attempts to mitigate any adverse affects on the environment that emanate from tourism activity.

2. Understand the concept of an optimal level of pollution and describe the three approaches to its determination.

3. Discuss the different strategies for pollution control and apply them in a tourism context.

4. Evaluate the problems that arise from the use of economic instruments to mitigate any adverse affects of tourism.

18.1 INTRODUCTION

Chapter 17 discussed the potential adverse impacts of tourist activity on the environment and set out alternate ways to value these impacts. This chapter describes and evaluates actual economic instruments that we use to try to forestall, or at least lessen, the adverse environmental impacts of tourism activity.

As noted, the environmental impacts of visits to, say, a penguin colony, rainforest or heritage monument are all likely to be quite different. Moreover, the different resilience of different areas to tourism activity implies that similar activities will have different consequences in different locations. Such differential environmental impacts raise the question as to what is the best way to avoid or reduce them. A wide variety of economic instruments have been developed to address this question.

Much of our focus in this chapter will be on policies to reduce pollution resulting from tourism. The discussion allows us to introduce a number of concepts relevant to addressing other problems arising from the environmental effects of tourism activity and which are also relevant to the issues addressed in Chapter 19. We now ask two questions for any given tourism activity:

- How much pollution control is needed?
- What will be the cost of achieving this?

The economists' answer to each question is phrased in marginalist terms, namely, that the level of pollution should be reduced (i.e. environmental quality increased) until the marginal benefit from a further reduction in pollution equals the marginal costs of achieving it. This will give the 'optimal level' of pollution.

18.2   THE OPTIMAL LEVEL OF POLLUTION

We now consider three approaches to determining the optimal level of pollution in the context of a producer to consumer type of negative externality. Although much more complex analyses can be conducted, the simple models to be discussed here allow an appreciation of some basic issues and constitute the foundations for more sophisticated modelling of real-world pollution problems. Each approach can stand apart but we have linked them together as in Figures 18.1a, b and c.

The first approach (Figure 18.1a) uses supply and demand curves to determine an optimal level of output.

The second approach (Figure 18.1b) uses the marginal private gain curve to again determine the optimal output level.

The third approach (Figure 18.1c) uses the marginal damage to society curve and the firms' marginal pollution control cost curve to determine the optimal pollution level. For purposes of exposition we assume that each unit of output produces one unit of pollution. Thus E^* is the optimal level of pollution corresponding to the optimal level of output Q^*.

Where,

MPC is marginal private costs (firm's supply curve);

MSC is marginal social cost (MPC + MXC);

MXC is marginal external cost (marginal damage to society);

MAC is marginal abatement cost (marginal private gain);

MPB is marginal private benefit curve (demand curve).

Figure 18.1a (a variant of Figure 17.6) depicts a situation where, in a competitive industry, profit-maximising tourism firms equating price and marginal (private) costs of supply will produce output Q_0 and charge price P_0 (point D). If the production process imposes pollution costs on other firms and consumers, the social costs of supply will exceed the private costs of supply by the value of the negative externality. To determine the optimal level of output, it is the marginal social cost of supply rather than the firm's supply curve which is relevant. Since this intersects the demand curve at point A, the socially optimal output and price are Q^* and P^*, respectively.

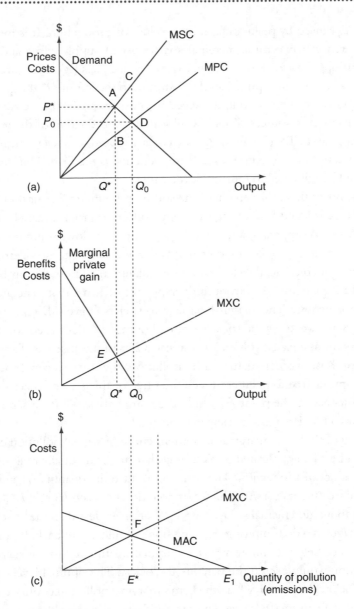

Figure 18.1 The optimal level of pollution

Figure 18.1b depicts a marginal private gain curve for the producer. This measures the difference between marginal revenue and marginal cost, that is, the marginal profit, for each additional unit of output. Since under perfect competition average revenue equals marginal revenue and the marginal cost curve is the supply curve (above minimum average variable cost), the marginal private gain curve measures the (vertical) difference between the demand and supply curves up to output Q_0. The marginal external cost (marginal damage to society) curve depicted in Figure 18.1b represents the external or incidental costs to society caused by pollution as a by-product of production. It is measured as the (vertical) difference between the marginal social cost of supply curve and the marginal private cost of supply curve. That is, AB in Figure 18.1a equals EQ^* in Figure 18.1b. Again, Q^* is seen to be the socially optimal level of output. To the left of Q^* the gains to the firm from producing an extra unit of output exceed the costs imposed on society through extra pollution. Thus more resources should be allocated to production of the good (i.e. more tourism development). To the right of Q^* the costs imposed on society from the pollution by-product of extra units of output exceed the benefits to the firm. Thus less of society's resources should be devoted to tourism development.

It should be noted that achievement of the social optimum implies nothing about equity or fairness. The costs and benefits attach to two different groups, namely, firms and the community. Also, in comparing output levels Q_0 and Q^*, the lower output level may result in some consumers losing while others gain. As economists well know, an efficient solution may not be an equitable one. Policies can be formulated to address this problem.

Figure 18.1c depicts the issue from the perspective of firms that generate pollution in their production activity. The marginal damage to society curve (MXC) is the same as in Figure 18.1b. Since we know the socially optimal output Q^* lies in relation to that curve, we can identify the associated volume of emissions E^*. In the absence of any requirement to compensate those who are damaged by pollution, the waste receptor services of the environment appear free to polluters. Since the price of this service is zero to them, they could expand its use to the point E_1 where the marginal value of the service to them is zero even though the damage to society may be great.

The meaning of the firm's marginal abatement curve (marginal pollution control curve) cost curve can best be appreciated by assuming that the firm initially pollutes the volume E_1 as a by-product of production. The firm can reduce the quantity of emissions but at rising marginal treatment cost. At volumes of pollution between E_1 and E^*, the treatment costs to bring about incremental reductions in pollution are less than the benefits to society by way of damages avoided, implying that emissions should be cut back. If pollution was to be further reduced below E^*, however, the marginal treatment costs of successive reductions in pollution would exceed the benefits to society. The optimal level of pollution is E^*, vertically below the point F where the firm's marginal pollution control cost curve cuts the marginal damage to society curve. This approach can also show the impact of changing pollution control technology. Any reductions in the firm's marginal pollution control costs (e.g. resulting from installation of pollution control technology) can be represented by a flatter curve from E_1 to the vertical axis, resulting in a lower optimal level of pollution.

18.3 INSIGHTS FROM ECONOMIC THEORY

While measurement problems must be acknowledged, economic theory enables several insights into the problem of pollution which are relevant to tourism firms.

- Where pollution is a by-product of production the actual level of output will be above, and actual price below, the socially optimal levels.
- The optimal level of output of a product which generates negative externalities will generally be greater than zero.
- Achieving the optimal level of output or pollution does not imply reduction of external costs to zero. At the optimal level of output Q^* and optimal level of emissions E^* the value of the negative externality (marginal damage to society) is $AB = EQ^* = FE^*$.

Unless we can provide incentives for firms to account for the marginal social costs, they will continue to produce at Q_0, beyond the optimal output level. Rational firms respond to price signals but in the above example the market price does not reflect all costs of production (internal and external).

The user-pays principle simply reflects the notion that users (rather than non-users) should pay full social costs in their use of an environmental amenity. This principle underpins the use of market-based economic instruments in their protection of the environment. The economic analysis is relevant to formulating policy to reduce the adverse environmental impacts of tourism development and associated tourism flows.

We now discuss some alternative strategies of pollution control.

18.4   STRATEGIES FOR POLLUTION CONTROL

Economic instruments are controls imposed on environmentally damaging activity in an attempt to avoid or lessen that damage. As we have seen, when externalities are present, the market mechanism is likely to fail to achieve an efficient allocation of societal resources. The Figures 18.1a, b and c can be used to provide different insights into how the negative impacts of tourism activity can be controlled. We will discuss several different strategies for pollution control. These are the following:

- voluntary agreements
- the bargaining solution
- merger
- direct controls
- subsidies
- tax on output
- tax on pollution
- market for pollution rights
- other (education and information, codes of conduct)

18.4.1   VOLUNTARY AGREEMENTS

Voluntary agreements between industry and governments to reduce pollution are politically attractive, raise awareness among stakeholders and have played a role in the

681

evolution of many national policies. One voluntary form of agreement that is becoming widely employed in tourism to help the industry reduce overall Greenhouse Gas (GHG) emissions is carbon offsetting. Indeed, in many destinations, this seems to have become the means used by the industry to 'reduce' emissions. Some airlines have introduced carbon offset schemes which are available to their customers. By paying extra, passengers contribute to a carbon-offset scheme which enables their flight to be carbon neutral.

While voluntary agreements have the potential to stimulate the application of best available technology, the majority have not achieved significant emissions reductions beyond 'business as usual'. As the UNWTO (2008b) points out, voluntary schemes effectively mean that producer responsibility is turned into customer responsibility with the result that industry does not pursue energy efficiency as actively as it might otherwise do under other policy instruments. Carbon offsetting can be ideal up to a point, but it potentially diverts from the real causes of the problems and therefore bypasses the structural and technological changes that need to be made to achieve longer-term reduction in GHGs. Relying as it does on customer willingness to incur extra costs, the 'free rider' problem again emerges limiting the effectiveness of carbon offsetting to reducing the adverse environmental impacts of economic activity.

18.4.2 THE BARGAINING SOLUTION

Some argue that when externalities exist, collective action may not be necessary because it is in the interest of private parties to voluntarily take the appropriate action. The Coase Theorem states that if property rights are fully assigned and if people can negotiate at low cost with one another, they will arrive at efficient solutions to problems caused by externalities without the need for explicit government intervention in the form of regulation and/or taxation (Coase, 1960). Optimality requires that the payment not exceed the value of the damage suffered.

We discuss the bargaining strategy with reference to Figure 18.2 (a variant of Figure 18.1b).

Assume a simple two-party situation – a polluting firm (e.g. a noisy hotel) and an affected household (or community of households). The bargaining strategy is to grant enforceable property rights to one of the parties and rely on market transactions to achieve the optimum.

With property rights to the environment vested in the hotel it will produce output Q_0 (Q_0 could be number of hours of opening per week (or numbers of customers admitted late at night)). Since at levels of output beyond Q^* the marginal damages to society exceed the marginal private gains to the firm, the household can bribe the hotel to cut production (hours of business) back to Q^*. The household would be prepared to pay a sum up to a maximum of c + d, that is, a sum equal to the total costs imposed on them at Q_0 minus the costs imposed on them at Q*. The hotel, on the other hand, would be prepared to reduce

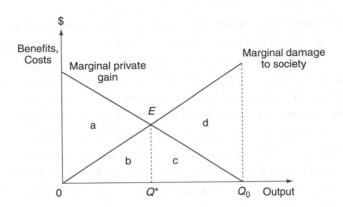

Figure 18.2 Bargaining strategy

output from Q_0 to Q^* for a payment of not less than area c which is the extent of the private benefits foregone from output reduction. The difference between the maximum sum that the household is prepared to pay and the minimum sum that the hotel is willing to accept equals area d. This represents the overall gain to the economy if bargaining brings about the optimal level of production.

With property rights to the environment vested in the household we can take the initial situation as one of zero output (zero noise from the hotel). The hotel can now compensate those adversely affected by its polluting activity to the full extent of costs imposed on them. Since at output levels less than Q^* the marginal private gain to the hotel from production exceeds the marginal damages to society, the firm can bribe the household to accept a level of output up to Q^*. The household would be prepared to allow increased production from O to Q^* for a payment of not less than area b which is the extent of the costs imposed on them by the hotel's activity. The hotel, on the other hand, would be prepared to pay a sum up to a maximum of areas a + b which is the extent of the gains available to it by increasing output to Q^*. The difference between the maximum sum the hotel is willing to pay and the maximum that the household is willing to accept is area a. This represents the overall gain to the economy if bargaining brings about the optimal level of production.

On this simple model, regardless of the allocation of property rights, the outcome is the same: bargaining results in achievement of the optimal level of output Q^*. Although the voluntary payment solution is consistent with Pareto Optimality (everyone is better off and no one is worse off), some problems exist. However, there are several problems with the bargaining strategy for pollution control.

- How is the community to value the externality? Converting environmental impacts into monetary values is always problematic.
- High transaction costs may deter households from taking action or seeking a bargaining solution. It is unlikely that bargaining will be a costless exercise especially when large numbers are involved. Transaction costs include the costs of identifying and arranging

meetings for members of a group (e.g. the community), agreeing in a joint offer to be made or on what offer would be acceptable, agreeing on individual contributions, negotiating with the other party and implementing and policing the agreement. Bargaining becomes even more complex if there are several emitters of a pollutant, as in the case of CO_2 emissions, with each located in different countries (e.g. international airlines).

- There is also the problem of free riding, especially among the sufferers of pollution damage. Since sufferers are often large in numbers and poorly organised, many individuals may not participate in collective community action to limit pollution because they expect others will act and they will benefit at no cost to themselves. This limits the amount that damaged parties can pay by way of bribes to firms to restrict output. In such circumstances, even if bargaining does take place, the level of output is likely to be greater than the optimal level.

- If there is unequal bargaining power between the polluting firms and affected households, outcomes may differ from the optimal solution as one side bluffs the other into a worse position.

- The bargaining approach can encourage blackmail. Firms may deliberately emit more pollution to obtain extra compensation or larger bribes.

- There is also the issue of equity or fairness. While, as far as *efficiency* is concerned, the optimal level of output can be achieved regardless of who possesses property rights, as far as *equity* is concerned, there is a differential effect on the distribution of income. Why should damaged parties (who often are poor) have to bribe the polluter to cease activity?

These considerations provide strong arguments for giving individuals the right to a clean environment rather than giving firms the right to pollute without compensation. One solution to market failure is to establish property rights. This means that individual people or communities of people are allocated land so they assume the responsibility for stewardship of the land. This provides the incentive to use the land to yield a financial return in the present and the future.

One unresolved equity issue is whether the creator of an adverse externality ('the polluter') should pay the full social costs of that externality. The issue is very relevant to tourism. On equity grounds, it may be felt that visitors who impose environmental costs, or who cause a need for local spending to avoid environmental costs, should pay for such costs, rather than the local community. To the extent that tourists use unpriced public goods (beaches, roads, national parks, street lighting, police services, etc.) and create congestion or pollution that reduces the value of an amenity to other residents, such costs reduce the overall economic and non-economic benefits of tourism. As discussed in Chapter 15, a host country, hoping to maximise net benefits from foreign tourism, might make overseas visitors meet the environmental costs that they impose on resident community.

The discussion also flags the case for public intervention. This case is based on the presumption that the resource costs of government action (e.g. gathering information, administration and enforcement) are small relative to the private transaction costs that tend to impede a bargaining solution and are small relative to the potential gains from intervention.

18.4.3 MERGER

When the entities generating externalities are firms, merger can result in addressing the problem 'in-house'. If waste from a resort hotel is polluting a river so that a downstream sporting complex must make large expenditures on water purification before using the water, the problem may be eliminated by a merger of the two firms. Similarly, a hotel whose patrons are disturbed at night by noise from a nearby disco could merge with the latter to 'internalise' the externality. In this way, the social costs are effectively internalised, forcing firms to treat them as a part of their relevant costs for decision-making purposes and to make appropriate responses to eliminate their influence. Of course, firms typically merge to share market and profit rather than to reduce externalities. Moreover, this solution doesn't work well in the case of consumption externalities (where the social costs are caused by consumers rather then by producers).

18.4.4 DIRECT CONTROLS

For government, a simple solution to a negative externality is simply to prohibit the action that generates the external effects.

There are several actual or proposed mandatory requirements which have the potential to impact on tourism. Some of these will affect tourism *directly* – for example, lower vehicle emissions standards, green fleet requirements, limits on air travel and bans on incandescent light globes. Others affect tourism *indirectly*. Thus, for example, renewal targets for electricity add to the cost of the electricity purchased by tourism businesses and bans on the use of certain insecticides in agricultural production affect food prices in restaurants.

In particularly sensitive areas, direct regulation of tourism activity can be imposed to mitigate potentially adverse effects. Destination managers at national, state or local level can adopt either prevention or cure techniques designed to impose qualitative and quantitative standards on development. *Preventative regulations* such as planning controls and effluent standards can be put in place before the tourism development begins while *curative regulations*, such as setting of maximum site visitor numbers, can be imposed when the tourism development is operational.

Thus, the destination manager can decide how much of an externality is allowed. Quantitative limits can be imposed either on *usage*, for instance, restrictions on the number of persons allowed entry to a limestone cavern, the number of cars allowed into a national park, or on the *amount* of waste emissions produced by some tourist activity, for instance, discharge by houseboats of sewage into a river. Quantitative limits cap the potential for adverse environmental affects by requiring firms or consumers to change their behaviour.

Many direct controls are, however, often non-optimal and impractical for many tourism-related businesses. Airline GHG emissions would be zero if flying were to be banned but at what cost globally to societies? An optimal solution does not require that externalities be completely eliminated, but rather that the right amount of them is eliminated.

Direct controls cover regulations or restrictions on output or on the quantity of pollution discharges. Standards are normally arrived at through scientific research and may prescribe general ambient and/or point source emission levels. Suppose, as shown in Figure 18.3 (a variant of Figure 18.1c), that firms are restricted from polluting more than quantity E^*. This is the optimal level of emissions since MAC = MXC.

- Since either the amount of usage is controlled or the amount of pollution generated is controlled, the imposition of quantitative limits results in precise physical environmental impacts.
- Direct controls are the surest way to prevent irreversible effects or totally unacceptable stock pollutants (e.g. mercury, cadmium, lead, radioactivity, etc.).
- Direct controls may be appropriate where there is uncertainty about the magnitude of the possible social costs, for example, the long-term effects of certain chemicals and pharmaceuticals on the environment and human health, the effects of continued GHG emissions on global warming or the effects of tourists encroaching on animal habitats and breeding areas.
- In certain cases, direct controls may be fairly easy to administer, for example, in the setting of standards for sulphur content of fuel, carbon content of coal, lead content of petrol or exhaust emission standards.
- Direct controls may be cheaper to implement and enforce than price-based instruments. Enforcement of direct controls is relatively straightforward. Rather than continuous

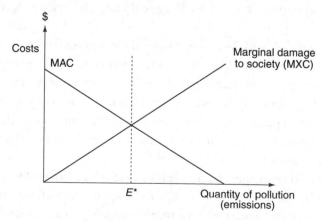

Figure 18.3 Direct control to reduce an externality

measurement of firm performance, which can be costly, technology regulation, for example, can be enforced through simple spot checks that the appropriate equipment is installed.

- Regulations and standards generally target more obvious sources of abatement. They generally provide some certainty about emission levels. They can be effective up to a point when abatement technologies are relatively standard and their environmental consequences known, as in the implementation of improved fuel standards or the phasing in of new lighting standards. Regulations and standards may be preferable to other instruments when information gaps or other barriers prevent producers and consumers from responding to price signals.

The general approach suffers from some serious weaknesses, however:

- Standards setting involves determining just how much of an externality should be permitted. Ideally, the standards should attempt to eliminate an externality up to the point where the marginal cost of further reductions are just equal to the marginal benefit derived, but in practice there is insufficient data to bring this about. If the set standards are too lenient, then pollution levels will exceed the optimal level. If they are overly restrictive, pollution discharges will be below the optimal level. In both cases there is a resource misallocation resulting in less benefits to society overall.
- Regulations and standards may also impose substantial costs on business. This approach typically requires affected parties to achieve specified outcomes irrespective of the costs, so there is little incentive to reduce emissions beyond the mandated level, or to do more than is absolutely necessary for compliance. In addition, the price impact of regulation is not immediately transparent to consumers and downstream producers.
- The imposition of quantitative controls on emissions may not induce innovations and the development of more advanced energy-efficient technologies.
- Fixed pollution quotas have income distributional consequences since some firms are financially more able to bear the costs of pollution control than others.
- The most efficient sources of abatement may not be pursued, with the consequence that the abatement burden is spread unevenly across industries and countries.

Figure 18.4 represents the marginal costs of pollution control for three firms on the assumption that they each initially emit the same level of pollution E_1. The cost of pollution treatment is lowest for firm 1 and highest for firm 3. Since optimality requires that the marginal effectiveness of the last dollar spent by each polluter be equal, this cannot be achieved in the absence of standards which vary from industry to industry and firm to firm. The costs of determining suitable pollution quotas for every firm and policing the situation become substantial.

For the above reasons it is difficult to see how direct controls are either efficient or equitable. To allocate quotas as a rational basis the government would need to know in detail

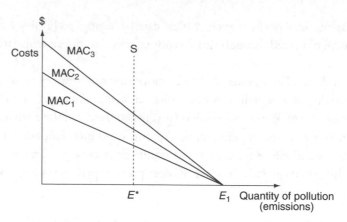

Figure 18.4 Direct controls and differences in firms' emissions abatement costs

the costs of pollution control, of changing production processes or of cutting output for all firms under its authority. In a tourism context this means that standards and regulations would need to be set so as to result in the optimal level of externalities from tourism activity.

18.4.5 SUBSIDIES

Governments often use fiscal measures, including grants, subsidies and rebates, to stimulate the development and diffusion of new energy-saving technologies There are calls from industry for subsidies (i.e. grants, tax concessions, etc) for pollution control activities. Tourism industries worldwide typically demand special consideration in mitigation policies to address climate change. Sometimes subsidies can increase social efficiencies. There are many different ways to classify subsidies, such as the reason behind them, the recipients of the subsidy, the source of the funds (government, consumer, general tax revenues, etc.). Direct subsidies (e.g. to prevent the decline of an industry, to encourage it to hire more labour (as in the case of a wage subsidy) or to promote the adoption of pollution control technology, the benefits of which can be attributed to the general public) often are more transparent than many alternative forms of government intervention. Subsidies to address adverse environmental effects typically have a number of disadvantages:

- Subsidies are often inefficient since they do not provide incentives to achieve pollution reduction at lowest cost to society. If the amount of the subsidy is determined in part by the cost of waste treatment undertaken, the firm has little incentive to reduce these costs.
- Where the subsidy reduces the average cost of production for the firm, it could possibly result in increased output of the product at lower price. Subsidies may even have the perverse effect of increasing pollution by encouraging entry of more firms.

- Subsidies are inequitable since they transfer the burden of control costs from the polluter to the taxpayer.
- Subsidies are inequitable to the extent that they penalise firms which have already invested in pollution control.
- Subsidies are often difficult to apply because of the inherent difficulty in distinguishing plant and equipment serving to control pollution from that installed to increase productive capacity.
- The financing of subsidies and specific project-based interventions also impose costs on society through the tax system. This issue was addressed in Chapter 15. If subsidies were to be used extensively to achieve large-scale abatement in tourism, the economy may well suffer substantial losses in economic and administrative efficiency.

Economists generally do not favour subsidies as a pollution control mechanism and would argue that reductions in pollution can be achieved more efficiently and equitably by using other instruments.

The exception to this involves subsidies for goods and services where the social benefits exceed the private benefits. Since consumers typically take into account only the expected private benefits from consumption of any good, it is likely that such goods will be under-consumed (and so under-produced). This leads to a market equilibrium quantity lower than the social optimum as we saw in Chapter 6. In the case of environmental protection measures and pollution control technology, individuals are typically myopic in that they are short-term utility maximisers not fully understanding or appreciating the long-term social benefits of producing or consuming certain goods in their purchasing choices. In such cases subsidies by government may help to bring about a social optimum. As an example governments worldwide are offering households financial incentives to reduce their carbon footprint.

18.4.6 TAX ON OUTPUT

One solution to externalities problems which has long been favoured by economists is to tax those whose activities generate substantial external costs. Price-based instruments are measures designed to place the cost of an adverse impact firmly back on to the actual consumers and producers of the good or service. Essentially, they are government fees and charges levied on market participants in order to incorporate the external cost back into the market price. Such charges raise the price of an activity and, depending on price sensitivity, reduce the demand for that activity.

A tax on output is sometimes referred to as the Pigou solution. We can show the effect of a tax on output with reference to Figure 18.5 (a variant of Figure 18.1a).

If the output of the industry is determined competitively, it can be reduced from Q_0 to Q^* by imposition of a tax T per unit of output. The tax helps to 'internalise' the externality

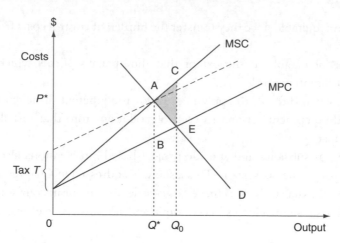

Figure 18.5 Tax on output to reduce a negative externality

by causing a parallel upward shift in the industry supply curve (which is the sum of firms' marginal (private) cost curves). If the tax is set at a level equal to AB, equal to the value of the external costs of pollution at the optimal level of output, then the new industry supply curve (following imposition of the tax) will cut the demand curve at A and the optimal price and output will be P^* and Q^*, respectively. This results in a saving to society of external costs equal to the shaded area ACE.

This price-based instrument is designed to place the cost of an adverse environmental impact from production firmly back on to the actual consumers and producers of the tourist activity. The tax raises the price of an activity and, depending on price sensitivity, reduces the demand for that activity. We also note that charging tourists for external costs is equivalent to charging tourism operators providing the tourism service. If the tax is related to the sale of some good or service (for instance, hotel rooms or rental cars), it makes no difference at all, in terms of incidence and economic effects, whether the tax is levied on the supplier or on the tourism consumer.

While the Pigovian tax is perhaps the standard instrument for pollution control approach, we may note several limitations to this approach:

- It is very difficult to determine the optimal level of output in practice, because it is difficult to estimate the externality costs and this complicates the determination of an appropriate tax per unit of output.
- This tax solution uses output as a proxy for the level of the externality produced. It may be, however, that the level of externality is directly associated with the use of a certain input (e.g. coal with high sulphur content). This tax on output approach will not in itself encourage a switch to 'cleaner' inputs but will merely result in a reduced level of production using the same pollution-generating inputs. In such cases it will be more

efficient to tax the input rather than the output in order to encourage input substitution thereby reducing external costs at every output level.

- The solution assumes perfect competition. Under imperfectly competitive conditions (monopoly, oligopoly, monopolistic competition), taxes may be less effective where firms may restrict their supply of the good in order to increase profits. In circumstances where output of the good is initially below the socially optimal output, the imposition of a Pigovian tax could promote an even greater misallocation of resources.
- The solution assumes that no changes occur in the demand curve which will affect the level of the social optimum. Tourism demand could be either low or high depending on the weather, for instance. If demand is greater than expected, the tax may not reduce output sufficiently and environmental costs may be high. If demand is lower than expected, the tax may result in an inefficiently high discouragement of visitation or use.

18.4.7 TAX ON EMISSIONS

Emission charges such as taxes on effluent discharge may be levied on the amount of actual pollution caused by the economic activity. For example, a hotel might be charged according to the type and amount of waste it produces or an airline may be required to pay taxes on its carbon emissions.

A tax on pollution discharges can be illustrated in Figure 18.6 (a variant of Figure 18.1c).

Suppose an airline is discharging quantity E_1 of pollution annually and that a tax of OT per unit is now imposed on these emissions. If the airline's marginal control costs of reducing pollution are less than the tax liability for the last unit discharged, the firm will reduce pollution to avoid paying the tax. In Figure 18.6 the airline will reduce quantity of discharges from E_1 to the level of E^* thus reducing the tax burden by F G $E_1 E^*$. Pollution discharges will not be reduced below E^* since it would cost the airline more by way of

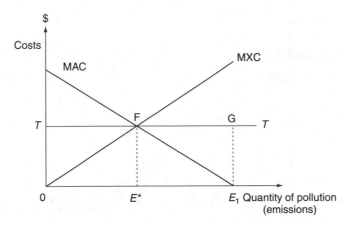

Figure 18.6 A tax on emissions

pollution control costs than the tax savings. Setting a charge appropriate to achieving the optimal level of pollution requires knowledge of the marginal social costs of pollution. If the charge is set below OT, there will be less resources directed to pollution control than is socially optimal. If the charge is set above OT, this will result in an over-allocation of resources to pollution control.

There are several reasons why economists are favourably disposed towards taxes as a pollution control strategy. These same reasons support the use of taxes for environmental protection against tourism activity

- Because of the economic incentives they create and the decentralised decision-making with respect to how much each firm reduces its discharges and how it does so, pollution taxes will yield a given level of pollution control at a lower total economic cost than alternative strategies. Some firms will find it much less costly to reduce pollution by a given amount than others and when a pollution charge is imposed they will reduce pollution to a greater extent.

    Suppose a carbon tax is levied on domestic flights in some country. As Figure 18.7 (a variant of Figure 18.1c) shows, the introduction of a pollution tax OT will result in airline 1 reducing the amount of pollution to E_1, airline 2 to E_2 and airline 3 to E_3. When all three firms have fully adjusted to the tax, the marginal abatement cost of pollution control will be the same for each, thus achieving a given reduction in pollution at less cost than direct controls.

- Emissions taxes are especially useful when the appropriate response varies between different regulated firms, and there are information problems so the regulator does not have the necessary knowledge about firm costs. Policy makers using this instrument of pollution control generally need less detailed information on individual polluters to achieve emissions reductions at lower cost. In climate change mitigation policy, for

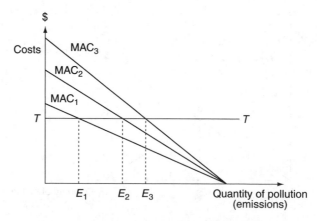

Figure 18.7 Emissions taxes and differences in firms' emissions abatement costs

example, government has highly imperfect information about the costs of reducing GHG emissions, and it is likely that some firms in some sectors can reduce emissions much more cheaply than others. Taxes on emissions are likely to be effective under these circumstances.

- Faced with pollution taxes, firms will seek the least costly combination of treatment, recycling, process changes and discharge pattern that can maximise tax savings from reduced pollution.
- Emissions taxes also provide an ongoing incentive for firms to undertake R&D into pollution control technology. The emissions taxes create a direct, powerful and continuing incentive to control discharges since the more the firms reduce pollution, the less taxes they pay. The aviation industry is particularly concerned to reduce its carbon footprint through the introduction of new more energy-efficient technology.
- Since each alternative of introducing pollution control measures or paying pollution taxes is costly, the price of the product (e.g. air fares, ferry tickets, ski lifts and car fuel) will tend to rise to cover these costs. In this way the costs of pollution and pollution control tend to be borne by those who produce and consume the good. This accords with the polluter-pays principle. The effect of the rise in price is to reduce the consumption of the product relative to substitutes.
- Emissions taxes raise revenue which can be used either to compensate the affected partners, to substitute for existing taxes or to increase expenditure in areas such as health, education or R&D on pollution control technology. The amount of revenue raised in Figure 18.6, for example, is OT F E^* if firms reduce pollution to the optimal level.
- Administrative costs are generally lower for a pollution tax scheme than for other pollution control strategies since the scheme can operate within existing taxation systems.

There are weaknesses to emissions taxes which must be recognised. These relate to uncertainty (see below). Direct controls are capable of achieving their environmental objectives quicker and with greater certainty than tax policies.

The real advantages of emissions charges are realised only over time, because they provide a continual incentive to reduce emissions, thus promoting new technology, and permit maximum flexibility in achieving emissions reductions.

18.4.8   A MARKET FOR POLLUTION RIGHTS

An increasingly popular approach to the problem of pollution is the sale of pollution rights or emissions trading. The authorities decide upon the level of pollution to be permitted during each period in order to maintain an acceptable standard of environmental quality,

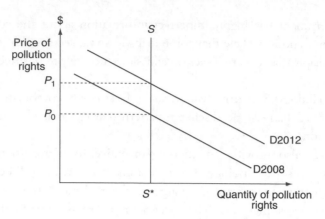

Figure 18.8 Emissions trading scheme (simplified representation)

and then issue licences or rights to pollute up to this fixed amount, the licences being sold at auction to the highest bidder. These licences can be freely traded in an organised market permitting their price to fluctuate according to market demand. Firms which don't use up their full quotas can sell the rights to other 'dirtier' companies and so gain a competitive advantage. In theory, each firm will pay the price to expand its right to pollute only as long as doing so is a cheaper option than achieving marginal reductions in pollution. Thus the desired level of pollution would be achieved at minimum social cost.

A market for pollution rights is a hybrid instrument – a tailored combination of price and quantity instruments. As such, a hybrid instrument is neither a pure price nor a pure quantity instrument, but a mixture of both. Creating this market involves at least three elements: (i) an aggregate quantity is fixed, (ii) licenses are allocated between individuals and firms and (iii) a mechanism is established for enforcing compliance with the scheme (Hepburn, 2006).

Figure 18.8 shows a fixed supply S^* of pollution rights as determined by some (local, state, national) authority. Presumably, S^* quantity of pollution rights would be selected to correspond to an estimated optimal volume of pollution E^*. The curves D2008 and D2012 show the demand for pollution rights in 2008 and 2012, respectively. The intersection of supply and demand at a particular time will determine the price of a pollution right.

There are a number of advantages in establishing a market for pollution rights.

• Under idealised conditions, if the regulated quantity is allocated and then licenses are traded, the resulting license price will equal the optimum price instrument (e.g. a tax). A greater quantity of licenses is equivalent to setting a lower tax, and vice versa. As such, under idealised conditions, there is a one-to-one correspondence between price and quantity instruments. As Weitzman has emphasised, 'generally speaking it is neither easier nor harder to name the right prices than the right quantities because in principle exactly the *same* information is needed to correctly specify either' (Weitzman, 1974).

- The approach is essentially market-oriented, forcing pollution costs to be internalised by firms. Potential polluters are confronted with an explicit financial incentive to reduce pollution. The effect of the scheme is to make the environment a scarce resource with a positive price.
- Since the price of pollution rights can be expected to increase over time, due to income and population growth, firms have increasing incentives to pollute less by installing pollution control technology.
- Environmentalists and conservation groups can fight pollution by buying up and withholding pollution rights thus reducing actual pollution levels below the government-determined standards.
- The scheme is a revenue-earner for the government. As the demand for pollution rights increases over time, the growing revenue from the sale of the fixed quantity of pollution rights can be devoted to environmental improvements, other government programmes or reductions in other taxes.
- A tradeable permits scheme can work in tourism contexts other than emissions from production. For example, limits could be placed on the number of four-wheel drive trips made into a rainforest, and licences to operate such trips could be allocated (perhaps auctioned). Ideally, these supply-limiting licences would be tradeable, that is, able to be sold on the private market.

Some limitations of such schemes may be noted.

- Pollution standards are difficult to establish because of incomplete and disputed technological, biological information and the marginal damages to society from discharged wastes. To the extent that the quantity of pollution rights S^* offered for sale corresponds to a level of pollution above or below the optimal level E^*, a misallocation of resources results.
- Schemes involving the sale of pollution rights are limited to circumstances where emissions are measurable. The quantity of pollution rights offered for sale must correspond to a measurable quantity of pollution discharges.
- The approach is inherently biased against smaller firms which lack the financial resources of larger companies. This serves to remind us again of the possible trade-offs between environmental quality and other ends.

Despite these shortcomings (which also apply to other pollution control strategies) this scheme, in its various forms, seems superior to alternative strategies. In Chapter 19 we shall explore in some detail how such a scheme is being used to mitigate the effects of climate change.

18.4.9 OTHER INSTRUMENTS OF ENVIRONMENTAL PROTECTION

As we have discussed, market-based instruments are designed to influence either the *price* of an environmentally adverse activity (which in turn will affect the quantity of that activity) or its *quantity* (which in turn will affect the price of that activity). As complements to the types of market instruments discussed above, there are broader approaches that can be taken to lessen any potentially adverse impacts that tourism activity may have on the environment. Three types of instruments are technology development for energy efficiency, information and education, and codes of conduct.

18.4.9.1 Technology development for energy efficiency

There is a growing demand for energy efficiency due to increasing demand for energy services combined with the need to reduce greenhouse emissions, and other energy supply limitations (e.g. infrastructure). Additional investment in R&D can stimulate technological advances to reduce emissions of pollutants. For example, in the tourism industry technological change is taking place in all sectors aimed at reducing the industry's carbon footprint.

Innovation in product design and production processes can help to conserve energy, by developing products that require less energy to manufacture, deliver, maintain and eventually recycle and that allow us to consume less energy to get the same level of services. Many innovations that improve energy efficiency also bring a range of other benefits to the community.

All instruments require enforcement and some instruments (e.g. technology standards) may be simpler and cheaper to enforce than others. However, the more rapid introduction of new technologies depends on environmentally pro-active management decisions influenced by market solutions (taxes or as emission trading).

18.4.9.2 Education and information

Environmental impacts are critically dependent on both tourist numbers and tourist behaviour. While tourist numbers can be controlled through price and quantity controls, the monitoring and control of *tourist behaviour* is more problematic. Price and quantity controls will have some effect on environmental outcomes through restrictions on total visitation but they may have no influence on the way visitors behave once they are using the amenity. Similarly, suppliers of tourism services may behave irresponsibly towards the very environment that attracts their clientele.

Environmental behaviour is closely linked to environmental attitudes. It may be possible to influence individual or group behaviour or operator behaviour through specific environmental education, suggesting that if people are informed about what is damaging and what is not, many are likely to avoid damaging behaviour, especially if doing so is costless to them.

Information and education campaigns can alert businesses and households to emissions abatement opportunities by providing information that may not otherwise be readily accessible. Thus awareness campaigns aimed at both industry and consumers may positively affect environmental quality and the cost of emissions abatement by promoting informed choices and possibly contribute to behavioural change.

However, to drive large-scale emissions reductions, substantial changes in production, consumption and relative prices are needed. These changes can be achieved by more direct market mechanisms which can drive larger-scale changes in production and consumption.

18.4.9.3 Codes of conduct

Behavioural codes of conduct are imposed on visitors through admonitions such as 'walk only on the marked trails', 'don't feed the native animals' and 'don't pick the wildflowers'. Self-regulation or enforcement by individuals and groups, though, may not be sufficient. It is often necessary to back up the code of conduct with sanctions imposed by the authorities responsible for the area.

Destinations must regulate the type of development that balances social, environmental and economic objectives. Whatever the type of development, influencing the behaviour of tourism operators is of prime importance. The routes they take, where they stay, their general care for the environment and so on can influence the way tourists behave. Tour operators can educate tourists on appropriate behaviour, can monitor their actual behaviour and can discourage their damaging behaviour. Moreover, given that many earn their livelihood from the environment, it is in the interests of tour operators to encourage environmentally responsible behaviour by their patrons, and to be responsible themselves. The best monitors of behaviour of individual operators are often the other operators themselves who will not wish to see maverick or 'cowboy' operators behaving in a way that damages the environment. They will have an incentive to report poor behaviour to the authority which will be able to impose sanctions such as exclusion of particular operators.

Industry stakeholders sometimes develop codes of conduct which operators commit to as conditions of 'certification'. Thus, for example, EC3 Global has accreditation programmes for operators wishing to be 'certified' as environmentally friendly in their operations (www.ec3global.com). The Rainforest Alliance has developed a code of conduct for tour operators (www.rainforestalliance.org) while the World Wildlife Fund has developed various codes of conduct for the different tourism industry stakeholders (www.wwf.org), as have specific destinations (e.g. Holy Land, and Kokoda Track in Papua New Guinea). Industry associations whose members commit to responsible conduct regarding interactions with the environment can play an important role in fashioning appropriate operator behaviour.

It is most likely that these other instruments will be more effective when they address all sources of impacts on the environment, not just those emanating from tourism. Codes of conduct, whether voluntary or enforced by an authority, can be combined effectively with other control instruments, such as user charges.

18.5   ASSESSING ECONOMIC INSTRUMENTS TO PROTECT THE ENVIRONMENT

There has been a gradual trend towards the use of market-based instruments for environmental policy, probably because efficiency considerations are increasingly important as environmental targets become more ambitious. In determining the best policy mix for any destination, the primary aim should be to achieve any given level of emissions abatement at least cost. Market-based approaches – involving the explicit pricing of emissions and industry choice of which abatement opportunities to exploit – are superior in achieving large-scale abatement at least cost to the economy. Market-based instruments provide a strong ongoing incentive for investment in abatement technology research, development and deployment, and in business efforts to improve energy efficiency. Since firms have an incentive to abate whenever a unit of abatement is cheaper than the price of emissions, this promotes the efficient deployment of all abatement opportunities.

There are several issues that create problems for the use of economic instruments in protecting the environment from any adverse effects of tourism. These problems relate to uncertainty, boundary problems, transaction costs and public goods (Dwyer *et al.*, 1995).

18.5.1   UNCERTAINTY

If for any given type of emissions the marginal costs of abatement are known with certainty, the policy maker should set the rate of the emission tax to equal the marginal benefits of abatement, also assumed to be known. The optimal quantity of emissions allocated would also be given by this intersection, resulting in the establishment of an equilibrium price in a perfectly competitive market. These situations are shown in Figures 18.3 and 18.6. The choice of quota or tax would not matter in this case.

Uncertainties have always created problems for economic theory. In many economic analyses, demand is often assumed to be known and external costs are assumed to be measured precisely so that the optimal price and quantity can be determined exactly. Uncertainty makes the choice of best instrument much more complex.

In the case of tourism's effects on the environment, there is likely to be substantial uncertainty surrounding the timing and scale of impacts, as well as the costs of abatement of emissions. In such circumstances, policy instruments will need to be chosen with care. The appropriate choice of an instrument to protect an amenity depends on what is known about the relevant demand and cost structures. This makes the optimal level of pollution extremely difficult to determine in practice.

Uncertainty in the tourism context manifests itself in three ways:

Demand uncertainty. There always tends to be considerable uncertainty on the demand side, even though it may not be as difficult to resolve as uncertainty on the cost side.

The demand for visits to a particular amenity may be quite variable and uncertain and its elasticity difficult to determine. The number of visits to a national park, for example, may depend on the weather, and this is unpredictable. While uncertainty can be reduced by collecting, sometimes costly, information on the structure and elasticity of demand, the setting of price to control usage is still problematic. If demand levels are inherently uncertain, this must be taken into account in the choice of instruments.

Impact uncertainty. There is also uncertainty about the ways in which tourism will impact on the environment. Ecological systems are complex, physical impacts can be difficult to determine let alone measure and unpredictable consequences often arise. Measurement of marginal social costs involves identifying the effects of different types of pollution as they impact on humans, flora and fauna. There is limited knowledge of the physical and biological effects of pollution on the environment. The exercise is further complicated by the fact that discharge damage varies by location and over time. Some pollutants affect us in a cumulative way and so many have noticeably serious effects only in the long term (e.g. asbestos dust, lead poisoning, radiation and GHG emissions). Some pollutants may not become a significant problem until a certain threshold is reached after which marginal social costs increase rapidly (e.g. acid rain, concentrations of GHGs). Some activities may exhibit cumulative threshold or lagged effects that become noticeable only when they are too late to reverse. Some effects of tourism growth may be irreversible, for example, extinction of species.

Cost uncertainty. It is often difficult to determine the size of environmental costs. Consider the problems involved in estimating the costs of climate change. Both the marginal social cost curve and the marginal abatement cost curve are difficult to estimate. Even when consequences can be identified, attaching monetary values to these consequences is often extremely subjective. Estimates of the benefits of production of goods and services where pollution is a by-product will themselves change according to the distribution of income and wealth in society. Further, since the size of marginal social costs depends on the method of pollution control, the relevant curves cannot be estimated independently of each other. Uncertainty regarding the costs to firms makes it hard to strike a balance between environmental objectives and other objectives, impinging on how effective, in the sense of being efficient, the different instruments are.

When conditions are uncertain – as they always are – price instruments do not guarantee that a particular quantity target will be achieved. Similarly, the use of a quantity instrument will not guarantee that a particular price target will be achieved (Hepburn, 2006).

Under uncertainty, price instruments are more efficient than quantity instruments when the marginal benefit curve is flat relative to the marginal social cost curve, but quantitative limits are more efficient the steeper is the marginal benefit curve relative to the marginal social cost curve.

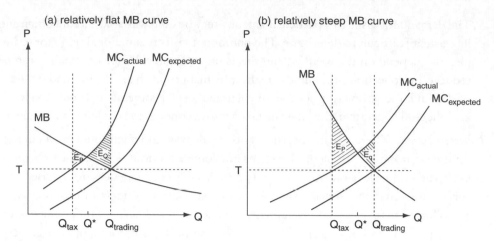

Figure 18.9 Use of market instruments under uncertainty
Source: Hepburn (2006), Figures 1a, b, p 232

Weitzman (1974) demonstrated that when the marginal costs of supplying a good are uncertain, using a price instrument is more (less) efficient than a quantity instrument when the marginal benefits of that good are relatively flat (steep) compared with the marginal costs. This is because the price instrument is intended to internalise the marginal benefit curve.

In Figure 18.9 the actual marginal costs of supplying the good are higher than expected. Here, the price instrument (tax T) generates under-provision of the good ($Q_{tax} < Q^*$) leading to efficiency loss E_P, while the quantity instrument (trading scheme with cap $Q_{trading}$) leads to over-provision of the good ($Q_{trading} > Q^*$) with efficiency loss E_Q.

As Figure 18.9 shows, the price instrument is preferable to the quantity instrument ($E_P < E_Q$) when the marginal benefit curve is relatively flat, and vice versa. In Chapter 19 we will discuss the relevance of this finding to the issue of preferred instruments for mitigating the effects of climate change.

While attempting to make the market bear the costs of its harm-producing activity is the basic advantage for any price-based instrument, the downside is that such harmful activity will still take place, even if to a lesser extent.

In perfectly competitive markets with perfect information and certainty, and no transaction costs, both taxes and quantity controls, if correctly designed, can establish a common price signal across individual firms and sectors.

18.5.2 BOUNDARY PROBLEMS

Where people can get around controls, a boundary problem arises. When boundary problems arise, both price and quantitative solutions lose their effectiveness and sometimes may be counter-productive. Unfortunately, many environmentally sensitive areas favoured by tourists face boundary problems. They tend not to have clearly defined boundaries in physical terms, and even when they do, the boundaries may not be clearly drawn in economic terms. Such circumstances make it difficult to include or exclude specific users.

Where areas are defined in physical terms, barriers such as fences and gates may make it is possible to determine who enters and who does not. Here, it is feasible to charge for entry or to impose conditions on entry. However, where barriers cannot be erected, exclusion can prove difficult. Charging for entry or imposing conditions in such cases can induce some visitors to take alternative routes into the area, resulting in the control methods being less effective, perhaps even counter-productive if visitors use more environmentally damaging routes into the area than the official routes. In extreme cases, the optimal charge for use of the area may be zero (or negative).

Problems also arise where there are clear barriers to an area, but they do not include the whole of the environmentally sensitive area. For example, if entry is quantity limited or if a fee applies, potential visitors will have an incentive to visit similar areas outside the defined boundaries. This again reduces the effectiveness of the control, and can prove counter-productive.

Piecemeal approaches to the boundary problem will prove to be ineffective. Economic instruments, such as user-pays, will only be useful for protecting a particular amenity if they can also be applied to all other amenities that could be substituted for the competing amenity. For example, suppose that the cost to a waterfront restaurant to dispose of its garbage at the local rubbish dump is $150. However, the owner of the restaurant may choose a substitute option. For $100 and very little risk of detection because of the high transaction costs associated with policing the ocean, he or she might be able to pay someone to dump the rubbish illegally in the ocean, therein imposing a social cost of, say, $300. Under these circumstances the best price to charge the restaurant owner for garbage disposal might be something less than $150, in the hope of eliminating illegal activity. With different disposal and damage costs, the optimal price could be zero or even negative.

If the boundary problem is one of not being able to exclude visitors, there is the possibility that both price and quantitative controls will result in a less efficient solution overall than would be the case if no controls were imposed. This could occur if the environmental costs of overuse of the uncontrolled region were high.

Consider an environmentally sensitive area for which exclusion of visitors is difficult. It may be feasible to exclude visitors from one part of the area but not others, or it may be feasible to exclude some visitors (e.g. organised groups of operators) but not others (visitors using their own vehicles, boats or aircraft). Prices and quantitative limits will be only partly effective at controlling visitor flows. In the latter case, it may be possible to influence total actual visitation through prices charged to, or restrictions placed on, the controlled group of visitors. This cannot be guaranteed, as there may be more of the uncontrolled visitors than the desired total.

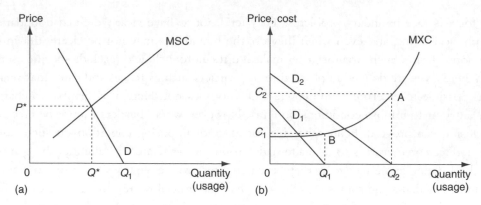

Figure 18.10 (a) Optimum use of a controlled areas (b) Boundary problems in uncontrolled areas

Figures 18.10a and 18.10b set out the boundary problem for controlled and uncontrolled areas.

Figure 18.10a is a variant of Figures 18.3 and 18.6. By imposing a price of P^* in the controlled region, or a quantitative limit of Q^*, the use of this area is optimised. There is a welfare gain over the alternative situation where the price is zero and the usage is Q_1.

However, as shown in Figure 18.10b, a charge for use of the controlled area will push visitors towards use of the uncontrolled area, thereby increasing demand for the uncontrolled area from D_1 to D_2.

A tourist-related example would be camping permits, where the cost of a permit is set on a user-pays basis equal to the cost of maintaining campsites. The imposition of fees in controlled areas might encourage illegal camping in environmentally sensitive areas where pricing cannot be enforced. As shown in Figure 18.10b, at zero price, this would increase uncontrolled campsite usage from Q_1 to Q_2 resulting in higher marginal external costs from C_1 to C_2. In the case where illegal camping extends to uncontrolled areas, the external costs have increased by $Q_1 BA Q_2$. Additional usage in the controlled areas, which are often developed for visitors through tracks, boardwalks, fences and so on, will impose lower costs than usage of the uncontrolled areas. In some circumstances, it may be optimal to forego simple user-pays principles and charge nothing for controlled campsites.

Taxes or charges are sometimes levied on complementary goods and services – products that accompany tourism activity, for example, an accommodation tax within a national park or car parking metres located near access to public beaches. Taxes levied on complementary goods or services only work well if complementarity is high. The more indirect the pricing solution, the less efficient it is likely to be. For example, visitors to an environmentally sensitive area may not purchase complementary goods and services such as accommodation. Also, those who do buy such items may not visit the sensitive area when the tax creates unwarranted distortions, reducing the welfare gains from such control.

Education and codes of conduct, as less formal methods of control, can play an important part in resolving boundary problems. If visitors are educated in the damage they might do to uncontrolled areas, some at least will be less inclined to visit them. Codes of conduct among operators may mean that they are less likely to visit uncontrolled areas, especially if other operators are *de facto* monitors of their behaviour. How well this works, of course, depends on the effectiveness of the codes.

18.5.3 TRANSACTIONS COSTS

Transaction costs refer to the administrative and add-on costs associated with the implementation of a control instrument. They lie behind the problems of monitoring and determining boundaries. Even when monitoring and boundary problems do not exist, it may be that the administrative transactions costs of controlling usage make such control not worthwhile. The imposition of quantitative limits, for instance, can attract substantial costs in establishing and policing barriers so that exclusion is possible, especially in areas that are seldom visited. There can also be costs of allocating rights to use and in setting up markets in which such rights can be traded. High transaction costs may make education and codes of conduct more effective than market-based instruments as means of limiting environmental costs in rarely used but environmentally highly sensitive areas.

Transaction costs pose problems for tourism for at least three reasons. First, tourism is a pervasive industry. Most activities that tourists are involved in, such as travelling, eating, enjoying recreational pursuits and the like, are also enjoyed by all sections of the resident community and thus their environmental costs may be difficult to address directly because of the costs involved in monitoring and pricing such environmental usage. Second, tourist-attracting amenities, such as physical environment, tend to be non-marketed amenities. Third, many adverse tourism-related environmental impacts stem from bad *individual* behaviour. While monitoring may lessen adverse behaviour, it will be expensive. There can be substantial costs in establishing and policing barriers that deter adverse behaviour and exclude undesired visitors.

On the other hand, as increasing numbers of consumers enjoy an environmental amenity, the fixed transactions costs per capita decline. Since the costs of collecting fees (and in some cases monitoring behaviour) include a substantial fixed component, efficient pricing of a currently unpriced amenity may become more viable as numbers increase, particularly so if external costs increase as numbers increase. It then becomes cheaper in a transactions cost sense to price according to numbers, and it becomes more costly from the viewpoint of external costs not to do so.

18.5.4 PUBLIC GOODS

The provision of environmental amenities gives rise to public goods problems. To allow tourists to use these amenities, governments can invest in capital infrastructure in order to head off, reduce or eliminate environmental externalities arising from that amenity's use. Once the infrastructure is in place, the amenity's marginal cost of use may be zero or negligible. Even when the exclusion of additional users is possible, on efficiency grounds, exclusion will not be desirable. A zero price for the provision of public goods may, however, reduce the amount of revenue raised and made available for environmental improvement. To illustrate, once a boardwalk is constructed over a marsh, it may be able to cater for different numbers of visitors at zero marginal cost. As in the case with public goods generally, it is inefficient to restrict use, whether by price or by quantitative instruments. This, of course, will give rise to cost recovery problems, and the question of who should pay for the cost of the public good needs to be addressed.

Once they have undertaken expenditures of this kind, authorities often wish to set prices (user-pays) so as to recover costs. User-pays, however, may not be efficient, here, especially if the new charges reduce the number of users significantly, reducing economic benefits for no saving in cost. Obviously, the cost of the amenity does have to be recovered and one way is through general taxation. If raising revenue through taxation is distortionary, however, as it is likely to be, there may be a case for charging a fee for use. The other problem with public goods is that if no charge for use is made, it is difficult to know potential users' willingness to pay (WTP) for the amenity.

18.6   CONCLUSIONS AND POLICY

- Tourism activity may cause environmental pollution (damage). In theory, there is an optimal level of such environmental pollution. Graphically, this optimal level may be determined and shown through any of three approaches: the intersection of demand and supply curves for the final product; the intersection of the firm's marginal private gain curve and the marginal damage to society curve; and the intersection of the firm's marginal abatement cost curve and the marginal damage to society curve.
- Economic instruments may be used to try to forestall, or at least lessen, any adverse environmental impacts associated with tourism activity. Among such instruments are voluntary agreements; bargaining; merger; direct controls; tax on output; tax on pollution; subsidies; market for pollution rights; and others such as technology development and energy efficiency, education and information, and codes of conduct.
- There has been a gradual trend towards the use of market-based instruments for environmental policy. Market-based instruments are designed to influence either the *price* of an environmentally adverse activity (which in turn will affect the quantity of that activity) or its *quantity* (which in turn will affect the price of that activity).
- In determining the best policy mix for any destination, the overriding objective should be to achieve any given level of emissions abatement at least cost. Market-based instruments provide a strong ongoing incentive for investment in abatement technology

research, development and deployment, and in business efforts to improve energy efficiency.

- There are several issues that attend the use of economic instruments in their protection of the environment from any adverse effects of tourism, including uncertainty, boundary problems, transaction costs and public good considerations.
- In perfectly competitive markets with perfect information and certainty, and no transaction costs, both taxes and quantity controls, if correctly designed, can be used to establish a common price signal across firms and sectors. Under uncertainty, price instruments are more efficient than quantity instruments when the marginal benefit curve is flat relative to the marginal social cost curve, but quantitative limits are more efficient the steeper is the marginal benefit curve relative to the marginal social cost curve.

SELF-REVIEW QUESTIONS

1. What is meant by the concept of the optimal level of pollution? Choose a tourism context and describe three approaches to determining the optimal level of pollution within that context.

2. Using a tourism example, explain the difference between marginal private costs and marginal social costs.

3. Achieving the optimal level of output or pollution does not imply reduction of external costs to zero. Why not?

4. Use diagrams to explain the difference in approach between the use of bargaining and direct controls to solve problems associated with negative externalities generated by tourism activity.

5. A tax on output and a tax on emissions must necessarily achieve the same result. Discuss this statement in the context of any negative externalities that may emanate from the development and operation of a tourism resort.

6. Evaluate the advantages and disadvantages of using subsidies as opposed to taxes to mitigate any adverse effects of tourism.

7. Describe how a market for pollution rights might work in the tour operating industry.

8. What is meant by the term *economic instrument* in an environmental context? Outline the issues that create problems for the use of economic instruments in protecting the environment from any adverse effects of tourism.

9. Describe the ways in which uncertainty manifests itself in the choice of best instrument to lessen any environmental problems associated with tourism.

10. How do transaction costs accompany the implementation of control instruments chosen to mitigate the adverse environmental effects of tourism?

ESSAY QUESTIONS

1. Where pollution is a by-product of production, why will the actual level of output be above, and actual price be below, the socially optimal levels? Show the negative externality implications of this situation on a diagram. Discuss ways in which these negative externalities may be mitigated.

2. The optimal level of output of a tourism product which generates negative externalities will generally be greater than zero. How so?

3. Evaluate the use of property rights and bargaining between affected parties as a solution to the problem of pollution within a tourism context.

4. Direct controls such as prohibition are always a better solution to overcoming any negative externalities associated with tourism than other options such as the imposition of taxes or the entering into of voluntary agreements or bargaining. Discuss.

5. Notwithstanding all the different types of economic instruments that may be applied to mitigate the adverse environmental effects associated with tourism, it is the market-based instruments that have the most potential to reduce these negative externalities at least cost. Discuss.

6. The only real long-term way to mitigate any adverse effects associated with tourism activity is through education, information and adherence to strict codes of conduct. Discuss.

7. While economic theory assumes perfect certainty, reality suggests that uncertainty makes the choice of best instrument to mitigate the adverse environmental effects of tourism much more complex. How so?

8. 'When boundary problems arise, both price and quantitative solutions lose their effectiveness and sometimes may be counter-productive.' Is this so, and if it is, how then might the adverse environmental effects of tourism be mitigated?

CHAPTER 19

CLIMATE CHANGE AND TOURISM

LEARNING OBJECTIVES

After reading this chapter, you should be able to:

1. Appreciate the fact that climate change can impact on tourism and tourism activities can impact on climate.

2. Discuss how tourism can respond to climate change through adaptation strategies.

3. Appreciate that tourism activity can leave a carbon footprint on the environment.

4. Evaluate climate change mitigation policies available to tourism, understand their complexity and explain how their implementation will impact back on tourism.

5. Explain why the aviation industry should not receive differential treatment in relation to climate change.

19.1 INTRODUCTION

Climate change will have increasing substantial effects on tourism flows worldwide. A process of global warming is caused by the growth in emissions of greenhouse gases (GHG), particularly carbon dioxide (CO_2), but also including other gases such as methane and nitrogen oxides. Natural and human factors both affect global climate. Natural causes include interactions between the ocean and the atmosphere, changes in the Earth's orbit and volcanic eruptions. Humans influence global climate by releasing GHGs into the atmosphere. This growth in GHGs is increased as a result of human activity, especially from the burning of fossil fuels such as coal and oil. These gases absorb energy that is radiated from the Earth's surface, warming the atmosphere and increasing temperatures globally.

   Climate change is a global challenge that requires a long-term global solution in order to avoid environmental, social and economic dislocation. GHG emissions cause damage both within and also well outside the country in which they occur. Once emitted into the atmosphere, their impact is substantial and long-lasting, for both developed and developing economies. Climate change threatens the basic elements of life for people around the world – access to water, food, health and use of land and the environment. Hundreds of millions of people could suffer hunger, water shortages and coastal flooding as the world warms. The adverse consequences of climate change, and their amelioration, will last for generations and will require fundamental shifts in consumer and business behaviour.

Climate change will affect the world's rate of economic growth. Using the results from formal economic models, the Stern Report estimates that if the world does not act immediately, the overall costs and risks of climate change will be equivalent to losing at least 5% of global GDP each year, now and forever. If a wider range of risks and impacts is taken into account, the estimates of damage could rise to 20% of GDP or more. It is claimed that the poorest countries will be especially hard-hit by climate change, with millions potentially pushed deeper into poverty. In contrast, the costs of action – reducing GHG emissions to avoid the worst impacts of climate change – can be limited to around 1% of global GDP each year (Stern, 2006).

Given the importance of economic growth as a driver of tourism, the tourism industry globally will undoubtedly suffer. Not only will climate change impact on the total volume of tourism flows, but it will affect destination market shares as some destinations will be adversely affected more than others. Economic analysis has an important role to play in contributing to our understanding of the different types of issues raised by climate change and in policy formulation. While climate change is a physical phenomenon, there is a critical role of economics in analysing the implications for tourism.

Human-induced climate change is an example of market failure involving externalities and public goods (Stern, 2006).

- Human-induced climate change is an externality on a global scale which, in the absence of policy intervention, is not 'corrected' through any institution or market. GHGs are negative externalities from industrial activity (including tourism). Economic activities that produce GHG emissions bring about climate change, thereby imposing costs on the world and on future generations. However, emitters typically do not directly face the full consequences of the costs of their actions.
- The climate is a public good. As discussed in Chapter 17, markets do not automatically provide the right type and quantity of public goods, since in the absence of public policy there are limited or no returns to private investors for doing so. Those who fail to pay for it cannot be excluded from enjoying its benefits and one person's enjoyment of the climate does not diminish the capacity of others to enjoy it also. Markets for relevant goods and services (energy, land use, innovation, etc.) do not reflect the full costs and benefits of different consumption and investment choices for the climate.

The seriousness of the climate change problem is captured in Stern's comment that 'All in all, it must be regarded as market failure on the greatest scale the world has seen' (Stern, 2006: x).

19.2 CLIMATE CHANGE AND TOURISM: A TWO-WAY INTERACTION

Tourism and climate change can be considered as 'a two-way street' with climate influencing tourism, and tourism influencing climate (Figure 19.1).

As the top arrow indicates, tourism industries are not just potential victims of climate change but also part of the climate change problem. Tourism firms contribute to emissions, either directly (e.g. through transport use of fuels) or indirectly (e.g. through a hotel's use of electricity generated by fossil fuels). And since tourism demand extends over a large range of goods and services, firms outside of the tourism industry generate GHG in their production processes to meet tourist needs.

Climate change mitigation is aimed at reducing the severity of the levels and impacts of GHGs. Tourism's impact on climate implies that tourism will be affected by the various types of mitigation policies that are being formulated to address the carbon emissions associated with economic activity.

Economics can help to determine how climate change mitigation policies will work in the context of the tourism industry. From a policy perspective, governments will be interested in determining which policies are effective in reducing emissions at minimum costs. From the industry perspective, there is interest in how specific policies will impact on particular sectors or destinations.

In respect of the bottom arrow, the attractiveness of many of the most popular tourist destinations globally relies heavily on the natural environment. Coastal resorts, tropical rainforests, wildlife reserves, wilderness regions, alpine ski resorts and so on all rely on a mixture of natural beauty, ideal weather and safe conditions to attract tourists.

Climate change will result in shifting market shares of domestic and international destinations. Destination managers and individual operators will need to adapt to the changes

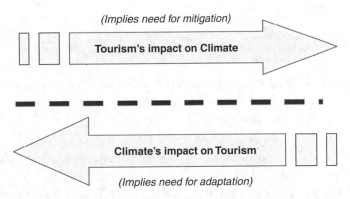

Figure 19.1 Climate affects tourism and tourism affects climate

Source: Patterson *et al.* (2006)

709

brought about by global warming. Adaptation refers to the ability of a system to adjust to climate change (including climate variability and extremes), to moderate potential damages, to take advantage of opportunities or to cope with the consequences. Adaptation, together with mitigation, is an important response strategy to global warming. Without early and strong mitigation, the costs of adaptation will rise, and countries' and individuals' ability to adapt effectively will be constrained (Gossling 2002; Stern, 2006). Mitigation involves reducing the severity of impacts while adaptation involves adjusting to the impacts.

19.3 CLIMATE CHANGE IMPACTS ON TOURISM

Because of the importance of weather and environment to leisure demand, it is not surprising that tourism is one of the sectors most likely to be affected by climate change. As discussed in Chapters 17 and 18, tourism is closely linked with the natural environment. Climate is a principal resource for tourism, as it influences the suitability of locations for a wide range of tourist activities. Climate already has a major influence on destination choice. As a result of changing climatic conditions, tourists are likely to entirely avoid some destinations in favour of others or else shift the timing of travel to avoid unfavourable climate conditions. As such, the response of tourists to the complexity of destination impacts will reshape demand patterns and play an important role in determining the impacts of climate change on the tourism industry (UNWTO, 2009b). Climate change will generate both negative and positive impacts on the tourism industry, varying substantially by market segment and geographic region. There will be 'winners and losers' at the business, destination and nation level.

Box 19.1 highlights some of the major anticipated effects of climate change on the tourism industry.

BOX 19.1 Major anticipated effects of climate change on tourism

- Altered climate conditions for tourist demand suggests that the geographic and seasonal redistribution of tourist demand may be very large for individual destinations and countries by mid- to late-21st century.
- Global economic growth will be adversely affected by climate change which will in turn impact upon global tourism numbers given the importance of income as a determinant of tourism growth.
- Regardless of its affect on overall tourism flows, climate change is most likely to affect market shares between and within destinations.

- Small island tourism destinations are particularly vulnerable to sea level rise and erosion of beaches and shorelines. Tropical islands will be susceptible to intense climatic events such as hurricanes, and these may become more frequent.
- Global warming will have serious consequences for tourism industries and attractions, especially those which rely heavily on the natural environment, such as beaches, ski fields, rainforests and reefs.
- Changes in weather patterns could severely damage or destroy tourism attractions. These include bushfires, hurricanes, leading to reductions in the benefits from tourism from key nature based markets.
- Reduced precipitation and increased evaporation will cause water shortages in some regions, competition between tourism and other industry sectors over water, desertification and increased bushfires threatening infrastructure.
- Increased frequency of heavy precipitation in some destinations could cause flood damage to historic architectural and cultural assets and damage tourism infrastructure.
- Soil changes occasioned by changing moisture levels, erosion and acidity could lead to loss of archaeological assets and other natural resources with impacts on destination attractions.
- Sea level rises can cause coastal erosion, loss of beach area, higher costs to protect and maintain waterfront tourism precincts.
- Sea surface temperature rises can cause coral bleaching and marine resource degradation and species extinction, reducing destination attractiveness.
- Tourism seasons will be altered with more tourists travelling in shoulder seasons, or in winter seasons, as climate will be more appealing. This shift in travel patterns may have important implications, including proportionally more tourism spending in temperate nations and proportionally less tourist spending in warmer nations.
- The direct effect of climate change might be significant enough to alter major intra-regional tourism flows where climate is particularly important, including Northern Europe to the Mediterranean and the Caribbean, North America to the Caribbean, and to a lesser extent North East Asia to Southeast Asia.
- Some tourist market segments will be unaffected. Business, convention and VFR tourism may be relatively unaffected by climate change, and holiday tourists more interested in visiting urban locations will not be particularly

affected. However, for many leisure destinations it is very likely that climate change will have adverse affects on tourist visitation.

- Some locations will cease to attract tourists. Lower visitation implies a loss of tourism expenditure and economic contribution in the local region and in the wider economy.
- Many attractions may survive, but the quality of the visitor experience will decline resulting in reduced visitation and reduced economic impacts.
- Some attractions may be created or improved by climate change. For example, some beaches may become warmer and more attractive and some destinations may experience less severe climates and become more attractive to visitors.
- Some destinations will experience a reduction in some tourism markets but growth in others. In the Arctic, for example, longer summer seasons might benefit cruise tourism and activities such as whale-watching, but shorter winters could deplete the range of Arctic fauna and flora which attracts visitors.
- Climate change will affect operator costs as a result of both adaptation policies and conformance with climate change mitigation policies enacted by governments. When countries implement policies to reduce their GHGs, the profitability of tourism industries will be affected. Thus if a price is put on carbon, input costs for tourism will increase. Some types of tourism (e.g. long haul air trips) and destinations will be affected more than others.
- For some destinations climate change leads to increased outbound tourism by residents, leading to a loss of tourism expenditure in the home country, with an associated impact on the domestic tourism industry and the whole economy.

Source: UNWTO (2009b); IPCC (2007a, b)

Projecting tourism flows is important since estimates of the economic effects of climate change on tourism must use forecast changes in tourism flows (and associated expenditure) as inputs into modelling. Box 19.2 summarises some results of a study of the tourism-related economic impacts of climate change.

BOX 19.2 Modelling the economic impacts of climate change on tourism

Berrittellaa *et al.* (2006) investigated the economic implications of climate-change-induced variations in tourism demand. The authors take their estimates of changes in international tourist flows from an econometrically estimated simulation model of bilateral flows of tourists between 207 countries. To assess the systemic, general equilibrium effects of tourism impacts, induced by global warming, the authors employ a multi-country world CGE (GTAP) model. The GTAP model is a standard CGE static model, distributed with the GTAP database of the world economy (Hertel, 1996). The model is first re-calibrated at some future years, obtaining hypothetical benchmark equilibria, which are subsequently perturbed by shocks, simulating the effects of climate change. The impact of climate change on tourism flows is simulated by means of two sets of shocks occurring simultaneously.

The first set of shocks translates projected variations in tourist flows into changes of consumption preferences for domestically produced goods. The second set of shocks reallocates income across world regions, simulating the effect of higher or lower tourists' expenditure.

Table 19.1 shows the climate change impacts on private domestic demand and household income, in terms of variation from the baseline. For the European Union, shocks are positive in 2010 and 2030, but become negative in 2050. At the global (world) level, these shocks are neither positive nor negative, as they entail a redistribution of income both within a region (changes in consumption patterns) and across regions (income transfers). Therefore, in the model employed, aggregate results are solely due to structural composition effects.

Impacts on domestic demand and household income affect the rest of the economy through substitution with other goods and services, and through induced effects on primary factors demand and prices. Also, changes in the rate of return of capital influence investment flows, which affect income and welfare.

The main winners are projected to be the countries whose climate is currently too cold to attract many tourists, such as the former Soviet Union's countries and Canada (which is inside the Rest of Annex 1 group). Also, the USA, Japan, Australasia and Eastern Europe gain substantially. Tourism flows to China and India are not predicted to change in net terms. The EU enjoys a small welfare gain in 2010 and 2030, but suffers substantial losses in 2050. Welfare losses accrue mainly to the Rest of the World macro-region, which includes the poorest countries as well as the small island developing nations which are also more vulnerable to other negative climate change effects relevant for the tourism industry, such as sea-level rise. Net losers are Western Europe, energy exporting countries, and the rest of the world. The Mediterranean, currently the world's largest tourism destination, is projected to become substantially less attractive to tourists.

Table 19.1 Initial shocks of climate change on private domestic demand and private household income

Initial shocks on private domestic demand and private household income					
Region	Private domestic demand for Market Services (% change)			Private households' real income (1997 Millions US$)		
	2010	2030	2050	2010	2030	2050
USA	0.0004	0.047	0.110	10.833	2373.6	9279.3
EU	0.0005	0.008	−0.080	13.050	373.26	−9424.3
EEFSU	0.0027	0.310	0.712	7.652	1803.9	7419.0
JPN	0.0014	0.162	0.361	18.759	4013.0	15987.2
RoA1	0.0051	0.631	1.517	24.342	5312.9	21516.3
Eex	−0.0022	−0.243	−0.530	−34.377	−6348.9	−20576.5
CHIND	0.00002	0.003	0.008	0.033	9.221	39.660
RoW	−0.0025	−0.265	−0.568	−40.292	−7536.9	−24240.7

Note: USA [USA], European Union,[EU], Eastern Europe and Former Soviet Union [EEFSU], Japan, [JPN], Rest of Annex 1 (developed) countries [RoA1], Energy Exporters [EEx], China and India [CHIND], Rest of the World [RoW]

Source: Berrittella *et al.* (2006), Table 4

The authors conclude that while the global economic impact of a climate-change-induced change in tourism is quite small at present, by 2050, climate change will ultimately lead to a non-negligible global loss. It is concluded that climate change affects on tourism may affect world GDP by −0.3% to +0.5% in 2050. Thus, climate change will ultimately lead to a welfare loss on a global scale, unevenly spread across regions. They emphasise that the study includes only the direct effects of climate change on tourism. It ignores the effects of sea level rise, which may erode beaches, and which may submerge entire islands. It also neglects other indirect effects of climate change, such as those on the water cycle, and those on the spread of diseases both of which affect tourism flows. The study also ignores the adaptive behaviour of economic agents, with the associated costs of adaptation, and the effects of climate change mitigation policies on operator costs.

The concept of 'annual climate change' for a destination is meaningless to most tourists who for the most part focus on specific regions within countries. In geographically large countries (Russia, Canada, the USA, and Australia for example) climate change will differentially affect sub regions.

The authors assume that climate change will not affect the amount of money spent but rather where it is spent. This assumption may not be realistic given that climate change is likely to reduce rates of economic growth in the major origin markets which in turn will affect destination market shares in respect of both numbers and expenditure. As Stern (2006) has observed the impacts of climate change on economies and societies worldwide could be large relative to the global economy. Thus cannot be assumed that the global economy, net of the costs of climate change, will grow at a certain rate in the future, irrespective of whether countries follow a 'business as usual' path or take collective action to reduce GHG emissions.

Overall, it is very likely that the costs of climate change on tourism are underestimated. Even so, the economic ramifications of climate-change-induced tourism shifts are projected to be substantial.

Source: Berrittella, M., A. Bigano, R. Rosona and R.S.J. Tol (2006) 'A General Equilibrium Analysis of Climate Change Impacts on Tourism', *Tourism Management*, 27, 913–924

Individual tourism destinations need to interpret these global trends in the context of their own localities (UNWTO, 2009b). For accurate predictions of the specific effects on tourism flows, improved understanding of the potential geographic and seasonal shifts in tourist demand is needed. This implies a better understanding of tourist climate attitudes, tourist preferences and key thresholds (i.e. 'when is it too hot for a beach holiday?'), tourist perceptions of the environmental impacts of global climate change at destinations (i.e. perceptions of coral bleaching, degraded coastlines, depleted snow cover and reduced biodiversity or wildlife), elasticities of demand for travel and tourist perceptions of the environmental impacts of tourism related travel.

19.4 ADAPTATION POLICIES FOR TOURISM

Adaptation is a crucial part of the response of the tourist industry to the challenge of climate change. The aim of adaptation is to reduce vulnerability to climatic change and variability, thereby reducing their negative impacts. But adaptation strategies should also attempt to enhance a destination's capability to capture any of the benefits of climate change. Given existing levels of GHGs, adaptation is the only way to cope with their impacts over the next few decades.

Adaptation can operate at two broad levels – building adaptive capacity and delivering adaptive actions

Building adaptive capacity

This involves creating the information and conditions (regulatory, institutional and managerial) that are needed to support adaptation, reducing the destination's vulnerability to climate change. Developing the right policy frameworks will encourage and facilitate effective adaptation by households, communities and firms. Measures to build adaptive capacity range from understanding the potential impacts of climate change, and the options for adaptation (i.e. undertaking impact studies and identifying vulnerabilities), to piloting specific actions and accumulating the resources necessary to implement actions (Stern, 2006). Governments can support adaptation by providing both policy guidelines and economic and institutional support to the private sector and the community. The building of adaptive capacity will be a particular challenge for many tourist destinations and their host communities. The most vulnerable regions are in developing countries, which generally also have less financial resources and hence less adaptive capacity.

Delivering adaptation actions

This involves taking actions to reduce vulnerability to climate risks or to exploit opportunities. Examples include investing in physical infrastructure to protect against specific climate risks, such as flood defences, sea walls or new reservoirs; introducing new technologies; providing intensive training; investing in the creation of new products; nourishing beaches; creating artificial snow; and changing the attitudes of public authorities, entrepreneurs, host communities and tourists. Adaptation actions should be integrated into development policy and planning at every level, with climate change responses integrated into a broader risk management policy for the tourism sector.

The implications of climate change for any tourism business or destination will also partially depend on the types and extent of impacts on its competitors and their responses. A negative impact in respect of reduction in or loss of a particular market may open up opportunities for market growth elsewhere (UNWTO, 2009b).

The costs of climate change to a tourism destination or attraction can be illustrated as in Figure 19.2a and 19.2b.

An attraction enjoys domestic visitors as shown in Figure 19.2a, and international inbound visitors as shown in Figure 19.2b. If climate change lowers the quality of the tourism experience, the demand (or willingness to pay) curves will shift downwards, from D_{d1} to D_{d2}, in the case of domestic tourism (Figure 19.2a), and from D_{f1} to D_{f2} in the case of inbound tourism (Figure 19.2b). For simplicity, we assume that average and marginal

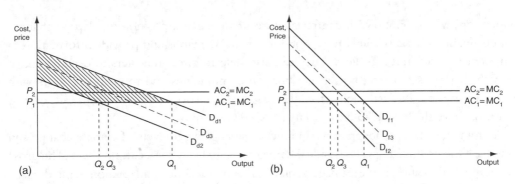

Figure 19.2 Costs of climate change to a destination

costs are constant at $AC_1 = MC_1$. For domestic tourism there will be a reduction in consumer surplus accruing to tourists when demand falls from D_{d1} to D_{d3}. This loss of consumer surplus is the shaded area in Figure 19.2a. While, as indicated in Figure 19.2b, international visitors will also suffer a loss of consumer surplus, this is not a cost to the home economy. The cost to the home economy is related to the loss in inbound expenditure (from $P_1 Q_1$ to $P_1 Q_2$). The size of this loss depends on how large are the benefits from inbound tourism relative to the expenditure.

Adaptation costs are hard to estimate, because of uncertainty about the precise impacts of climate change and its varied effects. They will vary on a case-by-case basis. For some attractions, it is possible to adapt to climate change. For example, a ski field can reduce the risks of loss of snow cover by investing in snowmaking. A process of adaptation is also shown in Figure 19.2. Adaptation results in costs rising to $AC_2 = MC_2$, but the payoff is that the demand (or willingness to pay) curves do not shift down by as much. In Figures 19.2a and 19.2b, they are shown as falling to D_{d3} and D_{f3} for domestic and inbound tourism, respectively. If the costs of adaptation are passed on to the tourists, the price of using the attraction rises to P_2. In this case, adaptation is worthwhile, since for domestic visitors, the reduction in consumer surplus is reduced, and the reduction in expenditure by international visitors is also smaller (the reduction is now $P_1 . Q_1 - P_2 . Q_3$ which may imply greater revenues. An attraction will need to undertake its own investment assessment to determine whether the expenditure on adaptation is worthwhile.

The capacity to adapt to climate change varies substantially between sub-sectors, destinations and individual businesses within the tourism industry. Tourists have the greatest adaptive capacity with relative freedom to avoid destinations impacted by climate change or shifting the timing of travel to avoid unfavourable climate conditions. Tour wholesalers know this and they can play an important role in destination choice as they shift their marketing activity towards particular destinations to the neglect of others. Tourism is, in a sense, a *footloose industry*. While the tourism plant may not shift from one country to another, production will, since tourists can choose which countries to visit. Suppliers of tourism services and tourism operators at specific destinations have less adaptive capacity. Large tour operators, who do not own the infrastructure, are in a better position to adapt to changes at destinations because they can respond to clients' demands and provide information to influence clients' travel choices. They can also help to direct travellers to destinations in which they posses market power. Destination communities and tourism operators with large investment in fixed capital facilities (e.g. hotel, resort complex, marina, airports or casinos) have the least adaptive capacity (UNWTO, 2009b).

For any destination, adaptation will reduce the negative impacts of climate change and increase the positive impacts. Residual damage is very likely to occur, however. The gross benefit of adaptation is the damage avoided. The net benefit of adaptation is the damage avoided less the cost of adaptation. The cost of climate change after adaptation is the residual cost of climate damage plus the cost of adaptation. Figure 19.3 indicates that ignoring climate change is not a rational option since inaction will be far more costly than adaptation.

In Figure 19.3 the relationship between rising temperatures and the different costs of climate change/adaptation is shown as linear. In reality, the costs of climate change are likely to accelerate with increasing temperature, while the net benefit of adaptation is likely to fall relative to the cost of climate change.

Adaptation will in most cases provide local benefits, realised without long lag times, in contrast to mitigation policies which typically take longer to have an effect. But there are limits to what adaptation can achieve. Adaptation can at best reduce the impacts, but cannot by itself solve the problem of climate change. As the magnitude and

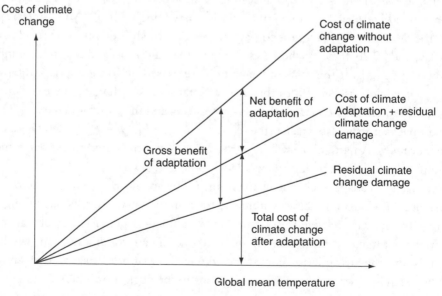

Figure 19.3 Gross and net benefits of adaptation to climate change

Source: Stern Report (2006), Figure 18.1, p. 405

speed of unabated climate change increase, the relative effectiveness of adaptation will diminish.

Without strong and early mitigation, the physical limits to – and costs of – adaptation will grow rapidly. This applies to developing countries in particular and attests to the importance of effective mitigation policies. We now discuss tourism impacts on GHGs and, hence, global warming before discussing types of mitigation policies affecting tourism.

19.5   TOURISM IMPACTS ON CLIMATE CHANGE

Tourism industries themselves are part of the climate change problem. Most tourism-related activities require energy directly in the form of fossil fuels or indirectly in the form of electricity often generated from petroleum, coal or gas. This consumption leads to the emission of GHGs, mainly CO_2.

Direct GHG emissions from tourism production include those from the fuel used by tour buses, rental cars, aviation, hotel operations, theme parks, restaurants and so on.

Indirect GHG emissions are associated with the outputs of industries that supply inputs to tourism, for example, GHGs emitted in production of electricity purchased by travel agencies or in construction of hotels, or manufacture of T-shirts, aircraft, cruise ships, agricultural produce and so on.

The Davos Declaration was adopted by the global Conference on Climate Change and Tourism convened by UNWTO jointly with the United Nations Environment Programme and the World Meteorological Organization, with the support of the World Economic Forum in October 2007. The Declaration (http://www.unwto.org/ climate/support/en/support.php) specifies that 'the tourism sector must rapidly respond to climate change, within the evolving UN framework, and progressively reduce its GHG contribution if it is to grow in a sustainable manner. This will require action to:

- mitigate its GHG emissions, derived especially from transport and accommodation activities
- adapt tourism businesses and destinations to changing climate conditions
- apply existing and new technology to improve energy efficiency
- secure financial resources to help poor regions and countries.'

19.5.1   MEASURING TOURISM'S CARBON FOOTPRINT

It is common nowadays to speak of tourism's 'carbon footprint'. A Carbon Footprint is essentially an accounting measure referring to the amount of GHG emissions (CO_2

equivalent (CO_2-eq.) associated with the production and consumption of goods and services at the level of an individual firm, industry or entire economy.

Because of the extensive use of energy-intensive technologies that deliver tourist amenities, and to construct and operate new infrastructure, accommodations and other facilities, energy use in tourism destinations is typically much greater than that associated with other similar-sized communities (Kelly & Williams, 2007). Tourism destinations also rely on substantial amounts of energy for importing food and other material goods, transporting water and disposing waste (Becken *et al.*, 2003; Gössling *et al.*, 2002). Tourist attractions, including theme parks with use of mechanised activities, also may generate substantial energy demands in destinations. Energy is also used in up- and down-stream business functions (e.g. tour office administration, marketing and goods transportation) that support the delivery of these activities (Becken & Simmons, 2002). GHG emissions from international air and sea transport are a substantial and growing component of global emissions. Air travel accounts for a major share of tourism-related energy use, particularly for developing countries and island destinations where the vast majority of tourists arrive by air (Becken, 2002; Gössling, 2000).

The Kyoto Protocol

Countries worldwide have obligations under the Kyoto Protocol. Kyoto imposes national caps on the emissions of Annex I (developed) countries. Under Kyoto, industrialised countries have agreed to reduce their collective GHG emissions by 5.2% compared to the year 1990, with varying reductions agreed to by the signatories. Most GHG emissions produced from within a destination are included under Kyoto accounting rules. However, there are GHG emissions from destination-based firms producing within the destination which are not included under Kyoto rules. While the Kyoto Protocol includes emissions from international aviation in principle, in reality this extends presently only to an obligation on parties to monitor these emissions. There also are GHG emissions which are produced in other countries as part of their production of goods and services which are subsequently imported for consumption by tourist in a destination. Individual countries do not assume any responsibility under the Kyoto agreement for the carbon footprint from goods produced outside of their jurisdiction. The next round of negotiations took place in Copenhagen late 2009.

In order to meet the objectives of the Kyoto Protocol, Annex I countries are required to prepare policies and measures for the reduction of GHGs in their respective countries. The tourism industry, alongside other industry sectors, is expected to play its role in reducing GHG emissions wherever possible. Among the tourism-specific strategies emphasised by UNWTO (2009b) are the mitigation of GHG emissions, the adaptation of tourism businesses and destinations to changing climate conditions, the application of existing and new technologies to improve energy efficiency, and securing financial resources to assist regions and countries in need. Tourism stakeholders are expected to play their role in the required strategy formulation and implementation to reduce tourism's carbon footprint. Essential for these tasks is accurate information on the carbon footprint of each the various sectors that comprise 'the tourism industry'.

Tourism's carbon footprint has been estimated globally, and also for particular destinations and also by type of tourist.

19.5.2 TOURISM'S GLOBAL CARBON FOOTPRINT

A report by UNWTO (2009b) represents the first attempt to calculate direct emissions of CO_2 from three main tourism sub-sectors – transportation, accommodations and activities – as well as the contribution to radiative forcing (i.e. including all GHGs) for the year 2005.

Table 19.2 shows the results of the emissions for world tourism in 2005. International and domestic tourism emissions from three main sub-sectors are estimated to represent between 4.0% and 6.0% of global emissions in 2005, with a best estimate of 5.0%. A globally averaged tourist journey is estimated to generate 0.25 tonnes of CO_2 emissions.

In 2005 transport (all forms) generated the largest proportion of CO_2 emissions (75%) from global tourism, with just under 40% of the total being caused by air transport alone. In sum:

- air transport accounts for an estimated 40% of the travel and tourism contribution of CO_2;
- air transport accounts for an estimated 60% of the *international* travel and tourism contribution of CO_2 and is overwhelmingly dominant for medium- and long-haul trips;
- a 'business as usual' forecast for travel and tourism for 2035 is for an increase over 2005 of 160% in CO_2, with the share of air transport emissions rising from 40% to just over 50% (UNWTO, 2009b).

Aviation is a relatively large generator of GHGs, which, per traveller, are high, especially for long trips. Long-haul travel by air between the five UNWTO world tourism regions represents only 2.7% of all tourist trips but contributes 17% to global tourism-related CO_2 emissions. In contrast, trips by coach and rail account for 34% of all trips, but contribute only 13% of all CO_2 emissions.

Apart from the transport sector, tourism is not a major direct producer of GHGs globally. Emissions from accommodation and activities were estimated to be substantially lower than transport emissions but still form one-quarter of tourism-related emissions.

While indicative of tourism's relative global carbon intensity, the UNWTO qualifies its findings. CO_2 emissions do not capture the full GHG emissions from economic activity of tourism or any other industry. Moreover, the estimates relate to direct emissions only. Tourism is also an indirect producer of GHGs through its purchases of goods and services

Table 19.2 Emissions from global tourism in 2005 (including same-day visitors)

	CO_2 *(Mt)*	%
Air Transport	517	39.6
Other Transport	468	35.8
Accommodation	274	16.6
Activities	45	8.0
TOTAL	1,307	100
Total World	26,400	
Share (%)	4.95	

Source: Adapted from UNWTO (2008a)

which use fossil fuels. A full accounting of tourism's global carbon footprint would require estimation of both the direct and indirect carbon intensity.

19.5.3 THE CARBON FOOTPRINT OF A DESTINATION

Carbon footprints are likely to vary greatly between destinations, reflecting climate, culture, energy sources, available technology, activities undertaken and the country of origin of the tourists. Thus each destination should be treated individually. As discussed in Chapter 7, TSA can be used to define the scope of the tourism industry to estimate its output and thence associated GHG emissions (Forsyth *et al.*, 2008; Jones & Munday, 2007; Jackson *et al.*, 2008; Patterson & McDonald, 2004; Dwyer *et al.*, 2010).

The development of a carbon footprint for any destination is not straightforward, however, as there are several different interpretations given to what the carbon footprint is, and what it should encompass. In their study of tourism's carbon footprint in New Zealand, Becken and Patterson (2006) suggest two approaches for accounting for CO_2 emissions from tourism: a bottom-up analysis involving industry and tourist analyses and a top-down analysis using environmental accounting. They demonstrate for New Zealand that both approaches result in similar estimates of the degree to which tourism contributes to national CO_2 emissions. The bottom-up analysis provides detailed information on energy end-uses and the main drivers of CO_2 emissions. These results can be used for the development of targeted industry-based GHG reduction strategies. The top-down analysis, including use of TSA, allows assessment of tourism as a sector within the wider economy, for example, with the purpose of comparing tourism's eco-efficiency with other sectors, or the impact of macroeconomic instruments such as carbon charges.

19.5.4 CARBON FOOTPRINT OF DIFFERENT TOURISM MARKETS

By origin market

Different types of tourists generate different economic, social and environmental impacts on destinations. These impacts, or 'footprints', vary across market segments depending on the mix of services utilised by the tourist. Lundie *et al.* (2007) estimated the environmental impacts of tourists to Australia from different origin markets. In this study, a hybrid approach is employed, combining input–output analysis with an on-site audit for tourist accommodation. The direct (on-site) requirements of different tourists were assessed, while all remaining higher-order requirements (for materials extraction, manufacturing and services) were addressed using input–output analysis. Other direct impacts, such as from transportation, were omitted due to the lack of data.

Environmental impacts included those on energy use, water use, GHG emissions and ecological footprint. The effects on GHG emissions are shown in Table 19.3.

Average GHG per trip in Australia was 4.3 tonnes of CO_2. The greatest GHG emissions per trip are associated with backpackers (a long-stay market), German holiday makers and Malaysian repeaters, while the lowest are associated with Japanese honeymooners and New Zealand over-55s. The average emissions per dollar spent in Australia was 1.81 kg. The largest emissions per dollar spent are associated with Japanese honeymooners and New Zealand over-55s and the lowest with Malaysian repeaters. The average emissions per visitor night were 213 kg CO_2. The different emissions generated by the different markets are related to their choice of accommodation and the types of goods and services purchased by the tourists. Per visitor night, by far the largest emissions are associated with Japanese honeymooners, convention visitors and business travellers.

From an economic viewpoint the preferred market segments will be those that generate higher expenditure per night (although we would argue that it is economy-wide economic impacts that are more important than expenditure; see below), while from an environmental viewpoint, the preferred markets are those that involve fewer GHG emissions. In Figure 19.4 the preferred markets from an economic viewpoint lie to the right of the vertical axis which indicates the average expenditure for a tourist to Australia ($93 per night), while from an environmental perspective the preferred markets lie below the average of 213 kg CO_2 per visitor night. Therefore, market segments which occupy the South East quadrant are preferred from both economic and environmental perspectives while those that occupy the North West quadrant are the least preferred on both perspectives.

Table 19.3 GHG emissions in Australia per visitor trip, per $A spent and per night, 2002–04

Environmental indicators	Unit	Japanese honey mooners	Convention	Business	Malaysia +55	NZ +55	Malaysian first timers	HK first timers	Canadian +55	UK repeats	German holidayers	Back packers	Malaysian repeats	Average (all tourism)
Per visitor trip	tCO_2-eq./trip	2.5	2.8	3.7	2.9	2.5	2.8	3.6	4.8	4.8	6.5	9.5	4.9	4.3
Per $A spent	kg CO_2/$	2.1	1.7	1.8	2.0	2.0	1.5	1.5	2.1	1.8	1.9	1.9	1.4	1.81
Per visitor night	kg CO_2/night	448	346	314	148	160	163	173	182	141	175	143	161	213

Source: Lundie *et al.* (2007)

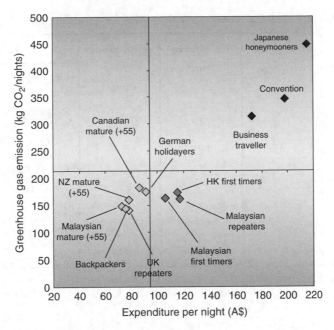

Figure 19.4 Daily expenditure and GHG emissions

The findings reveal that, for some inbound markets, simultaneous achievement of relatively high economic and environmental goals may be difficult, and that economic–environmental trade-offs may be necessary. The more tourists spend (high economic yield), the more likely it is that GHG are emitted in the associated production processes (high carbon footprint).

By travel mode

Becken and Simmons (2002) investigated carbon emissions for transport within New Zealand by transport type. While extensive travel and dispersion into less visited areas can be seen as beneficial for regional development, Becken and Simmons demonstrated that it comes at an environmental cost, measured here through CO_2 emissions. Their findings are in Table 19.4. Focusing on five types of travellers (coach; fully independent travellers (FIT); backpackers; campers; and visiting friends and relatives (home visitors)), they found that tourists' CO_2 costs vary between 177 kg and 267 kg per trip. Costed at $25 per tonne of CO_2, tourism's CO_2 costs vary between $2.65 and $6.67 per trip for the transport component. The largest CO_2 emissions per trip were associated with camping tourists. These tourists dominated road travel (3293 km per tourist). Coach tourists are by far the largest user of air transport (533 km per tourist trip). Home visitors travel the least distance, 1199 km in total.

Estimating the CO_2 emissions for different types of tourist can provide valuable information in the development of strategies to reduce their carbon footprints.

Table 19.4 CO_2 emissions for transport within New Zealand by tourist type

	CO_2 from air (kg)	CO_2 from road	CO_2 from other modes	Total	
				CO_2 kg	$ per trip $25/t
Coach	101	117	11	229	$5.70
FIT	45	125	7	177	$4.42
Backpackers	53	173	23	249	$6.22
Campers	33	225	9	267	$6.67
Home visitors (VFR)	43	60	4	106	$2.65

Source: Becken and Simmons (2002)

19.5.5 TOURISM'S CARBON FOOTPRINT: INTENSITY VERSUS IMPACT

There are two types of 'carbon footprint' that are associated with tourism. The first is an *intensity measure* and the second is an *impact measure*. In discussions of tourism and climate change policies, it is important that the distinctions be appreciated.

(1) The carbon *intensity* of tourism reflects an economic/technical relationship between tourism and carbon GHGs. Tourism is associated with economic activity which creates GHGs. A particular pattern of expenditure, for example, whether associated with an international or a domestic tourist, results in GHG emissions. For the most part, except for aviation and ground transport, tourism is mainly an indirect producer of GHGs, using electricity, aluminium, steel and food, and in doing so contributing indirectly to GHGs.

Carbon intensity measures (e.g. as measured in metric tonnes of emissions) can be developed at many levels. Thus they can be developed for individual tourists, individual operators, industry sectors, regions, entire destinations and internationally. While countries may focus on GHGs within the destination, global GHG emissions will exceed the sum of individual country's emissions, given the emissions from international transportation of goods and services.

(2) The carbon *impact* of tourism is the ultimate impact on GHGs associated with changes in tourism flows and expenditure after all inter-industry effects have taken place. This is different from the carbon intensity since, to measure the impact, it is necessary to specify

what further changes in GHG emissions are associated with changes in tourism due to the changing composition of industry following the demand shock.

- if there is an increase in domestic tourism for any reason, there will be less spending by residents on other goods and services – this reduction also affects GHGs. If there is an increase in foreign inbound tourism, there will be more GHGs directly associated with this tourism.
- there will be other changes taking place – as tourism exports rise, putting upward pressure on the exchange rate, the adverse impact on exports of non-tourism goods and services, along with a reduction in import-competing production, will reduce GHG emissions in these industries. As we discussed in Chapter 9, the net result of these industry interactive effects can only be determined through economic modelling.

Suppose a policy is enacted to discourage domestic aviation, perhaps by levying a carbon tax on it. There will be less domestic flying, but tourists will still spend more, perhaps, on surface transport, perhaps on overseas trips or perhaps on other goods and services. To estimate the impact on GHGs of the policy, it is necessary to specify what the discouraged air travellers do, and to model the expenditure changes and their impacts. This is to recognise that a carbon tax, if widely applied to industry, would change a number of technologies and prices throughout the economy. A higher-priced destination may also impact adversely on both domestic and inbound tourism flows increasing outbound tourism flows with effects on GHG emissions in other economies. The final impact on tourism prices, overall tourism demand and global GHG emissions can only be determined by economic modelling of the changes.

Measuring the economy-wide or country-wide environmental impacts is thus an important area for further research. Ideally, this would involve exploration of the use of Computable General Equilibrium (CGE) models in identifying the net environmental impacts of changes in industry composition.

19.6 CLIMATE CHANGE MITIGATION POLICIES

Several countries, and even entire regions (e.g. Europe – see Commission of the European Communities, 2006), are now moving towards implementing long-run comprehensive climate change mitigation policies. Climate change mitigation relates to technological, economic and socio-cultural changes that can reduce GHG emissions. They may do this by inducing less consumption of GHG-intensive goods or by encouraging GHG emitters to use less GHG-intensive technologies, where available.

Four major mitigation strategies for addressing GHG emissions from tourism can be distinguished (UNWTO, 2009b: 667):

- *Reducing energy use* (i.e. energy conservation). This can be achieved, for example, by changing transport behaviour (e.g. more use of public transport, shift to rail and coach instead of car and aircraft and choosing less distant destinations) as well as changing management practices (e.g. videoconferencing for business tourism).
- *Improving energy efficiency.* This refers to the use of new and innovative technology to decrease energy demand (i.e. carrying out the same operation with a lower-energy input).
- *Increasing the use of renewable or carbon neutral energy.* This involves substituting scarce fossil fuels with energy sources that are not finite and cause lower emissions, such as biomass, hydro-, wind- and solar energy.
- *Sequestering CO_2 through carbon sinks.* CO_2 can be stored in biomass (e.g. through afforestation and deforestation), in aquifers or oceans, and in geological sinks (e.g. depleted gas fields). The UNWTO points out that, indirectly, this option can have relevance to the tourism sector, considering that most developing countries and small island destinations that rely on air transport for their tourism-driven economies are biodiversity-rich areas with important biomass CO_2 storage function. Environmentally oriented tourism can play a key role in the conservation of these natural areas.

19.6.1   IMPACTS OF CLIMATE CHANGE MITIGATION POLICIES ON TOURISM FLOWS

The cost base of the tourism industry will rise as the result of the implementation of climate change mitigation policies. In addition, the cost base of other industries that are substitutes for tourism will increase. Granted the difficulties in the short run at least of passing on, in full, all of the higher cost, it is likely that the profitability of the tourism industry will suffer for a period, when a climate change mitigation policy is first introduced into any destination.

Mitigation policies will add to the cost of tourism and subsequent price rises make tourism less attractive. The home tourism product becomes more expensive. This will have a negative impact on a country's competitive position in international tourism. In the short run, during which time firms have little scope to adapt, some of the cost would fall on tourism firms. In the long run, most of the impact is likely to be passed on to the consumers/tourists.

A comprehensive assessment of the impacts on domestic tourism prices of climate change policies and ultimately on tourism flows, expenditures and impacts on the economy requires the use of CGE models, which can capture how other industries adapt to these policies (and vice versa).

Economic modelling enables the impact on tourism demand to be estimated for an ETS with a specific target, or a carbon tax set at a specific level. It will also be possible to determine how substitutes for tourism are affected by such policies. An important component of any modelling exercise will also involve assessment of the impacts on, and consequences of, inbound and outbound international tourism and the balance between these.

Domestic tourism

As a result of climate change mitigation policies such as the ETS, the price of domestic tourism will rise, as tourism firms pass on their higher costs, and as the costs of travel increase. The most significant price increases are likely to occur in the transport sector – car travel will become more expensive, and air fares will rise. The impact on prices depends partly on the GHG intensity of tourism (its carbon intensity footprint). It also depends on how other industries respond to the implementation of the ETS. For example, there is likely to be some switching away from coal in the electricity sector, which will moderate the impact of the ETS on electricity prices, and ultimately, tourism prices. The higher price of domestic tourism is likely to lead to a reduction in its demand.

Inbound tourism

Assessing the impacts on inbound tourism is a more complex exercise, requiring detail on how international air fares will change and how climate change policies affect other export industries prices and exchange rates. Again, a CGE approach is required for this.

Both the price of the component of an international inbound trip and the air fare to the region or country will rise. Air fares for outbound trips will rise, though the ground component price will not change if other countries do not implement similar climate change mitigation policies. However, the costs of all exports and the outputs of import-competing industries will increase due to the mitigation policy. Thus manufacturing industry costs will rise, and this will make manufactured products less competitive on international markets. Thus there will be downward pressure on the exchange rate, which will fall. This will counteract to some extent the effect of the rising ground component cost.

Climate change policies pose specific difficulties for international aviation, which is not controlled by any one country. The impact on tourism of the international air fare increases will depend very much on the particular aviation market, and the importance of air fares in trip costs. Travel to long-haul destinations can be particularly affected and destination managers in Southeast Asia, Australia, New Zealand and the Caribbean may well be particularly concerned that mitigation policies could adversely impact upon inbound travel. Thus the impact on UK travel to Argentina, for example, could be much greater than the impact on UK travel to Greece.

There is likely to be some impact on trip duration, with more distant visitors opting for fewer, longer trips. In analysing these effects of climate change policies, it is best to analyse major markets separately. The effects of carbon offsets and taxes on tourism flows will depend on the levels set, the impact on the air fare as well as the price elasticity of demand for air travel.

For any destination, the impacts on tourism will also depend on climate change policies enacted elsewhere. The impacts on a country that goes alone in implementing such policies will be more severe than if all other countries are also implementing them, since this would mean that the country's competitiveness as a destination would be less negatively affected.

Outbound tourism

While inbound tourism to particular destinations is likely to be reduced as the price of flying rises, so also will outbound tourism from those destinations. Depending on the extent to which outbound travellers divert to a domestic tourism experience as a result of higher air fares, this will offset losses to the host tourism industry. There are several unknowns here. One uncertainty involves the perception of travellers as to the 'substitutability' of domestic tourism for international tourism. The more highly regarded the domestic tourism experience, the more will holiday travellers be inclined to substitute one for the other. Conversely, the more unattractive the domestic destination as a result of climate change effects, the greater will be flows of outbound tourism. Another uncertainty involves the mode of travel taken for the domestic tourism experience. Flying domestic short haul will increase GHGs as will increased use of ground transport.

Tourism is a footloose industry

We have noted that tourism is very much a footloose industry. If one country raises the costs of visits to its shores, many travellers will switch to other countries. There is no need for the industry to shift plant and equipment, as would be the case with other industries such as manufacturing. Rather, the tourists simply change their travel plans – something that can be done very quickly. The tourists will switch to other destinations, at least some of which are not implementing climate change mitigation policies. Thus, if a destination imposes climate change policies which raise the cost of inbound tourism, but its competitors do not, then visitors will, to some extent, shift to competitor destinations. While the destination will lose out, global GHGs may not fall.

When climate change policies are proposed, they can pose particular problems for footloose export industries. Increasing the costs of the home export industry will render it less competitive on world markets, and customers will shift elsewhere. Production may actually shift offshore. While the home economy will reduce its production of GHGs, the global total GHGs may increase. Thus the economy imposes a cost on itself and achieves no reduction in global GHGs (these could actually increase).

A range of policy options to achieve emissions reductions is available to governments, each of which attempts to make consumers and producers take account of the full cost of their decisions. The different types of instruments were discussed in Chapter 18. Consistent with our discussion there, it is market-based instruments that have the most potential to reduce GHG emissions at least cost.

19.6.2 MARKET-BASED INSTRUMENTS

Where markets are well functioning, two conditions must hold to reduce GHG emissions efficiently within a destination (Stern, 2006):

- Mitigation (abatement) should take place up to the point where the benefits of further emission reductions are just balanced by the costs. This is where the marginal social cost of carbon is equal to the marginal cost of abatement. This indicates the appropriate level of emissions and also sets a long-term stabilisation target for GHG emissions.

- To deliver reductions at least cost, a common price signal is required across countries and different sectors of their economies at a given point in time. For example, if the marginal cost of reduction is lower in industry X than in industry Y, then abatement costs could be reduced by greater reductions in industry X than in industry Y.

Figure 19.5 displays the marginal social cost of carbon (MSCC) and the marginal abatement cost (MAC). The MSCC and the MAC are drawn as functions of emissions in this period (period 0). The MSCC curve indicates the total damage from now into the indefinite future of emitting an extra unit of GHGs. It corresponds to the marginal damage cost curve or marginal external cost curve (MXC) in Figures 18.1c and 18.4 in Chapter 18. In Figure 19.5, however, the MSCC slopes downwards with increasing abatement in any given period, reflecting the assumption that the lower the stock of GHGs at any point in the future, the less the marginal damage from additional emissions. As drawn, the MSCC curve is relatively flat, since extra emissions in this period do not greatly affect the total stock of GHGs. Nevertheless, extra abatement now implies a slightly lower stock in the future. On the other hand, the MAC curve slopes upwards abatement, since it will be more costly at the margin to undertake additional abatement as abatement increases in the given period. The optimum level of abatement is where the MAC equals the MSCC. If, for example, the MSCC is greater than the MAC, the social gain from one extra unit of abatement would be less than the cost and it would be better to undertake extra abatement. On the other hand, if abatement is so high that the MAC exceeds the MSCC, then a social gain can be experienced by cutting back on abatement. Thus, E^* represents the optimal level of GHG abatement in this period. The optimal price of carbon is thus T^*.

How can quantity of reduced emissions E^* be achieved? As we discussed in Chapter 18, Government cannot control both the price and the quantity of emissions reductions at the same time – control over one necessarily affects the other. Therefore, the choice of policy instrument will be guided by the relative importance placed on having greater control over the emissions outcome, or the price (cost) imposed (Australian Government, 2007b).

Although Figure 19.5 is a standard curve in the climate change literature, it greatly oversimplifies the difficulties involved in identifying the optimum price of carbon and the optimum quantity of emissions. The MSCC curve for any given period depends on the future stock and thus on the future path of emissions. This precludes estimation of the MSCC without assuming that future emissions and stocks follow some specified path. If increased future emissions are assumed, the entire MSCC curve shifts upwards, and so also do the costs of abatement in any given period. It is very likely that the MSCC will rise over time, since stocks of GHG will rise as further emissions take place, up to the point

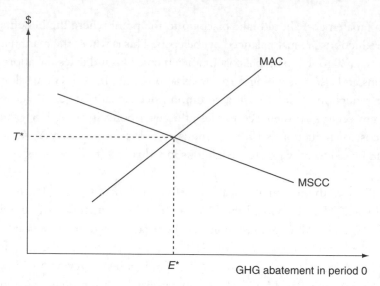

Figure 19.5 The optimum degree of abatement in a given period

Source: Adapted from Stern (2006), Figure 2.1

where stabilisation is reached. Thus the MAC at the optimum rises and the intersection of the MAC and MSCC curves will imply successively greater abatement. Thus, if we consider the optimum path over time, rather than simply an optimum emission for any given period it must be recognised that, for different specified paths, the MSCC will be different. For example, it will be much higher on a 'business as usual' path compared to one that cuts emissions strongly and eventually stabilises concentrations. MSCC calculations are often vague on this crucial point (Stern, 2006).

Delayed action on mitigating the effects of climate change will increase total costs and raise the whole trajectory for the MSCC. The difference between the MSCC on the 'business as usual' trajectory and the MSCC on stabilisation trajectories reflects the fact that a tonne of GHG emitted is more harmful and more costly, the higher are the concentration levels. Delays allow excessive accumulation of GHGs, giving decision-makers a worse starting position for implementing adaptation and mitigation strategies (Stern, 2006).

The issues are represented schematically in Figure 19.6, which compares two paths for an economy, one with mitigation and one without. Income on the 'path with mitigation' is below that on the path without ('business as usual') for the earlier time period, because costs of mitigation are incurred. Later, as the damages from climate change accumulate, growth on the 'path without mitigation' will slow and income will fall below the level on the other path. The analysis shows that the losses from mitigation in the near future are strongly outweighed by the later gains in averted damage. Without global action to mitigate climate change, both the impacts and adaptation costs will be much

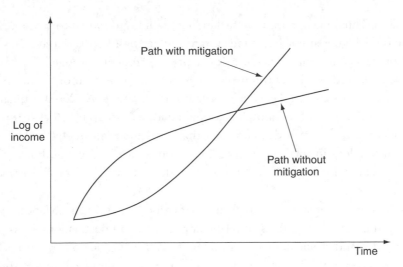

Figure 19.6 Comparing divergent growth paths of the economy over the long term

Source: Stern (2006), Figure 2.3

larger, and so will be the need for richer countries to help the poorer and most exposed countries.

There are two main types of market-based instruments that are widely regarded as having an important role to play in mitigating the effects of climate change on industry in general, including tourism. These are carbon taxes and tradable permits schemes.

19.6.2.1 Carbon taxes

Carbon taxes can be imposed on the output of GHG-intensive goods or taxes imposed on use of carbon-based fuels or on measured production of GHGs. As discussed in Chapter 18, this type of tax delivers emissions reductions by setting a price for each unit of emissions, and allowing the quantity of abatement to emerge from the market. The issues were discussed in Chapter 18 with reference to Figures 18.6 and 18.7.

Taxes deliver emissions reductions by setting a price for each unit of emissions (e.g. T^*) and allowing the quantity of abatement to emerge from the market. Taxes are an efficient way of internalising costs of GHG emissions. The tax should be set to reflect the marginal damage caused by emissions. Abatement should then occur up to the point where the marginal cost of abatement is equal to this tax. This would be a tax of T^*. A carbon tax would encourage firms to seek ways to reduce their emissions and their tax bill. Emissions would be at the optimal level E^*.

A tax on GHG emissions will induce a reduction in GHGs, partly by inducing users of the fuel to adopt less GHG-intensive technologies, possibly using other fuels, and partly by making more expensive the product the fuel is used to produce, inducing a reduction

733

in its demand. Thus, a tax on aviation fuel induces airlines to switch to more fuel-efficient aircraft, and the higher airline costs and air fares induce passengers to travel less by air.

A carbon tax is, like other taxes, a form of government revenue. The tax receipts can be used for improved environmental management or for various other projects or programmes, or to fund GHG-reducing technologies. Wit *et al.* (2002) estimated that a €50/tCO$_2$ tax imposed on aviation in Europe (equivalent to up to €9 charge per round-trip) would reduce air travel demand such that emissions fall by 4.9%. This is almost entirely due to a loss in total travel demand – modal shift is minimal. For a €10/tCO$_2$ tax, emissions drop 1%; for €30/tCO$_2$ tax, the reduction is 3.1%. Travel demand appears to be linear in price.

Destinations contemplating the imposition of carbon taxes on the aviation sector need improved estimates of the effects of relative price levels on destination choice and, very importantly, demand elasticities for air travel between the destination and its major tourist origin markets. Box 19.3 summarises a recent study of the impacts of a carbon tax on aviation.

BOX 19.3 Impacts of a carbon tax on tourism flows

Tol (2006) employed a simulation model of international tourist flows to estimate the impacts of a carbon tax on aviation fuel. Tol employs the Hamburg Tourism Model. This describes, at a reasonable level of geographic disaggregation, the reactions of tourists to climate change and climate policy.

In the base case, the effect of a carbon tax on international tourist travel is investigated for the year 2010 for three alternative taxes: $10/tC, $100/tC and $1000/tC. Tol first assumed that the tax is global in scope and then assumed (more realistically) that it is levied only in the European Union.

Global Effects
- The effect of the global tax on travel behaviour is small. A global $1000/tC would reduce carbon dioxide emissions from international aviation by 0.8% due to reduced demand for flights. This is because the imposed tax is probably small relative to the air fare and the price elasticities tend to be quite low. A $1000/tC tax would less than double air fares, and have a smaller impact on the total cost of the holiday.
- If applied to Annex 1 countries only, this falls to 0.40%; for the EU plus, this is 0.21%; for the EU, 0.19%.
- A carbon tax disproportionately increases the price of short flights, because take-off and landing are very energy-intensive. A carbon tax would induce a shift

from long flights to medium distance ones, and a shift from medium distance flights to short distance car and train holidays.

- Medium distance flights would be affected least. This implies that tourist destinations that rely heavily on short-haul flights (for example islands near continents, such as Ireland) or on intercontinental flights (e.g., Africa) will experience a decline in international tourism numbers, while other destinations may see international arrivals rise.

- Sensitivity analyses reveal that a carbon tax on aviation fuel would have little effect on international tourism, and little effect on emissions.

EU Effects

When the tax is applied only to flights to and from the EU, the findings are different. If the tax is applied regionally rather than globally, then market share shifts from the taxed region to the non-taxed regions.

- EU tourists would stay closer to home so that EU tourism would grow at the expense of other destinations. In particular, an EU tax would divert European travellers from the USA, Africa, and the Middle East to Europe.
- The Americas would benefit from US citizens holidaying domestically rather than travelling to Europe.
- South Asia, East Asia, and Australasia would benefit from tourists diverted from Europe to their destinations.
- Iceland, Ireland and the UK lose market share because they are heavily dependent on airborne tourists.
- Norway, and Switzerland, even though exempt from the tax, lose market share, Norway because it is relatively remote, Switzerland because it is central and therefore sees a relatively high price increase.
- Central and Eastern Europe gain – primarily from each other's custom but also from redirect Scandinavian and British travel.
- Countries that disproportionally rely on European visitors, such as Pakistan, South Korea and Japan, will lose market share.
- Countries that neighbour China and India all gain – a sign of the growing importance of these two countries in international tourism.

Tol's findings are based on several unrealistic assumptions. One is that the total demand for international travel is not affected by the tax (that is, the tax leads to shifts in market shares only). Another is that there is no substitution between domestic and international holidays, or indeed between holidays and no holidays. Another is that technical measures to reduce emissions are precluded. These assumptions all imply that emission reductions will be underestimated.

Tol now estimates the *average* travel cost of international tourism with and without the tax and, using price elasticity estimates based on the research literature derives a large effect: a €1000/tC tax would cut emissions by 7.6%, eight times larger than in the base case. However, this is a very large tax, while emission reduction is still small. For a €10/tC tax, emissions fall by 0.1%; for a €100/tC tax, emissions fall by 0.9%.

The results depend to a large extent on the assumed travel price elasticity of tourism demand – and on the assumed travel costs. Both are uncertain. Tol concludes that unless the tax induces technological and/or behavioural change it is unlikely to substantially reduce GHG emissions.

Source: Tol, R. (2006) 'The Impact of a Carbon Tax on International Tourism' *Working Paper FNU-120*, Hamburg: Hamburg University and Centre for Marine and Atmospheric Science

Carbon taxes can set a price for carbon but they cannot guarantee a particular level of emissions. A preferred option for many governments is an ETS.

19.6.2.2 Emissions trading scheme

An ETS sets a price by imposing a quantity constraint on aggregate emissions. A total quota (or ceiling) for emissions is set and tradable quotas can then determine market prices. In a tradable-quota scheme, the parameters of the scheme – notably the total quota allocation – should be set to generate a market price that is consistent with the MSCC. This would indicate a level of abatement of the amount E^* as in Figure 19.5.

The most common type of ETS is known as a 'cap and trade' scheme. Under such a scheme, the government determines limits on GHG emissions for the nation or region and issues tradable emissions permits up to this limit. Each permit represents the right to emit a specified quantity of GHG (e.g. 1 tonne of CO_2). Businesses must hold enough permits to cover the GHG emissions they wish to generate each year. The amount of allowed emissions determines their environmental effectiveness as firms can only generate GHGs to the extent that they have permits. Firms that create GHGs would need a permit to do so or else risk a potentially prohibitive fine. Permits can be bought and sold, with the price determined by the supply of and demand for permits. This establishes the price of carbon emissions. The mechanics of a cap and trade scheme is set out in Box 19.4.

BOX 19.4 Mechanics of a cap and trade emissions trading scheme

There are two distinct elements of a cap and trade scheme – the cap itself, and the ability to trade. The cap is the limit on GHG emissions imposed by the destination government. The cap will be effective, and the environmental objective met, as long as the compliance and enforcement mechanisms ensure emissions are consistent with the cap. The act of capping emissions creates a carbon price. The ability to trade ensures that emissions are reduced at the lowest possible cost.

Step 1: An emissions trading scheme involves the government issuing permits to achieve a measurable emissions reduction task. The number of permits issued (either auctioned or freely allocated) must be less than the amount required under normal 'business as usual' conditions. The price of each permit arises from its scarcity value. Significant emitters of GHG must acquire a 'carbon pollution permit' for every tonne of GHG that they emit.

Step 2: The quantity of emissions produced by firms will be monitored and audited.

Step 3: At the end of each year, each polluting firm must surrender a 'carbon pollution permit' for every tonne of emissions that they produced in that year. The number of permits issued by the Government in each year will be limited to the total carbon cap for the particular economy.

Step 4: Where firms have different capacities to reduce emissions, they can trade the emissions permits.

Firms that value carbon permits most highly will be prepared to pay most for them, either at auction, or on a secondary trading market. Firms buy permits on the market up to the point where the cost of purchasing a permit equals the cost of undertaking their own abatement activities. For other firms it will be cheaper to reduce emissions than to buy 'permits'.

Step 5: Firms can enhance their ability to reduce emissions by investing in emissions reduction technologies. Firms with low-cost abatement options will reduce their emissions until the cost of abatement equals the market price of the permits

Step 6: The price on emissions resulting from the ETS will increase the cost of those goods and services that are most emissions intensive in their production or use. This alters the relative prices of goods and services across the economy, making emissions-intensive goods and services become more expensive relative to goods and services with low emissions intensity. This provides businesses and consumers with incentives to adjust their behaviour, invest in low-emissions technologies and help the country to reduce emissions.

Suppose two firms, A and B, each emit 100,000 tonnes of CO_2-e each year. The government wants to cut emissions by 5 per cent, and it gives each firm an allowance to emit 95,000 tonnes. Each firm has the option of either reducing its emissions by 5,000 tonnes or buying permits to emit up to 5,000 tonnes of CO_2-e allowances from elsewhere.

Suppose the market price for the permits is $10 per tonne. Assume that firm A can reduce its emissions for half this cost per tonne. Thus it is reasonable for it to cut its emissions by 10,000 tonnes: if it sells the extra 5,000 tonnes of emissions reductions (for $50,000) it will be able to recover its expenditure.

Assume that, for firm B, making reductions is more expensive, at $15 per tonne. It decides not to reduce its emissions, but instead to buy the 5,000 tonnes of surplus allowances on offer from firm A. If firm B reduced its own emissions, it would cost $75,000, but if it buys them from firm A, the cost is significantly less, at $50,000.

The end result is that both firms are better off by $25,000 compared to their costs without trading. If they are the only two firms in the destination, this means the country's business sector is able to cut emissions by 5 per cent for $50,000 less than if the government forced both firms to reduce their emissions by the same amount. In a scheme with full international linkages, this example could equally apply to trade between firms in different countries.

Source: Australian Government (2007b) *Report of the Task Group on Emissions Trading*, Prime Ministerial Task Group on Emissions Trading, The Department of the Prime Minister and Cabinet, Canberra © Commonwealth of Australia, reproduced with permission

In a well-functioning market with an ETS, the firms that can reduce GHG for a lower cost than the permit cost will do so, while other firms, which find GHG reduction costly, will buy permits and not reduce their emissions as much – this would result in achieving a

GHG target at minimum cost to the economy. Possible fluctuations in the price of emissions may, however, generate uncertainty among business operators regarding their cost structures.

ETS is a widely based scheme, which can cover most large firms that directly produce GHG and which incorporates upstream suppliers of energy to firms not directly included in the ETS so that these are included indirectly. In some respects, an ETS works like a carbon-offset scheme. If one person, firm or industry emits GHG as a result of their economic activity, they know that this implies an 'offset' elsewhere given that the amount of total emissions is fixed. That is, if a firm emits more, it needs more permits, which it can only get if other firms emit less GHG.

A number of destinations, including Europe, Australia, the USA and New Zealand are exploring the use of ETS to mitigate the effects of GHG emissions. Adoption of ETS will affect tourism, both directly (e.g. if an ETS is imposed on aviation) and indirectly in all tourism sectors (e.g. through the price of inputs, such as electricity). Thus, a cost is imposed on a firm whenever it generates GHG and it will seek to pass these costs onto its customers. Not only will the prices of their products rise, other industries will have to pay more for these products if they use them as inputs. Overall, cost levels of the tourism industry will rise to an extent dependent on the industry's carbon intensiveness. Ultimately, directly or indirectly, prices to consumers and tourists will rise. The extent of 'pass through' (price rises) will have significant implications for the size of consumer responses to climate change mitigation policies.

The revenue implications of an ETS depend on how permits to generate GHG are allocated. If all the permits are auctioned, the revenue consequences are similar to those of a tax – the government receives all the revenue. However, the government could allocate some or all of the permits free of charge. The government would not gain any revenue but the firms which obtain the permits could be better off.

An important advantage of an ETS for a destination is that it possesses more options to link with global developments in a carbon-constrained environment. Emissions trading also provides for linkages to be established with other national schemes, allowing for cross-border trade in permits. Reductions in global GHG emissions are more likely to develop with linked trading schemes. An ETS provides the framework that will afford the greatest opportunity for a destination's engagement within a global effort (Prime Ministerial Task Group on Emissions Trading, 2007b). Climate change presents policy challenges such that all nation-states are better off if they can find a mechanism to support co-operation. Mitigation is a global public good, but free-rider problems make full participation and compliance in any agreement extremely difficult (Barrett & Stavins, 2002).

Box 19.5 summarises an investigation of the economic effects on tourism of an ETS proposed for Australia.

BOX 19.5 Economic effects of an emissions trading scheme on the Australian tourism industry

Hoque *et al.* (2009) have investigated the potential economic impacts of introduction by the Australian government of its proposed ETS (the so-called Carbon Pollution Reduction Scheme (CPRS)). The CPRS is intended to introduce a cap and trade mechanism for reducing Greenhouse Gas emissions in Australia to commence in 2011. The modelling focused on a scenario called the 'CPRS – 5' which targets aimed to achieve greenhouse gas emissions reduction by 2020 of 5 per cent below 2000 level. Effects on the Australian economy and in particular the tourism sector in Australia are examined.

The ETS Economic Impact: Macroeconomic Simulation Results

The major shocks that are employed in the modelling of ETS scenario were as follows:

- A cap on Australia's greenhouse emissions covered by the ETS is set at 475 Mt in 2020 i.e. 5 percent below year 2000 level (of 500 Mt) by year 2020;
- An initial emissions price of A$25 (nominal term) a tonne of carbon dioxide equivalent (tonnes CO_2-e) in 2011 is imposed;
- It is assumed that with a global scheme Australia industries can purchase global permits from a secondary market to cover their emissions obligation;
- Emissions from stationary energy, transport, industrial processes, waste, and fugitive emissions are covered from July 2010, and the Scheme excludes agriculture until 2015;
- Assistance, in the form of allocation of free permits, for most emissions-intensive trade-exposed (EITE) industries is provided to reduce the risk of carbon leakage and provide transitional support to industries affected by Australia's adoption of a carbon constraint prior to similar action by other countries; and
- Assistance for households is provided directly to low- and middle- income households through the tax and transfer system, amounting to $9.9 billion from 2010–11 to 2011–12 to meet the higher cost of living resulting from the Scheme's introduction.

The proposed ETS for Australia is projected to lead to changes in key macroeconomic variables as set out in Table 19.5.

Table 19.5 Australian macroeconomic variables selected years (percentage deviation from base case)

Variable	2011	2015	2020
1. Real household consumption	−0.48	−0.48	−0.98
2. Real investment	−1.56	−1.41	−2.12
3. Real state government consumption	−0.40	−0.13	−0.32
4. Real federal government consumption	−0.36	−0.10	−0.29
5. Export volumes	0.53	−0.76	−0.68
6. Non-traditional export volumes	3.30	0.93	3.60
7. Tourism export volumes	−0.79	−3.04	−2.85
8. Import volumes	−1.18	−1.13	−1.79
9. Real GDP	−0.42	−0.57	−0.87
10. Real gross national product	−0.52	−0.44	−0.91
11. Employment (wage weights)	−0.37	−0.15	−0.21
12. Capital stock	−0.17	−0.59	−0.87
13. Real wage index	−0.77	−1.49	−2.05
14. GDP deflator	0.53	1.28	1.68
15. Consumer price index	0.78	1.52	2.10
16. Terms of trade	−0.61	0.22	−0.31
17. Real exchange rate			

Note: The CPRS includes Agriculture only from 2015. Thus some variables such as terms of trade and real exchange rate are projected to reverse the direction after that year.

Source: CGE simulation results

The findings highlight the projected negative effect that the ETS has on the key variables of real GDP, real consumption and employment relative to base levels. Real GDP falls by 0.87 percent relative to its baseline value in 2020. Real GDP falls because, first, the emissions price under the ETS acts as a tax and thus introduces a distortion reducing economic efficiency. With less productive resources, real GDP will be lower than it otherwise would be. Second, the emissions price reduces the incentive for producers to use variable factors of production – labour and capital. Less variable factors are used because the emissions price increases the real cost of these factors.

The introduction of the ETS reduces real household consumption in 2020 by 0.98 percent relative to its baseline value. In the ETS simulations, the change in real consumption links to the change in real income which has as its main components: changes in income from wages and profits after income tax and disbursements from the ETS. The simulations indicate a fall in net real household income because the loss of real household income from labour and capital outweighs the gain of real household income from the ETS (directly through the tax and transfer system and through the dividend income paid to shareholders from permits allocated to emissions generators).

The impacts of the ETS on employment are relatively small. Australian national aggregate employment (wage weights) falls by only 0.21 percent relative to its baseline value in 2020 as the real wage falls. The reduction in real wage rate strengthens producers' incentives to substitute labour for capital and consequently, the economy experiences only a small fall in employment.

As a result of the ETS the consumer price index (CPI) in 2020 will be 2.10 per cent higher than the baseline value. An increased CPI is expected since the CPRS is an economic instrument that acts through the incentive of increased prices of goods and services to cut demand and production and the associated energy requirements.

Projected Effects on Tourism Industry
Table 19.6 shows, for the selected years, the deviations from the 'do nothing' option that are projected for the different tourism industries following imposition of the ETS. The tourism industries listed are those that comprise the category of tourism characteristic and connected industries in the Australian TSA.

Table 19.6 shows deviations (percent and $ million) from baseline values for real tourism GVA by industries nationally in selected years. The ETS reduces real tourism gross value added (GVA) relative to the baseline projection levels. As shown in the last row of Table 19.6, with the ETS in place, national real tourism GVA falls by 0.70 percent relative to its baseline value in 2020. This is equivalent to a reduction of about $361.42 million in 2009 dollars. The most negatively affected tourism industries include accommodation, cafes, restaurants and food outlets, air

Table 19.6 Deviations in real Australian tourism industry gross value added 2011–2020

Tourism Industry	Deviations from the Baseline Forecast					
	2011		2015		2020	
	%	$ m	%	$ m	%	$ m
Travel agency & tour operator services	−0.39	−6.50	−0.36	−7.23	−0.43	−10.77
Taxi transport	−0.45	−1.68	−1.00	−4.51	−1.48	−8.17
Air & water transport	−0.18	−8.66	−0.62	−37.45	−0.82	−62.26
Motor vehicle hiring	−0.39	−3.26	−0.36	−3.63	−0.43	−5.40
Accommodation	−0.61	−33.07	−0.79	−49.37	−1.32	−97.81
Cafes, restaurants & food outlets	−0.61	−22.38	−0.79	−33.40	−1.32	−66.18
Clubs, pubs, taverns & bars	−0.61	−7.08	−0.79	−10.57	−1.32	−20.94
Other road transport	−0.45	−4.70	−1.00	−12.61	−1.48	−22.82
Rail transport	0.40	2.45	0.20	1.60	1.28	12.70
Food manufacturing	0.28	2.84	0.03	0.35	−0.02	−0.29
Beverage manufacturing	0.23	1.76	0.17	1.53	0.40	4.12
Transport equipment manufacturing	−0.38	−0.62	−0.33	−0.63	0.29	0.61

Other manufacturing	−0.18	−1.72	−0.12	−1.34	0.36	4.32
Automotive fuel retailing	−0.46	−1.37	−0.42	−1.39	−0.61	−2.31
Retail trade	−0.46	−19.93	−0.42	−20.19	−0.61	−33.59
Casino & gambling	−0.62	−1.23	−0.56	−1.24	−1.03	−2.65
Library museum & art	−0.62	−3.14	−0.56	−3.17	−1.03	−6.77
Other entertainment	−0.62	−3.29	−0.56	−3.32	−1.03	−7.10
Education	−0.28	−7.51	−0.03	−0.92	−0.13	−4.68
Ownership of dwelling	−0.02	−0.53	−0.14	−4.13	−0.36	−12.05
Other industries	− 0.40	−14.02	−0.32	−13.33	−0.39	−19.37
Total	**−0.36**	**−133.63**	**−0.47**	**−204.97**	**−0.70**	**−361.42**

Source: Authors' calculations based on CGE simulation results and TSA industry data

and water transport, retail trade, clubs, pubs, taverns and bars and other road transport. The simulation results indicate that while most tourism industries experience at least a small contraction in their real value added relative to baseline values, there are some that experience expansion. The most favourably affected is the rail transport industry, real GVA of this industry which grows by 12.70 percent relative to baseline values in 2020. This is because the emissions price causes substitution toward the rail transport industry against the high-emissions transport industries (air and water transport, and other road transport industry). The reductions in contribution to TGVA experienced by the tourism characteristic industries in particular far outweighs the gains to less 'core' tourism industries.

Table 19.7 Shows deviations (percentage and '000 person) from baseline values for tourism employment by tourism industries in Australia in 2020

Tourism Industry	2007–08 Tourism employment (actual estimate), '000	2020			
		Baseline forecast (business-as-usual case), '000	Policy forecast (with ETS in place), '000	Deviations from baseline, number of persons	Deviations from baseline, %
Travel agency & tour operator services	23.1	32.7	32.7	− 61	− 0.19
Road transport & motor vehicle hiring	26.6	28.1	27.8	− 323	− 1.15
Air & water transport	34.3	42.1	41.9	−143	− 0.34
Accommodation	71.7	94.1	93.1	− 1064	− 1.13
Cafes & restaurants	53.0	69.6	68.8	− 787	− 1.13
Clubs, pubs, taverns & bars	23.2	30.5	30.1	− 344	− 1.13
Rail transport	3.4	4.5	4.6	131	2.90
Manufacturing	32.8	34.3	34.6	236	0.69
Retail trade	125.6	132.0	131.5	−494	− 0.37
Casino & gambling	2.1	2.6	2.6	−17	−0.66
Library museum & art	10.9	13.5	13.5	− 090	− 0.66

Other entertainment	13.1	16.3	16.2	−108	−0.66
Education	36.4	43.4	43.4	5	0.01
Other industries	41.7	51.3	51.3	−44	−0.09
Total	**497.9**	**595.0**	**591.9**	**−3,104**	**−0.52**

With the ETS in place, tourism employment falls by 0.52 per cent relative to baseline levels in 2020. This is equivalent to a reduction of about 3,100 jobs. The greatest job losses are in accommodation, cafes and restaurants and retail trade. Similar to the tourism GVA results, employment in most tourism industries decreases relative to baseline levels, while employment in some industries (manufacturing, rail transport) increases.

Conclusion

If the proposed ETS is approved by the Australian parliament, the tourism sector will contract. Falls will occur in real tourism gross value added and tourism employment. The largest falls are projected to be in accommodation, air and water industries and in cafes, restaurants and food outlets. While most tourism industries experience contraction in their real value added relative to baseline values, the rail transport industry experiences an expansion because the emissions price causes substitution toward this industry against the high-emissions transport industries such as air, water and other road transport industries. Overall, the gains experienced by some tourism industries will be heavily outweighed by contractions in some of the tourism characteristic industries.

Source: Hoque, S., P. Forsyth, L. Dwyer, R. Spurr, D. Pambudi (2009) 'Economic Effects of an Emissions Trading Scheme on the Australian Tourism Industry: A Dynamic CGE Analysis', Paper presented at conference of International Association for Tourism Economics (IATE), Chiang Mai, Thailand, December 2009

19.7 CLIMATE CHANGE AND AVIATION

Of all tourism industries, aviation is the one which has attracted the greatest attention in the climate change debate.

Aviation only accounts for a small proportion of total global carbon emissions, around 2%–3%. Aviation also produces non-carbon emissions which are of concern, in particular nitrogen oxides, and condensation trails from aircraft are also considered to contribute to global warming. Thus aviation might account for 5%–6% of damage from global warming.

Air travel is growing faster than other modes, and thus its contribution to GHG is growing. As a result it is expected to account for a growing proportion of GHGs.

Over time, aircraft technology is improving, and fuel use and emissions per passenger kilometre are falling. However, to a significant extent, the aviation industry is locked into existing and future technologies which determine the amount of GHGs that are emitted. However, there is some limited scope to lessen GHGs though improved flight paths, or less running of engines on the ground.

Overall, long-haul air travel does create significant GHGs, and the climate change costs of these emissions are mostly not factored in to decisions by travellers. Confronting travellers with the GHG cost consequences of their travel decisions will raise the cost of air travel and will discourage this travel somewhat. These costs are minimised if aviation is included within a comprehensive climate change policy.

The implementation of an ETS which includes aviation is likely to give rise to a situation under which the reduced GHGs in aviation will be smaller than in other industries. The strong demand for air travel, combined with the limited ability of airlines to switch to less GHG-intensive technologies, implies that the introduction of the ETS has only a small impact on aviation-related GHGs initially. As a result, GHGs from aviation will continue to grow. Nevertheless, there is a strong economic argument for including aviation within a broadly based tax or permit system, and not imposing different or additional measures on the industry. Once aviation is included, there is no case for further action. Additional measures directed at aviation in general, or long-haul air travel, will simply reduce the benefits from aviation and tourism to the economy, with no benefit in terms of lower GHGs. The supporting arguments are set out in Box 19.6.

BOX 19.6 Aviation – A special case for exemption from an ETS?

Aviation is sometimes suggested to be a 'special case', even within the context of an ETS, in that special measures are warranted to target its emissions. Some ministers of religion have told their congregations that given aviation's contribution to global warming, 'it is a sin to fly,' and there are suggestions to ban or limit short-haul flights, or to restrict the number of flights individuals can take. Others, with less religious fervour, have argued for a special tax on aviation passengers, along with arguments that air travel will have to be stabilised or reduced. In the UK a carbon tax has been imposed on domestic and international flights. Aviation bodies are concerned that there are now strong pressures for measures to be taken to restrict aviation.

We can make three responses to such calls:

First, calls for special restrictions on aviation fail to appreciate the role of aviation in promoting the economic development objectives of low-income countries and small island destinations in particular. Many developing destinations look to the tourism industry to provide incomes and jobs and to alleviate poverty. The costs of special measures affecting aviation that will be incurred by many destinations must be considered in any policy measures to address climate change.

Second, they fail to appreciate the rationale of the ETS. The purpose of the ETS is to impose the same carbon price on all industries and induce them to reduce their GHGs. Aviation-targeted special measures would be a very costly, and possibly a counter-productive, means of addressing the problem of climate change. Once appropriate targets are set for GHG reductions, it makes good sense to seek to achieve these at minimum cost to the economy and to the environment. Measures directed to aviation (or any other sector) will not achieve this. It is a standard proposition of economics that the costs of adaptation to a change are minimised if the burden of adaptation is spread as widely as possible. The implication is that all activities which lead to GHG emissions should be treated equally – all should be charged the same per unit of damage created. Some activities can be adapted more easily and cheaply than others, and thus should be relied on more heavily than others which cannot adapt easily. With an ETS, permits should be required at the same rate for all GHG-producing activities. It is neither important nor desirable that the proportional reduction of GHGs be the same for all industries. As long as the system as a whole is achieving the target set for it, it does not matter if one industry, such as aviation, is reducing emissions by less than the average. This will be consistent with GHG-reduction objectives, at whatever level they are set, being met at minimum cost.

Third, the case against special measures applied to aviation is even stronger than this general argument implies. In the context of an effective ETS, special measures directed against aviation (or any other industry included in the ETS) would be, at best, ineffective. An ETS sets an absolute limit on the amount of GHGs for the specified period. If aviation is subjected to a special tax, or restrictions are placed on the number of long-haul flights people may take, the demand for air travel will fall, and the GHGs from aviation will also fall. However, this will achieve nothing, since other industries will increase their emissions to take up the slack. If airlines need fewer permits, they will sell them to other industries. Since the number of permits is fixed, the reduction in GHGs from aviation will be exactly matched by the increase from other industries. Imposing special measures on aviation will simply increase its costs and discourage air travel and tourism, with no benefit in the form of reduced GHGs.

To illustrate, if a person chooses to fly from Paris to Rio, in the context of an ETS he or she will not add to global GHGs. To enable the flight, the airline will have to use permits, which are in fixed supply. The more permits airlines use, the less other industries can use. While increased air travel leads to more GHGs from aviation, it is accompanied by an equal reduction in emissions from other industries. This should appeal to the responsible traveller, who effectively can make a carbon neutral flight. Including aviation along with other industries in the ETS, this should allay the public concern that aviation is creating emissions – additional air travel does not add to GHG emissions. The overall impacts, of course, will depend upon the type of ETS that is formulated.

19.8 CONCLUSIONS AND POLICY

- Human-induced climate change is an externality on a global scale which, in the absence of policy intervention, is not 'corrected' through any institution or market. Climate change is the greatest market failure the world has seen. It presents a global challenge that requires a long-term global solution in order to avoid environmental, social and economic dislocation.
- The climate is a public good. Those who fail to pay for contributing to GHG emissions cannot be excluded from enjoying climatic benefits and one person's enjoyment of the climate does not diminish the capacity of others to enjoy it. Markets for relevant goods and services (energy, land use, innovation, etc.) do not reflect the full costs and benefits of different consumption and investment choices for the climate.
- Economic analysis can contribute to our understanding of the different types of issues raised by climate change, in policy formulation, and in analysing the implications for tourism.
- Tourism can and must play a significant role in addressing climate change as part of its broader commitment to sustainable development and the United Nations Millennium Development Goals.

- Climate change will directly impact on a country's tourism and the benefits it creates through loss or degradation of attractions, the costs of adaptation and replacement of capital infrastructure.
- Climate has a major influence on destination choice. As a result of changing climatic conditions, tourists are likely to entirely avoid some destinations in favour of others or else shift the timing of travel to avoid unfavourable climate conditions. Countries which rely heavily on nature-based tourism are likely to be net losers from changing international patterns of tourism as a result of climate change.
- Climate change generates both negative and positive impacts in the tourism sector and these impacts will vary substantially by market segment and geographic region. There are 'winners and losers' at the business, destination and nation level. Tourism is a footloose export industry, and tourism will shift offshore to the extent that a destination becomes less attractive due to climate change.
- The same as for other industries, the tourism industry is recognised to be a contributor to climate change through its generation of GHGs to meet tourist needs. Climate change, in turn though, will also have increasing substantial effects on tourism flows, shifting market shares of domestic and international destinations.
- Adaptation is a vital part of the response by the tourist industry to the challenge of climate change. Its objectives are to reduce tourism's vulnerability to climatic change and variability (thereby reducing their negative impacts) and to enhance tourism's capability to capture any benefits from climate change.
- Adaptation operates at two broad levels: building adaptive capacity (creating the information and regulatory, institutional and managerial conditions needed to support adaptation) and delivering adaptive actions (taking steps to help reduce vulnerability to climate risks or to exploit opportunities). Ignoring climate change is not a viable option for tourism stakeholders – over the long term inaction will be far more costly than adaptation.
- Tourism generates a carbon footprint both directly (through GHG emissions associated with production of a tourism service) and indirectly (through GHG emissions associated with the supply of inputs into tourism production).
- The carbon *intensity* footprint of tourism refers to the GHGs directly and indirectly associated with tourism activity.
- The carbon *impact* footprint of tourism refers to how changes in tourism impact on overall GHGs – this depends on its carbon intensity and also on how other industries are impacted on by changes in tourism activity. Estimation of tourism's carbon impact requires CGE modelling to determine the net changes in the outputs of different industries in the economy. Most policy questions are questions about impact, not just intensity.
- We distinguished four major mitigation strategies for addressing GHG emissions from tourism, namely, reducing energy use, improving energy efficiency, increasing the use of

renewable or carbon neutral energy and sequestering CO_2. Tourism will be affected by the different types of climate change mitigation policies, all of which will increase the cost base of tourism firms.

- There are two main types of market-based instruments that play an important role in mitigating the effects of climate change on tourism: *carbon taxes* (in which a tax is imposed for each unit of emissions, thus setting a price and allowing the quantity of abatement to emerge from the market) and *emissions trading schemes* (in which a total quota or ceiling for emissions is set, individual quota permits within that set are sold and the individual quotas are allowed to be traded, thereby setting their price). An ETS involves setting a target for the number of permits to be allocated, allocating them among conflicting users, and then policing their use to ensure that firms only create GHGs to the extent that they have permits.

- In practice there are difficulties involved in identifying the optimum price of carbon and the optimum quantity of emissions. Over a particular time horizon, the most efficient market-based instrument for climate change mitigation policy will depend on how the total costs of abatement change with the level of emissions; how the total benefits of abatement change with the level of emissions; and the degree of uncertainty about both costs and benefits of abatement.

- Although emissions trading is likely to be the key instrument used to reduce GHG emissions over time, complementary policies will be needed. There is a role for governments in setting regulatory standards, supporting innovation of new low-emission technology and encouraging changes in household behaviour. Destinations will tailor a package of measures that suits their specific circumstances, including the existing tax and governance system, participation in regional initiatives to reduce emissions (e.g. via trading schemes) and the structure of the economy and characteristics of specific sectors.

- No convincing case has been made for treating aviation differently, either more or less favourably (other than under general arrangements for footloose industries). Special taxes or restrictions on aviation, if they are included in the ETS, will be ineffective in reducing GHGs. When an effective and comprehensive ETS is in place, mandatory requirements or taxes imposed on specific industries such as aviation will be ineffective in reducing GHGs, given the quota imposed by the cap.

SELF-REVIEW QUESTIONS

1. Explain how the interaction of tourism and climate change may be considered to be a two-way street.

2. List ways in which tourism can be affected by climate change and ways in which climate can be affected by tourism activity.

3. In respect of tourism's response to climate change, distinguish between mitigation policies and adaptation strategies.

4. Adaptation by tourism to climate change can operate at two broad levels: building adaptive capacity and delivering adaptive actions. Explain each.

5. In relation to tourism's carbon footprint, differentiate carbon intensity from carbon impact.

6. How does the literature suggest that tourism's carbon footprint might differ between origin markets and between travel modes.

7. Outline the four major mitigation strategies for addressing GHG emissions from tourism.

8. Distinguish between carbon taxes and ETSs as means to abate the GHG emissions associated with tourism.

9. In what ways might climate change mitigation policies impact on tourism?

ESSAY QUESTIONS

1. 'The tourism industry is now recognised through aviation and energy use to be a significant contributor to climate change.' Argue for or against this statement.

2. In tourism's response to climate change, mitigation policies and adaptation strategies must proceed hand-in-hand. Discuss.

3. Evaluate the major anticipated effects of climate change on tourism.

4. The capacity to adapt to climate change varies substantially between sub-sectors, destinations and individual businesses within the tourism industry. Discuss.

5. 'For any destination, adaptation will reduce the negative impacts of climate change and increase the positive impacts.' How so?

6. The complexities associated with policies to mitigate the impacts of climate change make those policies largely unworkable. Discuss.

7. In his report, Stern (2006) has concluded that without global action to mitigate climate change, both the impacts and adaptation costs will be much larger, and so will be the need for richer countries to help the poorer and most exposed countries. Explain what led him to this conclusion.

8. Discuss the potential use of carbon offsetting by the aviation industry to mitigate any negative environmental effects it may create.

9. Because tourism depends on aviation, aviation should be given special treatment in the fight against climate change. Discuss.

DESTINATION COMPETITIVENESS

CHAPTER 20

DESTINATION COMPETITIVENESS

LEARNING OBJECTIVES

After reading this chapter, you should be able to:

1. Define destination competitiveness and explain the factors that underpin it.

2. Describe the Travel and Tourism Competitiveness Index and explain how it allows countries to identify key obstacles to competitiveness and understand its construction.

3. Distinguish between the different measures of destination price competitiveness, understanding which one might be used in what context.

4. Describe the nature of both the Tourism Trade Weighted Index and the Aviation Trade Weighted Index.

5. Explain the relevance of the various tourism price competitiveness indices for policy.

20.1 INTRODUCTION

We can distinguish two groups of determinants of the demand for tourism:

1. Factors that determine *market volume*. These include population, income in origin country, leisure time, education, occupation and so on. These factors underpin outbound tourism and determine the total tourism flows worldwide. As we discussed in Chapter 2, income has by far the greatest influence on tourism flows worldwide.

2. Factors that determine *market shares* of different destinations. These include the following:

- The *cost of tourism* to the visitor. This includes (i) the cost of *transport services* to and from the destination and (ii) the cost of *ground content* (accommodation, tour services, food and beverage, entertainment, etc.). Changing costs in particular destinations relative to others are an important economic influence on destination shares of total travel abroad.
- *Qualitative Factors*. These include such variables as transport access, health and safety issues, political stability, tourist appeal, destination image, quality of service, nature of

attractions, effectiveness of tourism promotion and so on. The strength of some of these factors often reflects changing fashions and tastes.

Destination competitiveness is increasingly becoming an important issue since competition from emerging tourist destinations and the changing tastes of tourists, who are now increasingly better informed and harder to satisfy, are posing a challenge to developed tourist destinations. Existing and potential visitation to any destination is inextricably linked to that destination's overall competitiveness, however that is defined or measured.

There are several definitions of competitiveness in the literature. The following are indicative:

- 'A country's ability to create, produce, distribute and/or service products in international economy, while earning rising returns on its sources' (Scott & Lodge, 1985: 3).
- 'The ability of entrepreneurs (of a country) to design, produce and market goods and services, the price and non-price characteristics of which form a more attractive package than that of competitors' (Porter, 1990).
- '... the degree to which a country can, under free and fair market conditions, produce goods and services which meet the tests of international markets while simultaneously maintaining and expanding the real incomes of its people over the longer term' (OECD, 1997).

To achieve competitive advantage for its tourism industry, a destination must ensure that its overall attractiveness, and the tourist experience, is superior to that of the many alternative destinations available to potential visitors. Destination competitiveness is linked to the ability of a country or region to deliver goods and services that perform better than other destinations on those aspects of the tourism experience considered to be important by tourists (Crouch & Ritchie, 1999).

It is important to understand the factors that determine the competitiveness of the tourism industry. Industry stakeholders and government need to understand where a destination's competitive position is weakest and strongest. All stakeholders need to know how destination competitiveness (price and non-price) is changing and why these changes are occurring. Patterns of changes in demand need to be assessed in the light of changes in destination competitiveness.

For such reasons, there has been an increasing amount of attention by tourism researchers to develop a model and indicators of destination competitiveness (Dwyer & Kim, 2003; Enright & Newton, 2004, 2005; Gooroochurn & Sugiyarto, 2005; Hassan, 2000; Mazanec et al., 2007; Ritchie & Crouch, 2000, 2003). The development of a model of destination competitiveness allows tourism stakeholders in both the private and the public sector to

- Identify key strengths and weaknesses of their destination from the visitor perspective;
- Highlight opportunities for tourism development; and
- Develop strategies to counter possible threats to future tourism.

Competitiveness frameworks have been used to rank destinations globally (Blanke *et al.*, 2009; Gooroochurn & Sugiyarto, 2005) as well as to explore the competitiveness of particular destinations such as Australia (Dwyer & Kim, 2003; Dwyer *et al.*, 2003, 2004), Korea (Kim & Dwyer, 2003), Hong Kong and Asia Pacific cities (Enright & Newton, 2004, 2005) and Slovenia (Omerzel & Mihalic, 2008). Other studies have focused on the development of price competitiveness indices for selected destinations (Dwyer *et al.*, 2000a, b, c).

20.2 FACTORS UNDERPINNING DESTINATION COMPETITIVENESS

Destination competitiveness is a general concept that encompasses price differentials coupled with exchange rate movements, productivity levels of various components of the tourist industry and qualitative factors affecting the attractiveness or otherwise of a destination. The competitiveness of an industry is a critical determinant of how well it performs in world markets.

The model displayed as Figure 20.1 brings together the main elements of competitiveness as proposed in the wider economics and management literature (Moon & Peery, 1995;

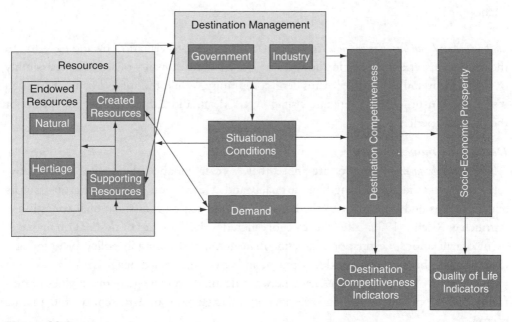

Figure 20.1 Integrated model of destination competitiveness

Source: Dwyer *et al.* (2004)

Narashimbha, 2000; Porter, 1990; Waheeduzzan & Ryans, 1996) and the main elements of destination competitiveness as proposed by tourism researchers. The model contains many of the variables and category headings identified by Crouch and Ritchie (1999) and Ritchie and Crouch (2000, 2003) in their comprehensive framework of destination competitiveness. This model, in turn, builds upon Porter's well-known framework of the 'diamond of national competitiveness' which claims that success in international competition in a given industry depends on the relative strength of an economy in a set of business-related features or 'drivers' of competitiveness. These drivers relate to 'factor conditions'; 'demand conditions'; 'related and supporting industries'; and 'firm strategy, structure and rivalry' (Porter, 1990).

Resources

Core Resources and *Supporting Factors and Resources* comprise the basic foundations of a sustainable tourism industry (Crouch & Ritchie, 1999). Together, they provide the resource base, attracting visitors and underpinning destination competitiveness.

Core Resources can be divided into two types – *Endowed* (*Inherited*) and *Created*.

– *Endowed* resources can be classified as *Natural* (mountains, lakes, beaches, rivers, climate, etc.) or *Cultural/Heritage* (cuisine, handicrafts, language, customs, belief systems, etc.).
– *Created* resources include attributes such as accommodation, restaurants, organised tours, transportation, special events, the range of available activities, entertainment and shopping.

Supporting or Enabling Factors and Resources enable or facilitate visitation by adding value to the tourism experience. They include general infrastructure, quality of service, accessibility of destination and hospitality of resident community. While the mere existence of such resources is insufficient to generate visitation to a destination, they enhance the quality of the visitor experience.

Destination management

Destination Management factors are those that '…can enhance the appeal of the core resources and attractors, strengthen the quality and effectiveness of the supporting factors and resources and best adapt to the constraints imposed by the (situational conditions)' (Crouch & Ritchie, 1999: 149). The category includes the activities of destination management organisations, destination marketing management, destination policy, planning and development, human resource development and environmental management.

In Figure 20.1, a distinction is made between destination management activities undertaken by the public sector and destination management undertaken by the private sector.

Included among the activities of the public sector are the development of national tourism strategies, marketing by the National Tourism Organisation, national and regional manpower programmes, environmental protection legislation, climate change mitigation and adaptation policies and so on. Included among the activities of the private sector are those of tourism/hospitality industry associations, industry involvement in and funding of destination marketing programmes, industry training programmes, industry adoption of 'green' tourism operations, environmental certification programmes and so on. Together, the activities of public and private sector tourism organisations influence types of products and services developed to match visitor preferences.

Demand Conditions comprise three main elements of tourism demand – awareness, perception and preferences. Awareness can be generated by various means including destination marketing activities and market ties (religious, sporting, ethnic, etc.). Destination image can influence perceptions and hence affect visitation. Actual visitation will depend on the match between tourist preferences and perceived destination product offerings. The nature of demand conditions, specifically tourist preferences and motives for travel, influences the types of products and services developed within a destination.

Situational Conditions are forces in the wider external environment that impact upon tourism flows and hence destination competitiveness. Situational conditions relate to economic, social, cultural, demographic, environmental, political, legal, governmental, regulatory, technological and competitive trends and events that impact on the way firms and other organisations in the destination do business, and present both opportunities and threats to their operations (Dwyer *et al.*, 2009). These conditions correspond to the Qualifying and Amplifying determinants as identified by Ritchie and Crouch (2003).

The situational conditions can be thought of as falling within one of two interactive and interrelated contexts of organisations operating in the destination – the operating environment and the remote environment.

The *operating environments* of the different private and public sector institutions in a destination are important because, to a large extent, the conduct and performance of these institutions depend on the overall structure of the industry in which they are situated.

The *remote environment* comprises those forces and events outside the destination that constrain the strategic options of organisation managers but over which management has no control, for example, exchange rates movements, government fiscal policy, world economic conditions, demographic trends, political stability or global warming (Dwyer *et al.*, 2009).

Destination competitiveness

Destination competitiveness, the outcome of the process, is linked backwards to the various determinants of competitiveness and forwards to socio-economic prosperity, or quality of life, indicating that destination competitiveness is itself an intermediate goal towards a more fundamental aim. Each of these objectives is associated with a set of indicators. Dwyer and Kim (2003) identify 83 competitiveness attributes in their study of the destination competitiveness of Australia and Korea, Enright and Newton (2005) employ

52 attributes for their study of Hong Kong, while Omerzel and Mihalic (2008) identify 85 attributes for their study of Slovenia. The World Economic Forum (WEF) in 2009 ranked 133 countries on 73 different indicators (WEF, 2009).

A major problem, underlying all attempts to establish indices of competitiveness, involves the integration of objective and subjective attributes of competitiveness. An important issue for further research is to attempt to incorporate qualitative factors into the construction of destination competitiveness indexes. There is no method available that can be used to integrate 'hard' and 'soft' factors into a single index. 'Hard' measures are those that are 'objectively' or 'quantitatively' measurable. These would include economic performance indicators (e.g. inbound numbers, expenditure and market share). 'Soft' measures of a destination's competitiveness in natural resources would be those relating to 'aesthetics', 'grandeur', 'beauty' and so on. More research needs to be undertaken as to how 'objective' and 'subjective' attributes of competitiveness are to be given due weight in determining overall destination competitiveness.

It is widely held that the ultimate goal of destination competitiveness is to maintain and increase the real income of its citizens, usually reflected in the standard of living of residents of the country. From this perspective, destination competitiveness is not an end in itself but a means to an end. The ultimate goal of industry development is to increase the standard of living of the resident of a destination (Ritchie & Crouch, 2003).

Several attempts have been made to 'measure' or 'rank' the destination competitiveness of particular countries. However, there is no single or unique set of competitiveness indicators that apply to all destinations at all times. Thus, for example, it makes little sense in general to ask tourists questions such as how important are natural resources compared with, say, heritage resources? And, within the category of natural resources, how important is, say, climate, compared with pristine environments? How important is service quality compared with price competitiveness? Such questions are unable to be answered in the abstract. For any given element of destination competitiveness, any number of attributes or indicators may be employed as measures. The importance of competitiveness indicators will vary across locations, depending on product mix and target market segments. Further research needs to incorporate consumer input and perceptions in the context of a specific destination being studied and for specific visitor market segments to that destination. The resulting gains will be more informed policy making regarding the type of tourism development most likely to enhance both visitor experiences and resident socio-economic quality of life.

20.3 THE TRAVEL AND TOURISM COMPETITIVENESS INDEX

A comprehensive framework incorporating indicators that are widely agreed upon to be important to destination competitiveness has been developed under the auspices of the

WEF with input from the World Travel and Tourism Council (WTTC). The WEF has, for some years, actively been engaged in an investigation of national competitiveness to better understand the drivers of growth and prosperity. The objective is to provide benchmarking tools that enable countries to identify key obstacles to competitiveness, and to provide a platform for dialogue among government, business and the community to discuss the best ways of removing them. Within this context, building upon the work of Gooroochurn and Sugiyarto (2005), the WEF has developed Travel and Tourism Competitiveness Index (TTCI). The fundamental objective of the TTCI is to help explore the factors driving travel and tourism (T&T) competitiveness worldwide, thus providing a basis for implementing policies on a country-by-country basis. The TTCI for 2009 covers 133 countries, accounting for 90% of world population and 98% of world GDP (Blanke *et al.*, 2009).

The TTCI is composed of 14 'pillars' of T&T competitiveness. The pillars are organised into three sub-indexes capturing broad categories of variables that facilitate or drive T&T competitiveness. These categories are (1) T&T regulatory framework, (2) T&T business environment and infrastructure and (3) T&T human, cultural and natural resources. These indices are based on 'hard' or numerical or empirical data and on surveys of expert opinion (see below). Figure 20.2 summarises the structure of the overall Index, showing how the 14 component pillars are allocated within the three sub-indexes. Each pillar comprises a number of individual variables.

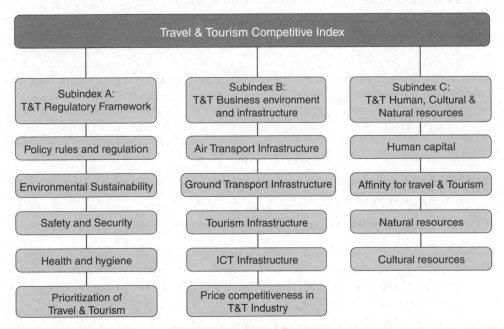

Figure 20.2 Composition of the three sub-indexes of the TTCI

Source: Blanke *et al.* (2009)

Sub-index A: T&T regulatory framework

This sub-index captures those elements that are policy-related and generally under the purview of the government.

> Pillar 1: *Policy rules and regulation*: Foreign ownership restrictions; Property rights; Rules governing Foreign Direct Investment (FDI); Visa requirements; Openness of bilateral Air Service Agreements.

> Pillar 2: *Environmental sustainability*: Stringency of environmental regulation; Clarity and stability of environmental regulations; Government prioritisation of sustainable T&T.

> Pillar 3: *Safety and security*: Business costs of terrorism; Reliability of police services; Business costs of crime and violence.

> Pillar 4: *Health and hygiene*: Government efforts to reduce health risks from pandemics; Physician density; Access to improved sanitation; Access to improved drinking water.

> Pillar 5: *Prioritisation of T&T*: Government prioritisation of the T&T industry; T&T government expenditure; Effectiveness of marketing and branding to attract tourists; T&T fair attendance.

Sub-index B: T&T business environment and infrastructure

This sub-index captures elements of the business environment and the infrastructure of each economy.

> Pillar 6: *Air transport infrastructure*: Quality of air transport infrastructure; Available seat kilometres; Departures per 1000 population; Airport density; Number of operating airlines; International air transport network.

> Pillar 7: *Ground transport infrastructure*: Road infrastructure; Railroad infrastructure; Port infrastructure; Domestic transport network.

> Pillar 8: *Tourism infrastructure*: Hotel rooms; Presence of major car rental companies; ATMs accepting Visa cards.

> Pillar 9: *ICT infrastructure*: Extent of business Internet use; Internet users; Telephone lines.

> Pillar 10: *Price competitiveness in the T&T industry*: Ticket taxes and airport charges; Purchasing Power Parity (PPP); Extent and effect of taxation; Fuel price levels.

Sub-index C: T&T human, cultural and natural resources

This sub-index captures the human and cultural elements of each country's resource endowments.

Pillar 11: *Human capital*: Primary education enrolment ; Secondary education enrolment; Quality of the educational system; Local availability of specialised research and training services; Extent of staff training; Availability of qualified labour; Hiring-and-firing practices; Ease of hiring foreign labour; Workforce wellness; HIV prevalence; Malaria incidence; Tuberculosis incidence; Life expectancy.

Pillar 12: *Affinity for T&T*: Tourism openness; Attitude towards tourists; Recommendation to extend business trips.

Pillar 13: *Natural resources*: Carbon dioxide (CO_2) damage; Nationally protected areas; Business concern for ecosystems; Risk of malaria and yellow fever.

Pillar 14: *Cultural resources*: The number of UNESCO world heritage sites; Sports stadia seating capacity; Number of international fairs and exhibitions in country.

Construction of the TTCI

The dataset used to construct the TTCI includes both hard data and survey data from the WEF's annual Executive Opinion Survey. The hard data were obtained from publicly available sources, international T&T institutions and T&T experts (e.g. International Air Traffic Association (IATA), the International Civil Aviation Organisation (ICAO), UNWTO, WTTC and the United Nations Educational, Scientific and Cultural Organization (UNESCO)). The Survey is carried out among CEOs and top business leaders making the investment decisions in each of the 133 economies covered. The Survey data comprise the responses to the WEF's Executive Opinion Survey, with additional questions relevant to tourism. The responses range from 1 to 7 with higher values indicating better performance. A standard formula is used to convert each hard data variable to the 1-to-7 scale. Each of the pillars has been calculated as an unweighted average of the individual component variables. The sub-indexes are then calculated as unweighted averages of the included pillars. The overall TTCI is then the unweighted average of the three sub-indexes.

The data requirements are comprehensive and many countries lack the types of statistics that underpin many of the component indexes. Nevertheless, the very awareness of these data needs can lead tourism stakeholders in these countries (including government agencies) to put pressure on their national statistical agencies to collect the data. Inevitably, there is subjectivity in the development of the rankings, a problem which pervades all competitiveness indexes which range over variables that are not, by their nature, able to be quantified precisely.

Although some of the factors appear to be necessary for high-income economies, they might not yet be essential for developing countries. Indeed, the importance of the various factors that make up the TTCI is likely to vary depending on each country's stage of development. Political stability, for example, is important for any destination wishing to attract FDI and inbound tourism. Government policies and regulations concerning environmental protection and new technologies, on the other hand, might become relevant only when basic infrastructure is in place. A less developed country (LDC) that is in the process of building up its air and ground transport network may consider environmental regulations a secondary priority, possibly to the detriment of its long-term tourism sustainability. In this respect, the growing pressure for all countries to initiate mitigation and adoptive measures to combat global warming will be of particular relevance to Less Developed Countries (LDCs) as such measures will inevitably involve costs to tourism suppliers.

20.4 DESTINATION COMPETITIVENESS BY NICHE MARKET

There are difficulties in developing any measurements of overall destination competitiveness applicable to all destinations. Destinations may be competitive in some respects but may lack competitiveness in other respects. Thus, regarded as a beach destination, Las Vegas performs poorly since it is surrounded by desert. As a gambling and night entertainment location, it is very competitive. In contrast, Samoa has attractive beaches but no casinos.

However, for specified market segments, it is possible to identify the most important attributes as perceived by tourists and to compare the performance of different destinations. A framework developed by Enright and Newton (2004, 2005) is useful in this context.

Enright and Newton adopt a two-stage approach, which explores both the importance of each factor and the destination's competitiveness in respect of that factor relative to its main competitors. Respondents are asked to rate the factors for both importance and relative competitiveness, in a method consistent with Importance Performance Analysis (IPA). The IPA approach can display measures of importance and performance in a two-dimensional grid to facilitate data interpretation and the implications for policy. The overall mean scores of importance and performance are then used to create four quadrants as

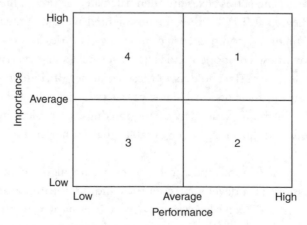

Figure 20.3 Destination attribute competitiveness and importance

Source: Enright and Newton (2004)

displayed in Figure 20.3. A matrix such as Figure 20.3 can be constructed for a particular destination either for a particular special interest tourism market (e.g. adventure tourism, nature-based tourism and heritage tourism) or for travel motivation (e.g. business travel and conventions market).

Quadrant 1 includes those attributes that are considered to be important for the niche market and also in which the destination performs relatively well. Thus, for nature-based tourism, viewing a diversity of wildlife may be considered to be important. If, for example, the destination has facilities that allow tourists to view the wildlife, then the destination may be considered to perform well on this attribute.

Quadrant 2 includes destination attributes that are low in importance but high in relative competitiveness. For nature-based tourism, the availability of five star hotel accommodation may rank low in importance but the destination as a whole may be regarded as relatively competitive in this respect.

Quadrant 3 identifies attributes in which the destination is not particularly competitive but which are low in importance. For nature-based tourism, this might relate to entertainment and night life. Inclusion of the attribute in Quadrant 3 indicates that the destination ranks relatively low on an attribute of low importance for nature-based tourism.

Quadrant 4 includes attributes that are high in importance but in which the destination has low relative competitiveness. For nature-based tourism, this attribute might relate to transport links connecting tourism gateways to wildlife areas.

The matrix has policy significance for all industry stakeholders.

Quadrant 1 represents areas of destination strength that should be supported to ensure their ongoing competitiveness.

Quadrant 2 represents areas that can be monitored to ensure that the destination competitiveness is maintained.

Quadrant 3 represents attributes of lowest policy priority.

Quadrant 4 represents destination attributes that could receive special attention for improvements to enhance their competitiveness.

An important advantage of this model is that it can incorporate consumer input and perceptions in the context of a specific destination being studied and for specific visitor market segments to that destination. The approach also offers a basis for strategy development and policy formulation for the different market segments of the destination tourism industry. The approach reinforces the fact that both private sector and public sector decision makers can play important roles in tourism planning and development.

In particular, by recognising the importance of each attribute, the approach provides practitioners and policy makers with the means to prioritise decisions by taking account of the weighting ascribed to the attributes.

20.5 DESTINATION PRICE COMPETITIVENESS

Price competitiveness is one of the core aspects of destination competitiveness. This is reflected in the TTCI, where, in pillar 10, price competitiveness is assessed using four sets of hard data – on ticket taxes and airport charges, national PPP prices, fuel price levels and the hotel price index.

20.5.1 DETERMINANTS OF DESTINATION PRICE COMPETITIVENESS

Tourism price competitiveness is essentially a matter of the prices of the goods and services that tourists buy, expressed in some common currency. Several factors impinge in different ways on tourism price competitiveness (Forsyth & Dwyer, 2009).

Exchange rates: Exchange rates are an obvious factor influencing tourism competitiveness. Other things being equal, if a country's exchange rate rises, its tourism competitiveness falls. Exchange rates do tend to reflect relative price levels at home and in other countries: when a country's prices rise relative to those of competitors, its exchange rate tends to fall. However, many other factors influence exchange rates, especially in the short term. Exchange rates can be quite volatile, even for industrial countries with stable trading patterns, as experience with the Global Financial Crisis (GFC) shows.

Inflation and overall price levels: Higher general price levels in a country tend to be cancelled out by exchange rate depreciations – but only up to a point. General prices – and the prices that tourists are paying – may be rising, but export prices may not increase to the same extent. In such a situation, a country's exchange rate may not move much, and it may lose price competitiveness in tourism.

Labour prices: These prices are a key determinant of long-term price competitiveness in tourism. Countries with low wages tend to have low prices for goods and services, even when these are converted into other currency terms using market exchange rates. Prices in US dollar terms are lower in China than in the USA, for example – as a result of this, international comparisons need to use PPP measures, not just market exchange rates. PPP measures the relative purchasing power of different countries' currencies over the same types of goods and services. Low-income countries thus tend to be price competitive in tourism. Over time, growth in per capita incomes alters patterns of tourism price competitiveness; in this way, the tourism price competitiveness of Asian tiger countries such as Singapore has been eroded over time.

Productivity performance of tourism industries: The more productive a tourism industry is, the lower will be its output prices given its input prices. Output prices will reflect input prices (especially labour) as well as industry productivity. A high-income country could be quite price competitive in tourism if its tourism industries are productive relative to those of its low-income competitors. To some extent, high-income countries have been able to achieve high tourism price competitiveness because their industries are productive. The relative productivity performance of different countries' tourism industries is a relatively under-researched area.

Export booms and Dutch disease: Structural shifts can impact tourism competitiveness through changes in the exchange rate. A well-known effect is the Dutch disease, whereby an export boom in one industry pushes up the exchange rate and makes other export industries less competitive (see Chapter 9). This effect is very relevant for a country's tourism price competitiveness. Over the 5 years from mid-2003 to mid-2008, Australia experienced a mineral export boom, which pushed up its exchange rate. This made its tourism industry less competitive, and inbound tourism fell – well before the effects of the GFC.

Tax levels and structures: Taxes, and especially indirect taxes, can influence the prices of the goods and services that tourists buy, and thus they can impact price competitiveness. If taxes result in price rises of a country's goods and services for export and home markets, they will tend to be counteracted by exchange rate depreciation, and the country's tourism price competitiveness will be relatively unchanged. However, taxes often impact different industries unevenly. Taxes such as the Value Added Tax (VAT) or Goods and Services Tax (GST) are typically levied on goods and services sold at home, but not on exports. When the rate of these taxes is increased, it will not affect most export industries – but tourism is the exception. The exchange rate will not alter much, but prices to tourists will rise and the country will lose competitiveness. Thus the ways taxes are levied will be a significant determinant of tourism competitiveness. Countries that rely heavily on taxes such as the VAT/GST will be less tourism competitive than other countries with similar per capita incomes and industry structures.

Infrastructure charges: Infrastructure charges can take many forms, such as road pricing, airport levies and developer contributions to resort developments. These charges push up the prices charged to tourists, and thus they will reduce a country's tourism competitiveness.

Fuel prices and taxation: Fuel is an important input into tourism goods and services, and fuel prices can have a significant impact on tourism price competitiveness. Fuel prices are dominated by the price of oil, which is much the same for all countries. However, countries differ considerably in the way that they tax (or sometimes subsidise) fuels. Thus higher fuel taxes in European countries lessen their tourism competitiveness.

Environmental charges: Tourism industries are increasingly subject to environmental charges. These may be either specific, such as a noise levy on an airport, or very general, such as higher costs due to the implementation of an Emissions Trading Scheme (ETS). The impact on competitiveness will depend on how general the charge is, and how it affects other trading industries. If an ETS raises costs to all industries, it will make exports more expensive; this will tend to lead to exchange rate depreciation, which in turn will tend to (partially) cancel out the cost increase.

However, if some export industries are exempted from the ETS, as is proposed in some countries, the impact on the exchange rate will be limited, and the competitiveness of industries that are not exempted, such as tourism, will suffer. Specific duties, such as the air passenger duties of the UK and the Netherlands (which, dubiously, are claimed to be environmental levies) will not have any appreciable impact on the exchange rate, and thus they will reduce tourism competitiveness.

Destination competitiveness is sensitive to both government policy and the general macroeconomic environment. We discuss these in turn.

20.5.2 TOURISM COMPETITIVENESS AND GOVERNMENT POLICY

Government policy can affect tourism competitiveness through both general and specific policies. General policies, such as the implementation of an ETS to mitigate the effects of climate change, can impact a country's tourism competitiveness, as discussed in Chapter 19. In addition, some policies, such as an aviation tax, may be quite specific; these policies may have unintended impacts on tourism. Objectives for policies differ: sometimes the objective of a policy may be to increase the price competitiveness of tourism (e.g. when improved infrastructure lowers the cost to tourism) and sometimes the intention is to achieve some other objective, which incidentally has some cost to tourism competitiveness (e.g. when an aviation tax is levied to raise revenue or correct for an environmental external cost).

Policy can thus impact the determinants of tourism competitiveness in a number of ways. These are summarised in Table 20.1.

The exchange rate is a variable that governments can, and do, use to increase the competitiveness of their export industries. However, there are costs to using exchange rates in this way, by way of the uncertainties and distortions introduced, and most advanced countries now prefer floating exchange rates.

Governments can influence price levels through their monetary policies, but this is not a very well-targeted way of influencing tourism competitiveness, especially since low home prices tend to be associated with higher exchange rates.

Table 20.1 Government policy and the determinants of tourism competitiveness

Determinant	Open to Policy?	Sensitivity to Policy	Impact on Tourism Competitiveness	Comments
Exchange Rate	Yes	High	Low/Moderate	Often not recommended
Price Level	Yes	Moderate	Low	Not easy to target tourism
Real Wage Levels	No	Low	Low	Depends on labour market
Tourism Industry Productivity	Yes	Low	Low	Some scope to improve productivity in longer term
Export Booms	No	NA	Moderate	Governments can mitigate effects of sudden booms
General Taxes	Yes	High	Low	Tax structure important
Specific Taxes	Yes	High	High	Other objectives important
Infrastructure Charges	Yes	High	High	Other objectives important
General Environmental Policies	Yes	High	Low	Policy design critical
Specific Environmental Policies	Yes	High	High	Other objectives important

Governments have little influence over real wage rates, which reflect the country's stage of development and the workings of the labour market.

Governments can have some influence over the productivity of different industries, including the tourism industry. In the main this influence is indirect, through the implementation of policies, such as competition policy, which stimulate efficiency. Again, however, economy-wide productivity improvements will tend to result in exchange rate rises and no gain in export competitiveness.

Governments cannot really control export booms, although they can introduce policies to limit the effects (e.g. industry assistance packages for sectors that become less competitive). These booms do, however, have an impact on the competitiveness of non-boom export industries, such as tourism. Where booms are sharp and temporary, governments can mitigate their effects on exchange rates, and thus on non-boom industries, through encouraging the saving of the temporary income gains (as Norway does with its booms in its oil revenues).

Tax policies can have a direct impact on tourism prices, and thus on competitiveness. But it is important to distinguish between taxes that apply to all export industries and those that apply only to some. While VAT/GST taxes are general, they are not applied to most export industries. Since they are, however, applied to tourism exports, they reduce tourism price competitiveness in much the same way as do specific taxes on tourism. If a tax is a general one and it affects all trading industries in the same way (say, an increase in corporation tax), the impact on competitiveness of any industry, such as tourism, will be limited since it will set in train compensating movements in exchange rates.

Infrastructure charges are like specific taxes – when they are increased, they lessen tourism competitiveness, and when they are reduced, they enhance competitiveness. Fuel prices, and especially those of oil-based fuels that are critical to tourism, are sensitive to government policy – countries differ considerably as to how they tax fuels.

Environmental policies can affect tourism competitiveness. Specific environmental measures, such as levies on aviation, will reduce tourism competitiveness. To the extent that general measures, such as the implementation of an ETS, apply to all trading industries, they will set in train compensating exchange rate shifts, which will at least partially cancel out the initial impact on competitiveness. Again, the exact design of the policy is important, because if exemptions are granted to some industries, the loss of competitiveness experienced by other industries will be greater.

20.5.3 TOURISM COMPETITIVENESS AND THE MACROECONOMIC ENVIRONMENT

Destination competitiveness is sensitive to the general macroeconomic environment. In normal times of macro-stability, the effects are not great. However, in times of macroeconomic stress, such as in the current GFC or during the 1997 Asian Financial Crisis, macro-conditions can have a considerable impact on patterns of tourism competitiveness.

One of the most obvious ways in which this can happen is through changes in exchange rates. Exchange rates have shifted, for some countries quite substantially, and they show considerable volatility. The results are shifts in, and volatility of, patterns of tourism competitiveness. Recession in several countries brought on by the GFC impacted upon the prices paid for tourism inputs, especially labour. This reduction leads to some reductions in product prices with hotels and airlines cutting prices to win business. This, in turn, brought about at least temporary changes in patterns of tourism competitiveness, with some high-cost countries (in North America and Europe) increasing their tourism price competitiveness vis-à-vis other countries, such as those of Asia. The GFC also had a large impact on oil prices. While this reduced the prices of tourism across the board, it did not have a large impact on the *relative* competitiveness of countries since they all pay much the same prices for their oil.

In response to the GFC, some governments altered their tax, infrastructure and environmental policies. Thus postponing the introduction of their ETS proposals could have some impact on patterns of tourism competitiveness but with longer-term consequences for the world's environments. Some individual countries choose to stimulate their economies through tax reductions. Depending on how this is done, their tourism competitiveness could be affected. With tax reductions putting pressure on governments' budgets, governments may look for 'easy' sources of revenue – and taxes on tourism, paid by non-residents, may be appealing. Already the UK Government in 2008 announced sharp increases in aviation taxes, designed to reduce its fiscal deficit, making the UK less competitive in tourism.

20.6   DIFFERENT MEASURES OF DESTINATION PRICE COMPETITIVENESS

There are several measures of price competitiveness that have been and are employed by researchers. We next describe several indicators, some of which are simple and quick to calculate, while others are more complex and require more measurement effort, but which are more accurate and give greater detail on the factors behind price competitiveness. The main ones are the following:

* The Consumer Price Index
* Price index of tourist bundles purchased
* Package tour prices
* The Big Mac Index
* Purchasing power parity
* Comprehensive Destination Price Competitiveness Index
* Tourism Trade Weighted Index
* Aviation Trade Weighted Index

20.6.1   THE CONSUMER PRICE INDEX

The majority of researchers have used the Consumer Price Index (CPI) as a measure of destination price competitiveness (Divisekera, 2003). The limitations of this measure are as follows: (1) it is excessively aggregate (and need not reflect the prices that tourists pay) and (2) it can only capture changes in price levels, not the levels themselves.

On the first point, this price competitiveness measure is only as good as its implicit assumption that the goods and services purchased by tourists are similar to those purchased by the representative household on which the CPI is constructed. However, the CPIs of the origin country and the destination may not reflect the prices of goods which tourists actually purchase, because the expenditure pattern of a tourist is quite different from that of the average household (Dwyer *et al.*, 2000a). Indeed, the basket of goods and services included in the price indices of a given country could differ significantly from the one consumed by its short-term tourists.

Another assumption underlying the use of the CPI is that prices of tourism goods and services tend to move in the same direction as overall consumer prices. However, as Divisekera (2003) points out, trends in general price levels as implied by CPI measures may not necessarily coincide with that of tourism. Moreover, there is no uniformity among countries in the coverage, weights and/or the components included in the relevant price indices, depending as they do on the particular socio-economic characteristics and consumption habits of the residents of the destination in question.

The second limitation is that CPI statistics provide no information on the *levels* of prices in different country or destination – it is not possible to use them to determine whether a country is more or less price competitive than another.

While the CPI can serve as a proxy for the change in cost of tourism at a destination, given lack of more suitable data, it would be more appropriate to use data relating to the price of the tourist's basket of goods and services that tourists actually purchase if this is available.

20.6.2   PRICE INDEXES OF TOURISM BUNDLES

A preferable measure of destination price competitiveness involves estimating the prices of the specific goods and services that tourists purchase. As Lim (2006) notes, since there are likely to be substantial measurement errors associated with the use of the CPI as a proxy for relative tourism prices, some researchers have preferred to use a specific tourist cost of living variable, such as drink and tobacco price indices, shopping/ meals/entertainment and hotel price indices, or weighted prices of food, accommodation, transport, entertainment and other variables, as proxies, or the average spending on travel goods and services as the composite tourism price. Kwack (1972) and Kliman (1981) use the implicit consumer expenditure deflator to measure the disparity between the origin, destination and competing destinations' prices.

While the tourism price index approach is preferable to the use of the CPI, in that it more accurately reflects the ways tourism prices are changing, it still faces that limitation that it can only be used to measure changes in price competitiveness between different countries or destinations over time, and cannot measure whether prices in one country are higher or lower than in another country.

20.6.3 PACKAGE TOUR PRICES

The costs of package tours have been used in some studies as proxies for tourism prices. This involves a major data-gathering exercise, since prices are not readily obtainable from comprehensive sources. Rather, they must be obtained from brochures and advertisements for tours. Once collated, it must be recognised that package tours are not a standardised product – they differ in duration, accommodation standard, tours included and amount of internal travel. With such information it would be possible to regress price on these factors and estimate the price of a standardised package.

It is also possible to use a synthetic approach, using actual price data to estimate how much a package tour of particular characteristics would cost in different countries (Dwyer *et al.*, 2000b). In this study the authors used a 'bottom-up' approach, which involved getting information about the cost shares of the various components, which make up a tour package. However, data used were economy-wide data, and there are significant variations in tourism prices across countries. Thus, hotel prices in Nice differ from hotel prices in Paris. It is also not the case that rates for every hotel in every region in Thailand are lower than for every hotel in every region in Canada. Nevertheless, rates in Thailand are, on average, lower than for Canada (and for similar types of accommodation, Thai rates will be lower than Canada's). All aggregate, economy-wide statistics have this problem.

20.6.4 BIG MAC INDEX

The most frequently quoted index of price competitiveness of different countries is the 'Big Mac Index'. *The Economist* magazine regularly publishes the price of 'Big Mac' hamburgers in about 60 different countries. These prices are converted into a single currency and give an indication of the cost of buying a standardised product in different countries.

It is tempting to read more into the 'Big Mac' Index than there really is to see it as an indicator of the general price competitiveness of the country. In fact, the index tells us little more than the price of a particular type of hamburger in the different countries. The 'Big Mac' is a simple product with ingredients in fixed proportions, whereas the tourism product is a very complex one comprising different components depending on tourist expenditure patterns. There is no equivalent tourism product offered across countries, as the nature of the product is tailored to the origin market, expenditure levels and the length of the trip involved. The key issue is that of how to standardise the products being compared, so as to determine their relative price competitiveness.

20.6.5 PURCHASING POWER PARITY

Another indicator of price competitiveness is the ratio of Purchasing Power Parity (PPP) conversion factor to the official exchange rate. PPP theory states that the exchange rate between one currency and another is in equilibrium when their domestic purchasing powers at that rate of exchange are equivalent. The simplest way to calculate PPP between two countries is to compare the price of a 'standard' good that is, in fact, identical across countries. If a 'representative' consumption basket costs $1200 in the USA and £800 in the UK, the PPP exchange rate would be $1.50/£. If the actual nominal rate was $1.80/£, this would indicate that the pound is overvalued by 20%, or equivalently the dollar is undervalued by 16.7%. PPPs can be used to estimate the amount of adjustment needed on the exchange rate between countries in order for the exchange to be equivalent to each currency's purchasing power.

The PPP theory is based on the assumption that, in ideally efficient markets, identical goods should have only one price. In the absence of transportation and other transaction costs, competitive markets will equalize the price of an identical good in two countries when the prices are expressed in the same currency. The main reasons why different measures do not perfectly reflect destination price competitiveness are that PPP numbers can vary with the specific basket of goods used, making it a rough estimate of destination competitiveness. One of the key problems is that people in different countries consume very different sets of goods and services, making it difficult to compare the purchasing power between countries. Also, variations in the qualities of goods and services are not sufficiently reflected in PPP.

20.6.6 A COMPREHENSIVE DESTINATION PRICE COMPETITIVENESS INDEX

Visitors from different origin markets spend different amounts of money on their trip and have different expenditure purchasing patterns within any destination. Once we know the bundle of goods and services purchased by a tourist, we can ask the basic question: what would the same bundle of goods and services cost if the tourist purchased it in another destination? The answer to this question determines whether one destination is more or less price competitive than another.

Both the cost of transport services to and from the destination and the cost of ground content (accommodation, tour services, food and beverage, entertainment, etc.) are relevant to the travel decision and can be taken into account in constructing price competitiveness indices. A destination price competitiveness index compares the prices in different destinations of the goods and services that tourists actually buy, as opposed to general price indices that include goods and services that tourists seldom or never purchase. Price competitiveness indices can be used to explore questions of how the competitiveness of destinations change over time and what causes these changes.

A comprehensive destination price competitive index has been developed by Dwyer *et al.* (2000a, b, c, 2002). The method used provides more information on the relative price competitiveness of different destinations than any of the alternatives, since they compare tourist expenditure on the same bundle of goods and services in different destinations. Unlike earlier approaches, the approach enables the construction of price competitiveness indices which indicate the level of price competitiveness of a destination as well as allowing for measurement of changes in these indices. The method of index construction recognises that changes in destination competitiveness can occur because of changes in exchange rates, differences in inflation rates and changes in the ratio of prices within the tourism sector to prices in other (non-tourism) sectors. The price competitiveness indices are more accurate and detailed than others since it is based on direct comparison of the (exchange rate adjusted) expenditure outlay in one destination as compared to competitor destinations, to purchase the exact same bundle of goods and services.

The steps involved in constructing a destination price competitiveness index are set out in Box 20.1.

BOX 20.1 Constructing a destination price competitiveness index

The construction of price competitiveness indexes for tourism in a selected destination involves several steps:

1. The origin markets are chosen. Since visitors from different origins will have different purchasing patterns, a set of origin markets must be identified. The major current and emerging origin markets for the selected destination can be used to construct the set of origin countries.

2. The destination markets are chosen. These include the major competitors of the selected destination. A destination's price competitiveness can be fully understood only in comparison to alternative destinations that the visitor can choose.

3. Price data must be collected for each of the items purchased by tourists. Ideally, the price data should be sufficiently detailed so as to include all of the different types of goods and services that tourists purchase. This detailed information is impossible to obtain in practice except at more aggregated level.

4. Expenditure patterns of tourists from different origin markets must be identified for the selected destination. In order to compute price competitiveness indexes it is necessary to attach weights to different goods and services consumed by

tourists to reflect purchasing patterns. Visitor expenditure, in total and in pattern, varies depending upon the origin market of the visitor, the purpose of travel and the types of goods and services available in the destination.

In order to compute price competitiveness indices it is necessary to attach weights to different products and services consumed by tourists to reflect purchasing patterns. The weights used are the share of expenditure of each of the items in the tourist basket.

5. Purchasing power parities (PPPs) for tourism expenditure are calculated. Establishment of a correspondence between tourist purchasing patterns and price data enables derivation of PPPs for each category of tourist expenditure. PPPs indicate the levels of expenditure required in different destinations to purchase the same basket of tourism goods and services.

6. The PPPs are adjusted by exchange rates to derive price competitiveness indexes. The index measures the level of prices of goods and services in a competitor destination, relative to prices in a selected destination and then adjust for exchange rates, as follows:

Price Competitive Index = PPP/Exchange Rate $\times$ 100/1

7. Interpretation of the price competitiveness index is straightforward. A particular destination is taken as base and its index is 100. For any destination, a price competitiveness index less than 100 indicates that this destination is more price competitive than the selected destination. Similarly, a figure above 100 indicates that this destination is less price competitive than the selected destination.

8. The values of the indexes allow destinations to be ranked according to their price competitiveness. The absolute values of the indexes can also be compared to determine the extent to which different destinations vary in price competitiveness in tourism. Both types of information can thus be used to measure the destination's price competitiveness in tourism in *relative* and *absolute* terms.

By way of example, suppose that Singapore wishes to compare its tourism price competitiveness with competitor destinations. Singapore's price competitiveness index is thus set at 100. For the purpose of illustration, consider the price competitiveness of Singapore and a competitor destination, Korea, from the viewpoint of a representative Japanese tourist. When the Japanese tourist compares prices in Singapore and Korea, he/she finds that what one Singapore dollar (or $S1000) buys in Singapore costs 596 (or 596,000) Korean won if the same bundle of goods and services is purchased in Korea (PPP). This figure is then compared with the exchange rate between the Singapore dollar and Korean won. The exchange rate as at 30 June 2008 was SGD $1 = 744 KRW.

Price Competitiveness Index for Korea = purchasing power parity/exchange rate
$$\times 100 = 596/744 \times 100 = 80.1$$

This means that the particular bundle of goods and services purchased by the Japanese tourist is less costly in Korea than in Singapore, when adjusted for the exchange rate. The index of 80.1 for Korea means that, for the typical Japanese tourist, given the costs of a particular bundle of goods and services consumed in each destination country, Korea is 20% more price competitive than Singapore (100).

Source: Based on Dwyer *et al.* (2000)

Dwyer *et al.* (2000a) estimated price competitiveness indices for 19 destination countries, and for 13 origin countries, both for the ground component of trips and for travel to Australia. A sample of the results is shown in Table 20.2.

In Table 20.2 Australia is the base destination with its price competitiveness index set at 100. The price competitiveness indices are estimated from the perspective of tourists from the UK, Japan and Singapore assuming that they would purchase the same bundle of goods and services in Australia, USA and Thailand. For each origin country Australia is more price competitive as a destination than is the USA (10%–15% more competitive depending on the origin market), but is much less price competitive than Thailand.

Table 20.2 Competitiveness indexes, ground component and selected countries

Destination/origin	UK	Japan	Singapore
Australia	100	100	100
US	110	116	111
Thailand	31	26	33

Source: Dwyer *et al.* (2000a, 2002)

The Comprehensive Price Competitiveness Indices have substantial policy relevance:

- Destination price competitiveness in absolute and relative terms can be estimated from the perspective of visitors from different national origin markets, and from the perspective of visitors having different journey purpose or special interest (Dwyer *et al.*, 1999, 2000a, b, c; Dwyer *et al.*, 2001).
- Price competitiveness indices can be disaggregated in respect of key tourism products and services so as to provide information on a destination's price competitiveness in different sectors of its tourism industry. This is to recognise that a tourism destination's overall price competitiveness depends on the price competitiveness of each of the sectors that deliver goods and services to visitors (accommodation, entertainment, conventions, etc.). These sub-indexes can provide the basis for tourist industry policy to enhance destination price competitiveness through studies of the productivity and efficiency of different tourism industry sectors (Dwyer *et al.*, 2000c).
- Destination Price Competitiveness indices can be used to explore questions of how the price competitiveness of destinations changes over time, and what causes this change. This is because they enable the changing sources of tourism price competitiveness to be identified and analysed. They can be decomposed to determine the relative influences on destination competitiveness of exchange rate changes and domestic inflation rates (Dwyer *et al.*, 2002). It is helpful for both industry and government to know how price competitiveness is changing and why these changes are occurring.
- Industry stakeholders can employ these results to help assess the impacts of alternative government policies on destination price competitiveness, for example, impacts of tourist taxes, or climate change adaptation policies on the prices of tourism-related goods and services.
- The price competitiveness indices also have particular relevance for destination marketing. They indicate that a destination may be price competitive from the perspective of some tourists, but not for others, depending on the purpose of visit and associated purchasing patterns.

Construction of the indices requires good price data and data on tourist purchasing patterns. Destinations vary considerably in the comprehensiveness and accuracy of the visitor expenditure data that they collect. The more comprehensive is the visitor expenditure data, and the price levels of the goods and services purchased, the more detailed and accurate will be the price competitiveness indices that can be constructed for that destination.

Where the data used are economy-wide data, there may well be significant variations in tourism prices across regions within a country. For example, the prices charged to tourists in Goa may differ considerably from those charged elsewhere in India, or prices along the coast may vary from those of locations inland. But all aggregate, economy-wide statistics have this problem. The methodology for constructing price competitiveness indices allows such indices to be completed for different regions within a tourist destination.

20.6.7 TOURISM TRADE WEIGHTED INDEX

As we have seen, changes in the exchange rate are likely to have a considerable impact on price competitiveness of different countries. This would be picked up in indices such as the Comprehensive Destination Price Competitiveness Index as discussed above. However, what is often needed is a simpler, but more easy and quick to calculate measure of how changes in exchange rates are impacting on a country's tourism price competitiveness.

The best known international measure of the competitiveness of a country's industries is the Trade Weighted Index of exchange rates (TWI). The TWI is a general index of the competitiveness of the country, weighting different countries' exchange rates according to their relative importance in trade, in terms of both exports and imports. For example, in Australia, the Reserve Bank of Australia publishes the index three times daily as a measure of the average movement of the $A against the currencies of Australia's trading partners (www.rba.gov.au). Most other countries publish an index of the average value of their currency. For Australia, the exchange rates vis-à-vis the USA and Japan (and increasingly China) have high weights in the TWI reflecting their importance in Australia's trade patterns.

The TWI gives a better indication of the competitive pressure on a country's export- and import-competing industries than the exchange rate with any one country in particular. Typically, it is the nominal TWI which is quoted – real effective exchange rates can be calculated, but only with a lag, since they require adjusting exchange rates by the relative rates of price change, as measured by the CPI or GDP deflator in the different countries. Generally, however, it will be the real TWI which is more reliable as an indicator of the competitive position of the countries – if a country has a depreciating exchange rate, which has been the case for Turkey, this will not be an indicator of improved competitiveness if it is also experiencing rapid inflation, as Turkey has. Real TWIs can be calculated.

The standard TWI is not an accurate measure of competitiveness for the tourism industry because tourism trade patterns are different from overall trade patterns. A particular country might be an important destination for a country's residents, or it might be an important source of tourists, but it may not be an important source of imports and exports of goods and services in general. Since it is quite possible that a country's exchange rate will appreciate, on average, relative to its trading partners, but depreciate relative to those countries that are the sources of its tourists, or the destinations for its outbound travellers, the TWI need not be a very good indicator of the competitive pressure on the tourism industry.

A simple and easy way to update measure of a country's tourism competitiveness can be obtained by developing a tourism-specific TWI, the Tourism Trade Weighted Index (TTWI). The TTWI is an index of exchange rates with the weights being determined by the importance of the different countries in tourism inbound and outbound expenditures. The TTWI is a new indicator of effective exchange rates that provides policy makers with an ongoing monitor of the home country's price competitiveness.

The TTWI is similar in structure to the TWI, which is a readily available and well-understood indicator of the trading position of a country. It is a simple, aggregate, measure of the change in the home country's general price level relative to those in a group of source countries or competitor countries. The TTWI can be calculated in either real or nominal terms, just as the standard TWI can be. As an indicator of how a country compares in price terms with its source or destination markets, a real TTWI will be more useful.

The TTWI differs importantly from two other measures developed in recent years. In a recent report, Global Insight (2003) has developed a measure called the 'Tourism-Weighted Exchange Rate' (TWER). This is simply the average exchange rate for a destination weighted by each of its origin market's share of total arrivals. This then is adjusted for relative inflation in the origin and destination to calculate a measure of the average change in prices for tourists to each destination. While similar in intent to the TTWI, the TWER measure is based on visitor flow data, whereas the TTWI is based on tourism expenditure data. In this respect, the TTWI is more consistent with the standard TWI measure which is estimated from expenditure on imports and exports rather than the flows of goods and services. The TTWI developed herein also differs from a 'TTWI' developed independently by Tourism Research Australia (2006) which also uses visitor flow data, rather than expenditure data.

While the TTWI index is less detailed than the price competitiveness indices based on comparisons of real exchange rates and PPPs, the TTWI has the advantage of timely (daily) relevance to destination managers as an index of tourism competitiveness and leading indicator of future tourism flows to and from the home country.

The method of constructing and interpreting a TTWI is set out in the Box 20.2.

BOX 20.2 Construction of a TTWI

Forsyth and Dwyer have developed a TTWI for Australia covering the years 1990–2008. The TTWI was estimated based on the exchange rates for fourteen major tourist origin countries (inbound TTWI) and twelve major tourist destination countries (outbound TTWI). The weights are based on the expenditure share that each country represents in Australia's total inbound and outbound tourism expenditure volume.

The TTWI consists of two arithmetically weighted average indicators.

- The *Inbound TTWI* consists of exchange rates for those countries or currency areas, representing the main sources of visitors to a destination, weighted by the total expenditure in that destination from each of the source countries.
- The *Outbound TTWI* reflects patterns of expenditure by a country's outbound travelers in different destinations.

- The *Overall TTWI* averages these two but it does not provide as much information as the separate inbound and outbound TTWI.

To estimate real TTWI, the nominal TTWI was divided by the ratio of the index of source or destination country prices, relative to the home country price index. The nominal and real TTWIs for Inbound and Outbound travel are presented in Table 20.3.

Table 20.3 Nominal and real tourism trade weighted indexes of exchange rates for Australia, selected periods 2000–2008

Period	Nominal TTWI		Real TTWI	
	Inbound	*Outbound*	*Inbound*	*Outbound*
2000 (June)	111.814	115.550	106.325	103.782
2005 (Dec)	128.086	132.102	129.325	119.268
2006 (Dec)	130.607	132.821	134.397	121.280
2007 (Dec)	139.483	143.109	142.392	127.993
2008 (March)	140.031	153.657	142.493	129.803
2008 (June)	149.151	133.853	154.401	141.275
2008 (Sept)	130.303	123.798	135.515	124.252
2008 (Dec)	116.598	126.778	118.122	111.942

Note: The Index was expressed using the base year of 1995

Source: Authors' estimates

Interpretation of the TTWI is straightforward. The TTWI is a weighted average of exchange rates. If the inbound TTWI increases by 10 percent, this means that prices in the home country have risen by 10 percent relative to those of a weighted average of source country prices. On average, the home country has become 10 percent more expensive to visit. To this extent, the TTWI, and especially the real TTWI, is a measure of competitiveness in tourism markets. When the inbound TTWI rises, this can be taken as a leading indicator of a fall in inbound tourism. When the outbound TTWI increases, the cost of overseas travel falls and more residents of a country will make overseas trips; these overseas trips are made to some extent at the expense of domestic tourism.

Between 2003 and 2005 the $A rose by 38% relative to the $US (Reserve Bank of Australia, 2005 (www.rba.com.au)). Three drivers behind the upward shift were slightly higher interest rates in Australia attracting capital inflow into the market and pushing the exchange rate higher; the weakness of the US dollar because of concerns about its trade performance and budget deficit and uncertainties about economic recovery; and a big lift in commodity prices – as the world economy recovered demand for commodities increased. While the $A did not rise as much relative to other currencies (in 2003 and 2004 it rose by 5.8% against the Euro, 19.1% against the Yen and 14.5% against the British Pound) (Reserve Bank of Australia, 2005), the rising $A implied a substantial drop in the price competitiveness of the Australian tourism industry. Between June 2000 and June 2008 the real TTWI for inbound tourism rose by 21.6%, while that for outbound tourism increased by 14.9%. This resulted in a flattening of the demand for inbound tourism and encouraged growth in outbound tourism, which was at least in part, at the expense of domestic tourism.

Both the nominal and real TTWI for inbound travel rose from June 2000 until June 2008. The rise in the TTWI indicates a significant loss in competitiveness by the Australian tourism industry. This was very much associated with the appreciation of the Australian dollar, particularly relative to the US dollar. In the third and fourth quarters of 2008, the TTWI fell substantially. This was associated with a dramatic fall in the value of the Australian dollar, particularly against the US dollar. This indicates a substantial gain in the competitiveness of Australian tourism. In real terms, the cost of visiting Australia, excluding airfares, fell by 21.8 percent over this period. During the same six-month period in late 2008, the real outbound TTWI fell by 20.8 percent, indicating the increased competitiveness of an overseas holiday for residents compared with a domestic tourism experience.

The TTWI indicates that, during the period investigated, Australia lost and then regained its price competitiveness as a tourism destination, while outbound tourism also lost and then rapidly regained its competitiveness relative to domestic tourism.

One of the key properties of the TTWI is that it can be calculated very quickly – in fact, almost instantaneously for the nominal index. The real index depends on data on prices that are only published with a lag, but good estimates of price indexes can be projected for a quarter or two using recent inflation rates. The result is that the TTWI provides an up-to-the-minute summary measure of the international competitive position of a country's tourism industry.

Source: Forsyth, P. and L. Dwyer (2009) 'Tourism Price Competitiveness', in *The Travel & Tourism Competitiveness Report 2009*, WEF, Geneva, Switzerland

20.6.8   AVIATION TRADE WEIGHTED INDEX

Of all industries, international aviation is among the most exposed to international trade. On international routes, airlines from one country compete directly with airlines from other countries. As liberalisation of international aviation markets has proceeded, this competition has intensified.

Airline profitability is affected by exchange rates in a number of ways. Three important ways are as follows:

- Changes in exchange rates affect the flows of passengers and hence revenues. If a country's exchange rate rises, it is likely to attract fewer inbound visitors, but outbound travel is likely to increase. The airlines of the country might gain or lose passengers, on balance, from this.
- Exchange rate changes can also impact on airlines through their capital structure – the impact depends on what countries' currencies they have borrowed in, and in which currencies they hold investments. In addition, the pricing of assets matters – an appreciation will decrease the value of assets, such as aircraft, purchased on international markets, in home currency terms.
- Exchange rate changes will affect the prices that airlines pay for inputs relative to the prices their competitors are paying. The ability of an airline to compete depends critically on its costs relative to those of other airlines. A key determinant of the relative costs faced by an airline, and thus its cost competitiveness, is the exchange rate in the home economy. If the exchange rate of the home country appreciates, the competitive pressure on the airline will increase, since its costs rise relative to those of its competitors. This loss of cost competitiveness comes about because international airlines buy some of their inputs, such as fuel, on international markets, but others, such as most of their labour, in home markets. Thus their costs rise relative to those of their international competitors. While the first two effects could go either way, this effect will be unambiguously negative for an airline in a country whose exchange rate has appreciated.

In reality, a country's exchange rate may be rising relative to some currencies, and falling relatively to others. Thus, if the objective is to gain an indicator of the relative cost competitiveness of its airlines, it becomes important to specify the countries where the exchange rate is changing. If these countries are strong competitors in airline markets, the effect on the airline cost competitiveness is greatest. Thus, to obtain an indicator of how a country's airlines' cost competitiveness position is changing overall, it is necessary to develop an index which weights countries by the strength of the competition they provide in relevant aviation markets.

The Aviation Trade Weighted Index of exchange rates (ATWI) developed by Forsyth and Dwyer seeks to provide an indicator of the change in the international competitive pressure on a country's aviation sector resulting from exchange rate changes. It weights different currencies according to how important different countries' airlines are as competitors in markets operated in by home country airlines. An airline's relative cost competitiveness may have changed, but the impact on its competitive position will depend on how its cost competitiveness has altered relative to those of the airlines with which it competes closely. Cost competitiveness indexes can be aggregated in the same way as the ATWI components are aggregated.

The ATWI is a measure of the changes in relative cost competitiveness which come about as a result of changes in nominal and real exchange rates. A rise in the exchange rate will make the airlines less cost competitive – if their competitiveness position is to be restored, they will have to improve their efficiency or lower the input cost they face (perhaps by sourcing inputs offshore).

The method of constructing and interpreting the ATWI is set out in the Box 20.3.

BOX 20.3 Constructing and interpreting the ATWI

The ATWI is a relative measure that gives an overall measure of competitiveness by weighting all the country's airlines competitiveness by their market shares in the country's routes. Forsyth and Dwyer have developed an ATWI for Australia covering the years 1990–2008. Table 20.4 contains estimates for selected quarters in selected years, providing a measure of how the real exchange rates of Australia and the 16 most important competitor countries on Australia's international air routes have varied over this decade.

Table 20.4 Aviation trade weighted index, nominal and real, Australia, 2000–2008, selected periods (1995 = 100. 0)

Period	Real ATWI	Nominal ATWI
2000 (June)	106.324	115.550
2005 (Dec)	129.325	132.012
2006 (Dec)	134.397	132.821
2007 (Dec)	142.392	143.109
2008 (March)	142.493	145.496
2008 (June)	154.401	153.657
2008 (Sept)	135.515	133.853
2008 (Dec)	118.122	123.798

The ATWI is calculated for Australian international airlines. It reveals that there has been a significant loss of competitiveness in recent years – the result of the appreciation of the Australian dollar relative to currencies of key airline competitor countries. The results indicate that, from June 2000 to June 2008, the Australian dollar appreciated relative to those countries whose airlines the home airlines are in close competition. This made Australia-based airlines progressively less competitive relative to airlines based elsewhere. Since June 2008, the situation has reversed, with Australia's international airlines becoming more competitive than rival airlines. Between June and December 2008, the competitiveness of Australian-owned airlines increased by 23.5 percent, an increase that would, other things equal, have been expected to have boosted inbound travel, albeit with a lag. Unfortunately the global financial crisis intervened to depress numbers.

These figures confirm that an Australian international airline such as Qantas has generally faced a difficult operating environment since late 2002, since its input costs have risen significantly compared to those of its competitors. The ATWI indicates that, except for the December quarter of 2008, the change in the real index over the period is slightly higher than the nominal index, implying that the nominal index understates the competitive pressure. This highlights the need for productivity increases and cost reductions. During this period, Qantas has acted to improve its cost competitiveness. It has increased its hiring of staff on international rather than home markets, it has contracted maintenance offshore, and it has introduced a low cost subsidiary, Jetstar International, shifting marginal international routes to it. These initiatives have placed Qantas in a sound position to weather the tourism downturn resulting from the global financial crisis.

Source: Forsyth and Dwyer (2010)

The ATWI provides an additional perspective to that provided by the TTWI. For example, Emirates is a major competitor of Qantas and any loss of competitiveness of Qantas relative to Emirates may be expected to result in lost market share of inbound passenger numbers. However, the currency of the United Arab Emirates (Dirham, AED) would be inconsequential in any trade weighted index calculation for Australia.

20.7   HORSES FOR COURSES: WHICH PRICE COMPETITIVENESS INDICATOR?

We have outlined a range of different tourism price competitiveness indicators. Which one should be used, and in what context? Depending on the exact question at hand, different indicators are suitable for different purposes. It is a matter of horses for courses.

Some questions relevant to the choice of indicators are the following:

- How detailed and tourism-specific need the indicator be?
- What is the trade-off between accuracy and timeliness and ease of access?
- Are cross-country comparisons of the level of tourism prices needed?
- Is specific sectoral information of interest?
- Are patterns of change over time in relative tourism competitiveness needed?
- Is it useful to have an overall measure of changes in a country's tourism competitiveness?

The performance of the different indicators in terms of these aspects is summed up in Table 20.5.

The Tourism Competitiveness Index is the most comprehensive indicator of tourism price competitiveness. It measures only prices that enter the tourism bundle, and thus is highly reflective of tourism. It enables cross-country comparisons at a point in time and can be calculated over time to indicate trends. With appropriate weights, it can be used to develop an indicator of changes in a country's overall tourism competitiveness. It is, however, the most data intensive of the measures. Detailed and accurate measures involve more data collection and processing, and thus they take longer to produce. If timeliness is important, it may be necessary to rely on broader proxies that can be obtained readily for price competitiveness.

A simple PPP comparison is much more readily available, but it is a measure of prices for whole economies, and it does not take any specific account of the prices that tourists actually pay, though these are likely to be correlated with the PPP prices.

If tourism-specific information is not regarded as necessary, then estimates of real exchange rate changes derived using CPI changes will be sufficient. However, if it is felt that CPI changes may not accurately reflect tourism price changes, then exchange rate changes can be adjusted using a tourism price index.

The Big Mac Index of *The Economist* is a popular device for illustrating PPP, but it is not to be regarded as a reliable indicator of tourism competitiveness. In contrast to the Big Mac, the tourism product is quite complex, comprising different components depending on tourist expenditure patterns.

Sectoral measures, such as hotel price surveys, can give a high degree of accuracy about a specific sector, though they do involve collection costs. If cross-country comparisons are not needed, and all that is needed are changes in the patterns of price competitiveness over time, then it is possible to adjust changes in exchange rates by changes in prices.

Over time, a country's competitiveness will rise relative to some competitors and fall relative to others. If an overall indicator of how a country's competitiveness fits in comparison with other countries is required, it is necessary to develop some measure such as the widely used TWI. In contrast, the TTWI is an index that reflects the importance

Table 20.5 Comparison of price competitiveness indexes

Indicator	Accuracy-reflectiveness of tourism	Data gathering	Cross-country comparisons	Comparison over time	Overall indicator of competitiveness	Comments
Tourism Price Competitiveness Index (Dwyer et al. 2000a)	High	Extensive	Yes	Yes	Potential	Most detailed indicator available
Simple PPP	Moderate	Easy	Yes	Yes	Potential	Broad readily available indicator
Big Mac	Low	Moderate	Yes	Yes	No	Too specific – really a gimmick
Sectoral Measurement (e.g. Hotel Prices)	High	Extensive	Yes	Potential	No	Useful for specific purpose and in general indicators
Tourism price index/exchange rate	High	Extensive	No	Yes	Potential	Not used extensively
CPI/exchange rate	Moderate	Easy	No	Yes	No	Broad measure of changes
Tourism Trade Weighted Index	Moderate	Moderate	No	Yes	Yes	Summary measure of competitiveness changes over time
Aviation Trade Weighted Index	Moderate	Moderate	No	Yes	Yes	Summary measure of competitiveness changes over time for aviation sector

Source: Forsyth and Dwyer (2009)

of different countries for inbound and outbound tourism expenditure. It is thus more tourisms-specific than the general TWI. The concept can be extended to a sectoral context.

The ATWI takes account of the real exchange rate changes taking place in the countries whose airlines are competitors for the home country airline – it thus gives a more accurate measure of the competitive pressure an airline will be under from its competitors than a general TWI will provide.

It needs to be emphasised that while price competitiveness is important, product quality must also be considered. An important business strategy for firms is to improve the quality of the characteristics of goods and services that are offered to tourists. Such quality improvements often enable the products to be sold for higher prices. If firms add sufficient value to the products and services on offer in a destination, prices can be increased to gain more expenditure from tourists. These issues were discussed in Chapter 5.

20.8 CONCLUSIONS AND POLICY

- Destination competitiveness is linked to the ability of a country or region to deliver goods and services that perform better than other destinations on those aspects of the tourism experience considered to be important by tourists.
- There is increasing effort to develop an overall model and indicators of destination competitiveness. Such a model would help tourism stakeholders to identify key strengths and weaknesses of their destination, highlight opportunities for tourism development and develop strategies to counter possible threats to future visitation.
- Integrated models attempt to bring together the main elements of national and firm competitiveness into one such overall model of destination competitiveness. It is difficult, however, to develop such an overall model of destination competitiveness comprising both quantitative and qualitative variables.
- There is no single or unique set of competitiveness indicators that apply to all destinations at all times. For any given element of destination competitiveness, any number of attributes or indicators may be employed as measures. The importance of competitiveness indicators will vary across locations, depending on product mix and target market segments.
- For specified market segments, it is possible to identify the most important attributes as perceived by tourists and to compare the performance of different destinations on the selected attributes. The approach offers a basis for strategy development and policy formulation for the different market segments of the destination tourism industry.
- The TTCI is designed to help explore the factors that drive T&T competitiveness worldwide, so providing a basis for implementing policies on a country by-country-basis. It is composed of 14 pillars organised into three sub-indexes capturing broad categories of

variables that drive or facilitate T&T competitiveness: regulatory framework; business environment and infrastructure; and human, cultural and natural resources.

- Factors that impinge on price competitiveness include exchange rates, inflation, the price of labour, productivity, export booms, tax structures and levels, infrastructure charges, fuel prices and environmental charges.

- Measures of price competitiveness employed by researchers include: The consumer price index; price index of tourist bundles purchased; package tour prices; the Big Mac index; purchasing power parity; comprehensive destination price competitiveness index; tourism trade weighted index; aviation trade weighted index.

- Destination price competitiveness indices attempt to compare across different destinations the prices of goods and services that tourists actually buy (as opposed to general price indices that include goods and services that tourists seldom or never purchase).

- The TTWI is an index of exchange rates with the weights being determined by the relative importance of the different countries in tourism inbound and outbound expenditures. It indicates effective exchange rates and provides policy makers with an ongoing monitor of the home country's price competitiveness, acting as a leading indicator of future tourism flows to and from the home country.

- The ATWI provides an indicator of the change in the international competitive pressure on a country's aviation sector resulting from changes in exchange rates. It weights different currencies according to how important different countries' airlines are as competitors in markets operated in by home country airlines.

- The type of price competitiveness index employed depends on the research or policy needs at a given time. In some situations, quickly calculated, simple measures are most useful, while in others, more detailed and accurate measures are required. The measures used will also depend on the data available – some countries have very detailed tourism and price statistics, while statistics in other countries can be rudimentary.

- Destination competitiveness is a goal that is achievable through informed decision-making and strategic choice. If the limitations of the various competitiveness indices are recognised, they can be valuable tools for policy formulation for any tourism destination to achieve and maintain competitive advantage over competitors, as well as empirical studies of tourism demand. The outcomes will be more informed policy making regarding the type of tourism development most likely to enhance resident quality of economic and social life.

SELF-REVIEW QUESTIONS

1. Define the concept of destination competitiveness.

2. Highlight the main components of an integrated model of destination competitiveness.

3. Why is it difficult to develop any measure of overall destination competitiveness?

4. Briefly describe the rationale behind the construction of the TTCI and outline how it is constructed.

5. What are the main sources of destination price competitiveness?

6. Briefly describe the rationale behind the construction of a destination price competitiveness index and outline how one is constructed.

ESSAY QUESTIONS

1. 'The potential for any country's tourism industry to develop will depend substantially on its ability to maintain competitive advantage in its delivery of goods and services to visitors.' Discuss.

2. Use the niche market four-quadrant Importance Performance Analysis diagram to explain the importance of factors that might underlie heritage tourism.

3. Choose an LDC and discuss the factors that give it a low ranking on the TTCI. Through what practical ways might the country try to improve its ranking?

4. Changes in the exchange rate are likely to have the same impact on a tourist's destination choice as relative price changes. Do you agree? How might exchange rates be included in measures of destination competitiveness?

FUTURE DIRECTIONS

CHAPTER 21

FUTURE DIRECTIONS FOR RESEARCH IN TOURISM ECONOMICS

The topics discussed in the text are only some of the issues that could have been discussed in a book on tourism economics and policy. Clearly which topics to include and which to exclude come down to matters of judgement. We are aware of a number of important topics that have not been included in this edition. For example, despite discussion throughout the text on the importance of the workings of labour markets in estimating the impacts of shocks to tourism demand and supply, there is no chapter dedicated to a discussion of tourism employment. Another topic involves tourism transportation in modes other than air travel. The importance of land-based transport (train, bus, car, etc.) for tourist travel is well recognised as is the growing importance of cruise tourism globally. Others might point out that the book devotes insufficient space to issues of the role of tourism in the economic development of small countries and those with low Gross Domestic Product (GDP) per capita. We plead guilty, but one can do only so much in one text. What we have attempted to do is to consider each topic in some depth. This has rendered them each rather long but, we hope, of detailed content.

Another topic that might be regarded as relatively neglected in the book is that of sustainability. Increasingly, one finds this concept discussed in the tourism literature as an ideal that should guide destination management and industry operations. A reading of the text would confirm, however, that issues relevant to sustainability are discussed in some detail throughout the text. We do not regard ourselves as having adopted a narrow economic stance regarding any of the topics addressed in the text. We are well aware that social and environmental effects are invariably present alongside the more purely economic effects associated with tourism shocks including policy initiatives. Our view of sustainability is the traditional one that acknowledges the importance of considering the social, environmental and economic effects of tourism development strategies and policy formulation. While recognising this, the focus of the text is on the economic issues. Our broader concern with issues beyond those that are more narrowly 'economic' is evident from the material on cost benefit analysis (CBA) and impact assessment as well as the general approach adopted in our exploration of the issues in and around each topic.

Not surprisingly, a good number of the examples of economic analysis appearing in the text relate to Australian tourism. Over two decades of contribution to tourism research, Dwyer and Forsyth have addressed many different topics using Australia as a context for analysis and policy discussion. Inevitably much of this research is featured in the text, that said, the particular destination context is very often less important than the ideas advanced and the approaches used to address problems and issues. Throughout their writings, the authors have sought to emphasise the relevance of their investigations for economic analysis and policy formulation in both developed and developing destinations globally. Whatever the particular destination that is highlighted in the different discussions throughout the text, we would claim that lessons can be learned for other tourism destinations.

In each of the topics discussed in the preceding chapters, ongoing research is progressively expanding the boundaries of our knowledge. It would be an enormous task for this chapter to attempt to highlight the specific directions that research on any given topic area might take. For present purposes, we will herein outline some directions for future research that seem to us to have some importance.

TOURISM DEMAND AND FORECASTING

Over time, the modelling of tourism demand has become more sophisticated and more complex and different contexts of study, different data sets, use of different variables and different modelling techniques preclude generalisations. Given the importance of a better understanding of demand for destination management, marketing and policy purposes tourism demand modelling may be expected to continue to be refined with more input from the econometrics literature.

A recent event, the Global Financial Crisis (GFC), has substantial longer-term implications for demand modelling. The estimated income elasticities discussed in the text are averages, derived from analysis over a long run of years. Traditionally, the price elasticities of demand that have been estimated by demand modellers have been based on time-series data which tend to smooth over crises that change prices dramatically. They do not allow adequately for the sharp shocks reducing consumer and business confidence that the world is experiencing as a result of the GFC. Economic slow-downs or recessions, building as sharply as is currently the case, are likely to increase the negative effect on tourism spending from the measured slowing in economic growth. These confidence effects are likely to be particularly pronounced for discretionary spending such as tourism. The substantial falls in prices associated with the GFC call attention to the need to consider the price sensitivities of tourists in times where levels of wealth are being eroded and unemployment is rising at a rapid rate.

In the demand modelling literature, the focus on income as an influence on tourism flows has been associated with a relative neglect of wealth as a determining factor. The importance of wealth as a determinant of travel has been amply demonstrated as a result of GFC. While the GFC certainly reduced incomes on average for millions of people, perhaps the greatest effect was on their level of wealth due to the decline in value of their assets including superannuation payouts. While there has always been some recognition that wealth is important for some tourism markets, for example, seniors' tourism, the issue remains under-researched.

Another outcome of the GFC is recognition of the importance of domestic tourism as a substitute given the constraints on international and long-haul travel and possible reductions in the time people have to travel and the money they have to spend. While domestic tourism does not have the same positive impact on a country's foreign exchange earnings, it is a research area worthy of greater consideration by tourism economists. Domestic tourism as a substitute for outbound travel reduces the leakages that occur and has the potential to create income and employment in the home economy. For many tourism destinations, the domestic tourism industry provides much larger visitor numbers than do international markets. Unfortunately, destination managers and researchers often see domestic tourism as inferior to the more 'glamorous' international market. While increased marketing efforts in respect of domestic tourism markets will have no expansive effects internationally, they can, however, serve to enhance the viability of the home tourism products through crises such as the GFC, providing a basis for future recovery.

The relative neglect of wealth as a determinant of tourism demand has implications also for tourism forecasting. A better understanding of consumer behaviour and attitudes to travel is needed in times of economic recession. Our lack of knowledge about possible consumer responses to the crisis places great impediments in the way of forecasting its effects on the industry. Thus, consumers may spend less, and travel less, but to what extent they shift to other products, reduce debt or save more is not known. Typically, estimates of income elasticities of tourism demand are based on longitudinal data and are not applicable to the sharp falls associated with the GFC. The degree to which tourists switch to closer destinations, domestic destinations, shorter lengths of stay or 'trade-down' (e.g. lower cost carriers, lower standard hotels, business class to economy) are also important research areas. Whether crises make consumers more sensitive to price signals and differentials thereby increasing the elasticity of demand for tourism products is also worthy of research. The implications for particular destinations and tourism market segments (senior tourism, business tourism, visiting friends and relatives, cruise tourism, etc.) are unknown. To what extent price level and exchange rate falls offset income falls to maintain tourism flows needs to be researched also. We simply don't know enough about consumer travel behaviour to give definite answers to these questions. We can expect a greater emphasis on consumer behaviour as a topic in tourism research.

The same as for the area of demand modelling the forecasting literature is increasingly incorporating 'state-of-the-art' statistical techniques that traditionally lie outside of the tourism research methods. This is appropriate. However, a fruitful additional area of research involves efforts to enhance tourism forecasting accuracy through forecast combination and forecast integration of quantitative and qualitative approaches. Forecasts need to be justifiable with the forecasting process transparent and open to all to question and challenge. Combined forecasts tend to have greater explanatory power than single approach forecasts and tend to be more accurate. Future research in this area should reflect an understanding of this.

SUPPLY AND PRICING

As discussed in the text, supply-side definitions of tourism products and industries are listed in the Recommended Methodological Framework (TSA-RMF) developed by the Commission of the European Communities, the Organisation for Economic Cooperation and Development (OECD), the United Nations World Tourism Organisation (UNWTO) and the World Travel and Tourism Council (WTTC), and approved by the United Nations Statistical Commission. The recommended framework identifies tourism's component products and industries through the concepts of Tourism Characteristic and Tourism Connected products and industries. Tourism economists can play an important role in using these internationally agreed-upon definitions and concepts in their research. It is to be hoped that tourism economists use the definitions that are contained in the recommended framework in order to underpin the credibility of their research and to facilitate replication of results in other contexts and benchmarking generally. Use of the internationally agreed-upon definitions and concepts allows research on the tourism industry to be better included in the mainstream of economic analysis. In addition, consistent use of internationally endorsed concepts and definitions will also facilitate the policy relevance of the research outcomes. Research based on consistent use of comprehensive and reliable statistics is essential for policy makers to make effective decisions about resource allocation.

Progress made in the development of the recommended framework of statistics has now opened up a suite of research opportunities for tourism economists. These include measuring tourism's interrelationship with other industries as well as comparison of tourism activity with other major industries in terms of size, economic performance, employment and contribution to the national and regional economy, and comparisons between regions, countries or groups of countries. Researchers now have a better opportunity to help tourism stakeholders to better understand the economic importance of tourism activity and, by extension, its role in all the industries producing the various goods and services demanded by tourists. In this way, tourism economics can better serve as a tool for enhanced strategic management and planning for the tourism industry to achieve enhanced destination competitiveness in the context of broader policy agenda.

The tourism industry globally is comprised predominantly of small businesses. It seems fair to say that the conduct and performance of small business enterprises generally has been under-researched compared to the behaviour of the larger, more 'glamorous' players. On the other hand, the oligopolistic nature of some tourism markets has led firms to seek to control their supply chains through vertical and horizontal integration and through the formation of strategic alliances. It is expected that the larger tourism firms will increasingly seek to form strategic alliances and the advantages and limitations of these may vary sector to sector. This is an area deserving of future research. At the same time, all firms, large and small may be expected to pay closer attention to aspects of their value system with their value chains linking to the value chains of upstream and downstream suppliers. There are substantial opportunities for research in this area also.

The tourism industry has experienced many financial crises over the years, yet there remain large knowledge gaps about the financial behaviour and strategies of firms under financial stress. The implications for new product development, investment, marketing and staffing are not well understood. Likewise, the strategic options to help firms remain viable during economic downturns are not well researched. Additionally, little is known about the impacts of financial and economic crises on event sponsorship, business meetings and corporate travel. There is also scope for economic modelling of the impact of financial crises on sustainable tourism initiatives (especially with respect to climate change). Historical accounts and case studies of tourism stakeholder responses to previous economic recessions may also provide valuable lessons for the future.

As discussed in the text, the price that a tourism firm sets for its products is governed by the interplay of a number of factors that are internal and external to the firm. These include the firm's objectives and ownership pattern, the market structure in which it operates, the degree of competition within the market and the firm's position within the market, seasonality, government policy, the macroeconomic environment, the price of other goods, capacity constraints and the degree of perishability of its products. It seems fair to say that how tourism firms set prices is one that is under-researched. The issue is important since small businesses of the type that comprise the global tourism industry historically have operated with low profitability.

Marginal pricing approaches of the type most used in economic analysis work best when the firm is well informed and able to make effective use of the information available to it. Moreover, in the tourism industry generally some firms may be less focused on maximising profits than in achieving other objectives. Tourism firms can potentially adopt different pricing strategies according to their objectives (which may emphasise market share or lifestyle objectives). The pricing strategies adopted will have different implications for firm output, sales and profits. As discussed in Chapter 20, prices in a destination are an important factor in the destinations overall competitiveness. Tourism firms can adopt competitive strategies such as cost leadership, product differentiation and/or segment focus and set their prices by reference to one or a combination of these strategies. Contributions to our knowledge of how prices are set by firms in destinations can help in the formulation of strategies to improve destination competitiveness.

One area deserving of more attention by researchers is that of determining the importance of quality in firms' pricing strategies. As discussed in the text, the hedonic pricing method has been used by tourism researchers to show how various supply-related factors explain the variation in overall accommodation and package tour prices, presenting tourism managers with an opportunity to enhance their strategic pricing through quality improvements and innovation.

ECONOMIC CONTRIBUTION AND ECONOMIC IMPACTS

Given the development of Tourism Satellite Accounts (TSA) worldwide, it can be expected that more research will be undertaken on tourism's economic contribution to a destination. TSA allow the tourism industry to be better included in the mainstream of economic analysis. As discussed in the text, tourism's total economic contribution (both direct and indirect) measures the size and overall significance of the tourism industry within an economy. The research literature may now be expected to contain more studies that compare and analyse the contributions that tourism and its component industries make to key variables such as GDP, value added and employment. TSA provide policy makers with insights into tourism and its contribution to the economy providing an instrument for designing more efficient policies relating to tourism and its employment aspects. As a result of basing more of their research in analysing data from TSA, the outputs of tourism economists should become even more relevant to the information needs of destination managers.

TSA provide the basic information required for the development of models of the economic impact of tourism. For example, analysts may use data from TSA to estimate the direct effect of changes in tourism consumption on other industries or on employment. In helping governments and businesses determine the value of tourism to the economy, TSA can also aid in the formulation of strategies for ensuring competitive advantage in this sector.

National level TSA are generally of less relevance to regional destination management organisations and local businesses than a regional TSA. Worldwide, regional governments are developing tourism plans to maximise the opportunities for income and employment growth resulting from an expanding tourism industry. This presents tourism economists with opportunities to investigate tourism's contribution to sub-regions. This has traditionally been a neglected research area given previous data limitations. Tourism economists also have a role to play in analysis of the advantages and disadvantages of 'top-down', 'bottom-up' and 'hybrid' approaches to the construction of regional TSA.

TSA are not in themselves modelling tools for economic impact assessment. Tourism economists have a role to play in keeping other researchers and destination managers aware of the distinction between 'economic contribution' and 'economic impact'. As discussed in the text, *economic contribution* measures the size and overall significance of the industry within an economy, while *economic impact* refers to the *changes* in the economic contribution resulting from specific events or activities that comprise 'shocks' to the tourism system. Economic impact implies that the overall change in the economic contribution must take account of the extensive interactive effects which occur across the economy.

TSA can also be used to develop measures of tourism yield. The text discusses six yield measures – expenditure per tourist, return on capital, profitability, GDP, value added and employment. Researchers have substantial opportunities to develop and compare different measures of tourism yield using TSA. Given that TSA distinguish the numbers and expenditure of different tourist markets by origin, the yield contribution measures can be developed per tourist by origin market.

A relatively neglected research topic has been measures of tourism productivity at the industry level. TSA can be used to develop performance indicators such as measures of productivity, prices and profitability for the tourism industry as a whole. They can also be used to explore performance in individual sectors. Tourism researchers now have the data to explore the performance of individual tourism sectors or of the entire tourism industry relative to that of other industries, domestically and internationally.

One of the fundamental challenges for tourism into the future is to adapt to climate change and to meet the responsibilities that all industries have in respect of mitigating greenhouse gas (GHG) emissions. TSA provide the opportunity for tourism economists to contribute to our understanding of the 'carbon footprint' associated with the tourism industry. The advantage of using the TSA to estimate the carbon footprint is that it ensures that the measure is comprehensive, and incorporates all emissions from all industries which make up tourism. That is, if the relationship between industry production and GHG emissions is known, then it is possible to calculate the emissions which are due to tourism as measured by the TSA. In addition, since the TSA is extensively used as a measure of the economic contribution of size of the tourism industry, this carbon footprint is an environmental measure which is consistent, in terms of definition of the industry, with the economic measure.

The topic of economic impact analysis has engaged tourism economists for decades. An economic impact analysis estimates the changes that take place in an economy due to some existing or proposed project, action or policy. A major objective of such estimates has been to inform policy makers as to the appropriate allocation of resources both within the tourism sector itself and between tourism and other industry sectors. Unfortunately economic impact analyses continue to be published in the research literature despite their reliance on obsolete assessment techniques, specifically through the use of Input–Output (I–O) multipliers. Certainly, there has been insufficient awareness by researchers that the size of a tourism multiplier depends on the particular model employed as well as the specific circumstances of the case under study, including the structure of the local economy and particularly the degree to which its various sectors are inter-linked in their trading patterns and the existing factor constraints.

Given the advances in CGE modelling over the past decade and a half, tourism economists now have the opportunity to play a much more important role in providing information that destination managers can use in policy formulation. CGE models can guide policy makers in a variety of scenarios arising from a range of domestic or international shocks or alternative policy scenarios. They can be tailored to allow for alternative conditions such as flexible or fixed prices, alternative exchange rate regimes, differences in the degree of mobility of factors of production and different types of competition.

CGE models can be used to quantify the effects of actual policies, such as changes in taxation, subsidies or government borrowing, as well as predicting the effects of a range of alternative policies or exogenous expenditure shocks. CGE models are helpful to tourism policy makers who seek to use them to provide guidance about a wide variety of 'what if?' questions, arising from a wide range of domestic or international expenditure shocks or alternative policy scenarios. In tourism, very interesting results have emerged using this technique in areas as diverse as tourism taxation, the impacts of special events, policies in response to human-induced tourism crises (terrorism) and other crises affecting tourism destinations (e.g. SARS, foot and mouth disease). Tourism researchers have recently applied CGE modelling to determine who gains and who loses from tourism development together with analysis of the extent to which tourism growth alleviates poverty. Clearly, different research projects can be done in this area to improve our understanding of tourism's impacts on both developed and developing economies.

All of the limitations of I–O modelling apply also to its use in the economic impact assessment of special events. Perhaps more than in any other area, tourism economists seem still uncritically wedded to an assessment method based on I–O multipliers which gives exaggerated impacts for special events. Tourism economists have an important role to play in researching the effects of the workings of labour markets, government subsidies and taxes on event impacts as well as the distributional effects associated with large events. Given that government funding agencies are now demanding that event evaluation be undertaken using state of the art techniques, it can be expected that evaluation of special events will increasingly incorporate CGE modelling of the economic impacts and CBA of the wider economic, social and environmental effects.

Estimates of the economic impacts of an event provide, in themselves, an imperfect basis for decisions about resource allocation. Economic impacts, such as the change in Gross Regional Product (GRP) resulting from an event, are not the same thing as the economic benefits which arise. The change in GRP is an exaggeration of how much better off are destination residents. The measured impacts on economic activity of most tourism shocks, such as increases in tourism expenditure, may normally be expected to be much greater than the net benefits which they generate for the community (or in other words, the measure of the extent to which they make the community better off). Tourism researchers should demonstrate awareness of the policy implications of their findings.

Researchers in the special events area have tended to treat economic impact analysis and CBA as distinct techniques of assessment, with the potential to provide conflicting recommendations. Essentially, CBA is detailed but partial equilibrium, whereas CGE techniques are general equilibrium but less detailed. In principle, it would be possible to develop a CGE model which incorporates all the detail that one might include in a CBA, but in practice, this would be an impossibly demanding task. A CBA picks up a whole range of benefits and costs which would not be picked up in a CGE model. These include non-priced effects which do not get included in the markets which are modelled – for example, noise from an event, the consumers surplus of home patrons, loss of park amenity and traffic congestion associated with the event. The CGE modelling, in contrast picks up the increased income to households resulting from the event. Since neither technique is completely comprehensive, both have a role in a comprehensive evaluation of a project or event. Integrating the two techniques to provide a better basis for funding agencies to make informed decisions as to whether or not to subsidies special events is an important topic for research.

COSTS AND BENEFITS

It is important that the net benefits of tourism be assessed accurately for policy reasons. Issues of concern in the measurement of net benefits associated with a change in tourism expenditure relate to: terms of trade effects (Chapter 6); taxation (Chapter 15); government revenue and subsidies (Chapter 9); market power, underemployment; foreign exchange effects, and externalities (Chapters 6, 10, 17, 18 and 19). These are all areas where research is needed to estimate the net benefits associated with tourism development.

As argued, estimates of the economic impacts of events do not *per se* provide a basis for decisions about resource allocation. The failure to understand this arises from a failure to distinguish clearly between the *impacts* and the (net) *benefits* of the event. The failure to make the distinction clear, has, we believe, resulted in the situation where tourism stakeholders generally regard 'impacts' as synonymous with 'benefits'. 'Impacts' on economic activity are measured by changes in GDP or similar measures. The change in GDP is an exaggeration of how much better off the country, and, more precisely, its residents, are when additional resources are used to enable this activity. 'Net benefits' are a measure of the value of the gain in economic activity less the cost needed to enable this extra activity. Tourism economics should play their role in upholding the distinction between the different concepts in their research.

Some CGE models are explicitly designed to include a measure of resident welfare. Consistent with economic theory, these models measure a change in welfare by equivalent variation (EV), which indicates how much the change in welfare is worth to the economy at the pre-simulation set of prices. This measure takes the results from what may be quite complex effects of a simulation on a household and produces a single value to describe how much better (or worse) off the economy is as a result of such effects. The credibility of such estimates depends upon how robust they are to alternative specifications of the utility functions, production functions, ability of factors to move from jurisdiction to jurisdiction and many other assumptions inherent in the CGE model. There are opportunities for welfare measures to be given more emphasis in CGE modelling to improve their input into informed policy making.

INVESTMENT AND INFRASTRUCTURE

Issues regarding tourism investment have also been relatively under-researched. Strong, continuing tourism investment is vital to a strong, successful tourism industry. Destinations must continually monitor changing consumer values and needs in order to provide the types of goods and products that will be demanded into the future. Apart from the increase in capacity and profits that accrue to individual firms and the tourism sector in general from successful investment, the perceived national and regional benefits that come from a more favourable tourism investment climate include economic growth; job creation; utilisation of domestic resources, particularly renewable resources; skills acquisition; expansion of exports; development of remote areas of the country; and facilitation of increased ownership of investment by the nation's citizens. Unfortunately, these outcomes of investment are often taken for granted by researchers and insufficiently examined in particular cases.

The importance of tourism investment became particularly evident during the recent GFC. Declining asset values impacted on the ability of firms to fund debt or invest and many capital projects (including fleet expansion, hotel projects, attractions, etc.) were shelved due to financing difficulties. Credit availability and de-risking of bank balance sheets stifle the volume of tourism investment needed to support tourism growth over time with its attendant economic effects. The source of capital financing is an important issue in tourism investment decision-making, since it can substantially affect a tourism project's overall costs. We need greater understanding of the sources of finance available to support tourism investment including the extent of distortions that exist in different economies to restrict its volume.

Various theories of the basis of firms financing decisions have been proposed in the wider finance literature. These include the Pecking Order and Trade-off theories as well as right-financing and the Market Timing Hypothesis. There are opportunities for researchers to explore the implications of these different perspectives to increase our understanding of the conditions that support successful tourism investment.

There is a general recognition of the importance of infrastructure to support tourism development. Infrastructure is of course required for the development and growth of tourism capacity so that supply can match a growing demand. It is widely acknowledged that the infrastructure on which a country's tourism industry relies, such as its roads, railways, airports, terminals, accommodation facilities, shopping, entertainment, restaurants, currency exchange facilities, telecommunications and so on are major determinants of its overall destination competitiveness including destination 'experience' and perceived trip value. However, potentially important research involving infrastructure issues has tended to be neglected. The GFC has reminded us that public sector investment in 'tourism and community infrastructure' may have both counter-cyclical and longer-term merits in the current and prospective environment, provided its social return justifies the use of taxpayer funds involved. However, little effort seems to have been devoted to investigate the 'returns' to destinations from provision of infrastructure that is used by tourists, especially when tourist use is subsidised by resident ratepayers and taxpayers. Infrastructure provision also increases the efficiency of privately producing and distributing tourism services, facilitating the supply of tourism services at competitive prices. But there has been relatively little research addressing the implications of this for communities.

Infrastructure industries are often complex ones which pose a number of public policy problems which need to be addressed – for example, they are often monopolies, and governments will wish to limit the use of their market power. Infrastructure projects, which often involve large, capital-intensive investments, often have large environmental impacts, which mean that obtaining approval for them is a drawn out process. The text covered various economic problems associated with ensuring the supply of tourism infrastructure, all of which comprise potentially fruitful areas of research. These include investigation of the changes that have been taking place in the institutional structure of infrastructure – the move from public to private provision; the congestion problem which impedes the efficiency of infrastructure provision; problems in government regulation of tourism infrastructure; the effects of environmental constraints on infrastructure; how provision of good infrastructure can stimulate tourism; and the particular problems that developing countries face in ensuring that their infrastructure helps their tourism development.

Moves to privatisation appear to have resulted in improved performance of infrastructure generally, including tourism-oriented infrastructure. The establishment of public–private partnerships, and an increasing emphasis on user-pays are two initiatives that hold out the promise of further improvements over time. The benefits and costs of each and the implications of each for tourism industry performance by location have, however, been relatively neglected by tourism researchers.

Tourism industries worldwide (e.g. airlines, rail services, public transport, etc.) display the problems associated with regulated infrastructure such as inadequate investment, excessive investment, poor service quality, over-servicing, high-cost operation and ineffective use of available capacity. These problems also appear with tourism infrastructure. The positive side is that in many destinations the problems are being diagnosed, and regulation is being better designed to take account of the problems that have developed. Neither of the two broad approaches to monopoly regulation, namely, cost-plus regulation or price-cap or incentive regulation, have received the attention from researchers that they deserve given the importance of the issue to efficient resource use in tourism development. The extent of environmental constraints on the development of tourism infrastructure is also an area in need of the attention of researchers. Consideration of the trade-offs that must be made between economic and environmental attributes is a crucial task to achieve sustainable development of the tourism industry.

Provision of tourism infrastructure and its maintenance is a particular problem for developing countries given lack of local investment, limitations on local legal systems and pressure from donor countries. While researchers have addressed these issues, very often the type of economic modelling that has been employed will not give accurate results on the extent to which investment in tourism infrastructure will benefit a destination nor does it lead to a better understanding of who gains and who loses within the destination. As Chapter 9 makes clear in its discussion of the use of CGE modelling in developing countries, it cannot be assumed that investment in infrastructure to develop the tourism industry will reduce poverty within a destination.

There are various arguments both for and against Foreign Direct Investment (FDI) in the tourism industry particularly in developing countries. Since the determination of the net benefits (costs) for any country is an empirical there is potential for research on the effects of FDI particularly in emerging destinations.

TAXATION

Tourism taxes are unlike most other barriers to international trade. Most of these, such as tariffs on imports, impose net costs on the economy levying the tariff (home-country residents have to pay the tariff). Reducing tariffs around the world has been a slow and difficult business; reducing tourism taxes may be even more difficult. Most countries have some market power or the ability to raise prices to foreign tourists. Many destinations use their market power to levy taxes on foreign tourists. The result of such 'tourism tax exporting' is inefficiently high tourism taxes that may well be rational from the viewpoint of the individual country or jurisdiction, but too high from a more general, worldwide welfare perspective.

While much research on the effects of tourism taxes has been undertaken by researchers the great bulk of it has involved partial equilibrium analysis of specific sectors of the economy. A tax that directly affects tourism flows will have impacts across the entire economy as the reduced demand impedes employment growth in tourism and related industries. As we have emphasised throughout this text, to understand the full implications of any tourism shock it is necessary to move beyond partial equilibrium analysis to consider the general equilibrium (economy-wide) effects. It is hoped that more tourism economists will take up this research challenge.

In estimating the effects of tourism taxes on the economy, researchers must acknowledge that if the government does not tax tourism, or some other industry, it will have to raise the tax somewhere else resulting in similar negative effects on activity and employment. Alternatively, the government may not raise the tax revenue and may cut expenditure, but this too will have a negative impact on activity and employment. A tax on tourism will lower employment in the tourism industry and related industries, but not necessarily overall. To show that employment overall was lower than under an alternative revenue raising policy, it would be necessary to show that taxes on tourism were more harmful to employment, directly and indirectly, than the alternative policy.

There is no general reason why this should be the case, even if tourism is a labour-intensive industry. Claims that specific taxes, such as taxes on tourism services, will affect employment adversely may be superficially convincing, but they are based on incomplete and misleading analysis and must be treated with caution. It is necessary to use CGE models of the economy, with all direct and indirect linkages between sectors, to explore this issue and tourism economists can be expected to undertake research along these lines.

Given the increasing importance of tourism taxation in both developed and developing countries, greater understanding of the economic underpinnings of tourism taxation and its effects is necessary, so that modelling of tourism taxation can be undertaken and appropriate policies for tourism taxation can be formulated.

TRANSPORT

Despite the importance of transportation to tourism research generally, this seems to be a relatively neglected area by tourism economists. Tourism and Transportation have an essentially symbiotic relationship, each being essential to the development of the other. Transport is a key sector in tourism nationally and globally. Transportation modes supporting tourism include air travel, cruise shipping and various forms of ground transport. Transportation issues range across many areas of interest to research in tourism economics including provision of tourism supporting infrastructure, destination access and travel within destinations, tourism demand modelling and forecasting, tourism planning, destination competitiveness, inter-governmental regulatory environments and destination management. Additional challenges today involve managing the environmental consequences of travel and the implication for destinations of new forms of tourism-related transport.

Despite the important links between tourism and transportation research, at the interface of the two disciplines, such research is widely agreed to be underdeveloped. Researchers now face the challenge of bridging this gap, focusing on the role that economic theory and practice can play to improve our understanding of the diverse linkages between tourism and transportation.

This text focused on aviation. Changes in aviation have had profound implications for tourism. The availability of low fares has made air travel affordable for leisure tourism and has greatly stimulated international tourism. Aviation shapes tourism – changes in aviation prices, technology and constraints have determined where tourists go to, and have helped some destinations to grow and others to decline.

Aviation and tourism are complementary industries. Aviation depends on tourist travel and tourists depend on air transport. Yet, the two industries also exhibit a conflict of interest in that it is in the interests of the industry that the prices and perhaps profits of the other industry be low. This provides a policy dilemma for governments in their regulation and/or support of both industries. The issues arising from this conflict have been unduly neglected by tourism economists.

Another aspect of the aviation–tourism connection concerns aviation and tourism taxes. Does a country wish to encourage tourism, and maximise economic benefits of tourism, by keeping taxes, on both aviation and ground tourism, low? Or does it wish to make use of its market power and use foreign tourists as a source of revenue? Whichever of these options it chooses, it will need to determine at which level – aviation or ground tourism – such taxes are best levied. Furthermore, if there is already general taxation of tourism and aviation services, it will need to determine how best to counteract these if it wishes to keep taxes low. Aviation and tourism taxation need to be considered jointly – though they often are not. This is another area which presents challenges to tourism researchers.

ENVIRONMENT

The importance of environment to tourism is universally acknowledged. At the same time, much of the discussion of the interaction between the two has been uninformed by economic analysis. It is the 'public good' aspect of many environmental resources that leads to their under-provision. Private markets will fail to allocate sufficient resources to the production of so-called public goods, including environmental quality, resulting in a misallocation of resources. In view of this 'market failure', collective action is needed to provide such goods in sufficient quantities. In no other area, perhaps, is there a greater need for discussion to be informed by economic theory. Given the progress made in the environmental economics literature, tourism economists have the opportunity to make greater contributions to our understanding of how to preserve valued natural environments in the context of tourism development.

There has been a gradual trend towards the use of market-based instruments for environmental policy. Market-based instruments are designed to influence either the *price* of an environmentally adverse activity (which in turn will affect the quantity of that activity) or its *quantity* (which in turn will affect the price of that activity). Tourism economists have the opportunity to meet the challenge of addressing the issues that attend the use of economic instruments in their protection of the environment from any adverse effects of tourism, including: uncertainty; boundary problems; transaction costs; and public good considerations.

Human-induced climate change is an externality on a global scale which, in the absence of policy intervention, is not 'corrected' through any institution or market. Climate change is the greatest market failure the world has seen. It presents a global challenge that requires a long-term global solution in order to avoid environmental, social and economic dislocation. The climate is a public good. Those who fail to pay for contributing to GHG emissions cannot be excluded from enjoying climatic benefits, and one person's enjoyment of the climate does not diminish the capacity of others to enjoy it also. Markets for relevant goods and services (energy, land use, innovation, etc.) do not reflect the full costs and benefits of different consumption and investment choices for the climate.

Climate change will directly impact on a country's tourism and the benefits it creates through loss or degradation of attractions, the costs of adaptation and replacement of capital infrastructure. Climate also has a major influence on destination choice. As a result of changing climatic conditions, tourists are likely to entirely avoid some destinations in favour of others or else shift the timing of travel to avoid unfavourable climate conditions. Countries which rely heavily on nature based tourism are likely to be net losers from changing international patterns of tourism as a result of climate change. Climate change generates both negative and positive impacts in the tourism sector and these impacts will vary substantially by market segment and geographic region. There are 'winners and losers' at the business, destination and nation level. Tourism is a footloose export industry, and tourism will shift offshore to the extent that a destination becomes less attractive due to climate change. There is scope here for tourism economists to develop a substantial research agenda to investigate these issues.

The text made the distinction between the carbon *intensity* footprint of tourism which refers to the GHGs directly and indirectly associated with tourism activity, and the carbon *impact* footprint of tourism which refers to how changes in tourism impact on overall GHGs. The latter depends on how other industries are impacted on by changes in tourism activity. Estimation of tourism's carbon impact requires CGE modelling to determine the net changes in the outputs of different industries in the economy. Most policy questions are questions about impact not just intensity. Tourism will be affected by the different types of climate change mitigation policies, all of which will increase the cost base of tourism firms. There is substantial scope for researchers to investigate these issues, including the effects on the tourism industry of different policy measures to mitigate climate change.

Although emissions trading is likely to be the key instrument used to reduce GHG emissions over time, complementary policies will be needed. There is a role for governments in setting regulatory standards, supporting innovation of new low-emission technology and encouraging changes in household behaviour. Destinations will tailor a package of measures that suits their specific circumstances, including the existing tax and governance system, participation in regional initiatives to reduce emissions (e.g. via trading schemes) and the structure of the economy and characteristics of specific sectors.

No convincing case has been made for treating aviation differently, either more or less favourably (other than under general arrangements for footloose industries). Special taxes or restrictions on aviation, if they are included in the Emissions Trading Scheme (ETS), will be ineffective in reducing GHGs. When an effective and comprehensive ETS is in place, mandatory requirements or taxes imposed on specific industries such as aviation will be ineffective in reducing GHGs, given the quota imposed by the cap. Researchers have an important role to play also in the economic instruments that need to be applied to aviation in order to mitigate the effects of GHG emissions from this sector.

Tourism can and must play a significant role in addressing climate change as part of its broader commitment to sustainable development and the United Nations Millennium Development Goals. Tourism will be affected by the different types of climate change mitigation policies, all of which will increase the cost base of tourism firms. Economic analysis can contribute to our understanding of the different types of issues raised by climate change, in policy formulation and in analysing the implications for tourism. This is an area of research for tourism economists that will be relevant over the long term (yes, 'in which we are all dead').

DESTINATION COMPETITIVENESS

Destination competitiveness is linked to the ability of a country or region to deliver goods and services that perform better than other destinations on those aspects of the tourism experience considered to be important by tourists. There exists substantial scope for researchers to contribute to the development of an overall model and indicators of destination competitiveness. It has proved difficult, however, to develop an integrated model of destination competitiveness comprising both quantitative and qualitative variables. While some work has already been undertaken an increased research effort in this area would help tourism stakeholders to: identify key strengths and weaknesses of their destination; highlight opportunities for tourism development; and develop strategies to counter possible threats to future visitation.

There is no single or unique set of competitiveness indicators that apply to all destinations at all times. For specified market segments, it is possible to identify the most important attributes as perceived by tourists and to compare the performance of different destinations on the selected attributes. The approach offers a basis for strategy development and policy formulation for the different market segments of the destination tourism industry. More research along these lines would contribute to our knowledge of destination competitiveness in respect of niche market segments.

Tourism researchers generally appear to have placed greater effort on developing models of overall destination competitiveness rather than on price competitiveness. Factors that impinge on price competitiveness include exchange rates; inflation; the price of labour; productivity; export booms; tax structures and levels; infrastructure charges; fuel prices; and environmental charges. There is substantial opportunity to undertake research on the determinants of price competitiveness of different sectors of the tourism industry as well as the price competitiveness of the destination as a whole.

The type of price competitiveness index employed depends on the research or policy needs at a given time. In some situations, quickly calculated, simple measures are most useful, while in others, more detailed and accurate measures are required. The measures used will also depend on the data available – some countries have very detailed tourism and price statistics, while statistics in other countries can be rudimentary. In this area also, tourism economists can help to refine the existing price indicators or develop new ones while assessing their relevance to the different research needs in different destinations.

Destination competitiveness is a goal that is achievable through informed decision-making and strategic choice. If the limitations of the various competitiveness indices are recognised, they can be valuable tools for policy formulation for any tourism destination to achieve and maintain competitive advantage over competitors, as well as empirical studies of tourism demand. The outcomes will be more informed policy making regarding the type of tourism development most likely to enhance resident quality of economic and social life. Again, researchers can contribute to our understanding of how these goals can be achieved.

The directions for further research highlighted above are just some of those that arise in the topics covered in the book. The listing is in no way intended to be exhaustive and readers can add research topics of their own to the list. Other research topics relate to areas that are important but not covered in the book. Changing global trends (economic, social, demographic, political, technological and environmental) will continually pose challenges to economic theory and policy and the ways we analyse tourism activity. Whatever the specific topics that researchers will address in the coming years, it is clear that tourism economics provides a fertile ground for research with the potential to inform policy making to improve socio-economic prosperity in all destinations worldwide.

REFERENCES

ABS (1989) Australian Bureau of Statistics *Australian National Accounts, Introduction to Input-Output Multipliers* (Cat. no. 5246.0), Australian Bureau of Statistics, Canberra.

ABS (2000) Australian Bureau of Statistics Information Paper *Australian National Accounts Introduction to Input-Output Multipliers* Catalogue No. 5246.0.

ABS (2007) Tourism Satellite Account 2005–2006, 5249.0, Australian Bureau of Statistics, Canberra, May.

ABS (2009) Tourism Satellite Account 2007–2008, Australian Bureau of Statistics, Canberra, para 41, April.

ACT Auditor General (2002) *ACT Auditor General's Office Performance Audit Report V8 Car Races in Canberra – Costs and Benefits*, ACT, Canberra.

Acutt, M.Z. and J.S. Dodgson (1996) 'Cross-elasticities of Demand for Travel', *Transport Policy*, 2(4), 271–277.

Adams, P.D. and B.R. Parmenter (1995) 'An Applied General Equilibrium Analysis of the Economic Effects of Tourism in a Quite Small, Quite Open Economy', *Applied Economics*, 27(10), 985–994.

Adams, P.D. and B.R. Parmenter (1999) 'General Equilibrium Models', *Valuing Tourism. Methods and Techniques*, Canberra: Bureau of Tourism Research.

Aguilo, E., A. Rieri and J. Rossello (2005) 'The Short-term Price Effect of a Tourist Tax through a Dynamic Demand Model: The Case of the Balearic Islands', *Tourism Management*, 26, 359–365.

Aguilo, P.M., J. Alegre and A. Riera (2001) 'Determinants of the Price of German Tourist Packages on the Island of Mallorca', *Tourism Economics*, 7, 59–74.

Alperovich, G. and Y. Machnes (1994) 'The Role of Wealth in the Demand of International Air Travel', *Journal of Transport Economics and Policy*, 28, 163–173.

Alwaked, A. (2005) 'Estimating Fare and Expenditure Elasticities of Demand for Air Travel in the US Domestic market', Doctoral Dissertation, Texas A&M University.

Anastasopoulos, Petros G.E. (1984) 'Interdependence in International Travel: The Role of Relative Prices. A Case Study of the Mediterranean Region', Ph.D. Dissertation, New School for Social Research.

Andrew, B.P. (1997) 'Tourism and the Economic Development of Cornwall', *Annals of Tourism Research*, 24(3), 721–735.

Archer, B. (1973) *The Impact of Domestic Tourism*. Bangor Occasional Papers in Economics No. 2, Cardiff: University of Wales Press.

Archer, B. (1977) 'Tourism in the Bahamas and Bermuda: Two Case Studies', Occasional Papers in Economics No. 10, Bangor: University of Wales Press.

Archer, B. (1980) 'Forecasting Demand, Quantitative and Intuitive Techniques', *International Journal of Tourism Management*, 1, 5–12, March.

Archer, B. (1985) 'Tourism in Mauritius: An Economic Impact Study with Marketing Implications', *Tourism Management*, 6(1), 50–54.

Archer, B. (1994) 'Demand Forecasting and Estimation' in J.R. Brent Ritchie and Charles R. Goeldner (eds) *Travel, Tourism, and Hospitality Research: A Handbook for Managers and Researchers* (pp. 105–114), 2nd edition, New York: John Wiley and Sons Ltd.

Archer, B. (1995) 'Importance of Tourism for the Economy of Bermuda', *Annals of Tourism Research*, 22(4), 918–930.

Archer, B. and J. Fletcher (1996) 'The Economic Impact of Tourism in the Seychelles', *Annals of Tourism Research*, 23(1), 32–47.

Ashley, C., D. Meyer, D. Roe and H. Goodwin (2004) Pro-Poor Fact Sheet No. 10: International Tour Operators: Roles, Practices and Implications for Developing Countries, Pro-Poor Tourism Partnership.

Auerbach, A. (1985) 'The Theory of Excess Burden and Optimal Taxation' in A. Auerbach and M. Feldstein (eds) *Handbook of Public Economics*, Vol. 1, Amsterdam: North Holland.

Australian Competition and Consumer Commission (2003) *Draft Determination Applications for Authorization, Qantas and Air New Zealand*, 10 April.

Australian Government (2007a) Australian Government Response National Tourism Emerging Markets Strategy Report, *Investing Today for Tomorrow* National Tourism Investment Strategy Report, *Investing for Our Future*, Department of Industry, Tourism and Resources, January.

Australian Government (2007b) *Report of the Task Group on Emissions Trading*, Prime Ministerial Task Group on Emissions Trading, The Department of the Prime Minister and Cabinet, Canberra.

Australian Government National Aviation Policy (2008) Flight Path to the Future, Green Paper, Canberra, December.

Baade, Robert A. (1997) 'Professional Sports and Economic Impact: The View of the Judiciary', *State Tax Notes*, 1495–1505.

Baade, R., R. Baumann and V. Matheson (2006) 'Selling the Big Game: Estimating the Economic Impact of Mega-Events through Taxable Sales', Working Papers 0610, International Association of Sports Economists.

Baddeley, M.C. (2004) 'Are Tourist Willing to Pay for Aesthetic Quality? An Empirical Assessment from Krabi Province, Thailand', *Tourism Economics*, 10(1), 45–61.

Bailey, E.E., D.R. Graham and D.P. Kaplan (1985) *Deregulating the Airlines*, Cambridge: MIT Press.

Baker, M. and J. Wurgler (2002) 'Market Timing and Capital Structure', *The Journal of Finance*, 57(1), 1–32, February.

Bakkalsalihoglu, I. (1987) 'Analysis of Demand for International Tourism in Northern Mediterranean Countries', Ph.D. dissertation, Northern Illinois University.

Ballard, Charles L., John B. Shoven and John Whalley (1985) 'The Welfare Cost of Distortions in the United States Tax System: A General Equilibrium Approach' (June 1985), NBER Working Paper Series, Vol. w1043.

Bandara, J.S. (1991) 'Computable General Equilibrium Models for Development Policy, Analysis in LDCs' *Journal of Economic Surveys*, 7(1), 3–69.

Bandara, R. and C. Tisdell (2003) 'Use and Non-Use Values of Wild Asian Elephants: A Total Economic Valuation Approach', Economics, Ecology and the Environment, Working Paper No. 80, School of Economics, the University of Queensland, Brisbane.

Barrett, S. and R. Stavins (2002) 'Increasing Participation and Compliance in International Climate Change Agreements', Working Paper Series rwp02-031, Harvard University, John F. Kennedy School of Government.

Barrowclough D (2007) 'Foreign Investment in Tourism and Small Island Developing States, *Tourism Economics*, 13(4), 615–638.

Baum, T. (1991) 'Scope of the Tourism Industry and Its Employment Impact in Ireland', *Services Industry Journal*, 11, 140–151.

Baum, T. and Mudambi, R. (1995) 'An Empirical Analysis of Oligopolistic Hotel Pricing', *Annals of Tourism Research*, 22, 501–516.

Becken, S. (2002) 'Analysing International Tourist Flows to Estimate Energy Use Associated with Air Travel', *Journal of Sustainable Tourism*, 10(2), 114–131.

Becken, S. and D. Simmons (2002) 'Understanding Energy Consumption Patterns of Tourist Attractions and Activities in New Zealand', *Tourism Management*, 23(4), 343–354.

Becken, S., D. Simmons and C. Frampton (2003) 'Energy Use Associated with Different Travel Choices', *Tourism Management*, 24(3), 267–278.

Becken, S. and M. Patterson (2006) 'Measuring National Carbon Dioxide Emissions from Tourism as a Key Step Towards Achieving Sustainable Tourism', *Journal of Sustainable Tourism*, 14(4), 323–338.

Bedate, A., L.C. Herrero and J.Á. Sanz (2004) 'Economic Valuation of the Cultural Heritage: Application to Four Case Studies in Spain', *Journal of Cultural Heritage*, 5(1), 101–111, January–March.

Bell, Frederick, and Vernon Leeworth (1990) 'Recreational Demand by Tourists for Saltwater Beach Days,' *Journal of Environmental Economics and Management*, 18, 189–205.

Beltran, E. and M. Rojas (1996) 'Diversified Funding Methods in Mexican Archeology', *Annals of Tourism Research*, 23(2), 463–478.

Berrittellaa, M., A. Bigano, R. Rosona and R.S.J. Tol, (2006) 'A General Equilibrium Analysis of Climate Change Impacts on Tourism', *Tourism Management*, 27, 913–924.

Bhat, M. (2003) 'Application of Nonmarket Valuation to the Florida Keys Marine Reserve Management', *Journal of Environmental Management*, 67, 315–325.

Bhattacharyya, S.C. (1996) 'Applied General Equilibrium Models for Energy Studies: A Survey', *Energy Economics*, 18, 145–164.

Bigano, A., J.M. Hamilton and R.S.J. Tol (2005) 'The Impact of Climate Change on Domestic and International Tourism: A Simulation Study', Working paper FNU-58, p. 23.

Bille Hansen, T. (1997) 'The Willingness-To-Pay for the Royal Theatre in Copenhagen as a Public Good', *Journal of Cultural Economics*, 21, 1–28.

Bird, R. (1992) 'Taxing Tourism in Developing Countries', *World Development*, 20(8), 1145–1158.

Blake, A. (2005) 'The Economic Impact of the London 2012 Olympics', Research Report 2005/5, Christel DeHaan Tourism and Travel Research Institute, Nottingham University Business School, http://www.nottingham.ac.uk/ttri.

Blake, A., T. Sinclair and J. Gillham (2006) 'CGE Tourism Analysis and Policy Modeling' in L. Dwyer and P. Forsyth (eds) *International Handbook of Tourism Economics*, London: Edward Elgar.

Blake, A., R. Durbarry, M. Sinclair and G. Sugiyarto (2001) 'Modelling Tourism and Travel Using Tourism Satellite Accounts and Tourism Policy and Forecasting Models', TTRI Discussion Paper (4), UK: Nottingham.

Blake, A., J.S. Arbache, M.T. Sinclair and V. Teles (2008) 'Tourism and Poverty Relief', *Annals of Tourism Research*, 35(1), 107–126.

Blake, A., R. Durbarry, J.L. Eugenio-Martin, N. Gooroochurn, B. Hay, J. Lennon, G. Sugiyarto, M.T. Sinclair and I. Yeoman (2004) 'Tourism in Scotland: The Moffat Model for Forecasting and Policy in Complex Situations' *Christel DeHaan Tourism and Travel Research Institute Discussion Paper*, http://www.nottingham.ac.uk/ttri/series.html, 2004/2.

Blake, A.T. (2000) 'The Economic Effects of Tourism in Spain', *Christel DeHaan Tourism and Travel Research Institute Discussion Paper*, http://www.nottingham.ac.uk/ttri/series.html, 2000/2.

Blake, A.T. (2004) 'The Structure of the Moffat Scenario CGE Model', *Christel DeHaan Tourism and Travel Research Institute Discussion Paper*, http://www.nottingham.ac.uk/ttri/series.html, 2004/6.

Blake, A.T. and M.T. Sinclair (2003) 'Tourism Crisis Management: US Response to September 11', *Annals of Tourism Research*, 30(4), 813–832.

Blake, A.T., M.T. Sinclair and G. Sugiyarto (2003a) 'Quantifying the Impact of Foot and Mouth Disease on Tourism and the UK Economy', *Tourism Economics*, 9(4), 449–465.

Blake, A., M.T. Sinclair and G. Sugiyarto (2003b) 'Tourism and Globalisation: Economic Impact in Indonesia', *Annals of Tourism Research*, 30(3), 683–701.

Blake, A.T., M.T. Sinclair and G. Sugiyarto (2003c) 'Tourism and the Effects of EU Accession on Malta and Cyprus', *Conference on Tourism Modelling and Competitiveness*, Paphos, Cyprus, October. *Christel DeHaan Tourism and Travel Research Institute Discussion Paper*, http://www.nottingham.ac.uk/ttri/series.html, 2003/7.

Blanke, J., T. Chiesa and E. Trujillo Herrera (2009) 'The Travel & Tourism Competitiveness Index 2009: Measuring Sectoral Drivers in a Downturn WEF', Geneva, Switzerland.

Block, S. and G. Hirt (2008) *Foundations of Financial Management*, 12th edition, New York: McGraw-Hill Publishing.

Boadway, R. (1975) 'Cost Benefit Rules in General Equilibrium', *Review of Economic Studies*, 42, 361–374.

Bonham, C. and B. Gangnes (1996) 'Intervention Analysis with Cointegrated Time Series: The Case of the Hawaii Hotel Room Tax', *Applied Economics*, 28, 1281–1293.

Bonham, C., E. Fujii, E. Im and J. Mak (1992) 'The Impact of the Hotel Room Tax: An Interrupted Time Series Approach', *National Tax Journal*, 45, 433–441.

Bostedt, G. and L. Mattsson (1995) 'The Value of Forests for Tourism in Sweden', *Annals of Tourism Research*, 22(3), 671–680.

Box, G.E.P. and G.M. Jenkins (1976) *Time Series Analysis: Forecasting and Control*, San Francisco: Holden-Day.

Boyfield, K. (ed.) (2003) *A Market in Airport Slots*, London: Institute of Economic Affairs.

Briassoulis, H. (1991) 'Methodological Issues: Tourism Input-Output Analysis', *Annals of Tourism Research*, 18, 435–449.

Brohman, J. (1996) 'New Directions in Tourism for Third World Development', *Annals of Tourism Research*, 23, 48–70.

Brons, M, E. Pels, P. Nijkamp and P. Rietveld (2002) 'Price Elasticities of Demand for Passenger Air Travel: A Meta-analysis', *Journal of Air Transport Management*, 8, 165–175.

Brown, J.R., Dev, D.S. and Zhou, Z. (2003) 'Broadening the Foreign Market Entry Mode Decision: Separating Ownership and Control', *Journal of International Business Studies*, 34, 473–488.

Brueckner, J.K. (2002) 'Airport Congestion When Carriers Have Market Power', *American Economic Review*, 92, 1357–1375.

BTCE (1993) 'The Progress of Aviation Reform Bureau of Transport and Communications Economics', Canberra.

BTCE (1994) *Demand Elasticities for Air Travel To and from Australia*, Bureau of Transport and Communications Economics Working Paper 20, Australian Government Publications.

Buckley, P. (1987) 'Tourism – An Economic Transactions Analysis', *Tourism Management*, 8, 190–194.

Burgan, B. and T. Mules (2000) 'Event Analysis – Understanding the Divide between Cost Benefit and Economic Impact Assessment' in J. Allen, R. Harris, L. Jago and A. Veal (eds) *Events Beyond 2000: Setting the Agenda* (pp. 256–264), Sydney: Australian Centre for Event Management, University of Technology.

Burns, J., J. Hatch and T. Mules (eds) (1986) *The Adelaide Grand Prix: The Impact of a Special Event*, The Centre for South Australian Economic Studies, Adelaide, South Australia.

Butler R. (1980) 'The Concept of a Tourism Area Cycle of Evolution: Implications for Management Resources', *The Canadian Geographer*, 24(1), 5–16.

Calder, S. (2002) *No Frills: The Truth behind the Low Cost Revolution in the Skies*, London: Virgin Books.

Campbell, H. and K. Bond (1997) 'The Cost of Public Funds in Australia', *Economic Record*, 73(220), 230–234, March.

Carmody, G. (2009) *Australia Tourism: How Deep the Recession? How Will Tourism Fare during the 'Great Recession' of 2009*, Report prepared by Geoff Carmody & Associates for the Tourism and Transport Forum, GCA tourism analysis note no.2 – March 2009.

Carr, L. and R. Mendelsohn (2003) 'Valuing Coral Reefs: A Travel Cost Analysis of the Great Barrier Reef', *Ambio*, 32(2), 353–357.

Cassani, B. and K. Kemp (2003) *Go: An Airline Adventure*, London: Time Warner.

Chambers, C., P. Chambers and J. Whitehead (1998) 'Contingent Valuation of Quasipublic Good: Validity, Reliability, and Application to Valuing a Historic Site', *Public Finance Review*, 26(2), 137–154.

Chase, L., D. Lee, W. Schulze and D. Anderson (1998) 'Ecotourism Demand and Differential Pricing of National Park Access in Costa Rica', *Land Economics*, 74(4), 466–482.

Chen, R.J., P. Bloomfield and J.S. Fu (2003) 'An Evaluation of Alternative Forecasting Methods to Recreation Visitation', *Journal of Leisure Research*, 35(4), 441–454.

Chen, W., H. Hong, Y. Liu, L. Zhang, X. Hou and M. Raymond (2004) 'Recreation Demand and Economic Value: An Application of Travel Cost Method for Xiamen Island', *China Economic Review*, 15, 398–406.

Cho, V. (2001) 'Tourism Forecasting and its Relationship with Leading Economic Indicators, *Journal of Hospitality & Tourism Research*, 25(4), 399–420.

Chu, F.L. (1998) 'Forecasting Tourism Demand in Asian-Pacific Countries', *Annals of Tourism Research*, 25, 597–615.

Clarke, H., and Y. Ng (1993) 'Tourism, Economic Welfare and Efficient Pricing', *Annals of Tourism Research*, 20, 613–632.

Clewer, A., A. Pack and M.T. Sinclair (1992) 'Price Competitiveness and Inclusive Tour Holidays' in P. Johnson and B. Thomas (eds) *Choice and Demand in Tourism* (pp. 123–143), London: Mansell.

Coase, Ronald H. (1960) 'The Problem of Social Cost', *Journal of Law and Economics*, 3(1), 1–44.

Cockerell, N. and R. Spurr (2002) 'Overview', in N. Cockerell and R. Spurr (eds) *Best Practice in Tourism Satellite Account Development in APEC Member Economies*, Singapore: Asia-Pacific Economic Cooperation (APEC) Secretariat Publication #202-TR-01-1, June.

Collins, D., U. Salma and T. Suridge (2004) 'Economic Contribution by Inbound Market Segments', *Tourism Research Report*, 6(1), 83–94, Canberra: Tourism Research Australia. © 2010 Commonwealth of Australia. Reproduced with permission.

Combs, J. and B. Elledge (1979) 'Effects of Room Tax on Resort Hotels/Motels', *National Tax Journal*, 32, 201–207.

Commission of the European Communities (EU) (2006) *Commission Staff Working Document, Summary of the Impact Assessment: Inclusion of Aviation in the EU Greenhouse Gas Emissions Trading Scheme (EU ETS)*, Brussels, December.

Commonwealth Department of Finance (1992) *Introduction to Cost-Benefit Analysis for Program Managers*, AGPS, Canberra.

Copeland, B.R. (1991) 'Tourism, Welfare and De-industrialization in a Small Open Economy', *Economica*, 58, 515–529.

Corporate Partnering (2009) A How-To Handbook, An Executive's Guide to Key Partnering Practices, www.corporate-partnering.com.

Coshall, J.T. (2009) 'Combining Volatility and Smoothing Forecasts of UK Demand for International Tourism', *Tourism Management*, 30(4), 495–511, August.

Crompton, J.L. (1995) 'Economic Impact of Sports Facilities and Events: Eleven Sources of Misapplication', *Journal of Sport Management*, 9(1), 14–35.

Crompton, J.L. (1999) *Measuring the Economic Impact of Visitors to Sports Tournaments and Special Events*, National Recreation and Park Association, Division of Professional Services, Ashburn, Virginia, VA.

Crompton, J.L. (2006) 'Economic Impact Studies: Instruments for Political Shenanigans?', *Journal of Travel Research*, 45, 67–82.

Crompton, J.L., and S.L. McKay (1994) 'Measuring the Economic Impact of Festivals and Events: Some Myths, Misapplications and Ethical Dilemmas', *Festival Management and Event Tourism*, 2(1), 33–43.

Crompton, J.L., S. Lee and T. Shuster (2001) 'A Guide for Undertaking Economic Impact Studies: The Springfest Festival', *Journal of Travel Research*, 40(1), 79–87.

Crouch, G.I. (1992) 'Effects of Income and Price on International Tourist Demand', *Annals of Tourism*, 19(4), 643–664.

Crouch, G.I. (1994a) 'The Study of International Tourism Demand: A Review of Findings', *Journal of Travel Research*, 33, 12–23.

Crouch, G.I. (1994b) 'The Study of International Tourism Demand: A Review of Practice', *Journal of Travel Research*, 33, 41–54.

Crouch, G. (1995) 'A Meta-Analysis of Tourism Demand', *Annals of Tourism Research*, 22(1), 103–118.

Crouch, G.I. and J.R. Ritchie (1999) 'Tourism, Competitiveness, and Societal Prosperity', *Journal of Business Research*, 44, 137–152.

Crouch, G.I., L. Schultz and P. Valerio (1992) 'Marketing International Tourism to Australia: A Regression Analysis', *Tourism Management*, 13, 196–208.

Cummings, R.G. and L.O. Taylor (1999) 'Unbiased Value Estimates for Environmental Goods: A Cheap Talk Design for the Contingent Valuation Method', *The American Economic Review*, 89(3), 649–655.

Czerny, A. (2008) 'Airport Slots' in A. Czerny, P. Forsyth, D. Gillen and Hans-Martin Niemeier (eds) *Airport Slots International Experiences and Options for Reform*, Aldershot, England: Ashgate Publishing.

Dargay, J. and M. Hanly (2001) 'The Determinants of the Demand for International Air Travel to and from the UK', Paper presented at the 9th World Conference on Transport Research.

Davies, B. and P. Downward (2006) 'Structure Conduct Performance and Industrial Organisation in Tourism' in L. Dwyer and P. Forsyth (eds) *International Handbook on the Economics of Tourism*, UK: Edward Elgar.

De Mello, M., A. Pack and M.T. Sinclair (2002) 'A System of Equations Model of UK Tourism Demand in Neighbouring Countries', *Applied Economics*, 34, 509–521.

de Melo, J. (1988) 'SAM-Based Models: An Introduction', *Journal of Policy Modelling*, 10, 321–325.

Delpy, L. and M. Li (1998) 'The Art and Science of Conducting Economic Impact Studies', *Journal of Vacation Marketing*, 4(3), 230–254.

Department for Transport (2009) 'Adding Capacity at Heathrow Airport: Impact Assessment', London: DfT Publications, January.

Department of Transport and Communications (Australia) (1988) *Negotiating International Aviation Rights*, Consultants' Report, June.

Dharmaratne, G.S., F. Yee Sang and L.J. Walling (2000) 'Tourism Potentials for Financing Protected Areas', *Annals of Tourism Research*, 27(3), 590–610.

Divisekera, S. (2003) 'A Model of International Tourism Demand', *Annals of Tourism Research*, 30(1), 31–49.

Dixon, P. and B. Parmenter (1996) 'Computable General Equilibrium Modelling for Policy Analysis and Forecasting', in H. Aman, D. Kendrick and J. Rust (eds), *Handbook of Computational Economics*, Vol. 1 (pp. 4–85), Melbourne: Elsevier Science B.V.

Dixon, P, M. Picton and M. Rimmer (2002) *Effects of Changes in Commonwealth Grants to the States: An Applied General Equilibrium Analysis*, Centre of Policy Studies, Monash University, March.

Doganis, R. (1986) *Flying Off Course: The Economics of International Airlines*, London: Routledge.

Doganis, R. (2001) *The Airline Business in the Twenty-First Century*, London: Routledge.

Doganis, R (2002) *Flying Off Course*, 3rd edition, London and New York: Routledge.

Doyle, P. (2000) Value-based Marketing: Marketing Strategies for Corporate Growth and Shareholder Value, London: John Wiley & Sons.

Drummond, G. and J. Ensor (1999) *Strategic Marketing: Planning and Control*, Oxford: Butterworth-Heinemann.

Duc Pham, T., L. Dwyer and R. Spurr (2009) 'Constructing a Regional Tourism Satellite Account: The Case of Queensland', *Tourism Analysis*, 13, 445–460.

Dunning, J. (2001) 'The Eclectic (OLI) Paradigm of International Production: Past, Present and Future', *International Journal of the Economics of Business*, 8(2), 173–190.

Dwyer, L. (2000) 'Economic Contribution of Tourism to Andhra Pradesh', *Tourism Recreation Research*, 25(3), 1–11.

Dwyer, L. (2005) 'Tourism Investment in the South Pacific: Barriers and Opportunities' in C. Cooper and M. Hall (eds) *Oceania: A Tourism Handbook*, UK: Channel View Publications.

Dwyer, L. and D. Edwards (2009) 'Managing Tourism to Avoid "Strategic Drift" ', *International Journal of Tourism Research*, 11, 321–335.

Dwyer, L., I. Burnley, P. Forsyth and P. Murphy (1993) 'Tourism–Immigration Inter-relationships', Bureau of Immigration and Population Research, Canberra, June, pp. 1–135.

Dwyer, L., D. Edwards, N. Mistilis, N. Scott and C. Roman (2009) 'Destination and Enterprise Management for a Tourism Future', *Tourism Management*, 30, 63–74.

Dwyer, L. and P. Forsyth (1992) 'The Case for Tourism Promotion: An Economic Analysis', *Revue de Tourisme*, AIEST, 43, 16–26.

Dwyer, L. and P. Forsyth (1993a) 'Foreign Investment in Australian Tourism: A Framework for Assessing Impacts', *Journal of Tourism Studies*, 4(1), 26–37, May.

Dwyer, L. and P. Forsyth (1993b) 'Assessing the Benefits and Costs of Inbound Tourism', *Annals of Tourism Research*, 20(4), 751–768. (This paper also appears in Tisdell, C.A. (ed.) (2000) *The Economics of Tourism*, Vol. II, International Library of Critical Writings in Economics (pp. 286–303) Cheltenham: Edward Edgar Publishing).

Dwyer, L. and P. Forsyth (1994a) 'Government Support for Inbound Tourism Promotion: Some Neglected Issues', *Australian Economic Papers*, 32, 355–373. (This paper also appears in Tisdell, C.A. (ed.) (2000) *The Economics of Tourism*, Vol. II, International Library of Critical Writings in Economics (pp. 304–323), Cheltenham: Edward Edgar Publishing).

Dwyer, L. and P. Forsyth (1994b) 'Motivation and Impacts of Foreign Tourism Investment' *Annals of Tourism Research*, 21(3), 512–537.

Dwyer, L. and P. Forsyth (1998) 'Estimating the Employment Impacts of Tourism to a Nation', *Tourism Recreation Research*, 23(2), 3–12.

Dwyer, L. and P. Forsyth (1999) 'Should Accommodation Providers Pay for the Olympics? A Critique of the Sydney Bed Tax', *Tourism and Hospitality Research: The Surrey Quarterly Review*, 1(3), 253–264.

Dwyer, L. and P. Forsyth (2008) 'Economic Measures of Tourism Yield: What Markets to Target?', *International Journal of Tourism Research*, 10, 155–168.

Dwyer, L., P. Forsyth and R. Spurr (2004) 'Evaluating Tourism's Economic Effects: New and Old Approaches', *Tourism Management*, 25, 307–317.

Dwyer, L., P. Forsyth and R. Spurr (2007a) 'Contrasting the Uses of TSAs and CGE Models: Measuring Tourism Yield and Productivity', *Tourism Economics*, 13(4), 537–551, December.

Dwyer, L., P. Forsyth and R. Spurr (2007b) 'Productivity and Yield Measurement in Australian Inbound Tourism Using Tourism Satellite Accounts and Computable General Equilibrium Models' in J. Tribe and D. Airey (eds) *Advances in Tourism Research*, UK: University of Surrey.

Dwyer, L., P. Forsyth and H. Clarke (1995) 'Problems in the Use of Economic Instruments to Reduce Adverse Environmental Impacts of Tourism' *Tourism Economics*, 1(3), 265–282, September.

Dwyer, L., P. Forsyth and P. Rao (1999) 'Tourism Price Competitiveness and Journey Purpose', *Turizam*, Special Issue on Competitiveness in *Hospitality and Tourism*, 47(4), 283–299.

Dwyer, L., P. Forsyth and P. Rao (2000a) 'The Price Competitiveness of Travel and Tourism: A Comparison of 19 Destinations', *Tourism Management*, 21(1), 9–22.

Dwyer, L., P. Forsyth and P. Rao (2000b) 'Price Competitiveness of Package Tourism: Beyond the Big Mac Approach', *Asia Pacific Journal of Tourism Research*, 5(2), 50–56.

Dwyer, L., P. Forsyth and P. Rao (2000c) 'Sectoral Analysis of Price Competitiveness of Tourism: An International Comparison', *Tourism Analysis*, 5(1), 1–12.

Dwyer, L., P. Forsyth and P. Rao (2002) 'Destination Price Competitiveness: Exchange Rate Changes versus Inflation Rates', *Journal of Travel Research*, 40(3), 340–348.

Dwyer, L., P. Forsyth and R. Spurr (2005) 'Estimating the Impacts of Special Events on the Economy', *Journal of Travel Research*, 43, 351–359, May.

Dwyer, L., P. Forsyth and R. Spurr (2006a) 'Assessing the Economic Impacts of Events: A Computable General Equilibrium Approach', *Journal of Travel Research*, 45, 59–66.

Dwyer, L., P. Forsyth and R. Spurr (2006b) 'Assessing the Economic Impacts of Special Events' in L. Dwyer and P. Forsyth (eds) *International Handbook of Tourism Economics*, London: Edward Elgar.

Dwyer, L., P. Forsyth, R. Spurr and S. Hoque (2010) 'Estimating the Carbon Footprint of Australian Tourism', *Journal of Sustainable Tourism*, 18(3), 355–366.

Dwyer, L., P. Forsyth and W. Dwyer (2009) 'Tourism and Economic Development: Three Tools of Analysis', *Tourism Recreation Research*. Special Issue Project Planning and Development, 34(3).

Dwyer, L., P. Forsyth, J. Madden and R. Spurr (2000) 'Economic Impacts of Inbound Tourism under Different Assumptions Regarding the Macroeconomy', *Current Issues in Tourism*, 3(4), 325–363.

Dwyer, L., P. Forsyth, R. Spurr and T. Van Ho (2003) 'The Contribution of Tourism to a State and National Economy: A Multi-regional General Equilibrium Analysis', *Tourism Economics*, 9(4), 431–448.

Dwyer, L., P. Forsyth, R. Spurr and T. Van Ho (2006) 'Economic Effects of the World Tourism Crisis on Australia', *Tourism Economics*, 12(2), 171–186.

Dwyer, L., P. Forsyth, L. Fredline, L. Jago, M. Deery and S. Lundie (2007) 'Yield Measures for Australia's Special Interest Inbound Tourism Markets', *Tourism Economics*, 13(3), 421–440.

Dwyer, L., Z. Livaic and R. Mellor (2003) 'Competitiveness of Australia as a Tourism Destination', *Journal of Hospitality and Tourism Management*, 10(1), 60–78.

Dwyer, L. and C.W. Kim (2003) 'Destination Competitiveness: A Model and Indicators', *Current Issues in Tourism*, 6(5), 369–413.

Dwyer, L., R. Mellor, N. Mistilis and T. Mules (2000) 'A Framework for Assessing "Tangible" and "Intangible" Impacts of Events and Conventions', *Event Management*, 6(3), 175–191.

Dwyer, L., R. Mellor, Z. Livaic, D. Edwards and C.W. Kim (2004) 'Attributes of Destination Competitiveness: A Factor Analysis', *Tourism Analysis*, 9(1–2), 91–102.

Dwyer, L., N. Mistilis, P. Forsyth and P. Rao (2001) 'International Price Competitiveness of Australia's MICE Industry', *International Journal of Tourism Research*, 3(2), 123–140.

Dwyer, L. and R. Spurr (2009) 'Critique of Productivity Commission Report on Assistance to Australian Tourism', *Tourism Economics*, 15(1), 181–192, March.

Endo, K. (2006) 'Foreign Direct Investment in Tourism – Flows and Volumes', *Tourism Management*, 27, 600–614.

Ennew, C. (2003) 'Understanding the Economic Impact of Tourism' Discussion Paper 2003/5, Tourism and Travel Research Institute (www.nottingham.ac.uk/ttri/).

Enright, M.J. and J. Newton (2004) 'Tourism Destination Competitiveness: A Quantitative Approach', *Tourism Management*, 25(6), 777–788.

Enright, M.J. and J. Newton (2005) 'Determinants of Tourism Destination Competitiveness in Asia Pacific: Comprehensiveness and Universality', *Journal of Travel Research*, 43, 339–350.

ESCAP (1994) 'Economic and Social Commission for Asia and the Pacific Investment and Economic Cooperation in the Tourism Sector in Pacific Island Countries', United Nations, New York, ST/ESCAP/1386.

ESCAP (2001) Economic and Social Commission for Asia and the Pacific Promotion of Investment in Tourism Infrastructure, United Nations, New York, ST/ESCAP/2133.

Espey, M. and H. Lopez (2000) 'The Impact of Airport Noise and Proximity on Residential Property Values', *Growth and Change*, 31(22), 408–419, Summer.

European Commission (2004) Commission Decision of 12 February 2004, *Official Journal of the European Union*, 30 April.

Evans, N., D. Campbell and G. Stonehouse (2003) *Strategic Management for Travel and Tourism*, Oxford: Butterworth-Heinemann.

Evans, N.G. and M.J. Stabler (1995) 'A Future for the Package Tour Operator in the 21st Century', *Tourism Economics*, 1(3), 245–264.

Fama, E. and K.R. French (2002) 'Testing Trade-Off and Pecking Order Predictions about Dividends and Debt', *Review of Financial Studies*, 15, 1–33.

Fane, D. (1991) 'The Social Opportunity Cost of Foreign Exchange: A Partial Defence of Harburger et al.', *Economic Record*, 67, 307–316.

Faulkner, B. and P. Valerio (1995) 'An Integrative Approach to Tourism Demand Forecasting', *Tourism Management*, 16(1), 29–37.

Faulkner, B. and P. Valerio (2000) 'An Integrative Approach to Tourism Demand Forecasting' in C. Ryan and S. Page (eds) *Tourism Management: Toward the New Millennium* (pp. 45–58), Chapter 3, Oxford, UK: Pergamon, Elsevier Science Ltd.

Findlay, C. (1985) *The Flying Kangaroo: An Endangered Species? An Economic Perspective of Australian International Civil Aviation Policy*, Sydney: Allen and Unwin.

Fish, M. (1982) 'Taxing International Tourism in West Africa', *Annals of Tourism Research*, 9, 91–103.

Fisher, Ronald C. (1996) *State and Local Public Finance*, 2nd edition, Chicago: Irwin.

Fleischer, A. and D. Felsenstein (2002) 'Cost-Benefit Analysis Using Economic Surpluses: A Case Study of a Televised Event', *Journal of Cultural Economics*, 26(2), 139–156, May.

Fletcher, J. and B. Archer (1991) 'The Development and Application of Multiplier Analysis' in C. Cooper (ed.) *Progress in Tourism, Recreation and Hospitality Management*, Vol. 1, London: Bellhaven.

Fletcher, J. and J. Westlake (2006) 'Globalisation' in L. Dwyer and P Forsyth (eds) *International Handbook on the Economics of Tourism*, Chapter 21, Cheltenham, UK and Northampton, MA, USA: Edward Elgar.

Flyvbjerg, Bent, Nils Bruzelius and Werner Rothengatter (2003) *Megaprojects and Risk: An Anatomy of Ambition*, Cambridge, UK: Cambridge University Press.

Forsyth, P. (1991) 'The Regulation and Deregulation of Australia's Domestic Airline Industry' in K. Button (ed.) *Airline Deregulation: International Experiences* (pp. 48–84), London: David Fulton Publishers.

Forsyth, P. (2005a) 'Promoting Competition in Trans-Pacific Tourism', unpublished.

Forsyth, P. (2005b) 'Air Transport Liberalisation and Tourism Benefits: The Case of the Australia–US Route', Monash University, Mimeo, June.

Forsyth, P. (2006) 'Estimating the Costs and Benefits of Regional Airport Subsidies: A Computable General Equilibrium Approach'. Presented at German Aviation Research Society Workshop, Amsterdam, June–July.

Forsyth, P. and L. Dwyer (2002) 'Market Power and the Taxation of Domestic and International Tourism', *Tourism Economics*, 8(4), 377–399.

Forsyth, P. and L. Dwyer (2009) 'Tourism Price Competiveness' in J. Blanke and T. Chiesa (eds) *The Travel and Tourism Competitiveness Report* (pp. 77–90), Geneva: Managing in a Time of Turbulence, World Economic Forum.

Forsyth, P. and L. Dwyer (2010) 'Exchange Rate Changes and the Cost Competitiveness of International Airlines: The Aviation Trade Weighted Index', *Research in Transport Economics*, 26, 12–17.

Forsyth, P., S. Hoque, L. Dwyer, R. Spurr, T.V. Ho and D. Pambudi (2008) 'The Carbon Footprint of Australian Tourism, Centre for Economics and Policy', Gold Coast: Sustainable Tourism Cooperative Research Centre.

Frank, M.Z. and V.K. Goyal (2008) 'Trade-off and Pecking Order Theories of Debt' in B. Espen Eckbo (ed.) *Handbook of Corporate Finance: Empirical Corporate Finance, Volume 2*, Chapter 12, North-Holland: Handbooks in Finance Series, Elsevier.

Frechtling, D. (1999) 'The Tourism Satellite Account: Foundations, Progress and Issues', *Tourism Management*, 20, 163–170.

Frechtling, D. and E. Horvath (1998) 'Estimating the Multiplier Effects of Tourism Expenditures on a Local Economy through a Regional Input–Output Model', *Journal of Travel Research*, 37(4), 324–332.

Frechtling, D.C. (2001) *Forecasting Tourism Demand: Methods and Strategies*, Oxford, UK: Butterworth-Heinemann.

Fredline, E., T. Mules, M. Raybould and R. Tomljenovic (1999) 'Sweet Little Rock and Roller: The Economic Impact of the 1998 Wintersun Festival' in J. Molloy and J. Davis (eds) *Tourism and Hospitality: Delighting the Senses* (pp. 12–21), Proceedings of the Ninth Australian Tourism and Hospitality Research Conference, Part Two, Canberra Bureau of Tourism Research.

Fujii, E., M. Khaled and J. Mak (1985) 'The Exportability of Hotel Occupancy and Other Tourist Taxes', *National Tax Journal*, 38, 169–177.

Fyall, A. and B. Garrod (2005) *Tourism Marketing: A Collaborative Approach*, UK: Channel View Publications.

García-Ferrer, A. and R.A. Queralt (1997) 'A Note on Forecasting International Tourism Demand in Spain', *International Journal of Forecasting*, 13(4), 539–549.

Getz, D. (1994) 'Events Tourism: Evaluating the Impacts' in J.R.B. Ritchie and C.R. Goeldner (eds) *Travel, Tourism and Hospitality Research – A Handbook for Managers and Researchers*, New York: John Wiley and Sons.

Gillen, D., R. Harris and T. Oum (1996) *Assessing the Benefits and Costs of International Air Transport Liberalisation*, Ottawa: Transport Canada.

Gillen, D., W.G. Morrisson and C. Stewart (2003) *Air Travel Elasticities: Concepts, Issues and Measurement*, Canada: Department of Finance.

Gillen, D., H. Hinsch, B. Mandel and H. Wolf (2001) *The Impact of Liberalizing International Aviation Bilaterals: The Case of the North German Region*, Aldershot: Ashgate.

Giraud, K., B. Turcin, J. Loomis and J. Cooper (2002) 'Economic Benefit of the Protection Program for the Steller Sea Lion', *Marine Policy*, 26, 451–458.

Global Tourism Insight (2003) Global Tourism Report, Issue 3, www.globalinsight.com.

Gooroochurn, N. and G. Sugiyarto (2005) 'Competitiveness Indicators in the Travel and Tourism Industry', *Tourism Economics*, 11(1), 25–43.

Gooroochurn, N. and T. Sinclair (2005) 'The Economics of Tourism Taxation: Evidence from Mauritius', *Annals of Tourism Research*, 32(2), 478–498.

Gössling, S. (2000) 'Sustainable Tourism Development in Developing Countries: Some Aspects of Energy-use', *Journal of Sustainable Tourism*, 8(5), 410–425.

Gössling, S. (2002) 'Global Environmental Consequences of Tourism', *Global Environmental Change*, Part A, 12(4), 283–302.

Graham (2003) *Managing Airports: An International Perspective*, 2nd edition, Oxford: Butterworth-Heinemann.

Gramlich, Edward M. (1994) 'Infrastructure Investment: A Review Essay' *Journal of Economic Literature*, 32, 1176–1196, September.

Gudmundsson, S. (1998) *Flying too Close to the Sun: The Success and Failure of the New-entrant Airlines*, Aldershot: Ashgate.

Han, Z., R. Durbarry and M.T. Sinclair (2006) 'Modelling US Tourism Demand for European Destinations', *Tourism Management*, 27, 1–10.

Hanley, N., S. Maurato and R. Wright (2001) 'Choice Modelling Approaches: A Superior Alternative for Environmental Valuation?', *Journal of Economic Surveys*, 15(3), 435–462.

Harrison, D., Jr. and D.L. Rubinfeld (1978) 'Hedonic Housing Prices and the Demand for Clean Air', *Journal of Environmental Economics and Management*, 5, 81–102.

Harrison, G., S. Jensen, L. Pedersen and T. Rutherford (2000) 'Using Dynamic General Equilibrium Models for Policy Analysis' in G. Harrison, S. Jensen, L. Pedersen and T. Rutherford (eds) *Contributions to Economic Analysis* Vol. 248, North Holland, Oxford and New York: Elsevier.

Hassan, S. (2000) 'Determinants of Market Competitiveness in an Environmentally Sustainable Tourism Industry', *Journal of Travel Research*,38(3), 239–245, February.

Haveman, R. (1970) *The Economics of the Public Sector*, New York: John Wiley and Sons. Reproduced with permission of John Wiley & Sons, Inc.

Hesseln, H., John B. Loomis, A. Gonzalez-Caban and S. Alexander (2003) 'Wildfire Effects on Hiking and Biking Demand in New Mexico: A Travel Cost Study', *Journal of Environmental Management*, 69, 359–368.

Heng, T.M. and L. Low (1990) 'The Economic Impact of Tourism in Singapore', *Annals of Tourism Research*, 17(2), 246–249.

Henry, E.W. and B. Deane (1997) 'The Contribution of Tourism to the Economy of Ireland in 1990 and 1995', *Tourism Management*, 18(8), 535–553.

Hepburn, C. (2006) 'Regulation by Prices, Quantities, or Both: A Review of Instrument Choice', *Oxford Review of Economic Policy*, 22(2), 226–247.

Hertel, T.W. (1997) *Global Trade Analysis: Modelling and Applications*, Cambridge: Cambridge University Press.

Hiemstra, S. and J. Ismail (1992) 'Analysis of Room Taxes Levied on the Lodging Industry', *Journal of Travel Research*, 31(1), 42–49.

Hiemstra, S.J. and J.A. Ismail (1993) 'Incidence of the Impacts of Room Taxes in the Lodging Industry', *Journal of Travel Research*, 31(4), 22–26.

Hines, J.R. (1999) 'Three sides of Harberger Triangles', *Journal of Economic Perspectives*, 13, 167–188.

Hines, J.R. (2007) 'Excess Burden of Taxation' in Lawrence E. Blume and Steven N. Durlauf (eds) *The New Palgrave Dictionary of Economics*, 2nd edition, London, UK: Bureau of Industry Economics.

Hollander, G. (1982a) 'Determinants of Demand for Travel and from Australia', Working Paper No. 26, Canberra: Bureau of Industry.

Hollander, G. (1982b) 'Measuring Economic Impacts of Tourism', Working Paper No. 24, Canberra: Bureau of Industry Economics.

Hoque, S., P. Forsyth, L. Dwyer, R. Spurr and D. Pambudi (2009) 'Economic Effects of an Emissions Trading Scheme on the Australian Tourism Industry: A Dynamic CGE Analysis', Paper presented at conference of International Association for Tourism Economics (IATE), Chiang Mai, Thailand, December 2009.

Howarth, G. and T. Kirsebom (1999) *The Future of Airline Alliances: Current Thinking, Strategic Directions and Implications*, Sutton, UK: Gemini Consulting and Reed Business Information.

Hughes, H.L. (1981) 'A Tourism Tax – the Cases for and Against', *International Journal of Tourism Management*, 2, 196–206, September.

Humphreys, J.M. and M.K. Plummer (1995) 'The Economic Impact on the State of Georgia of Hosting the 1996 Summer Olympic Games', Mimeograph, Athens, GA: Selig Center for Economic Growth, University of Georgia.

ICAO (2009) *Manual on the Regulation of International Air Transport* (Doc 9626, Part 4), www.*icao.int/icao/en/trivia/freedoms_air.htm*.

Im, E. and M. Sakai (1996) 'A Note on the Effect of Changes in Ad Valorem Tax Rates on Net Revenue of Firms: An Application to the Hotel Room Tax', *Public Finance Quarterly*, 24, 397–402.

IMPLAN (2000) 'Elements of the Social Accounting Matrix', Technical report TR-98002. www.implan.com/reports.

Industry Commission (1996) *State Territory and Local Government Assistance to Industry Report 55*, October, Canberra: AGPS.

IPCC (2007a) Intergovernmental Panel on Climate Change (IPCC) *Climate Change 2007: Synthesis Report*, An Assessment of the Intergovernmental Panel on Climate Change, December 2007, http://www.ipcc.ch/ipccreports/ar4-syr.htm.

IPCC (2007b) 'Intergovernmental Panel on Climate Change (IPCC), Summary for Policymakers' in M.L. Parry et al. (eds) *Climate Change 2007: Impacts, Adaptation and Vulnerability. Contribution of Working Group II to the Fourth Assessment Report of the IPCC*, Cambridge and New York: Cambridge University Press.

IRTS (2008) United Nations World Tourism Organization, 2008 International Recommendations for Tourism Statistics, New York, Madrid.

Jackson, C., D. Kotsovos and C. Morissette (2008) 'Linking the Canadian Tourism Satellite Account and the Canadian System of Environmental and Resource Accounts to Measure the Environmental Impact of Tourism in Canada: An Exploratory Study for Two Pilot Industries', 9th International Forum on Tourism Statistics, Paris, 19–21 November.

Jackson, R.T. (1990) 'VFR Tourism: Is it Underestimated', *The Journal of Tourism Studies*, 1(2), 10–17, November.

Jago, L. and L. Dwyer (2006) *Economic Evaluation of Special Events: A Practitioners Guide*, Altona, Australia: Common Ground Publishing Pty. Ltd.

Jago, L. and R. Shaw (1998) 'Special Events: A Conceptual and Definitional Framework', *Festival Management and Event Tourism*, 5, 21–32.

Jenkins, G.P. and C.Y. Kuo (1985) 'On Measuring the Social Opportunity Cost of Foreign Exchange', *Canadian Journal of Economics*, 18, 400–415.

Johnson, R. (1999) 'Input-output Models with and without the Multiplier Effect' *Valuing Tourism: Methods and Techniques*, Occasional Paper No. 28, Canberra: Bureau of Tourism Research.

Johnson, R. and E. Moore (1993) 'Tourism Impact Estimation', *Annals of Tourism Research*, 20, 279–283.

Jones, C., A. Munday and A. Roberts (2003) Regional Tourism Satellite Accounts: A Useful Policy Tool? *Urban Studies*, 40(13), 2777–2794.

Jones C. and A. Munday (2007) 'Tourism Satellite Accounts and Impact Assessments: Some Considerations', *Tourism Analysis*, 13(1), 53–69.

Kahn, H., C. Seng and W. Cheong (1989) 'The Economic and Social Impact of Tourism on Singapore' in C. Tisdell, C. Aislabee and J.Stanton (eds) *Economics of Tourism: Case Study and Analysis*, Australia: University of Newcastle.

Kahnemann, D. and J.L. Knetsch (1992) Valuing Public Goods: The Purchase of Moral Satisfaction, *Journal of Environmental Economics and Management*, 22, 57–70.

Kasper, D. (1988) *Deregulation and Globalization: Liberalizing International Trade in Air Services*, Ballinger: American Enterprise Institute.

Keat, P. and P. Young (2009) *Managerial Economics: Economic Tools for Today's Decision Makers*, 6th edition, New Jersey: Pearson International Edition.

Kelly, J. and P.W. Williams (2007) 'Modelling Tourism Destination Energy Consumption and Greenhouse Gas Emissions: Whistler, British Columbia, Canada', *Journal of Sustainable Tourism*, 15(1), 67–90.

Kim, C.W. and L. Dwyer (2003) 'Destination Competitiveness and Bilateral Tourism Flows between Australia and Korea', *Journal of Tourism Studies*, 14(2), 55–67, December.

Kim, S. and H. Song (1998) 'Analysis of Inbound Tourism Demand in South Korea: A Cointegration and Error Correction Approach', *Tourism Analysis*, 3, 25–41.

Kliman, M.L. (1981) 'A Quantitative Analysis of Canadian Overseas Tourism', *Transportation Research*, 15A, 487–497.

Kraft, D., T. Oum and M. Tretheway (1986) 'Airline Seat Management', *Logistics and Transportation Review*, 22(2), 115–130, June.

Kulendran, N. and S. Divisekera (2007) 'Measuring the Economic Impact of Australian Tourism Marketing Expenditure', *Tourism Economics*, 13(2), 261–274.

Kulendran, N. and L. Dwyer (2009) 'Measuring the Return from Australian Tourism Marketing Expenditure in Asia', *Journal of Travel Research*, 47, 275–284, February.

Kulendran, N. and S. Witt (2003a) 'Forecasting the Demand for International Business Tourism', *Journal of Travel Research*, 41, 265–271, February.

Kulendran, N. and S.F. Witt (2003b) 'Leading Indicator Tourism Forecasts', *Tourism Management*, 24(5), 503–510.

Kusluvan, S. and K. Karamustafa (2001) 'Multinational Hotel Development in Developing Countries: An Exploratory Analysis of Critical Policy Issues', *International Journal of Tourism Research*, 3, 179–197.

Kwack, S.Y. (1972) 'Effects of Income and Prices on Travel Spending Abroad, 1960 III–1967 IV', *International Economic Review*, 13, 245–256.

Kweka, J., O. Morrissey and A. Blake (2001) 'Is Tourism a Key Sector in Tanzania? Input-Output Analysis of Income, Output, Employment and Tax Revenue', Discussion paper 2001/1.

Lancaster, K.J. (1966) 'A New Approach to Consumer Theory', *Journal of Political Economy*, 74, 132–157.

Lansford, N.H. Jr. and L.L. Jones (1995) 'Recreational and Aesthetic Value of Water Using Hedonic Price Analysis', *Journal of Agricultural and Resource Economics*, 20(2), 341–355.

Lawton, T. (2002) *Cleared for Take-Off: Structure and Strategy in the Low Fare Airline Business*, Aldershot: Ashgate.

Lee, C. (1997) 'Valuation of Nature-Based Tourism Resources Using Dichotomous Choice Contingent Valuation Method', *Tourism Management*, 18, 587–591.

Lee, C., J. Lee and S. Han (1998) 'Measuring the Economic Value of Ecotourism Resources: The Case of South Korea, *Journal of Travel Research*, 36, 40–47, Spring.

Lee, C-K. and T. Taylor (2005) 'Critical Reflections on the Economic Impact Assessment of a Mega-event: The Case of 2002 FIFA World Cup', *Tourism Management*, 26, 595–603.

Lei, Z. (2006) 'Theoretical Pillars of Industrial Organization in Tourism' in A. Papatheodorou (ed.) *Corporate Rivalry and Market Power: Competition Issues in the Tourism Industry*, London: I.B. Tauris.

Levine, M.E. (2007) 'Congestion Pricing at New York Airports: Right Idea, But Can We Really Start Here and Now?', Policy Brief No. 66, Los Angeles: Reason Foundation, November, www.reason.org/pb66_nycongestion.pdf.

Li, G., H. Songand S.F. Witt (2005) 'Recent Developments in Econometric Modeling and Forecasting', *Journal of Travel Research*, 44, 82–99.

Li, G., H. Song, and S.F. Witt (2006) 'Time Varying Parameter and Fixed Parameter Linear AIDS: An Application to Tourism Demand Forecasting', *International Journal of Forecasting*, 22, 57–71.

Libreros, M., A. Massieu and S. Meis (2006) 'Progress in Tourism Satellite Account Implementation and Development', *Journal of Travel Research*, 45, 83.

Lim, C. (1999) 'A Meta Analysis Review of International Tourism Demand', *Journal of Travel Research*, 37, 273–284.

Lim, C. (2006) 'Tourism Demand Modelling: Issues and Implications' in L. Dwyer and P. Forsyth (eds) *International Handbook of Tourism Economics*, London: Edward Elgar.

Lim, C. and M. McAleer (2001) 'Forecasting Tourist Arrivals', *Annals of Tourism Research*, 28(4), 965–977.

Lin, T. and Y-W. Sung (1983) 'Hong Kong' in E.A. Pye and T. Lin (eds) *Tourism in Asia: the Economic Impact*, Singapore: Singapore University Press.

Lindberg, K. (1991) *Policies for Maximizing Nature Tourism's Ecological and Economic Benefits*, USA: World Resources Institute, February.

Liston-Heyes, C. and A. Heyes (1999) Recreational Benefits from the Dartmoor National Park, *Journal of Environmental Management*, 55, 69–80.

Little, J.S. (1980) 'International Travel in the UK Balance of Payments', *New England Economic Review*, 42–55, May.

Lockwood, M. and K. Tracy (1995) 'Nonmarket Economic Valuation of an Urban Recreation Park', *Journal of Leisure Research*, 27(2), 155–167.

Lockwood, M., K. Tracey and N. Klomp (1996) 'Analyzing Conflict between Cultural Heritage and Nature Conservation in the Australian Alps: A CVM Approach', *Journal of Environmental Planning and Management*, 39(3), 357–370.

Louvier, J., D. Henscher and J. Swait (2000) *Stated Choice Methods: Analysis and Applications*, Cambridge, UK: Cambridge University Press.

Lundie, S., L. Dwyer and P. Forsyth (2007) 'Environmental-Economic Measures of Tourism Yield', *Journal of Sustainable Tourism*, 15(5), 1–18.

Mabugu, R. (2002) 'Short-term Effects of Policy Reform on Tourism and the Macroeconomy in Zimbabwe: Applied CGE Analysis', *Development Southern Africa*, 19, 419–430.

Madden, J. (2006) 'Economic and Fiscal Impacts of Mega Sporting Events: A General Equilibrium Assessment', *Public Finance and Management*, 6(3), 346–394.

Mahan, B.L., S. Polasky and R.M. Adams (2000) 'Valuing Urban Wetlands: A Property Price Approach', *Land Economics*, 76(1), 100–113.

Mak, J. (1988) 'Taxing Hotel Room Rentals in the US', *Journal of Travel Research*, 27(1), 10–15, Summer.

Mak, J. (2006) 'Taxing Travel and Tourism' in L. Dwyer and P. Forsyth (eds) *International Handbook of Tourism Economics*, UK: Edward Elgar, July.

Mak, J. (2008) 'Taxing Cruise Tourism: Alaska's Head Tax on Cruise Ship Passengers', *Tourism Economics*, 14(3), 599–614.

Mangion, D., R. Durbarry and T. Sinclair (2005) 'Tourism Competitiveness: Price and Quality', *Tourism Economics*, 11(1), 45–68.

Martin, C.A. and S.F. Witt (1988) 'Substitute Prices in Models of Tourism Demand', *Annals of Tourism Research*, 15, 255–268.

Matheson, V. (2002) 'Upon Further Review: An Examination of Sporting Event Economic Impact Studies', *The Sport Journal*, 5(1), 1–3.

Matheson, V. and R. Baade (2003a) 'Bidding for the Olympics: Fools Gold?' in C. Barros, M. Ibrahim and S. Szymanski (eds) *Transatlantic Sport*, London: Edward Elgar Publishing.

Matheson, V. and R. Baade (2003b) 'Mega-Sporting Events in Developing Nations: Playing the Way to Prosperity?', *South African Journal of Economics*, 72(5), 1084–1095, December.

Mazanec, J.A., K. Wöber and A.H. Zins (2007) 'Tourism Destination Competitiveness: From Definition to Explanation?', *Journal of Travel Research*, 46, 86.

McDougall, R. (1995) 'Computable General Equilibrium Modelling: Introduction and Overview', *Asia-Pacific Economic Review*, 1(1), 88–91, April.

McKercher, B. and H. du Cros (2002) *Cultural Tourism: the Partnership between Tourism and Cultural Heritage Management*, New York: Haworth Press.

McNulty, R. and P. Wafer (1990) 'Transnational Corporations and Tourism Issues', *Tourism Management*, 11(4), 291–295.

McQueen, M. (1989) 'Multinationals in Tourism' in S. Witt and L. Moutinho (eds) *Tourism, Marketing and Management*, New York: Handbook Prentice Hal.

Meagher G. and B. Parmenter (1990) *ORANI-NT: A Multisectoral Model of the Northern Territory Economy*, Darwin: The Australian National University, North Australia Research Unit.

Meis, S. (1999) 'The Canadian Experience in Developing and Using the Tourism Satellite Account', *Tourism Economics*, 5(4), 315–330.

Middleton, V. and J. Clarke (2001) *Marketing in Travel and Tourism: Butterworth-Heinemann*, Oxford: Linacre House, Jordan Hill.

Mitra-Kahn, Benjamin H. (2008) 'Debunking the Myths of Computable General Equilibrium Models', *SCEPA Working Paper* 01-2008.

Monty, B. and M. Skidmore (2003) 'Hedonic Pricing and Willingness to Pay for Bed and Breakfast Amenities in Southeast Wisconsin', *Journal of Travel Research*, 42, 195–199.

Moon, H.C. and N. Peery (1995) 'Competitiveness of Product, Firm, Industry, and Nation in a Global Business', *Competitiveness Review*, 5(1), 37–43.

Morey, E.R. and William S. Breffle (2006) 'Valuing a Change in a Fishing Site without Collecting Characteristics Data on All Fishing Sites: A Complete but Minimal Model', *American Journal of Agricultural Economics*, 88(1), 150–161.

Moriarty, J. (2006) 'Enhancing Financial and Economic Yield in Tourism: Analysing New Zealand's Tourism Satellite Accounts for Measures of Sector Performance and Business Benchmarks', Tourism Recreation Research and Education Centre (TRREC) Yield Report No. 2.

Morley, C.L. (2003) 'Impacts of International Airline Alliances on Tourism', *Tourism Economics*, 9, 31–51.

Morley, C.L. (2006) 'Airline Alliances and Tourism' in L. Dwyer and P. Forsyth (eds) *International Handbook on the Economics of Tourism*, Chapter 9, Cheltenham: Edward Elgar Publishing.

Mules, T. (1999) 'Estimating the Economic Impact of an Event on a Local Government Area, Region, State or Territory', *Valuing Tourism: Methods and Techniques*, Occasional Paper No. 28, Canberra: Bureau of Tourism Research.

Mules, T. and B. Faulkner (1996) 'An Economic Perspective on Special Events', *Tourism Economics*, 2, 2.

Mules, T. and L. Dwyer (2005) 'Public Sector Support for Sport Tourism Events: The Role of Cost-benefit Analysis', *Sport in Society*, 8(2), 338–355, June.

Musgrave, R.A. and P.B. Musgrave (1989) *Public Finance*, 5th edition, New York: McGraw-Hill.

Narashimbha, S. (2000) 'Organisation Knowledge, Human Resource Management, and Sustained Competitive Advantage: Toward a Framework', *Competitiveness Review*, 10(1), 123–135.

Narayan, P. and B.C. Prasad (2007) 'The Long-run Impact of Coups on Fiji's Economy: Evidence from a Computable General Equilibrium Model', *Journal of International Development*, 19(2), 149–160.

Narayan, P.K. (2004) 'Economic Impact of Tourism on Fiji's Economy: Empirical Evidence from the Computable General Equilibrium Model', *Tourism Economics*, 10(4), 419–433.

Naudé, W. A. and A. Saayman (2005), 'Determinants of Tourist Arrivals in Africa: A Panel Data Regression Analysis', *Tourism Economics*, 11, 365–391.

Nellis, J.G. and D. Parker (2006) *Principles of Business Economics*, 2nd edition, London: Pearson Education.

New Zealand Commerce Commission (2003) *Final Determination: Qantas Air New Zealand Application*, 23 October.

New Zealand Treasury (2008) 'Public Sector Discount Rates for Cost Benefit Analysis, Wellington', July http://www.treasury.govt.nz/publications/guidance/ costbenefit-analysis/discountrates.

Newell, G. and R. Seabrook (2006) 'Factors Influencing Hotel Investment Decision Making', *Journal of Property Investment and Finance*, 24(4), 279–294.

NIEIR (1989) *The Economic Impact and Tourism Value of the 1989 Australian Motorcycle Grand Prix on Phillip Island*', National Institute of Economic and Industry Research report prepared for the Department of Sport and Recreation and the Victorian Tourism Commission, Melbourne, Victoria.

NIEIR (2005) *Economic Impact Evaluation of the 2005 Foster's Australian Grand Prix*. National Institute of Economic and Industry Research: A Report for the Australian Grand Prix Corporation, Melbourne.

Njegovan, N. (2006) 'Elasticities of Demand for Leisure Air Travel: A System Modelling Approach', *Journal of Air Transport Management*, 12, 33–39.

NSW Treasury (2007) *NSW Government Guidelines for Economic Appraisal*, Office of Financial Management Policy and Guideline Paper, Sydney, July.

Nunes, P. and E. Schokkaert (2003) 'Identifying the Warm Glow Effect in Contingent Valuation', *Journal of Environmental Economics and Management*, 45, 231–245.

Nunes, P. and P. Nijkamp (2009) 'Contingent Valuation Method' Encora Coastal Portal http://www.coastalwiki.org.

O'Connell, J.F. and G. Williams (2005) 'Passengers' Perceptions of Low Cost Airlines and Full Service Carriers: A Case Study Involving Ryanair, Aer Lingus, Air Asia and Malaysia Airlines', *Journal of Air Transport Management*, 11, 259–272.

OECD (1997) 'Industrial Competitiveness: Benchmarking Business Environments', Paris.

OECD (2000) Organisation for Economic Cooperation and Development, *Measuring the Role of Tourism in OECD Economies: The OECD Manual on Tourism Satellite Accounts and Employment.*

Oh, C.-O. and B.J. Morzuch (2005) 'Evaluating Time-series Models to Forecast the Demand for Tourism in Singapore', *Journal of Travel Research*, 43(4), 404–413.

Omerzel, D. and T. Mihalic (2008) 'Destination Competitiveness – Applying Different Models, the Case of Slovenia', *Tourism Management*, 29, 294–307.

Oum, T.H. and C. Yu (2000) *Shaping Air Transport in Asia Pacific*, Aldershot: Ashgate Publications.

Oum, T.H., J.H. Park and A. Zhang (2001) *Globalization and Strategic Alliances: The Case of the Airline Industry*, Amsterdam: Elsevier Science.

Oum, T.H., W.T. Stanbury and M.W. Tretheway (1991) 'Airline Deregulation in Canada' in K. Button (ed.) *Airline Deregulation: International Experiences* (pp. 124–179), London: David Fulton Publishers.

Oum, T.H., W.G. Waters and J.S. Yong (1992) 'Concepts of Price Elasticities of Transport Demand and Recent Empirical Estimates', *Journal of Transport Economics and Policy*, 26(2), 139–154.

Pambudi, D., N. McCaughey and R. Smyth (2009) 'Computable General Equilibrium Estimates of the Impact of the Bali Bombing on the Indonesian Economy', *Tourism Management*, 30, 232–239.

Papatheodorou, A. (1999) 'The Demand for International Tourism in the Mediterranean Region', *Applied Economics*, 31, 619–630.

Papatheodorou, A. (2002) 'Exploring Competitiveness in Mediterranean Resorts', *Tourism Economics*, 8, 133–150.

Park, T., J.M. Bowker and V.R. Leeworthy (2002) 'Valuing Snorkeling Visits to the Florida Keys with Stated Revealed Preference Models', *Journal of Environmental Management*, 65, 301–312.

Patterson, T., S. Bastianoni and M. Simpson (2006) 'Tourism and Climate Change: Two-Way Street, or Vicious/Virtuous Circle?', *Journal of Sustainable Tourism*, 14(4), 339–348.

Patterson, M.G. and G. McDonald (2004) *How Clean and Green Is New Zealand's Tourism? Lifecycle and Future Environmental Impacts*, Landcare Research Series No. 24, Lincoln: Maanaki Whenua Press, p. 183.

Pavaskar, M. (1987) 'Employment Effects of Tourism and the Indian Experience', *Journal of Travel Research*, 26(1), 32–38, Fall.

Perdue, R. (2002) 'Perishability, Yield Management, and Cross Product Elasticity: A Case Study of Deep Discount Season Passes in the Colorado Ski Industry', *Journal of Travel Research*, 41(1), 15–23.

Persson, M. (2008) 'Socio-economic Evaluation Encora Coastal Portal', http://www.coastalwiki.org.

Peterson, T. (1975) 'Cost-Benefit Analysis for Evaluating Transportation Proposals: Los Angeles Case Study', *Land Economics*, 51(1), 72–79, February.

Pindyck, R., D. Rubinfeld and W. Koh (2006) *Microeconomics: An Asian Perspective*, Singapore: Prentice Hall.

Pollard, G. (1976) 'Antigua, West Indies: An Example of the Operation of the Multiplier Process Arising from Tourism', *Revue de Tourisme*, 3, 30–34.

Pollicino, M. and D. Maddison (2001) 'Valuing the Benefits of Cleaning Lincoln Cathedral', *Journal of Cultural Economics*, 25, 131–148.

Polo, C. and E. Vaile (2008) 'A General Equilibrium Assessment of the Impact of a Fall in Tourism Under Alternative Closure Rules: The Case of the Balearic Islands', *International Regional Science Review*, 31(1), 3–34.

Poole, R.W. and B. Dachis (2007) 'Congestion Pricing for New York Airports Reducing Delays while Promoting Growth and Competition' Policy Study 366, Los Angeles: Reason Foundation, November, www.reason.org/pb66_nycongestion.pdf.

Porter, M. (1980) *Competitive Strategy: Techniques for Analysing Industries and Competitors*, New York: Free Press.

Porter, Michael E. (1990) *The Competitive Advantage of Nations*, New York: The Free Press.

Porter, P. (1999) 'Mega-Sports Events as Municipal Investments: A Critique of Impact Analysis' in J.L. Fizel, E. Gustafson and L. Hadley (eds) *Sports Economics: Current Research*, New York: Praeger Press.

Price Waterhouse (1989) 'Economic Impact Assessment of the 1988 Australian Formula 1 Grand Prix', A report prepared for the Australian Formula I Grand Prix Board, Adelaide, Victoria.

Prime Ministerial Task Group on Emissions Trading (2007) *Report of the Task Group on Emissions Trading*, Barton, ACT, Department of the Prime Minister and Cabinet.

Productivity Commission (1998) *International Air Services: Report No 2*, Ausinfo, Canberra, September.

Property Council of Australia (2003) *New Investment Frontiers: An Industry Action Plan For Reshaping Hotel Investment*, Sydney: PCA.

Pyatt, G. and J.I. Round (1977) 'Social Accounting Matrices for Development Planning', *Review of Income and Wealth*, Series 23, No. 4, 339–364.

Pyatt, G. and J.I. Round (1985) *Social Accounting Matrices: A Basis for Planning*, Washington DC: The World Bank.

Raghbendra, J. (1998) *Modern Public Economics*, London: Routledge.

Rahim, K.A. (2008) 'Non-Market Valuation Techniques', Economic Valuation of the Goods and Services of Coastal Habitats' *The Regional Training Workshop*, 24–28 March, Samut Songkram Province, Thailand.

Rahmatian, M. and L. Cockerill (2004) 'Airport Noise and Residential Housing Valuation in Southern California: A Hedonic Pricing Approach', *International Journal of Environmental Science & Technology*, 1(1), 17–25, Spring.

Ray, A. (1984) *Cost Benefit Analysis*, Washington DC: The World Bank.

Read, S. (2009) 'The Hidden Costs of Snapping up a Bargain', *The Independent*, Saturday, 17 October, http://www.independent.co.uk/money/spend-save/simon-read-the-hidden-costs-of-snapping-up-a-bargain-1804203.html.

Ritchie, J.R. and G.I. Crouch (2000) 'The Competitive Destination: A Sustainability Perspective', *Tourism Management*, 21(1), 1–7.

Ritchie, J.R.B. and G.I. Crouch (2003) *The Competitive Destination: A Sustainable Tourism Perspective*, Cambridge: Cabi Publishing.

Robinson, S. and D.W. Roland-Holst (1988) 'Macroeconomic Structure and Computable General Equilibrium Models', *Journal of Policy Modeling*, 10(3), 353–375, Fall.

Rosen, S. (1974) 'Hedonic Prices and Implicit Markets: Product Differentiation in Pure Competition', *Journal of Political Economy*, 82, 34–55.

Rosensweig, J.A. (1986) 'Exchange Rates and Competition for Tourists', *New England Economic Review*, July/August, 57–67.

Rosato, P. (2008) 'Travel Cost Method', Encora Coastal Portal, http://www.coastalwiki.org.

Rossello-Nadal, J. (2001) 'Forecasting Turning Points in International Visitor Arrivals in the Balearic Islands, *Tourism Economics*, 7(4), 365–380.

Ruiz, A.L. (1985) 'Tourism and the Economy of Puerto Rico: An Input-output Approach', *Tourism Management*, 6(1), 61–65.

Rutherford, T. and S. Paltsev (1999) 'From an Input-Output Table to a General Equilibrium Model: Assessing the Excess Burden of Indirect Taxes in Russia', Department of Economics, University of Colorado, mimeo.

Ryan, C. and Lockyer, T. (2001) 'An Economic Impact Case Study: The South Pacific Masters Games', *Tourism Economics*, 7(3), 267–275.

Saayman, A. and M. Saayman (2008) 'The Determinants of Inbound Tourism to South Africa', *Tourism Economics*, 14(1), 81–96.

Sadler, P., B. Archer and C. Owen (1973) *Regional Income Multipliers*, Occasional Papers in Economics, No. 1, Bangor: University of Wales Press.

Sakai, M. (1985) *A Micro-Analysis of Demand for Travel Goods: An Application to the Business Traveler*, Ph.D. dissertation in economics, Honolulu: University of Hawaii-Manoa.

Sakai, M. (1988) 'Micro-Analysis of Business Travel Demand', *Applied Economics*, 20, 1481–1493.

Sakai, M. (2006) 'Public Sector Investment in Tourism Infrastructure' in L. Dwyer and P. Forsyth (eds) *International Handbook of Tourism Economics*, UK: Edward Elgar, July.

Salazar, S. and J. Marques (2005) 'Valuing Cultural Heritage: The Social Benefits of Restoring an Old Arab Tower', *Journal of Cultural Heritage*, 6, 69–77.

Salma, U. (2004) 'Indirect Economic Contribution of Tourism to Australia, 2001/02', Tourism Research Report, Vol. 5, Number 2, Canberra: Bureau of Tourism Research. © 2010 Commonwealth of Australia. Reproduced with permission.

Salma, U. and L. Heaney (2004) 'Proposed Methodology for Measuring Yield', *Tourism Research Report*, 6(1), 73–81, Canberra: Tourism Research Australia.

Salvatore, D. (1989) *Managerial Economics*, New York: McGraw-Hill.

Sanford, D.M. and H. Dong (2000) 'Investment in Familiar Territory: Tourism and New Foreign Direct Investment', *Tourism Economics*, 6(3), 205–219.

Scott, B. and H.C. Lodge (1985) *United States Competitiveness in World Economy*, Boston: Harvard Business School Press.

Seaton, A.V. and M.M. Bennett (1999) *The Marketing of Tourism Products*, London: Centage Learning.

Seetaram, N. and L. Dwyer (2009) 'Immigration and Tourism Demand in Australia: A Panel Data Analysis', *ANATOLIA*, 20(1), 212–222.

Shaffer, M., A. Greer and C. Mauboules (2003) 'Olympic Costs and Benefits', Canadian Centre for Policy Alternatives Publication, February.

Sheldon, P.J., and T. Var (1985) 'Tourism Forecasting: A Review of Empirical Research', *Journal of Forecasting*, 4(2), 183–195.

Shoven, J. and J. Whalley (1992) *Applying General Equilibrium*, Cambridge Surveys of Economic Literature, Cambridge: Cambridge University Press.

Sinclair, M.T. (1998) 'Tourism and Economic Development: A Survey', *Journal of Development Studies*, 34(5), 1–51, June.

Sinclair, T. and M. Stabler (1997) *The Economics of Tourism*, London: Routledge.

Sinclair, M.T., A. Clewer and A. Pack (1990) 'Hedonic Prices and the Marketing of Package Holidays: The Case of Tourism Resorts in Malaga' in G. Ashworth and B. Goodall (eds) *Marketing Tourism Places* (pp. 85–103), London: Routledge.

Skalpe, O. (2003) 'Hotels and Restaurants – Are the Risks Rewarded? Evidence from Norway', *Tourism Management*, 24(6), 623–634.

Smith, A.B. and J.N. Toms (1978) 'Factors Affecting Demand for International Travel to and from Australia', Occasional Paper 11, Canberra: Bureau of Transport Economics.

Solomon, B., C. Corey-Luse and K. Halvorsen (2004) 'The Florida Manatee and Eco-tourism: Toward a Safe Minimum Standard', *Ecological Economics*, 50, 101–115.

Song, B. N. and C-Y. Ahn (1983) 'Korea' in E.A. Pye and T-b. Lin (eds) *Tourism in Asia: the Economic Impact*, Singapore: Singapore University Press.

Song, H. and G. Li (2008) 'Tourism Demand Modelling and Forecasting – A Review of Recent Research', *Tourism Management*, 29(2), 203–220.

Song, H. and L. Turner (2006) 'Tourism Demand Forecasting' in L. Dwyer and P. Forsyth (eds) *International Handbook on the Economics of Tourism*, Cheltenham: Edward Elgar.

Song, H. and S.F. Witt (2000) *Tourism Demand Modelling and Forecasting: Modern Econometric Approaches*, Cambridge: Pergamon.

Song, H. and S.F. Witt (2003) 'Tourism Forecasting: The General-to-specific Approach, *Journal of Travel Research*, 42(1), 65–74.

Song, H., P. Romilly and X. Liu (2000) 'An Empirical Study of Outbound Tourism Demand in the UK', *Applied Economics*, 32(5), 611–624.

Song, H., S.F. Witt and T.C. Jensen (2003a) 'Tourism Forecasting: Accuracy of Alternative Econometric Models', *International Journal of Forecasting*, 19(1), 123–141.

Song, H., S.F. Witt and G. Li (2003b) 'Modelling and Forecasting the Demand for Thai Tourism', *Tourism Economics*, 9(4), 363–387.

Spengler, J. and M. Uysal (1989) 'Considerations in the Hotel Taxation Process', *International Journal of Hospitality Management*, 8(4), 309–316.

Spinet, J.M.E., M.S. Aez, G.C. Oenders and M.F. Luvià (2003) 'Effect on Prices of the Attributes of Holiday Hotels: A Hedonic Prices Approach', *Tourism Economics*, 9(2), 165–177.

Spreen, M. and E. Mot (2008) *Een rookverbod in deNederlandse horeca, Een kosten-batenanalyse* (A smoking ban in the Dutch hotel and catering sector, a cost-benefit analysis), Netherlands Bureau for Economic Analysis, Document 159, February (English summary, main report only in Dutch).

Spurr, R. (2006) 'Tourism Satellite Accounts' in L. Dwyer and P. Forsyth (eds) *International Handbook on the Economics of Tourism*, Cheltenham, UK and Northampton, MA: Edward Elgar.

Statistics New Zealand (2008) Tourism Satellite Account 2007, Wellington: Statistics New Zealand.

STCRC (2009) 'Tourism within Communities: The Flow of Expenditure through Economies and Industries', Sustainable Tourism Cooperative Research Centre, Australia: Griffith University.

Stern, N. (2006) *Stern Review. The Economics of Climate Change*, London: UK Treasury.

Stynes, D.J. (2006) 'Economic Impacts of Tourism Economic Impacts of Recreation & Tourism', http://web4.canr.msu.edu/mgm2/econ/pdf/ecimpvol1.pdf.

Sugiyarto, G., A. Blake and M.T. Sinclair (2003) 'Tourism and Globalization: Economic Impact in Indonesia', *Annals of Tourism Research*, 30(3), 683–701.

Tang, S., E.A. Selvanathan and S. Selvanathan (2007) 'The Relationship between Foreign Direct Investment and Tourism: Empirical Evidence from China', *Tourism Economics*, 13(1), 25–39.

Taylor, P. (1995) 'Measuring Changes in the Relative Competitiveness of Package Tour Destinations', *Tourism Economics*, 1(2), 169–182.

Thrane, C. (2005) 'Hedonic Price Models and Sun-and-Beach Package Tours: The Norwegian Case', *Journal of Travel Research*, 43(3), 302–308.

Tisdell, C. (1982) *The Microeconomics of Markets*, Sydney: John Wiley and Sons.

Tisdell, Clem A. (1983) 'Public Finance and the Appropriation of Gains from International Tourists: Some Theory with ASEAN and Australian Illustrations', *Singapore Economic Review*, 28, 3–20.

Tisdell, C. (1987) 'Tourism, the Environment and Profit', *Economic Analysis and Policy*, 17(1), 13–20, March.

Tisdell, C. (2001) *Tourism Economics, the Environment and Development: Analysis and Policy*, Cheltenham, UK: Edward Elgar.

Tisdell, C. (2006) 'Valuation of Tourism's Natural Resources' in L. Dwyer and P. Forsyth (eds) *International Handbook on the Economics of Tourism* (pp. 359–378), Cheltenham, UK and Northampton, MA: Edward Elgar.

Tohmo, T. (2005) 'Economic Impacts of Cultural Events on Local Economies: An Input–output Analysis of the Kaustinen Folk Music Festival', *Tourism Economics*, 11(3), 431–451.

Tol, R. (2006) 'The Impact of a Carbon Tax on International Tourism', *Working Paper FNU-120*, Hamburg: Hamburg University and Centre for Marine and Atmospheric Science.

Tourism Forecasting Council (1998) 'Inbound Tourism Short-term Scenarios', Research Report No. 2, Canberra, Australia: Tourism Forecasting Council.

Tourism Research Australia (2006) *Forecast*, Canberra: Tourism Forecasting Committee, Tourism Australia, October.

Treasury Board of Canada (1998) *Benefit-Cost Analysis Guide*, Ottawa: Treasury Board of Canada Secretariat, July.

Tremblay, P. (1989) 'Pooling International Tourism in Western Europe', *Annals of Tourism Research*, 16, 477–491.

Tretheway, M.W. and T.H. Oum (1992) *Airline Economics: Foundations for Strategy and Policy*, Centre for Transportation Studies, Vancouver: University of British Columbia.

TSA RMF (2008) *Tourism Satellite Account: Recommended Methodological Framework*. Jointly presented by the United Nations Statistics Division (UNSD), the Statistical Office of the European Communities (EUROSTAT), the Organisation for Economic Co-operation and Development (OECD) and the World Tourism Organisation (UNWTO).

Turner, L.W., N. Kulendran and H. Fernando (1997) 'The Use of Composite National Indicators for Tourism Forecasting', *Tourism Economics*, 3(4), 309–317.

UNCTAD (2008a) World Investment Report 2008, *Transnational Corporations and the Infrastructure Challenge: An Overview*, p. 42, http://www.unctad.org/en/docs//wir2008overview_en.pdf.

UNCTAD (2008b) *FDI and Tourism: The Development Dimension East and Southern Africa*, New York: United Nations.

UNCTAD Investment Brief Number 1 2009 (01/02/09) http://www.unctad.org/en/docs/webdiaeia20095_en.pdf.

United Nations (1989) 'Foreign Direct Investment and Transnational Corporations in Services', New York: United Nations Centre on Transnational Corporations.

United Nations (2001) 'Tourism Satellite Accounts', Tables 1–7 and 10, chapter 4, 75–84.

United Nations Department for Economic and Social Affairs Statistics Division (1999) 'Handbook of Input-output Table Compilation and Analysis Studies in Methods Series F, No. 74', Handbook of National Accounting, United Nations, New York.

United Nations World Tourism Organisation and United Nations Environment Programme [WTO-UNEP] (2008) *Climate Change and Tourism – Responding to Global Challenges*, Madrid, Spain: World Tourism Organisation.

UNWTO (1998) *Tourism Taxation: Striking a Fair Deal*, Madrid: World Tourism Organization.

UNWTO (2008a) *2008 International Recommendations for Tourism Statistics*, New York and Madrid: United Nations World Tourism Organisation.

UNWTO (2008b) United Nations World Tourism Organisation, www.unwto.org.

UNWTO (2009a) *United Nations World Tourism Barometer*, Vol. 7, No. 2, June, available at www. unwto.org.

UNWTO (2009b) 'Discussion Paper on Climate Change Mitigation Measures for International Air Transport', Madrid: United Nations World Tourism Organisation, August.

Van Der Merwe, P., M. Saayman and W.F. Krugell (2007) 'The Determinants of the Spending of Biltong Hunters', *South African Journal of Economics and Management Sciences*, 10(2), 184–194.

van Doorn, J.W.M. (1984) 'Tourism Forecasting and the Policy-maker: Criteria and Usefulness', *Tourism Management*, 5(1), 24–39.

Veloce, W. (2004) 'Forecasting Inbound Canadian Tourism: An Evaluation of Error Corrections Model Forecasts', *Tourism Economics*, 10(3), 263–280.

Victorian Auditor General (2007) *State Investment in Major Events*, Victoria: Victorian Government Printer, May.

Vu, J. and Turner, L. (2006) 'Regional Data Forecasting Accuracy: The Case of Thailand', *Journal of Travel Research*, 45, 186.

Wagner, J. (1997) 'Estimating the Economic Impacts of Tourism', *Annals of Tourism Research*, 24(3), 592–608.

Waheeduzzan, A. and J. Ryans (1996) 'Definition, Perspectives, and Understanding of International Competitiveness: A Quest for a Common Ground', *Competitiveness Review*, 6(2), 7–26.

Wanhill, S. (1988) 'Tourism Multipliers under Capacity Constraints', *Service Industries Journal*, 8, 136–142.

Ward, F.A. and D. Beal (2000) *Valuing Nature with Travel Cost Method: A Manual*, Northampton: Edward Elgar.

Wattanakuljarus, A. and I. Coxhead (2008) 'Is Tourism-based Development Good for the Poor? A General Equilibrium Analysis for Thailand', *Journal of Policy Modeling*, 30(6), 929–955.

WEF (2009) *The Travel & Tourism Competitiveness Report 2008: Managing in a Time of Turbulence*, Geneva, Switzerland: World Economic Forum.

Weitzman, M. (1974) 'Prices vs Quantities', *Review of Economic Studies*, 41(4), 477–491.

West, G. and A. Gamage (2001) 'Macro Effects of Tourism in Victoria: A Nonlinear Input-output Approach', *Journal of Travel Research*, 40(1), 101–109.

Wilkinson, P. (1989) 'Strategies for Tourism in Island Microstates', *Annals of Tourism Research*, 16(2), 153–177.

Williams, G. (2002) *Airline Competition: Deregulation's Mixed Legacy*, Aldershot: Ashgate.

Wilton, D. (1998) 'Recent Developments in Tourism as Revealed by the National Tourism Indicators, Canadian Tourism Commission, Research Report 1998-1', www.canadatourism.com.

Wit, R.C.N., J.W.M. Dings, P. Mendes de Leon, L. Thwaites, P. Peeters, D. Greenwood and R. Doganis (2002) 'Economic Incentives to Mitigate Greenhouse Gas Emissions from Air Transport in Europe', CE Delft, Delft, 02.4733.10.

Witt, S.F. (1987) 'Economic Impact of Tourism on Wales', *Tourism Management*, 8, 306–316.

Witt, S.F. and C.A. Martin (1987) 'Econometric Models for Forecasting International Tourism Demand', *Journal of Travel Research*, 25, 23–30.

Witt, S.F. and C.A. Witt (1995) 'Forecasting Tourism Demand: A Review of Empirical Research', *International Journal of Forecasting*, 11(3), 447–475.

Witt, S., H. Song and P. Louvieris (2003) 'Statistical Testing in Forecasting Model Selection', *Journal of Travel Research*, 42, 151–158, November.

Witt, S.F., H. Song and S. Wanhill (2004) 'Forecasting Tourism-generated Employment: The Case of Denmark', *Tourism Economics*, 10(2), 167–176.

WTTC (2001) *Tax Proposal Dossier*, No 1, October, London: World Travel & Tourism Council Taxation Policy Taskforce.

WTTC (2009) *Economic Impact Research*, www.wttc.org.

Wu, J. (2004) 'Influence of Market Orientation and Strategy on Travel Industry Performance: An Empirical Study of E-commerce in Taiwan', *Tourism Management*, 25(3), 368–365.

Yamauchi, H. (1997) 'Air Transport Policy in Japan: Limited Competition under Regulation' in C. Findlay, C. Lin Sien and K. Singh (eds) *Asia Pacific Air Transport Challenges and Policy Reforms* (pp. 106–122), Singapore: Institute of Southeast Asian Studies.

Zhou, D., J.F. Yanagida, U. Chakravorty and P. Leung (1997) 'Estimating Economic Impacts of Tourism', *Annals of Tourism Research*, 24(1), 76–89.

ABOUT THE AUTHORS

Larry Dwyer and Peter Forsyth are internationally reputed tourism economists who have made substantial contributions to the discipline over many years particularly in the area of tourism policy analysis. Larry Dwyer is Qantas Professor of Tourism Economics at the University of New South Wales, Australia while Peter Forsyth is Professor of Economics at Monash University, Australia. Wayne Dwyer, formerly senior lecturer in economics and finance at the University of Western Sydney specialises in managerial economics.

Larry Dwyer

Peter Forsyth

Wayne Dwyer

INDEX